Lecture Notes in Compu)2

Commenced Publication in 1973
Founding and Former Series Editors:
Gerhard Goos, Juris Hartmanis, and Jan van Leeuwen

Editorial Board

David Hutchison
Lancaster University, UK

Takeo Kanade
Carnegie Mellon University, Pittsburgh, PA, USA

Josef Kittler
University of Surrey, Guildford, UK

Jon M. Kleinberg
Cornell University, Ithaca, NY, USA

Friedemann Mattern
ETH Zurich, Switzerland

John C. Mitchell
Stanford University, CA, USA

Moni Naor
Weizmann Institute of Science, Rehovot, Israel

Oscar Nierstrasz
University of Bern, Switzerland

C. Pandu Rangan
Indian Institute of Technology, Madras, India

Bernhard Steffen
University of Dortmund, Germany

Madhu Sudan
Massachusetts Institute of Technology, MA, USA

Demetri Terzopoulos
New York University, NY, USA

Doug Tygar
University of California, Berkeley, CA, USA

Moshe Y. Vardi
Rice University, Houston, TX, USA

Gerhard Weikum
Max-Planck Institute of Computer Science, Saarbruecken, Germany

Wei-Ngan Chin (Ed.)

Programming Languages and Systems

Second Asian Symposium, APLAS 2004
Taipei, Taiwan, November 4-6, 2004
Proceedings

 Springer

Volume Editor

Wei-Ngan Chin
National University of Singapore
Department of Computer Science
School of Computing
3, Science Drive 2, Singapore 117543
E-mail: chinwn@comp.nus.edu.sg

Library of Congress Control Number: 2004113831

CR Subject Classification (1998): D.3, D.2, F.3, D.4, D.1, F.4.1

ISSN 0302-9743
ISBN 3-540-23724-0 Springer Berlin Heidelberg New York

This work is subject to copyright. All rights are reserved, whether the whole or part of the material is concerned, specifically the rights of translation, reprinting, re-use of illustrations, recitation, broadcasting, reproduction on microfilms or in any other way, and storage in data banks. Duplication of this publication or parts thereof is permitted only under the provisions of the German Copyright Law of September 9, 1965, in its current version, and permission for use must always be obtained from Springer. Violations are liable to prosecution under the German Copyright Law.

Springer is a part of Springer Science+Business Media

springeronline.com

© Springer-Verlag Berlin Heidelberg 2004
Printed in Germany

Typesetting: Camera-ready by author, data conversion by Scientific Publishing Services, Chennai, India
Printed on acid-free paper   SPIN: 11341635   06/3142   5 4 3 2 1 0

Foreword

On behalf of the organizing committee I would like to welcome you all to the second Asian Symposium on Programming Languages and Systems (APLAS 2004) held in Taipei on November 4–6, 2004. Since the year 2000, researchers in the area of programming languages and systems have been meeting annually in Asia to present their most recent research results, thus contributing to the advancement of this research area. The last four meetings were held in Singapore (2000), Daejeon (2001), Shanghai (2002), and Beijing (2003). These meetings were very fruitful and provided an excellent venue for the exchange of research ideas, findings and experiences in programming languages and systems. APLAS 2004 is the fifth such meeting and the second one in symposium setting. The first symposium was held in Beijing last year.

The success of the APLAS series is the collective result of many people's contributions. For APLAS 2004, first I would like to thank all the members of the Program Committee, in particular the Program Chair Wei-Ngan Chin, for their hard work in putting together an excellent program. I am most grateful to invited speakers, Joxan Jaffar, Frank Pfenning, and Martin Odersky, who have traveled a long way to deliver their speeches at APLAS 2004. I would like to thank all the referees, who helped review the manuscripts, the authors, who contributed to the proceedings of APLAS 2004, the members of the Organizing Committee, who made considerable effort to organize this event, and all the participants present at this meeting. Without your support this symposium would not have been possible. Finally I would like to acknowledge the support of the Asian Association for Foundation of Software and Academia Sinica, Taiwan.

I am sure you will enjoy this meeting, and I hope you will also find time to do some sightseeing in Taipei and take back some fond memories of your visit after this meeting is over.

September 2004   D. T. Lee

Preface

This volume contains the proceedings of the 2nd Asian Symposium on Programming Languages and Systems (APLAS 2004). The symposium was held in Taipei, Taiwan and was sponsored by the Asian Association for Foundation of Software (AAFS) and the Academia Sinica.

Following our call for papers, 97 full submissions were received. Almost all the papers were reviewed by three (or more) program committee members with the help of external reviewers. The program committee met electronically over a 10-day period and accepted 26 papers after careful deliberations. I would like to thank members of the APLAS 2004 Program Committee, for the tremendous effort they put into their reviews and deliberations, and all the external reviewers for their invaluable contributions.

The final program covered both foundational and practical issues in programming languages and systems. Apart from the 26 accepted papers, the symposium also featured invited talks from three distinguished speakers, Joxan Jaffar (National University of Singapore), Frank Pfenning (Carnegie Mellon University, USA) and Martin Odersky (École Polytechnique Fédérale de Lausanne, Switzerland).

Many people helped to promote APLAS as a high-quality forum in Asia to serve programming language researchers worldwide. Following a series of well-attended workshops that were held in Singapore (2000), Daejeon (2001), and Shanghai (2002), the first formal symposium was successfully held in Beijing in 2003. The present symposium benefited from the past momentum, and was also due to the contributions of many people.

Foremost, I am grateful to the General Chair, D. T. Lee, for his invaluable support and guidance, making our symposium in Taipei possible. I am also indebted to our Local Arrangements Chair, Tyng-Ruey Chuang, for the considerable effort he put into planning and organizing the meeting itself. Hidehiko Masuhara kindly agreed to act as Poster Chair, and Shengchao Qin helped with publicity matters. From the AAFS Committee, I would like to especially thank Atsushi Ohori and Tetsuo Ida for providing sound advice. Last but not least, I thank Florin Craciun for his dedication in handling the CyberChair submissions system and other administrative matters.

September 2004   Wei-Ngan Chin

Organization

General Chair

D.T. Lee (Academia Sinica, Taiwan)

Program Chair

Wei-Ngan Chin (National University of Singapore)

Program Committee

Jifeng He (United Nations University, Macau)
Thomas Henzinger (University of California, Berkeley, USA)
Yuh-Jzer Joung (National Taiwan University, Taiwan)
Gabriele Keller (University of New South Wales, Australia)
Jenq-Kuen Lee (National Tsinghua University, Taiwan)
Luc Maranget (INRIA, France)
Hidehiko Masuhara (University of Tokyo, Japan)
Luke Ong (University of Oxford, UK)
Tamiya Onodera (IBM Research, Japan)
Zongyan Qiu (Peking University, China)
Martin Rinard (Massachusetts Institute of Technology, USA)
David Sands (Chalmers University of Technology, Sweden)
Akihiko Takano (National Institute of Informatics, Japan)
Kazunori Ueda (Waseda University, Japan)
Chengyong Wu (Chinese Academy of Science, China)
Hongwei Xi (Boston University, USA)
Kwangkeun Yi (Seoul National University, Korea)

Local Arrangements Chair

Tyng-Ruey Chuang (Academia Sinica, Taiwan)

Poster Chair

Hidehiko Masuhara (University of Tokyo, Japan)

Publicity

Shengchao Qin (National University of Singapore)

External Referees

Seika Abe	William Greenland	Masataka Sassa
Joonseon Ahn	Hai-Feng Guo	Sean Seefried
Ki-yung Ahn	Hwansoo Han	Sunae Seo
Wolfgang Ahrendt	Pao-Ann Hsiung	Rui Shi
C. Scott Ananian	Ming-Yu Hung	K. Y. Shieh
Stefan Andrei	Tatsushi Inagaki	Yuan-Shin
Thomas Arts	Wu Jiajun	Donald Bruce Stewart
Martin Berger	Jang-Wu Jo	Eijiro Sumii
Manuel Chakravarty	Hyun-Goo Kang	Josef Svenningsson
Byeong-Mo Chang	Paul Kennedy	Munehiro Takimoto
Rong-Guey Chang	Siau-Cheng Khoo	Feng Tang
Chiyan Chen	Youil Kim	C. L. Tang
Chung-Kai Chen	Jaejin Lee	Akihiko Tozawa
Gang Chen	Oukseh Lee	Yih-Kuen Tsay
Woongsik Choi	James Leifer	Jerome Vouillon
Tyng-Ruey Chuang	Young-Jia Lin	Ken Wakita
Koen Claessen	Tao Liu	Bow-Yaw Wang
Florin Craciun	Zhanglin Liu	Jason Wu
Huimin Cui	Tom Melham	Dana N. Xu
Xie Haibin	Francois Metayer	Hongseok Yang
Fritz Henglein	Oege de Moor	Wuu Yang
Kohei Honda	Andrzej Murawski	Masahiro Yasugi
Gwan-Hwang Hwang	Keisuke Nakano	Handong Ye
Chung-Wen Hwang	Huu Hai Nguyen	Yi-Ping You
D. Doligez	Susumu Nishimura	Shoji Yuen
Derek Dreyer	Jeff Polakow	Patrick Zadarnowski
Kai Engelhardt	Corneliu Popeea	Naijun Zhan
Hyunjun Eo	Shengchao Qin	Xiaogang Zhang
Jacques Garrigue	Julian Rathke	Dengping Zhu
Martin Giese	Masahiko Sakai	

Sponsoring Institutions

Asian Association for Foundation of Software (AAFS)
Academia Sinica, Taiwan

Table of Contents

Invited Talk

Session 5

Session 6

Session 7

Invited Talk

Session 8

Session 9

Author Index

A CLP Approach to Modelling Systems

Joxan Jaffar*

School of Computing, National University of Singapore,
Republic of Singapore 117543
joxan@comp.nus.edu.sg

We present a formal method for modelling the operational behavior of various kinds of systems of concurrent processes. A first objective is that the method be broadly applicable. A system can be described in terms of its processes written in a traditional syntax-based manner, or in some non-traditional form such as a timed automaton. The number of processes may be fixed, or parameterized, or, because of dynamic process creation, unbounded. The communication and synchronization between processes may be synchronous or not, and via shared variables or some form of channels. We may have a traditional interleaving of processes, or use a specific scheduling strategy. The observables modelled should not be restricted to just the values of the program variables, but possibly other attributes of the system such as its registers and cache, its clock and battery values, etc. An example application area which touches upon these characteristics is that of determining worst-case execution time.

We choose to model a generic system S in the form of a CLP program P. The model-theoretic semantics of P shall characterize the "collecting" semantics of S, that is, those states that are observable. The proof-theoretic semantics of P, on the other hand, further characterize the "trace" semantics of S. An advantage of this CLP approach is that intricate details of the system can be captured in a familiar logical framework.

We then present a specification language for an extensive class of system behaviors. In addition to the traditional safety and liveness properties which specify the universality or eventuality of certain predicates on states, we introduce the notions of relative safety and relative progress. The former extends traditional safety assertions to accommodate non-behavioral properties such as symmetry, serializability and commutativity between processes. The latter provides for specifying progress properties. Our specification method is not just for stating the property of interest, but also for the assertion of properties held at various program points.

Finally, we present an inference method, based upon a notion of inductive tabling, for proving an assertion A. This method can use assertions that have already been proven, use the assertion A itself, in a manner prescribed by induction principles, and dynamically generate new assertions. All these properties are shown to be useful in preventing redundant computations, which then can lead to efficient proofs. Our proof method thus combines the search characteristic of model-checking and abstract interpretation, and methods of inductive assertions.

We demonstrate a prototype implementation on some benchmark examples.

---

* Joint work with Andrew Santosa and Răzvan Voicu.

W.-N. Chin (Ed.): APLAS 2004, LNCS 3302, p. 1, 2004.
© Springer-Verlag Berlin Heidelberg 2004

An Algebraic Approach to Bi-directional Updating

Shin-Cheng Mu, Zhenjiang Hu, and Masato Takeichi

Department of Information Engineering,
University of Tokyo,
7-3-1 Hongo, Bunkyo-ku, Tokyo 113, Japan
{scm,hu,takeichi}@ipl.t.u-tokyo.ac.jp

Abstract. In many occasions would one encounter the task of maintaining the consistency of two pieces of structured data that are related by some transform — synchronising bookmarks in different web browsers, the source and the view in an editor, or views in databases, to name a few. This paper proposes a formal model of such tasks, basing on a programming language allowing injective functions only. The programmer designs the transformation as if she is writing a functional program, while the synchronisation behaviour is automatically derived by algebraic reasoning. The main advantage is being able to deal with duplication and structural changes. The result will be integrated to our structure XML editor in the Programmable Structured Document project.

1 Introduction

In many occasions would one encounter the task of maintaining consistency of two pieces of structured data that are related by some transform. In some XML editors, for example [3, 15], a source XML document is transformed to a user-friendly, editable *view* through a transform defined by the document designer. The editing performed by the user on the view needs to be reflected back to the source document. Similar techniques can also be used to synchronise several bookmarks stored in formats of different browsers, to maintain invariance among widgets in an user interface, or to maintain the consistency of data and view in databases.

As a canonical example, consider the XML document in Figure 1(a) representing an article. When being displayed to the user, it might be converted to an HTML document as in Figure 1(b), with an additional table of contents. The conversion is defined by the document designer in some domain-specific programming language. We would then wish that when the user, for example, adds or deletes a section in (b), the original document in (a) be updated correspondingly. Further more, the changes should also trigger an update of the table of contents in (a). We may even wish that when an additional section title is added to the table of contents, a fresh, empty section will be added to the article bodies in both (a) and (b). All these are better done without too much effort, other than specifying the transform itself, from the document designer.

W.-N. Chin (Ed.): APLAS 2004, LNCS 3302, pp. 2–20, 2004.
© Springer-Verlag Berlin Heidelberg 2004

View-updating [5, 7, 10, 14, 1] has been intensively studied in the database community. Recently, the problem of maintaining the consistency of two pieces of structured data was brought to our attention again by [12] and [11]. Though developed separately, their results turn out to be surprisingly similar, with two important features missing. Firstly, it was assumed that the transform is total and surjective, which ruled out those transforms that duplicate data. Secondly, structural changes, such as inserting to or deleting from a list or a tree, were not sufficiently dealt with.

```
<article>                                <html>
 <title>Program inversion                 <h1>Program inversion</h1>
    </title>
 <section>                                 <ol><li>Our first effort</li>
   <title>Our first effort</title>            <li>Our second effort</li>
   <p>...</p>                              </ol>
 </section>
 <section>                                 <div>
   <title>Our second effort</title>       <h3>Our first effort</h3>
    <p>...</p>                                <p>...</p></div>
 </section>                               <div>
</article>                                <h3>Our second effort</h3>
                                              <p>...</p></div>
                                         </html>

         (a)                                      (b)
```

Fig. 1. An XML article and its HTML view with a table of contents

In this paper we will address these difficulties using a different approach inspired by previous studies of program inversion [2, 8]. We extend the injective functional language designed in [13], in which only injective functions are definable and therefore every program is trivially invertible. The document designer specifies the transform as if she were defining an injective function from the source to the view. A special operator for duplication specifies all element-wise dependency. To deal with inconsistencies resulting from editing, however, we define an alternative semantics, under which the behaviour of programs can be reasoned by algebraic rules. It will be a good application of program inversion [8] and algebraic reasoning, and the result will soon be integrated into our XML editor in the Programmable Structured Document project [15].

In Section 2 we give a brief introduction of the injective functional language in which the transforms are specified, and demonstrate the view-updating problem more concretely. An alternative semantics of the language is presented in Section 3, where we show, by algebraic reasoning, how to solve the view-updating problem. Section 4 shows some more useful transform, before we conclude in Section 5.

2   An Injective Language for Bi-directional Updating

Assume that a relation X, specifying the relationship between the source and the view, is given. In [11], the updating behaviour of the editor is modelled by two functions $get_X :: S \to V$ and $put_X :: (S \times V) \to S$. The function get_X transforms the source to the view. The function put_X, on the other hand, returns an updated source. It needs both the edited view and the *original* source, because some information might have been thrown away. For example, if the source is a pair and get_X simply extracts the first component, the second component is lost. The cached original source is also used for determining which value is changed by the user. A more symmetrical approach was taken in [12], where both functions take two arguments. The relation X is required to be bi-total (total and surjective), which implies that duplicating data, which would make the relation non-surjective, is not allowed.

In this paper we will explore a different approach. We make $get_X :: S \to V$ and $put_X :: V \to S$ take one argument only, and the transform has got to be injective — we shall lose no information in the source to view transform. A point-free language allowing only injective functions has been developed in [13] with this as one of the target applications. Duplication is an important primitive of the language.

Restricting ourselves to injective functions may seem like a severe limitation, but this is not true. In [13], it was shown that for all possibly non-injective functions $f :: A \to B$, we can automatically derive an injective function $f' :: A \to (B, H)$ where H records book-keeping information necessary for inversion. The extra information can be hidden from the user (for example, by setting the CSS visibility if the output is HTML). In fact, one can always make a function injective by copying the input to the output, if duplication is allowed. Therefore, the key extension here is duplication, while switching to injective functions is merely a change of presentation – rather than separating the original source and the edited view as two inputs to put_X, we move the burden of information preserving to X. This change, however, allows put_X itself to be simpler, while making it much easier to expose expose its properties, limitation, and possibly ways to overcome the limitation.

In this section we will introduce the language, Inv with some examples, and review the view-updating problem in our context. Extensions to the language and its semantics to deal with the view-updating problem will be discussed in Section 3. Some readers may consider the use of a point-free language as "not practical". We will postpone our defend to Section 5.

2.1   Views

The View datatype defines the basic types of data we deal with.

$$
\begin{aligned}
View \ ::= \ &Int \mid String \mid () \\
&\mid (View \times View) \mid L\,View \mid R\,View \\
&\mid ListView \mid TreeView \\
List\,a \ ::= \ &[\,] \mid a : List\,a \\
Tree\,a \ ::= \ &Node\,a\,(List\,(Tree\,a))
\end{aligned}
$$

The atomic types include integer, string, and unit, the type having only one value (). Composite types include pairs, sum (L View and R View), lists and rose trees. The (:) operator, forming lists, associates to the right. We also follow the common convention writing the list $1 : 2 : 3 : []$ as $[1, 2, 3]$. More extensions dealing with editing will be discussed later. For XML processing we can think of XML documents as rose trees represented by the type Tree. This very simplified view omits features of XML which will be our future work. In fact, for the rest of this paper we will be mostly talking about lists, since the techniques can easily be generalised to trees.

2.2   An Injective Language Inv

The syntax of the language Inv is defined as below. We abuse the notation a bit by using X_V to denote the union of X and the set of variable names V . The $*$ operator denotes "a possibly empty sequence of".

$$
\begin{aligned}
X ::= &\ X^\vee \mid \text{nil} \mid \text{zero} \mid C \\
&\mid \delta \mid \text{dup}\,P \mid \text{cmp}\,B \mid \text{inl} \mid \text{inr} \\
&\mid X\,;X \mid \text{id} \mid X \cup X \\
&\mid X \times X \mid \text{assocr} \mid \text{assocl} \mid \text{swap} \\
&\mid \mu(V : X_V) \\
C ::= &\ \text{succ} \mid \text{cons} \mid \text{node} \\
B ::= &\ < \mid \le \mid \ne \mid \ge \mid > \\
P ::= &\ \text{nil} \mid \text{zero} \mid \text{str}\,String \mid (S;)^*\text{id} \\
S ::= &\ C^\vee \mid \text{fst} \mid \text{snd}
\end{aligned}
$$

The semantics of each Inv construct is given in Figure 2. A relation of type $A \to B$ is a set of pairs whose first components have type A and second components type B, while a function[1] is one such that a value in A is mapped to at most one value in B. A function is injective if all values in B are mapped to at most one value in A as well. The semantics of every Inv program is an injective function from View to View. That is, the semantics function $[\![]\!]$ has type $Inv \to View \to View$. For example, nil is interpreted as a constant function always returning the empty list, while zero always returns zero. Their domain is restricted to the unit type, to preserve injectivity.

The function id is the identity function, the unit of composition. The semi-colon (;) is overloaded both as functional composition and as an Inv construct. It is defined by $(f; g)\,a = g\,(f\,a)$.

Union of functions is simply defined as set union. To avoid non-determinism, however, we require in $f \cup g$ that f and g have disjoint domains. To ensure injectivity, we require that they have disjoint ranges as well. The *domain* of a function $f :: A \to B$, written dom f, is the partial function (and a set) $\{(a, a) \in A \mid \exists b \in B :: (a, b) \in f\}$. The *range* of f, written ran f, is defined symmetrically. The product $(f \times g)$ is a function taking a pair and applying f and g to the two components respectively. We make composition bind tighter than product. Therefore $(f; g \times h)$ means $((f; g) \times h)$.

---

[1] For convenience, we refer to possibly partial functions when we say "functions".

$$\begin{array}{ll}
[\![nil]\!]\,() & = [\,] \\
[\![zero]\!]\,() & = 0 \\
[\![succ]\!]\,n & = n+1 \\
[\![cons]\!]\,(a,x) & = a\!:\!x \\
[\![node]\!]\,(a,x) & = Node\ a\ x \\
[\![inl]\!]\,a & = L\,a \\
[\![inr]\!]\,a & = R\,a \\
[\![id]\!]\,a & = a
\end{array}$$

$$[\![swap]\!]\,(a,b) \quad = (b,a)$$
$$[\![assocr]\!]\,((a,b),c) = (a,(b,c))$$

$$[\![assocl]\!]\,(a,(b,c)) = ((a,b),c)$$

$$\begin{array}{ll}
[\![cmp \trianglelefteq]\!]\,(a,b) = (a,b),\ \text{if}\ a \trianglelefteq b \\
[\![\delta]\!]\,a \qquad\qquad = (a,a)
\end{array}$$

$$\begin{array}{ll}
[\![f;g]\!]\,x & = [\![g]\!]\,([\![f]\!]\,x) \\
[\![f \times g]\!]\,(a,b) & = ([\![f]\!]\,a, [\![g]\!]\,b) \\
[\![f \cup g]\!] & = [\![f]\!] \cup [\![g]\!], \\
\multicolumn{2}{l}{\quad\text{if}\ dom\,f \cap dom\,g = ran\,f \cap ran\,g = \emptyset} \\
[\![f^{\,\smallsmile}]\!] & = [\![f]\!]^{\,\square} \\
[\![\mu F]\!] & = [\![F\,\mu F]\!]
\end{array}$$

Fig. 2. Functional semantics of Inv constructs apart from *dup*

The fixed-point of F, a function from Inv expressions to Inv expressions, is denoted by μF. We will be using the notation $(X : \mathsf{expr})$ to denote a function taking an argument X and returning expr.

The *converse* of a relation R is defined by

$$(\mathsf{b},\mathsf{a}) \in \mathsf{R}^{\circ} \equiv (\mathsf{a},\mathsf{b}) \in \mathsf{R}$$

The *reverse* operator $^{\smallsmile}$ corresponds to converses on relations. Since all functions here are injective, their converses are functions too. The reverse of cons, for example, decomposes a non-empty list into the head and the tail. The reverse of nil matches only the empty list and maps it to the unit value. The reverse operator distributes into composition, products and union by the following rules, all implied by the semantics definition $[\![\mathsf{f}^{\smallsmile}]\!] = [\![\mathsf{f}]\!]^{\circ}$:

$$\begin{array}{l}
[\![(\mathsf{f};\mathsf{g})^{\smallsmile}]\!] = [\![\mathsf{g}^{\smallsmile}]\!]; [\![\mathsf{f}^{\smallsmile}]\!] \\
[\![(\mathsf{f} \times \mathsf{g})^{\smallsmile}]\!] = [\![(\mathsf{f}^{\smallsmile} \times \mathsf{g}^{\smallsmile})]\!] \\
[\![(\mathsf{f} \cup \mathsf{g})^{\smallsmile}]\!] = [\![\mathsf{f}^{\smallsmile}]\!] \cup [\![\mathsf{g}^{\smallsmile}]\!]
\end{array}$$

$$\begin{array}{l}
[\![\mathsf{f}^{\smallsmile\smallsmile}]\!] = [\![\mathsf{f}]\!] \\
[\![(\mu F)^{\smallsmile}]\!] = [\![\mu(X : (F\ X^{\,\smallsmile})^{\smallsmile})]\!]
\end{array}$$

The δ operator is worth our attention. It generates an extra copy of its argument. Written as a set comprehension, we have $\delta_A = \{(\mathsf{n},(\mathsf{n},\mathsf{n})) \,|\, \mathsf{n} \in A\}$, where A is the type δ gets instantiated to. We restrict A to atomic types (integers, strings, and unit) only, and from now on use variable n and m to denote values of atomic types. To duplicate a list, we can always use $\mathsf{map}\,\delta; \mathsf{unzip}$, where map and unzip are to be introduced in the sections to come. Taking its reverse, we get:

$$\delta_A{}^{\smallsmile} = \{((\mathsf{n},\mathsf{n}),\mathsf{n}) \,|\, \mathsf{n} \in A\}$$

That is, $\delta^{\smallsmile}$ takes a pair and lets it go through only if the two components are equal. That explains the observation in [8] that to "undo" a duplication, we have to perform an equality test.

In many occasions we may want to duplicate not all but some sub-component of the input. For convenience, we include another Inv construct dup which takes a sequence of "labels" and duplicates the selected sub-component. The label is either fst, snd, cons˘, and node˘. Informally, think of the sequence of labels as the composition of selector functions (fst and snd) or deconstructors, and dup can be understood as:

$$[\![dup\ f]\!]\ x = (x, [\![f]\!]\ x)$$

If we invert it, (dup f)˘ becomes a partial function taking a pair (x, n), and returns x unchanged if f x equals n. The second component n can be safely dropped because we know its value already. We write (dup f)˘ as eq f. For example, dup (fst; snd) ((a, n), b) yields (((a, n), b), n), while eq (fst; snd) (((a, n), b), m) returns ((a, n), b) if $n = m$. Formally, dup is defined as a function taking a list of function names and returns a function:

$$
\begin{aligned}
&dup\ id &&= \delta \\
&dup\ (fst; P) &&= (dup\ P \times id); subl \\
&dup\ (snd; P) &&= (id \times dup\ P); assocl \\
&dup\ (cons˘; P) &&= cons˘; dup\ P; (cons \times id) \\
&dup\ (node˘; P) &&= node˘; dup\ P; (node \times id)
\end{aligned}
$$

Here, $[\![subl]\!]\ ((a, b), c) = ((a, c), b)$, whose formal definition is given in Section 2.3.

Another functionality of dup is to introduce constants. The original input is kept unchanged but paired with a new constant:

$$
\begin{aligned}
&[\![dup\ nil]\!]\ a &&= (a, [\,]) \\
&[\![dup\ zero]\!]\ a &&= (a, 0) \\
&[\![dup\ (str\ s)]\!]\ a &&= (a, s)
\end{aligned}
$$

Their reverses eliminates a constant whose value is known. In both directions we lose no information.

The cmp construct takes a pair of values, and let them go through only if they satisfy one of the five binary predicates given by non-terminal B.

2.3   Programming Examples in Inv

All functions that move around the components in a pair can be defined in terms of products, assocr, assocl, and swap. We find the following functions useful:

$$
\begin{aligned}
subr &= assocl; (swap \times id); assocr \\
subl &= assocr; (id \times swap); assocl \\
trans &= assocr; (id \times subr); assocl
\end{aligned}
$$

Their semantics, after expanding the definition, is given below:

$$
\begin{aligned}
&[\![subr]\!]\ (a, (b, c)) &&= (b, (a, c)) \\
&[\![subl]\!]\ ((a, b), c) &&= ((a, c), b) \\
&[\![trans]\!]\ ((a, b), (c, d)) &&= ((a, c), (b, d))
\end{aligned}
$$

$$
\begin{aligned}
mktoc &= denode\ \texttt{article}; cons^{\smile}; (h1 \times cont); cons; ennode\ \texttt{html} \\
h1 &= denode\ \texttt{title}; ennode\ \texttt{h1} \\
cont &= extract; (enlist \times body); cons \\
extract &= map\ (denode\ \texttt{section}; cons^{\smile}; (denode\ \texttt{title} \times id); dup\ fst; swap); unzip \\
enlist &= map\ (ennode\ \texttt{li}); ennode\ \texttt{ol} \\
body &= map\ ((ennode\ \texttt{h3} \times id); cons; ennode\ \texttt{div})
\end{aligned}
$$

$$
\begin{aligned}
denode\ s &= node^{\smile}; swap; eq\ (str\ s) \\
ennode\ s &= (denode\ s)^{\smile}
\end{aligned}
$$

Fig. 3. An Inv program performing the transform from Figure 1(a) to Figure 1(b). String constants are written in typewriter font

Many list-processing functions can be defined recursively on the list. The function map applies a function to all elements of a list; the function unzip takes a list of pairs and splits it into a pair of lists. They can be defined by:

$$
\begin{aligned}
map\ f &= \mu(X : nil^{\smile}; nil \cup \\
&\qquad cons^{\smile}; (f \times X); cons) \\
unzip &= \mu(X : nil^{\smile}; \delta; (nil \times nil) \cup \\
&\qquad cons^{\smile}; (id \times X); trans; (cons \times cons))
\end{aligned}
$$

This is what one would expect when we write down their usual definition in a point-free style. The branches starting with $nil^{\smile}$ are the base cases, matching empty lists, while $cons^{\smile}$ matches non-empty lists. It is also provable from the semantics that $(map\ f)^{\smile} = map\ f^{\smile}$.

The function merge takes a pair of sorted lists and merges them into one. However, by doing so we lose information necessary to split them back to the original pair. Therefore, we tag the elements in the merged list with labels indicating where they were from. For example, $merge\ ([1, 4, 7], [2, 5, 6]) = [\mathsf{L}\ 1, \mathsf{R}\ 2, \mathsf{L}\ 4, \mathsf{R}\ 5, \mathsf{R}\ 6, \mathsf{L}\ 7]$. It can be defined in Inv as below:

$$
\begin{aligned}
merge = \mu(X :\ &eq\ nil; map\ inl \cup \\
&swap; eq\ nil; map\ inr \cup \\
&(cons^{\smile} \times cons^{\smile}); trans; \\
&((leq \times id); assocr; (id \times subr; (id \times cons); X); (inl \times id) \cup \\
&\ \ ((gt; swap) \times id); assocr; (id \times assocl; (cons \times id); X); (inr \times id)); \\
&cons)
\end{aligned}
$$

where $leq = cmp\ (\leq)$ and $gt = cmp\ (>)$.

As a final example, the program in Figure 3 performs the transform from Figure 1(a) to Figure 1(b). It demonstrates the use of map, unzip and dup. For brevity, the suffixing id in $dup\ (fst; id)$ will be omitted.

2.4   The View-Updating Problem

Now consider the scenario of an editor, where a source document is transformed, via an Inv program, to a view editable by the user. Consider the transform $toc = map\ (dup\ fst); unzip$, we have:

$$\text{toc}\,[(1, \text{``a''}), (2, \text{``b''}), (3, \text{``c''})] = ([(1, \text{``a''}), (2, \text{``b''}), (3, \text{``c''})], [1, 2, 3])$$

Think of each pair as a section and the numbers as their titles, the function toc is a simplified version of the generation of a table of contents, thus the name.

Through a special interface, there are several things the user can do: change the value of a node, insert a new node, or delete a node. Assume that the user changes the value 3 in the "table of contents" to 4:

$$([(1, \text{``a''}), (2, \text{``b''}), (3, \text{``c''})], [1, 2, 4])$$

Now we try to perform the transformation backwards. Applying the reverse operator to toc, we get $(\text{map}\,(\text{dup fst}); \text{unzip})^{\vee} = \text{unzip}^{\vee}; \text{map}\,(\text{eq fst})$. Applying it to the modified view, $\text{unzip}^{\vee}$ maps the modified view to:

$$[((1, \text{``a''}), 1), ((2, \text{``b''}), 2), ((3, \text{``c''}), 4)]$$

pairing the sections and the titles together, to be processed by $\text{map}\,(\text{eq fst})$. However, $((3, \text{``c''}), 4)$ is not in the domain of eq fst because the equality check fails. We wish that eq fst would return $(4, \text{``c''})$ in this case, answering the user's wish to change the section title.

Now assume that the user inserts a new section title in the table of contents:

$$([(1, \text{``a''}), (2, \text{``b''}), (3, \text{``c''})], [1, 2, 4, 3])$$

This time the changed view cannot even pass $\text{unzip}^{\vee}$, because the two lists have different lengths. We wish that $\text{unzip}^{\vee}$ would somehow know that the two 3's should go together and the zipped list should be

$$[((1, \text{``a''}), 1), ((2, \text{``b''}), 2), (\bot, 4), ((3, \text{``c''}), 3)]$$

where $\bot$ denotes some unconstrained value, which would be further constrained by $\text{map}\,(\text{dup fst})$ to $(4, \bot)$. The Inv construct eq fst should also recognise $\bot$ and deal with it accordingly.

In short, we allow the programmer to write Inv transforms that are not surjective. Therefore it is very likely that a view modified by the user may fall out of the range of the transform. This is in contrast of the approach taken in [12] and [11]. The two problems we discussed just now are representative of the view-updating problem. There are basically two kinds of dependency we have to deal with: element-wise dependency, stating that two pieces of primary-typed data have the same value, and structural dependency, stating that two pieces of data have the same shape.

One possible solution is to provide an alternative semantics that extends the ranges of Inv constructs in a reasonable way, so that the unmodified, or barely modified programs can deal with the changes. We will discuss this in detail in the next section.

3   Alternative Semantics

We will need some labels in the view, indicating "this part has been modified by the user." We extend the View data type as described below:

$$\mathsf{View} ::= \ldots \mid *\mathsf{Int} \mid *\mathsf{String}$$
$$\mathsf{Lista} ::= \ldots \mid a \oplus \mathsf{Lista} \mid a \ominus \mathsf{Lista}$$

Here the $*$ mark applies to atomic types only, indicating that the value has been changed. The view $a \oplus x$ denotes a list $a : x$ whose head a was freshly inserted by the user, while $a \ominus x$ denotes a list x which used to have a head a but was deleted. The deleted value a is still cached for future use. The two operators associate to the right, like the cons operator $(:)$. A similar set of operators can be introduced for Tree but they are out of the scope of this paper.

The original semantics of each Inv program is an injective function. When the tags are involved, however, we lost the injectivity. Multiple views may be mapped to the same source. For example, the value 1 is mapped to $(1,1)$ by δ. In the reverse direction, $(n, *1)$ and $(*1, n)$, for all numerical n, are all mapped to 1. Similarly, all these views are mapped back to $[1, 2, 3]$ when the transform is $\mathsf{map\,succ}: [2, 3, 4]$, $a \ominus [2, 3, 4]$, $2 : a \ominus [3, 4]$, $2 \oplus [3, 4]$, $2 : 3 \oplus [4]$ for all a.

We define two auxiliary functions $\mathsf{notag?}$ and ridtag. The former is a partial function letting through the input view unchanged if it contains no tags. The latter gets rid of the tags in a view, producing a normal form. Their definitions are trivial and omitted. The behaviour of the editor, on the other hand, is specified using two functions get_X and put_X, both parameterised by an Inv program X:

$$\mathsf{get}_X = \mathsf{notag?}; [\![X]\!]$$
$$\mathsf{put}_X \mathbin{\dot{\subseteq}} [\![X^{\smallsmile}]\!]; \mathsf{ridtag}$$

The function get_X maps the source to the view by calling X. The function put_X, on the other hand, maps the (possibly edited) view back to the document by letting it go though $X^{\smallsmile}$ and removing the tags in the result. Here $\dot{\subseteq}$ denotes "functional refinement", defined by $f \dot{\subseteq} g$ if and only if $f \subseteq g$ and $\mathsf{dom}\,f = \mathsf{dom}\,g$. In general $[\![X^{\smallsmile}]\!]; \mathsf{ridtag}$ is not a function since $[\![X^{\smallsmile}]\!]$ may leave some values unspecified. However, any functional refinement of $[\![X^{\smallsmile}]\!]; \mathsf{ridtag}$ would satisfy the properties we want. The implementation can therefore, for example, choose an "initial value" for each unspecified value according to its type. The initial view is obtained by a call to get_X. When the user performs some editing, the editor applies put_X to the view, obtaining a new source, before generating a new view by calling get_X again.

In the original semantics of Inv, the $^{\smallsmile}$ operator is simply relational converse. In the extended semantics, the $^{\smallsmile}$ operator deviates from relational converse for three constructs: δ, **cons** and sync, to be introduced later. For other cases we still have $[\![f^{\smallsmile}]\!] = [\![f]\!]^{\circ}$. The distributivity rules of $^{\smallsmile}$ given in Section 2.2 are still true.

In the next few sub-sections we will introduce extensions to the original semantics in the running text. A summary of the resulting semantics will be given in the end of Section 3.2.

3.1   Generalised Equality Test

The simple semantics of $\delta_A^\vee$, where A is an atomic type, is given by the set $\{((n,n),n) \mid n \in A\}$. To deal with editing, we generalise its semantics to:

$$\llbracket \delta^\vee \rrbracket\,(n,n) = n \qquad\qquad \llbracket \delta^\vee \rrbracket\,(*n, *n) = *n$$
$$\llbracket \delta^\vee \rrbracket\,(*n, m) = *n \qquad\qquad \llbracket \delta^\vee \rrbracket\,(m, *n) = n$$

When the two values are not the same but one of them was edited by the user, the edited one gets precedence and goes through. Therefore $(*n, m)$ is mapped to $*n$. If both values are edited, however, they still have to be the same. Note that the semantics of δ does not change. Also, we are still restricted to atomic types. One will have to call $map\,\delta; unzip$ to duplicate a list, thereby separate the value and structural dependency.

The syntax of dup can be extended to allow, a possibly non-injective function. The results of the non-injective function, and those derive from them, are supposed to be non-editable. It is a useful functionality but we will not go into its details.

3.2   Insertion and Deletion

Recall $unzip$ defined in Section 2.3. Its reverse, according to the distributivity of $\vee$, is given by:

$$unzip^\vee = \mu(X : (nil^\vee \times nil^\vee); \delta^\vee; nil \cup$$
$$(cons^\vee \times cons^\vee); trans; (id \times X\,); cons)$$

The puzzle is: how to make it work correctly with the presence of $\ominus$ and $\oplus$ tags? We introduce several new additional operators and types:

- two new Inv operators, del and ins, both parameterised by a view. The function $del\,a :: [A] \to [A]$ introduces an $(a \ominus)$ tag, while $ins\,a :: [A] \to [A]$ introduces an $(a \oplus)$ tag.
- two kinds of pairs in $View$: positive $(a, b)^+$ and negative $(a, b)^-$. They are merely pairs with an additional label. They can be introduced only by the reverse of $fst_b^\pm$ and $snd_a^\pm$ functions to be introduced below. The intention is to use them to denote pairs whose components are temporary left there for some reason.
- six families of functions $fst_a^\square$ and $snd_a^\square$, where $\square$ can be either $+$, $-$, or nothing, defined by

$$fst_b^\square\,(a, b)^\square = a$$
$$snd_a^\square\,(a, b)^\square = b$$

That is, fst_b^+ eliminates the second component of a positive pair only if it equals b. Otherwise it fails. Similarly, snd_a eliminates the first component of an ordinary pair only of it equals a. When interacting with existing operators, they should satisfy the algebraic rules in Figure 4. In order to shorten the presentation, we use $\square$ to match $+$, $-$ and nothing, while $\pm$ matches only $+$ and $-$. The $\square$ and $\pm$ in the same rule must match the same symbol.

With the new operators and types, an extended unzip capable of dealing with deletion can be extended from the original unzip by (here "..." denotes the original two branches of unzip):

$$
\begin{aligned}
\mathsf{unzip}^\vee = \mu(X : \ldots \forall a, b \cdot \\
((\mathsf{ins}\,a)^\vee \times (\mathsf{ins}\,b)^\vee); X \; ; \mathsf{ins}\,(a, b) \; \cup \\
((\mathsf{ins}\,a)^\vee \times \mathsf{isList}); X \; ; \mathsf{ins}\,(a, b) \; \cup \\
(\mathsf{isList} \times (\mathsf{ins}\,b)^\vee); X \; ; \mathsf{ins}\,(a, b) \; \cup \\
((\mathsf{del}\,a)^\vee \times (\mathsf{del}\,b)^\vee); X \; ; \mathsf{del}(a, b) \; \cup \\
((\mathsf{del}\,a)^\vee \times \mathsf{cons}^\vee; \mathsf{snd}_b^-); X \; ; \mathsf{del}(a, b) \; \cup \\
(\mathsf{cons}^\vee; \mathsf{snd}_a^- \times (\mathsf{del}\,b)^\vee); X \; ; \mathsf{del}(a, b))
\end{aligned}
$$

where a and b are universally quantified, and $\mathsf{isList} = \mathsf{nil}^\vee; \mathsf{nil} \cup \mathsf{cons}^\vee; \mathsf{cons}$, a subset of id letting through only lists having no tag at the head.

Look at the branch starting with $((\mathsf{ins}\,a)^\vee \times (\mathsf{ins}\,b)^\vee)$. It says that, given a pair of lists both starting with insertion tags $a\oplus$ and $b\oplus$, we should deconstruct them, pass the tails of the lists to the recursive call, and put back an $((a, b) \oplus)$ tag. If only the first of them is tagged (matching the branch starting with $((\mathsf{ins}\,a)^\vee \times \mathsf{isList})$), we temporarily remove the $a \oplus$ tag, recursively process the lists, and put back a tag $((a, b) \oplus)$ with a freshly generated b. The choice of b is non-deterministic and might be further constrained when unzip is further composed with other relations. The situation is similar with deletion. In the branch starting with $(\mathsf{del}\,a \times \mathsf{snd}_b^{+\circ}; \mathsf{cons})$ where we encounter a list with an a deleted by the user, we remove an element in the other list and remember its value in b. Here universally quantified b is used to match the value — all the branches with different b's are unioned together, with only one of them resulting in a successful match.

It would be very tedious if the programmer had to explicitly write down these extra branches for all functions. Luckily, these additional branches can be derived automatically using the rules in Figure 4. In the derivations later we will omit the semantics function $[\![\,]\!]$ and use the same notation for the language and its semantics, where no confusion would occur. This is merely for the sake of brevity.

In place of ordinary cons, we define two constructs addressing the dependency of structures. Firstly, the *bold* **cons** is defined by::

$$
\mathbf{cons} = \mathsf{cons} \; \cup \; \bigcup_{a::A}(\mathsf{snd}_a^-; \mathsf{del}\,a) \; \cup \; \bigcup_{a::A}(\mathsf{snd}_a^+; \mathsf{ins}\,a)
$$

$$
\begin{aligned}
(f \times g); fst^\square_{(g\,b)} &= fst^\square_b; f, \ \text{if } g \text{ total} & assocl; (fst^\square_b \times id) &= (id \times snd^\square_b) \\
(f \times g); snd^\square_{(f\,a)} &= snd^\square_a; g, \ \text{if } f \text{ total} & assocl; (snd^\square_a \times id) &= (snd^\square_a \cup snd_a) \\
swap; snd^\square_a &= fst^\square_a & assocl; snd^\square_{(a,b)} &= snd^\square_a; (snd^\square_b \cup snd_b) \\
snd^\square_a{}^\vee; eq\ nil &= (\lambda\,[\,] \to a)
\end{aligned}
$$

Fig. 4. Algebraic rules. Here $(\lambda\,[\,] \to a)$ is a function mapping only empty list to a. Only rules for *assocl* are listed. The rules for *assocr* can be obtained by pre-composing *assocr* to both sides and use *asscor*; *assocl* = *id*. Free identifiers are universally quantified

Secondly, we define the following sync operator:

$$\mathsf{sync} = (\mathsf{cons} \times \mathsf{cons})$$
$$\mathsf{sync}^{\smallsmile} = (\mathsf{cons}^{\smallsmile} \times \mathsf{cons}^{\smallsmile})$$
$$\cup \bigcup_{a,b \in A} (((\mathsf{dela})^{\smallsmile}; \mathsf{snd}_a^{-\smallsmile} \times (\mathsf{delb})^{\smallsmile}; \mathsf{snd}_b^{-\smallsmile})$$
$$\cup ((\mathsf{dela})^{\smallsmile}; \mathsf{snd}_a^{-\smallsmile} \times \mathsf{cons}^{\smallsmile}; \mathsf{snd}_b; \mathsf{snd}_b^{-\smallsmile})$$
$$\cup (\mathsf{cons}^{\smallsmile}; \mathsf{snd}_a; \mathsf{snd}_a^{-\smallsmile} \times (\mathsf{delb})^{\smallsmile}; \mathsf{snd}_b^{-\smallsmile}))$$
$$\cup \bigcup_{a,b \in A} (((\mathsf{insa})^{\smallsmile}; \mathsf{snd}_a^{+\smallsmile} \times (\mathsf{insb})^{\smallsmile}; \mathsf{snd}_b^{+\smallsmile})$$
$$\cup ((\mathsf{insa})^{\smallsmile}; \mathsf{snd}_a^{+\smallsmile} \times \mathsf{isList}; \mathsf{snd}_b^{+\smallsmile})$$
$$\cup (\mathsf{isList}; \mathsf{snd}_b^{+\smallsmile} \times (\mathsf{insb})^{\smallsmile}; \mathsf{snd}_b^{+\smallsmile}))$$

In the definition of unzip, we replace every singular occurence of cons with **cons**, and every $(\mathsf{cons} \times \mathsf{cons})$ with sync. The definition of $\mathsf{sync}^{\smallsmile}$ looks very complicated but we will shortly see its use in the derivation. Basically every product corresponds to one case we want to deal with: when both the lists are cons lists, when one or both of them has a $\ominus$ tag, or when one or both of them has a $\oplus$ tag.

After the substitution, all the branches can be derived by algebraic reasoning. The rules we need are listed in Figure 4. To derive the first branch for insertion, for example, we reason:

$\mathsf{unzip}^{\smallsmile}$

$\supseteq$ {fixed-point}

  $\mathsf{sync}^{\smallsmile}; \mathsf{trans}; (\mathsf{id} \times \mathsf{unzip}); \mathbf{cons}$

$\supseteq$ {since $\mathsf{sync}^{\smallsmile} \supseteq ((\mathsf{insa})^{\smallsmile}; \mathsf{snd}_a^{+\smallsmile} \times (\mathsf{insb})^{\smallsmile}; \mathsf{snd}_b^{+\smallsmile})$ for all a, b}

  $((\mathsf{insa})^{\smallsmile} \times (\mathsf{insb})^{\smallsmile}); (\mathsf{snd}_a^{+\smallsmile} \times (\mathsf{insb})^{\smallsmile}); \mathsf{trans}; (\mathsf{id} \times \mathsf{unzip}); \mathbf{cons}$

$\supseteq$ {claim: $(\mathsf{snd}_a^{+\smallsmile} \times \mathsf{snd}_b^{+\smallsmile}); \mathsf{trans} \supseteq (\mathsf{snd}_{(a,b)}^{+})^{\smallsmile}$}

  $((\mathsf{insa})^{\smallsmile} \times (\mathsf{insb})^{\smallsmile}); (\mathsf{snd}_{(a,b)}^{+})^{\smallsmile}; (\mathsf{id} \times \mathsf{unzip}); \mathbf{cons}$

$=$ {since $(\mathsf{f} \times \mathsf{g}); \mathsf{snd}_{f \cdot a}^{+} = \mathsf{snd}_a^{+}; \mathsf{g}$ for total f}

  $((\mathsf{insa})^{\smallsmile} \times (\mathsf{insb})^{\smallsmile}); \mathsf{unzip}; (\mathsf{snd}_{(a,b)}^{+})^{\smallsmile}; \mathbf{cons}$

$\supseteq$ {since $\mathbf{cons} \supseteq \mathsf{snd}_{(a,b)}^{+}; \mathsf{ins}(a,b)$}

  $((\mathsf{insa})^{\smallsmile} \times (\mathsf{insb})^{\smallsmile}); \mathsf{unzip}; (\mathsf{snd}_{(a,b)}^{+})^{\smallsmile}; \mathsf{snd}_{(a,b)}^{+}; \mathsf{ins}(a,b)$

$=$ {since $\mathsf{snd}_x^{+\smallsmile}; \mathsf{snd}_x^{+} = \mathsf{id}$}

  $((\mathsf{insa})^{\smallsmile} \times (\mathsf{insb})^{\smallsmile}); \mathsf{unzip}; \mathsf{ins}(a,b)$

We get the first branch. The claim that $\mathsf{trans}^{\smallsmile}; (\mathsf{snd}_a^{\square} \times \mathsf{snd}_b^{\square}) = \mathsf{snd}_{(a,b)}^{\square}$ can be verified by the rules in Figure 4 and is left as an exercise. The introduction of two kinds of pairs was to avoid the suffix being reduced to $(\mathsf{del}(a,b))^{\smallsmile}$ in the last two steps. To derive one of the branches for deletion, on the other hand, one uses the inclusion $\mathsf{sync}^{\smallsmile} \supseteq ((\mathsf{dela})^{\smallsmile}; \mathsf{snd}_a^{-\smallsmile} \times \mathsf{cons}^{\smallsmile}; \mathsf{snd}_b; \mathsf{snd}_b^{-\smallsmile})$ for the first step, and $\mathbf{cons} \supseteq \mathsf{snd}_{(a,b)}^{-}; \mathsf{del}(a,b)$ and $(\mathsf{snd}_{(a,b)}^{-})^{\smallsmile}; \mathsf{snd}_{(a,b)}^{-} = \mathsf{id}$ fort the last step. All the branches can be derived in a similar fashion.

$$\llbracket nil \rrbracket\,() = []$$
$$\llbracket zero \rrbracket\,() = 0$$
$$\llbracket succ \rrbracket\,n = n + 1$$
$$\llbracket cons \rrbracket\,(a, x) = a : x$$
$$\llbracket node \rrbracket\,(a, x) = Node\ a\ x$$
$$\llbracket inl \rrbracket\,a = L\,a$$
$$\llbracket inr \rrbracket\,a = R\,a$$
$$\llbracket id \rrbracket\,a = a$$

$$\llbracket swap \rrbracket\,(a,b)^\square = (b,a)^\square$$
$$\llbracket assocr \rrbracket\,((a,b)^\pm, c)^\pm = (a,(b,c)^\pm)^\pm$$
$$\llbracket assocr \rrbracket\,((a,b)^\pm, c) = (a,(b,c)^\pm)$$
$$\llbracket assocr \rrbracket\,((a,b),c)^\pm = (a,(b,c))^\pm$$
$$assocl = assocr^{\smallsmile}$$

$$(f^{\smallsmile})^{\smallsmile} = f$$

$$\llbracket \delta \rrbracket\,n = (n, n)$$
$$\llbracket \delta^{\smallsmile} \rrbracket\,(n, n)^\square = n$$
$$\llbracket \delta^{\smallsmile} \rrbracket\,(*n, *n)^\square = *n$$
$$\llbracket \delta^{\smallsmile} \rrbracket\,(*n, m)^\square = *n$$
$$\llbracket \delta^{\smallsmile} \rrbracket\,(m, *n)^\square = *n$$

$$\llbracket dup\ nil \rrbracket\,a = (a, [])$$
$$\llbracket (dup\ nil)^{\smallsmile} \rrbracket\,(a, [])^\square = a$$
$$\llbracket dup\ zero \rrbracket\,a = (a, 0)$$
$$\llbracket (dup\ zer0)^{\smallsmile} \rrbracket\,(a, 0)^\square = a$$
$$\llbracket dup\,(str\ s) \rrbracket\,a = (a, s)$$
$$\llbracket (dup\,(str\ s))^{\smallsmile} \rrbracket\,(a, s)^\square = a$$

$$\mathbf{cons} = cons$$
$$\cup\ \bigcup_{a::A}(snd_a^-; del\ a)$$
$$\cup\ \bigcup_{a::A}(snd_a^+; ins\ a)$$

$$\llbracket cmp\ \trianglelefteq \rrbracket\,(a, b)^\square = (a, b)^\square,\ \text{if } a \trianglelefteq b$$
$$\llbracket f; g \rrbracket\,x = \llbracket g \rrbracket\,(\llbracket f \rrbracket\,x)$$
$$\llbracket f \times g \rrbracket\,(a, b)^\square = (\llbracket f \rrbracket\,a, \llbracket g \rrbracket\,b)^\square$$
$$\llbracket f \cup g \rrbracket = \llbracket f \rrbracket \cup \llbracket g \rrbracket,$$
$$\qquad \text{if } dom\ f \cap dom\ g = ran\ f \cap ran\ g = \emptyset$$
$$\llbracket \mu F \rrbracket = \lceil F\ \mu F \rceil$$

$$\llbracket f^{\smallsmile} \rrbracket = \llbracket f \rrbracket^{\blacksquare}$$
$$\llbracket f; g^{\smallsmile} \rrbracket = \llbracket g^{\smallsmile} \rrbracket; \llbracket f^{\smallsmile} \rrbracket$$
$$\llbracket (f \times g)^{\smallsmile} \rrbracket = \llbracket (f^{\smallsmile} \times g^{\smallsmile}) \rrbracket$$
$$\llbracket (f \cup g)^{\smallsmile} \rrbracket = \llbracket f^{\smallsmile} \rrbracket \cup \llbracket g^{\smallsmile} \rrbracket$$
$$\llbracket \mu F^{\smallsmile} \rrbracket = \llbracket \mu(X \to (F\ X^{\smallsmile})^{\smallsmile}) \rrbracket$$

$$\llbracket fst_a^\square \rrbracket\,(a, b)^\square = b$$
$$\llbracket snd_b^\square \rrbracket\,(a, b)^\square = a$$
$$\llbracket del\ a \rrbracket\,(a \ominus x) = (a, x)^-$$
$$\llbracket ins\ a \rrbracket\,(a \oplus x) = (a, x)^+$$

$$dup\ id = \delta$$
$$dup\,(fst; P) = (dup\ P \times id); subl$$
$$dup\,(snd; P) = (id \times dup\ P); assocl$$
$$dup\,(cons^{\smallsmile}; P) = cons^{\smallsmile}; dup\ P; (cons \times id)$$
$$dup\,(node^{\smallsmile}; P) = node^{\smallsmile}; dup\ P; (node \times id)$$

$$sync = (cons \times cons)$$
$$sync^{\smallsmile} = (cons^{\smallsmile} \times cons^{\smallsmile})$$
$$\cup\ \bigcup_{a,b\,\blacksquare\,A}(((del\ a)^{\smallsmile}; snd_a^{-\,\smallsmile} \times (del\ b)^{\smallsmile}; snd_b^{-\,\smallsmile})$$
$$\cup\,((del\ a)^{\smallsmile}; snd_a^{-\,\smallsmile} \times cons^{\smallsmile}; snd_b; snd_b^{-\,\smallsmile})$$
$$\cup\,(cons^{\smallsmile}; snd_a; snd_a^{-\,\smallsmile} \times (del\ b)^{\smallsmile}; snd_b^{-\,\smallsmile}))$$
$$\cup\ \bigcup_{a,b\,\blacksquare\,A}(((ins\ a)^{\smallsmile}; snd_a^{+\,\smallsmile} \times (ins\ b)^{\smallsmile}; snd_b^{+\,\smallsmile})$$
$$\cup\,((ins\ a)^{\smallsmile}; snd_a^{+\,\smallsmile} \times isList; snd_b^{+\,\smallsmile})$$
$$\cup\,(isList; snd_a^{+\,\smallsmile} \times (ins\ b)^{\smallsmile}; snd_b^{+\,\smallsmile}))$$

Fig. 5. Summary of the alternative semantics. The patterns should be matched from the top-left to bottom-left, then top-right to bottom-right

3.3   The Put-Get-Put Property and Galois Connection

A *valid* Inv program is one that does not use $fst_a^\square$ and $snd_b^\square$ apart from in **cons** and **sync**. The domain of get_X, for a valid X, is restricted to tag-free views, so is its range. In fact, $notag?; \llbracket X \rrbracket$ reduces to the injective function defined by the original semantics. Therefore, $get_X; get_X^{\circ} = dom\ get_X$. Furthermore, $notag?; ridtag = notag?$. As a result, for all valid Inv programs X we have the following *get-put* property:

$$get_X; put_X = dom\ get_X \qquad\qquad (1)$$

This is a desired property for our editor: mapping an unedited view back to the source always gives us the same source document.

On the other hand, $put_X ; get_X \subseteq id$ is not true. For example, $(put_\delta ; get_\delta) (*a, b) = (a, a) \neq (*a, b)$. This is one of the main differences between our work and that of [12] and [11]. They both assume the relation X to be bi-total, and that the *put-get* property $put_X ; get_X = id$ holds. It also implies that duplication cannot be allowed in the language.

Instead, we have a weaker property. First of all, for all valid X we have $dom\ get_X \subseteq ran\ put_X$. That is, every valid source input to get_X must be a result of put_X for at least one view, namely, the view the source get mapped to under the original semantics. Pre-composing $putX$ to (1) and use $put_X ; dom\ get_X \subseteq put_X ; ran\ put_X = put_X$, we get the following *put-get-put* property:

$$put_X ; get_X ; put_X \subseteq put_X \qquad (2)$$

When the user edits the view, the editor calls the function $putX$ to calculate an updated source, and then calls get_X to update the view as well. For example, $(*a, b)$ is changed to (a, a) after $put_\delta ; get_\delta$. With the *put-get-put* property we know that another put_X is not necessary, because it is not going to change the view — the result of $put_X ; get_X ; put_X$, if anything, is the same as that of put_X.

It is desirable to have $put_X ; get_X ; put_X = put_X$. However, this is not true, and $dom\ get_X \neq ran\ put_X$. For a counter-example, take $X = (\delta \times id); assocr; (id \times \delta)$. The function get_X takes only pairs with equal components and returns it unchanged. Applying put_X to $(*b, a)$ results in (b, a), which is not in the domain of get_X. Such a result is theoretically not satisfactory, but does not cause a problem for our application. The editor can signal an error to the user, saying that such a modification is not allowed, when the new source is not in the domain of get_X. The domain check is not an extra burden since we have to call get_X anyway.

A Galois connection is a pair of functions $f :: A \rightarrow B$ and $g :: B \rightarrow A$ satisfying

$$f x \trianglelefteq y \equiv x \preceq g y \qquad (3)$$

Galois connected functions satisfy a number of properties, including $f; g; f = f$. For those X that $dom\ get_X = ran\ put_X$ do hold, get_X and put_X satisfy (3), if we take $\preceq$ to be equality on tag-free V iew s and $\trianglelefteq$ to be $(put_X ; get_X)°$. That is, $s \preceq s'$ if and only if the two sources s and s' are exactly the same, while a view v is no bigger than v' under $\trianglelefteq$ if there exists a source s such that $v = get_X$ s and $s = put v'$. For example, (n, n) is no bigger than $(*n, m)$, $(m, *n)$, $(*n, *n)$, and (n, n) itself under $\trianglelefteq$, when the transform is δ. The only glitch here is that $\trianglelefteq$ is not reflexive! In fact it is reflexive only in the range of get_X — the set of tag-free views. However, this is enough for get_X and put_X to satisfy most properties of a Galois connection.

3.4   Implementation Issues

In our experimental implementation, we have a simple interpreter for Inv. One way to incorporate the algebraic rules in the previous section in the implementation is to call a pre-processor before the program is interpreted. Another possibility is to build the rules implicitly in the interpreter. In this section we will talk about how.

The abstract syntax tree of Inv is extended with new constructs **cons** and sync. The "intermediate" functions introduced in the last section, namely ins,del, fst$^\pm$s and snd$^\pm$s, are not actually represented in the abstract syntax. Instead, we extend the value domain View with additional constructs:

$$\mathrm{View} ::= \ldots \mid (\mathrm{View}, {}_+\mathrm{View}) \mid ({}_+\mathrm{View}, \mathrm{View})$$
$$\mid (\mathrm{View}, {}_-\mathrm{View}) \mid ({}_-\mathrm{View}, \mathrm{View})$$
$$\mid \bot \mid \mathrm{NilTo\,View}$$

Conceptually, after we apply $\mathrm{snd}_a^{+\vee}$ to a value b, we get $({}_+a, b)$, while $({}_-a, b)$ is the result of applying $\mathrm{snd}_a^{-\vee}$ to b. The reader can think of them as a note saying "the value should have been b only, but we temporarily pair it with an a, just to allow the computation to carry on." Or one can think of it as a pending application of snd_a^+ or snd_a^-. The $\bot$ symbol denotes an unconstrained value. Finally, NilTo a denotes a function taking only [] and returns a.

To implement the sync operator, we add the following definitions (some cases are omitted):

$$\llbracket \mathrm{sync}^\vee \rrbracket\,(a\!:\!x, b\!:\!y) = ((a, x), (b, y)) \qquad \llbracket \mathrm{sync}^\vee \rrbracket\,(a \oplus x, y) = (({}_+a, x), ({}_+\bot, y))$$
$$\llbracket \mathrm{sync}^\vee \rrbracket\,(a \ominus x, b\!:\!y) = (({}_-a, x), ({}_-b, y)) \qquad \llbracket \mathrm{sync}^\vee \rrbracket\,(x, b \oplus y) = (({}_+\bot, x), ({}_+b, y))$$
$$\llbracket \mathrm{sync}^\vee \rrbracket\,(a\!:\!x, b \ominus y) = (({}_-a, x), ({}_-b, y))$$

The first clause is simply what $(\mathrm{cons} \times \mathrm{cons})^\circ$ would do. The second clause shows that when there is a deletion in the first list, we throw away an element in the second list as well, while keeping note of the fact by the $(-, -)$ tag. It corresponds to the $(\mathrm{del}a^\circ; \mathrm{snd}_a^{-\circ} \times \mathrm{cons}^\circ; \mathrm{snd}_b^-; \mathrm{snd}_b^{-\circ})$ branch of $(\mathrm{cons} \times \mathrm{cons})^\circ$. The fourth branch, on the other hand, corresponds to $((\mathrm{ins}\,a)^\circ; \mathrm{snd}_a^{+\circ} \times \mathrm{isList}; \mathrm{snd}_b^{+\circ})$. The newly introduced, unconstrained value b is represented by $\bot$.

Now we build in some extra rules for cons and cons$^\vee$:

$$\llbracket \mathrm{cons} \rrbracket\,({}_-a, x) = a \ominus x \qquad\qquad \llbracket \mathrm{cons}^\vee \rrbracket\,(a \ominus x) = ({}_-a, x)$$
$$\llbracket \mathrm{cons} \rrbracket\,({}_+a, x) = a \oplus x \qquad\qquad \llbracket \mathrm{cons}^\vee \rrbracket\,(a \oplus x) = ({}_+a, x)$$

They correspond to the fact that $\mathrm{snd}^\vee; \mathbf{cons} = \mathrm{del}$ and $\mathrm{snd}_a^\vee; \mathbf{cons} = \mathrm{ins}\,a$. Also, some additional rules for assocr:

$$\llbracket \mathrm{assocr} \rrbracket\,((a, {}_+b), c) = (a, ({}_+b, c)) \qquad\qquad \llbracket \mathrm{assocr} \rrbracket\,({}_+(a, b), c) = ({}_+a, ({}_+b, c))$$
$$\llbracket \mathrm{assocr} \rrbracket\,(({}_+a, b), c) = ({}_+a, (b, c))$$

The three clauses correspond to the rules for assocl in the left column of Figure 4. Finally we need some rules for dupnil and its inverse eqnil:

$$\llbracket (\mathrm{eqnil}) \rrbracket\,({}_-a, []) = \mathrm{NilTo\,a} \qquad\qquad \llbracket (\mathrm{dupnil}) \rrbracket\,(\mathrm{NilTo\,a}) = ({}_-a, [])$$

which corresponds to the rule $\mathrm{snd}_a^{\square\vee}; \mathrm{eqnil} = (\lambda\,[] \to a)$ in Figure 4.

4   More Examples

In this section we will show more transforms defined in Inv that do satisfy dom $\mathrm{get}_X = \mathrm{ran}\,\mathrm{put}_X$ and how they react to user editing.

4.1   Snoc and List Reversal

The function $snoc :: (a, \text{List}\,a) \to \text{List}\,a$, appending an element to the end of a list, can be defined recursively as:

$$snoc = \mu(X : \textbf{eq}\,nil;\,dup\,nil;\,\textbf{cons} \cup$$
$$(id \times \textbf{cons}°);\,subr;\,(id \times X\,);\,\textbf{cons})$$

For example $[\![snoc]\!]\,(4, [1, 2, 3]) = [1, 2, 3, 4]$. Conversely, $snoc^{\vee}$ extracts the last element of a list. But what is the result of extracting the last element of a list whose last element was just removed? We expand the base case:

$$snoc^{\vee}$$
$$\sqsupseteq \quad \{\text{fixed-point}\}$$
$$\textbf{cons}^{\vee};\,\textbf{eq}\,nil;\,dup\,nil$$
$$\sqsupseteq \quad \{\text{specialising } \textbf{cons} \sqsupseteq snd_a^-;\,del\,a\}$$
$$(del\,a)^{\vee};\,snd_a^{-\,\vee};\,\textbf{ea}\,nil;\,dup\,nil$$
$$= \quad \{\text{since } snd_a^{-\,\vee};\,\textbf{eq}\,nil = (\lambda[\,] \to a)\}$$
$$(del\,a)^{\vee};\,(\lambda[\,] \to a);\,dup\,nil$$
$$= \quad \{\text{since } snd_a^{-\,\vee};\,\textbf{eq}\,nil = (\lambda[\,] \to a) \Rightarrow snd_a^{-\,\vee} = (\lambda[\,] \to a);\,dup\,nil\}$$
$$(del\,a)^{\vee};\,snd_a^{-\,\vee}$$

That is, for example, $eval\,snoc^{\vee}\,(4 \ominus [\,]) = (\text{-}4, [\,])$. Inductively, we have $eval$ $snoc^{\vee}\,(1 : 2 : 3 : 4 \ominus [\,]) = (\text{-}4, 1 : 2 : 3 : [\,])$, which is reasonable enough: by extracting the last element of a list whose last element, 4, is missing, we get a pair whose first element should not have been there.

The ubiquitous fold function on lists can be defined by

$$fold\,f\,g = \mu(X : nil^{\vee};\,g \cup \textbf{cons}^{\vee};\,(id \times X\,);\,f)$$

The function $reverse$, reverting a list, can be defined in terms of fold as $reverse = fold\,snoc\,nil$. Unfolding its definition, we can perform the following refinement:

$$reverse^{\vee}$$
$$\sqsupseteq \quad \{\text{unfolding the definitions}\}$$
$$snoc^{\vee};\,(id \times reverse^{\vee});\,\textbf{cons}$$
$$\sqsupseteq \quad \{\text{by the reasoning above, } snoc^{\vee} \sqsupseteq (del\,a)^{\vee};\,snd_a^{-\,\vee}\}$$
$$(del\,a)^{\vee};\,snd_a^{-\,\vee};\,(id \times reverse^{\vee});\,\textbf{cons}$$
$$= \quad \{\text{since } (f \times g);\,snd_{f\,a}^- = snd_a^-;\,g \text{ for total } f\}$$
$$(del\,a)^{\vee};\,reverse^{\vee};\,snd_a^{-\,\vee};\,\textbf{cons}$$
$$\sqsupseteq \quad \{\text{since } \textbf{cons} \sqsupseteq snd_a^-;\,del\,a \text{ and } snd_a^{-\,\vee};\,snd_a^- = id\}$$
$$(del\,a)^{\vee};\,reverse^{\vee};\,del\,a$$

which shows that $reverse^{\vee}$ regenerates the $\ominus$ tags (and, similiarly, $\oplus$ tags) upon receipt of the "partial" pairs returned by $snoc$. For example, we have $eval\,reverse\,(1 : 2 : 3 \ominus 4 : [\,]) = 4 : 3 \ominus 2 : 1 : [\,]$ which is exactly what we want. A lesson is that to deal with lists, we have to first learn to deal with pairs.

4.2   Merging and Filtering

Recall the function merge defined in Section 2.3, merging two sorted lists into one, while marking the elements with labels remembering where they were from:

$$\mathrm{merge}\,([1,4,7],[2,5,6]) = [\mathsf{L}\,1, \mathsf{R}\,2, \mathsf{L}\,4, \mathsf{R}\,5, \mathsf{R}\,6, \mathsf{L}\,7]$$

Filtering is an often needed feature. For example, in a list of (author, article) pairs we may want to extract the articles by a chosen author. The Haskell Prelude function filter :: $(\mathsf{a} \to \mathsf{Bool}) \to \mathsf{List}\,\mathsf{a} \to \mathsf{List}\,\mathsf{a}$, returning only the elements in the list satisfying a given predicate, however, is not injective because it throws away some items. A common scenario of filtering is when we have a list of sorted items to filter. For example, the articles in the database may be sorted by the date of creation, and splitting the list retains the order. If we simplify the situation a bit further, it is exactly the converse of what merge does, if we think of L and R as true and false!

To make merge work with editing tags, we simply replace every occurrence of cons with **cons**, including the cons in (cons × cons). This time the latter shall not be replaced by sync because we certainly do not want to delete or invent elements in one list when the user edits the other! This merge does behave as what we would expect. For example, when an element is added to the split list:

$$\mathrm{merge}\,(1:3 \oplus 4:7:[\,],[2,5,6]) = \mathsf{L}\,1:\mathsf{R}\,2:\mathsf{L}\,3 \oplus [\mathsf{L}\,4, \mathsf{R}\,5, \mathsf{R}\,6, \mathsf{L}\,7]$$

the new element is inserted back to the original list as well.

5   Conclusion

Bi-directional updating, though an old problem[5, 7, 10, 14, 1], has recently attracted much interests, each took a slightly different approach according to their target application. We have developed a formalisation of bi-directional updating which is able to deal with duplication and structural changes like insertion and deletion. From a specification X , written as an injective function, we induce two functions get_X and put_X that satisfy the important *get-put* and *put-get-put* properties. To find out how put_X reacts to user editing, one can make use of algebraic reasoning, which also provides a hint how the formalisation can be implemented in an interpreter.

Our formalisation deals with duplication and structural changes at the cost of introducing editing tags, which is okay for our application — to integrate it to our structural editor in [15]. The complementary approach taken by [11], on the other hand, chooses not to use any information how the new view was constructed. Upon encountering inconsistency, the system generates several possible ways to resolve the inconsistency for the user to choose from. It would be interesting to see whether there is a general framework covering both approaches.

Another feature of our work is the use of an injective language, and various program derivation and inversion techniques. The injective language Inv has been introduced in [13], where it is also described how to automatically derive an injective variant for every non-injective program. So far we have a primitive implementation. For an efficient implementation, however, the techniques described in [9] based on parsing may be of help.

The history of point-free functional languages many be traced to Backus's FP [4], although our style in this paper is more influenced by [6]. A number of well-established libraries adopt a point-free style, such as the XML processing library HaXml [16]. Furthermore, there is a tedious, uninteresting way of converting a certain class of pointwise functional programs into Inv. The class of programs is essentially the same as the source language in [9], that is, first-order functional programs with linear patterns in case expressions, where every variable is used at least once.

Acknowledgements

The idea of using algebraic rules and program transformation to guide the processing of editing tags was proposed by Lambert Meertens during the first author's visit to Kestrel Institute, CA. The authors would like to thank Johan Jeuring for useful improvements to an earlier draft of this paper, and the members of the Programmable Structured Document in Information Processing Lab, Tokyo University for valuable discussions. This research is partly supported by the e-Society Infrastructure Project of the Ministry of Education, Culture, Sports, Science and Technology, Japan.

References

1. S. Abiteboul. On views and XML. In *Proceedings of the 18th ACM SIGPLAN-SIGACT-SIGART Symposium on Principles of Database Systems*, pages 1–9. ACM Press, 1999.
2. S. M. Abramov and R. Glück. The universal resolving algorithm and its correctness: inverse computation in a functional language. *Science of Computer Programming*, 43:193–299, May-June 2002.
3. Altova Co. Xmlspy. `http://www.xmlspy.com/products_ide.html`.
4. J. Backus. Can programming be liberated from the von Neumann style? a functional style and its algebra of programs. *Communications of the ACM*, 21(8):613–641, August 1978.
5. F. Bancilhon and N. Spyratos. Update semantics of relational views. *ACM Transactions on Database Systems*, 6(4):557–575, December 1981.
6. R. S. Bird and O. de Moor. *Algebra of Programming*. International Series in Computer Science. Prentice Hall, 1997.
7. U. Dayal and P. A. Bernstein. On the correct translation of update operations on relational views. *ACM Transactions on Database Systems*, 7(3):381–416, September 1982.
8. R. Glück and M. Kawabe. A program inverter for a functional language with equality and constructors. In A. Ohori, editor, *Programming Languages and Systems. Proceedings*, number 2895 in Lecture Notes in Computer Science, pages 246–264. Springer-Verlag, 2003.

9. R. Glück and M. Kawabe. Derivation of deterministic inverse programs based on LR parsing (extended abstract). In Y. Kameyama and P. J. Stuckey, editors, *Proceedings of Functional and Logic Programming*, number 2998 in Lecture Notes in Computer Science, pages 291–306, Nara, Japan, 2004. Springer-Verlag.

10. G. Gottlob, P. Paolini, and R. Zicari. Properties and update semantics of consistent views. *ACM Transactions on Database Systems*, 13(4):486–524, December 1988.

11. M. B. Greenwald, J. T. Moore, B. C. Pierce, and A. Schmitt. A language for bi-directional tree transformations. Technical Report, MS-CIS-03-08, University of Pennsylvania, August 2003.

12. L. Meertens. Designing constraint maintainers for user interaction. `ftp://ftp.kestrel.edu/ pub/papers/meertens/dcm.ps`, 1998.

13. S.-C. Mu, Z. Hu, and M. Takeichi. An injective language for reversible computation. In *Seventh International Conference on Mathematics of Program Construction*. Springer-Verlag, July 2004.

14. A. Ohori and K. Tajima. A polymorphic calculus for views and object sharing. In *Proceedings of the 13th ACM SIGACT-SIGMOD-SIGART Symposium on Principles of Database Systems*, pages 255–266. ACM Press, 1994.

15. M. Takeichi, Z. Hu, K. Kakehi, Y. Hayashi, S.-C. Mu, and K. Nakano. TreeCalc:towards programmable structured documents. In *The 20th Conference of Japan Society for Software Science and Technology*, September 2003.

16. M. Wallace and C. Runciman. Haskell and XML: generic combinators or type-based translation? . In *Proceedings of the 1999 ACM SIGPLAN International Conference on Functional Programming*, pages 148–159. ACM Press, September 1999.

Network Fusion[*]

Pascal Fradet[1] and Stéphane Hong Tuan Ha[2]

[1] INRIA Rhône-Alpes,
655, av. de l'Europe, 38330 Montbonnot, France
Pascal.Fradet@inria.fr
[2] IRISA/INRIA Rennes,
Campus de Beaulieu, 35042 Rennes, France
Stephane.Hong_Tuan_Ha@irisa.fr

Abstract. Modular programming enjoys many well-known advantages but the composition of modular units may also lead to inefficient programs. In this paper, we propose an invasive composition method which strives to reconcile modularity and efficiency. Our technique, network fusion, automatically merges networks of interacting components into equivalent sequential programs. We provide the user with an expressive language to specify scheduling constraints which can be taken into account during network fusion. Fusion allows to replace internal communications by assignments and alleviates most time overhead. We present our approach in a generic and unified framework based on labeled transition systems, static analysis and transformation techniques.

1 Introduction

Modular programming enjoys many well-known advantages: readability, maintainability, separate development and compilation. However, the composition of modular units (components) gives rise to efficiency issues. Sequential composition poses space problems: the producer delivers its complete output before the consumer starts. Parallel composition relies on threads, synchronization and context switches which introduce time overhead.

In this paper, we propose an invasive composition method, network fusion, which strives to reconcile modularity and efficiency. Our technique automatically merges networks of interacting components into equivalent sequential programs. Our approach takes two source inputs: a network of components and user-defined scheduling constraints. Networks are formalized as Kahn Process Networks (KPNs) [7] a simple formal model expressive enough to specify component programming and assembly. Scheduling constraints allow the user to choose the scheduling strategy by specifying a set of desired executions. The operational semantics of KPNs and scheduling constraints are both formalized as guarded labeled transition systems (LTS).

---

[*] This work has been supported in part by the ACI DISPO and Région Bretagne

Network fusion is an automatic process which takes a KPN and scheduling constraints and yields a sequential program respecting the constraints. Note that constraints may introduce artificial deadlocks, in which case the user will be warned. The resulting program must be functionally equivalent to the KPN modulo the possible deadlocks introduced by constraints. Fusion alleviates most time overhead by allowing the suppression of context switches, the replacement of internal communications by assignments to local variables and optimizations of the resulting sequential code using standard compiling techniques. Network fusion can be seen as a generalization of filter fusion [12] to general networks using ideas from aspect-oriented programming [8] (scheduling constraints can be seen as an aspect and their enforcement as weaving).

The four main steps of the fusion process are represented in Figure 1.

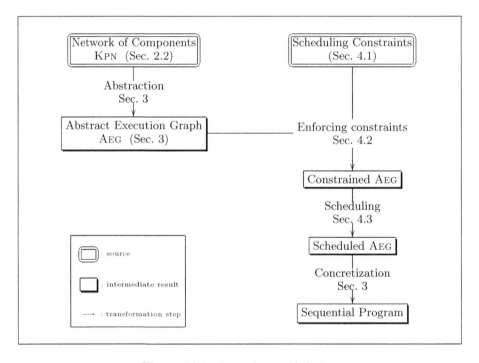

Fig. 1. Main steps of network fusion

– The first step is the abstraction of the network into a finite model called an Abstract Execution Graph (AEG). An AEG over-approximates the set of possible executions traces. We do not present this step in details since it relies on very standard analysis techniques (e.g., abstract interpretation) and many different abstractions are possible depending on the desired level of precision. Instead, we focus on the properties that an AEG must satisfy.
– The second step consists in enforcing constraints. This is expressed as a synchronized product between guarded LTS (the AEG and the constraints).

In general, this step does not sequentialize completely the execution and leaves scheduling choices.

- The third step completes the scheduling of the constrained AEG. Several strategies can be used as long as they are fair. Again, these strategies can be expressed as guarded LTS and scheduling as a synchronized product.
- The fourth step, concretization, maps the scheduled (serialized) AEG to a single sequential program. Further transformations (e.g., standard optimizations) can then be carried out on the resulting program.

We have chosen to present fusion in an intuitive and mostly informal way. In particular, we do not provide any correctness proofs. They would require a complete description of the operational semantics of KPN too long to fit space limits. This paper is organized as follows. Section 2 presents the syntax and semantics of KPNs. Section 3 describes AEGs and defines the abstraction and concretization steps which both relate AEG to concrete models (programs and KPNs). Section 4 presents the language of constraints and the two main transformation steps of fusion: constraints enforcement and scheduling. We propose three extensions of the basic technique in Section 5 and, finally, we review related work and conclude in Section 6.

2   Networks

We start by providing the syntax of components and networks. We just outline their semantics and provide some intuition using an example. A complete structural operational semantics for KPNs can be found in [6].

2.1   Basic Components

Components are made of commands c of the form:

$$l_1 : g \mid a \rightsquigarrow l_2$$

where l_1 and l_2 denote labels, g a guard and a an action. An action is either a read operation on an input channel $f?x$, a write operation on an output channel $f!x$, or an internal action i (left unspecified). A component (or process) p is a set of commands $\{c_1, \ldots, c_n\}$. If the current program point of a component p is l_1, if $l_1 : g \mid a \rightsquigarrow l_2$ is a command of p and the guard g is true, then the action a can be executed and the program point becomes l_2.

The components we consider in this paper represent valid, sequential and deterministic programs. They have the following restrictions:

- A component has a unique entry point denoted by the label l_0.
- All the labels used in p are defined in the lhs of commands.
- Two commands with the same label have mutually exclusive guards.

The program P in Figure 2 sends the set $\mathbb{N}$ in increasing order on channel f. Program C assigns a with the value read on channel f if $a < b$ or assigns b with

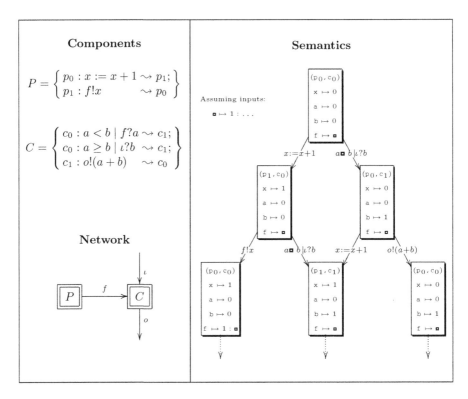

Fig. 2. A Simple Kpn and its trace semantics

the value read on the channel ι otherwise. Then, it sends $a + b$ on the channel o and loops. Note that guards are omitted when they are true.

The semantics of a component p is expressed as a LTS $(\Sigma_p, (l_0, s_0), \mathcal{E}_p, \longrightarrow_p)$ where:

- Σ_p is an (infinite) set of states (l, s) where l a label and s a store mapping variables to their values.
- (l_0, s_0) is the initial state made of the initial label l_0 and store s_0. We assume that the initial label is always indexed by 0 and that the initial store initializes integer variables by the value 0,
- $\mathcal{E}_p$ is the set of commands of p,
- $\longrightarrow_p$ is the transition relation (actually, a function) on states labeled with the current command.

The initial labels of programs P and C (Figure 2) are p_0 and c_0 respectively and the variables x, a and b are initialized to 0. In the remaining, we use $c|_g$ and $c|_a$ to denote the guard and the action of the command c respectively. To simplify the presentation, we consider only non-terminating programs. Termination could always be represented by a final looping command such as $l_{end} : skip \rightsquigarrow l_{end}$.

2.2   Networks of Components

A KPN k is made of a set of processes $\{p_1, \ldots, p_n\}$ executed concurrently. Networks are build by connecting output channels to input channels of components. Such channels are called internal channels whereas the remaining (unconnected) channels are the input and output channels of the network. The communication on internal channels is asynchronous (non blocking writes, blocking reads) and is modeled using unbounded fifos. In order to guarantee a deterministic behavior, KPNs require the following conditions [7]:

- An internal channel is written by and read from exactly one process.
- An input channel is read from exactly one component (and written by none).
- An output channel is written by exactly one component (and read from none).
- A component cannot test the absence of values on channels.

In order to simplify technical developments, we assume that networks have a single input and output channels denoted by ι and o respectively and that the input channel never remains empty.

The global execution state of a KPN is called a configuration. It is made of the local state of each component and the internal channel states i.e., finite sequences of values $v_1 : \ldots : v_n : \epsilon$.

The operational semantics of KPN is expressed as a LTS $(\Sigma_k, \alpha_0, \mathcal{E}_k, \longrightarrow_k)$ where:

- Σ_k is a (infinite) set of configurations,
- the initial configuration α_0 is such that each component is in its initial state and each internal channel is empty,
- $\mathcal{E}_k$ is the union of the sets of commands of components; these sets are supposed disjoint,
- the transition relation $\longrightarrow_k$ is defined as performing (non deterministically) any enabled command of any process. A command is enabled when the current program point is its lhs label, its guard is true in the current configuration/state and it is not a blocking read (i.e., a read on an empty channel).

The transition relation gives rise to an infinite graph representing all the possible execution traces. A small part of the transition relation $\longrightarrow_p$ for our example is depicted in Figure 2. Here, no global deadlock is possible and all traces are infinite.

An infinite execution trace is said to be fair if any enabled action at any point in the trace is eventually executed. The denotational semantics of a KPN is given by the function from the input values (the input channel) to the output values (the output channel) generated by fair executions. We will write $Traces(k)$ and $IO(k)$ to denote the set of traces and the denotational semantics of the KPN k respectively. KPNs of deterministic components are deterministic [7]. Also, all fair executions with the same input yield the same output [6]. An important corollary for us is that KPNs are serializable: they can always be implemented sequentially.

3   Abstract Execution Graphs

Network fusion necessitates to find statically a safe and sequential scheduling. This step relies upon an abstract execution graph (AEG), a finite model upper-approximating all the possible executions of the KPN. We present in this section the key properties than an AEG should satisfy and present an example.

An AEG $k^\sharp$ is a finite LTS $(\Sigma_{k^\sharp}, \alpha_0^\sharp, \mathcal{E}_{k^\sharp}, \longrightarrow_{k^\sharp})$ with:

- $\Sigma_{k^\sharp}$ a finite set of abstract configurations,
- $\alpha_0^\sharp$ is the initial abstract configuration,
- $\mathcal{E}_{k^\sharp}$ a (finite) set of commands,
- $\longrightarrow_{k^\sharp}$ a labeled transition relation.

The idea behind abstraction is to summarize in an abstract configuration a (potentially infinite) set of concrete configurations [10]. This set is given by the function $\text{conc} : \Sigma_{k^\sharp} \to \mathcal{P}(\Sigma_k)$ defined as:

$$\text{conc}(\alpha^\sharp) = \{\alpha \mid \alpha \approx \alpha^\sharp\}$$

where $\approx$ is a safety relation relating k and $k^\sharp$ (and we write $k \approx k^\sharp$).

There can be many possible abstractions according to their size and accuracy. Network fusion is generic w.r.t. abstraction as long as the AEG respect two key properties: safety and faithfulness. To be safe, the initial abstract configuration of an AEG must safely approximate the initial concrete configuration. Furthermore, if a configuration α_1 is safely approximated by $\alpha_1^\sharp$ and the network evolves in the configuration α_2, then there exists a transition from $\alpha_1^\sharp$ to $\alpha_2^\sharp$ in the AEG such that α_2 is safely approximated by $\alpha_2^\sharp$. These two points ensure that any execution trace of the KPN is safely simulated by one in the AEG. Formally:

Definition 1 (Safety). Let $k \approx k^\sharp$, then $k^\sharp$ is a safe approximation of k iff

$$\alpha_0 \approx \alpha_0^\sharp$$

$$\alpha_1 \approx \alpha_1^\sharp \wedge \alpha_1 \xrightarrow{c}_k \alpha_2 \Rightarrow \exists \alpha_2^\sharp. \; \alpha_2 \approx \alpha_2^\sharp \wedge \alpha_1^\sharp \xrightarrow{c}_{k^\sharp} \alpha_2^\sharp$$

A key property of safe abstractions is that they preserve fairness. Of course, since they are upper approximations they include false paths (abstract traces whose concretization is empty). However, for abstract traces representing feasible concrete traces, fair abstract traces represent fair concrete traces. Safety also implies that all fair concrete traces are represented by fair abstract traces.

An AEG is said to be faithful if each abstract transition corresponds to a concrete transition modulo the non-satisfiability of guards or a blocking read. In other words, faithfulness confines approximations to values. A false path can only be an abstract trace with a transition whose concrete image would be a transition with a false guard or a blocking read. Formally:

Definition 2 (Faithfulness). Let $k \approx k^\sharp$, then $k^\sharp$ is a faithful approximation of k iff

$$\alpha_1^\sharp \xrightarrow{c}_{k^\sharp} \alpha_2^\sharp \; \wedge \; \alpha_1 \approx \alpha_1^\sharp \Rightarrow \exists \alpha_2. \alpha_2 \approx \alpha_2^\sharp \; \wedge \; \alpha_1 \xrightarrow{c}_k \alpha_2$$
$$\vee \; \neg \mathcal{G}[\![c|_g]\!]\alpha_1$$
$$\vee \; (c|_a = f?x \; \wedge \; \alpha_1[f \mapsto \epsilon])$$

Faithfulness rules out, for instance, the (highly imprecise but safe) abstraction made of a unique abstract state representing all concrete states. In practice, the same abstract state cannot represent different program points (label configurations).

In order to provide some intuition we give here a crude but straightforward abstraction:

— Each process state is abstracted into the program point it is associated to. So, variables are not taken into account and process stores are completely abstracted away,
— Each internal channel state is represented by an interval approximating the length of its file.

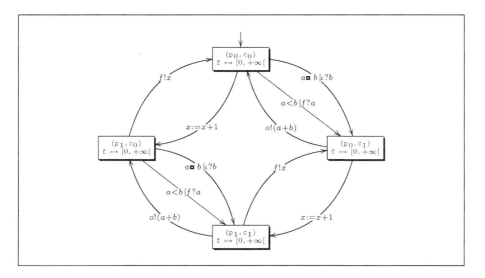

Fig. 3. Example of an AEG

It is the control flow graph of the KPN where each node holds a collection of intervals approximating the lengths of internal channels at the configuration of program points the node represents. The AEG for our running example is given in Figure 3. In this particular example, the state of f is always approximated by the interval $[0, +\infty[$ (the most imprecise information). More precise AEGs could be designed (see Section 5.2).

An AEG bears enough information to be translated back into a program. Commands (guards and actions) label edges and nodes represent labels. The concretization of finite LTS $k^\sharp = (\Sigma_{k^\bullet}, \alpha_0^\sharp, \mathcal{E}_{k^\bullet}, \longrightarrow_{k^\bullet})$ into a program is formalized by the following straightforward translation:

$$Concretization(k^\sharp) = \{l_{\alpha_1^\bullet} : c \rightsquigarrow l_{\alpha_2^\bullet} \mid \alpha_1^\sharp \xrightarrow{c}_{k^\bullet} \alpha_2^\sharp\}$$

An important property of safe and faithful abstractions is that their concretization has the same semantics as the network they approximate.

Property 1. If $k^\sharp$ is a safe and faithful approximation of k then $\mathrm{Traces}(k) = \mathrm{Traces}(Concretization(k^\sharp))$

4   Fusion

The user can specify scheduling constraints defining a subset of execution traces. Constraints impose implementation choices; they serve to guide and to optimize the fusion process. Constraints respect the black box nature of components. They are expressed w.r.t. IO operations, liveness properties or sizes of files. When constraints completely sequentialize the execution (no choice remains), they specify a scheduler. In general, however, constraints are incomplete and leave implementation choices.

4.1   Scheduling Constraints

We specify constraints by finite state LTS labeled with guarded actions. Of course, a more user-friendly language for declaring constraints should be studied but this is not the purpose of this article. The formalism used in Sections 2 and 3 is also well-suited to expressing constraints. We enrich the language of guards with two additional constructs dedicated to the expression of scheduling strategies:

$$g_c ::= \overline{f} \ominus k \mid \mathcal{B}_p \mid g \quad \text{where } \ominus \text{ is any comparison operator}$$

The size of a channel can be compared against an integer. For instance, $\overline{f} < 5$ is true if the file f has less than 5 elements. The guard $\mathcal{B}_p$ is true if the process p is blocked (by a read on an empty channel or by other scheduling constraints).

Constraints are more easily specified using sets of actions. We use the following notations:

$$\mathcal{A} ::= \star \mid [f]? \mid [f]! \mid \neg\mathcal{A} \mid \mathcal{A}_1 \cap \mathcal{A}_2 \mid \mathcal{A}_p$$

where

- $\star$ represents any action of the network,
- ? (resp. !) represents any read (resp. write) and f? (resp. f!) any read (resp. write) on file f,
- $\neg\mathcal{A}$ is the complementary set of $\mathcal{A}$,
- $\mathcal{A}_1 \cap \mathcal{A}_2$ is the intersection of the sets $\mathcal{A}_1$ and $\mathcal{A}_2$,
- $\mathcal{A}_p$ represents the projection of the set of actions $\mathcal{A}$ onto the commands of the component p.

For instance, $(\neg?)_p$ represents all non-read actions of component p. Using sets is just more convenient; constraints can be automatically translated into a standard LTS labeled by standard commands afterward.

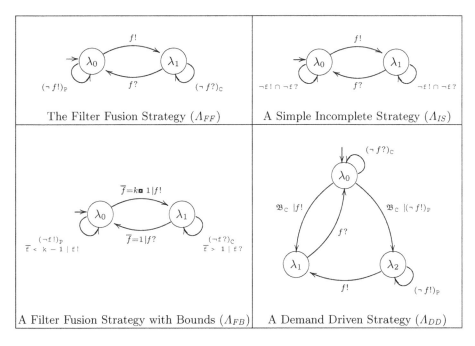

Fig. 4. Examples of Scheduling Constraints

Figure 4 gathers a few examples of constraints for a network with (at least) two components P (writing a file f) and C (reading the file f).

- The constraint Λ_{FF} summarizes in a small automaton the strategy used by Filter Fusion [12]. The producer P starts until it writes on f? The control is passed to the consumer C until it reads f and so on. This strategy bounds the size of the fifo f to be at most 1 and therefore it may introduce artificial deadlocks from some networks. Λ_{FF} sequentializes completely the execution of P and C (no scheduling choice remains).
- The constraint Λ_{IS} is similar to Λ_{FF} except that both P and C can be executed between writes and reads on f. Λ_{IS} leaves some scheduling choices.
- The constraint Λ_{FB} is a generalization of Λ_{FF} to a file f with k places (i.e., P writes k times before the control is passed to C). This is the formalization of the extension of filter fusion proposed in [3]
- A demand driven strategy is specified by Λ_{DD}. The consumer C is executed until it blocks i.e., is about to read the empty channel f. Then, P is executed until it produces a value in f. The control is passed to C which immediately reads f and continues.

These constraints can be applied to any network as long as it has two components P and C connected at least with a channel f. Of course, constraints can be specified for any number of components and channels.

4.2   Enforcing Constraints

Enforcing a constraint $\Lambda = (\Sigma_\lambda, \lambda_0, \mathcal{E}_\lambda, \longrightarrow_\lambda)$ to an Abstract Execution Graph $k^\sharp = (\Sigma_{k^\square}, \alpha_0^\sharp, \mathcal{E}_{k^\square}, \longrightarrow_{k^\square})$ can be expressed as a parallel composition $(k^\sharp \parallel \Lambda)$. This operation can be defined formally as follows. We assume that all shorthands (like $(\neg ?)_p$) used in constraints are replaced by the actions of the AEG they represent.

$$k^\sharp \parallel \Lambda = (\Sigma_{k^\square} \times \Sigma_\lambda, (\alpha_0^\sharp, \lambda_0), \mathcal{E}_{k^\square}, \longrightarrow_{k\lambda})$$

with

$$\frac{\alpha^\sharp \xrightarrow{g|a}_{k^\square} \alpha^{\sharp\prime} \quad \lambda \xrightarrow{g'|a} \lambda'}{(\alpha^\sharp, \lambda) \xrightarrow{g \wedge g'|a}_{k\lambda} (\alpha^{\sharp\prime}, \lambda')} \qquad \frac{\alpha^\sharp \xrightarrow{c}_{k^\square} \alpha^{\sharp\prime} \quad a \in \Sigma_{k^\square} \setminus \Sigma_\lambda}{(\alpha^\sharp, \lambda) \xrightarrow{c}_{k\lambda} (\alpha^{\sharp\prime}, \lambda)}$$

If an action a is taken into account by the constraints, the execution can proceed only if both LTS can execute a (i.e., they can both execute commands made of a and a true guard). The actions not taken into account by the constraints can be executed independently whenever possible. Constraints do not introduce new actions ($\mathcal{E}_\lambda \subseteq \mathcal{E}_k$). To simplify the presentation, we assumed in the above inference rules that the guards did not use the condition $\mathfrak{B}_p$. We now present the rule corresponding to this condition in isolation.

The $\mathfrak{B}_p$ construct serves to pass the control to another component when one is blocked. The condition $\mathfrak{B}_p$ is easily defined w.r.t. KPNs: p is blocked in configuration α if there is no outgoing transition labeled with a command of p. However, AEGs are approximations with false paths; a component p can be blocked even if the corresponding abstract state has outgoing transitions labeled with commands of p. Actually, p is blocked in an abstract state if any outgoing p transition has either a false guard or is a read on an empty channel (i.e., is not enabled). Formally, let $c_1, \ldots, c_n$ all the commands of p such that $\alpha^\sharp \xrightarrow{c_i}_{k^\square} \alpha_i^\sharp$

and $g_i = \begin{cases} \neg(c_i|_g) \vee \overline{f} = 0 \text{ if } c_i|_a = f?x \\ \neg(c_i|_g) \qquad\qquad \text{otherwise} \end{cases}$

then the necessary and sufficient condition for p to be blocked in $\alpha^\sharp$ is

$$b_p(\alpha^\sharp) = \bigwedge_{i=1,\ldots,n} g_i$$

The product of an AEG with a transition guarded by $\mathfrak{B}_p$ is defined as follows:

$$\frac{\alpha^\sharp \xrightarrow{g|a}_{k^\square} \alpha^{\sharp\prime} \quad \lambda \xrightarrow{\mathfrak{B}_p|a}_\lambda \lambda'}{(\alpha^\sharp, \lambda) \xrightarrow{g \wedge b_p(\alpha^\square)|a}_{k\lambda} (\alpha^{\sharp\prime}, \lambda')}$$

Figure 5 represents the product of the AEG of Figure 3 with Λ_{FF}. The component P is executed until it produces a value on f then C is executed until it

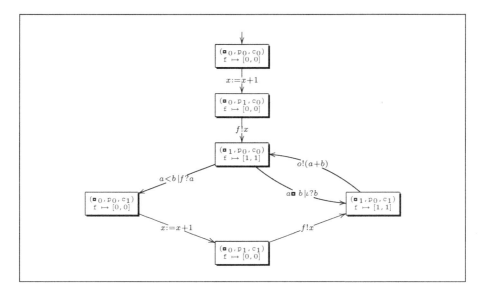

Fig. 5. Fusion with Λ_{FF}

reads a value on f. Note that if $a \geq b$ remains always true then P will never be executed. So, the execution is not fair but it is nevertheless correct and yields the same output as the network (P is never executed only when its production is not needed). The strategy does not use guards, so no new test appears in the constrained AEG. The result is completely sequentialized.

After the constrained AEG is produced, the size of files is reestimated using standard static analysis techniques. We have indicated in Figure 5 the new approximations for $\overline{f}$. They show that the AEG is now bounded (the size of f is at most 1).

It is easy to check that the AEG can be translated by Concretization (see Section. 3) into a sequential program. As already mentioned, one goal of fusion is to suppress internal communications. For unbounded AEG, internal reads and writes are replaced by assignments to lists or fifos. Here, the channel f can be implemented by a single variable v_f and writes $f!x$ and reads $f?a$ by assignments $v_f := x$ and $x := v_f$. These assignments can then be suppressed using standard optimization techniques [1]. Finally, after a renaming of labels, we get:

$$
PC = \left\{
\begin{array}{ll}
pc_0 : x := x + 1 & \leadsto pc_1; \\
pc_1 : a < b \mid a := x & \leadsto pc_2; \\
pc_1 : a \geq b \mid \iota?b & \leadsto pc_3; \\
pc_2 : x := x + 1 & \leadsto pc_3; \\
pc_3 : o!a + b & \leadsto pc_1;
\end{array}
\right\}
$$

We have presented the parallel composition as a fairly standard automata product. Depending on the size of the LTS, this may cause an unacceptable state explosion. We present a solution to this problem in Section 5.3.

4.3   Scheduling

In general, constraints enforcement leaves implementation choices which must be taken to produce a sequential program. The fusion process makes these choices automatically by scheduling the execution of components. A valid schedule must be fair (all enabled components must be eventually executed) and sequential (the scheduled execution must correspond to a sequential program).

We choose here a simple and fair policy: round-robin scheduling. Components are ordered in a circular queue and the scheduler activates them in turn. Either the current active component is blocked (by a read or a user defined constraint) either one of its command is executed. In both cases, the control is passed to the next component. Figure 6 formalizes round-robin for networks with two components P and C as a guarded LTS. It would be easy to generalize such a round-robin LTS for any network with a fixed number of processes.

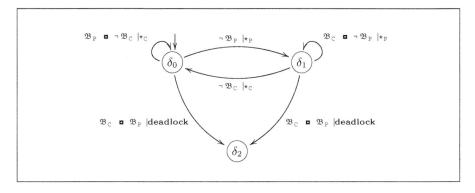

Fig. 6. Round-Robin Scheduling

The schedule is fair and ensures a complete serialization of the execution. It starts by enforcing the execution of one instruction of P, then one instruction of C and so on. If one of the two processes is blocked at its turn, then an instruction of the other process is executed instead. When both processes are blocked then it is a global deadlock denoted by the special instruction **deadlock**.

Constrained AEGs are composed in parallel with the automaton of Figure 6 to obtain sequential programs. The composition is the same as before except that the **deadlock** action does not belong to the set of actions of components. The product will therefore introduce a new **deadlock** transition along with a new state in the AEG. This new transition, which detects a global deadlock, will be implemented by printing an error message and terminating the program. When such a transition appears in the result of fusion, the user is warned of a possibility of deadlock.

Let us consider the scheduling of the original AEG of Figure 3. This situation would arise if the user does not provide any constraint. The AEG obtained after product (and simplifications) is given in Figure 7. Simplifications are needed

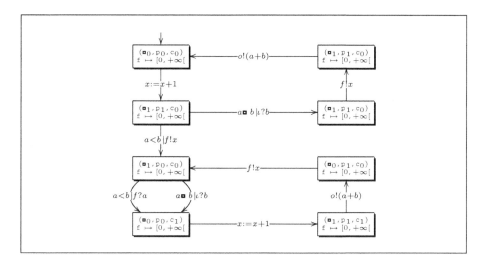

Fig. 7. Sequentialization with Round-Robin

since the product of transitions guarded by $\mathfrak{B}_X$ produces many dummy transitions (i.e., with false guards).

The process P is never blocked (it never reads), so the execution can start by $x := x + 1$. The execution must proceed by C if it is not blocked ($\neg\mathfrak{B}_C$). There are two cases: either $a \geq b$ and C is not blocked and its action ($\iota?b$) can be executed, either $a < b$ and C is blocked by a read of the empty file f. In the latter case, round-robin scheduling passes the control to P and executes the action $f!x$. The transition $a < b \mid f!x$ corresponds to "if C is blocked then execute the next P's command". We do not describe any further the product which proceeds similarly. Contrary to the product with Λ_{FF}, the result is fair but unbounded: the data produced by P may accumulate in the channel f without bounds.

The correctness of the scheduling process comes from the fact that the product with Δ_{RR} yields a sequential, fair and faithful AEG. Note that network fusion is generic w.r.t. the scheduling strategy. More sophisticated policies (e.g., using several queues, based on static or dynamic priorities, etc.) could be considered as well. As in Section 4.2, we have presented scheduling as an LTS product; scheduling could also be implemented by the technique outlined in Section 5.3.

4.4   Semantic Issues

User-defined constraints can change the semantics of the KPN. For example, a constraint which bounds communication channels would cause an artificial deadlock into an unbounded KPN. The user may want to enforce properties even at the price of deadlocks. We consider that a change of semantics is acceptable as long as it depends on the user and remains under her or his control. However, this requires to restrict the class of acceptable constraints. Consider the following constraint:

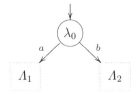

where a and b are two non-mutually exclusive commands and Λ_1 and Λ_2 represents distinct constraints. Since a and b can be executed indifferently, a choice will be made by scheduling. However, depending on this choice, the constraints that are enforced afterwards (Λ_1 or Λ_2) are different. For example, Λ_1 may imply an artificial deadlock in some (non statically determined) cases and Λ_2 in some other cases. In other words, the semantics of the resulting program will depend on a blind choice made by fusion. This semantic change is not acceptable since it would be out of the control of the user.

Our solution is to restrict the class of acceptable constraints. Namely, if a constraint leaves a non deterministic choice such as a or b above then the constraints must ensure that all processes can still evolve in the same way (an artificial deadlock in one side implies that we have the same artificial deadlock on the other side). Each choice a or b correspond to set (language) of acceptable traces ($a.\mathcal{L}(\Lambda_1)$ and $b.\mathcal{L}(\Lambda_2)$). A constraint is acceptable if for each choice, the projection of the corresponding languages to the commands of any process are equivalent. For the above example we must enforce that

$$\forall p. \ \ a.\mathcal{L}(\Lambda_1) \downarrow p = b.\mathcal{L}(\Lambda_2) \downarrow p$$

With this condition, the choices made by the scheduling step do not have any semantic impact.

All the constraints of Figure 4 are acceptable. It is obvious for Λ_{FF}, Λ_{FB}, Λ_{DD} since they do not leave any non deterministic choice. In Λ_{IS}, the two transitions labeled by $\neg f! \cap \neg f?$ leave the choice between executing P or C. However, in both states, they lead to the same state (and therefore accept the same language).

5 Extensions

The preceding sections have presented the main ideas of network fusion. We hint here at three ways of extending the basic technique: providing more linguistic support to the user, working on more precise abstractions, avoiding products between LTS. These three extensions all aim at getting more efficient fused programs.

5.1 Linguistic Support

Scheduling constraints allow users to control network fusion. Other linguistic support could be provided to users as well. We focus here on special commands allowing to alleviate the false path problem. False paths arise when data depending controls are abstracted by non deterministic choices [2]. This standard approximation makes fusion consider infeasible paths and spurious deadlocks.

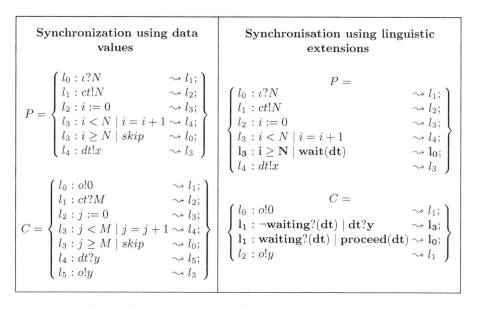

Synchronization using data values	Synchronisation using linguistic extensions

Fig. 8. A false path problem (left) and its solution (right)

The left part of figure 8 shows a simple but characteristic example of the problem. The process P begins by sending on channel ct the number of items it will produce on channel dt. Then, P and C respectively writes and reads the same number of items on dt ($M = N$). However, this information is lost in the AEG which abstracts away values. The fusion process must therefore consider the case where P produces not enough values and C is blocked and also the case where P produces unconsumed values and the size of dt cannot be bounded.

This problem can be alleviated using commands making synchronization or termination explicit. The languages of actions and guards are extended with the following constructs:

$$a ::= \mathbf{wait}(f) \mid \mathbf{proceed}(f) \mid \ldots$$
$$g ::= \mathbf{waiting?}(f) \mid \ldots$$

- The commands $\mathbf{wait}(f)$ and $\mathbf{proceed}(f)$ permit to express a rendezvous between the producer and the consumer of a file f. The producer blocks on $\mathbf{wait}(f)$ until the consumer emits $\mathbf{proceed}(f)$.
- The predicate $\mathbf{waiting?}(f)$ evaluates to true if the producer is waiting on $\mathbf{wait}(f)$ and all data has been consumed on f. It evaluates to false if there is some available data. It blocks if there is no available data and the producer is not waiting.

These instructions are just syntactic sugar and **waiting**?(f) do not affect the determinism of KPNs. They could be implemented by writing/reading a special value on an additional channel. On the other hand, they do provide more information to the fusion process and permit to avoid false paths.

The right part of Figure 8 shows how to take profit of these instructions on the previous example. Instead of communicating via ct the number of items written on dt, P finishes its emission by waiting to C. The consumer reads until it has consumed all data produced by P; it then releases P and both processes may proceed. Such explicit rendezvous can be taken into account by the abstraction step to avoid the problematic false paths mentioned above.

Others instructions could be considered as well. For example, an instruction **close**(f), indicating that a process will not write or read on f anymore, would also be useful.

5.2 More Precise Abstractions

In section 2, we presented an abstraction representing the control flow graph of the KPN. This abstraction gives a very imprecise approximation for the size of file f at each state $([0; +\infty[)$. As long as they respect the safety and faithfulness properties, many other abstractions could be used. We present here a new abstraction aimed at finding bounded schedules when they exist. A bounded schedule ensures that the size of fifo files remain bounded throughout the execution. In this case, fifo can implemented (after fusion) by local variables (instead of dynamically allocated data structures). Furthermore, when the precise size of a channel is known there is no need to test for its emptiness before reading it.

In some contexts, such as embedded systems, it is crucial to find bounded schedules and lot of work has been devoted to this issue ([11], [5], [13]). In the context of Petri Nets, Cortadella et al. presented a new criterion which limits the search state for schedules [5] . They conjectured that if a bounded schedule exists then it will be found in the delimited search space. We can adapt the criterion to our context to produce abstractions suited to the discovery of bounded schedule.

The idea is to have precise abstract states associating an integer to each size (not an interval anymore). The same set of control points (e.g., (p_0, c_1)) may appear several times in the AEG with different sizes of files. The finiteness of the AEG is ensured by the irrelevance criterion. A state s_2 is said irrelevant if the AEG contains another state s_1 such that:

- s_2 is reachable from s_1,
- all fifo have their size in s_2 greater or equal than their size in s_1,
- each fifo whose size is greater in s_2 than in s_1 has a non-zero size in s_1.

The idea behind this criterion is that a irrelevant state cannot enable any new action (e.g., it does not enable a blocked read). It is no use to continue unfolding the graph. It can be closed using a state where the size of channels are approximated by $[0; +\infty[$. A small part of the AEG obtained using the irrelevance criterion on our running example is shown on Figure 9. A bounded schedule can be found in the part shown. This improved precision allows to find bounded schedules automatically; it also involves larger AEGs.

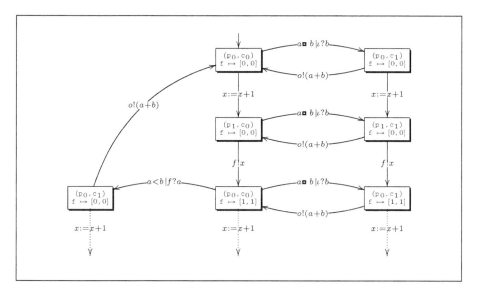

Fig. 9. AEG with irrelevance criterion (excerpt)

5.3   Instrumented Product

Two steps of network fusion are described as a synchronized product between guarded LTS. Obviously, in some cases, this could cause a state explosion and produce too large programs. A solution to avoid this space problem is to implement the product by instrumenting the AEG. The LTS representing the constraints or the schedule is taken into account by the AEG by introducing a variable (to represent the state of the LTS) and new instructions (to represent state transitions).

We have used such a technique in [4] to enforce safety properties (expressed as finite state automata) on programs. We have shown that the instrumentation can be made very efficient using simple techniques (specialization, minimization and reachability analysis). This instrumented product introduces at worst an assignment (a state transition) at each if and while command.

This technique is easily extended to guarded LTS. Figure 10 represents the result of the instrumented product between the AEG of Figure 3 and Λ_{FF}. It has the same number of states as the original AEG. On the other hand, instructions ($l := \{0, 1\}$) and tests ($l = \{0, 1\}$) have been inserted to encode the state transitions of Λ_{FF}. Compared to the LTS of Figure 5 which represents the standard synchronized product, some states like (λ_0, p_0, c_0) and (λ_1, p_0, c_0) are now merged into a single state (p_0, c_0). Transitions from this state must now test whether underlying LTS Λ_{FF} is in the state λ_0 or λ_1.

On this example, the smaller number of states is certainly not worth the overhead. In general, however, instrumented product is at most linear in size whereas synchronized product may entail a quadratic blowup. A small time overhead is preferable to a space explosion. In any case, the user should be given

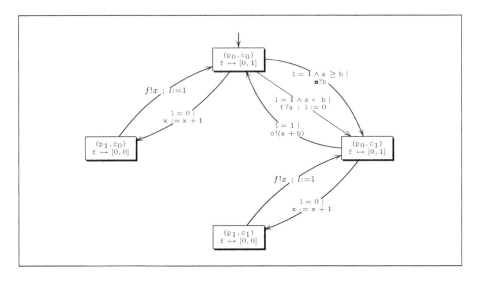

Fig. 10. Instrumented product with Λ_{FF}

the opportunity to specify on which LTS (or on which parts of a LTS) using standard or instrumented product.

6   Conclusion

The inspiration and motivation for this work came from two main sources:

- Filter fusion [12], a simple algorithm to merge a producer connected by a single channel to a consumer. Filter fusion is restricted to very specific networks (pipelines) and to a fixed strategy. Our work can be seen as a formalization of filter fusion using synchronized product and as well as a generalization to arbitrary networks and user-defined strategies. The application of our technique on pipelined filters with the constraint Λ_{FF} (Figure 4) is equivalent to filter fusion. The extension of filter fusion with a more sophisticated scheduling strategy proposed in [3] is formalized in our framework by the scheduling constraints Λ_{FB} (Figure 4).
- Aspect-Oriented Programming (AOP) [8] whose goal is to isolate aspects (e.g., security, synchronization, etc.) that cross-cut the basic functionality of the program. Our scheduling constraints can be seen as a scheduling/synchronization aspect and their enforcement as aspect weaving. As in [4], we consider aspects specified as temporal formulas on the trace semantics of programs. In network fusion, aspects express scheduling and synchronization choices by filtering unwanted (or selecting desired) execution traces. This restricted and formal view permits to describe and control precisely the semantic impact of weaving (usually, a very difficult task in AOP).

Some functional program transformations bear similarities with network fusion. As fusion aims at removing values produced on channels by the composition of components, Listlessness [15] and deforestation [16] aim at removing the intermediate data structures produced by the composition of functions. As filter fusion, these transformations consider producer-consumer pairs and have a fixed fusion strategy.

The area of embedded/reactive systems has produced a large body of work on static scheduling. Lin [9] studies the static scheduling of synchronously communicating processes. Cortadella et al. [5] and Strehl et al. [13] consider scheduling of asynchronous process networks. They all use petri nets as their underlying formalism. Like Parks [11], they focus on bounded scheduling and do not consider user-defined constraints even if some integrate a form of fusion. Strehl et al. [14] propose a design model that permits the specification of components and scheduling constraints. They derive a scheduler but do not consider fusion.

We have presented a generic and flexible framework for merging networks of interacting components. It is based on guarded labeled transition systems, synchronized product, static analysis and transformation techniques. Fusion can be applied to a large class of networks (KPNs) and can take into account user-defined scheduling constraints. The technique can be parameterized by different abstractions, constraints and scheduling strategies. Still, a lot of work remains to be done.

The formalization and the correctness proofs should be completed. A prototype needs to be implemented in order to validate the approach experimentally. We expect that large programs can be abstracted into small automata since fusion focuses on I/O instructions (blocks of internal instructions can be represented by a single action). Along with the use of instrumented product in problematic cases, we are confident that efficient and reasonable sized programs can be produced.

More generally we see network fusion as part of a more general framework to assemble and fuse components. A first feature of such a framework would consist in an architecture description language to specify the assembly (i.e., the ports and their connections). Another useful feature would be the ability to specify the synchronization instructions. They do not have to be IO instructions as supposed previously. By considering some actions of two components as IO operations on a (conceptual) channel f (i.e., $f!x$ and $f?x$), it becomes possible to impose constraints on their interleaving.

References

1. A. V. Aho, R. Sethi, and J. D. Ullman. *Compilers. Principles, Techniques, and Tools.* Addison-Wesley, 1986.
2. Arrigoni, Duchini, and Lavagno. False path elimination in quasi-static scheduling. In *Automation and Test in Europe Conference and Exhibition (DATE'02)*, pages 964–970, 2002.
3. R. Clayton and K. Calvert. Augmenting the proebsting-watterson filter fusion algorithm, 1997. http://citeseer.ist.psu.edu/186288.html.

4. T. Colcombet and P. Fradet. Enforcing trace properties by program transformation. In *Symposium on Principles of Programming Languages (POPL'00)*, pages 54–66, 2000.

5. J. Cortadella, A. Kondratyev, L. Lavagno, M. Massot, S. Moral, C. Passerone, Y. Watanabe, and A. L. Sangiovanni-Vincentelli. Task generation and compile-time scheduling for mixed data-control embedded software. Technical Report LSI-99-47-R, Dept. of Software, Universitat Politecnica de Catalunya, 1999.

6. M. Geilen and T. Basten. Requirements on the execution of Kahn process networks. In *European Symposium on Programming (ESOP'03)*, 2003.

7. G. Kahn. The semantics of a simple language for parallel programming. In *Proceedings of the IFIP Congress (Information Processing'74)*, pages 471–475, 1974.

8. G. Kiczales, J. Lamping, A. Mendhekar, C. Maeda, C. Lopes, J.-M. Loingtier, and J. Irwin. Aspect-oriented programming. In *Proc. of the European Conference on Object-Oriented Programming*, June 1997.

9. B. Lin. Software synthesis of process-based concurrent programs. In *Proceedings of the 1998 Conference on Design Automation (DAC-98)*, pages 502–505, 1998.

10. F. Nielson, H. R. Nielson, and C. L. Hankin. *Principles of Program Analysis*. Springer-Verlag, 1999.

11. T. M. Parks. *Bounded scheduling of process networks*. PhD thesis, University of California, Berkeley, 1995.

12. T. A. Proebsting and S. A. Watterson. Filter fusion. In *Symposium on Principles of Programming Languages (POPL'96)*, pages 119–130, 1996.

13. K. Strehl, L. Thiele, D. Ziegenbein, and R. Ernst. Scheduling hardware/software systems using symbolic techniques. In *Proceedings of the seventh international workshop on Hardware/software codesign (CODES '99)*, pages 173–177, 1999.

14. L. Thiele, K. Strehl, D. Ziegenbein, R. Ernst, and J. Teich. Funstate - an internal design representation for codesign. In *International Conference on Computer-Aided Design (ICCAD '99)*, pages 558–565, 1999.

15. P. Wadler. Listlessness is better than laziness. In *Conference Record of the 1984 ACM Symposium on Lisp and Functional Programming*, pages 45–52, 1984.

16. P. Wadler. Deforestation: transforming programs to eliminate trees. *Theoretical Computer Science*, 73(2):231–248, 1990.

Translation of Tree-Processing Programs into Stream-Processing Programs Based on Ordered Linear Type

Koichi Kodama*, Kohei Suenaga**, and Naoki Kobayashi***

*,***Tokyo Institute of Technology,
{kodama, kobayasi}@kb.cs.titech.ac.jp
**University of Tokyo,
kohei@yl.is.s.u-tokyo.ac.jp

Abstract. There are two ways to write a program for manipulating tree-structured data such as XML documents and S-expressions: One is to write a tree-processing program focusing on the logical structure of the data and the other is to write a stream-processing program focusing on the physical structure. While tree-processing programs are easier to write than stream-processing programs, tree-processing programs are less efficient in memory usage since they use trees as intermediate data. Our aim is to establish a method for automatically translating a tree-processing program to a stream-processing one in order to take the best of both worlds. We define a programming language for processing binary trees and a type system based on ordered linear type, and show that every well-typed program can be translated to an equivalent stream-processing program.

1 Introduction

There are two ways to write a program for manipulating tree-structured data such as XML documents [3] and S-expressions: One is to write a tree-processing program focusing on the logical structure of the data and the other is to write a stream-processing program focusing on the physical structure. For example, as for XML processing, DOM (Document Object Mode) API and programming language XDuce [5] are used for tree-processing, while SAX (Simple API for XML) is for stream-processing.

Figure 1 illustrates what tree-processing and stream-processing programs look like for the case of binary trees. The tree-processing program f takes a binary tree t as an input, and performs case analysis on t. If t is a leaf, it increments the value of the leaf. If t is a branch, f recursively processes the left and right subtrees. If actual tree data are represented as a sequence of tokens (as is often the case for XML documents), f must be combined with the function parse for parsing the input sequence, and the function unparse for unparsing the result tree into the output sequence, as shown in the figure. The stream-processing program g directly reads/writes data from/to streams. It reads an element from

W.-N. Chin (Ed.): APLAS 2004, LNCS 3302, pp. 41–56, 2004.
© Springer-Verlag Berlin Heidelberg 2004

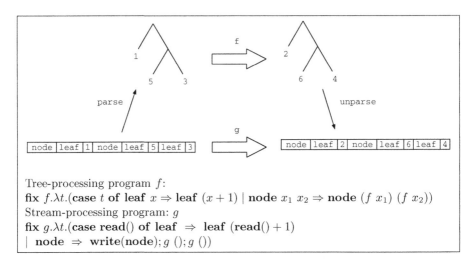

Tree-processing program f:
fix $f.\lambda t.(\textbf{case } t \textbf{ of leaf } x \Rightarrow \textbf{leaf } (x+1) \mid \textbf{node } x_1\ x_2 \Rightarrow \textbf{node } (f\ x_1)\ (f\ x_2))$
Stream-processing program: g
fix $g.\lambda t.(\textbf{case read}() \textbf{ of leaf } \Rightarrow \textbf{leaf } (\textbf{read}()+1)$
$\mid \textbf{node} \Rightarrow \textbf{write}(\textbf{node}); g\ (); g\ ())$

Fig. 1. Tree-processing and stream-processing

the input stream using the **read** primitive and performs case-analysis on the element. If the input is the **leaf** tag, g outputs **leaf** to the output stream with the **write** primitive, reads another element, adds 1 to it, and outputs it. If the input is the **node** tag, g outputs **node** to the output stream and recursively calls the function g twice with the argument ().

Both of the approaches explained above have advantages and disadvantages. Tree-processing programs are written based on the logical structure of data, so that it is easier to write, read, and manipulate (e.g. apply program transformation like deforestation [14]) than stream-processing programs. On the other hand, stream-processing programs have their own advantage that intermediate tree structures are not needed, so that they often run faster than the corresponding tree-processing programs if input/output trees are physically represented as streams, as in the case of XML.

The goal of the present paper is to achieve the best of both approaches, by allowing a programmer to write a tree-processing program and automatically translating the program to an equivalent stream-processing program. To clarify the essence, we use a λ-calculus with primitives on binary trees, and show how the translation works.

The key observation is that: (1) stream processing is most effective when trees are traversed and constructed from left to right in the depth-first manner and (2) in that case, we can obtain from the tree-processing program the corresponding stream-processing program simply by replacing case analysis on an input tree with case analysis on input tokens, and replacing tree constructions with stream outputs. In fact, the stream-processing program in Figure 1, which satisfies the above criterion, is obtained from the tree-processing program in that way.

In order to check that a program satisfies the criterion, we use the idea of ordered linear types [11, 12]. Ordered linear types, which are an extension of

Tree-processing program:
fix $f.\lambda t.(\textbf{case } t \textbf{ of leaf } x \Rightarrow \textbf{leaf } x \mid \textbf{node } x_1\ x_2 \Rightarrow \textbf{node } (f\ x_2)\ (f\ x_1))$

Fig. 2. A program that swaps children of every node

linear types [2, 13], describe not only how often but also in which order data are used. Our type system designed based on the ordered linear types guarantees that a well-typed program traverses and constructs trees from left to right and in the depth-first order. Thus, every well-typed program can be translated to an equivalent stream-processing program. The tree-processing program f in Figure 1 is well-typed in our type system, so that it can automatically be translated to the stream-processing program g. On the other hand, the program in Figure 2 is not well-typed in our type system since it accesses the right sub-tree of an input before accessing the left sub-tree. In fact, we would obtain a wrong stream-processing program if we simply apply the above-mentioned translation to the program in Figure 2.

The rest of the paper is organized as follows: To clarify the essence, we first focus on a minimal calculus in Section 2–4. In Section 2, we define the source language and the target language of the translation. We define a type system of the source language in Section 3. Section 4 presents a translation algorithm, shows its correctness and discuss the improvement gained by the translation. The minimal caclulus is not so expressive; especially, one can only write a program that does not store input/output trees on memory at all. (Strictly speaking, one can still store some information about trees by encoding it into lambda-terms.) Section 5 describes several extensions to recover the expressive power. With the extensions, one can write a program that selectively buffers input/output trees on memory, while the type system guarantees that the buffering is correctly performed. After discussing related work in Section 6, we conclude in Section 7.

For the restriction of space, proofs are omitted in this paper. They are found in the full version [7].

2   Language

We define the source and target languages in this section. The source language is a call-by-value functional language with primitives for manipulating binary trees. The target language is a call-by-value, impure functional language that uses imperative streams for input and output.

Source Language. The syntax and operational semantics of the source language is summarized in Figure 3.

The meta-variables x and i range over the sets of variables and integers respectively. The meta-variable W ranges over the set of values, which consists of integers i, lambda-abstractions $\lambda x.M$, and binary-trees V. A binary tree V is either a leaf labeled with an integer or a tree with two children. ($\textbf{case } M \textbf{ of leaf } x \Rightarrow M_1 \mid \textbf{node } x_1\ x_2 \Rightarrow M_2$) performs case analysis on a

Terms, values and evaluation contexts:

M (terms) $::= i \mid \lambda x.M \mid x \mid M_1\ M_2 \mid M_1 + M_2 \mid \textbf{fix}\ f.M$
                                     $\mid \textbf{leaf}\ M \mid \textbf{node}\ M_1\ M_2$
                                     $\mid (\textbf{case}\ M\ \textbf{of leaf}\ x \Rightarrow M_1 \mid \textbf{node}\ x_1\ x_2 \Rightarrow M_2)$

V (tree values) $::= \textbf{leaf}\ i \mid \textbf{node}\ V_1\ V_2$

W (values) $::= i \mid \lambda x.M \mid V$

E_s (evaluation contexts) $::= [\,] \mid E_s\ M \mid (\lambda x.M)\ E_s \mid E_s + M \mid i + E_s$
                                     $\mid \textbf{leaf}\ E_s \mid \textbf{node}\ E_s\ M \mid \textbf{node}\ V\ E_s$
                                     $\mid (\textbf{case}\ E_s\ \textbf{of leaf}\ x \Rightarrow M_1 \mid \textbf{node}\ x_1\ x_2 \Rightarrow M_2)$

Reduction rules:

$$E_s[i_1 + i_2] \longrightarrow E_s[plus(i_1, i_2)] \qquad \text{(Es-Plus)}$$

$$E_s[(\lambda x.M)W] \longrightarrow E_s[[W/x]M] \qquad \text{(Es-App)}$$

$$E_s[\textbf{fix}\ f.M] \longrightarrow E_s[[\textbf{fix}\ f.M/f]M] \qquad \text{(Es-Fix)}$$

$$E_s[\textbf{case leaf}\ i\ \textbf{of leaf}\ x \Rightarrow M_1 \mid \textbf{node}\ x_1\ x_2 \Rightarrow M_2] \longrightarrow E_s[[i/x]M_1] \ \text{(Es-Case1)}$$

$$E_s[\textbf{case node}\ V_1\ V_2\ \textbf{of leaf}\ x \Rightarrow M_1 \mid \textbf{node}\ x_1\ x_2 \Rightarrow M_2] \longrightarrow$$
$$E_s[[V_1/x_1, V_2/x_2]M_2]$$
$$\text{(Es-Case2)}$$

Fig. 3. The syntax, evaluation context and reduction rules of the source language. $plus(i_1, i_2)$ is the sum of i_1 and i_2

tree. If M is a leaf, x is bound to its label and M_1 is evaluated. Otherwise, x_1 and x_2 are bound to the left and right children respectively and M_2 is evaluated. **fix** $f.M$ is a recursive function that satisfies $f = M$. Bound and free variables are defined as usual. We assume that α-conversion is implicitly applied so that bound variables are always different from each other and free variables.

We write **let** $x = M_1$ **in** M_2 for $(\lambda x.M_2)\ M_1$. Especially, if M_2 contains no free occurrence of x, we write $M_1; M_2$ for it.

Target Language. The syntax and operational semantics of the target language is summarized in Figure 4. A stream, represented by the meta variable S, is a sequence consisting of **leaf**, **node** and integers. We write $\emptyset$ for the empty sequence and write $S_1; S_2$ for the concatenation of the sequences S_1 and S_2.

read is a primitive for reading a token (**leaf**, **node**, or an integer) from the input stream. **write** is a primitive for writing a value to the output stream. The term (**case** e **of leaf** $\Rightarrow e_1 \mid \textbf{node} \Rightarrow e_2$) performs a case analysis on the value of e. If e evaluates to **leaf**, e_1 is evaluated and if e evaluates to **node**, e_2 is evaluated. **fix** $f.e$ is a recursive function that satisfies $f = e$. Bound and free variables are defined as usual.

We write **let** $x = e_1$ **in** e_2 for $(\lambda x.e_2)\ e_1$. Especially, if e_2 does not contain x as a free variable, we write $e_1; e_2$ for it.

Figure 5 shows programs that take a tree as an input and calculate the sum of leaf elements. The target program assumes that the input stream represents

Terms, values and evaluation contexts:

$$e \text{ (terms)} ::= v \mid x \mid e_1 \ e_2 \mid e_1 + e_2 \mid \textbf{fix } f.e$$
$$\mid \textbf{read } e \mid \textbf{write } e \mid (\textbf{case } e \textbf{ of leaf} \Rightarrow e_1 \mid \textbf{node} \Rightarrow e_2)$$
$$v \text{ (values)} ::= i \mid \textbf{leaf} \mid \textbf{node} \mid \lambda x.e \mid ()$$
$$E_t \text{ (evaluation contexts)} ::= [] \mid E_t \ e \mid (\lambda x.e) \ E_t \mid E_t + e \mid i + E_t$$
$$\mid \textbf{read } E_t \mid \textbf{write } E_t$$
$$\mid (\textbf{case } E_t \textbf{ of leaf} \Rightarrow e_1 \mid \textbf{node} \Rightarrow e_2)$$

Reduction rules:

$$(E_t[v_1 + v_2], S_i, S_o) \longrightarrow (E_t[plus(v_1, v_2)], S_i, S_o) \qquad \text{(ET-Plus)}$$
$$(E_t[(\lambda x.M)v], S_i, S_o) \longrightarrow (E_t[[v/x]M], S_i, S_o) \qquad \text{(ET-App)}$$
$$(E_t[\textbf{fix } f.e], S_i, S_o) \longrightarrow (E_t[[\textbf{fix } f.e/f]e], S_i, S_o) \qquad \text{(ET-Fix)}$$
$$(E_t[\textbf{read}()], v; S_i, S_o) \longrightarrow (E_t[v], S_i, S_o) \qquad \text{(ET-Read)}$$
$$(E_t[\textbf{write } v], S_i, S_o) \longrightarrow (E_t[()], S_i, S_o; v) \quad (\text{when } v \text{ is an integer, } \textbf{leaf or node})$$
$$\text{(ET-Write)}$$
$$(E_t[\textbf{case leaf of leaf} \Rightarrow e_1 \mid \textbf{node} \Rightarrow e_2], S_i, S_o) \longrightarrow (E_t[e_1], S_i, S_o) \ \text{(ET-Case1)}$$
$$(E_t[\textbf{case node of leaf} \Rightarrow e_1 \mid \textbf{node} \Rightarrow e_2], S_i, S_o) \longrightarrow (E_t[e_2], S_i, S_o) \ \text{(ET-Case2)}$$

Fig. 4. The reduction rules of the target language

A source program:
fix *sumtree*.$\lambda t.$(**case** t **of leaf** $x \Rightarrow x \mid$ **node** $x_1 \ x_2 \Rightarrow (sumtree \ x_1) + (sumtree \ x_2))$
A target program:
fix *sumtree*.$\lambda t.$(**case read**() **of leaf** $\Rightarrow$ **read**() $\mid$ **node** $\Rightarrow$ *sumtree* () + *sumtree* ())

Fig. 5. Programs that calculate the sum of leaf elements of an binary tree

a valid tree. If the input stream is in a wrong format (e.g., when the stream is **node**; 1; 2), the execution gets stuck.

3   Type System

In this section, we present a type system of the source language, which guarantees that a well-typed program reads every node of an input tree exactly once from left to right in the depth-first order. Thanks to this guarantee, any well-typed program can be translated to an equivalent, stream-processing program without changing the structure of the program, as shown in the next section. To enforce the depth-first access order on input trees, we use ordered linear types [12, 11].

3.1   Type and Type Environment

Definition 1 (Type). The set of types, ranged over by τ, is defined by:

$$\tau \text{ (type)} ::= \textbf{Int} \mid \textbf{Tree}^d \mid \tau_1 \to \tau_2$$
$$d \text{ (mode)} ::= - \mid +.$$

Int is the type of integers. For a technical reason, we distinguish between input trees and output trees by types. We write **Tree$^-$** for the type of input trees, and write **Tree$^+$** for the type of output trees. $\tau_1 \to \tau_2$ is the type of functions from τ_1 to τ_2.

We introduce two kinds of type environments for our type system: ordered linear type environments and (non-ordered) type environments.

Definition 2 (Ordered Linear Type Environment). An ordered linear type environment is a sequence of the form $x_1:\textbf{Tree}^-, \ldots, x_n:\textbf{Tree}^-$, where $x_1, \ldots, x_n$ are different from each other. We write Δ_1, Δ_2 for the concatenation of Δ_1 and Δ_2.

An ordered linear type environment $x_1 : \textbf{Tree}^-, \ldots, x_n : \textbf{Tree}^-$ specifies not only that $x_1, \ldots, x_n$ are bound to trees, but also that each of $x_1, \ldots, x_n$ must be accessed exactly once in this order and that each of the subtrees bound to $x_1, \ldots, x_n$ must be accessed in the left-to-right, depth-first order.

Definition 3 (Non-ordered Type Environment). A (non-ordered) type environment is a set of the form $\{x_1:\tau_1, \ldots, x_n:\tau_n\}$ where $x_1, \ldots, x_n$ are different from each other and $\{\tau_1, \ldots, \tau_n\}$ does not contain **Tree^d**.

We use the meta-variable Γ for non-ordered type environments. We often write $\Gamma, x:\tau$ for $\Gamma \cup \{x:\tau\}$, and write $x_1:\tau_1, \ldots, x_n:\tau_n$ for $\{x_1:\tau_1, \ldots, x_n:\tau_n\}$.

Note that a non-ordered type environment must not contain variables of tree types. **Tree$^-$** is excluded since input trees must be accessed in the specific order. **Tree$^+$** is excluded in order to forbid output trees from being bound to variables. For example, we will exclude a program like **let** $x_1 = t_1$ **in let** $x_2 = t_2$ **in node** x_1 x_2 when t_1 and t_2 have type **Tree$^+$**. This restriction is convenient for ensuring that trees are constructed in the specific (from left to right, and in the depth-first manner) order.

3.2   Type Judgment

A type judgement is of the form $\Gamma \mid \Delta \vdash M : \tau$, where Γ is a non-ordered type environment and Δ is an ordered linear type environment. The judgment means "If M evaluates to a value under an environment described by Γ and Δ, the value has type τ and the variables in Δ are accessed in the order specified by Δ." For example, if $\Gamma = \{f : \textbf{Tree}^- \to \textbf{Tree}^+\}$ and $\Delta = x_1 : \textbf{Tree}^-, x_2 : \textbf{Tree}^-$,

$$\Gamma \mid \Delta \vdash \textbf{node} \ (f \ x_1) \ (f \ x_2) : \textbf{Tree}^+$$

holds, while

$$\Gamma \mid \Delta \vdash \textbf{node} \ (f \ x_2) \ (f \ x_1) : \textbf{Tree}^+$$

$$\Gamma \mid x : \textbf{Tree}^- \vdash x : \textbf{Tree}^- \qquad \text{(T-VAR1)}$$

$$\Gamma, x : \tau \mid \emptyset \vdash x : \tau \qquad \text{(T-VAR2)}$$

$$\Gamma \mid \emptyset \vdash i : \textbf{Int} \qquad \text{(T-INT)}$$

$$\frac{\Gamma \mid x : \textbf{Tree}^- \vdash M : \tau}{\Gamma \mid \emptyset \vdash \lambda x.M : \textbf{Tree}^- \to \tau} \qquad \text{(T-ABS1)}$$

$$\frac{\Gamma, x : \tau_1 \mid \emptyset \vdash M : \tau_2}{\Gamma \mid \emptyset \vdash \lambda x.M : \tau_1 \to \tau_2} \qquad \text{(T-ABS2)}$$

$$\frac{\Gamma \mid \Delta_1 \vdash M_1 : \tau_2 \to \tau_1 \qquad \Gamma \mid \Delta_2 \vdash M_2 : \tau_2}{\Gamma \mid \Delta_1, \Delta_2 \vdash M_1 M_2 : \tau_1} \qquad \text{(T-APP)}$$

$$\frac{\Gamma \mid \Delta_1 \vdash M_1 : \textbf{Int} \qquad \Gamma \mid \Delta_2 \vdash M_2 : \textbf{Int}}{\Gamma \mid \Delta_1, \Delta_2 \vdash M_1 + M_2 : \textbf{Int}} \qquad \text{(T-PLUS)}$$

$$\frac{\Gamma, f : \tau_1 \to \tau_2 \mid \emptyset \vdash M : \tau_1 \to \tau_2}{\Gamma \mid \emptyset \vdash \textbf{fix } f.M : \tau_1 \to \tau_2} \qquad \text{(T-FIX)}$$

$$\frac{\Gamma \mid \Delta \vdash M : \textbf{Int}}{\Gamma \mid \Delta \vdash \textbf{leaf } M : \textbf{Tree}^+} \qquad \text{(T-LEAF)}$$

$$\frac{\Gamma \mid \Delta_1 \vdash M_1 : \textbf{Tree}^+ \qquad \Gamma \mid \Delta_2 \vdash M_2 : \textbf{Tree}^+}{\Gamma \mid \Delta_1, \Delta_2 \vdash \textbf{node } M_1 \ M_2 : \textbf{Tree}^+} \qquad \text{(T-NODE)}$$

$$\frac{\Gamma \mid \Delta_1 \vdash M : \textbf{Tree}^- \qquad \Gamma, x : \textbf{Int} \mid \Delta_2 \vdash M_1 : \tau \qquad \Gamma \mid x_1 : \textbf{Tree}^-, x_2 : \textbf{Tree}^-, \Delta_2 \vdash M_2 : \tau}{\Gamma \mid \Delta_1, \Delta_2 \vdash \textbf{case } M \textbf{ of leaf } x \Rightarrow M_1 \mid \textbf{node } x_1 \ x_2 \Rightarrow M_2 : \tau} \qquad \text{(T-CASE)}$$

Fig. 6. Rules of typing judgment

does not. The latter program violates the restriction specified by Δ that x_1 and x_2 must be accessed in this order.

$\Gamma \mid \Delta \vdash M : \tau$ is the least relation that is closed under the rules in Figure 6. We explain only main rules below. T-VAR1, T-VAR2 and T-INT are the rules for variables and integer constants. As in ordinary linear type systems, these rules prohibit variables that do not occur in a term from occurring in the ordered linear type environment. (In other words, weakening is not allowed on an ordered linear type environment.) That restriction is necessary to guarantee that each variable in an ordered linear type environment is accessed exactly once.

T-ABS1 and T-ABS2 are rules for lambda abstraction. Note that the ordered type environments of the conclusions of these rules must be empty. This restriction prevents input trees from being stored in function closures. That makes it easy to enforce the access order on input trees. For example, without this restriction, the function

$$\lambda t.\textbf{let } g = \lambda f.(f \ t) \textbf{ in } (g \ \text{sum\_tree}) + (g \ \text{sum\_tree})$$

would be well-typed where sum_tree is the function given in Figure 5. However, when a tree is passed to this function, its nodes are accessed twice because the function g is called twice. The program above is actually rejected by our type system since the closure $\lambda f.(f\ t)$ is not well-typed due to the restriction of T-ABS2.[1]

T-APP is the rule for function application. The ordered linear type environments of M_1 and M_2, Δ_1 and Δ_2 respectively, are concatenated in this order because when $M_1\ M_2$ is evaluated, (1) M_1 is first evaluated, (2) M_2 is then evaluated, and (3) M_1 is finally applied to M_2. In the first step, the variables in Δ_1 are accessed in the order specified by Δ_1. In the second and third steps, the variables in Δ_2 are accessed in the order specified by Δ_2, On the other hand, because there is no restriction on usage of the variables in a non-ordered type environment, the same type environment (Γ) is used for both subterms.

T-CASE is the rule for case expressions. If M matches **node** $x_1\ x_2$, subtrees x_1 and x_2 have to be accessed in this order after that. This restriction is expressed by $x_1 : \mathbf{Tree}^-, x_2 : \mathbf{Tree}^-, \Delta_2$, the ordered linear type environment of M_2.

3.3   Examples of Well-Typed Programs

Figure 7 shows more examples of well-typed source programs. The first and second programs (or the catamorphism [8]) apply the same operation on every node of the input tree. (The return value of the function tree_fold cannot, however, be a tree because the value is passed to g.) One can also write functions that process nodes in a non-uniform manner, like the third program in Figure 7 (which increments the value of each leaf whose depth is odd).

The fourth program takes a tree as an input and returns the right subtree. Due to the restriction imposed by the type system, the program uses subfunctions copy_tree and skip_tree for explicitly copying and skipping trees.[2] (See Section 7 for a method for automatically inserting those functions.)

4   Translation Algorithm

In this section, we define a translation algorithm for well-typed source programs and prove its correctness.

---

[1] We can relax the restriction by controlling usage of not only trees but also functions, as in the resource usage analysis [6]. The resulting type system would, however, become very complex.

[2] Due to the restriction that lambda abstractions cannot contain variables of type $\mathbf{Tree}^d$, we need to introduce sequential composition (;) as a primitive and extend typing rules with the following rule:

$$\frac{\Gamma \mid \Delta_1 \vdash M_1 : \tau' \qquad \Gamma \mid \Delta_2 \vdash M_2 : \tau \qquad \tau' \neq \mathbf{Tree}^d}{\Gamma \mid \Delta_1, \Delta_2 \vdash M_1; M_2 : \tau.} \quad \text{(T-SEQ)}$$

---

fix $tree\_map.\lambda f.\lambda t.(\textbf{case } t \textbf{ of leaf } x \Rightarrow \textbf{ leaf } (f\ x)$
$|\ \textbf{node } x_1\ x_2\ \Rightarrow \textbf{node } (tree\_map\ f\ x_1)\ (tree\_map\ f\ x_2))$
fix $tree\_fold.\lambda f.\lambda g.\lambda t.$
$(\textbf{case } t \textbf{ of leaf } n\ \Rightarrow\ (f\ n)$
$|\ \textbf{node } t_1\ t_2\ \Rightarrow\ (g\ (tree\_fold\ f\ g\ t_1)(tree\_fold\ f\ g\ t_2)))$
fix $inc\_alt.\lambda t.(\textbf{case } t \textbf{ of leaf } x \Rightarrow \textbf{leaf } x\ |\ \textbf{node } x_1\ x_2 \Rightarrow \textbf{node}$
$\qquad (\textbf{case } x_1 \textbf{ of leaf } y \Rightarrow \textbf{leaf } (y+1)$
$\qquad\qquad\qquad |\ \textbf{node } y_1\ y_2 \Rightarrow \textbf{node } (inc\_alt\ y_1)\ (inc\_alt\ y_2))$
$\qquad (\textbf{case } x_2 \textbf{ of leaf } z \Rightarrow \textbf{leaf } (z+1)$
$\qquad\qquad\qquad |\ \textbf{node } z_1\ z_2 \Rightarrow \textbf{node } (inc\_alt\ z_1)\ (inc\_alt\ z_2))$

let $copy\_tree =$
$\qquad \textbf{fix } copy\_tree.\lambda t.(\textbf{case } t \textbf{ of leaf } x\ \Rightarrow\ \textbf{leaf } x$
$\qquad\qquad\qquad\qquad\qquad |\ \textbf{node } x_1\ x_2\ \Rightarrow\ \textbf{node } (copy\_tree\ x_1)\ (copy\_tree\ x_2))\ \textbf{in}$
let $skip\_tree =$
$\qquad \textbf{fix } skip\_tree.\lambda t.(\textbf{case } t \textbf{ of leaf } x\ \Rightarrow\ 0$
$\qquad\qquad\qquad\qquad\qquad |\ \textbf{node } x_1\ x_2\ \Rightarrow\ (skip\_tree\ x_1);(copy\_tree\ x_2)\ \textbf{in}$
$\lambda t.(\textbf{case } t \textbf{ of leaf } x \Rightarrow \textbf{leaf } x\ |\ \textbf{node } x_1\ x_2 \Rightarrow (skip\_tree\ x_1);(copy\_tree\ x_2))$

Fig. 7. Examples of well-typed programs

4.1 Definition and Correctness of Translation

The translation algorithm $\mathcal{A}$ is shown in Figure 8. $\mathcal{A}$ maps a source program to a target program, preserving the structure of the source program and replacing operations on trees with operations on streams.

The correctness of the translation algorithm $\mathcal{A}$ is stated as follows.

Definition 4. A function $[\![\cdot]\!]$ from the set of trees to the set of streams is defined by:

$$[\![\textbf{leaf } i]\!] = \textbf{leaf};i$$
$$[\![\textbf{node } V_1\ V_2]\!] = \textbf{node};[\![V_1]\!];[\![V_2]\!]\ .$$

Theorem 1 (Correctness of Translation).
If $\emptyset\ |\ \emptyset \vdash M : \textbf{Tree}^- \to \tau$ and τ is **Int** or **Tree**$^+$, the following properties hold for any tree value V:

(i) $M\ V\ \longrightarrow^*\ i$ if and only if $(\mathcal{A}(M)(), [\![V]\!], \emptyset) \longrightarrow^* (i, \emptyset, \emptyset)$
(ii) $M\ V\ \longrightarrow^*\ V'$ if and only if $(\mathcal{A}(M)(), [\![V]\!], \emptyset) \longrightarrow^* ((), \emptyset, [\![V']\!])\ .$

The above theorem means that a source program and the corresponding target program evaluates to the same value. The clause (i) is for the case where the result is an integer, and (ii) is for the case where the result is a tree.

We give an outline of the proof of Theorem 1 below. Full proofs are found in the full version of this paper [7]. We define another reduction semantics of the source language and prove that (1) for well-typed programs, the new semantics is equivalent to the one in Section 2 and (2) each reduction step based on the new semantics has the corresponding one in the target program.

$$\mathcal{A}(x) = x$$
$$\mathcal{A}(i) = i$$
$$\mathcal{A}(\lambda x.M) = \lambda x.\mathcal{A}(M)$$
$$\mathcal{A}(M_1 M_2) = \mathcal{A}(M_1)\ \mathcal{A}(M_2)$$
$$\mathcal{A}(M_1 + M_2) = \mathcal{A}(M_1) + \mathcal{A}(M_2)$$
$$\mathcal{A}(\textbf{fix } f.M) = \textbf{fix } f.\mathcal{A}(M)$$
$$\mathcal{A}(\textbf{leaf } M) = \textbf{write}(\textbf{leaf}); \textbf{write}(\mathcal{A}(M))$$
$$\mathcal{A}(\textbf{node } M_1\ M_2) = \textbf{write}(\textbf{node}); \mathcal{A}(M_1); \mathcal{A}(M_2)$$
$$\mathcal{A}(\textbf{case } M \textbf{ of leaf } x \Rightarrow M_1 \mid \textbf{node } x_1\ x_2 \Rightarrow M_2) =$$
$$\textbf{case } \mathcal{A}(M); \textbf{read}() \textbf{ of leaf} \Rightarrow \textbf{let } x = \textbf{read}() \textbf{ in } \mathcal{A}(M_1)$$
$$\mid \textbf{node} \Rightarrow [()/x_1, ()/x_2]\mathcal{A}(M_2)$$

Fig. 8. Translation Algorithm

$$
\begin{array}{ccccccc}
-(Mx, x \mapsto V) & \to & (M', \delta') & \to & \cdots & \to & (V', \emptyset) \\
\wr & & \wr & & & & \wr \\
(\mathcal{A}(M), [\![V]\!], \emptyset) \to^* (e, [\![V]\!], S_o) & \to^+ & (e', S_i', S_o') & \to^+ & \cdots & \to^+ & ((), \emptyset, [\![V']\!])
\end{array}
$$

Fig. 9. Evaluation of a source and the target program

The new reduction relation is of the form $(M, \delta) \longrightarrow (M', \delta')$ where δ is a sequence of binding of the form $x \mapsto V$. The formal definition is given in the full version [7]. The only difference from the one defined in Section 2 is that input trees are bound in δ and must be accessed in the order specified by δ. So, evaluation based on the new rules can differ from the one in Section 2 only when the latter one succeeds while the former one gets stuck due to the restriction on access to input trees. The following theorem guarantees that this does not happen if the program is well-typed.

Theorem 2 (soundness of the type system). If $\emptyset \mid x : \textbf{Tree}^- \vdash M : \tau$ and $(M, x \mapsto V) \longrightarrow^* (M', \delta')$ hold, then M' is a value or a variable, or $(M', \delta') \longrightarrow (M'', \delta'')$ holds for some M'', δ''.

Using the new semantics, we can prove that each reduction step of a source program has the corresponding one in the target program. Figure 9 illustrates the idea of the proof (for the case where the result is a tree). In the relation $(M, \delta) \sim (e, S_i, S_o)$, e represents the rest of computation, S_i is the input stream, and S_o is the already output streams. For example, $(\textbf{node}(\textbf{leaf } 1)(\textbf{leaf } (2+3)), \emptyset)$ corresponds to $(2+3, \emptyset, \textbf{node}; \textbf{leaf}; 1; \textbf{leaf})$. The formal definition of $\sim$ is found in the full version [7].) We can show that (1) the target program $\mathcal{A}(M)$ can always be reduced to a state corresponding to the inital state of the source program M and that (2) reductions and the correspondence relation commute.

Those imply that the whole diagram in Figure 9 commutes, so that the source program and the target program evaluates to the same value.

4.2   Efficiency of Translated Programs

Let M be a source program of type $\textbf{Tree}^- \rightarrow \textbf{Tree}^+$. We argue below that the target program $\mathcal{A}(M)$ runs more efficiently than the source program $\mathsf{unparse} \circ M \circ \mathsf{parse}$, where parse is a function that parses the input stream and returns a binary tree, and $\mathsf{unparse}$ is a function that takes a binary tree as an input and writes it to the output stream. Note that the fact that the target program is a stream-processing program does not necessarily imply that it is more efficient than the source program: In fact, if the translation $\mathcal{A}$ were defined by $\mathcal{A}(M) = \mathsf{unparse} \circ M \circ \mathsf{parse}$, obviously there would be no improvement.

Intuitively, the target program being more efficient follows from the fact that the translation function $\mathcal{A}$ preserves the structure of the source program, with only replacing tree constructions with stream outputs, and case analyses on trees with stream inputs and case analyses on input tokens.

In fact, by looking at the proof of Theorem 1, we know (see the full version for the reason):

- The memory space allocated by $\mathcal{A}(M)$ is less than the one allocated by $\mathsf{unparse} \circ M \circ \mathsf{parse}$, by the amount of the space for storing the intermediate trees output by parse and M (except for an implementation-dependent constant factor).
- The number of computation steps for running $\mathcal{A}(M)$ is the same as the one for running $\mathsf{unparse} \circ M \circ \mathsf{parse}$ (up to an implementation-dependent constant factor).

Thus, our translation is effective especially when the space for evaluating M is much smaller than the space for storing input and output trees.

5   Extensions

So far, we have focused on a minimal calculus to clarify the essence of our framework. This section briefly shows how to extend the framework to be used in practice. More details are found in the full version [7].

5.1   Constructs for Storing Trees on Memory

By adding primitives for constructing and destructing trees on memory, we can allow programmers to selectively buffer input/output trees at the cost of efficiency of target prgorams. Let us extend the syntax of the source and target languages as follows:

$$
\begin{aligned}
M ::= & \cdots \mid \textbf{mleaf } M \mid \textbf{mnode } M_1 \ M_2 \\
      & \mid (\textbf{mcase } M \textbf{ of mleaf } x \Rightarrow M_1 \mid \textbf{mnode } x_1 \ x_2 \Rightarrow M_2) \\
e ::= & \cdots \mid \textbf{mleaf } e \mid \textbf{mnode } e_1 \ e_2 \\
      & \mid (\textbf{mcase } e \textbf{ of mleaf } x \Rightarrow e_1 \mid \textbf{mnode } x_1 \ x_2 \Rightarrow e_2) \ .
\end{aligned}
$$

---

fix $strm\_to\_mem$.
$\lambda t.$**case** t **of leaf** $x \Rightarrow$ **mleaf** x
$\mid$ **node** $x_1 \ x_2 \Rightarrow$ **mnode** $(strm\_to\_mem \ x_1) \ (strm\_to\_mem \ x_2)$ **fix** mem_to_strm.
$\lambda t.$**mcase** t **of mleaf** $x \Rightarrow$ **leaf** x
$\mid$ **mnode** $x_1 \ x_2 \Rightarrow$ **node** $(mem\_to\_strm \ x_1) \ (mem\_to\_strm \ x_2)$

Fig. 10. Definition of $strm\_to\_mem$ and mem_to_strm

---

let $mswap =$
fix $f.\lambda \ t.$**mcase** t **of mleaf** $x \Rightarrow$ **leaf** x
$\mid$ **mnode** $x_1 \ x_2 \Rightarrow$ **node** $(f \ x_2) \ (f \ x_1)$ **in**
fix $swap\_deep.\lambda n.\lambda t.$
$\qquad$ **if** $n = 0$ **then** $mswap \ (strm\_to\_mem \ t)$
$\qquad$ **else**
$\qquad\qquad$ **case** t **of**
$\qquad\qquad\qquad$ **leaf** $x \Rightarrow$ **leaf** x
$\qquad\qquad\qquad \mid$ **node** $x_1 \ x_2 \Rightarrow$ **node** $(swap\_deep \ (n-1) \ x_1) \ (swap\_deep \ (n-1) \ x_2)$

Fig. 11. A program which swaps children of nodes whose depth is more than n

Here, **mleaf** M and **mnode** $M_1 \ M_2$ are constructors of trees on memory and **mcase** $\cdots$ is a destructor.

We also add type **MTree**, the type of trees stored on memory. The type system imposes no restriction on access order between variables of type **MTree** like type **Int** (so **MTree** is put in the ordinary type environment, not the ordered linear type environment). The translation algorithm $\mathcal{A}$ simply translates a source program, preserving the structure:

$$\mathcal{A}(\textbf{mleaf } M) = \textbf{mleaf } \mathcal{A}(M)$$
$$\mathcal{A}(\textbf{mnode } M_1 \ M_2) = \textbf{mnode } \mathcal{A}(M_1) \ \mathcal{A}(M_2)$$
$$\cdots$$

With these primitives, a function $strm\_to\_mem$, which copies a tree from the input stream to memory, and mem_to_strm, which writes a tree on memory to the output stream, can be defined as shown in Figure 10.

Using the functions above, one can write a program that selectively buffers only a part of the input tree, while the type system guarantees that the selective buffering is correctly performed. For example, the program in Figure 11, which swaps children of nodes whose depth is more than n, only buffers the nodes whose depth is more than n.

The proof of Theorem 1 can be easily adapted for the extended language.

5.2   Side Effects and Multiple Input Trees

Since our translation algorithm preserves the structure of source programs, the translation works in the presence of side effects other than stream inputs/outputs.

Our framework can also be easily extended to deal with multiple input trees, by introducing pair constructors and refining the type judgment form to $\Gamma \mid \{s_1 : \Delta_1, \ldots, s_n : \Delta_n\} \vdash M : \tau$ where $s_1, \ldots, s_n$ are the names of input streams and each of $\Delta_1, \ldots, \Delta$ is an ordered linear type environment.

5.3 Extention for Dealing with XML

We discuss below how to extend our method to deal with XML documents.

The difference between binary trees and XML documents is that the latter ones (i) are rose trees and (ii) contain end tags that mark the end of sequences in the stream format. The first point can be captured as the difference between the following types (we use ML-style type declarations):

```
datatype tree = leaf of int | node of tree*tree;
datatype xmltree = leaf of pcdata
                 | node of label * attribute * treelist
and treelist = nil | cons of xmltree * treelist;
```

While the type `tree` represents binary trees, `xmltree` represents rose trees. Based on the difference between these types, we can replace the **case**-construct of the source language with the following two **case**-constructs.

$$\textbf{caseElem } t \textbf{ of } \textbf{leaf}(x) \Rightarrow M_1 \mid \textbf{node}(l, attr, tl) \Rightarrow M_2$$
$$\textbf{caseSeq } tl \textbf{ of } \textbf{nil} \Rightarrow M_1 \mid \textbf{cons}(x, xl) \Rightarrow M_2.$$

Typing rules can also be naturally extended. For example, the typing rule for the latter construct is:

$$\frac{\Gamma \mid \Delta_1 \vdash tl : \textbf{treelist} \qquad \Gamma \mid \Delta_2 \vdash M_1 : \tau \qquad \Gamma \mid x : \textbf{xmltree}, xl : \textbf{treelist}, \Delta_2 \vdash M_2 : \tau}{\Gamma \mid \Delta_1, \Delta_2 \vdash \textbf{caseSeq } tl \textbf{ of } \textbf{nil} \Rightarrow M_1 \mid \textbf{cons}(x, xl) \Rightarrow M_2 : \tau.}$$

The restriction on the access order is expressed by $x : \textbf{xmltree}, xl : \textbf{treelist}, \Delta_2$ as in T-NODE.

The translation algorithm (1) maps the pattern **nil** in the source language to the pattern for closing tags. (2) prepares a stack and confirms well-formedness of input documents.

6   Related Work

Nakano and Nishimura [10, 9] proposed a method for translating tree-processing programs to stream-processing programs using attribute grammars. In their method, programmers write XML processing with an attribute grammar. Then, the grammar is composed with parsing and unparsing grammars by using the descriptional composition [4] and translated to a grammar that directly deals with streams. Quasi-SSUR condition in [10] and single use requirement in [9], which force attributes of non-terminal symbols to be used at most once, seems to correspond to our linearity restriction on variables of tree types, but there seems

$N \rightarrow \mathbf{node} \ N_1 \ N_2$
  $N_1.inh = f_1 \ N.inh; \ N_2.inh = f_2 \ N.inh \ N_1.syn \ N_1.inh$
  $N.syn = f_3 \ N.inh \ N_1.syn \ N_1.inh \ N_2.syn \ N_2.inh$
$N \rightarrow \mathbf{leaf} \ i$
  $N.syn = f_4 \ N.inh \ i$

$\mathbf{fix} \ f.\lambda inh.\lambda t.\mathbf{case} \ t \ \mathbf{of}$
    $\mathbf{leaf} \ x \Rightarrow f_4 \ inh \ x$
    $\mathbf{node} \ x_1 \ x_2 \Rightarrow \quad \mathbf{let} \ N_1.inh = f_1 \ inh \ \mathbf{in}$
                    $\mathbf{let} \ N_1.syn = f \ N_1.inh \ x_1 \ \mathbf{in}$
                    $\mathbf{let} \ N_2.inh = f_2 \ N.inh \ N_1.syn \ N_1.inh \ \mathbf{in}$
                    $\mathbf{let} \ N_2.syn = f \ N_2.inh \ x_2 \ \mathbf{in}$
                        $f_3 \ N.inh \ N_1.syn \ N_1.inh \ N_2.syn \ N_2.inh$

Fig. 12. L-attributed grammar over binary trees and corresponding program

to be no restriction that corresponds to our order restriction. As a result, their method can deal with programs (written as attribute grammars) that violate the order restriction of our type system, although in that case, generated stream-processing programs store a part of trees in memory, so that the translation may not improve the efficiency. On the other hand, an advantage of our method is that programs are easier to read and write since one can write programs as ordinary functional programs except for the restriction imposed by the type system, rather than as attribute grammars. Another advantage of our method is that we can deal with source programs that involve side-effects (e.g. programs that print the value of every leaf) while that seems difficult in their method based on attribute grammars (since the order is important for side effects).

The class of well-typed programs in our language seems to be closely related to the class of L-attributed grammars [1]. In fact, any L-attributed grammar over the binary tree can be expressed as a program as shown in Figure 12. If output trees are not used in attributes, the program is well-typed. Conversely, any program that is well-typed in our language seems to be definable as an L-attribute grammar. The corresponding attribute grammar may, however, be awkward, since one has to encode control information into attributes.

There are many studies on program transformation [14, 8] for eliminating intermediate data structures of functional programs, known as deforestation or fusion. Although the goal of our translation is also to remove intermediate data structures from unparse∘ f ∘parse, the previous methods are not directly applicable since those methods do not guarantee that transformed programs access inputs in a stream-processing manner. In fact, swap in Figure 2, which violates the access order, can be expressed as a treeless program [14] or a catamorphism [8], but the result of deforestation is not an expected stream-processing program.

Actually, there are many similarities between the restriction of treeless program [14] and that of our type system. In treeless programs, (1) variables have to occur only once, and (2) only variables can be passed to functions. (1) corresponds to the linearity restriction of our type system. (2) is the restriction for prohibiting trees generated in programs to be passed to functions, which corresponds to the restriction that functions cannot take values of type $\mathbf{Tree}^+$ in our type system. The main differences are:

– Our type system additionally imposes a restriction on the access order. This is required to guarantee that translated programs read input streams sequentially.
– We restrict programs with a type system, while the restriction on treeless programs is syntactic. Our type-based approach enables us to deal with higher-order functions. The type-based approach is also useful for automatic inference of selective buffering of trees, as discussed in Section 7.

The type system we used in this paper is based on the ordered linear logic proposed by Polakow [12]. He proposed a logic programming language Olli, logical framework OLF and ordered lambda calculus based on the logic. There are many similarities between our typing rules and his derivation rules for the ordered linear logic. For example, our type judgment $\Gamma \mid \Delta \vdash M : \tau$ corresponds to the judgment $\Gamma; \cdot; \Delta \vdash A$ of ordered linear logic. The rule T-ABS1 corresponds to a combination of the rules for an ordered linear implication and the modality (!). However, we cannot use ordered linear logic directly since it would make our type system unsound. Petersen et al. [11] used ordered linear types to guarantee correctness of memory allocation and data layout. While they used an ordered linear type environment to express a spatial order, we used it to express a temporal order.

7   Conclusion

We have proposed a type system based on ordered linear types to enable translation of tree-processing programs into stream-processing programs, and proved the correctness of the translation.

As we stated in Section 3 and 5, one can write tree-processing programs that selectively skip and/or buffer trees by using skip_tree, copy_tree, strm_to_mem and mem_to_strm. However, inserting those functions by hand is sometimes tedious. We are currently studying a type-directed, source-to-source translation for automatically inserting these functions.

In addition to application to XML processing, our translation framework may also be useful for optimization of distributed programs that process and communicate complex data structures. Serialization/unserialization of data correspond to unparsing/parsing in Figure 1, so that our translation framework can be used for eliminating intermediate data structures and processing serialized data directly.

Acknowledgement. We thank members of "Programming Language Principles" group at University of Tokyo and Tokyo Institute of Technology.

References

1. Alfred V. Aho, Ravi Sethi, and Jeffrey D. Ullman. *Compilers*. Addison-Wesley Pub Co, 1986.
2. Henry G. Baker. Lively linear lisp – look ma, no garbage! *ACM SIGPLAN Notices*, 27(8):89–98, 1992.
3. Tim Bray, Jean Paoli, C.M.Sperberg-McQueen, and Eve Maler. Extensible markup language (XML) 1.0 (second edition). Technical report, World Wide Web Consortium, October 2000. http://www.w3.org/TR/REC-xml.
4. Harald Ganzinger and Robert Giegerich. Attribute coupled grammars. In *Proceedings of the ACM SIGPLAN '84 Symposium on Compiler Construction*, 1984.
5. Haruo Hosoya and Benjamin C. Pierce. XDuce: A typed XML processing language. *ACM Transactions on Internet Technology (TOIT)*, 3(2):117–148, 2003.
6. Atsushi Igarashi and Naoki Kobayashi. Resource usage analysis. In *Proceedings of ACM SIGPLAN-SIGACT Symposium on Principles of Programming Languages*, pages 331–342, 2002.
7. Koichi Kodama, Kohei Suenaga, and Naoki Kobayashi. Translation of tree-processing programs into stream-processing programs based on ordered linear type. Full paper. Available from http://www.yl.is.s.u-tokyo.ac.jp/ kohei /doc/paper/translation.pdf
8. Erik Meijer, Maarten Fokkinga, and Ross Paterson. Functional programming with bananas, lenses, envelopes and barbed wire. In *Proceedings of the 5th ACM conference on Functional programming languages and computer architecture*, pages 124 – 144, 1991.
9. Keisuke Nakano. Composing stack-attributed tree transducers. Technical Report METR–2004–01, Department of Mathematical Informatics, University of Tokyo, Japan, 2004.
10. Keisuke Nakano and Susumu Nishimura. Deriving event-based document transformers from tree-based specifications. In Mark van den Brand and Didier Parigot, editors, *Electronic Notes in Theoretical Computer Science*, volume 44. Elsevier Science Publishers, 2001.
11. Leaf Petersen, Robert Harper, Karl Crary, and Frank Pfenning. A type theory for memory allocation and data layout. In *Proceedings of the 30th ACM SIGPLAN-SIGACT Symposium on Principles of Programming Languages*, 2003.
12. Jeff Polakow. *Ordered linear logic and applications*. PhD thesis, Carnegie Mellon University, June 2001. Available as Technical Report CMU-CS-01-152.
13. David N. Turner, Philip Wadler, and Christian Mossin. Once upon a type. In *Proceedings of Functional Programming Languages and Computer Architecture*, pages 1–11, San Diego, California, 1995.
14. P. Wadler. Deforestation: Transforming programs to eliminate trees. In *ESOP '88. European Symposium on Programming, Nancy, France, 1988 (Lecture Notes in Computer Science, vol. 300)*, pages 344–358. Berlin: Springer-Verlag, 1988.

An Implementation of Subtyping Among Regular Expression Types

Kenny Zhuo Ming Lu and Martin Sulzmann

School of Computing, National University of Singapore,
S16 Level 5, 3 Science Drive 2, Singapore 117543
{luzm,sulzmann}@comp.nus.edu.sg

Abstract. We introduce a novel implementation of subtyping among regular expression types in terms of Haskell-style type classes by making use of some modest type class extensions. We assume that each regular expression type has some underlying structured runtime representation. Hence, we not only check for the containment problem among regular expressions, but also automatically derive some appropriate casting functions among the underlying structured values. We believe that this work is the first step in adding type-safe XML support to languages such as Haskell.

1 Introduction

Regular expression types and regular expression pattern matching have been introduced in XML processing languages to provide type-safe transformation of XML documents. Languages based on these ideas such as XDuce [11,10] and CDuce [3] provide for some static safety guarantees. For example, assume function f is of type $R_1 \rightarrow R_2$ where R_1 and R_2 refer to some regular expression types. Assume that we apply f to some value v of another regular expression type R_3. For this application to be safe we need to verify that $L(R_3)$, the language denoted by R_3, is a subset of $L(R_1)$. Hence, (sub)type checking in XDuce and CDuce boils down to checking for containment among regular expressions. Commonly, this is referred to as sem antic subtyping.

Traditionally, at runtime the structure imposed on values by regular expression types is lost. XDuce and CDuce make use of a uniform (a.k.a. "flat") runtime representation for values. The downside of such an approach is that a flat representation of values might incur some performance penalties. Furthermore, it becomes harder to introduce XDuce features into languages such as Haskell [17] unless we enforce that all Haskell values obey the flat representation.

Here, we consider a novel approach to implement semantic subtyping such that we retain a structured runtime representation of values defined by regular expression types. A key feature is that our implementation can be encoded in terms of Haskell type classes. Thus, Haskell's type system and compilation scheme is expressive enough to integrate regular expression types into Haskell

W.-N. Chin (Ed.): APLAS 2004, LNCS 3302, pp. 57–73, 2004.
© Springer-Verlag Berlin Heidelberg 2004

without any significant changes to existing Haskell programming systems such as GHC [7].

The problem we are facing is as follows. Consider a structured value v1 of regular expression type R_1. Assume that we intend to use v1 in a context where v1 is expected to have type R_2, $L(R_1) \subseteq L(R_2)$. Such uses of v1 are safe. The standard method to check for containment among regular expression proceeds by converting regular expressions to DFAs, minimizing the DFAs etc. This gives us a proof method to check whether $L(R_1) \subseteq L(R_2)$ holds. However, we need more than the proof. The challenge here is that in order to use v1 in type context R_2 we need to change the structure of v1. That is, we need to (up)cast value v1 defined by R_1 into a value v2 defined by R_2. Such an upcast function must exist because $L(R_1) \subseteq L(R_2)$ holds. However, the standard method for checking containment among regular expressions does not give us any clues how to construct the appropriate upcast function.

Our idea is to make use of a mostly overlooked algebraic proof method to check for language containment among regular expressions. Antimirov [2] introduced a proof system with judgments of the form $\vdash R_1 \leq R_2$ to decide whether $L(R_1) \subseteq L(R_2)$. We model such judgments in terms of the following Haskell class declaration

```
class UCast r1 r2 h1 h2 | r1 r2 -> h1 h2 where ucast::h1->h2
```

Our task is to define the set of valid instances such that UCast r1 r2 h1 h2 is valid iff $\vdash$ r1 $\leq$ r2 is provable in Antimirov's system. As a side product, the type class resolution mechanism [8] generates some "evidence" for ucast::h1->h2 where h1 and h2 refer to the underlying representations of r1 and r2. That is, out of the proof for UCast r1 r2 h1 h2 we obtain a proof term for ucast::h1->h2. Note that in the above class declaration we make use of a functional dependency [12] | r1 r2 -> h1 h2 which states that h1 and h2 are uniquely determined by r1 and r2. Antimirov describes the set of valid judgments $\vdash R_1 \leq R_2$ in terms of rules of the form

$$(r) \frac{\vdash R_1 \leq R_1' \quad \ldots \vdash R_n \leq R_n'}{\vdash R \leq R'}$$

Such rules can directly be expressed in terms of Haskell instance declarations. Here is a type class encoding of the above rule (r). For simplicity, we have left out the instance body which describes the shape of the corresponding ucast function.

```
instance (UCast R₁ R′₁ H₁ H′₁, ...,UCast Rₙ R′ₙ Hₙ H′ₙ)
  ⇒ UCast R R′ H H′
```

Of course, there are some tricky parts behind our type class encoding of Antimirov's algorithm. There will be more about this in later sections.

We continue in Section 2 where we introduce Antimirov's algorithm. In Section 3 we show how to model semantic subtyping among regular expression types using type classes. In Section 4 we consider regular hedges (i.e., sequences of trees) which requires a novel adaption of Antimirov's algorithm. In Section 5 we discuss related work and conclude. We assume that the reader is familiar with Haskell type classes [7].

2   Background: Antimirov's Algorithm

We assume that the reader is familiar with the basics of regular expressions. E.g., we consider R^+ as a short-hand for (R, R^*) and $R?$ as a short-hand for $(()|R)$ where $()$ denotes the empty word. Regular expressions are defined as follows.

$$\text{Literals}\ \ l ::= A_1\ \|\ \ldots$$
$$\text{Regular Expression}\ R ::= ()\ \|\ l\ \|\ R^*\ \|\ (R|R)\ \|\ (R,R)$$

Note that we use $\|$ in BNF to eliminate the confusion with regular expression operator $|$. Antimirov's algorithm to check containment among regular expressions is defined in terms of a co-inductive term-rewriting system among judgments $\vdash R_1 \leq R_2$ where regular expressions R_1 and R_2 are put into "normal form" if necessary. Before providing a formal account of Antimirov's algorithm we take a look at an example.

Example 1. Consider the goal $\vdash ((A^*, B^*), B^*) \leq (A^*, B^*)$ plus some proof rules.

$$(,\text{-},1)\ \frac{\vdash (R_1, R_2)\ \leq\ R_3 \quad \vdash ()\ \leq\ R_4}{\vdash (R_1, R_2)\ \leq\ (R_3, R_4)} \quad (,\text{-},2)\ \frac{\vdash R_1\ \leq\ R_3 \quad \vdash R_2\ \leq\ R_4}{\vdash (R_1, R_2)\ \leq\ (R_3, R_4)}$$

$$(,\text{-},3)\ \frac{\vdash ()\ \leq\ R_3 \quad \vdash (R_1, R_2)\ \leq\ R_4}{\vdash (R_1, R_2)\ \leq\ (R_3, R_4)} \quad (()\text{-}*)\ \frac{True}{\vdash ()\ \leq\ R^*}$$

We have that $L((A^*, B^*), B^*) \subseteq L(A^*, B^*)$. However, the above rules are not strong enough to derive this statement. In the following, we write $C \longrightarrow_r C'$ to denote application of rule (r) to a set of judgments C yielding another set of judgments C'. E.g., we find that

$$\vdash ((A^*, B^*), B^*) \leq (A^*, B^*) \longrightarrow_{,\text{-},1} \vdash ((A^*, B^*), B^*) \leq A^*, \vdash ()\leq B^* \longrightarrow^* Fail$$
$$\longrightarrow_{,\text{-},2} \vdash (A^*, B^*) \leq A^*, \vdash B^* \leq B^* \longrightarrow^* Fail$$
$$\longrightarrow_{,\text{-},3} \vdash ()\leq A^*, \vdash ((A^*, B^*), B^*) \leq B^* \longrightarrow^* Fail$$

In the first step, we encounter three alternatives. After exploring all possibilities none of the derivations can be reduced to the empty store. Hence, we report $Fail$ure. Of course, we could now simply add more proof rules. Currently, we do not exploit the following equivalences $((A^*, B^*), B^*) = (A^*, (B^*, B^*)) = (A^*, B^*)$. However, incorporating all such equivalences into the reduction system would lead to non-termination. We cannot impose a definite order (e.g. from left to right) on our rewrite rules.

Apply if all other $\vdash R_1 \leq R_2$ failed:

$$(\text{Last}) \; \frac{N_1 = \mathtt{norm}(R_1) \quad N_2 = \mathtt{norm}(R_2) \quad \vdash_{\mathsf{Inf}} N_1 \leq N_2}{\vdash R_1 \leq R_2}$$

Containment rules among deterministic LNFs:

$$(\text{()-()}) \; \frac{True}{\vdash_{\mathsf{Inf}} () \leq ()} \qquad (|\text{-}\text{-}) \; \frac{\vdash_{\mathsf{Inf}} N_1 \leq N_3 \quad \vdash_{\mathsf{Inf}} N_2 \leq N_3}{\vdash_{\mathsf{Inf}} (N_1 | N_2) \leq N_3} \qquad (\text{m-m1}) \; \frac{l_1 = l_2 \quad \vdash R_1 \leq R_2}{\vdash_{\mathsf{Inf}} (l_1, R_1) \leq (l_2, R_2)}$$

$$(\text{-}|1) \; \frac{\vdash_{\mathsf{Inf}} N_1 \leq N_2}{\vdash_{\mathsf{Inf}} N_1 \leq (N_2 | N_3)} \qquad (\text{-}|2) \; \frac{\vdash_{\mathsf{Inf}} N_1 \leq N_3}{\vdash_{\mathsf{Inf}} N_1 \leq (N_2 | N_3)}$$

Fig. 1. Essence of Antimirov's Algorithm

To address this problem, Antimirov's idea is to normalize regular expressions to Linear Normal Forms(LNF) in case a judgement $\vdash R_1 \leq R_2$ cannot be verified.

$$\begin{aligned}
(\text{Monomial}) \; M &::= (l, R) \\
(\text{Sum}) \; S &::= M \;\|\; (M|S) \\
(\text{LNF}) \; N &::= S \;\|\; (()|S)
\end{aligned}$$

A LNF N is deterministic iff none of the monomials in N shares a common leading literal. In [2], Antimirov shows that every regular expression can be rewritten into a deterministic LNF. E.g., $\mathtt{norm}((l, R_1)|(l, R_2)) = (l, (R_1|R_2))$ where function $\mathtt{norm}$ turns regular expressions into deterministic LNF. Details can be found in [15].

Antimirov's proof system has two layers. The first layer consists of proof rules among "ordinary" expressions. Often, we call these rules "ordinary" proof rules. We refer to [2] for a description of these rules. As already observed, we cannot find a finite set of ordinary proof system such that we obtain a complete proof system. Therefore, Antimirov introduces a second proof system among normalized expressions. We refer to Figure 2 for details. Rule (Last) allows us to switch from the ordinary proof system $\vdash$ to the normalized proof system $\vdash_{\mathsf{Inf}}$. We assume that we have exhaustively applied all $\vdash$ proof rules. In the $\vdash_{\mathsf{Inf}}$ system we only need to consider normalized regular expressions. In rule (m-m1), we assume that the leading literals of the monomial on the lhs and rhs are equal. We drop the literals and switch back to the $\vdash$ proof system. In case the leading literals differ we need to backtrack. Rule (()-()) deals with the empty type (). Rules (|--), (-|1) and (-|2) deal with the union type |. Note that N_i's are in LNF. Hence, we make use of the $\vdash_{\mathsf{Inf}}$ proof system in the premise of these rules.

Note that Antimirov's proof rules have to be interpreted co-inductively. That is, if we encounter a judgement which we are trying to verify we simply assume that the judgement holds.

Example 2. Consider $\vdash ((A^*, B^*), B^*) \leq (A^*, B^*)$ which cannot be verified with the ordinary proof rules. Note that throughout the following derivation, we always pick the first judgment in the constraint store for reduction. We find that

$$
\begin{array}{ll}
& \vdash ((A^*, B^*), B^*) \leq (A^*, B^*) \\
\longrightarrow_{Last} & \vdash_{\text{Inf}} ()|(A, ((A^*, B^*), B^*))|(B, ((B^*, B^*)|B^*)) \leq ()|(A, (A^*, B^*))|(B, B^*) \\
\longrightarrow_{|--} & \vdash_{\text{Inf}} () \leq ()|(A, (A^*, B^*))|(B, B^*) \\
& \vdash_{\text{Inf}} (A, ((A^*, B^*), B^*))|(B, ((B^*, B^*)|B^*)) \leq ()|(A, (A^*, B^*))|(B, B^*) \\[6pt]
\longrightarrow_{--|1} & \vdash_{\text{Inf}} () \leq () \\
& \vdash_{\text{Inf}} (A, ((A^*, B^*), B^*))|(B, ((B^*, B^*)|B^*)) \leq ()|(A, (A^*, B^*))|(B, B^*) \\
\longrightarrow_{()-()} & \vdash_{\text{Inf}} (A, ((A^*, B^*), B^*))|(B, ((B^*, B^*)|B^*)) \leq ()|(A, (A^*, B^*))|(B, B^*) \\
\longrightarrow_{|--} & \vdash_{\text{Inf}} (A, ((A^*, B^*), B^*)) \leq ()|(A, (A^*, B^*))|(B, B^*) \\
& \vdash_{\text{Inf}} (B, ((B^*, B^*)|B^*)) \leq ()|(A, (A^*, B^*))|(B, B^*) \\
& \longrightarrow_{--|1} Fail \\
& \longrightarrow_{--|2} \vdash_{\text{Inf}} (A, ((A^*, B^*), B^*)) \leq (A, (A^*, B^*))|(B, B^*) \\
& \qquad \vdash_{\text{Inf}} (B, ((B^*, B^*)|B^*)) \leq ()|(A, (A^*, B^*))|(B, B^*) \\
\longrightarrow_{--|1} & \vdash_{\text{Inf}} (A, ((A^*, B^*), B^*)) \leq (A, (A^*, B^*)) \\
& \vdash_{\text{Inf}} (B, ((B^*, B^*)|B^*)) \leq ()|(A, (A^*, B^*))|(B, B^*) \\
\longrightarrow_{m-m1} & \vdash ((A^*, B^*), B^*) \leq (A^*, B^*) \\
& \vdash_{\text{Inf}} (B, ((B^*, B^*)|B^*)) \leq ()|(A, (A^*, B^*))|(B, B^*) \\
\longrightarrow_{CoInd} & \vdash_{\text{Inf}} (B, ((B^*, B^*)|B^*)) \leq ()|(A, (A^*, B^*))|(B, B^*) \\
\longrightarrow & \quad \ldots \\
\longrightarrow & \quad True
\end{array}
$$

Note that during the derivation we encounter the judgment $\vdash ((A^*, B^*), B^*) \leq (A^*, B^*)$ again which is resolved by applying the co-induction principle.

Theorem 1 (Antimirov). Let R_1 and R_2 be two regular expressions. Then, $L(R_1) \subseteq L(R_2)$ ▪ $\vdash R_1 \leq R_2$ is derivable in Antimirov's proof system.

3   Regular Expressions

We show how to encode Antimirov's algorithm in terms of Haskell type classes. First, we need to define an appropriate Haskell representation for regular expression types and their underlying structured representation. We employ the following singleton types.

```
data A = A
data B = B
data STAR x = STAR x
data OR x y = OR x y
```

E.g., we represent the regular expression $(A|B)^*$ in terms of the Haskell type (STAR (OR A B)). For convenience, we often make use of the more familiar regular expression notation.

The translation function $[\![\_]\!]$ from regular expression types to underlying structured representation types is adopted from Wallace and Runciman [22].

$$
\begin{array}{ll}
[\![()]\!] = [\texttt{Phi}] & [\![R^*]\!] & = [\,[\![R]\!]\,] \\
[\![l]\!] \; = \texttt{l\_H} & [\![(R_1|R_2)]\!] = \texttt{Or}\ [\![R_1]\!]\ [\![R_2]\!] \\
[\![B]\!] = B & [\![(R_1,R_2)]\!] = ([\![R_1]\!],[\![R_2]\!])
\end{array}
$$

where `data Phi` and `data Or a b = L a | R b`. Note that () is represented by the Haskell list type [Phi] where `Phi` has no associated value. Hence, the only Haskell value belonging to [Phi] is the empty list []. For each literal l we introduce `data l_H = l_H`. E.g., A is translated to `data A_H = A_H`.

We note that function $[\![\_]\!]$ can be modelled via type classes.

```
class REtoHT r h | r -> h
instance REtoHT () [Phi]
...
```

Our type class representation of judgments $\vdash R_1 \leq R_2$ is as follows.

```
class ( REtoHT r1 h1, REtoHT r2 h2
      ) => UCast r1 r2 h1 h2 | r1 r2 -> h1 h2 where
  ucast :: r1 -> r2 -> h1 -> h2
```

In contrast to the Introduction function `ucast` expects now two additional input values which refer to regular expressions.

Encoding of the $\vdash$ proof system in terms of instance declarations is straightforward. E.g., consider rules (,-,1), (,-,2) and (,-,3) from Example 1. Immediately, we obtain

```
instance ( UCast (r1,r2) r3 (h1,h2) h3, UCast () r4 [Phi] h4
         ) => UCast (r1,r2) (r3,r4) (h1,h2) (h3,h4) where    -- (1)
  ucast (r1,r2) (r3,r4) (h1,h2) =
      ((ucast (r1,r2) r3 (h1,h2)), (ucast () r4 []))
instance ( UCast r1 r3 h1 h3 , UCast r2 r4 h2 h4
         ) => UCast (r1,r2) (r3,r4) (h1,h2) (h3,h4) where    -- (2)
  ucast (r1,r2) (r3,r4) (h1,h2)=((ucast r1 r3 h1),(ucast r2 r4 h2))
instance ( UCast () r3 [Phi] h3, UCast (r1,r2) r4 (h1,h2) h4
         ) => UCast (r1,r2) (r3,r4) (h1,h2) (h3,h4) where    -- (3)
  ucast (r1,r2) (r3,r4) (h1,h2) =
      ((ucast () r3 []), (ucast (r1,r2) r4 (h1,h2)))
```

The experienced Haskell programmer will notice that the above instances are overlapping. Note that we can unify the instance heads (rhs of =>). In Haskell the common assumption is that instance declarations must be non-overlapping. This usually guarantees that there is a unique evidence translation for each type class constraint. In order to encode Antimirov's algorithm we require for a modest extension of type classes.

Definition 1 (Alternative Instances). For each instance TC t1 ... tm we allow for a number of alternatives such as

```
instance C1 => TC t1 ... tm where ... -- (1)
...
instance Cn => TC t1 ... tm where ... -- (n)
```

We assume that type class resolution proceeds by first considering instance (1). In case of failure we try instance (2) and so on.

Informally, type class resolution applies rule specified by instance and class declarations to a set of constraints yielding another set. A set of constraint is called final if no further rules can be applied. A path is a sequence rule applications yielding from an initial constraint store to some final store. A set of constraints is called successful if $False$ (the always unsatisfiable constraint) is not part of the set.

Assume that $TC_1,...,TC_k$ is the set of constraint symbols with an alternative number of instances. We say a set of constraints fails iff the set is unsuccessful, or we find TC_i $\overline{t_i}$ for some i in the set. Type class resolution fails if the final constraint store fails.

We note that the alternative instance extension will be problematic in case of separate compilation. However, we assume that all "alternative" instances are kept in the same module.

Example 3. Consider verifying $\vdash A \leq (A|A)$. Here are the relevant ordinary proof rules

$$(\_ - |1) \frac{\vdash R_1 \leq R_2}{\vdash R_1 \leq R_2|R_3} \quad (\_ - |2) \frac{\vdash R_1 \leq R_3}{\vdash R_1 \leq R_2|R_3} \quad (\text{Taut}) \frac{\vdash True}{\vdash R \leq R}$$

There are two possible proof trees.

$$\vdash A \leq (A|A) \longrightarrow_{\_-|1} \vdash A \leq A \longrightarrow_{Taut} True \qquad (1)$$

or

$$\vdash A \leq (A|A) \longrightarrow_{\_-|2} \vdash A \leq A \longrightarrow_{Taut} True \qquad (2)$$

In terms of our type class encoding, we can derive two versions of ucast on the same type. Here are the type class encodings of rules $(\_ - |1)$ and $(\_ - |2)$.

```
instance ( UCast r1 r2 h1 h2
         ) => UCast r1 (r2|r3) h1 (Or h2 h3) where    -- (1)
  ucast r1 (r2|r3) h1 = L (ucast r1 r2 h1)

instance ( UCast r1 r3 h1 h3
         ) => DCast r1 (r2|r3) h1 (Or h2 h3) where    -- (2)
  ucast r1 (r2|r3) h2 = R (ucast r1 r3 h1)
```

Depending on which instances we pick, we can either inject the value into the left or right component. To avoid such ambiguity problems we impose a textual order among instances. Based on this assumption, proof-term construction is deterministic.

To encode the $\vdash_{Inf}$ system we introduce an additional type class.

```
class ( REtoHT n1 h1 , REtoHT n2 h2
      ) => NUCast n1 n2 h1 h2 | n1 n2 -> h1 h2 where
  nucast :: n1 -> n2 -> h1 -> h2
```

The encoding of the $\vdash_{Inf}$ proof rules is yet again fairly straightforward. E.g. , we have the following instance to express rule (()-()) in Figure 1,

```
instance NUCast () () [Phi] [Phi] where
  nucast () () [] = []
```

However, the encoding of rule (Last) turns out to be more tricky. The instance UCast r1 r2 h1 h2 modeling rule (Last) must imply the existence of a ucast::h1->h2 function. So far, our encoding of the the premise $\vdash_{Inf}$ n1 $\leq$ n2 only guarantees the existence of nucast::h1'->h2' where h1' and h2' are the structured representation of the LNFs n1 and n2 of r1 and r2. Fortunately, we have that there is a bijection between the structured representations of regular expressions and their LNFs. Hence, we first compute the LNFs n1 and n2 of r1 and r2. We then apply the bijection function between r1 and n1 and convert h1 into h1'. Finally we apply the nucast::h1'->h2' and convert h2' into h2 by applying the bijection function between n2 and r2. In terms of type classes, this can be phrased as follows.

```
-- norm(r)=n
class Norm r n | r -> n where
  norm :: r -> n

-- bijection among underlying representation of r and norm(r)
class ( REtoHT r h , REtoHT n h' , Norm r n
      ) => NormV r n h h' | r -> n, r n -> h h' where
  toNorm :: r -> n -> h -> h'
  fromNorm :: n -> r -> h' -> h

-- last instance
instance ( Norm r1 n1, Norm r2 r2', NormV r1 n1 h1 h1'
         , NormV r2 n2 h2 h2', NUCast n1 n2 h1' h2''
         ) => UCast r1 r2 h1 h2 where
    ucast r1 r2 h1 = let n1 = norm r1
                         n2 = norm r2
                         h1' = toNorm r1 n1 h1
                         h2' = nucast n1 n2 h1'
                     in fromNorm n2 r2 h2'
```

Of course, we yet have to provide the appropriate instances for Norm and NormV. Note that both functions can readily be defined in terms of some first-order functional programs. Via some type class acrobatic we can easily encode their functionality on the level of types. The observant reader will notice that the above instance violates the "termination" condition imposed on functional dependencies [5]. Potentially, this might lead to undecidable type inference. However, the above use of "non-terminating" instances does not endanger decidable type inference in case of our particular type class application.

What remains is to extend type class resolution with the co-inductive proof principle.

Definition 2 (Co-inductive Type Class Resolution). Informally, whenever we encounter a constraint we have seen before on the path yielding the current constraint store, we simply remove this constraint.

Such an extension can be easily incorporated into existing implementations and is already available in the CVS version of GHC [7].

A complete description of all instances to encode Antimirov's algorithm can be found in [15].

Theorem 2. Antimirov's algorithm can be fully and faithfully encoded in terms of Haskell type classes by making use of alternative instances and co-inductive type class resolution. Additionally, we are able to construct proof terms representing the appropriate casting functions.

Analogue to `UCast` we can also describe down-casting in terms of type classes.

```
class ( REtoHT r1 h1, REtoHT r2 h2
      ) => DCast r1 r2 h1 h2 | r1 r2 -> h1 h2 where
  dcast :: r1 -> r2 -> h1 -> Maybe h2
```

We assume that `DCast r1 r2 h1 h2` is valid iff $\vdash$ r2 $\leq$ r1 and we can "down-cast" `h1` into `h2`. Note that there is no difference on the level of types. However, there is a crucial difference on the value level. Down-casting may not be always successful. Hence, we introduce `data Maybe a = Just a | Nothing` to report failure if necessary.

Example 4. Consider the derivation $\vdash A \leq ((\emptyset)|A) \longrightarrow_{--|2} \vdash A \leq A \longrightarrow_{Taut}$ *True* which makes use of the rules from Example 3, The corresponding `DCast` instances are as follows,

```
instance ( DCast r2 r3 h2 h3
         ) => DCast (r1|r2) r3 (Or h1 h2) h3 where
  dcast (r1|r2) r3 (R h2) = dcast r2 r3 h2 h3
  dcast _ _ (L _) = Nothing
instance DCast r r h h where
  dcast _ _ h = Just h
```

Then, `dcast (()|A) A (L [])` yields `Nothing` whereas `dcast (()|A) A (R A_H)` yields `Just A_H`.

An important property is that the down-casting of an upcasted value yields back the original value. i.e. `dcast R1 R2 (ucast R2 R1 v) = Just v`. In order to guarantee this property we simply put the `DCast` instances in the exact same order as their `UCast` counter part.

4   Regular Hedges

In the context of type-safe XML processing languages such as XDuce and CDuce types are described in terms of regular hedges (sequences of trees) rather than regular expressions.

Example 5. Here is a XDuce example [10] defining an address book type.

```
type Addrbook = addrbook[Person*]
type Person = person[Name, Tel?, Email*]
type Name = name[String]
type Tel = tel[String]
type Email = email[String]
```

Note that regular expressions types can appear under labels. e.g. The type `Person*` denotes a sequence of trees of type `Person`.

In the following we show how the results from Section 3 can be extended to deal with regular hedges.

The language of regular hedges is as follows.

$$\text{Regular Hedge } R ::= () \parallel l[R] \parallel R^* \parallel (R|R) \parallel (R,R)$$

A regular hedge $l[R]$ refers to a regular expression R under a label l. It is common to say that the regular expression R is guarded by label l. For simplicity, we omit base types like String, but they can be easily incorporated. The Haskell translation of regular hedge requires a minor change in the translation of regular expression, E.g., $l[R]$ is translated to `data l_H = l_H H` where `H` is the translation of R.

In order to accommodate regular hedges we first need to extend Antimirov's proof system. We replace all occurrences of literal l by label type $l[R]$ in the ordinary proof rules. This change implies that we need the following additional rule

$$(1[]\text{-}1[]) \ \frac{l_1 = l_2 \quad \vdash R_1 \leq R_2}{\vdash l_1[R_1] \ \leq \ l_2[R_2]}$$

The changes required for the $\vdash_{\text{Inf}}$ proof system are more substantial. Regular hedges make it necessary to adapt to our notion of deterministic LNF.

Example 6. Consider

$$\vdash \underbrace{(l_1[R_1|R_3], (R_1'|R_3'))}_{lhs} \ \leq \ \underbrace{(l_1[R_1], R_1')|(l_2[R_2], R_2')|(l_1[R_3], R_3')|(l_2[R_4], R_4')}_{rhs}$$

Assume that we extend the definition of monomials by replacing $l[R]$ for l. Note that there is no deterministic LNF for the rhs. E.g., $(l_1[R_1], R_1')$ and $(l_1[R_3], R_3')$ on the rhs share the same label. Relaxing the notion of deterministic LNF is not an option. Otherwise, Antimirov's algorithm becomes incomplete.

As a solution we assume that all monomials with a common label are grouped under a union. We refer to the resulting expression as the Common-Labelled Union (CLU). Here is the extended definition of normal forms.

$$
\begin{array}{llll}
\text{Monomial} & M & ::= & (l[R], R') \\
\text{Sum} & S & ::= & M \parallel (M|S) \\
\text{LNF} & N & ::= & S \parallel (()|S) \\
\text{CLU } CLU(l) & ::= & |_{j \in J}(l[R_j], R'_j) \\
\text{CLU-Sum} & C & ::= & CLU(l_1) \parallel (CLU(l_2)|C) \\
\text{CLU-Sum-LNF} & B & ::= & C \parallel (()|C)
\end{array}
$$

We say a CLU-Sum-LNF is deterministic iff none of the CLUs shares a common label. Note that we do not require LNFs to be deterministic anymore.

E.g., the deterministic CLU-Sum-LNF of the rhs in the above example is as follows

$$
\underbrace{((l_1[R_1], R'_1)|(l_1[R_3], R'_3))}_{CLU(l_1)} \mid \underbrace{((l_2[R_2], R'_2)|(l_2[R_4], R'_4))}_{CLU(l_2)}
$$

What remains is to check each monomial on the lhs against the CLU sum. That is,

$$
\vdash_{\text{Inf}} lhs \ \leq \ CLU(l_1) \ \vee \ \vdash_{\text{Inf}} lhs \ \leq \ CLU(l_2)
$$

Additionally, we rephrase rule (m-m1) from Figure 1 as follows.

$$
\text{(m-m1)} \ \frac{l_1 = l_2 \quad \vdash R_1 \leq R_2 \quad \vdash R'_1 \leq R'_2}{\vdash_{\text{Inf}} (l_1[R'_1], R_1) \ \leq \ (l_2[R'_2], R_2)}
$$

However, the resulting proof system is still not strong enough.

Example 7. Consider the following inequality,

$$
(l[R_1|R_2], (R'_1|R'_2)) \leq (l[R_1], R'_1)|(l[R_2], R'_2)
$$

The lhs is contained in the rhs, but neither in $(l[R_1], R'_1)$ nor $(l[R_2], R'_2)$. Hence, our current adaption of Antimirov's proof system fails, in other words. it is still incomplete.

Applying the distributivity law on the lhs might help in this example. However, in case there is a "*" type guarded by the label on the lhs, this potentially leads to non-termination.

Such problems have already been recognized by Hosoya [9] in the context of a slightly different algorithm for containment checking. Hosoya established a powerful law (originally from a lemma in [1]) which allowed him to establish completeness for his algorithm.

Apply if all other $\vdash R_1 \leq R_2$ failed:

$$\text{(Last)} \frac{N_1 = \texttt{norm}'(R_1) \quad B_2 = \texttt{clu} \circ \texttt{norm}'(R_2) \quad \vdash_{\mathsf{lnf}} N_1 \leq B_2}{\vdash R_1 \leq R_2}$$

Containment rules among LNFs and CLUs:

$$\text{(m-c1)} \frac{\begin{array}{c} l_1 = l_2 \quad \tau = S|T|R_1|\dots|R_n \\ \text{for each } I \subseteq [1,\dots,n], \bar{I} = [1,\dots,n]\backslash I \\ \vdash (l_1[S], T) \leq (l_2[|_{i\in I} R_i], \tau)|(l_2[\tau], |_{i\in\bar{I}} R_i') \end{array}}{\vdash_{\mathsf{lnf}} (l_1[S], T) \leq (l[R_1], R_1')|\dots|(l[R_n], R_n')}$$

$$\text{(()-())} \frac{True}{\vdash_{\mathsf{lnf}} () \leq ()} \qquad \text{(|-_)} \frac{\vdash_{\mathsf{lnf}} N_1 \leq B_3 \quad \vdash_{\mathsf{lnf}} N_2 \leq B_3}{\vdash_{\mathsf{lnf}} (N_1|N_2) \leq B_3}$$

$$\text{(\_-|1)} \frac{\vdash_{\mathsf{lnf}} N_1 \leq B_2}{\vdash_{\mathsf{lnf}} N_1 \leq (B_2|B_3)} \qquad \text{(\_-|2)} \frac{\vdash_{\mathsf{lnf}} N_1 \leq B_3}{\vdash_{\mathsf{lnf}} N_1 \leq (B_2|B_3)}$$

Fig. 2. Essence of Antimirov's Algorithm extended with Hosoya's Law

Theorem 3 (Hosoya2000). For any regular expression $S, T, R_1, \dots R_n$. We have that

$$L(l[S], T) \subseteq L((l[R_1], R_1')|\dots|(l[R_n], R_n'))$$
$$\text{iff}$$
for each $I \subseteq \{1, \dots, n\}, \bar{I} = \{1, \dots, n\}\backslash I$ we have that
$$L(l[S], T) \subseteq L((l[|_{i\in I} R_i], \tau)|(l[\tau], |_{i\in\bar{I}} R_i'))$$

where $\tau = S|T|R_1|\dots|R_n$ is the maximal type.

Based on the above Theorem we extend Antimirov's algorithm to regular hedges. We refer to Figure 2 for details. In rule (Last) we compute the deterministic CLU-Sum-LNF of the rhs via function clu. Function norm' is a simplified version of function norm where we do not require LNFs to be deterministic.

In rule (m-c1) we make use of Hosoya's Theorem. Rule (()-()) deals with the empty type (). Rules (|-_), (_-|1) and (_-|2) deal with the union type |. Note that $(B_1|B_2)$ denotes a union of unions (i.e. a union of CLUs), and $CLU(l)$ denotes a union of monomials. Hence there is no overlap with rules (m-c1) and (m-c2).

In fact, as we have learnt recently, a similar extension of Antimirov's algorithm has been considered by Kempa and Linnemann [13]. However, the crucial difference is that they do not consider how to derive proof terms, i.e., casting functions out of proofs. Note that it is by no means obvious how to define Antimirov's extended proof system in terms of type classes. Fortunately, we can apply a trick to achieve a type class encoding.

Example 8. Consider $\vdash_{\text{Inf}} l[S], T \leq (l[R_1], R_1')|(l[R_2], R_2')$ (0). The only rule applicable is (m-c1). We conclude that the above holds iff we can verify that

$$
\begin{array}{ll}
\vdash l[S], T \leq (l[\phi], \tau)|(l[\tau], (R_1'|R_2')) \wedge & (1) \\
\vdash l[S], T \leq (l[R_1], \tau)|(l[\tau], R_2') \wedge & (2) \\
\vdash l[S], T \leq (l[R_2], \tau)|(l[\tau], R_1') \wedge & (3) \\
\vdash l[S], T \leq (l[R_1|R_2], \tau)|(l[\tau], \phi) & (4)
\end{array}
$$

where $\tau = S|T|R_1|R_1'|R_2|R_2'$ and ϕ denotes the empty language. Silently, we assume that none of the regular expressions S, T, R_1, R_1', R_2 and R_2' denotes the empty language. We can enforce this assumption via a emptiness check. Note that (0) has been transformed into four sub-statements. The question is which of the sub-proof terms corresponding to (1-4) shall we pick to construct `nucast0` $::$ $(l[S], T) \rightarrow ((l[R_1], R_1')|(l[R_2], R_2')) \rightarrow [\![(l[S], T)]\!] \rightarrow [\![((l[R_1], R_1')|(l[R_2], R_2'))]\!]$?

It seems we are stuck. But wait! Consider statements (1) and (4). We have that neither $\vdash (l[S], T) \leq (l[\phi], (R_1'|R_2'))$ nor $\vdash (l[S], T) \leq (l[R_1|R_2], \phi)$ holds. Hence, (1) and (4) are equivalent to $\vdash ((l[S], T) \leq (l[\tau], (R_1'|R_2')))$ and $\vdash ((l[S], T) \leq (l[R_1|R_2], \tau))$. Hosoya observed that $(l[R], \tau) \cap (l[\tau], R') = (l[R], R')$ holds in general[1]. Hence, (1) and (4) are in fact equivalent to $\vdash (l[S], T) \leq (l[R_1|R_2], (R_1'|R_2'))$. In summary, (1-4) are equivalent to

$$
\begin{array}{ll}
\vdash l[S], T \leq l[R_1|R_2], (R_1'|R_2') \wedge & (1\&4) \\
\vdash l[S], T \leq (l[R_1], \tau)|(l[\tau], R_2') \wedge & (2) \\
\vdash l[S], T \leq (l[R_2], \tau)|(l[\tau], R_1') \wedge & (3) \\
\vdash (l[R_1], R_1')|(l[R_2], R_2') \leq (l[R_1|R_2], (R_1'|R_2')) & (5)
\end{array}
$$

Note that we added the somewhat redundant statement (5) (which is is a tautology). This assumption will become essential to construct `nucast0`.

In the following reasoning steps, we neglect the underlying representation types for simplicity. Assumption (1&4) implies the existence of a

`ucast1And4`$:: (l[S], T) \rightarrow (l[R_1|R_2], (R_1'|R_2'))$

Assumption (5) implies

`dcast5`$:: (l[R_1|R_2], (R_1'|R_2')) \rightarrow (l[R_1], R_1')|(l[R_2], R_2')$

The remaining assumptions (2) and (3) guarantee that down-casting via `dcast5` will never fail. Hence,

```
nucast0 v = let Just v' = dcast5 (ucast1And4 v)
            in v'
```

We conclude that for proof term construction of (0), we only make use of the proof terms resulting from (1&4) and (5). We do not make use of the proof

---

[1] Silently, we introduce binary operator $\cap$ to our regular hedge language, where $\cap$ denotes the intersection of two regular hedges. We have that $\vdash R_1 \leq (R_2 \cap R_3)$ iff $\vdash R_1 \leq R_2 \wedge \vdash R_1 \leq R_3$.

terms resulting from (2) and (3). However, the fact that their proofs exist allows us to conclude that down-casting never fails.

The above "trick" works in general. Consider the general case

$$\vdash_{\mathrm{Inf}} (l[S], T) \leq (l[R_1], R'_1)|...|(l[R_n], R'_n) \quad (0)$$

According to Hosoya's Law, (0) holds iff

$$\vdash (l[S], T) \leq \bigcap_I (l[|_{i \in I} R_i], \tau)|l[\tau], |_{i \in \bar{I}} R'_i)$$
$$\text{where } I \subseteq [1, \ldots, n], \bar{I} = [1, \ldots, n] \setminus I$$

where $\tau = S|T|R_1|...|R_n|R'_1|...|R'_n$. Each instance of I is an element of the powerset $P([1, \ldots, n])$. Hence in general, there are 2^n instances of I. Following our reasoning in Example 8, we can rephrase rule (m-c1) in Figure 2 as follows.

$$l_1 = l_2 \quad \tau = S|T|R_1|\ldots|R_n$$
$$\vdash (l[S], T) \leq (l[R_1|...|R_n], (R'_1|...|R'_n)) \quad (1\&2^n)$$
$$\vdash (l[S], T) \leq (l[R_1], \tau)|(l[\tau], (R'_2|...|R'_n)) \quad (2)$$
$$\cdots \qquad\qquad\qquad\qquad\qquad\qquad\qquad\qquad\qquad \cdots$$
$$\vdash (l[S], T) \leq (l[R_1|...|R_{n-1}], \tau)|(l[\tau], R'_n) \quad (2^n - 1)$$
$$\underline{\vdash (l[R_1], R_1)|...|(l[R_n], R_n) \leq (l[R_1|...|R_n], (R'_1|...|R'_n)) \;\;(\text{Taut})}$$
$$\vdash_{\mathrm{Inf}} (l_1[S], T) \leq (l[R_1], R'_1)|\ldots|(l[R_n], R'_n)$$

To implement the rephrased rule (m-c1) we introduce a new type class to to compute the rhs of $(1\&2^n)$ (the "key"), and the sequence of rhs of (2), ..., $(2^n - 1)$ (the "guards").

```
data KAG k gs = KAG k gs
-- k represents the key and gs represents the list of guards
class CLUtoKAG clu kag | clu -> kag where clutokag :: clu -> kag
```

Here is the encoding rule (m-c1).

```
-- ((l[r1],r1')|rs) is the CLU.
instance ( REtoHT gs hgs, REtoHT k h3, REtoHT (l[s],t) (h,h')
         , CLUtoKAG ((l[r1],r1')|rs) (KAG k gs)          -- (L1)
         , UCast (l[s],t) k (h,h') h3                    -- (L2)
         , UCasts (l[s],t) gs (h,h') hgs                 -- (L3)
         , DCast k ((l[r1],r1')|rs) h3 (Or (h1,h1') hs)) -- (L4)
=> NUCast (l[s],t) ((l[r1],r1')|rs) (h,h') (Or (h1,h1') hs) where
  nucast (l[s],t) ((l[r1],r1')|rs) (h,h') =
         let (KAG k gs) = clutokag ((l[r1],r1')|rs)      -- (L5)
             h3 = ucast (l[s],t) k (h,h1')
         in case (dcast k ((l[r1],r1')|rs) h3) of        -- (L6)
            Just hr -> hr
            Nothing -> error "This will never happen."
```

At location (L1) we compute the key and the list of guards. Note that the key value k will be requested in the instance body (see locations (L5) and (L6)) whereas the guards are only present on the level of types. At location (L2) we verify assumption $(1\&2^n)$. At location (L3) we verify assumptions (2), ...,$(2^n - 1)$. Type class UCasts is a variant of UCast, allowing us to verify a set of assumptions. At location (L4) we verify assumption (Taut). The instance body should not contain any more surprises.

The remaining rules in Figure 2 can be straightforwardly encoded in terms of type classes. Note that we need to introduce type classes Norm' and Clu to model functions norm' and clu. Full details can be found in [15].

Theorem 4. We can fully and faithfully encode Antimirov's algorithm extended to deal with regular hedges in terms of type classes. Additionally, we are able to construct proof terms representing the appropriate casting functions.

5   Related Work and Conclusion

Our use of type classes to model subtyping among regular expressions appears to be novel. To deal with regular hedges we make use of a novel adaption of Antimirov's algorithm. Such an extension of Antimirov's algorithm has already been considered by Kempa and Linnemann [13]. They also exploit Antimirov's algorithm for containment checking. But, they do not consider how to derive proof terms to represent casting functions. As we have seen this becomes non-trivial in case of regular hedges.

Thiemann [21] makes use of type classes to check for correctness of constructed XML values in the context of the combinator library WASH. However, he does not consider destruction of values, i.e. how to generate the appropriate casting functions.

Crary [4] implements a calculus with higher-order subtyping and subkinding by replacing uses of implicit subsumption with explicit coercions. Coercion functions are derived out of the proof from subkinding judgments. At this stage we do not know whether his proof system can be adapted to the setting of regular expression types, nor whether type classes can be used to encode his proof system. We plan to pursue these questions in the future.

Frisch and Cardelli [6] introduce a linear-time regular pattern matching algorithm over structured run-time values to avoid the exponential explosion in case of the "local longest match" policy. We conjecture that such problems can be circumvented altogether in our implementation of semantic subtyping based on Antimirov's algorithm. We refer to [15] for details.

We see the current work as the first step in adding type-safe XML support to languages such as Haskell. We are near to completion in the design of XHaskell [14], a variant of Haskell to support regular expression types, regular expression pattern matching and semantic subtyping. Our implementation of semantic subtyping in terms of type classes is crucial to achieve this goal. XHaskell is translated to Haskell by a source-to-source transformation. Then, XDuce-style type checking and insertion of casting functions is performed by type class resolution. The "alternative instance" extension is currently not available in any known Haskell extension. In fact, such an extension is straightforward given the close connection between type class programming and logic programming [16,18] We plan to incorporate alternative instances into the Chameleon system [20] – our own experimental version of Haskell. An important issue will be how to map type class errors back to meaningful type error messages in XHaskell. We expect that we can rely on our own work on type debugging [19]. We plan to pursue this topic in future work. We already conducted some initial experiments which show that XHaskell's run-time performance is competitive in comparison with XDuce and CDuce. We intend to provide a more detailed comparison in the future. To enable full XML support we yet need to add recursive types to our type language. We refer the interested reader to [15] for more details.

Acknowledgements

We thank Jeremy Wazny and the reviewers for their comments.

References

1. A. Aiken and B. Murphy. Implementing regular tree expressions. In *Proc. of FPCA'91*, volume 523 of *LNCS*, pages 427–447. Springer, 1991.
2. V. M. Antimirov. Rewriting regular inequalities. In *Proc. of FCT'95*, volume 965 of *LNCS*, pages 116–125. Springer-Verlag, 1995.
3. V. Benzaken, G. Castagna, and A. Frisch. Cduce: An XML-centric general-purpose language. In *Proc. of ICFP '03*, pages 51–63. ACM Press, 2003.
4. K. Crary. Foundations for the implementation of higher-order subtyping. In *Proc. of ICFP'97*, pages 125–135. ACM Press, 1997.
5. G. J. Duck, S. Peyton-Jones, P. J. Stuckey, and M. Sulzmann. Sound and decidable type inference for functional dependencies. In *Proc. of ESOP'04*, volume 2986 of *LNCS*, pages 49–63. Springer-Verlag, 2004.
6. A. Frisch and L. Cardelli. Greedy regular expression matching. In *In PLAN-X '04 Informal Proceedings*, 2004.
7. Glasgow Haskell compiler home page. http://www.haskell.org/ghc/.
8. C. V. Hall, K. Hammond, S. Peyton Jones, and P. Wadler. Type classes in Haskell. In *Proc. of ESOP'94*, volume 788 of *LNCS*, pages 241–256. Springer, April 1994.
9. H. Hosoya. *Regular Expression Types for XML*. PhD thesis, The University of Tokyo, December 2000.
10. H. Hosoya and B. C. Pierce. Regular expression pattern matching for XML. In *Proc. of POPL '01*, pages 67–80. ACM Press, 2001.
11. H. Hosoya, J. Vouillon, and B. C. Pierce. Regular expression types for XML. *ACM SIGPLAN Notices*, 35(9):11–22, 2000.
12. M. P. Jones. Type classes with functional dependencies. In *Proc. of ESOP 2000*, volume 1782 of *LNCS*. Springer, March 2000.
13. M. Kempa and V. Linnemann. Type checking in XOBE. In *Proc. Datenbanksysteme fur Business, Technologie und Web, BTW '03*, LNI, page 227-246 GI, 2003.

14. K. Z. M. Lu and M. Sulzmann. XHaskell, 2004. `http://www.comp.nus.edu.sg/~luzm/xhaskell`.
15. K.Z.M. Lu and M. Sulzmann. An implementation of subtyping among regular expression types. Technical report, The National University of Singapore, 2004. `http://www.comp.nus.edu.sg/~luzm/xhaskell/tr-impsubtype.ps`.
16. M. Neubauer, P. Thiemann, M. Gasbichler, and M. Sperber. Functional logic overloading. In *Proc. of POPL'02*, pages 233–244. ACM Press, 2002.
17. S. Peyton Jones et al. Report on the programming language Haskell 98, February 1999. http://haskell.org.
18. P. J. Stuckey and M. Sulzmann. A theory of overloading. In *Proc. of ICFP'02*, pages 167–178. ACM Press, 2002.
19. P.J. Stuckey, M. Sulzmann, and J. Wazny. Interactive type debugging in Haskell. In *Proc. of Haskell Workshop'03*, pages 72–83. ACM Press, 2003.
20. M. Sulzmann and J. Wazny. The Chameleon system, July 2004. `http://www.comp.nus.edu.sg/~sulzmann/chameleon`.
21. P. Thiemann. A typed representation for HTML and XML documents in Haskell. *Journal of Functional Programming*, 12(4 and 5):435–468, July 2002.
22. M. Wallace and C. Runciman. Haskell and XML: Generic combinators or type-based translation? In *ICFP '99*, pages 148–159. ACM Press, 1999.

An Implementation Scheme for XML Transformation Languages Through Derivation of Stream Processors

Keisuke Nakano

Department of Mathematical Engineering and Information Physics,
University of Tokyo
ksk@mist.i.u-tokyo.ac.jp

Abstract. We propose a new implementation scheme for XML transformation languages through derivation of stream processors. Most of XML transformation languages are implemented as tree manipulation, where input XML trees are completely stored in memory. It leads to inefficient memory usage in particular when we apply a facile transformation to large-sized inputs. In contrast, XML stream processing can minimize memory usage and execution time since it begins to output the transformation result before reading the whole input. However, it is much harder to program XML stream processors than to specify tree manipulations because stream processing frequently requires 'stateful programming'. This paper proposes an implementation scheme for XML transformation languages, in which we can define an XML transformation as tree manipulation and also we can obtain an XML stream processor automatically. The implementation scheme employs a framework of a composition of attribute grammars.

1   Introduction

In recent years, various languages specialized for XML transformation have been proposed [25, 28, 10, 3]. Since XML documents have tree structure, these languages support various functions of pattern matching for paths in order to access particular nodes. These node accessing methods are generally implemented as *tree manipulation* that requires the whole tree structure of an input XML document to be stored in memory. This implementation might be inefficient in memory usage in particular when a facile transformation, such as tag renaming and element filtering, is applied to large-sized XML documents because it does not require all information about the tree structure.

XML stream processing has been employed as one of solutions to reduce memory usage[22, 5]. XML stream processing completes a transformation by storing no tree structure of XML documents in memory. While taking advantage in memory usage, XML stream processing has a problem that programs are quite complicated because XML stream processing is defined by 'stateful program' in the sense that programmers need to consider what to memorize on reading a start tag, what to output on reading an end tag, and so on. It imposes a burden on programmers and causes error-prone unreadable programs.

To release programmers from the bother of stream processing, two kinds of approaches have been proposed. The first approach is to add various primitive combinators or functions for stream processing[11, 27]. Though it helps us to make stream

W.-N. Chin (Ed.): APLAS 2004, LNCS 3302, pp. 74–90, 2004.
© Springer-Verlag Berlin Heidelberg 2004

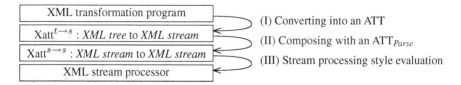

Fig. 1. Derivation of stream processing programs

processing programs, we still need to write programs with the prospect that the input XML is not a tree but a stream. The second approach is to give a mechanism deriving a stream processing program from a specification of a tree manipulation or node accessing[1, 17, 19, 4, 15]. We can write the program in tree manipulation style and need not to bear in mind that the input XML is a stream. However, the derivation mechanism can be applied to only a restricted class of XML transformations.

This paper basically takes the second approach, provided that the derivation method can deal with a wider class of XML transformations than before. Our derivation mechanism is based on a framework of *attributed tree transducer*(ATT) [6] which is a formal computational model for *attribute grammar*(AG) [12]. The mechanism is summarized by dividing it into three steps (Fig. 1). In the first step (I), a given XML transformation is converted into an ATT specialized for XML transformation, called Xatt$^{t \to s}$. The Xatt$^{t \to s}$ represents a transformation from XML trees to XML streams. This paper roughly shows how to convert an XML transformation into Xatt$^{t \to s}$ through two kinds of practical XML transformation: XPath querying [24] and partial modification. The former returns the collection of all elements specified by a given XPath expression. It is useful in the case that the input XML is regarded as a database. The latter returns an XML with a similar structure to the input XML where several fragments in the input are replaced with different ones. We can write a variety of XML transformations by combination of these basic transformations, though they are only a subset of the class of XML transformation specified by Xatt$^{t \to s}$. However, it does not show the limitation of this approach. This paper claims that we can derive an XML stream processor from every XML transformation program defined by Xatt$^{t \to s}$ which can deal with a wide class of XML transformation as well as non-circular AG. If one wants to implement an XML transformation language intended for stream processing, all he has to do is to give a conversion method into Xatt$^{t \to s}$ for the language. The stream processor is derived from an Xatt$^{t \to s}$ by the following two steps.

In the second step (II), we can obtain an Xatt$^{s \to s}$, which represents a transformation from XML streams to XML streams, from an Xatt$^{t \to s}$. We employ a *descriptional composition*[8], which is a composition method for AGs. If two AGs are given, where one represents a transformation from a language L_A to a language L_B and another represents a transformation from a language L_B to a language L_C, then we can obtain a single AG from L_A to L_C by descriptional composition. The obtained AG does not create any expressions in L_B even as intermediate result. The method can also be applied to ATT [14, 16]. In our framework, we use this method to compose a given Xatt$^{t \to s}$ with the other ATT representing a parsing function for XML and obtain an Xatt$^{s \to s}$. When more appropriate, the original descriptional composition cannot be applied to the parsing ATT because of the restriction of the method. For this reason, we use an extended descriptional composition[16] which can deal with ATTs with stack devices required in the parsing ATT.

In the third step (III), from the $Xatt^{s \to s}$ derived in the previous step, we can obtain an XML stream processor by specifying evaluation order for attributes in stream processing style. The XML stream processor can be derived by dividing the computation by $Xatt^{s \to s}$ into the computation for each input symbol. This generation method is similar to Nakano and Nishimura's method in [17, 19]. However, they failed to deal with a large class of ATTs because they sticked to derivation of finite state transition machines with dependency analysis.

This paper also shows benchmark results to illustrate effectiveness of our framework. The author has implemented an XML transformation language XTiSP (an abbreviation for XML Transformation language intended for Stream Processing) based on our framework. Using XTiSP, we can program an XML transformation as tree manipulation with XPath and obtain the corresponding XML stream processor for free. We compare an implementation of XTiSP with two XSLT processors, Xalan [26] and SAXON [23].

Related Work

The issue of automatic generation of stream processors has been studied for various languages. Most of these studies, however, targeted for only query languages such as XPath[1, 4, 9] and a subset of XQuery [15]. These querying languages have few expressibility to specify XML transformation. For example, they could not define the structure-preserved transformation, such as renaming a tag name a into b. Our framework allows not only querying functions but also ability to specify such transformation.

Our framework is based on the previous work [17, 19]. They succeeds in deriving a stream processing program from the specification of XML tree transformation defined by an ATT. However, in their framework, a set of ATTs we can deal with and input XMLs for them are quite restricted because of the weak applicability of AG composition method [8]. Our framework solves this problem by using the extended composition method [16].

Additionally, there are several work using a framework of attribute grammars for XML transformation. Whereas we use binary representation for XML trees, [18, 2] improve a traditional attribute grammar for unranked representation. However, their attribute grammars do not have a framework of descriptional composition we require. Although [13] employs an attribute grammar for XML stream processing, they uses only L-attribute grammars. In our framework, attribute grammars for XML stream processing are non-circular, which is wider class than L-attribute, and they are automatically derived from tree manipul ation programs.

Outline

The rest of this paper is comprised of seven sections, including introduction. Section 2 gives basic notations and a brief introduction of attributed tree transducers. In Section 3, we show how to specify XML transformation by using $Xatt^{t \to s}$. Section 4 presents a composition method of $Xatt^{t \to s}$ and an XML parser. In Section 5, we mention how to obtain an XML stream processor from $Xatt^{s \to s}$. Then Section 6 shows several benchmark results to illustrate effectiveness of our framework. Finally we conclude this paper in Section 7.

2 Preliminaries

2.1 Basic Notions

The empty set is denoted by $\emptyset$. The set of natural numbers including 0 by $\mathbb{N}$ and the set of natural numbers excluding 0 by $\mathbb{N}_+$. For every $n \in \mathbb{N}$, the set $\{1, \ldots, n\}$ is denoted by $[n]$. In particular, $[0] = \emptyset$. We denote a set of finite strings over a set P of symbols by P^*. A null string is denoted by ε.

A *ranked alphabet* Σ is a finite set in which every symbol is associated with a non-negative integer called *rank*. We denote the rank of a symbol σ by $rank(\sigma)$. We may write $\sigma^{(n)}$ to indicate that $rank(\sigma) = n$. Let Σ be a ranked alphabet and A be a set of variables disjoint with Σ. The set of Σ-*labeled trees indexed by* A, denoted by $T_\Sigma(A)$ (or T_Σ, if A is empty), is the smallest superset T of A such that $\sigma(t_1, \cdots, t_n) \in T$ for every $\sigma^{(n)} \in \Sigma$ and $t_1, \cdots, t_n \in T$.

We denote by $t[x := s]$ the *substitution* of occurrences of a variable x by s. Let $t, s_1, \ldots, s_n, u_1, \ldots, u_n$ be trees in $T_\Sigma(X)$ such that every u_i for $i \in [n]_+$ is a subtree of t, provided that u_i is not a subtree of u_j for any i and j with $i \neq j$. The tree $t[u_1, \ldots, u_n := s_1, \ldots, s_n]$, or $t[u_i := s_i]_{i \in [n]_+}$ is obtained from t by simultaneously *replacing* every subtree at the points of occurrences of $u_1, \ldots, u_n$ by the trees $s_1, \ldots, s_n$, respectively. If $\rho = [u_1, \ldots := s_1, \ldots]$, then we may write $\rho(t)$ for $t[u_1, \ldots := s_1, \ldots]$.

The prefix-closed set of all *paths* of t, denoted by $path(t)(\subseteq \mathbb{N}_+^*)$, is defined by $path(\sigma(t_1, \cdots, t_k)) = \{\varepsilon\} \cup \{iw \mid i \in [k], w \in path(t_i)\}$ if $\sigma^{(k)} \in \Sigma$. We write $t|_w$ for a subtree of a tree t at a path $w \in path(t)$. Every path $w \in path(t)$ refers to a corresponding label of t, denoted by $label(t, w)$, which is defined by $label(\sigma(t_1, \cdots, t_n), \varepsilon) = \sigma$ and $label(\sigma(t_1, \cdots, t_n), iw) = label(t_i, w)$ for every $i \in [n]$ and $w \in path(t_i)$.

A *reduction system* is a system $(A, \Rightarrow)$ where A is a set and $\Rightarrow$ is a binary relation over A. We write $a_1 \Rightarrow^n a_{n+1}$ if $a_i \Rightarrow a_{i+1}(i \in [n])$ for some $a_1, \cdots, a_{n+1} \in A$. In particular, $a \Rightarrow^0 a$. $a \in A$ is *irreducible* with respect to $\Rightarrow$ if there is no $c \in A$ such that $b \Rightarrow c(\neq b)$. If b is irreducible where $a \Rightarrow^i b$ for some $i \in \mathbb{N}$ and there is no pair of irreducible term $b'(\neq b)$ and $i' \in \mathbb{N}$ such that $a \Rightarrow^{i'} b'$, we say b is a *normal form* of a and write $nf(\Rightarrow, a)$ for b.

2.2 Attributed Tree Transducers

We give a brief introduction of *attributed tree transducer*(ATT) which has been introduced by Fülöp [6] as a formal computational model of attribute grammar(AG). See [7] for detail. The ATT M is defined by a tuple $M = (Syn, Inh, \Sigma, \Delta, s_{in}, \sharp, R)$, where

- *Syn* is a set of *synthesized attributes*. *Inh* is a set of *inherited attributes*. We denote $\{s(\pi k) \mid s \in Syn, k \in [n]\}$ and $\{i(\pi) \mid i \in Inh\}$ by $\Pi_{syn}(n)$ and Π_{inh}, respectively.
- Σ and Δ are ranked alphabets, called the *input and output alphabet*, respectively.
- s_{in} is the initial (synthesized) attribute and $\sharp$ is the root symbol with rank 1. These are used for specifying the computation result.
- R is a set of attribute rules such that $R = \cup_{\sigma \in \Sigma \uplus \{\sharp\}} R^\sigma$ with finite sets R^σ of σ-rules satisfying the following conditions:

- For every $s \in Syn$ and $\sigma \in \Sigma$, R^{σ} contains exactly one attribute rule of the form of $s(\pi) \to \eta$ where $\eta \in T_{\Sigma}(\Pi_{syn}(rank(\sigma)) \cup \Pi_{inh})$.
- For every $i \in Inh$ and $\sigma \in \Sigma$, R^{σ} contains exactly one attribute rule of the form of $i(\pi k) \to \eta$ where $k \in [rank(\sigma)]$ and $\eta \in T_{\Sigma}(\Pi_{syn}(rank(\sigma)) \cup \Pi_{inh})$.
- $R^{\sharp}$ contains exactly one attribute rule of the form of $s_{in}(\pi) \to \eta$ where $\eta \in T_{\Sigma}(\Pi_{syn}(1))$.
- For every $i \in Inh$, $R^{\sharp}$ contains exactly one attribute rule of the form of $i(\pi 1) \to \eta$ where $\eta \in T_{\Sigma}(\Pi_{syn}(1))$.

where we use $\pi, \pi 1, \pi 2, \cdots$ for *path variables*.

The computation by M for input tree $t \in T_{\Sigma}$ is defined by a reduction system $(U, \Rightarrow_{M,\sharp(t)})$ where $U = T_{\Delta}(\{a(w) \mid a \in Syn \cup Inh, w \in path(t)\}$ and $\Rightarrow_{M,t}$ is defined by

- $s(w) \Rightarrow_{M,t} \eta[\pi := w]$ where $s \in Syn$, $s(\pi) \to \eta \in R^{\sigma}$ and $\sigma = label(t, w)$.
- $i(wk) \Rightarrow_{M,t} \eta[\pi := w]$ where $i \in Inh$, $s(\pi k) \to \eta \in R^{\sigma}$ and $\sigma = label(t, w)$.
- $\delta(\ldots, \eta_k, \ldots) \Rightarrow_{M,t} \delta(\ldots, \eta'_k, \ldots)$ where $\delta \in \Delta$ and $\eta_k \Rightarrow_{M,t} \eta'_k$.

where $[\pi := w]$ with $w \in \mathbb{N}^*$ stands for a substitution $[i(\pi), s(\pi 1), s(\pi 2), \cdots := i(w)$, $s(w1), s(w2), \cdots]_{i \in Inh, s \in Syn}$. The *transformation result by M for the input tree t* is defined by $nf(\Rightarrow_{M,\sharp(t)}, s_{in}(\varepsilon))(\in T_{\Delta})$.

3 Attributed Tree Transducers for XML Transformation

Our framework requires XML transformations to be defined by specialized ATTs in order to obtain the corresponding XML stream processor. In this section, we first introduce a model of XML trees and XML streams as annotated trees. Next we extend ATTs to ones that deal with annotated trees, called *attributed tree transducers for XML*($Xatt^{t \to s}$). Then we show several examples of $Xatt^{t \to s}$ which represent basic XML transformations.

For simplicity, we deal with XML documents with no character data and no attribute. Our framework can be easily extended with them and the actual implementation supports them. In the rest of paper, a bare word 'attribute' is not used for XML attributes but for synthesized/inherited attributes in ATTs.

3.1 XML Trees and XML Streams

We use a binary representation for XML trees in which each left branch points to the leftmost child and each right branch to the first sibling node to follow in the tree structure of XML. For example, consider a fragment of XML `<a><b/><c/><d/></a>`. It has tree structure as shown in the upper-right figure. In binary representation, the XML tree is figured as shown in the lower-right one where a black bullet stands for a leaf which means the end of siblings. Every tree in binary representation is defined by a tree over $\Sigma_{tree} = \{N^{(2)}, L^{(0)}\}$ where N is a binary symbol annotated with a label and L is a nullary symbol corresponding a leaf. For instance,

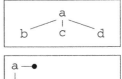

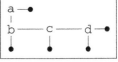

we write $N_a(N_b(L, N_c(L, N_d(L, L))), L)$ for the XML tree above. The set of trees in binary representation is denoted by $T_{\Sigma_{tree}}$.

XML streams are defined by monadic trees over $\Sigma_{stream} = \{S^{(1)}, E^{(1)}, Z^{(0)}\}$ where S and E are unary symbols corresponding a start tag and an end tag, respectively, each of them is annotated with a label as well as N, and Z is a nullary symbol standing for the end of stream. For instance, we write $S_a(S_b(E_b(S_c(E_c(E_a(Z))))))$ for a fragment of XML `<a><b/><c/></a>`. The set of streams is denoted by $T_{\Sigma_{stream}}$.

3.2   Extension of Attributed Tree Transducers with Annotation

$Xatt^{t \to s}$ deals with annotated trees such as XML trees and XML streams as ATT deals with trees. An $Xatt^{t \to s}$ is defined by a tuple of $M = (Syn, Inh, \Sigma, \Delta, R)^1$ in similar way to an ATT, where $\Sigma = \Sigma_{tree}$ and $\Delta = \Sigma_{stream}$ since an $Xatt^{t \to s}$ represents a transformation from XML trees to XML streams. The major difference from ATT is that R is defined by $\cup_{\sigma \in \Sigma_{tree}} R^{\sigma x}$ with finite sets $R^{\sigma x}$ of σ_x-rules in which we can use the annotation x in a right-hand side of an attribute rule. For example, R^{Nx} may contain an attribute rule $s(\pi) \to S_x(s(\pi 1))$. We show a simple example of $Xatt^{t \to s}$ which represents an identity XML transformation that takes an XML tree and returns the corresponding XML stream. The $Xatt^{t \to s}$ $M_{id} = (Syn, Inh, \Sigma, \Delta, R)$ is defined by

- $Syn = \{s\}$ and $Inh = \{i\}$
- $R = R^{\sharp} \cup R^{Nx} \cup R^L$ where
  - $R^{\sharp} = \{s_{in}(\pi) \to s(\pi 1), i(\pi 1) \to Z\}$
  - $R^{Nx} = \{s(\pi) \to S_x(s(\pi 1)), i(\pi 1) \to E_x(s(\pi 2)), i(\pi 2) \to i(\pi)\}$
  - $R^L = \{s(\pi) \to i(\pi)\}$.

Letting $t = N_a(N_b(L, N_a(L, L)), L)$ be a given input XML tree and $\Rightarrow$ stand for $\Rightarrow_{M, \sharp(t)}$, the transformation result of M_{id} is computed by

$$s_{in}(\varepsilon) \Rightarrow s(1) \Rightarrow S_a(s(11)) \Rightarrow S_a(S_b(s(111))) \Rightarrow S_a(S_b(i(111)))$$
$$\Rightarrow S_a(S_b(E_b(s(112)))) \Rightarrow S_a(S_b(E_b(S_a(s(1121))))) \Rightarrow S_a(S_b(E_b(S_a(i(1121)))))$$
$$\Rightarrow S_a(S_b(E_b(S_a(E_a(s(1122)))))) \Rightarrow S_a(S_b(E_b(S_a(E_a(i(1122))))))$$
$$\Rightarrow S_a(S_b(E_b(S_a(E_a(i(112)))))) \Rightarrow S_a(S_b(E_b(S_a(E_a(i(11))))))$$
$$\Rightarrow S_a(S_b(E_b(S_a(E_a(E_a(s(12))))))) \Rightarrow S_a(S_b(E_b(S_a(E_a(E_a(i(12)))))))$$
$$\Rightarrow S_a(S_b(E_b(S_a(E_a(E_a(i(1))))))) \Rightarrow S_a(S_b(E_b(S_a(E_a(E_a(Z)))))).$$

Fig. 2 visualizes the above computation. It shows the input XML tree t annotated with attributes and their dependencies. For example, $i(1121)$ is computed by $E_a(s(1122))$ because of the attribute rule $(i(\pi 1) \to E_x(s(\pi 2))) \in R^{Nx}$ with $\pi = 112$ and $x = a$ from $label(\sharp(t), 112) = N_a$.

The $Xatt^{t \to s}$ M_{id} transforms from XML trees into the corresponding XML stream. Using two attributes s and i, we can make an evaluation in depth-first right-to-left order. Note that we do not directly use this $Xatt^{t \to s}$ for stream processing. Since we use an ATT obtained by the composition of the original $Xatt^{t \to s}$ and parsing transformation,

---

[1] The initial attribute s_{in} and the root symbol $\sharp$ are omitted for simplicity.

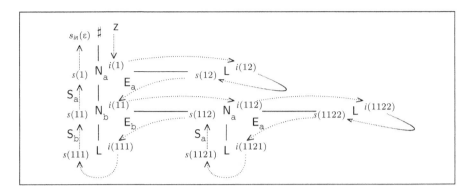

Fig. 2. The computation by M_{id} for the input $N_a(N_b(L, N_a(L, L)), L)$

the above evaluation does not mean that stream processing cannot start to output any result before it reads the complete input.

$Xatt^{t \to s}$ can deal with symbols other than output symbols in Σ_{stream} in right-hand sides of the attribute rules. Let us consider an $Xatt^{t \to s}$ M'_{id} has the same definition as M_{id} except that R^{N_x} is a set of the following rules:

$$s(\pi) \to \mathsf{Cat}(\mathsf{S}_x, s(\pi 1)), \quad i(\pi 1) \to \mathsf{Cat}(\mathsf{E}_x, s(\pi 2)), \quad i(\pi 2) \to i(\pi).$$

The computation by M'_{id} is done in similar to that by M_{id}. For example, if M_{id} outputs $\mathsf{S}_a(\mathsf{S}_b(\mathsf{E}_b(\ldots)))$ for an input, M'_{id} outputs $\mathsf{Cat}(\mathsf{S}_a, \mathsf{Cat}(\mathsf{S}_b, \mathsf{Cat}(\mathsf{E}_b, \ldots)))$ for the same input. The symbols S_x and E_x are used as nullary symbols and the binary symbol Cat means a concatenation of outputs and In the rest of paper we use these symbols instead of unary symbols S_x and E_x for output symbols. It will be helpful for us to obtain XML stream processors.

Furthermore, our framework allows the output alphabet of $Xatt^{t \to s}$ to include the other symbols such as Str_x, Eq_x, And, Or and If: the nullary symbol Str_x means a string value x; the unary symbol Eq_x means a boolean value representing whether the argument matches a string value x or not; the binary symbols And and Or represent boolean operations in usual way; the 3-ary symbol If means a conditional branch by the first argument. These symbols are useful for us to define a wide variety of XML transformations.

3.3 Conversion from Practical XML Transformations to $Xatt^{t \to s}$

This section gives practical examples and several hints for converting XML transformation into $Xatt^{t \to s}$. A basic idea of the conversion is that we give a number of pairs of synthesized attribute s and inherited attributes i whose attribute rules for N_x have the following form:

$$s(\pi) \to \mathsf{If}(e_{test}, e_{s1}, e_{s2}), \qquad i(\pi 1) \to \mathsf{If}(e_{test}, e_{i1}, e_{i2}), \qquad i(\pi 2) \to i(\pi) \quad (1)$$

where $e_{test}, e_{s1}, e_{s2}, e_{i1}$ and e_{i2} are right-hand side expressions for $Xatt^{t \to s}$. By adjusting these expressions we can convert a variety of XML transformations into $Xatt^{t \to s}$. For example, let us consider an $\text{Xatt}^{t \to s}$ M_{fil} which has the same definition as M'_{id} except that R^{N_x} has attribute rules of the form (1) where

$$e_{test} = \text{Eq}_x(\text{Str}_b), \; e_{s1} = s(\pi2), \; e_{s2} = \text{Cat}(S_x, s(\pi1)), \; e_{i1} = e_{i2} = \text{Cat}(E_x(s(\pi2)))^2.$$

The $\text{Xatt}^{t \to s}$ M_{fil} gives a transformation which outputs the input tree with no b element, which can be figured out as follows. If $x \neq b$, then R^{N_x} of M_{fil} equals to that of M'_{id} because we take the second branch $\text{Cat}(S_x, s(\pi1))$ for If. Suppose that $x = b$. Since we take the first branch $s(\pi2)$, the dotted arrow which points to $s(11)$ in Fig. 2 comes from $s(112)$ instead of $s(111)$. It implies that all nodes under the first branch of N_b is skipped in the evaluation. Therefore we get the transformation result which is the input tree with no b element. In the following, we show how to convert XML transformations to $\text{Xatt}^{t \to s}$ for two practical examples, *XPath querying* and *partial modification*. Each transformation is defined by a pair of synthesized and inherited attributes. A number of XML transformation programs can be regarded as the combination of these basic transformations.

XPath Querying and Its Extension. XPath [24] is a syntax for defining parts of an XML tree by using paths on the XML tree. For example, /child::a/descendant::b [child::c] designates b elements each of which is descendant of an a node and has a c node as its child. XPath querying collects all elements satisfying the XPath expression.

A part of XPath querying can be converted into $\text{Xatt}^{t \to s}$. We consider querying by absolute XPath expressions in which only forward axes are used, *i.e.*, the expression cannot contain backward axes such as parent and ancestor. Note that this restriction is not too excessive. All backward axes in absolute XPath can be removed by the method introduced by Olteanu et al. [21].

XPath querying is converted into $\text{Xatt}^{t \to s}$ M_{que} which contains conditional branches of the form (1) where

$$e_{s1} = \text{Cat}(S_x, s(\pi1)), \quad e_{s2} = s(\pi1), \quad e_{i1} = \text{Cat}(E_x, s(\pi2)), \quad e_{i2} = s(\pi2).$$

In the computation by M_{que}, the node is copied if e_{test} is evaluated to true at the node. Otherwise, no copy is created for the node. Thus we need to specify how to give e_{test} for each XPath expression in order to convert the XPath querying into $\text{Xatt}^{t \to s}$[3].

The conversion is defined by associating all subexpressions of a given XPath expression. with a synthesized or inherited attribute in an $\text{Xatt}^{t \to s}$. Subexpressions in bracketed qualifiers (also called predicates) in the XPath are associated with synthesized attributes. The other subexpressions are related with inherited attributes. Consider an absolute XPath expression $\overbrace{\underbrace{\underbrace{\text{/child::a/descendant}}_{u2}::b}_{u1}\underbrace{[\text{child::c}]}_{v1}}$. We take three subexpressions as shown by curly braces each of which is associated with an

---

[2] The conditional branch If is useless for $i(\pi1)$-rule because $e_{i1} = e_{i2}$.

[3] This conversion assumes that the node whose ancestor is queried is not queried by a given XPath expression. In order to query such nested nodes, the other conversion is required.

attribute assigned to the brace. The attributes $u1$ and $u2$ are inherited and $v1$ is synthesized. To complete the conversion, we use one more attribute $u3$ to propagate information about whether the node is a descendant of the node satisfying the XPath expression. The following attribute rules define the relation of the attributes:

$$R^{\sharp} = \{u1(\pi1) \rightarrow \mathsf{True},\ u2(\pi1) \rightarrow \mathsf{False},\ u3(\pi1) \rightarrow \mathsf{False},\ \ldots\}$$
$$R^{N_x} = \{v1(\pi) \rightarrow \mathsf{Or}(\mathsf{Eq}_x(\mathsf{Str}_c), v1(\pi2)),\ u1(\pi1) \rightarrow \mathsf{False},\ u1(\pi2) \rightarrow u1(\pi),$$
$$u2(\pi1) \rightarrow \mathsf{Or}(u2(\pi), \mathsf{And}(u1(\pi), \mathsf{Eq}_x(\mathsf{Str}_a))),\ u2(\pi2) \rightarrow u2(\pi),$$
$$u3(\pi1) \rightarrow \mathsf{Or}(u3(\pi), \mathsf{And}(u2(\pi), \mathsf{And}(\mathsf{Eq}_x(\mathsf{Str}_b), v1(\pi1)))),$$
$$u3(\pi2) \rightarrow,\ \mathsf{Or}(u3(\pi), \mathsf{And}(u2(\pi), \mathsf{And}(\mathsf{Eq}_x(\mathsf{Str}_b), v1(\pi1)))),\ \ldots\}$$
$$R^{L} = \{v1(\pi) \rightarrow \mathsf{False},\ \ldots\}.$$

where several attribute rules are omitted. We use the same attribute rules as R^L and $R^{\sharp}$ of M_{id} for attributes s_{in}, s and i. The value of an attribute $u1$ represents whether the node is the child of the root; The value of $u2$ represents whether the node is the descendant of an a node which is the child of the root; The value of $v1$ represents whether either the node or one of the following sibling node is a c node. An $\mathrm{Xatt}^{t \rightarrow s}$ representing the intended XPath querying is defined by M_{que} with $e_{test} = \mathsf{Or}(u3(\pi), \mathsf{And}(u2(\pi), \mathsf{And}(\mathsf{Eq}_x(\mathsf{Str}_b), v1(\pi1))))$. The expression e_{test}, which equals to the right-hand side of the attribute rules for $u3$, represents whether either the node or one of its ancestors satisfies the XPath.

Partial Modification. Whereas XPath querying leaves the designate elements and strips their contexts, partial modification leaves the context of the the designate elements and replaces the elements with the other elements. The partial modification is converted into an $\mathrm{Xatt}^{t \rightarrow s}$ in similar way to XPath querying. Let us consider an $\mathrm{Xatt}^{t \rightarrow s}$ M_{mod} which has the same definition as M'_{id} except that R^{N_x} is a set of the following rules:

$$e_{s1} = \mathsf{Cat}(\mathsf{S}_x, \mathsf{Cat}(\mathsf{E}_x, s(\pi2))), \quad e_{s2} = \mathsf{Cat}(\mathsf{S}_x, s(\pi1)), \quad e_{i1} = e_{i2} = \mathsf{E}_x(s(\pi2)).$$

where e_{test} is a certain expression for specifying the designate node. The element is replaced with a no-child element if e_{test} is evaluated to true at the node. Otherwise, the node does not change since the attribute rules equals to that of M'_{id}.

Let us see the other example of partial modification. Consider an $\mathrm{Xatt}^{t \rightarrow s}$ M'_{mod} which has the same definition as M_{mod} except that the first two rules of R^{N_x} is as follows:

$$e_{s1} = \mathsf{Cat}(\mathsf{S}_a, s(\pi1)),\ e_{s2} = \mathsf{Cat}(\mathsf{S}_x, s(\pi1)),\ e_{i1} = \mathsf{Cat}(\mathsf{E}_a, s(\pi2)),\ e_{i2} = \mathsf{Cat}(\mathsf{E}_x, s(\pi2)).$$

The name of the node changes into a if e_{test} is evaluated to true at the node. Otherwise, the node does not changed. This procedure is applied to every node of the input XML. Now we show an example of $\mathrm{Xatt}^{t \rightarrow s}$ M_{JkS} that plays a role of partial modification. The attribute rules of M_{JkS} are comprised of

$$R^\sharp = \{s_{in}(\pi) \rightarrow s(\pi1),\ i(\pi1) \rightarrow Z\}$$
$$R^{N_x} = \{v1(\pi) \rightarrow \mathsf{Or}(\mathsf{Eq}_x(\mathsf{Str}_k), v1(\pi2)),$$
$$s(\pi) \rightarrow \mathsf{Cat}(\mathsf{If}(\mathsf{And}(\mathsf{Eq}_x(\mathsf{Str}_J), v1(\pi1)), \mathsf{S}_\mathsf{S}, \mathsf{S}_x), s(\pi1)),$$
$$i(\pi1) \rightarrow \mathsf{Cat}(\mathsf{If}(\mathsf{And}(\mathsf{Eq}_x(\mathsf{Str}_J), v1(\pi1)), \mathsf{E}_\mathsf{S}, \mathsf{E}_x), s(\pi2)),$$
$$i(\pi2) \rightarrow i(\pi)\}$$
$$R^\mathsf{L} = \{s(\pi) \rightarrow i(\pi),\ v1(\pi) \rightarrow \mathsf{False}\}$$

where we use $\mathsf{Cat}(\mathsf{If}(e_{test}, e_1, e_2), e_3)$ instead of $\mathsf{If}(e_{test}, \mathsf{Cat}(e_1, e_3), \mathsf{Cat}(e_2, e_3))$ to obtain efficient stream processors. The name of every node changes into S by M_{JkS} only if the node satisfies an XPath expression `/descendant-or-self::J[child::k]` $(= //\mathsf{J[k]})$, *i.e.*, M_{JkS} changes the name of the J node having a k node as its child into S. For example, an XML `<h><I><k/></I><J><k/></J><J><c/></J></h>` is transformed into `<h><I><k/></I><S><k/></S><J><c/></J></h>` by M_{JkS}. It uses no inherited attribute associated with the subexpression `/descendant-or-self::` since the expression should be satisfied at any node.

Combination of Basic Transformations. The conversion of basic transformations is easily extended by the other XML transformations. For instance, consider an XML transformation T_{comb} which returns the collection of results of partial modification only for nodes specified by an XPath. We need two pairs of synthesized and inherited attributes: one pair $\langle s_1, i_1 \rangle$ is used for a partial modification; another pair $\langle s_2, i_2 \rangle$ is used for collecting results for each nodes specified by XPath. The XML transformation T_{comb} is defined by $\mathrm{Xatt}^{t \rightarrow s}$ with these attributes. The conversion of combination of basic transformation into $\mathrm{Xatt}^{t \rightarrow s}$ has been automatically done in the implementation of an XML transformation language XTiSP introduced in Appendix B (see also [29]).

4   Composition with an XML Parsing Attributed Tree Transducer

This section introduces a method for obtaining an ATT which represents a transformation from XML streams to XML streams, denoted by $\mathrm{Xatt}^{s \rightarrow s}$. An $\mathrm{Xatt}^{t \rightarrow s}$ in the previous section represents a transformation from XML trees to XML streams. In order to derive $\mathrm{Xatt}^{s \rightarrow s}$, we compose the $\mathrm{Xatt}^{t \rightarrow s}$ with an XML-parsing ATT M_{parse} to synthesize a single ATT, where M_{parse} represents a transformation from XML streams to trees. The composition employs a composition method for *stack-attributed tree transducers*(SATT) [16] because the parsing ATT requires a stack device which was harmful for the original composition method [8, 14]. Since the composition method is rather involved, we introduce the method specialized for the case of the composition an $\mathrm{Xatt}^{t \rightarrow s}$ and the parsing ATT M_{parse} whose definition is presented in Appendix A. By applying the composition method to a given $\mathrm{Xatt}^{t \rightarrow s}$ and M_{parse}, the following composition method is obtained. Although the composition method does not deal with annotations of nodes, we can easily make extension of the method for them.

Let $M = (Syn, Inh, \Sigma_{tree}, \Delta, s_{in}, \sharp, R)$ be an $\mathrm{Xatt}^{t \rightarrow s}$ where Δ includes primitive functions such as Cat, S_x, True, and so on. The corresponding $\mathrm{Xatt}^{s \rightarrow s}$ is defined by $M = (Syn', Inh', \Sigma_{stream}, \Delta', s_{in}, \sharp, R')$ where

- $Syn' = \{\langle s',s \rangle \mid s' \in Syn, \ s \in \{p,l\}\}, \ Inh' = \{\langle i',s \rangle \mid i' \in Inh, \ s \in \{p,l\}\}$
- $\Delta' = \Delta \cup \{Head^{(1)}, Tail^{(1)}, Cons^{(2)}, Nil^{(0)}\}$,
- and $R' = R'^{\sharp} \cup R'^{S_x} \cup R'^{E_x} \cup R'^{Z}$ with

$$
\begin{aligned}
R'^{\sharp} = \ & \{s_{in} \to \varphi[s'(\pi 1) := \langle s',p \rangle(\pi 1)]_{s' \in Syn} \mid (s_{in}(\pi) \to \varphi) \in R^{\sharp}\} \\
& \cup \{\langle i',p \rangle \to \varphi[s'(\pi 1) := \langle s',p \rangle(\pi 1)]_{s' \in Syn} \mid (i'(\pi 1) \to \varphi) \in R^{\sharp}\} \\
& \cup \{\langle i',l \rangle \to Nil \mid i' \in Inh\} \\
R'^{S_x} = \ & \{\langle s',p \rangle(\pi) \to \rho(\varphi) \mid (s'(\pi) \to \varphi) \in R^{N_x}, s' \in Syn\} \\
& \cup \{\langle s',l \rangle(\pi) \to Tail(\langle s',l \rangle(\pi 1)) \mid s' \in Syn\} \\
& \cup \{\langle i',p \rangle(\pi 1) \to \rho(\varphi) \mid (i'(\pi 1) \to \varphi) \in R^{N_x}, i' \in Inh\} \\
& \cup \{\langle i',l \rangle(\pi 1) \to Cons(\rho(\varphi), \langle i',l \rangle(\pi)) \mid (i'(\pi 2) \to \varphi) \in R^{N_x}, i' \in Inh\} \\
R'^{E_x} = \ & \{\langle s',p \rangle(\pi) \to \varphi[i'(\pi) := \langle i',p \rangle(\pi)]_{i' \in Inh} \mid (s'(\pi) \to \varphi) \in R^{L}, s' \in Syn\} \\
& \cup \{\langle s',l \rangle(\pi) \to Cons(\langle s',p \rangle(\pi 1), \langle s',l \rangle(\pi 1)) \mid s' \in Syn\} \\
& \cup \{\langle i',p \rangle(\pi 1) \to Head(\langle i',l \rangle(\pi)) \mid i' \in Inh\} \\
& \cup \{\langle i',l \rangle(\pi 1) \to Tail(\langle i',l \rangle(\pi)) \mid i' \in Inh\} \\
R'^{Z} = \ & \{\langle s',p \rangle(\pi) \to \varphi[i'(\pi) := \langle i',p \rangle(\pi)]_{i' \in Inh} \mid (s'(\pi) \to \varphi) \in R^{L}, s' \in Syn\} \\
& \cup \{\langle s',l \rangle(\pi) \to Nil \mid s' \in Syn\}
\end{aligned}
$$

where $\rho = [s'(\pi 1), s'(\pi 2), i'(\pi) := \langle s',p \rangle(\pi 1), Head(\langle s',l \rangle(\pi 1)), \langle i',p \rangle(\pi)]_{s' \in Syn, i' \in Inh}$.

The added output symbols $Head, Tail, Cons$ and Nil are caused by a stack operator in M_{parse}. Each of them has a meaning with respect to stack operation: $Head(e)$ represents the top-most element of a stack e; $Tail(e)$ represents a stack e whose top-most element is removed; $Cons(e_1, e_2)$ represents a stack obtained by pushing a value e_1 to a stack e_2; Nil represents an empty stack.

For example, we obtain $\text{Xatt}^{s \to s}$ M'_{JkS} from the definition of the $\text{Xatt}^{t \to s}$ M_{JkS} by the above method. The attribute rules of M'_{JkS} are comprised of

$$
\begin{aligned}
R'^{\sharp} = \ & \{s_{in}(\pi) \to \langle s,p \rangle(\pi 1), \ \langle i,p \rangle(\pi 1) \to Z, \ \langle i,l \rangle(\pi 1) \to Nil\}, \\
R'^{S_x} = \ & \{\langle s,p \rangle(\pi) \to \mathsf{Cat}(\mathsf{If}(\mathsf{And}(\mathsf{Eq}_x(\mathsf{Str}_J), \langle v1,p \rangle(\pi 1)), \mathsf{S}_S, \mathsf{S}_x), \langle s,p \rangle(\pi 1)), \\
& \ \langle s,l \rangle(\pi) \to Tail(\langle s,l \rangle(\pi 1)), \\
& \ \langle i,p \rangle(\pi 1) \to \mathsf{Cat}(\mathsf{If}(\mathsf{And}(\mathsf{Eq}_x(\mathsf{Str}_J), \langle v1,p \rangle(\pi 1)), \mathsf{E}_S, \mathsf{E}_x), Head(\langle s,l \rangle(\pi 1))), \\
& \ \langle i,l \rangle(\pi 1) \to Cons(\langle i,p \rangle(\pi), \langle i,l \rangle(\pi)), \\
& \ \langle v1,p \rangle(\pi) \to \mathsf{Or}(\mathsf{Eq}_x(\mathsf{Str}_k), Head(\langle v1,l \rangle(\pi 1))), \ \langle v1,l \rangle(\pi) \to Tail(\langle v1,l \rangle(\pi 1))\}, \\
R'^{E_x} = \ & \{\langle s,p \rangle(\pi) \to \langle i,p \rangle(\pi), \ \langle s,l \rangle(\pi) \to Cons(\langle s,p \rangle(\pi 1), \langle s,l \rangle(\pi 1)), \\
& \ \langle i,p \rangle(\pi 1) \to Head(\langle i,l \rangle(\pi)), \ \langle i,l \rangle(\pi 1) \to Tail(\langle i,l \rangle(\pi)), \\
& \ \langle v1,p \rangle(\pi) \to \mathsf{False}, \ \langle v1,l \rangle(\pi) \to Cons(\langle v1,p \rangle(\pi 1), \langle v1,l \rangle(\pi 1))\}, \\
R'^{Z} = \ & \{\langle s,p \rangle(\pi) \to \langle i,p \rangle(\pi), \ \langle s,l \rangle(\pi) \to Nil, \ \langle v1,p \rangle(\pi) \to \mathsf{False}, \ \langle v1,l \rangle(\pi) \to Nil\}.
\end{aligned}
$$

5   Attribute Evaluation in Stream Processing Style

We show a method deriving an XML stream processor from an $\text{Xatt}^{s \to s}$. The main idea of the method is that attribute values the $\text{Xatt}^{s \to s}$ are evaluated in stream processing style.

In the attribute evaluation for $\text{Xatt}^{s \to s}$, we use extra rules for primitive functions as well as the reduction rules specified by the definition of ATT. The definition of $\text{Xatt}^{t \to s}$ allows to use primitive functions such as If, And and Cat. At the previous stage, they have been regarded as constructor symbols since the composition method for ATTs cannot be applied to primitive functions destroying tree structures. The attribute evaluation deals with them as meaningful functions to obtain the transformation result. For instance, we have the following rules:

$$\text{If}(\text{True}, e_1, e_2) \Rightarrow e_1, \qquad \text{If}(\text{False}, e_1, e_2) \Rightarrow e_2, \qquad \text{Eq}_x(\text{Str}_x) \Rightarrow \text{True},$$
$$\text{And}(\text{True}, e_1) \Rightarrow e_1, \qquad \text{And}(\text{False}, e_1) \Rightarrow \text{False}, \qquad \cdots$$

It is obvious that these rules do not conflict with the reduction rules defined by ATT.

We use a running example of the $\text{Xatt}^{s \to s}$ M'_{JkS} to show a method for deriving an XML stream processor. Suppose that an input for M'_{JkS} is $t = S_J(S_k(E_k(S_1(E_1(E_J(Z))))))$ corresponding to an XML <J><k/><l/></J>. Let $\Rightarrow$ stand for $\Rightarrow_{M'_{JkS}, \sharp(t)}$ in the rest of this section. From the definition by ATT, we obtain the transformation result r by $r = nf(\Rightarrow, s_{in}(\varepsilon))$. An XML stream processor for M'_{JkS} computes the normal form by integrating a partial result for each input symbol, S_J, S_k, E_k, S_1, E_1, E_J and Z.

Before any input symbol is read, we find that r is computed as $nf(\Rightarrow, \langle s,p \rangle(1))$. since we have $s_{in}(\varepsilon) \Rightarrow \langle s,p \rangle(1)$ from the attribute rule of $R'^{\sharp}$ in M'_{JkS}. We cannot progress the computation until the first symbol is read. Additionally, in preparation for the following computation, we evaluate two attribute values $\langle i,p \rangle(1)$ and $\langle i,l \rangle(1)$ which may be needed when the next symbol is read. These values are computed into Z and Nil, respectively, by the attribute rules of $R'^{\sharp}$.

When an input symbol S_J is read, we find that r is computed as $nf(\Rightarrow, \langle s,p \rangle(1))$. since we have

$$\langle s,p \rangle(1) \Rightarrow \text{Cat}(\text{If}(\text{And}(\text{Eq}_J(\text{Str}_J), \langle v1,p \rangle(11)), S_S, S_J), \langle s,p \rangle(11))$$
$$\Rightarrow \text{Cat}(\text{If}(\text{And}(\text{True}, \langle v1,p \rangle(11)), S_S, S_J), \langle s,p \rangle(11))$$
$$\Rightarrow \text{Cat}(\text{If}(\langle v1,p \rangle(11), S_S, S_J), \langle s,p \rangle(11))$$

from the attribute rule of $R'^{\sharp}$ in M'_{JkS}, $\text{Eq}_x(\text{Str}_x) \Rightarrow \text{True}$ and $\text{And}(\text{True}, e_1) \Rightarrow e_1$. We cannot progress the computation until the next symbol is read for computing the value of $\langle s,p \rangle(11)$ and $\langle v1,p \rangle(11)$. Additionally, in preparation for the following computation, we evaluate two attribute values $\langle i,p \rangle(11)$ and $\langle i,l \rangle(11)$ which may be needed when the next symbol is read. These values are computed as follows:

$$\langle i,p \rangle(11) \Rightarrow^* \text{Cat}(\text{If}(\langle v1,p \rangle(11), E_S, E_J), Head(\langle s,l \rangle(11)))$$
$$\langle i,l \rangle(11) \Rightarrow Cons(\langle i,p \rangle(1), \langle i,l \rangle(1)) = Cons(Z, Nil)$$

where we use the values of $\langle i,p \rangle(1)$ and $\langle i,l \rangle(1)$ that is prepared by the last step. The attribute value of $\langle i,p \rangle(11)$ is just partially computed since it requires the following input symbol to know the values of $\langle v1,p \rangle(11)$ and $\langle s,l \rangle(11)$.

When the next input symbol S_k is read, we find that r is computed as $nf(\Rightarrow, \langle s,p \rangle(1))$. since we have

$$
\begin{aligned}
&\mathsf{Cat}(\mathsf{If}(\langle v1,p \rangle(11), \mathsf{S_S}, \mathsf{S_J}), \langle s,p \rangle(11)) \\
\Rightarrow\ &\mathsf{Cat}(\mathsf{If}(\mathsf{Or}(\mathsf{Eq_k}(\mathsf{Str_k}), Head(\langle v1,l \rangle(111))), \mathsf{S_S}, \mathsf{S_J}), \langle s,p \rangle(11)) \\
\Rightarrow\ &\mathsf{Cat}(\mathsf{If}(\mathsf{Or}(\mathsf{True}, Head(\langle v1,l \rangle(111))), \mathsf{S_S}, \mathsf{S_J}), \langle s,p \rangle(11)) \\
\Rightarrow\ &\mathsf{Cat}(\mathsf{If}(\mathsf{True}, \mathsf{S_S}, \mathsf{S_J}), \langle s,p \rangle(11)) \Rightarrow \mathsf{Cat}(\mathsf{S_S}, \langle s,p \rangle(11)) \\
\Rightarrow\ &\mathsf{Cat}(\mathsf{S_S}, \mathsf{Cat}(\mathsf{If}(\mathsf{And}(\mathsf{Eq_k}(\mathsf{Str_J}), \langle v1,p \rangle(111)), \mathsf{S_S}, \mathsf{S_k}), \langle s,p \rangle(111))) \\
\Rightarrow\ &\mathsf{Cat}(\mathsf{S_S}, \mathsf{Cat}(\mathsf{If}(\mathsf{And}(\mathsf{False}, \langle v1,p \rangle(111)), \mathsf{S_S}, \mathsf{S_k}), \langle s,p \rangle(111))) \\
\Rightarrow\ &\mathsf{Cat}(\mathsf{S_S}, \mathsf{Cat}(\mathsf{If}(\mathsf{False}, \mathsf{S_S}, \mathsf{S_k}), \langle s,p \rangle(111))) \\
\Rightarrow\ &\mathsf{Cat}(\mathsf{S_S}, \mathsf{Cat}(\mathsf{S_k}, \langle s,p \rangle(111))).
\end{aligned}
$$

Note that two Cat applications in $\mathsf{Cat}(\mathsf{S_S}, \mathsf{Cat}(\mathsf{S_k}, \ldots))$ will not be modified by the following computation. Therefore the XML stream processor can output the string $\mathsf{S_S}$ and $\mathsf{S_k}$, corresponding <S><k>, and the rest of result is computed by $\langle s,p \rangle(111)$. The output is a desirable behavior for XML stream processing. The transformation by M_{JkS} replaces every J element into S only when the node has a k element as its child. Thought the transformation cannot return any symbol even if an input symbol <J> is read, the symbol <S> and its children are output once an input symbol <k> is found at the child position. If no <k> element is found at the child position of a J element, then the J element are output without changing the element name.

The XML stream processor computes the transformation result by repeating the similar procedure to above for the following input. Letting $\#Inh$ be the number of inherited attributes of an Xatt$^{s \to s}$ M, the stream processor computes the fixed number $\#Inh + 1$ of values for each input symbol: one is used for the transformation result to be output afterward, the others may be needed at the next computation as values of inherited attributes.

6   Experimental Results

We have implemented our framework as an XML transformation language XTiSP[29], in which we can use two kinds of primitive transformations: XPath iteration and partial modification. See Appendix B for summary of XTiSP. The implemented system takes an XTiSP program and returns a stream processing program written in Objective Caml [20]. The system itself is also written in Objective Caml.

We compared a program in XTiSP, which is converted into M_{JkS}, with the corresponding program written in XSLT [25]. We used Xalan [26] and SAXON [23] as XSLT processors. The comparison was done for an input XML generated randomly such that each tag name is I, J or k. The experiments were conducted on a PC (PowerMacintosh G5/Dual 2GHz, 1GB memory). We measured execution time and memory usage for several inputs whose size are 1MB, 2MB, 4MB and 8MB. Fig. 3(a) and Fig. 3(b) show the comparison results. Our implementation is much faster and much more memory-efficient than the others. We also tried more complicated examples of XML transformation such as XML database into XHTML and then our implementation won definitely.

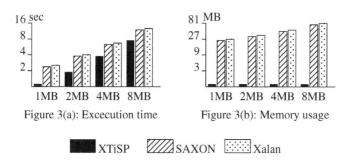

Figure 3(a): Excecution time   Figure 3(b): Memory usage

■ XTiSP   ▨ SAXON   ▦ Xalan

Fig. 3. Benchmark results

However we cannot always benefit from automatic derivation of stream processors. As an extreme example, $Xatt^{t \to s}$ can define a mirror transformation which reverses the order of child elements at every node. In this case, the program cannot output anything except for the start tag of the root until the end tag of the last child of the root is read whose next tag is the end tag of the root, that is the last token event of the input. This kind of transformation is not appropriate to stream processing. Although we have no way to find whether a given XML transformation is appropriate or not, we can easily add a mechanism to measure growth of stacks required by stream processing.

7   Conclusion

We have shown an implementation scheme for XML transformation language intended for stream processing. If one wants to implement an XML transformation language, all he has to do is to give a conversion method into $Xatt^{t \to s}$ for the language. The programmer can obtain an efficient stream processing program without writing stateful programs like SAX.

Additionally, we have implemented an XML transformation language XTiSP, which has its encoding method into $Xatt^{t \to s}$, and have compared with other XML tree transformation languages to confirm effectiveness of our system. XTiSP works much faster than the other implementations. because that it can output until the whole input is read.

Recently the author is addressing automatic generation from programs written in XSLT into $Xatt^{t \to s}$. If we automatically obtain $Xatt^{t \to s}$ from XSLT programs, we can also obtain the corresponding XML stream processor for XSLT.

Acknowledgment

This work is partially supported by the *Comprehensive Development of e-Society Foundation Software* program of the Ministry of Education, Culture, Sports, Science and Technology, Japan. The author also thanks anonymous reviewers for their comments.

References

1. M. Altinel and M. J. Franklin. Efficient filtering of XML documents for selective dissemination of information. In *International Conference on Very Large Databases*, 2000.
2. M. Benedikt, C. Y. Chan, W. Fan, R. Rastogi, S. Zheng, and A. Zhou. Dtd-directed publishing with attribute translation grammars. In *International Conference on Very Large Databases*, 2002.
3. V. Benzaken, G. Castagna, and A. Frisch. CDuce: an XML-centric general-purpose language. In *International Conference on Functional Programming*. ACM Press, 2003.
4. Y. Diao, P. Fischer, M. J. Franklin, and R. To. YFilter: Efficient and scalable filtering of XML documents. In *International Conference on Data Engineering*, 2002.
5. Expat XML parser. `http://expat.sourceforge.net`.
6. Z. Fülöp. On attributed tree transducers. *Acta Cybernetica*, 5:261–280, 1980.
7. Z. Fülöp and H. Vogler. *Syntax-directed semantics—Formal models based on tree transducers*. Monographs in Theoretical Computer Science. Springer-Verlag, 1998.
8. H. Ganzinger and R. Giegerich. Attribute coupled grammars. In *Symposium on Compiler Construction*, SIGPLAN Notices, 1984.
9. T. J. Green, G. Miklau, M. Onizuka, and D. Suciu. Processing XML streams with deterministic automata. In *International Conference of Database Theory*, volume 2572 of *LNCS*, 2003.
10. H. Hosoya and B. C. Pierce. XDuce: A statically typed XML processing language. *ACM Transactions on Internet Technology*, 3(2):117–148, May 2003.
11. O. Kiselyov. A better XML parser through functional programming. In *Practical Aspects of Declarative Languages*, volume 2257 of *LNCS*, 2002.
12. D. E. Knuth. Semantics of context-free languages. *Mathematical Systems Theory*, 2(2), 1968.
13. C. Koch and S. Scherzinger. Attribute grammars for scalable query processing on XML streams. In *International Workshop on Database Programming Languages*, 2003.
14. A. Kühnemann. *Berechnungsstärken von Teilklassen primitiv-rekursiver Programmschemata*. PhD thesis, Technical University of Dresden, 1997. Shaker Verlag, Aachen.
15. B. Ludäscher, P. Mukhopadhayn, and Y. Papakonstantinou. A transducer-based XML query processor. In *International Conference on Very Large Databases*, 2002.
16. K. Nakano. Composing stack-attributed tree transducers. Technical Report METR–2004–01, Department of Mathematical Informatics, University of Tokyo, Japan, 2004.
17. K. Nakano and S. Nishimura. Deriving event-based document transformers from tree-based specifications. In *Workshop on Language Descriptions, Tools and Applications*, volume 44-2 of *Electronic Notes in Theoretical Computer Science*, 2001.
18. F. Neven. Extensions of attribute grammars for structured document queries. In *International Workshop on Database Programming Languages*, volume 1949 of *LNCS*, 1999.
19. S. Nishimura and K. Nakano. XML stream transformer generation through program composition and dependency analysis. *Science of Computer Programming*. To appear.
20. The Caml language homepage. `http://caml.inria.fr/`.
21. D. Olteanu, H. Meuss, T. Furche, and F. Bry. XPath: Looking forward. In *EDBT Workshop on XML Data Management*, volume 2490 of *LNCS*, 2002.
22. SAX: The simple API for XML. `http://www.saxproject.org/`.
23. SAXON: The XSLT and XQuery processor. `http://saxon.sourceforge.net/`.
24. XML path language (XPath). `http://www.w3c.org/TR/xpath/`.
25. XSL transformations (XSLT). `http://www.w3c.org/TR/xslt/`.
26. Xalan-Java homepage. `http://xml.apache.org/xalan-j/`.
27. XP++: XML processing plus plus. dfdfdsfdsaf `http://www.alphaworks.ibm.com/tech/xmlprocessingplusplus`.

28. XQuery 1.0: An XML query language. `http://www.w3.org/TR/xquery/`.
29. XTiSP: An implementation framework of XML transformation languages intended for stream processing. `http://xtisp.psdlab.org/`.

A   Stack-Attributed Tree Transducers M_{parse}

Stack-attributed tree transducer(SATT) is an extension of attributed tree transducer(ATT). See [16] for detail. The major difference from ATT is that SATT can deal with a stack device for attribute values. Roughly speaking, SATT can simulate an ATT with an arbitrary number of attributes. In SATT, attributes are divided into two kinds of attributes, stack attributes and output attributes. Only stack attributes have a stack value which can be operated by *Head*, *Tail* and *Cons*. An XML parsing transformation M_{parse} is an example of SATT. An SATT M_{parse} is defined by

$$M_{parse} = (Syn, Inh, StSyn, StInh, \Sigma_{stream}, \Sigma_{tree}, s_{in}, \sharp, R)$$

where $Syn = \{p\}$, $Inh = \emptyset$, $StSyn = \{l\}$, $StInh = \emptyset$ and $R = R^{\sharp} \cup R^{S_x} \cup R^{E_x} \cup R^Z$ with

$$R^{\sharp} = \{s_{in}(\pi) \to p(\pi 1)\}, R^{S_x} = \{p(\pi) \to N_x(p(\pi 1), Head(l(\pi 1))), l(\pi) \to Tail(l(\pi 1))\}$$
$$R^{E_x} = \{p(\pi) \to L, l(\pi) \to Cons(p(\pi 1), l(\pi 1))\}, R^Z = \{p(\pi) \to L, l(\pi) \to Nil\}$$

B   Summary of XTiSP

We summarize our language XTiSP[29]. A program written in XTiSP specifies a transformation from an XML to an XML. A simplified syntax of XTiSP is defined by

$$exp = f(exp, \cdots, exp) \mid <exp>[exp] \mid exp; exp \mid xpath$$
$$\mid \texttt{if } exp \texttt{ then } exp \texttt{ else } exp \texttt{ endif}$$
$$\mid \texttt{invite } xpath \texttt{ do } exp \texttt{ done}$$
$$\mid \texttt{visit } xpath \texttt{ do } exp \texttt{ done}$$

A symbol *f* represents a function which takes a fixed number of strings or boolean values and returns a string or a boolean value. An expression *<e1>[e2]* is used for constructing an element whose tag name and children are given by evaluation of *e1* and *e2*, respectively. An expression *e1;e2* returns a concatenation of evaluation results for *e1* and *e2*. A symbol *xpath* stands for an XPath expression which returns a collection of elements satisfying the XPath. An `if` clause represents a conditional branch in a usual way. `invite` and `visit` are used for XPath-based iteration mentioned below. An expression between `do` and `done` is called *iteration body*.

The transformation by XTiSP is defined by changing the *current node*. Initially, the current node is the root node of an input XML. When an iteration body for `invite`/ `visit` is evaluated, the current node is changed into a node specified by XPath assigned with the iteration. An `invite` iteration returns a collection of results returned by evaluating the iteration body where the current node is changed into every node satisfying the XPath. An `visit` iteration returns a subtree of the input XML whose root is the current node, provided that every node v satisfying the XPath is replaced with the result returned by the iteration body where the current body is changed into v.

All XTiSP programs can be converted into $\text{Xatt}^{t \to s}$. Roughly speaking, an XTiSP program is converted by associating each subexpression of the program, in particular invite/visit iteration, with a pair of synthesized and inherited attributes.

Detecting Software Defects in Telecom Applications Through Lightweight Static Analysis: A War Story

Tobias Lindahl and Konstantinos Sagonas

Computing Science, Dept. of Information Technology, Uppsala University, Sweden
{Tobias.Lindahl,Konstantinos.Sagonas}@it.uu.se

Abstract. In safety-critical and high-reliability systems, software development and maintenance are costly endeavors. The cost can be reduced if software errors can be identified through automatic tools such as program analyzers and compile-time software checkers. To this effect, this paper describes the architecture and implementation of a software tool that uses lightweight static analysis to detect discrepancies (i.e., software defects such as exception-raising code or hidden failures) in large commercial telecom applications written in Erlang. Our tool, starting from virtual machine bytecode, discovers, tracks, and propagates type information which is often implicit in Erlang programs, and reports warnings when a variety of type errors and other software discrepancies are identified. Since the analysis currently starts from bytecode, it is completely automatic and does not rely on any user annotations. Moreover, it is effective in identifying software defects even in cases where source code is not available, and more specifically in legacy software which is often employed in high-reliability systems in operation, such as telecom switches. We have applied our tool to a handful of real-world applications, each consisting of several hundred thousand lines of code, and describe our experiences and the effectiveness of our techniques.

Keywords: Compile-time program checking, software development, software tools, defect detection, software quality assurance.

1 Introduction

All is fair in love and war, even trying to add a static type system in a dynamically typed programming language. Software development usually starts with love and passion for the process and its outcome, then passes through a long period of caring for (money making) software applications by simply trying to maintain them, but in the end it often becomes a war, the *war against software bugs*, that brings sorrow and pain to developers. In this war, the software defects will use all means available to them to remain in their favorite program. Fortunately, their primary weapon is concealment, and once identified, they are often relatively easy to kill.

In the context of statically typed programming languages, the type system aids the developer in the war against software bugs by automatically identifying type errors at compile time. Unfortunately, the price to pay for this victory is the compiler rejecting all programs that cannot be proved type-correct by the currently employed type system. This starts another war, the *war against the type system*, which admittedly is a milder

W.-N. Chin (Ed.): APLAS 2004, LNCS 3302, pp. 91–106, 2004.
© Springer-Verlag Berlin Heidelberg 2004

one. The only way for programmers to fight back in this war is to rewrite their programs. (Although occasionally the programming language developers help the programmers in fighting this war by designing a bigger weapon, i.e., a more refined type system).

Dynamically typed programming languages avoid getting into this second war. Instead, they adopt a more or less "anything goes" attitude by accepting all programs, and relying on type tests during runtime to prevent defects from fighting back in a fatal way. Sometimes these languages employ a less effective weapon than a static type system, namely a *soft type system*, which provides a limited form of type checking. To be effective, soft type systems often need guidance by manual annotations in the code. Soft typing will not reject any program, but will instead just inform the user that the program could not be proved type-correct. In the context of the dynamically typed programming language ERLANG, attempts have been made to develop such soft type systems, but so far none of them has gained much acceptance in the community. We believe the main reasons for this is the developers' reluctance to invest time (and money) in altering their already existing code and their habits (or personal preferences). We remark that this is not atypical: just think of other programming language communities like e.g., that of C.

Instead of devising a full-scale type checker that would need extensive code alterations in the form of type annotations to be effective, we pragmatically try to adapt our weapon's design to the programming style currently adhered to by ERLANG programmers. We have developed a lightweight type-based static analysis for finding *discrepancies* (i.e., software defects such as exception-raising code, hidden failures, or redundancies such as unreachable code) in programs without having to alter their source in any way. The analysis does not even need access to the source, since its starting point is virtual machine bytecode. However, the tool has been developed to be extensible in an incremental way (i.e., with the ability to take source code into account and benefit from various kinds of user annotations), once it has gained acceptance in its current form.

The actual tool, called DIALYZER,[1] allows its user to find discrepancies in ERLANG applications, based on information both from single modules and from an application-global level. It has so far been applied to programs consisting of several thousand lines of code from real-world telecom applications, and has been surprisingly effective in locating discrepancies in heavily used, well-tested code.

After briefly introducing the context of our work in the next section, the main part of the paper consists of a section which explains the rationale and main methods employed in the analysis (Sect. 3), followed by Sect. 4 which describes the architecture, effectiveness, and current and future status of DIALYZER. Section 5 reviews related work and finally this paper finishes in Sect. 6 with some concluding remarks.

2   The Context of Our Work

The Erlang Language and Erlang/OTP. ERLANG [1] is a strict, dynamically typed functional programming language with support for concurrency, communication, dis-

---

[1] DIALYZER: Discrepancy analyzer of erlang programs. (From the Greek $\delta\iota\alpha\lambda\acute{\upsilon}\omega$: to dissolve, to break up something into its component parts.) System is freely available from `www.it.uu.se/research/group/hipe/dialyzer/`.

tribution and fault-tolerance. The language relies on automatic memory management. ERLANG's primary design goal was to ease the programming of soft real-time control systems commonly developed by the telecommunications (telecom) industry.

ERLANG's basic data types are atoms, numbers (floats and arbitrary precision integers), and process identifiers; compound data types are lists and tuples. A notation for objects (*records* in the ERLANG lingo) is supported, but the underlying implementation of records is the same as tuples. To allow efficient implementation of telecommunication protocols, ERLANG nowadays also includes a *binary* data type (a vector of byte-sized data) and a notation to perform pattern matching on binaries. There are no destructive assignments of variables or mutable data structures. Functions are defined as ordered sets of guarded clauses, and clause selection is done by pattern matching. In ERLANG, clause guards either succeed or silently fail, even if these guards are calls to builtins which would otherwise raise an exception if used in a non-guard context. Although there is a good reason for this behavior, this is a language "feature" which often makes clauses unreachable in a way that goes unnoticed by the programmer. ERLANG also provides a `catch`/`throw`-style exception mechanism, which is often used to protect applications from possible runtime exceptions. Alternatively, concurrent programs can employ so called *supervisors* which are processes that monitor other processes and are responsible for taking some appropriate clean-up action after a software failure.

Erlang/OTP is the standard implementation of the language. It combines ERLANG with the Open Telecom Platform (OTP) middleware. The resulting product, Erlang/OTP, is a library with standard components for telecommunications applications (an ASN.1 compiler, the Mnesia distributed database, servers, state machines, process monitors, tools for load balancing, etc.), standard interfaces such as CORBA and XML, and a variety of communication protocols (e.g., HTTP, FTP, SMTP, etc.).[2]

Erlang Applications and Real-World Uses. The number of areas where ERLANG is actively used is increasing. However, its primary application area is still in large-scale embedded control systems developed by the telecom industry. The Erlang/OTP system has so far been used quite successfully both by Ericsson and by other companies around the world (e.g., T-Mobile, Nortel Networks, etc.) to develop software for large (several hundred thousand lines of code) commercial applications. These telecom products range from high-availability ATM servers, ADSL delivery systems, next-generation call centers, Internet servers, and other such networking equipment. Their software has often been developed by large programming teams and is nowadays deployed in systems which are currently in operation. Since these systems are expected to be robust and of high availability, a significant part of the development effort has been spent in their (automated) testing. On the other hand, more often than not, teams which are currently responsible for a particular product do not consist of the original program developers. This and the fact that the code size is large often make bug-hunting and software maintenance quite costly endeavors. Tools that aid this process are of course welcome.

Our Involvement in Erlang and History of This Work. We are members of the HiPE (High Performance Erlang) group and over the last years have been developing the

---

[2] Additional information about ERLANG and Erlang/OTP can be found at `www.erlang.org`.

HiPE native code compiler [10, 16]. The compiler is fully integrated in the open source Erlang/OTP system, and translates, in either a just-in-time (JIT) or ahead-of-time fashion, BEAM virtual machine bytecode to native machine code (currently UltraSPARC, x86, and AMD64). The system also extends the Erlang/OTP runtime system to support mixing interpreted and native code execution, at the granularity of individual functions.

One of the means for generating fast native code for a dynamically typed language is to statically eliminate as much as possible the (often unnecessary) overhead that type tests impose on runtime execution. During the last year or so, we have been experimenting with type inference and an aggressive type propagator, mainly for compiler optimization purposes. In our engagement on this task, we noticed that every now and then the compiler choked on pieces of ERLANG code that were obviously bogus (but for which the rather naïve bytecode compiler happily generated code). Since in the context of a JIT it does not really make much sense to stop compilation and complain to the user, and since it is a requirement of HiPE to preserve the observable behavior of the bytecode compiler, we decided to create a separate tool, the DIALYZER, that would statically analyze ERLANG (byte)code and report defects to its users. We report on the methods we use and the implementation of the tool below. However, we stress that the DIALYZER is not just a type checker or an aggressive type propagator.

3   Detecting Discrepancies Through Lightweight Static Analysis

3.1   Desiderata

Before we describe the techniques used in DIALYZER, we enumerate the goals and requirements we set for its implementation before we embarked on it:

1. The methods used in DIALYZER should be *sound*: they should aim to maximize the number of reported discrepancies, but should not generate any false positives.
2. The tool should request minimal, preferably no, effort or guidance from its user. In particular, the user should not be *required* to do changes to existing code like providing type information, specifying pre- or post-conditions in functions, or having to write other such annotations. Instead the tool should be completely automated and able to analyze legacy ERLANG code that (quite often) no current developer is familiar with or willing to become so. On the other hand, if the user *chooses* to provide more information, the tool should be able to take it into consideration and improve the precision of the results of its analysis.
3. The tool should be able to do something reasonable even in cases where source code is not available, as e.g., could be the case in telecom switches under operation.
4. The analysis should be *fast* so that DIALYZER has a chance to become an integrated component of ERLANG development.

All these requirements were pragmatically motivated. The applications we had in mind as possible initial users of our tool are large-scale software systems which typically have been developed over a long period and have been tested extensively. This often creates the illusion that they are (almost) bug-free. If the tool reported to their maintainers 1,000 possible discrepancies the first time they use it, of which most are false alarms, quite possibly it would not be taken seriously and its use would be considered a waste of time and effort.[3] In short, what we were after for DIALYZER version 1.0 was to create a lightweight static analysis tool capable of locating discrepancies that are errors: i.e., software defects that are easy to inspect and are easily fixed by an appropriate correcting action.[4] We could relax these requirements only once the tool gained the developers' approval; more on this in Sect. 4.4.

Note that the 2nd requirement is quite strong. It should really be obvious, but it also implies that there are no changes to the underlying philosophy of the language: ERLANG is dynamically typed and there is nothing in our method that changes that.[5]

3.2   Local Analysis

To satisfy the requirement that the analysis is fast, the core of the method is an *intra-procedural, forward* dataflow analysis to determine the set of possible values of live variables at each program point using a *disjoint union of prime types*. The underlying type system itself is based on an extension of the Hindley-Milner static type discipline that incorporates recursive types and accommodates a limited form of union types without compromising its practical efficiency. In this respect, our type system is similar to that proposed by Wright and Cartwright for Soft Scheme [18].

The internal language of the analysis to which bytecode is translated, called Icode, is an idealized ERLANG assembly language with unlimited number of temporaries and an implicit stack. To allow for efficient dataflow analyses and to speed up the fixpoint computation which is required when loops are present, Icode is represented as a control-flow graph (CFG) which has been converted into static single assignment (SSA) form [3]. In Icode, most computations are expressed as function calls and all temporaries survive these. The function calls are divided into calls to primitive operations (primops), built-in functions (bifs), and user-defined functions. Furthermore, there are assignments and control flow operations, including switches, type tests, and comparisons. The remainder of this section describes the local analysis; in Sect. 3.3 we extend it by describing the handling of user-defined functions and by making it inter-modular.

Although ERLANG is a dynamically typed language, type information is present both explicitly and implicitly at the level of Icode. The explicit such information is in the form of type tests which can be translations of explicit type guards in the ERLANG source code, or tests which have been introduced by the compiler to guard unsafe primitive operations. The implicit type information is hidden in calls to primops such as in e.g. addition, which demands that both its operands are numbers. Note that non-trivial types for arguments and return values for all primops and bifs can be known *a priori* by the analyzer. These

---

[3] This was not just a hunch; we had observed this attitude in the past. Apparently, we are not the only ones with such experiences and this attitude is not ERLANG-specific; see e.g. [5, Sect. 6].

[4] Despite the conservatism of the approach, we occasionally had hard time convincing developers that some of the discrepancies identified by the tool were indeed code that needed some correcting action. One reaction we got was essentially of the form: "*My program cannot have bugs. It has been used like that for years!*". Fortunately, the vast majority of our users were more open-minded.

[5] This sentence should *not* be interpreted as a religious statement showing our conviction on issues of programming language design; instead it simply re-enforces that we chose to follow a very pragmatic, down-to-earth approach.

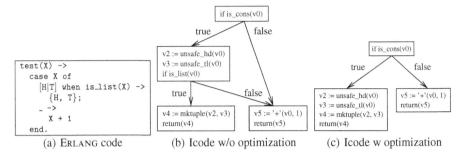

(a) ERLANG code   (b) Icode w/o optimization   (c) Icode w optimization

Fig. 1. ERLANG code with a redundant type guard

types can be propagated forward in the CFG to jump-start the discrepancy analysis. For example, if a call to addition succeeds, we know for sure that the return value must be a number. We also know that, from that point forward in the CFG the arguments must be numbers as well, or else the operation would have failed. Similarly, if an addition is reached and one of its arguments has a type which the analysis has already determined is not a number, then this is a program point where a discrepancy occurs.

More specifically, the places where the analysis changes its knowledge about the types of variables are:

1. At the *definition point* of each variable[6]. At such a point, the assigned type depends on the operation on the right-hand side. If the return type of the operation is unknown, or if the operation statically can be determined to fail, the variable gets assigned the type *any* (the lattice's top) or *undefined* (its bottom), respectively.
2. At *splits* in the CFG, such as in nodes containing type tests and comparisons. The type propagated in the success branch is the *infimum* (the greatest lower bound in the lattice) of the incoming type and the type tested for. In the fail branch, the success type is subtracted from the incoming set of types.
3. At a point where a variable is used as an *argument* in a call to a primop or a bif with a known signature. The propagated type is the *infimum* of the incoming type and the demanded argument type for the call. If the call is used in a guard context, then this is a split in the CFG and the handling will be as in case 2 above.

When paths join in the CFG, the type information from all incoming edges is unioned, making the analysis *path-insensitive*. Moreover, when a path out of a basic block cannot be taken, the dead path is removed to simplify the control flow. In Fig. 1 the is_list/1 guard in the first clause of the case statement can be removed since the pattern matching compiler has already determined that X is bound to a (possibly non-proper) list. This removal identifies a possible discrepancy in the code.

The analysis, through such local type propagation aided by liveness analysis and by applying aggressive global sparse conditional constant propagation and dead code elimination [13], tries to reason about the intent of the programmer. If the most likely path out of a node with a type test is removed, or if a guard always fails, this is re-

---

[6] Note that since Icode is on SSA form there can be only one definition point for each variable.

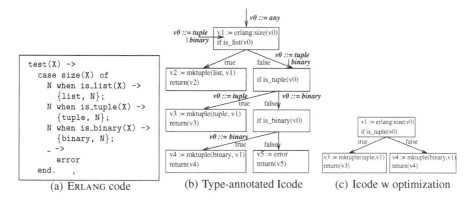

Fig. 2. An ERLANG program with two discrepancies due to a misuse of the bif `size/1`

ported to the user as a discrepancy. Other discrepancies that are identified by local static analysis include function calls that always fail, pattern matching operations that will raise a runtime exception, and dead clauses in switches (perhaps due to an earlier more general clause). For example, on the program of Fig. 2(a), given that the signature of the `erlang:size/1` built-in function is

$$\texttt{size(tuple | binary) -> integer}$$

the analysis first annotates the Icode control-flow graph with type information. This can be seen in Fig. 2(b) which shows the result of propagating types for variable v0 only. Given such a type-annotated CFG, it is quite easy to discover and report to the user that both the first `case` clause and the catch-all clause are dead, thereby removing these clauses; see Fig. 2(c). In our example, finding code which is redundant, especially the first clause, reveals a subtle programming error as the corresponding 'measuring' function for lists in ERLANG is `length/1`, not `size/1`.

3.3   Making the Analysis Intra- and Inter-modular

Currently, the only way to provide the compiler with information about the arguments to a function is by using non-variable terms and guards in clause heads. (This information is primarily used by pattern matching to choose between the function clauses.) Since DIALYZER employs a forward analysis, when analyzing only one function, there can be no information at the function's entry point, but at the end of the analysis there is information about the type of the function's return value. By unioning all proper (i.e., non-exception) type values at the exit points of a function, we get additional type information that can then be used at the function's call sites. The information is often non-trivial since most functions are designed to return values of a certain type and do not explicitly fail (i.e., raise an exception). To take advantage of this, the local analysis is extended with a *persistent lookup table*, mapping function names to information about their return values. The table is used both for intra-modular calls and for calls across module boundaries, but since the table only contains information about functions which have already been analyzed, some kind of iterative analysis is needed.

First consider intra-modular calls. One approach is to iteratively analyze all functions in a module until the information about their return values remains unchanged (i.e., until a fixpoint is reached). The possible problem with this approach is that the fixpoint computation can be quite expensive. Another approach, which is currently the default, is to construct a static call graph of the functions in a module, and then perform one iteration of the analysis by considering the strongly connected components of this graph in a bottom-up fashion (i.e., based on a reversed topological sort). If all components consist of only one function, this will find the same information as an iterative analysis. If there are components which consist of mutually recursive functions, we can either employ fixpoint computation or heuristically compute a safe approximation of the return value types in one pass (for example, the type *any*). Note that this heuristic is acceptable in our context; the discrepancy analysis remains sound but is not complete (i.e., it is not guaranteed to find all discrepancies).

Now consider function calls across module boundaries. In principle, the call graph describing the dependencies between modules can be constructed *a priori*, but this imposes an I/O-bound start-up overhead which we would rather avoid. Instead, we construct this graph as the modules are analyzed for the first time, and use this information only if the user requests a complete analysis which requires a fixpoint computation.

A Final Note: So far, the analysis has been applied to code of projects which are quite mature. However, as mentioned, our intention is that the tool becomes an integrated component of the program development cycle. In such situations, the code of a module changes often, so the information in the lookup table may become obsolete. When a project is in a phase of rapid prototyping, it might be convenient to get reports of discrepancies discovered based on the code of a single module. The solution to this is to analyze one module till fixpoint, using a lookup table that contains function information from only the start of the analysis of that module. The tool supports such a mode.

4   DIALYZER

4.1   Architecture and Implementation

Figure 3 shows the DIALYZER in action, analyzing the application **inets** from the standard library of the Erlang/OTP R9C-0 distribution.

In DIALYZER v 1.0, the user can choose between different modes of operation. The *granularity* option controls whether the analysis is performed on a single module or on all modules of an application. The *iteration* option selects between performing the analysis till fixpoint or doing a quick-and-dirty, one-pass analysis. The meaning of this option partly depends on the selected granularity. For example, if the granularity is per application and the one-pass analysis is selected, each module is only analyzed once, but fixpoint iteration is still applied inside the module. Finally, the *lookup table re-init* option specifies when the persistent lookup table is to be re-initialized, i.e., if the information is allowed to leak between the analysis elements specified by the granularity. Combinations of options whose semantics is unclear are automatically disabled.

While the analysis is running, a log displays its progress, and the discrepancies which are found are reported by descriptive warnings in a separate window area; see

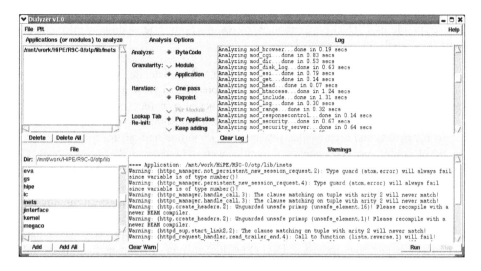

Fig. 3. The DIALYZER in action

Fig. 3. When the analysis is finished, the log and the warnings can be saved to files. As described in Sect. 3.3, the module-dependency graph is calculated during the first iteration of the analysis of an entire application. If a fixpoint analysis on the application level is requested, DIALYZER uses this information to determine the order in which the modules are analyzed in the next iteration to reduce the number of iterations needed to reach a fixpoint. In fact, even in the one-pass mode the module-dependency graph is constructed, just in case the user decides to request a fixpoint analysis on completion. Requesting this is typically not burdensome as the analysis is quite fast; this can also be seen in the figure. On a 2GHz laptop running Linux, the DIALYZER analyzes roughly 800 lines of ERLANG code per second, including I/O. (For example, the sizes of **mod_cgi**, **mod_disk_log**, and **mod_htaccess** modules are 792, 405, and 1137 lines, respectively. As another example, one run of the analysis for the complete Erlang/OTP standard library, comprising of about 600,000 lines of code, takes around 13 minutes.)

The DIALYZER distribution includes the code for the graphical user interface and the analyzer, both written in ERLANG. As its analyzer depends on having access to a specific version of the HiPE native code compiler, on whose infrastructure (the BEAM bytecode disassembler, the translator from BEAM to Icode, and the Icode supporting code such as SSA conversion and liveness analysis) it relies, the presence of a recent Erlang/OTP release is also required. Upon first start-up, DIALYZER will automatically trigger the fixpoint-based analysis of the Erlang/OTP standard library, **stdlib**, to construct a persistent lookup table which can be used as a basis for all subsequent analyses.

4.2   The DIALYZER in Anger

In order to show that our analysis is indeed effective in identifying software defects, we present some results obtained from using the DIALYZER to analyze code from large-scale telecom applications written in ERLANG. These applications all have in common that they are heavily used and well-tested commercial products, but as we will see, DIALYZER still exposed problems that had gone unnoticed by testing. Some brief additional information about these applications appears below:

- AXD301 is an asynchronous transfer mode (ATM) switching system from Ericsson [2]. The project has been running for more than eight years now and its team currently involves 200 people (but this number also includes some support staff; not only developers or testers). The ATM switch is designed for non-stop operation, so robustness and high availability are very important and taken seriously during development. As a consequence, a significant effort (and part of the project's budget) has been spent on testing its safety-critical components; see also [17].
- GPRS (General Packet Radio Service) is a telecom system from Ericsson. A large percentage of its code base is written in ERLANG. The project has been running for more than seven years now and its testing includes extensive test suites, automated daily builds, and code coverage analysis. Since this was a pilot-study for the applicability and effectiveness of DIALYZER in identifying discrepancies, only part of GPRS's ERLANG code has so far been analyzed. Although only part of the total code base, the analyzed code is rather big: it consists of 580,000 lines of ERLANG code, excluding comments.
- Melody is a control system for a "Caller Tunes" ringbacktone service developed by T-Mobile. It is an implementation of a customer database with interfaces to media players, short message service centers, payment platforms, and provisioning systems. The core of Melody is significantly smaller than the other telecom products which were analyzed; however, it includes parts of T-Mobile's extensively used and well-tested standard telecom library.

In addition to these commercial applications of ERLANG, we also analyzed the complete set of standard libraries from Erlang/OTP release R9C-0 from Ericsson and code from Jungerl,[7] which is an open-source code repository for ERLANG developers.

In order to have a more refined view of the kinds of discrepancies DIALYZER found, we can manually divide them into the following categories:

Explosives. These are places in the code that would raise a run-time exception. Examples of this are calls to ERLANG built-in functions with the wrong type of arguments, operators not defined on certain operands, faulty (byte) code, etc. An explosive can of course be conditional (e.g., firing on some execution paths only, rather than in all paths).

Camouflages. These are programming errors that for example make clauses or branches in the control flow graph unreachable — although the programmer did not intend them as such — without causing the program to stop or a supervisor process being notified that something is wrong. The most common error of this kind is a guard that will always silently fail.

Cemeteries. These are places of dead code. Such code is of course harmless, but code that can never be executed often reveals subtle programming errors. A common kind

---

[7] A Jungle of ERLANG code; see `sourceforge.net/projects/jungerl/`.

Table 1. Number of discrepancies of different kinds found in the analyzed projects

Project	Lines of code (total)	Discrepancies (total)	Classification Explosives	Camouflages	Cemeteries
OTP R9C-0	600,000	57	38 (31)	5	14
AXD301	1,100,000	132	26	2	104
GPRS	580,000	44	10	2	32
Jungerl	80,000	12	5	2	5
Melody	25,000	9	8 (7)	1	0

of cemeteries are clauses in `case` statements which can never match (because of previous code) and are thus redundant.

For example, in the code of Fig. 2(a) if the analysis encounters, in this or in some other module, a call of the form `test([_|_])`, this is classified as an explosive since it will generate a runtime exception. In the same figure, both the first and the last clause of the `case` statement are cemeteries, as they contain dead code. On the other hand, the code fragment below shows an example of a camouflage: the silent failure of the `size(X)` call in a guard context will prevent this clause from ever returning, although arguably the programmer's intention was to handle big lists.

```
test(X) when is_list(X), size(X) > 10 ->
    {list, big_size};
...    %% Other clauses
```

Table 1 shows the number of discrepancies found in the different projects[8]. The numbers in the column titled "lines of code" show an indication of the size of each project (comments and blank lines have been excluded) and justify our reasoning why requiring type information or any other user annotations *a posteriori* in the development cycle is not an option in our context. Although we would actually strongly prefer to have any sort of information that would make the analysis more effective, we are fully convinced that it would be an enormous task for developers to go through all this code and provide type information — especially since this would entail intimate knowledge about code that might have been written by someone else years ago. Realistically, the probability of this happening simply in order to start using DIALYZER in some commercial project, is most certainly zero.

Despite these constraints, DIALYZER is quite effective in identifying software defects in the analyzed projects; see Table 1. Indeed, we were positively surprised by the amount of discrepancies DIALYZER managed to identify, given the amount of testing effort already spent on the safety-critical components of these projects and the conservatism of the methods which DIALYZER version 1.0 currently employs.

In addition to finding programming errors in ERLANG code, DIALYZER can also expose software errors which were caused by a rather flawed translation of record expressions by the BEAM bytecode compiler. In Table 1, 31 of the reported explosives

---

[8] Actually, DIALYZER also warns its user about the use of some archaic ERLANG idioms and code relics; these warnings are not considered discrepancies and are not reported in Table 1.

for Erlang/OTP R9C-0 and 7 for Melody (indicated in parentheses) are caused by the BEAM compiler generating unsafe instructions that fail to be guarded by an appropriate type test. This in turn could result in buffer overruns or segmentation faults if the instructions' arguments were not of the (implicitly) expected type. This compiler bug has been corrected in release R9C-1 of Erlang/OTP.

4.3   Current Features and Limitations

The tool confuses programming errors with errors in the BEAM bytecode. Typically this is not a problem as DIALYZER has built-in knowledge about common discrepancies caused by flawed BEAM code. When such a discrepancy is encountered, DIALYZER recommends its user to re-generate the bytecode file using a newer BEAM compiler and re-run the analysis. As a matter of fact, we see this ability to identify faulty BEAM code as an advantage rather than as a limitation.

Starting from bytecode unfortunately means that warning messages cannot be descriptive enough: in particular they do not precisely identify the clause/line where the discrepancy occurs; see also Fig. 3. This can often be confusing. Also, since soundness currently is a major concern, the DIALYZER only reports warnings when it is clear that these are discrepancies. For example, if a switch contains a clause with a pattern that cannot possibly match then this is reported since it is a clear discrepancy. On the other hand, if the analysis finds that the patterns in the cases of the switch fail to cover all possible type values of the incoming term, this is not reported since it might be due to over-approximation caused by the path-insensitivity of the analysis. Of course, we could easily relax this and let the programmer decide, but as explained in Sect. 3.1 soundness is a requirement which DIALYZER religiously follows at this point.

4.4   Planned Future Extensions

One of the strengths of DIALYZER version 1.0 is that no alterations to the source code are needed. In fact, as we have pointed out, the tool does not even need access to it. However, if the source code is indeed available, it can provide the analysis with additional information. Work is in progress to generate Icode directly from CORE ERLANG, which is the official core language for ERLANG and the language used internally in the BEAM compiler. Since CORE ERLANG is on a level which is closer to the original source, where it is easier to reason about the programmer's intentions, it can provide DIALYZER with means to produce better warning messages; in particular line number information can be retained at this level. The structure of CORE ERLANG can also help in deriving, in a more precise way, information about the possible values used as arguments to functions that are local to a module.

We also plan to extend DIALYZER with the possibility that its user incrementally adds optional type annotations to the source code. The way to do this is not yet decided, but the primary goal of these annotations, besides adding valuable source code documentation, is to aid the analysis in its hunt for discrepancies, not to make ERLANG a statically typed language. If a type signature is provided for a function, and this signature can be verified by DIALYZER as described below, it can be used by the analysis in the same way as calls to bifs and primops are used in the current version. The way to verify a signature is as follows: instead of trying to infer the types at each call site (as would be the case in most type systems), the signature would be trusted until the function is analyzed. At this point the signature would be compared to the result of the analysis and checked for possible violations. Since DIALYZER is not a compiler, no programs would be rejected, but if violations of user-defined signatures are discovered, this would be reported to the user together with a message saying that the results of the discrepancy analysis could not be trusted.

Taking this idea further, we also plan to experiment with relaxing soundness by allowing the user to specify annotations that in general cannot be statically verified (for example, that a certain argument is a non-negative integer). This is similar to the direction that research for identifying defects such as buffer overruns and memory leaks in C (see e.g. [6, 4]) or for detecting violations of specifications in Java programs [8] has recently taken.

5 Related Work

Clearly, we are not the first to notice that compiler and static analysis technology can be employed for identifying defects in large software projects.[9] Especially during the few last years, researchers in the programming language community have shown significant interest in this subject; see e.g. the work mentioned in the last paragraph of the previous section and the references therein. Most of that work has focused on detecting errors such as buffer overruns, memory access errors such as accessing memory which has already been freed or following invalid pointer references in C, race detection in multi-threaded Java programs, etc. These software defects are simply not present in our context, at least not directly so.[10] Similarly to what we do, some of these analyses do not need source code to be present, since they start from the binary code of the executable. On the other hand, we are not aware of any work that tries to detect flaws at the level of virtual machine bytecode caused by its flawed generation.

During the late 80's and the beginning of the 90's, the subject of automatic type inference without type declarations received a lot of attention; see e.g. [12] for an early work on the subject. A number of soft type systems have been developed, most of them for the functional languages Lisp and Scheme, and some for Prolog. The one closest to our work is that of Soft Scheme [18]. Perhaps sadly, only a few of them made it into actual distributions of compilers or integrated development environments for these languages. Some notable exceptions are DrScheme [7], a programming environment for Scheme which uses a form of set-based analysis to perform type inference and to mark potential errors, and the NUDE (the NU-Prolog Debugging Environment [14]) and Ciao Prolog [9] systems which also incorporate type-annotation-guided static debuggers.

In the context of ERLANG, two type systems have been developed before: one based on subtyping [11] and a recent one based on soft types [15]. To the best of our knowledge, the latter has not yet been used by anybody other than its author, although time might of course change this. The former ([11]) allows for declaration-free recursive types using subtyping constraints, and algorithms for type inference and checking are also

---

[9] We are also willing to bet our fortunes that we will not be the last ones to do so either!

[10] They can only occur in the VM interpreter which is written in C, not in ERLANG code.

given in the same paper. It is fair to say that the approach has thus far not been very successful in the ERLANG community. Reasons for this include the fact that the type system constrains the language by rejecting code that does not explicitly handle cases for failures, that its inference algorithm fails to infer types of functions depending on certain pattern matching constructs, and that it demands a non-trivial amount of user intervention (in the form of type annotations in the source code). Stated differently, what [11] tries to do is to impose a style of programming in ERLANG which is closer to that followed in statically typed languages, in order to get the benefits of static type-error detection. Clearly this goal is ambitious and perhaps worthwhile to pursue, but then again its impact on projects which already consist of over a million lines of code is uncertain. Our work on the other hand is less ambitious and more pragmatically oriented. We simply aim to locate (some of the) software defects in already developed ERLANG code, *without imposing a new method for writing programs, but by trying to encourage an implicit philosophy for software development* (namely, the frequent use of a static checker tool rather than just relying on testing) which arguably is better than the practice the (vast majority of the) ERLANG community currently follows.

6   Concluding Remarks

DIALYZER version 1.0 represents a first attempt to create a tool that uses lightweight static analysis to detect software defects in large telecom applications and other programs developed using ERLANG. While we believe that our experiment has been largely successful, there are several aspects of the tool that could be improved through either better technology or by relaxing its requirements (e.g., no false warnings), which are currently quite stringent. Given support, we intend to work in these directions.

On a more philosophical level, it is admittedly the case that most of the software defects identified by DIALYZER are not very deep. Moreover, this seems to be an inherent limitation of the method. For example, problems such as deadlock freedom of ERLANG programs cannot be checked by DIALYZER. One cannot help being a bit skeptical about the *real* power of static analysis or type systems in general, and wonder whether a tool that used techniques from software model checking would, at least in principle, be able to check for a richer set of properties and give stronger correctness guarantees. On the other hand, there is enough evidence that neither static analysis nor software model checking are currently at the stage where one dominates the other; see also [5].

More importantly, one should *not* underestimate the power of simplicity and ease of use of a (software) tool. In a relatively short time and with very little effort, DIALYZER managed to identify a large number of software defects that had gone unnoticed after years of testing. Moreover, it managed to identify bugs that are relatively easy to correct — in fact some of them have been already — which brings software in a state closer to the desired goal of total correctness. One fine day, some projects might actually win their war!

Acknowledgments

This research has been supported in part by VINNOVA through the ASTEC (Advanced Software Technology) competence center as part of a project in cooperation with Ericsson and T-Mobile. The research of the second author was partly supported by a grant by Vetenskapsrådet (the Swedish Research Council). We thank Ulf Wiger and Hans Nilsson from the AXD301 team at Ericsson, Kenneth Lundin from the Erlang/OTP team, and Sean Hinde from T-Mobile for their help in analyzing the code from commercial applications and for their kind permission to report those results in this paper.

References

1. J. Armstrong, R. Virding, C. Wikström, and M. Williams. *Concurrent Programming in Erlang.* Prentice Hall Europe, Herfordshire, Great Britain, second edition, 1996.
2. S. Blau and J. Rooth. AXD 301—A new generation ATM switching system. *Ericsson Review*, 75(1):10–17, 1998.
3. R. Cytron, J. Ferrante, B. K. Rosen, M. N. Wegman, and F. K. Zadeck. Efficiently computing static single assignment form and the control dependence graph. *ACM Trans. Prog. Lang. Syst.*, 13(4):451–490, Oct. 1991.
4. N. Dor, M. Rodeh, and M. Sagiv. CSSV: Towards a realistic tool for statically detecting all buffer overflows in C. In *Proceedings of the ACM SIGPLAN 2003 Conference on Programming Language Design and Implementation*, pages 155–167. ACM Press, June 2003.
5. D. Engler and M. Musuvathi. Static analysis versus software model checking for bug finding. In B. Steffen and G. Levi, editors, *Verification, Model Checking, and Abstract Interpretation. Proceedings of the 5th International Conference*, number 2937 in LNCS, pages 191–210. Springer, Jan. 2004.
6. D. Evans and D. Larochelle. Improving security using extensible lightweight static analysis. *IEEE Software*, 19(1):42–51, Jan./Feb. 2002.
7. R. B. Findler, J. Clements, C. Flanagan, M. Flatt, S. Krishnamurthi, P. Steckler, and M. Felleisen. DrScheme: A programming environment for Scheme. *Journal of Functional Programming*, 12(2):159–182, Mar. 2002.
8. C. Flanagan, K. R. M. Leino, M. Lillibridge, G. Nelson, J. B. Saxe, and R. Stata. Extended static checking for Java. In *Proceedings of the ACM SIGPLAN 2002 Conference on Programming Language Design and Implementation*, pages 234–245. ACM Press, June 2002.
9. M. V. Hermenegildo, G. Puebla, F. Bueno, and P. López-García. Program development using abstract interpretation (and the Ciao system preprocessor). In R. Cousot, editor, *Static Analysis: Proceedings of the 10th International Symposium*, number 2694 in LNCS, pages 127–152, Berlin, Germany, June 2003. Springer.
10. E. Johansson, M. Pettersson, and K. Sagonas. HiPE: A High Performance Erlang system. In *Proceedings of the ACM SIGPLAN Conference on Principles and Practice of Declarative Programming*, pages 32–43, New York, NY, Sept. 2000. ACM Press.
11. S. Marlow and P. Wadler. A practical subtyping system for Erlang. In *Proceedings of the ACM SIGPLAN International Conference on Functional Programming*, pages 136–149. ACM Press, June 1997.
12. P. Mishra and U. S. Reddy. Declaration-free type checking. In *Proceedings of the Twelfth Annual ACM Symposium on the Principles of Programming Languages*, pages 7–21. ACM Press, 1984.
13. S. S. Muchnick. *Advanced Compiler Design & Implementation.* Morgan Kaufman Publishers, San Fransisco, CA, 1997.
14. L. Naish, P. W. Dart, and J. Zobel. The NU-Prolog debugging environment. In A. Porto, editor, *Proceedings of the Sixth International Conference on Logic Programming*, pages 521–536. The MIT Press, June 1989.

15. S.-O. Nyström. A soft-typing system for Erlang. In *Proceedings of ACM SIGPLAN Erlang Workshop*, pages 56–71. ACM Press, Aug. 2003.

16. M. Pettersson, K. Sagonas, and E. Johansson. The HiPE/x86 Erlang compiler: System description and performance evaluation. In Z. Hu and M. Rodríguez-Artalejo, editors, *Proceedings of the Sixth International Symposium on Functional and Logic Programming*, number 2441 in LNCS, pages 228–244, Berlin, Germany, Sept. 2002. Springer.

17. U. Wiger, G. Ask, and K. Boortz. World-class product certification using Erlang. *SIGPLAN Notices*, 37(12):25–34, Dec. 2002.

18. A. Wright and R. Cartwright. A practical soft type system for Scheme. *ACM Trans. Prog. Lang. Syst.*, 19(1):87–152, Jan. 1997.

History Effects and Verification

Christian Skalka and Scott Smith

The University of Vermont
skalka@cs.uvm.edu
The Johns Hopkins University
scott@cs.jhu.edu

Abstract. This paper shows how type effect systems can be combined with model-checking techniques to produce powerful, automatically verifiable program logics for higher-order programs. The properties verified are based on the ordered sequence of events that occur during program execution—an *event history*. Our type and effect systems automatically infer conservative approximations of the event histories arising at runtime, and model-checking techniques are used to verify logical properties of these histories.

Our language model is based on the λ-calculus. Technical results include a powerful type inference algorithm for a polymorphic type effect system, and a method for applying known model-checking techniques to the *history effects* inferred by the type inference algorithm, allowing static enforcement of history- and stack-based security mechanisms.

1 Introduction

Safe and secure program execution is crucial for modern information systems, but is difficult to attain in practice due to both programmer errors and intentional attacks. Various programming language-based techniques increase program safety, by verifying at compile- and/or run-time that programs possess certain safety properties. This paper proposes a foundation for automated verification of program properties, by defining a process for automatically predicting *event histories* of program executions at compile-time, and for specifying and statically verifying properties of these histories. Our particular focus is on security applications, but the techniques apply broadly.

An *event* is a record of some program action, explicitly inserted into program code either manually (by the programmer) or automatically (by the compiler). Events are conceived of broadly, and can be a wide array of program actions— *e.g.* opening a file, an access control privilege activation, or entry to or exit from a critical region. *Histories* are ordered sequences of events; whenever an event is encountered during program execution, it is appended to the current history stream, and thus histories record the sequence of program events in temporal order. Program event histories are similar to audit trails, and provide many of the same benefits for monitoring system activity.

W.-N. Chin (Ed.): APLAS 2004, LNCS 3302, pp. 107–128, 2004.
© Springer-Verlag Berlin Heidelberg 2004

Verification consists of checking to make sure that histories are well-formed, i.e. the sequence of events prior to a check conforms to specifications. For example, if the program is sending and receiving data over an SSL socket, the relevant events are opening and closing of sockets, and reading and writing of data packets. An example event history produced by a program run could be:

```
ssl_open("snork.cs.jhu.edu",4434); ssl_hs_begin(4434);
ssl_hs_success(4434); ssl_put(4434); ssl_get(4434);
ssl_open("moo.cs.uvm.edu",4435); ssl_hs_begin(4434);
ssl_put(4435); ssl_close(4434); ssl_close(4435)
```

Here, `ssl_open` is a sample event with two arguments, a url and a port. Event histories can then be used to detect logical flaws or security violations. For SSL, sockets must first be opened, handshake begun, handshake success, and only then can data be get/put over the socket. For example, The above history is illegal because data is put on socket 4435 before notification has been received that handshake was successful on that socket.

The previous paragraph informally defines the well-formed event histories for SSL connections; codifying this assertion as a local check in a decidable logic would provide a rigorous definition of well-formedness, and would allow mechanical verification of it. Such a mechanical verification increases the reliability and security of programs.

1.1   Overview

Several systems have been developed along these general lines; perhaps the principal division between them is run-time [20, 1] vs. compile-time [3, 7, 4] verification. The focus of this paper is on the latter.

The systems all have in common the idea of extracting an abstract interpretation of some form from a program, and verifying properties of that abstraction. The MOPS system [7] compiles C programs to Push-down Automata (PDAs) reflecting the program control flow, where transitions are program transitions, and the automaton stack abstracts the program call stack. [14, 4] assume that some (undefined) algorithm has already converted a program to a control flow graph, expressed as a form of PDA.

These aforementioned abstractions work well for procedural programs, but are not powerful enough to fully address advanced language features such as higher-order functions or dynamic dispatch. Our approach is to develop a type and effect system to extract abstract interpretations from higher-order programs.

Most type systems predict the class of values to which a program will evaluate, but type and effect systems [25, 2] predict program side-effects as well. In our system, history effects capture the history events generated by programs, with the property that the effect of a program should conservatively approximate the history generated by that program during execution. History effects accomplish this by specifying a set of possible histories containing at least the realized execution history. History effects yield history streams via an LTS (Labelled Transition System) interpretation: the LTS transitions produce a label stream from a history effect.

The intepretation of history effects as LTSs allows the expression of program assertions as temporal logical formulae, and the automated verification of assertions via model-checking techniques [23]. Some of the aforecited systems also automatically verify assertions at compile-time via model-checking, including [3, 7, 4]. (None of these works however defines a rigorous process for extracting an LTS from higher-order programs; there are a few more closely related systems, discussed in the conclusion.) In these works, the specifications are temporal logics, regular languages, or finite automata, and the abstract control flow is extracted as an LTS in the form of a finite automaton, grammar, or PDA. These particular formats are chosen because these combinations of logics and abstract interpretations can be automatically model-checked.

Security automata [20] use finite automata for the specification and run-time enforcement of language safety properties. Systems have also been developed for statically verifying correctness of security automata using dependent types [26], and in a more general form as refinement types [18]. These systems do not extract any abstract interpretations, and so are in a somewhat different category than the aforementioned (and our) work. These systems also lack type inference, and do not use a logic that can be automatically verified.

Logical assertions can be local, concerning a particular program point, or global, defining the whole behavior required. However, access control systems [27, 1, 9], use local checks. Since we are interested in the static enforcement of access control mechanisms (see section 6), the focus in this paper is on local, compile-time checkable assertions, though in principle the verification of global properties is also possible in our system.

1.2   The Technical Development

In the remaining text, we formalize our ideas in the system λ_{hist}: we define the type and effect system, and develop a type inference algorithm. We next show how the μ-calculus can be integrated as a static verification logic. A stack-history variant is also developed, by redefining the history as those events in active frames only. As an extended example of the system, we show how a rich model of Java stack inspection with first-class privilege parameters can be expressed via embedded μ-calculus formulae in this latter variant.

2   The Language λ_{hist}

In this Section we develop the syntax, semantics, and logical type theory for our language model, called λ_{hist}. History effect approximation and type safety results are stated in Theorem 1 and Theorem 2, respectively.

2.1   Syntax

The syntax of the theory λ_{hist} is given in Fig. 1. The base values include booleans and the unit value (). Expressions let $x = v$ in e are included to implement let-polymorphism in the type system (subsection 2.3). Functions, written $\lambda_z x.e$,

$$c \in \mathcal{C} \qquad\qquad\qquad\qquad\qquad\qquad\qquad \textit{atomic constants}$$
$$b ::= \mathsf{true} \mid \mathsf{false} \qquad\qquad\qquad\qquad\qquad\qquad \textit{boolean values}$$
$$v ::= x \mid \lambda_z x.e \mid c \mid b \mid \neg \mid \vee \mid \wedge \mid () \qquad\qquad\qquad \textit{values}$$
$$e ::= v \mid e\,e \mid ev(e) \mid \phi(e) \mid \mathsf{if}\,e\,\mathsf{then}\,e\,\mathsf{else}\,e \mid \mathsf{let}\,x = v\,\mathsf{in}\,e \qquad \textit{expressions}$$
$$\eta ::= \epsilon \mid ev(c) \mid \eta; \eta \qquad\qquad\qquad\qquad\qquad\qquad \textit{histories}$$
$$E ::= [\,] \mid v\,E \mid E\,e \mid ev(E) \mid \phi(E) \mid \mathsf{if}\,E\,\mathsf{then}\,e\,\mathsf{else}\,e \qquad \textit{evaluation contexts}$$

Fig. 1. λ_{hist} language syntax

$$\eta, (\lambda_z x.e)v \rightsquigarrow \eta, e[v/x][\lambda_z x.e/z] \qquad\qquad (\beta)$$
$$\eta, \neg\mathsf{true} \rightsquigarrow \eta, \mathsf{false} \qquad\qquad (notT)$$
$$\eta, \neg\mathsf{false} \rightsquigarrow \eta, \mathsf{true} \qquad\qquad (notF)$$
$$\eta, \wedge\,\mathsf{true} \rightsquigarrow \eta, \lambda x.x \qquad\qquad (andT)$$
$$\eta, \wedge\,\mathsf{false} \rightsquigarrow \eta, \lambda\_.\mathsf{false} \qquad\qquad (andF)$$
$$\eta, \vee\,\mathsf{true} \rightsquigarrow \eta, \lambda\_.\mathsf{true} \qquad\qquad (orT)$$
$$\eta, \vee\,\mathsf{false} \rightsquigarrow \eta, \lambda x.x \qquad\qquad (orF)$$
$$\eta, \mathsf{if}\,\mathsf{true}\,\mathsf{then}\,e_1\,\mathsf{else}\,e_2 \rightsquigarrow \eta, e_1 \qquad\qquad (ifT)$$
$$\eta, \mathsf{if}\,\mathsf{false}\,\mathsf{then}\,e_1\,\mathsf{else}\,e_2 \rightsquigarrow \eta, e_2 \qquad\qquad (ifF)$$
$$\eta, \mathsf{let}\,x = v\,\mathsf{in}\,e \rightsquigarrow \eta, e[v/x] \qquad\qquad (let)$$
$$\eta, ev(c) \rightsquigarrow \eta; ev(c), () \qquad\qquad (event)$$
$$\eta, \phi(c) \rightsquigarrow \eta; ev_\phi(c), () \quad \mathsf{if}\, \Pi(\phi(c), \hat{\eta}\,ev_\phi(c)) \quad (check)$$
$$\eta, E[e] \rightarrow \eta', E[e'] \quad \mathsf{if}\, \eta, e \rightsquigarrow \eta', e' \qquad (context)$$

Fig. 2. λ_{hist} language semantics

possess a recursive binding mechanism where z is the self variable. We assume the following syntactic sugarings:

$$e_1 \wedge e_2 \triangleq \wedge e_1 e_2 \qquad e_1 \vee e_2 \triangleq \vee e_1 e_2 \qquad \lambda x.e \triangleq \lambda_z x.e \quad z \text{ not free in } e$$

$$\lambda\_.e \triangleq \lambda x.e \quad x \text{ not free in } e \qquad e_1; e_2 \triangleq (\lambda\_.e_2)(e_1)$$

Events ev are named entities parameterized by constants c (we treat only the unary case in this presentation, but the extension to n-ary events is straightforward). These constants $c \in \mathcal{C}$ are abstract; this set could for example be strings or IP addresses. Ordered sequences of these events constitute histories η, which maintain the sequence of events experienced during program execution. We let $\hat{\eta}$ denote the string obtained from this sequence by removing delimiters (;). History assertions ϕ, also parameterized by constants c, may be used to implement history checks. These assertions are in a to-be-specified logical syntax (section 4). We presuppose existence of a meaning function Π such that $\Pi(\phi(c), \hat{\eta})$ holds iff $\phi(c)$ is valid for $\hat{\eta}$; we also leave the meaning function Π abstract until later (section 4).

Parameterizing events and predicates with constants c allows for a more expressive event language; for example, in section 6 we show how the parameterized privileges of Java stack inspection can be encoded with the aid of these parameters.

2.2   Semantics

The operational semantics of λ_{hist} is defined in Fig. 2 via the call-by-value small step reduction relations $\rightsquigarrow$ and $\rightarrow$ on configurations η, e, where η is the history of run-time program events. We write $\rightarrow^\star$ to denote the reflexive, transitive closure of $\rightarrow$. Note that in the event reduction rule, an event $ev(c)$ encountered during execution is added to the end of the history. The check rule specifies that when a configuration η, ϕ is encountered during execution, the "check event" $ev_\phi(c)$ is appended to the end of η, and $\phi(c)$ is required to be satisfied by the current history η, according to our meaning function Π. The reasons for treating checks as dynamic events is manifold; for one, some checks may ensure that other checks occur historically. Also, this scheme will simplify the definition of Π, as well as history typing and verification, as discussed in section 4. In case a check fails at runtime, execution is "stuck"; formally:

Definition 1. We say that a configuration η, e is stuck if e is not a value and there does not exist η' and e' such that $\eta, e \rightarrow \eta', e'$. If $\epsilon, e \rightarrow^\star \eta, e'$ and η, e' is stuck, then e is said to go wrong.

The following example demonstrates the basics of syntax and operational semantics.

Example 1. Let the function f be defined as:

$$f \triangleq \lambda_z x.\mathsf{if}\ x\ \mathsf{then}\ ev_1(c)\ \mathsf{else}\ (ev_2(c); z(\mathsf{true}))$$

Then, in the operational semantics, we have:

$$\epsilon, f(\mathsf{false}) \rightarrow^\star ev_2(c); ev_1(c), ()$$

since the initial call to f will cause ev_2 to be added to the history, followed by a recursive call to f that hits its basis, where event ev_1 is encountered.

2.3   Logical Type System

In the type analysis, we are challenged to statically identify the histories that result during execution, for which purpose we introduce history effects H. In essence, history effects H conservatively approximate histories η that may develop during execution, by representing a set of histories containing at least η. A history effect may therefore be an event $ev(c)$, or a sequencing of history effects $H_1; H_2$, a nondeterministic choice of history effects $H_1 | H_2$, or a μ-bound

$$\begin{aligned}
&\alpha \in \mathcal{V}_s, t \in \mathcal{V}_\tau, h \in \mathcal{V}_H, \beta \in \mathcal{V}_s \cup \mathcal{V}_\tau \cup \mathcal{V}_H && \textit{variables} \\
&s \;::=\; \alpha \mid c && \textit{singletons} \\
&\tau \;::=\; t \mid \{s\} \mid \tau \xrightarrow{H} \tau \mid bool \mid unit && \textit{types} \\
&\sigma \;::=\; \forall \bar{\beta}.\tau && \textit{type schemes} \\
&H \;::=\; \epsilon \mid h \mid ev(s) \mid H;H \mid H|H \mid \mu h.H && \textit{history effects} \\
&\Gamma \;::=\; \varnothing \mid \Gamma; x : \sigma && \textit{type environments}
\end{aligned}$$

Fig. 3. λ_{hist} type syntax

history effect $\mu h.H$ which finitely represents the set of histories that may be generated by a recursive function. History types may contain predicate events $ev_\phi(c)$, allowing us to verify predicate checks at the right points in history effect approximations of "historical developments". Noting that the syntax of histories η is the same as linear, variable-free history effects: We abuse syntax and let η also range over linear, variable-free history effects, interpreting histories η as the same history effect.

The syntax of types for λ_{hist} is given in Fig. 3. In addition to histories, we include function types $\tau_1 \xrightarrow{H} \tau_2$, where H represents the histories that may result by use of the function. Events are side-effects, and so these function types are a form of effect type [25, 2]. Additionally, since events and predicates are parameterized in history types, we must be especially accurate with respect to our typing of constants. Thus, we adopt a very simple form of singleton type $\{c\}$ [24], where only atomic constants can have singleton type. Types contain three sorts of variables; regular type variables t, singleton type variables α, and history effect type variables h; β ranges over all sorts of variables. Universal type schemes $\forall \bar{\beta}.\tau$ bind any sort of type variable in τ. We write τ as syntactic sugar for $\forall \bar{\beta}.\tau$ with $\bar{\beta} \cap \mathrm{fv}(\tau) = \varnothing$.

Source code type derivation rules for judgements of the form $\Gamma, H \vdash e : \tau$ are given in Fig. 4, where Γ is an environment of variable typing assumptions. Intuitively, the history effect H in judgements represents the set of histories that may arise during execution of e (this intuition is formalized in the upcoming Theorem 1). For example:

Example 2. Let f defined as in Example 1, and let:

$$H \triangleq (\mu h.ev_1(c) \mid ev_2(c); h); ev_3(c')$$

Then, the following judgements are derivable[1]:

$$\varnothing, \epsilon \vdash f : bool \xrightarrow{\mu h.\,ev_1(c)|ev_2(c);h} unit \qquad \varnothing, H \vdash f(\mathsf{false}); ev_3(c') : unit$$

---

[1] These and following examples simplify history effects according to the equivalences specified in [22].

$$
\begin{array}{l}
\text{VAR} \\
\dfrac{\Gamma(x) = \forall \bar{\beta}.\tau}{\Gamma, \epsilon \vdash x : \tau[\bar{\tau}/\bar{\beta}]}
\end{array}
\qquad
\begin{array}{l}
\text{BOOL} \\
\Gamma, \epsilon \vdash b : bool
\end{array}
\qquad
\begin{array}{l}
\text{UNIT} \\
\Gamma, \epsilon \vdash () : unit
\end{array}
\qquad
\begin{array}{l}
\text{AND} \\
\Gamma, \epsilon \vdash \wedge : bool \xrightarrow{\epsilon} bool \xrightarrow{\epsilon} bool
\end{array}
$$

$$
\begin{array}{l}
\text{OR} \\
\Gamma, \epsilon \vdash \vee : bool \xrightarrow{\epsilon} bool \xrightarrow{\epsilon} bool
\end{array}
\qquad
\begin{array}{l}
\text{NOT} \\
\Gamma, \epsilon \vdash \neg : bool \xrightarrow{\epsilon} bool
\end{array}
\qquad
\begin{array}{l}
\text{CONST} \\
\Gamma, \epsilon \vdash c : \{c\}
\end{array}
$$

$$
\begin{array}{l}
\text{WEAKEN} \\
\dfrac{\Gamma, H \vdash e : \tau}{\Gamma, H|H' \vdash e : \tau}
\end{array}
\qquad
\begin{array}{l}
\text{EVENT} \\
\dfrac{\Gamma, H \vdash e : \{s\}}{\Gamma, H; ev(s) \vdash ev(e) : unit}
\end{array}
\qquad
\begin{array}{l}
\text{CHECK} \\
\dfrac{\Gamma, H \vdash e : \{s\}}{\Gamma, H; ev_\phi(s) \vdash \phi(e) : unit}
\end{array}
$$

$$
\begin{array}{l}
\text{IF} \\
\dfrac{\Gamma, H_1 \vdash e_1 : bool \qquad \Gamma, H_2 \vdash e_2 : \tau \qquad \Gamma, H_2 \vdash e_3 : \tau}{\Gamma, H_1; H_2 \vdash \text{if } e_1 \text{ then } e_2 \text{ else } e_3 : \tau}
\end{array}
$$

$$
\begin{array}{l}
\text{ABS} \\
\dfrac{\Gamma; x : \tau_1; z : \tau_1 \xrightarrow{H} \tau_2, H \vdash e : \tau_2}{\Gamma, \epsilon \vdash \lambda_z x.e : \tau_1 \xrightarrow{H} \tau_2}
\end{array}
\qquad
\begin{array}{l}
\text{APP} \\
\dfrac{\Gamma, H_1 \vdash e_1 : \tau' \xrightarrow{H_3} \tau \qquad \Gamma, H_2 \vdash e_2 : \tau'}{\Gamma, H_1; H_2; H_3 \vdash e_1 e_2 : \tau}
\end{array}
$$

$$
\begin{array}{l}
\text{LET} \\
\dfrac{\Gamma, \epsilon \vdash v : \tau' \qquad \bar{\beta} \cap \mathrm{fv}(\Gamma) = \varnothing \qquad \Gamma; x : \forall \bar{\beta}.\tau', H \vdash e : \tau}{\Gamma, H \vdash \text{let } x = v \text{ in } e : \tau}
\end{array}
$$

Fig. 4. λ_{hist} logical typing rules

Note that let-polymorphism over types, singletons, and history effects is included in our system. A typing $\Gamma, H \vdash e : \tau$ is valid iff it is derivable, and if H is valid in the interpretation defined in the next section. Additionally, typing judgements are identified modulo equivalence of history effects, as characterized in the next section. We observe that the addition of history effects is a conservative extension to the underlying type system: by using weakening before each if-then-else typing, any derivation in the underlying history-effect-free type system may be replayed here.

2.4 Interpretation of History Effects and Type Safety

As alluded to previously, the interpretation of a history effect is, roughly, a set of histories. More accurately, we define the Labelled Transition System (LTS) interpretation of history effects as sets of traces, which include a $\downarrow$ symbol to denote termination. Traces may be infinite, because programs may not terminate.

Definition 2. Our interpretation of histories will be defined via strings (called traces) denoted θ, over the following alphabet:

$$
a ::= ev(c) \mid \epsilon \mid \downarrow
$$

We let Θ range over prefix-closed sets of traces.

Sets of traces are obtained from history effects by viewing the latter as programs in a simple nondeterministic transition system:

Definition 3. The history effect transition relation is defined as follows:

$$ev(c) \xrightarrow{ev(c)} \epsilon \qquad H_1|H_2 \xrightarrow{\epsilon} H_1 \qquad H_1|H_2 \xrightarrow{\epsilon} H_2 \qquad \mu h.H \xrightarrow{\epsilon} H[\mu h.H/h]$$

$$\epsilon; H \xrightarrow{\epsilon} H \qquad\qquad H_1; H_2 \xrightarrow{a} H_1'; H_2 \text{ if } H_1 \xrightarrow{a} H_1'$$

We may formally determine the sets of traces Θ associated with a closed history effect in terms of the transition relation:

Definition 4. The interpretation of history effects is defined as follows:

$$\llbracket H \rrbracket = \{a_1 \cdots a_n \mid H \xrightarrow{a_1} \cdots \xrightarrow{a_n} H'\} \cup \{a_1 \cdots a_n {\downarrow} \mid H \xrightarrow{a_1} \cdots \xrightarrow{a_n} \epsilon\}$$

Any history effect interpretation is clearly prefix-closed. In this interpretation, an infinite trace is viewed as the set of its finite prefixes.

History effect equivalence is defined via this interpretation, i.e. $H_1 = H_2$ iff $\llbracket H_1 \rrbracket = \llbracket H_2 \rrbracket$. This relation is in fact undecidable: histories are equivalent to BPA's (basic process algebras) [22], and their trace equivalence is known to be undecidable [6].

We then base the validity of a history effect on validity of the assertion events that occur in traces in its interpretation. In particular, for any given predicate event in a trace, that predicate must hold for the immediate prefix trace that precedes it:

Definition 5. A history effect H is valid iff for all $\theta ev_\phi(c) \in \llbracket H \rrbracket$ it is the case that:

$$\Pi(\phi(c), \theta ev_\phi(c))$$

holds. A type judgement $\Gamma, H \vdash e : \tau$ is valid iff it is derivable and H is valid.

An important aspect of this definition is that $\llbracket H \rrbracket$ contains prefix traces. Essentially, if $\Gamma, H \vdash e : \tau$ is derivable, then $\llbracket H \rrbracket$ contains "snapshots" of e's potential run-time history at every step of reduction, so that validity of H implies validity of any check that occurs at run-time, "part-way through" the full program history as approximated by H. This is formally realized in our primary approximation result for history effects:

Theorem 1. If $\Gamma, H \vdash e : \tau$ is derivable for closed e and $\epsilon, e \rightarrow^\star \eta, e'$ then $\hat{\eta} \in \llbracket H \rrbracket$.

which in turn is the basis of a type safety result for λ_{hist}:

Theorem 2 (λ_{hist}^c Type Safety). If $\Gamma, H \vdash e : \tau$ is valid for closed e then e does not go wrong.

Proofs and details of these results are given in [22].

3   Polymorphic Type and Effect Inference

We implement our type and effect system using a constraint-based technique. This allows us to adopt existing methods [10] for realizing let-polymorphism, with appropriate modifications in the presence of history effects– in particular, the addition of effect constraints HC to capture weakening in inference. We define the new categories of type and effect constraints, constraint sets, constrained types, and constrained type schemes for the algorithm in Fig. 5. We write τ as syntactic sugar for $\forall \bar{\beta}.\tau/\varnothing, \varnothing$ when $\bar{\beta} \cap \mathrm{fv}(\tau) = \varnothing$.

Substitutions ψ are fundamental to our inference method. Substitutions are mappings from type variables β to types, extended to types constraints and environments in the obvious manner. We define substitutions as solutions of constraints via interpretation in a partially ordered universe of monotypes:

Definition 6 (Interpretation). Monotypes are types τ such that $\mathrm{fv}(\tau) = \varnothing$. We let $\hat{\tau}$ range over monotypes, and define $\preccurlyeq$ to be a partial ordering over monotypes such that $\hat{\tau}_1 \xrightarrow{H} \hat{\tau}_2 \preccurlyeq \hat{\tau}_1' \xrightarrow{H'} \hat{\tau}_2'$ implies $\hat{\tau}_1' \preccurlyeq \hat{\tau}_1$ and $\hat{\tau}_2 \preccurlyeq \hat{\tau}_2'$ and $H \preccurlyeq H'$, and $H \preccurlyeq H'$ implies $[\![H]\!] \subseteq [\![H']\!]$. An interpretation ρ is a total mapping from type variables to monotypes, extended to types and constraints in the usual manner (e.g. [19]).

Then, in addition to equality constraints on types, we posit a notion of $\sqsubseteq$ constraints on types; while type inference only treats such constraints on effects, a generalization of the relation to types is useful for characterizing type principality, as in Theorem 4:

Definition 7 (Constraint Solution). We say that a substitution ψ solves or satisfies a constraint $\tau \sqsubseteq \tau'$, and we write $\psi \vdash \tau \sqsubseteq \tau'$, if $\rho(\psi(\tau)) \preccurlyeq \rho(\psi(\tau'))$ for all ρ. We write $\vdash \tau \sqsubseteq \tau'$ if $\varnothing \vdash \tau \sqsubseteq \tau'$. Finally, ψ solves an effect constraint set HC if it solves every constraint in HC.

The type inference rules are given in Fig. 6. These rules are nondeterministic only in the choice of type variables introduced in various rules; without loss of generality, we assume that all inference derivations are in canonical form, wherein fresh type variables are chosen wherever possible.

$\tau = \tau' \in C$	*constraints*
$H \sqsubseteq H' \in \mathcal{HC}$	*effect constraints*
$C \in 2^C$	*constraint sets*
$HC \in 2^{\mathcal{HC}}$	*effect constraint sets*
$k ::= \tau/C, HC$	*constrained types*
$\varsigma ::= \forall \bar{\beta}.k$	*constrained type schemes*
$\Gamma ::= \varnothing \mid \Gamma; x : \varsigma$	*constrained type environments*

Fig. 5. Constained types and environments

$$
\begin{array}{l}
\text{VAR} \\
\dfrac{\Gamma(x) = \forall \bar{\beta}.k}{\Gamma, \epsilon \vdash_W x : k[\bar{\beta}'/\bar{\beta}]}
\end{array}
\qquad
\begin{array}{l}
\text{CONST} \\
\Gamma, \epsilon \vdash_W c : \{c\}/\varnothing, \varnothing
\end{array}
$$

$$
\text{EVENT} \\
\dfrac{\Gamma, H \vdash_W e : \tau/C, HC}{\Gamma, H; ev(\alpha) \vdash_W ev(e) : unit/C \cup \{\tau = \{\alpha\}\}, HC}
$$

$$
\text{CHECK} \\
\dfrac{\Gamma, H \vdash_W e : \tau/C, HC}{\Gamma, H; ev_\phi(\alpha) \vdash_W \phi(e) : unit/C \cup \{\tau = \{\alpha\}\}, HC}
$$

IF
$$
\dfrac{\begin{array}{c}\Gamma, H_1 \vdash_W e_1 : \tau_1/C_1, HC_1 \\ \Gamma, H_2 \vdash_W e_2 : \tau_2/C_2, HC_2 \qquad \Gamma, H_3 \vdash_W e_3 : \tau_3/C_3, HC_3\end{array}}{\begin{array}{c}\Gamma, H_1; H_2|H_3 \vdash_W \text{if } e_1 \text{ then } e_2 \text{ else } e_3 : t/C_1 \cup C_2 \cup C_3 \cup \{\tau_1 = bool, \tau_2 = t, \tau_3 = t\}, \\ HC_1 \cup HC_2 \cup HC_3\end{array}}
$$

$$
\text{APP} \\
\dfrac{\Gamma, H_1 \vdash_W e_1 : \tau_1/C_1, HC_1 \qquad \Gamma, H_2 \vdash_W e_2 : \tau_2/C_2, HC_2}{\Gamma, H_1; H_2; h \vdash_W e_1\, e_2 : t/C_1 \cup C_2 \cup \left\{\tau_1 = \tau_2 \xrightarrow{h} t\right\}, HC_1 \cup HC_2}
$$

$$
\text{FIX} \\
\dfrac{\Gamma; x : t; z : t \xrightarrow{h} t', H \vdash_W e : \tau/C, HC}{\Gamma, \epsilon \vdash_W \lambda_z x.e : t \xrightarrow{h} \tau/C \cup \{\tau = t'\}, HC \cup \{H \sqsubseteq h\}}
$$

$$
\text{LET} \\
\dfrac{\begin{array}{c}\Gamma, \epsilon \vdash_W v : \tau'/C', HC' \qquad \Gamma; x : \forall \bar{\beta}.\tau'/C', HC', H \vdash_W e : \tau/C, HC \\ \bar{\beta} = \text{fv}(\tau', C', HC') - \text{fv}(\Gamma) \qquad \psi = [\bar{\beta}'/\bar{\beta}]\end{array}}{\Gamma, H \vdash_W \text{let } x = v \text{ in } e : \tau/\psi(C') \cup C, \psi(HC') \cup HC}
$$

Fig. 6. Type constraint inference rules for λ_{hist}

The use of effect constraints HC in the type inference rules allows necessary weakening of effects to be inferred where allowable, while equality constraints C enforce invariance elsewhere, in keeping with the logical system. To solve equality constraints, a standard unification technique is defined in Fig. 7; unification of history effects on function types is trivial, since only variables h annotate function types in any inferred constraint set C. Otherwise, as observed in section 2, equality of history effects is undecidable. Solvability of effect constraint sets HC generated by inference is decidable as well, since these also adhere to a specific amenable form. In particular, the effect constraints generated by type inference will define a system of lower bounds on history effect variables:

Lemma 1. If $\varnothing, H \vdash_W e : \tau/C, HC$ is derivable and $\psi = \text{unify}(C)$, then for all $H_1 \sqsubseteq H_2 \in \psi(HC)$, H_2 is a history effect variable h.

$$unify(\varnothing) = \varnothing$$
$$unify(C \cup \{\tau = \tau\}) = unify(C)$$
$$unify(C \cup \{\beta = \tau\}) = \textbf{fail if } \beta \in \text{fv}(\tau), \text{ else}$$
$$unify(C[\tau/\beta]) \circ [\tau/\beta]$$
$$unify(C \cup \{\tau = \beta\}) = \textbf{fail if } \beta \in \text{fv}(\tau), \text{ else}$$
$$unify(C[\tau/\beta]) \circ [\tau/\beta]$$
$$unify(C \cup \{\{s_1\} = \{s_2\}\}) = unify(C \cup \{s_1 = s_2\})$$
$$unify\left(C \cup \left\{\tau_1 \xrightarrow{h} \tau_2 = \tau_1' \xrightarrow{h'} \tau_2'\right\}\right) = unify(C \cup \{h = h'\} \cup \{\tau_1 = \tau_1'\} \cup \{\tau_2 = \tau_2'\})$$

Fig. 7. Constraint set unification algorithm

$$MGS(C, HC) = \text{let } \psi_1 = unify(C) \text{ in } MGS_{\textbf{H}}(\psi_1(HC)) \circ \psi_1$$

$$bounds(h, HC) = H_1 | \cdots | H_n \quad \text{where } \{H_1, \ldots, H_n\} = \{H \mid H \sqsubseteq h \in HC\}$$

$$MGS_{\textbf{H}}(\varnothing) = \varnothing$$
$$MGS_{\textbf{H}}(HC) = \text{let } \psi = [(\mu h.bounds(h, HC))/h] \text{ in}$$
$$MGS_{\textbf{H}}(\psi(HC - \{H \sqsubseteq h \in HC\})) \circ \psi$$

Fig. 8. Most general solution algorithm

The result follows since H C is a system of lower bounds as a consequence of the inference rules, and ψ preserves this property since unification generates at most a renaming of any upper bound h in H C .

Thus, a most general solution algorithm M G S$_{\textbf{H}}$ for effect constraint sets is defined in Fig. 8, which joins the lower bounds inferred for any h, and μ-binds h on this join to account for the possibility of recursive effect constraints. Note that since each distinct upper bound h represents the effect of some function, μ-bound effects are function effects in inferred types, a fact that will become significant in section 5. The M G S$_{\textbf{H}}$ algorithm is composed with unification to obtain a complete solution for inferred type constraints. A soundness result is obtainable for this system, as follows:

Theorem 3 (Soundness). If the judgem ent $\varnothing, H \vdash_W e : \tau/C, HC$ is derivable and $\psi = $ M G S(C, HC), then $\varnothing, \psi(H) \vdash e : \psi(\tau)$ is derivable.

Completeness is also obtainable, comprising a principal types property, as follows:

Theorem 4 (Completeness). If $\varnothing, H \vdash e : \tau$ is derivable, then so is $\varnothing, H' \vdash_W e : \tau'/C, HC$ with M G S$(C, HC) = \psi$, where $\vdash \psi(H') \sqsubseteq H$ and $\vdash \psi' \circ \psi(\tau') \sqsubseteq \tau$ for som e ψ'.

We have developed a prototype implementation of type inference in OCaml, that has confirmed correctness of the algorithm. The implementation has also demonstrated the usefulness of simplification techniques for enhancing readability of history effects, e.g. tranforming $\mu h.H$ to H in case h does not appear free in H, transforming $\epsilon; H$ to H, etc.

4   Verification of History Checks

We have described the dynamic model of λ_{hist}, which includes a new event history component in configurations. We have also described a type system that conservatively approximates run-time histories. However, we have been abstract so far with respect to the form of history checks, basing safety of computation and validity of typing on a yet-to-be-defined notion of history check validity. To fill in these details, we first define a logic for run-time checks, including a syntax for expressing checks as predicates in the logic, together with a notion of validity for these checks that can be automatically verified in the run-time system. Secondly, we define a means of verifying validity of history effects, as defined in Definition 5, where check events that are predicted by the history effect analysis are automatically shown to either succeed or fail in the relevant context. The latter point is necessary to address because, even though validity of history effects has been defined, the notion is logical but not algorithmic; in particular, $[\![H]\!]$ may be an infinite set. We accomplish automated verification using a temporal logic and model-checking techniques, allowing us to reuse existing algorithms and results for history effect verification.

4.1   Verified Checks in the Linear μ-Calculus

While a plethora of model-checking logics are available, we use the μ-calculus [17] because it is powerful and is syntactically close to histories H. Further, efficient techniques for the automated verification of μ-calculus formulas on BPA processes have been developed [6, 11], and history effects are isomorphic to BPA's [22]. We use the linear variant of the μ-calculus [11] because at run-time only one linear trace of events is known, and so history effects H and runtime histories η can only be compared in a linear-time logic.

Definition 8. The syntax of the linear μ-calculus is:

$$\phi ::= x \mid \textbf{true} \mid \textbf{false} \mid (a)\phi \mid \boldsymbol{\mu} x.\phi \mid \boldsymbol{\nu} x.\phi \mid \neg\phi \mid \phi \vee \phi \mid \phi \wedge \phi$$

Here, a ranges over arbitrary transition labels; in particular, a may range over events $\text{ev}(c)$. The semantics of the linear μ-calculus is defined in Fig. 9. This semantics is defined over potentially infinite traces $\theta^\infty \in \Theta^\infty$ that, unlike sets of traces θ, may not be prefix-closed. V denotes a mapping from μ-calculus variables to sets of potentially infinite traces, $\varnothing$ denotes the empty mapping. $[\![\phi]\!]$ is shorthand for $[\![\phi]\!]_\varnothing$. Several formulae are not given in this figure because they can be defined in terms of the others: $\phi_1 \vee \phi_2$ is $\neg(\neg\phi_1 \wedge \neg\phi_2)$, $\textbf{false}$ is $\neg\textbf{true}$, and $\boldsymbol{\mu} x.\phi$ is $\neg(\boldsymbol{\nu} x.\neg\phi)$.

$$
\begin{aligned}
\llbracket \mathbf{true} \rrbracket_V &= \Theta^\infty \\
\llbracket x \rrbracket_V &= V(x) \\
\llbracket \neg\phi \rrbracket_V &= \Theta^\infty - \llbracket \phi \rrbracket_V \\
\llbracket \phi_1 \wedge \phi_2 \rrbracket_V &= \llbracket \phi_1 \rrbracket_V \cap \llbracket \phi_2 \rrbracket_V \\
\llbracket (a)\phi \rrbracket_V &= \{ \theta^\infty \in \Theta^\infty \mid \theta^\infty = a; \theta_1^\infty \text{ and } \theta_1^\infty \in \llbracket \phi \rrbracket_V \} \\
\llbracket \nu x.\phi \rrbracket_V &= \bigcup \{ W \subseteq \Theta^\infty \mid W \subseteq \llbracket \phi \rrbracket_{V[x \mapsto W]} \}
\end{aligned}
$$

Fig. 9. Semantics of the linear-time μ-calculus

Since our history effect semantics is prefix-closed, we will explicitly prefix-close $\llbracket \phi \rrbracket$ so the two sets are compatible.

Definition 9. The prefix closure $\Theta^\infty \downarrow$ of a set of infinite traces Θ^∞ is:

$$\{ \theta \mid \theta \text{ is a prefix of some } \theta^\infty \in \Theta^\infty \} \cup \{ \theta \downarrow \mid \theta \text{ is finite and } \theta \in \Theta^\infty \}$$

Definition 10. The formula ϕ is valid for H, written $H \Vdash \phi$, if $\llbracket H \rrbracket \subseteq \llbracket \phi \rrbracket \downarrow$.

This relation is decidable by known model-checking results [11] and the above mentioned equivalence of BPA processes and histories [22].

4.2   Relating History Effect and History Runtime Properties

We now instantiate the logic of history checks in λ_{hist} with linear μ-calculus formulae ϕ. As discussed above, the relation $H \Vdash \phi$ is decidable, so this will make a natural foundation for history effect verification.

One important requirement of this logic is that formulae must have truth values for a given history effect H, and for a history runtime η. The meaning of a formula ϕ under a run-time history η is taken by verifying $\hat{\eta} \in \llbracket \phi \rrbracket \downarrow$. We will define the history check interpretation function Π of Fig. 2 in terms of this relation (Definition 11).

In Theorem 1, history effects were shown to approximate dynamic histories—in particular, if $\epsilon, e \to^* \eta, e'$ and $H, \Gamma \vdash e : \tau$ is derivable, then $\hat{\eta} \in \llbracket H \rrbracket$. The key result linking the static and dynamic histories is the following:

Lemma 2. If $\hat{\eta} \in \llbracket H \rrbracket$ and $H \Vdash \phi$, then $\hat{\eta} \in \llbracket \phi \rrbracket \downarrow$.

Proof. Immediate from Definition 10 and Definition 4.

Theorem 1 ensures that by the above Lemma, verifying a history effect entails verifying all history checks that may occur at run-time, meaning a combination of type inference and automated verification yields a sound static analysis for λ_{hist}.

4.3   Soundness of Verification

We are close to a complete definition of our logical framework for history checks and history effect verification. However, a few small points remain: firstly, in

λ_{hist}, we are able to parameterize checks with constants with the syntax $\phi(c)$. To implement this, we specify a distinguished variable χ that may occur free in history checks, which is assumed to be instantiated with a history check parameter during verification.

Secondly, checks ϕ should express expected history patterns that may occur up to the point of the check. This is the same as requiring that if an event $\mathrm{ev}_\phi(c)$ occurs historically (resp. is predicted statically), the history η that precedes it (resp. any history that may precede it as predicted by typing) must exhibit the pattern specified by ϕ. However, there is an infinite regress lurking here: a property ϕ that mentions an event $\mathrm{ev}_\phi(c)$ suggests circularity in the syntax of ϕ. Thus, we introduce a distinguished label Now, that in any formula ϕ represents the relevant checkpoint of ϕ. This label is interpreted appropriately during verification.

We now stand ready to instantiate our logic and verification framework. In the dynamic system, this is accomplished by defining the language of history checks, and by defining the implementation of Π, our previously abstract representation of history check verification:

Definition 11 (Definition of Π). The framework of Section 2 is officially instantiated to let ϕ range over linear μ-calculus formulae, where labels a in ϕ are defined as follows:

$$a ::= \mathrm{ev}(s) \mid \mathrm{Now}$$

and, letting $\chi \in \mathcal{V}_s$ be a distinguished variable for parameterizing constants c in ϕ, we define Π as follows:

$$\Pi(\phi(c), \theta) \iff \theta \in [\![\phi[c/\chi][\mathrm{ev}_\phi(c)/\mathrm{Now}]]\!] \downarrow$$

Now, we specify what it means for a history effect to be verified; intuitively, it means that if a history effect H predicts the occurrence of a check event $\mathrm{ev}_\phi(c)$, then H semantically entails ϕ instantiated with c. Formally:

Definition 12 (History Effect Verification). A history effect H is verified iff for all subterms $\mathrm{ev}_\phi(c)$ of H it is the case that:

$$H \Vdash \phi[c/\chi][\mathrm{ev}_\phi(c)/\mathrm{Now}]$$

The preceding construction completes the definition of the framework. Lemma 2 and definition of Π together yield the desired formal property for history effect verification as a Corollary:

Corollary 1 (Verification Soundness). If H is verified, then H is valid.

Proof. Immediate by Definition 5, Definition 11, Definition 12, and Lemma 2.

5   The Stack-Based Variation

In this section we define a stack-based variation on the framework of the previous sections, allowing properties of the runtime stack at a program point to be verified at compile-time. Instead of keeping track of all events, only events for functions on the current call stack are maintained, in keeping with a general stack-based security model (as in e.g. [14]). Assertions ϕ in this framework are run-time assertions about the active event sequence, not all events. While the stack-based model is somewhat distinct from the history-based model, we show that this variation requires only a minor "post-processing" of inferred history effects for a sound analysis. There are results showing how it is possible to directly model-check stack properties of a Push-Down Automata (PDA) computation [12]; our approach based on post-processing history effects represents an alternative method, which may also prove useful for modeling features such as exceptions: the raising of an exception implies any subsequent effect is discarded.

We note that our system captures a more fine-grained stack-based model than has been previously proposed; in particular, the use of stacks of histories allows the ordering of events within individual stack frames to be taken into account, along with the ordering of frames themselves.

5.1   Syntax and Semantics

The values, expressions, and evaluation contexts of $\lambda_{\text{hist}}^{\text{S}}$ are exactly those of λ_{hist}, extended with an expression form $\cdot e \cdot$ and evaluation context form $\cdot E \cdot$ for delimiting the scope of function activations. We impose the requirement that in any function $\lambda_z x.e$, there exist no subexpressions $\cdot e' \cdot$ of e. The operational semantics of $\lambda_{\text{hist}}^{\text{S}}$, is a relation on configurations S, e, where S ranges over stacks of histories, defined in Fig. 10. The active security context for run-time checks is obtained from the history stack in configurations, by appending histories in the order they appear in the stack; to formalize this, we define the notation $\text{S}; \eta$ as follows:

$$\text{nil}; \eta = \eta \qquad\qquad \text{S} :: \eta; \eta' = \text{S}; \eta; \eta'$$

Selected rules for the reduction relations $\rightsquigarrow$ and $\rightarrow$ on configurations are then specified in Fig. 10 (those not specified are obtained by replacing metavariables η with S in reductions for other expression forms in Fig. 2). The history interpretation function Π is defined as for λ_{hist}.

5.2   Stackified History Effects

Although $\lambda_{\text{hist}}^{\text{S}}$ uses stack rather than history contexts at run-time, we are able to use the type and verification framework developed previously, assigning types to $\lambda_{\text{hist}}^{\text{S}}$ expressions in the same manner as λ_{hist} expressions. The only additional requirement will be to process history effects– to stackify them, yielding an approximation of the stack contexts that will evolve at run-time. The trick is to use μ-delimited scope in history types, since this corresponds to function scope in inferred types as discussed in section 3, and function activations and deactivations induce pushes and pops at run-time. The stackify algorithm is defined inductively in Figure 11. This algorithm works over histories that are sequences; for histories that are not sequences, the last clause puts it into sequence form.

$$S ::= \text{nil} \mid S :: \eta \qquad history\ stacks$$

$$S, (\lambda_z x.e)v \rightsquigarrow S :: \epsilon, \cdot e[v/x][\lambda_z x.e/z] \cdot \qquad (\beta)$$

$$S :: \eta, ev(c) \rightsquigarrow S :: \eta; ev(c), () \qquad (event)$$

$$S :: \eta, \phi(c) \rightsquigarrow S :: \eta; ev_\phi(c), () \qquad (check)$$

$$\text{if } \Pi(\phi(c), (\hat{S; \eta})\, ev_\phi(c))$$

$$S :: \eta, \cdot v \cdot \rightsquigarrow S, v \qquad (pop)$$

Fig. 10. Semantics of λ_{hist}^S (selected rules)

$$stackify(\epsilon) = \epsilon$$

$$stackify(\epsilon; H) = stackify(H)$$

$$stackify(ev(c); H) = ev(c); stackify(H)$$

$$stackify(h; H) = h \mid stackify(H)$$

$$stackify((\mu h.H_1); H_2) = (\mu h.stackify(H_1)) \mid stackify(H_2)$$

$$stackify((H_1 \mid H_2); H) = stackify(H_1; H) \mid stackify(H_2; H)$$

$$stackify((H_1; H_2); H_3) = stackify(H_1; (H_2; H_3))$$

$$stackify(H) = stackify(H; \epsilon)$$

Fig. 11. The *stackify* algorithm

The last three clauses use history effect equalities characterized in [22] to "massage" history effects into appropriate form. Observe that the range of stackify consists of history effects that are all tail-recursive; stacks are therefore finite-state transition systems and more efficient model-checking algorithms are possible for stacks than for general histories [12].

Example 3. With a, b, c, d representing arbitrary events:

$$stackify(a; (\mu h.b; c); (\mu h.c; (\epsilon \mid (d; h; a)))) = a; ((\mu h.b; c) \mid (\mu h.c; (\epsilon \mid (d; h) \mid (d; a))))$$

Validity of a type judgement $\Gamma, H \vdash e : \tau$, and type safety in the λ_{hist}^S, will hinge upon validity of stackify(H). We obtain the desired result indirectly, via an equivalent, but more immediately applicable and technically convenient type logic. Details, omitted here for brevity, are given in [22]. The main result is Type Safety for stackified history typings, as follows; the definition of e "going wrong" here is analogous to Definition 1. Note that we make an expected restriction on expressions to ensure that the empty stack is never popped:

Theorem 5 (λ_{hist}^S **Type Safety**). If the judgement $\Gamma, H \vdash e : \tau$ is derivable for closed e with no subexpressions of the form $\cdot e' \cdot$, and stackify(H) is valid, then e does not go wrong.

As a corollary of this result and Theorem 2, type inference and verification as developed for λ_{hist} may be re-used in the stack model.

6   Applications

In this section we show that our program logic is sufficiently expressive to be useful in practice for security applications. First, we show how access control decisions based on past events in a history-based model can be expressed and typechecked. Then, we solve an open problem by showing how Java's parameterized privileges can be statically modeled.

In our examples we will be interested in unparameterized events and predicates; in such cases we will write ev and ϕ for $ev(c_{\text{dummy}})$ and $\phi(c_{\text{dummy}})$ respectively, where c_{dummy} is a distinguished dummy constant. Also, we will abbreviate events ev_i by their subscripts i, and the notation:

$$(\vee \{ev_1(c_1), \ldots, ev_n(c_n)\})\phi \triangleq ev_1(c_1)\phi \vee \cdots \vee ev_n(c_n)\phi$$

will be convenient, as will:

$$(.*)\phi \triangleq ev_1(c_1)\phi \vee \cdots \vee ev_n(c_n)\phi$$

where $\{ev_1(c_1), \ldots, ev_n(c_n)\}$ for the latter definition is the set of events in a specified context.

6.1   History-Based Access Control

History-based access control is a generalization of Java's notion of stack inspection that takes into account all past events, not just those on the stack [1]. Our language is perfectly suited for the static typechecking of such security policies. In the basic history model of [1], some initial current rights are given, and with every new activation the static rights of that activation are automatically intersected with the current rights to generate the new current rights. Unlike stack inspection, removal of the activation does not return the current rights to its state prior to the activation.

Before showing how this form of assertion can be expressed in our language, we define the underlying security model. We assume all code is annotated with a "principal" identifier p, and assume an ACL policy $\mathcal{A}$ mapping principals p to resources $r(c)$ for which they are authorized. An event ev_p is issued whenever a codebase annotated with p is entered. A demand of a resource r with parameter c, $\phi_{\text{demand},r}(c)$, requires that all invoked functions possess the right for that resource. This general check may be expressed in our language as $\phi_{\text{demand},r}$, defined in Fig. 12, where we assume given for verification history effect H containing events $ev_1(c_1), \ldots, ev_n(c_n)$.

Assertion $\phi_{\text{demand},r}(c)$ forces all code principals invoked thus far to have the rights for $r(c)$. For example, validity of the following requires $r(c) \in \mathcal{A}(p_1) \cap \mathcal{A}(p_2)$:

$$\Gamma, p_1; p_2; \phi_{\text{demand},r}(c) \vdash p_1; (\lambda x.p_2; \phi_{\text{demand},r}(x))\, c : \text{unit}$$

The model in [1] also allows for a combination of stack- and history-based properties, by allowing the amplication of a right on the stack: it stays active even after function return. Such assertions can be expressed in our framework using a combination of stack- and history-based assertions.

6.2   Stack Inspection with Parameterized Privileges

Java stack inspection [27, 21, 19] uses an underlying security model of principals and resources as defined in the previous section. One additional feature of Java is that any principal may also explicitly enable a resource for which they are authorized. When a function is activated, its associated principal identifier is pushed on the stack, along with any resource enablings that occur in its body. Stack inspection for a particular resource $r(c)$ then checks the stack for an enabling of $r(c)$, searching frames from most to least recent, and failing if a principal unauthorized for $r(c)$ is encountered before an enabling of $r(c)$, or if no such enabling is encountered.

Stack inspection can be modeled in the stack-based variant of our programming logic defined in Section 5. Rather than defining the general encoding, we develop one particular example which illustrates all the issues. Consider the following function checkit:

$$\text{checkit} \triangleq \lambda x.p\text{:system}; \phi_{\text{inspect},r\text{:filew}}(x)$$

Every function upon execution first issues an owner (principal) event, in this case p:system indicating "system" is the principal p that owns checkit. The function takes a parameter x (a file name) and inspects the stack for the "filew" resource with parameter x, via embedded μ-calculus assertion $\phi_{\text{inspect},r\text{:filew}}(x)$. This assertion is defined below; it enforces the fact that all functions on the call stack back to the nearest enable must be owned by principals p that according to ACL $\mathcal{A}$ are authorized for the r:filew(x) resource.

Now, to model resource enabling we use a special parameterized event $\text{enable}_r(x)$, indicating resource $r(x)$ is temporarily enabled. We illustrate use of explicit enabling via an example "wrapper" function enableit, owned by say the "accountant" principal p:acct, that takes a function f and a constant x, and enables r:filew(x) for the application of f to x:

$$\text{enableit} \triangleq \lambda f.p\text{:acct}; (\lambda x.p\text{:acct}; \text{enable}_{r\text{:filew}}(x); \text{let } y = f(x) \text{ in } y)$$

The definition of $\phi_{\text{inspect},r}(c)$, for fixed $r(c)$, is generalized over parameterized resources $r(c)$. For history effect H containing only the events $\text{ev}_1(c_1), \ldots, \text{ev}_n(c_n)$, and parameterized resource $r(c)$, Fig. 12 gives the definition of $\phi_{\text{inspect},r}(c)$. ϕ_{inspect} has two parts: first, any $r(c)$ enabling must be valid via $\phi_{\text{enable-ok},r}(c)$; second, we must check that stack inspections for $r(c)$ are valid via $\phi_{\text{inspect-ok},r}(c)$.

Returning to our previous example expressions checkit and enableit, the following most general types are inferred in our system:

$$\text{checkit} : \forall \alpha.\{\alpha\} \xrightarrow{p\text{:system};\phi_{\text{inspect},r\text{:filew}}(\alpha)} \text{unit}$$

$$\text{enableit} : \forall \alpha h t.(\{\alpha\} \xrightarrow{h} t) \xrightarrow{p\text{:acct}} \{\alpha\} \xrightarrow{p\text{:acct};\text{enable}_{r\text{:filew}}(\alpha);h} t$$

$$(p_{\neg r(c)})\phi \triangleq (\vee \{p | r(c) \notin \mathcal{A}(p)\})\phi$$

$$\phi_{\text{demand},r}(c) \triangleq \neg((.*)(p_{\neg r(c)})(.*)(\text{Now})\textbf{true})$$

$$(\bar{p})\phi \triangleq (\vee(\{ev_1(c_1),\ldots,ev_n(c_n)\} \setminus \text{dom}(\mathcal{A})))\phi$$

$$(\neg ev(c))\phi \triangleq (\vee(\{ev_1(c_1),\ldots,ev_n(c_n)\} \setminus \{ev(c)\}))\phi$$

$$(a*)\phi \triangleq \mu x.(a)x \vee \phi \qquad \text{for } a \in \{\bar{p}, \neg ev(c)\}$$

$$\phi_{\text{enable-ok},r}(c) \triangleq \neg((.*)(p_{\neg r(c)})(\bar{p}*)(\text{enable}_r(c))\textbf{true})$$

$$\phi_{\text{inspect-ok},r}(c) \triangleq \neg((\neg \text{enable}_r(c)*)(\text{Now})\textbf{true}) \wedge \neg((.*)(p_{\neg r(c)})(\neg \text{enable}_r(c)*)(\text{Now})\textbf{true})$$

$$\phi_{\text{inspect},r}(c) \triangleq \phi_{\text{enable-ok},r}(c) \wedge \phi_{\text{inspect-ok},r}(c)$$

Fig. 12. Definitions of $\phi_{\text{demand},r}$ and $\phi_{\text{inspect},r}$

The stackification of the application (enableit checkit (/accts/ledger.txt)) will then generate the history effect p:acct$|H$, where:

$$H = p\text{:acct}; \text{enable}_{r:\text{filew}}(/\text{accts/ledger.txt}); p\text{:system}; \phi_{\text{inspect},r:\text{filew}}(/\text{accts/ledger.txt})$$

This reflects that the call and return of the application (enableit checkit) is assigned the effect p:acct, while the subsequent application to /accts/ledger.txt is assigned effect H. Assuming that both p:system and p:acct are authorized for r:filew(/accts/ledger.txt) in $\mathcal{A}$, verification will clearly succeed on this expression. On the other hand, stackification of the application checkit(/accts/ledger.txt) will generate the following history effect:

$$p\text{:system}; \phi_{\text{inspect},r:\text{filew}}(/\text{accts/ledger.txt})$$

for which verification will fail: there is no required $\text{enable}_{r:\text{filew}}(/\text{accts/ledger.txt})$ on the stack.

7   Conclusions

We have presented a new type effect system, an inference algorithm for inferring effects, and an algorithm for automatically verifying assertions made about the effects. With this system, users merely need to decorate code with logical assertions about past events, and the system will automatically verify those assertions without user intervention.

The original goal of our project was to build the first system to statically model the parameterized privileges of Java stack inspection, and also to allow the static checking of general runtime history assertions for enforcing access control policies. We believe we have succeeded in this regard. But, the system we have produced is not particularly biased toward access control properties, and thus will be useful in other domains: it can statically enforce a wide class of event-based runtime invariants.

The type system itself makes several contributions in its combination of expressiveness and completeness. The effect system conservatively extends effect-free typing, so the effects will not "get in the way" of typing. The inference algorithm merges history effect H in a sound and complete manner instead of attempting to unify them.

7.1   Related Work

Our type effect system shares much of the basic structure of the effect system in [2]; their system lacks our singletons and contextual assertions. Their approach has one significant drawback as compared to ours, in that their inference algorithm is not "sound enough"; it is formally proven sound, but the soundness property doesn't preclude inconsistent constraints such as $ev_{up} = ev_{down}$.

Perhaps the most closely related work is [15], which proposes a similar type and effect system and type inference algorithm, but their "resource usage" abstraction is of a markedly different character, based on grammars rather than LTSs. Their system lacks parametric polymorphism, which restricts expressiveness in practice, and verifies global, rather than local, assertions. Furthermore, their system analyzes only history-based properties, not stack-based properties as in our stackify transformation.

The system of [13] is based on linear types, not effect types. Their usages U are similar to our history effects H, but the usages have a much more complex grammar, and appear to have no real gain in expressiveness. Their specification logic is left abstract, thus they provide no automated mechanism for expressing or deciding assertions. Our history effects can easily be seen to form an LTS for which model-checking is decidable; their usages are significantly more complex, so it is unclear if model-checking will be possible.

The systems in [8, 5, 14, 4] use LTSs extracted from control-flow graph abstractions to model-check program security properties expressed in temporal logic. Their approach is close in several respects, but we are primarily focused on the programming language as opposed to the model-checking side of the problem. Their analyses assume the pre-existence of a control-flow graph abstraction, which is in the format for a first-order program analysis only. Our type-based approach is defined directly at the language level, and type inference provides an explicit, scalable mechanism for extracting an abstract program interpretation, which is applicable to higher-order functions and other features. Furthermore, polymorphic effects are inferrable, and events may be parameterized by constants so partial dataflow information can be included.We believe our results are critical to bringing this general approach to practical fruition for production programming languages such as ML and Java.

Acknowledgments

Thanks to David Van Horn for his useful comments, implementations, and testing.

References

1. Martín Abadi and Cédric Fournet. Access control based on execution history. In *Proceedings of the 10th Annual Network and Distributed System Security Symposium (NDSS'03)*, feb 2003.
2. T. Amtoft, F. Nielson, and H. R. Nielson. *Type and Effect Systems*. Imperial College Press, 1999.
3. Thomas Ball and Sriram K. Rajamani. Bebop: A symbolic model checker for boolean programs. In *SPIN*, pages 113–130, 2000.
4. F. Besson, T. Jensen, D. Le Métayer, and T. Thorn. Model checking security properties of control flow graphs. *J. Computer Security*, 9:217–250, 2001.
5. Frédéric Besson, Thomas de Grenier de Latour, and Thomas Jensen. Secure calling contexts for stack inspection. In *Proceedings of the Fourth ACM SIGPLAN Conference on Principles and Practice of Declarative Programming (PPDP'02)*, pages 76–87. ACM Press, 2002.
6. O. Burkart, D. Caucal, F. Moller, , and B. Steffen. Verification on infinite structures. In S. Smolka J. Bergstra, A. Pons, editor, *Handbook on Process Algebra*. North-Holland, 2001.
7. Hao Chen and David Wagner. MOPS: an infrastructure for examining security properties of software. In *Proceedings of the 9th ACM Conference on Computer and Communications Security*, pages 235–244, Washington, DC, November 18–22, 2002.
8. Thomas Colcombet and Pascal Fradet. Enforcing trace properties by program transformation. In *27th ACM SIGPLAN-SIGACT Symposium on Principles of Programming Languages*, pages 54–66, 2000.
9. Guy Edjlali, Anurag Acharya, and Vipin Chaudhary. History-based access control for mobile code. In *ACM Conference on Computer and Communications Security*, pages 38–48, 1998.
10. Jonathan Eifrig, Scott Smith, and Valery Trifonov. Type inference for recursively constrained types and its application to OOP. volume 1, 1995. `http://www.elsevier.nl/locate/entcs/volume1.html`.
11. J. Esparza. On the decidability of model checking for several mu-calculi and Petri nets. In *Proceeding of CAAP '94*, volume 787 of *Lecture Notes in Computer Science*, 1994.
12. J. Esparza, A. Kucera, and S. Schwoon. Model-checking LTL with regular valuations for pushdown systems. In *TACS: 4th International Conference on Theoretical Aspects of Computer Software*, 2001.
13. Atsushi Igarashi and Naoki Kobayashi. Resource usage analysis. In *Conference Record of POPL'02: The 29th ACM SIGPLAN-SIGACT Symposium on Principles of Programming Languages*, pages 331–342, Portland, Oregon, January 2002.
14. T. Jensen, D. Le Métayer, and T. Thorn. Verification of control flow based security properties. In *Proceedings of the 1999 IEEE Symposium on Security and Privacy*, 1999.
15. P. J. Stuckey K. Marriott and M. Sulzmann. Resource usage verification. In *Proc. of First Asian Programming Languages Symposium, APLAS 2003*, 2003.
16. Naoki Kobayashi. Time regions and effects for resource usage analysis. In *Proceedings of ACM SIGPLAN International Workshop on Types in Languages Design and Implementation (TLDI'03)*, 2003.
17. Dexter Kozen. Results on the propositional mu-calculus. *Theoretical Computer Science*, 27:333–354, December 1983.

18. Yitzhak Mandelbaum, David Walker, and Robert Harper. An effective theory of type refinements. In *Proceedings of the the Eighth ACM SIGPLAN International Conference on Functional Programming (ICFP'03)*, Uppsala, Sweden, August 2003.

19. François Pottier, Christian Skalka, and Scott Smith. A systematic approach to static access control. In David Sands, editor, *Proceedings of the 10th European Symposium on Programming (ESOP'01)*, volume 2028 of *Lecture Notes in Computer Science*, pages 30–45. Springer Verlag, April 2001.

20. Fred B. Schneider. Enforceable security policies. *Information and System Security*, 3(1):30–50, 2000.

21. Christian Skalka and Scott Smith. Static enforcement of security with types. In *Proceedings of the the Fifth ACM SIGPLAN International Conference on Functional Programming (ICFP'00)*, pages 34–45, Montréal, Canada, September 2000.

22. Christian Skalka and Scott Smith. History types and verification. Extended manuscript, `http://www.cs.uvm.edu/~skalka/skalka-smith-tr04.ps`, 2004.

23. B. Steffen and O. Burkart. Model checking for context-free processes. In *CONCUR'92, Stony Brook (NY)*, volume 630 of *Lecture Notes in Computer Science (LNCS)*, pages 123–137, Heidelberg, Germany, 1992. Springer-Verlag.

24. Chris Stone. Singleton types and singleton kinds. Technical Report CMU-CS-00-153, Carnegie Mellon University, 2000.

25. Jean-Pierre Talpin and Pierre Jouvelot. The type and effect discipline. In *Seventh Annual IEEE Symposium on Logic in Computer Science, Santa Cruz, California*, pages 162–173, Los Alamitos, California, 1992. IEEE Computer Society Press.

26. David Walker. A type system for expressive security policies. In *Conference Record of POPL'00: The 27th ACM SIGPLAN-SIGACT Symposium on Principles of Programming Languages*, pages 254–267, Boston, Massachusetts, January 2000.

27. Dan S. Wallach and Edward Felten. Understanding Java stack inspection. In *Proceedings of the 1998 IEEE Symposium on Security and Privacy*, May 1998.

Controlled Declassification Based on Intransitive Noninterference

Heiko Mantel[1] and David Sands[2]

[1] Information Security, ETH Zürich, Switzerland
Heiko.Mantel@inf.ethz.ch
[2] Chalmers University of Technology, Göteborg, Sweden
www.cs.chalmers.se/~dave

Abstract. Traditional noninterference cannot cope with common features of secure systems like channel control, information filtering, or explicit downgrading. Recent research has addressed the derivation and use of weaker security conditions that could support such features in a language-based setting. However, a fully satisfactory solution to the problem has yet to be found. A key problem is to permit exceptions to a given security policy without permitting too much. In this article, we propose an approach that draws its underlying ideas from *intransitive noninterference*, a concept usually used on a more abstract specification level. Our results include a new bisimulation-based security condition that controls tightly where downgrading can occur and a sound security type system for checking this condition.

1 Introduction

Research on secure information flow in a programming-language setting has flourished in recent years, with advances in both theory and practice [SM03b]. The basic problem is to determine: When can a program be trusted to access confidential data even when some of its actions can be observed by untrusted subjects? That is, information flow security goes beyond access control as it not only restricts the program's access to data but also the propagation of data within the program. In the simplest case there are two kinds of data: confidential (high) and public (low) data, where the only permitted flow of information is from low to high. In the general case there is a partial ordering of security levels (often a lattice [Den76]), representing different levels of security where the ordering relation expresses where information may legitimately flow.

Despite many recent advances in the theory and practice of secure information flow, some serious practical concerns remain. One problem is that secure information flow, although a worthy goal, is often an unrealistic one. The problem is that many programs must inevitably leak certain amounts of data.

For instance, a bank's IT system stores data about the financial transactions of its customers. Information about a transaction should be kept confidential to the parties involved and to authorized bank personnel. However, in the process of a criminal prosecution it might become necessary and allowable for a

W.-N. Chin (Ed.): APLAS 2004, LNCS 3302, pp. 129–145, 2004.
© Springer-Verlag Berlin Heidelberg 2004

prosecutor to analyze the data about a particular customer in the bank's IT system. Hence, the system must be able to reveal the secret data about a customer to the prosecutor, which can be seen as a form of declassification. Naturally, this does not mean that arbitrary parts of the system may be able to perform declassification. For example, there should be no danger that a procedure responsible for printing account statements causes declassification neither with a malicious intent nor due to a bug in the program. Rather, declassification should be limited to designated parts of a program whose execution can then be protected by an unmistakable request for a confirmation of the declassification or a request for another password (e.g. to implement a two-person rule). Moreover, permitting declassification does not mean that arbitrary data may be declassified. For example, it would not be allowable if data about transactions that are completely unrelated to the prosecuted customer were revealed to the prosecutor. In summary, one wants to tightly control where classification can occur in a program and where exceptions to the information flow ordering are permitted in the security policy. This is what intransitive noninterference [Rus92, Pin95, RG99, Man01, BPR04] provides.

Our goal here is to adapt intransitive noninterference to a programming-language setting. To our knowledge, this has not been achieved before. Prior work on language-based information flow security has addressed other aspects of declassification, namely controlling what or how much information is declassified [Coh78, VS00, SS01, CHM02, Low02, BP02, DHW02, SM03a, SM03b] and controlling who initiates the act of declassification [ZM01, Zda03, MSZ04]. These aspects are also important, but orthogonal to the localization of declassification in a program and in a security policy, i.e. the aspects that we investigate here.

Rather than re-inventing a new program analysis from scratch, we want to illustrate how an existing analysis technique (namely, the one developed in [SS00]) can be adapted for dealing with intransitive information flow. The specific contributions of our work are: (1) A state-based definition of security for simple concurrent programming languages that is suitable for information flow policies permitting forms of declassification and that exhibits good compositionality properties (Section 4). (2) A security type system for a toy language illustrating the utility of our security definition (Section 6). We illustrate our security definition also with several examples (in Section 5) and compare it to related work (in Section 7). Due to space restrictions, proofs of the main results are presented in an extended version of the paper.

2   Preliminaries

The definition of security to be introduced in the next section is formulated in terms of a "small-step" transition relation on commands and states. The specification of the transition relation is stratified into a deterministic layer for individual commands and a nondeterministic layer for command vectors.

Deterministic judgments have the form $\langle C, s \rangle \rightarrow \langle \vec{W}, t \rangle$ expressing that a thread with program C performs a computation step in state s, yielding a state

t and a vector of programs $\vec{W}$ that has length zero if C terminated, length n if $n > 1$ threads were spawned, and length one, otherwise. That is, a program vector of length n can be viewed as a pool of n threads that run concurrently. Nondeterministic judgments have the form $\langle \vec{V}, s \rangle \rightarrow \langle \vec{W}, t \rangle$ expressing that some thread C_i in the thread pool $\vec{V}$ performs a step in state s resulting in the state t and some thread pool $\vec{W}'$. The global thread pool $\vec{W}$ results then by replacing C_i with $\vec{W}'$.

We abstract from the details of scheduling and work with a purely nondeterministic semantics for thread pools. This has shortcomings in terms of security modeling as the way in which nondeterminism is resolved can be exploited to create additional covert channels (see [SS00]). We adopt this simplification to reduce technical overhead. However, we believe that it is not a fundamental limitation of our approach and that most of our results would carry over to a more scheduler-specific setting, i.e. one in which the scheduler is under the control of the attacker [SS00].

For the sake of concreteness, we introduce a minimalistic programming language that we will use for illustrating the basic principles. The language that we adopt is the multi-threaded while language (short: MWL) from [SS00]. It includes commands for assignment, conditional branching, looping, and dynamic thread creation. The complete set of commands $C \in \mathsf{Com}$ is:

$$C ::= \mathsf{skip} \mid \mathsf{Id} := \mathsf{Exp} \mid C_1; C_2 \mid \text{if } B \text{ then } C_1 \text{ else } C_2 \mid \text{while } B \text{ do } C \mid \mathsf{fork}(C\vec{V})$$

In the following (and above), the metavariable C denotes an individual command, and $\vec{V}$, $\vec{W}$ denote command vectors. The set of all command vectors is defined by $\mathsf{Com} = \bigcup_{n \in \mathbb{N}} \mathsf{Com}^n$. We assume a set Var of program variables and a (not further specified) set Val of values. States are mappings from variables to values being denoted by s or t. A configuration is a pair $\langle \vec{V}, s \rangle$ where $\vec{V}$ specifies the threads that are currently active and s defines the current state of the memory. Expressions are simply variables, constants, or binary operators applied to expressions. Our treatment of expressions is rather informal; we assume the existence of a subset of expressions that yield boolean results. These boolean expressions are ranged over by B. We use a judgement $\langle \mathsf{Exp}, s \rangle \downarrow n$ for specifying that the expression Exp evaluates to the value n in state s. Expression evaluation is assumed to be total and to occur atomically. For reasons of space, the transition relation for MWL is omitted in this version of the paper.

The operational semantics require an implementation that executes small-step transitions atomically.

3   Strong Security for Multi-level Policies

The strong security condition has been defined in [SS00] for a security policy with a high and a low domain. In the following, we generalize this definition to multi-level security policies with an arbitrary number of security domains.

Definition 1 (MLS Policy). A multi-level security policy is a pair $(\mathcal{D}, \leq)$ where $\mathcal{D}$ is a set of security domains and $\leq \subseteq \mathcal{D} \times \mathcal{D}$ is a partial ordering.

Definition 2 (Domain Assignment). A domain assignment is a function $\mathrm{dom} : \mathrm{Var} \to \mathcal{D}$ that assigns a security domain to each program variable.

In examples, we adopt the convention that names of variables reflect their domains. For example, in the context of a two-level security policy $(L \leq H)$, l and h denote typical variables of the domains L and H, respectively.

Security will be defined with reference to the way that an observer with a given clearance (i.e. a security domain) observes the behavior of the system. We assume, in a standard manner, that an observer at domain D can see the values of variables at domain D, and at all domains below D. However, we focus not on this projection, but rather on the equivalence relation that it induces on states:

Definition 3 (D-Equality). Let $D \in \mathcal{D}$. Two states s_1 and s_2 are D-equal (denoted by $s_1 =_D s_2$) iff $\forall \mathrm{var} \in \mathrm{Var} : \mathrm{dom} \, (\mathrm{var}) \leq D \implies s_1(\mathrm{var}) = s_2(\mathrm{var})$.

The intuition is: if $s_1 =_D s_2$ then the states s_1 and s_2 are indistinguishable for an observer with clearance D.

In [SS00] a strong low-bisimulation relation captures when two command vectors are indistinguishable (from the low observer's perspective). This is an auxiliary definition that is used to define when a program is secure. Here we generalize the definition to the multi-level case:

Definition 4 (Strong D-Bisimulation). The strong D-bisimulation $\cong_D$ (for $D \in \mathcal{D}$) is the union of all symmetric relations R on command vectors $\vec{V}, \vec{V}' \in \mathrm{Com}$ of equal size, i.e. $\vec{V} = (C_1, \dots, C_n)$ and $\vec{V}' = (C_1', \dots, C_n')$, such that

$$\forall s, s', t : \forall i \in \{1 \dots n\} : \forall \vec{W} : \vec{V} \, R \, \vec{V}' \wedge s =_D s' \wedge \langle C_i, s \rangle \twoheadrightarrow \langle \vec{W}, t \rangle$$
$$\Rightarrow \exists \vec{W}', t' : \langle C_i', s' \rangle \twoheadrightarrow \langle \vec{W}', t' \rangle \wedge \vec{W} \, R \, \vec{W}' \wedge t =_D t'$$

Intuitively, two programs C and C' are strongly D-bisimilar ($C \cong_D C'$) iff their behavior on D-equivalent states is indistinguishable by an observer with clearance D. The definition is "strong" in a number of senses:

1. The programs must be indistinguishable for D not only if being run in identical starting states, but also if being run in different states that are D-equal.
2. The programs must not only be indistinguishable for D in their complete runs, but they must be strongly D-bisimilar after each computation step.
3. The relationship requires that threads match one-for-one and step-by-step.

The first property relates to the standard noninterference view: Being strongly D-bisimilar to itself means for a program that an observer can infer the starting state at most up to D-equality. That is, such a program cannot leak to domain D any information that D is not permitted to access. The second property is crucial for making the security condition compositional. This is related to the well-known fact that a (standard) compositional semantics cannot be given to the language if we only model the uninterrupted traces of computation. The third property is justified by the fact that the semantics remains sound for particular choices of the scheduler (see [SS00] for the details.) Note that $\approx_D$ is not reflexive as some programs yield different observations if run in D-equal starting states:

Example 1. For the two-level security policy $L \leq H$, the program $l := h$ is not L-bisimilar to itself. For instance, the states s (defined by $s(l) = 0$, $s(h) = 0$) and t (defined by $t(l) = 0$, $t(h) = 1$) are L-equal, but the states s' and t' resulting after $l := h$ is run in s and t, respectively, are not L-equal ($s'(l) = 0 \neq 1 = t'(l)$).

The security of a given program is then defined by using self-bisimilarity.

Definition 5 (Strong D-Security). Let Pol $= (\mathcal{D}, \leq)$ be an MLS policy and $D \in \mathcal{D}$ be a security domain. A program $\vec{V}$ is strongly secure for D iff $\vec{V} \approx_D \vec{V}$.

Strong D-security says that the program does not leak information to an observer with clearance D. Strong security is then defined by requiring this at all levels:

Definition 6 (Strong Security). Let Pol $= (\mathcal{D}, \leq)$ be an MLS policy. A program $\vec{V}$ is strongly secure iff it is strongly secure for all $D \in \mathcal{D}$.

4   Permitting Controlled Declassification

Declassification features are needed for many applications, but, unfortunately, they cause a fundamental problem for the security analysis: On the one hand, it shall be enforced that the flow of information complies with the given MLS policy, but on the other hand, violations of the policy should be tolerated. Obviously, these goals are conflicting. There is a wide spectrum of possible solutions, each of which involving some compromise. For instance, the strong security condition in the previous section is at the one end of the spectrum as it does not tolerate any exceptions to the MLS policy. A solution at the other end of the spectrum is employed in the Bell/La Padula model [BL76] where processes are considered as trusted processes if they involve downgrading and to exempt such processes from the formal security analysis. Such an analysis investigates the system without trusted processes although the system will always run with these processes.[1] Since the system being formally analyzed differs, it is not entirely clear which guarantees such a security analysis can provide for the system in operation.

Our goal here is to move away from such extreme solutions. We are aiming for a security condition that provides formal guarantees regarding the security of the system as it is in operation, but, nevertheless, also permits declassification under certain conditions. That is, we do not want to permit arbitrary downgrading but

---

[1] The traditional terminology is somewhat confusing. The term *trusted processes* expresses that one *needs to trust* these processes for the overall system to be secure although they have only been informally inspected.

rather want to control tightly where downgrading can occur. In comparison to
the trusted-processes approach, our aims differ as follows:

– Rather than localizing declassification in a program at the level of entire
  processes, we want to localize it at the level of individual commands.
– Rather than granting rights for arbitrary exceptions to a program (or parts
  thereof), we want to restrict exceptions to certain parts of the security lattice.

In other words, we aim for a finer-grained localization of declassification in
the program as well as for a localization of declassification in the security policy.
This is what we mean by controlling tightly where declassification can occur.

To this end, we modify the definition of a security policy such that it becomes possible to specify permissible exceptions, enrich the programming language with designated downgrading commands, and relax the strong security
condition such that it becomes compatible with the extended language and the
modified definition of security policies (and such that it meets our above goals).

4.1   Permitting Exceptions to MLS-Policies

We introduce a relation $\rightsquigarrow$ between security domains for expressing where exceptions to the information flow ordering $\leq$ are permitted: $D_1 \rightsquigarrow D_2$ means that
information may flow from D_1 to D_2 even if $D_1 \leq D_2$ does not hold.

Definition 7 (MLS Policy with Exceptions). A multi-level security policy
with exceptions is a triple $(\mathcal{D}, \leq, \rightsquigarrow)$ where $\mathcal{D}$ is a set of security domains, $\leq \subseteq \mathcal{D} \times \mathcal{D}$ is a partial ordering, and $\rightsquigarrow \subseteq \mathcal{D} \times \mathcal{D}$ is a relation.

Adding the information flow relation $\rightsquigarrow$ to an MLS policy changes where
information flow is permitted, but does not affect visibility. An observer can still
only see the values of variables at his clearance and below (according to $\leq$). In
particular, the definition of D-equality remains unchanged.

Note that the flow of information permitted by an MLS policy with exceptions
does not constitute a transitive relation, i.e. neither $\leq \cup \rightsquigarrow$ nor $\rightsquigarrow$ is transitive, in
general. For example, a standard example of such a policy is information flow via
a trusted downgrader. Suppose we wish to allow information to flow from levels
A to B, but only if it is vetted by a trusted downgrader (representing a physical
audit, or a mechanical procedure such as encryption). This could be represented
by the intransitive information flow relation $A \rightsquigarrow D \rightsquigarrow B$. As a second example,
suppose we have a three level policy www $\leq$ Employee $\leq$ Webmaster with a
downgrading relation: Webmaster $\rightsquigarrow$ www; in this case it is the relation $\leq \cup \rightsquigarrow$
which is intransitive. Ultimately, the webmaster chooses what information is
released to the web, which means that employee-level information can only be
published to the web if the information passes through the webmaster.

4.2   Downgrading Commands

We extend our programming language with a downgrading command $[\text{Id} := \text{Id}']$.
This command has the same effect as the usual assignment command $\text{Id} := \text{Id}'$, but it is handled differently in the security analysis. It may violate the

$$\frac{\langle Id', s \rangle \downarrow n \quad dom(Id') = D_1 \quad dom(Id) = D_2}{\langle [Id := Id'], s \rangle \rightarrow_d^{D_1 \rightarrow D_2} \langle \langle \rangle, [Id = n]s \rangle}$$

Fig. 1. Downgrading transitions

information flow ordering $\leq$ as long as it complies with the information flow relation $\rightsquigarrow$. Differentiating between downgrading commands and assignment on the syntactic level allows a programmer to make explicit where he intends to downgrade information in a program. For the analysis, this makes it possible to distinguish intentional downgrading from accidental information leakage.

We deliberately extend the language with a rather simple command for declassification. The motivation for this choice will be discussed in Section 5 where we will also illustrate how to program with this downgrading command.

Transitions that involve downgrading are highlighted in the operational semantics: The transition relation $\rightarrow$ is split into a relation $\rightarrow_o$ (the ordinary transitions) and a family $\rightarrow_d^{D_1 \rightarrow D_2}$ of relations (the downgrading transitions). The commands in Section 2 cause ordinary transitions, which means that $\rightarrow_o$ corresponds to $\rightarrow$ in the standard semantics. In contrast, $[Id := Id']$ causes downgrading transitions (as specified in Figure 1). The operational semantics are also extended with variants of the rules for sequential composition and for thread pools that propagate the annotations of downgrading transitions from the premise to the conclusion in the obvious way. From now on, transitions are either ordinary or downgrading transitions, i.e. $\rightarrow = \rightarrow_o \cup \bigcup_{D_1, D_2 \in \mathcal{D}} \rightarrow_d^{D_1 \rightarrow D_2}$.

4.3   A Modified Strong Security Condition

The strong security condition enforces that the flow of information complies with the information flow ordering and does not tolerate any exceptions. In order to cope with downgrading, we need to weaken this condition. To this end, we modify the notion of a strong D-bisimulation that underlies the strong security condition, and then use the modified notion to define a new security condition.

Intuitively, we want this condition to provide the following guarantees:

1. The strong security condition holds for programs without downgrading.
2. Downgrading commands may violate $\leq$, but the programs resulting after downgrading again satisfy the modified strong security condition.
3. Downgrading obeys the information flow relation $\rightsquigarrow$:
   (a) If $D_1 \not\rightsquigarrow D_2$ then no declassification from D_1 to D_2 occurs.
   (b) A command that supposedly downgrades information to D_2 may only affect observations at D_2 or above D_2 in the security lattice.
   (c) A downgrading command that supposedly downgrades information from D_1 must not leak information from other domains.

Note that the first item above subsumes the guarantees provided by the trusted processes approach. The other items above go beyond what the trusted processes approach can achieve. Also note that (3c) is not a trivial requirement because executing [Id := Id′] might leak information beyond Id′. There is a danger of information leakage from other domains than dom (Id′) via the control flow:

Example 2. Consider [c1:=b1]; [c2:=b2]; if a==0 then [c0:=b1] else [c0:=b2] and the policy represented to the right assuming that variable names follow their security classification. If the program is run in a state where b1≠b2 then an observer at domain C can determine at the end of the run whether a is zero or not although the program was meant to downgrade only from B to C (and not from A to C). Intuitively, such a program is insecure due to the information leakage via the control flow and this should be captured by a sensible security definition.

Let us now try to formalize each of the three aspects. Formalizing property (1) is somewhat straightforward because this is the strong security condition restricted to ordinary transitions ($\vec{V}$ and $\vec{V}'$ shall be as in Definition 4):

$$\forall s, s', t \colon \forall i \in \{1 \ldots n\} \colon \forall \vec{W} \colon \vec{V} \, R \, \vec{V}' \land s =_D s' \land \langle C_i, s \rangle \to_o \langle \vec{W}, t \rangle \tag{1}$$
$$\Rightarrow \exists \vec{W}', t' \colon \langle C_i', s' \rangle \to_o \langle \vec{W}', t' \rangle \land \vec{W} \, R \, \vec{W}' \land t =_D t'$$

The remaining properties are concerned with downgrading transitions. Obviously, the analog of the strong security condition cannot hold for such transitions, in general. In particular, it cannot be guaranteed, in general, that the resulting states are D_2-equal if the starting states are D_2-equal (due to downgrading information from some domain D_1 to D_2). However, it can be guaranteed that downgrading commands are executed in lock step and that the resulting programs are in relation. Demanding that downgrading commands are executed in lock step prevents downgrading commands occurring in one branch of a conditional but not in the other. Otherwise, there would be a danger of information leakage in a branch without a downgrading command, which would violate the requirement that declassification in a given program shall be localized to its downgrading commands. That the programs resulting after downgrading are in relation is precisely what property (2) demands. We arrive at the following condition (leaving a place holder for property (3)).

$$\forall s, s', t \colon \forall i \in \{1 \ldots n\} \colon \forall \vec{W} \colon \vec{V} \, R \, \vec{V}' \land s =_D s' \land \langle C_i, s \rangle \to_d^{D_1 \to D_2} \langle \vec{W}, t \rangle \tag{2}$$
$$\Rightarrow \exists \vec{W}', t' \colon \langle C_i', s' \rangle \to_d^{D_1 \to D_2} \langle \vec{W}', t' \rangle \land \vec{W} \, R \, \vec{W}' \land (3)$$

Properties (3a)–(3c) express special cases where the resulting states must be D-equal although a downgrading command has occurred. Property (3a) says that downgrading must not have any effect if the information flow relation would be violated, i.e. $D_1 \not\rightsquigarrow D_2 \implies t =_D t'$. Property (3b) says that downgrading to D_2 may only affect the observations at D_2 and at domains being above D_2 in the lattice, i.e. $D_2 \not\leq D \implies t =_D t'$. Finally, property (3c) says that downgrading information from D_1 to D_2 in two states that are indistinguishable for D_1 should result in states that are also indistinguishable, i.e. $s =_{D_1} s' \implies t =_D t'$. In summary, we arrive at the following condition:

$$(D_1 \not\rightsquigarrow D_2 \vee D_2 \not\leq D \vee s =_{D_1} s') \implies t =_D t' \tag{3}$$

Let us summarize our variant of a strong D-bisimulation. The remaining definitions proceed along the same lines as those in Section 3.

Definition 8 (Strong D-Bisimulation). The strong D-bisimulation $\approx_D$ (for $D \in \mathcal{D}$) is the union of all symmetric relations R on command vectors $\vec{V}, \vec{V}' \in \overrightarrow{Com}$ of equal size, i.e. $\vec{V} = (C_1, \ldots, C_n)$ and $\vec{V}' = (C_1', \ldots, C_n')$, such that

$$\forall s, s', t : \forall i \in \{1, \ldots, n\} : \forall \vec{W} :$$
$$\left[\begin{array}{l} \vec{V} \, R \, \vec{V}' \wedge s =_D s' \wedge \langle C_i, s \rangle \rightarrow_o \langle \vec{W}, t \rangle \\ \implies \exists \vec{W}', t' : \langle C_i', s' \rangle \rightarrow_o \langle \vec{W}', t' \rangle \wedge \vec{W} \, R \, \vec{W}' \wedge t =_D t' \end{array} \right]$$
$$\wedge$$
$$\left[\begin{array}{l} \vec{V} \, R \, \vec{V}' \wedge s =_D s' \wedge \langle C_i, s \rangle \rightarrow_d^{D_1 \rightarrow D_2} \langle \vec{W}, t \rangle \\ \implies [\exists \vec{W}', t' : \langle C_i', s' \rangle \rightarrow_d^{D_1 \rightarrow D_2} \langle \vec{W}', t' \rangle \wedge \vec{W} \, R \, \vec{W}' \\ \quad \wedge ((D_1 \not\rightsquigarrow D_2 \vee D_2 \not\leq D \vee s =_{D_1} s') \implies t =_D t')] \end{array} \right]$$

Definition 9 (Strong D-Security). Let $\mathrm{Pol} = (\mathcal{D}, \leq, \rightsquigarrow)$ be an MLS policy with exceptions and $D \in \mathcal{D}$. A program $\vec{C}$ is strongly secure for D iff $\vec{C} \approx_D \vec{C}$.

Definition 10 (Strong Security). Let $\mathrm{Pol} = (\mathcal{D}, \leq, \rightsquigarrow)$. A program $\vec{V}$ is strongly secure iff it is strongly secure for all $D \in \mathcal{D}$.

The following two theorems justify our re-use of terminology. They show that our new definition of strong security is equivalent to the original one for programs without downgrading and also for policies that do not permit declassification.

Theorem 1. Let $\mathrm{Pol} = (\mathcal{D}, \leq, \rightsquigarrow)$. A program C without downgrading commands is strongly secure under Definition 10 if and only if it is strongly secure under Definition 6.

The proofs of this and all subsequently presented results are in the extended version of this paper.

Theorem 2. Let $\mathrm{Pol} = (\mathcal{D}, \leq, \rightsquigarrow)$ with $\rightsquigarrow = \emptyset$. Let C be an arbitrary program and C' be the program that results from C by replacing each downgrading command with the corresponding assignment statement. Then C is strongly secure under Definition 10 if and only if C' is strongly secure under Definition 6.

From now on, we will refer by the terms "strong D-bisimulation", "strong D-security", and "strong security" to Definitions 8, 9, and 10, respectively (rather than to Definitions 4, 5, and 6).

5   Applying the Strong Security Condition

Let us illustrate the strong security condition with some simple example programs that do or do not satisfy the modified strong security condition.

Example 3. For the policy in Example 2, the program c:=b1 is intuitively insecure because it leaks information outside a downgrading command. This information leakage is ruled out by the strong security condition because running the
program in any two C-equal starting states that differ in the value of b1 results
in states that are not C-equal. Hence, condition (1) is violated. The intuitively
secure program [c:=b0], however, satisfies the strong security condition.

Composing these two programs sequentially results in [c:=b0]; c:=b1, an intuitively insecure program. This is detected by our strong security condition. In
other words, the program is not strongly secure: for any two C-equal starting
states that differ in the value of b1 the resulting states are not C-equal. Note
that the proposition $\vec{W} \; R \; \vec{W'}$ in condition (2) ensures that the first downgrading
command does not mask the information leakage in the second command.

The security condition also rules out information leakage via the control flow.

Example 4. The program if a==0 then [c:=b1] else [c:=b2] is intuitively insecure
because it leaks information about the value of a to C (see Example 2). The
program is not strongly secure: Take two C-equal starting states s_1 and s_2
with $s_1(a)=0$, $s_2(a)=1$, and $s_1(b1)\neq s_2(b2)$. Less obviously, the program if b0
then [c:=b1] else [c:=b2] is also not strongly secure: Take two C-equal starting
states that differ in their value of b0. Condition (1) demands that the two downgrading commands are C-bisimilar to each other. Running these commands in
the same starting state (taking any state with b1$\neq$b2) results in two states that
are not C-equal. This contradicts condition (3c).

We have limited the declassification capabilities in our programming language to one very simple downgrading command, i.e. assignment of variables to
variables. This is a deliberate choice that shall prevent the programmer from
accidentally creating information leaks. Let us illustrate this aspect in the following example where we assume a language with more powerful declassification
capabilities. In this extended language, any program fragment can be marked
as a trusted piece of code that may declassify information from some domain to
another one.

Example 5. RSA encryption is based on computing $a^k \; mod \; n$, where a represents
the plaintext and k the encryption key. To efficiently compute $r := a^k \; mod \; n$
without first computing a^k the following exponentiation algorithm can be used:

```
w:=length(k); r:=1; while w > 0 do r:=r*r mod n
                          if k[w]==1 then r:=(r*a) mod n
                          w:=w-1
```

Here we have assumed a primitive function length that returns the number
of bits needed to encode the key, array indexing k[w] returning the wth bit of k
(where k[1] is the least significant bit), and an if-statement without else-branch
with the obvious semantics. Let us assume a two-level policy. In a typical context
of use, we expect the key k and the data a to be high. Therein lies the problem.
If w is secret, then the program is not strongly secure, since it loops over w, and
the duration of this loop may be indirectly observed by other threads.

We might want to mark the entire algorithm as a trusted piece of code, e.g. by surrounding it with brackets (assuming we had such a powerful declassification capability in our language). However, this is a rather course-grained solution and one might not want to trust a piece of code of this size (as we will see, mistrust is justified). Alternatively, one might only modify the assignment w:=length(k) into a downgrading command and change the security level of w into low. Interestingly, it turns out for this second solution that the resulting program is not strongly secure (take two low-equal starting states that differ in the number of ones in the value of k). The problem is that the number of small-step transitions not only differs depending on how often the loop is executed, but also depending on whether the body of the conditional is executed or not. Hence, observing the runtime may reveal to a *low*-level observer more information about the key k than only its length (namely, the number of ones in the key). This is a well-known problem for real implementations [Koc96].

This problem can be solved without significantly changing the algorithm by adding an else-branch with a skip-command, which results in an identical number of atomic computation steps no matter whether the guard of the conditional is true or false. Agat [Aga00] discusses variants for a finer-grained time model.

Downgrading commands where an expression is assigned to a variable are less troublesome than the ones we started out with at the beginning of the example. Though there still is a danger of accidental information leakage, in particular, if the expressions are complex. Therefore, we limit downgrading to even simpler commands that only permit the assignment of variables to variables. In order to meet this constraint, the above program fragment can be modified by replacing [w:=length(k)] with h:=length(k);[w:=h] (where h is a high-level variable).

In summary, we arrive at the following strongly secure program:

```
h:=length(k); [w:=h]; r:=1; while w > 0 do r:=r*r mod n
                            if k[w]==1 then r:=(r*a) mod n
                                        else skip
                          w:=w-1
```

6   Mechanizing the Analysis

Proving the strong security condition for a given program is rather tedious. Here, we develop a security type system that can be used to mechanize the information flow analysis. The type system is sound in the sense that any type correct program is also strongly secure. This soundness result provides the basis for mechanically analyzing that a program is strongly secure. Before presenting the (syntactic) type system, we derive some compositionality results that will be helpful for proving soundness.

6.1   Compositionality Properties

The strong security condition with downgrading satisfies a number of compositionality properties. The main compositionality properties are established based on the following reasoning principles for $\cong_D$:

Lemma 1. If $C_1 \cong_D C_1'$, $C_2 \cong_D C_2'$ and $\vec{V} \cong_D \vec{V'}$, then

1. $C_1; C_2 \cong_D C_1'; C_2'$
2. $fork(C_1\vec{V}) \cong_D fork(C_1'\vec{V'})$
3. If $\forall s =_D s' : \langle B, s \rangle \downarrow n \iff \langle B, s' \rangle \downarrow n$ then
   (a) $if\ B\ then\ C_1\ else\ C_2 \cong_D if\ B\ then\ C_1'\ else\ C_2'$
   (b) $while\ B\ do\ C_1 \cong_D while\ B\ do\ C_1'$

From here it is a small step to the following "hook-up" properties:

Theorem 3. If C_1, C_2 and $\vec{V}$ are strongly secure then so are

1. $C_1; C_2$
2. $fork(C_1\vec{V})$
3. $if\ B\ then\ C_1\ else\ C_2$ and $while\ B\ do\ C_1$ given that there is a least security domain, low, and $\forall s =_{low} s' : \langle B, s \rangle \downarrow n \iff \langle B, s' \rangle \downarrow n$

6.2   A Security Type System

We begin with the "proto" type system given in Figure 2. The typing rules can be used to deduce when a program is secure. The rules for expressions are quite simple: the security level of variables is determined by the domain assignment, constants may have any level, and the level of compound expressions must be an upper bound of the security levels of each subexpression. The statement $\mathtt{Exp} : D$ implies that $\mathtt{Exp}$ only depends on the part of the state at or below level D. This is captured by the following standard noninterference property for expressions.

Lemma 2. If $\mathtt{Exp} : D$ then $s =_D s' \implies (\langle \mathtt{Exp}, s \rangle \downarrow n \iff \langle \mathtt{Exp}, s' \rangle \downarrow n)$.

The rules for commands largely follow the compositionality properties for the strong security condition. The only point of note for the downgrading rule itself is that there is no "subtyping" permitted. This reflects the tight control of intransitive information flow enforced by the semantic condition. The thrust of

$$[\text{Var}] \quad Id : dom(Id) \qquad\qquad [\text{Const}] \quad n : D \qquad\qquad [\text{Skip}] \quad \vdash \mathsf{skip}$$

$$[\text{Arithm}] \quad \frac{Exp_1 : D_1 \quad Exp_2 : D_2 \quad D_1 \leq D \quad D_2 \leq D}{op(Exp_1, Exp_2) : D} \qquad [\text{Seq}] \quad \frac{\vdash C_1 \quad \vdash C_2}{\vdash C_1; C_2}$$

$$[\text{Assign}] \quad \frac{Exp : D \quad D \leq dom(Id)}{\vdash Id := Exp} \qquad\qquad [\text{Fork}] \quad \frac{\vdash C \quad \vdash \vec{V}}{\vdash fork(C\vec{V})}$$

$$[\text{DG}] \quad \frac{dom(Id') \rightsquigarrow dom(Id)}{\vdash [Id := Id']} \qquad\qquad [\text{While}] \quad \frac{B : low \quad \vdash C}{\vdash while\ B\ do\ C}$$

$$[\text{If}] \quad \frac{B : D \quad \vdash C_1 \quad \vdash C_2 \quad \forall D' \not\geq D : C_1 \cong_{D'} C_2}{\vdash if\ B\ then\ C_1\ else\ C_2}$$

Fig. 2. The Proto Type System

the "type" system is concentrated in the conditional rule. This rule has a semantic side condition – so the system is not decidable – but it serves as a starting point for a variety of refinements (to be presented later in this section), and helps to modularize the correctness argument. The rule says that a conditional is secure if each branch is typeable and if the branches have identical behavior for all observers who are not permitted to see the value of the guard. The latter condition ensures that we do not indirectly leak information via the control flow. Note that this also includes the leaking of the conditional test via a downgrading operation in the branches. We obtain the following soundness result:

Theorem 4. If $\vdash C$ then C is strongly secure.

6.3   A Syntactic Approximation of the Semantic Side Condition

It remains to mechanize the check of the semantic condition $\forall D' \not\sqsupseteq D : C_1 \approx_{D'} C_2$. Here, we provide a couple of approximations that can be easily mechanized. As the condition only occurs as a premise of the [If] rule, we may safely assume that the programs being compared, i.e. C_1 and C_2, are each strongly secure.

"Minimal" Typing Approximation. Assume the existence of a least security level, low. A simple approximation of the semantic rule is the conditional rule

$$\frac{B : \text{low} \quad \vdash C_1 \quad \vdash C_2}{\vdash \text{if } B \text{ then } C_1 \text{ else } C_2}$$

This is indeed a safe approximation of the semantic rule as there are no levels $D' \not\sqsupseteq$ low when $B :$ low and, hence, the semantic side condition is vacuous.

If we restrict our system to this special case, then the rules correspond, in essence, to the approach taken in the type system of [VS97] (ignoring other language features considered there). As pointed out in [Aga00], such a restriction is rather severe, since programs are not allowed to branch on other data than low data. In the presence of downgrading, however, the restriction is not nearly as severe because one can downgrade the data to the lowest level before branching.

Approximation Relations. In order to be more permissive than only permitting branching on low guards, we need to find a computable approximation of the condition $\forall D' \not\sqsupseteq D : C \approx_{D'} C'$ for an arbitrary level D. Before looking at a particular instance, let us clarify the requirements of a safe approximation.

Definition 11 (Safe Approximation Relation). A family $\{R_D\}_{D \in \mathcal{D}}$ of relations on commands is a safe approximation relation if given that C and C' are strongly secure and $C(R_D)C'$ holds for some level D then $\forall D' \not\sqsupseteq D : C \approx_{D'} C'$.

Theorem 5. Let $\{R_D\}$ be a safe approximation relation. Let $\vdash_R C$ be the predicate on commands obtained by replacing the [If] rule in Figure 2 with the rule

$$\text{If}_R \; \frac{B : D \quad \vdash C_1 \quad \vdash C_2 \quad C_1(R_D)C_2}{\vdash \text{if } B \text{ then } C_1 \text{ else } C_2}$$

Whenever $\vdash_R C$ then C is strongly secure.

A Safe Approximation Relation. The starting point for a variety of approximations is the syntactic identity relation, i.e. $C(R_D)C' \iff C = C'$. This is a safe
approximation, though not a too useful one as it amounts to the typing rule

$$\frac{B : D \vdash C}{\vdash \text{if } B \text{ then } C \text{ else } C}$$

However, we can derive more useful approximation relations by carefully relaxing syntactic equality while retaining D'-bisimilarity of the branches for all
levels D' that are not permitted to see D (i.e. $D' \not\geq D$). For instance, an observer at level D' cannot directly observe the changes caused by an assignment
$\text{Id} := \text{Exp}$ when $D' \not\geq \text{dom}(\text{Id})$ (due to transitivity of $\geq$). This fact motivates a
larger relation than the syntactic identity, which additionally relates $\text{Id} := \text{Exp}$
to skip and to assignments $\text{Id}' := \text{Exp}'$ with $\text{dom}(\text{Id}') = \text{dom}(\text{Id})$.

Definition 12 (Non k-Visible Equality). Let $\sim_k$ be the least pre-congruence
relation on commands (transitive, reflexive and symmetric relation closed under
the constructs of the language) satisfying the following rule:

$$\frac{\text{dom}(\text{Id}) \geq D}{(\text{Id} := \text{Exp}) \sim_D \text{skip}}$$

Theorem 6. $\{\sim_k\}$ is a safe approximation relation

Example 6. The modular exponentiation algorithm from the end of Example 5
is typeable using the above safe approximation relation, since to any non-high
observer, the two branches look identical, i.e., $r := (r * a) \mod n \sim_{high} \text{skip}$.

7   Related Work

Prior work on intransitive noninterference has focused on more abstract specifications of systems in terms of state machines [Rus92, Pin95, Ohe04], event systems
[Man01], or process algebras [RG99, BPR04]. In this article, we have demonstrated how the underlying ideas can be adapted to a programming-language
setting. The main objective in the derivation of our novel security condition has
been to provide tight control of where declassification can occur in a program
and where exceptions to the information flow ordering are permitted in a security
policy. Prior work on controlling declassification in a language-based setting has
focused on other aspects and can be classified into the following two categories:
What is downgraded? and Who can influence the downgrading decision?

What? Using Cohen's notion of selective dependency [Coh78], one would show,
e.g., that a program leaks no more than the least significant bit of a secret by
establishing the standard information flow property, firstly, for the case where the
secret is even and then for the case where the secret is odd, thereby proving that
no more than the least significant bit is leaked. A more compact formulation of

this idea can be made using equivalence relations to model partial information flow [SS01]. Sabelfeld and Myers [SM03a] have considered a condition which permits expressions in a program to be declassified if, roughly speaking, the entire program leaks no more than the declassified expressions would in isolation. An alternative to specifying exactly what is leaked, is to focus on the amount of information that is leaked [CHM02, Low02], or on the rate at which it is leaked. Complexity-theoretic and probabilistic arguments have been used to argue that leaks are "sufficiently small" or "sufficiently slow" (e.g. [VS00, BP02, DHW02]). An alternative is to modify the model of the attacker, making him less sensitive to small/slow information leaks [MRST01, Lau03].

W ho? Zdancewic and Myers [ZM01, Zda03] introduce robust declassification, a security condition focusing on the integrity of downgrading decisions, thereby limiting who can control downgrading. For example, in a two-level setting, a program exhibits robust declassification if decisions about downgrading of high-level data cannot be influenced by an attacker who controls and observes low-level data. A recent extension includes, amongst other things, also an account of endorsement, i.e. the controlled upgrading of low-integrity data [MSZ04].

Each the three broad approaches (W hat?, W ho?, W here?) has its merits – but also its limitations. Therefore, it would be desirable to combine these approaches with each other. However, this is outside the scope of the current paper.

8   Conclusion

Our main objective has been to localize possibilities for permitted declassification, both in the program and in the security policy. The basis for this has been the introduction of a designated downgrading command and of the information flow relation $\leadsto$ that co-exists with the usual information flow ordering $\leq$. These concepts allowed us to tightly restrict by our security condition where downgrading can occur. For checking the security condition mechanically, we have presented a security type system that is pleasingly simple, given that it can deal with controlled downgrading. Both, richer language features (from the point of view of the type system) and weaker definitions of security (e.g. without threads or termination sensitivity) deserve further investigation.

It would be desirable to integrate the different approaches for controlling declassification (W hat?, W ho?, W here?). As pointed out before, these approaches are largely orthogonal to each other and, e.g., an analysis of what is leaked in a given program can be performed independently from an analysis of where information is leaked. The benefit of a tighter integration of these analysis techniques would be that more complicated questions could be investigated like, e.g., W hat information is leaked where? or W ho can leak what information where?

Acknowledgments. Thanks to Andrei Sabelfeld for useful discussions and to Daniel Hedin and Boris Köpf for helpful comments. The first author thanks

Chalmers/Göteborg University for providing an inspiring working environment during his research stay. The work is partially funded by SSF and Vinnova.

References

[Aga00]   J. Agat. Transforming out Timing Leaks. In *Proceedings of the ACM Symposium on Principles of Programming Languages*, pages 40–53, 2000.

[BL76]   D. E. Bell and L. LaPadula. Secure Computer Systems: Unified Exposition and Multics Interpretation. Technical Report MTR-2997, MITRE, 1976.

[BP02]   M. Backes and B. Pfitzmann. Computational Probabilistic Non-interference. In *Proceedings of ESORICS*, LNCS 2502, pages 1–23, 2002.

[BPR04]   A. Bossi, C. Piazza, and S. Rossi. Modelling Downgrading in Information Flow Security. In *Proc. of IEEE CSFW*, 2004. to appear.

[CHM02]   D. Clark, S. Hunt, and P. Malacaria. Quantitative Analysis of the Leakage of Confidential Data. In *Quantitative Aspects of Programming Languages—Selected papers from QAPL 2001*, volume 59 of *ENTCS*, 2002.

[Coh78]   E. S. Cohen. Information Transmission in Sequential Programs. In *Foundations of Secure Computation*, pages 297–335. Academic Press, 1978.

[Den76]   D. E. Denning. A Lattice Model of Secure Information Flow. *Communications of the ACM*, 19(5):236–243, 1976.

[DHW02]   A. Di Pierro, C. Hankin, and H. Wiklicky. Approximate Non-Interference. In *Proceedings of IEEE CSFW*, pages 1–17, 2002.

[Koc96]   P. C. Kocher. Timing Attacks on Implementations of Diffie-Hellman, RSA, DSS, and Other Systems. In Neal Koblitz, editor, *Advances in Cryptology – CRYPTO'96*, volume 1109 of *LNCS*, pages 104–113. Springer-Verlag, 1996.

[Lau03]   P. Laud. Handling Encryption in an Analysis for Secure Information Flow. In *Proceedings of ESOP*, LNCS 2618, pages 159–173. Springer-Verlag, 2003.

[Low02]   G. Lowe. Quantifying Information Flow. In *Proceedings of IEEE CSFW*, pages 18–31, 2002.

[Man01]   H. Mantel. Information Flow Control and Applications – Bridging a Gap. In *Proceedings of Formal Methods Europe*, LNCS 2021, pages 153–172, 2001.

[MRST01]   J. Mitchell, A. Ramanathan, A. Scedrov, and V. Teague. A Probabilistic Polynomial-Time Calculus for Analysis of Cryptographic Protocols (Preliminary report). In *Proc. of the Conf. on the Math. Foundations of Programming Semantics*, volume 45 of *ENTCS*, 2001.

[MSZ04]   A. C. Myers, A. Sabelfeld, and S. Zdancewic. Enforcing Robust Declassification. In *Proc. of IEEE CSFW*, 2004. to appear.

[Ohe04]   David von Oheimb. Information flow control revisited: Noninfluence = Noninterference + Nonleakage. In *Proc. of the 9th European Symposium on Research in Computer Security*, LNCS. Springer, 2004. to appear.

[Pin95]   S. Pinsky. Absorbing Covers and Intransitive Non-Interference. In *Proceedings of the IEEE Symposium on Security and Privacy*, pages 102–113, Oakland, CA, USA, 1995.

[RG99]   A. W. Roscoe and M. H. Goldsmith. What is Intransitive Noninterference? In *Proceedings of IEEE CSFW*, pages 228–238, 1999.

[Rus92]   J. M. Rushby. Noninterference, Transitivity, and Channel-Control Security Policies. Technical Report CSL-92-02, SRI International, 1992.

[SM03a]   A. Sabelfeld and A. C. Myers. A Model for Delimited Information Release. In *International Symposium on Software Security*, 2003.

[SM03b] A. Sabelfeld and A. C. Myers. Language-Based Information-Flow Security. *IEEE Journal on Selected Areas in Communications*, 21(1):5–19, 2003.

[SS00]   A. Sabelfeld and D. Sands. Probabilistic Noninterference for Multi-threaded Programs. In *Proceedings of IEEE CSFW*, pages 200–214, 2000.

[SS01]   A. Sabelfeld and D. Sands. A Per Model of Secure Information Flow in Sequential Programs. *HOSC*, 14(1):59–91, 2001.

[VS97]   D. Volpano and G. Smith. Eliminating Covert Flows with Minimum Typings. In *Proceedings of IEEE CSFW*, pages 156–168, 1997.

[VS00]   D. M. Volpano and G. Smith. Verifying Secrets and Relative Secrecy. In *Proceedings of POPL*, pages 268–276, 2000.

[Zda03] S. Zdancewic. A Type System for Robust Declassification. In *Proc. of the Conf. on the Math. Foundations of Programming Semantics*, ENTCS, 2003.

[ZM01]   S. Zdancewic and A. C. Myers. Robust Declassification. In *Proceedings of IEEE CSFW*, pages 15–23, 2001.

A Concurrent System of Multi-ported Processes with Causal Dependency

Tatsuya Abe

Department of Computer Science, The University of Tokyo
abet@is.s.u-tokyo.ac.jp

Abstract. The π-calculus is a concurrent system invented by Milner et al. in which concurrent computation is expressed as interaction of processes through name-passing. Building on the concept of name-passing, we propose a new concurrent system based on multi-ports, whereas the π-calculus is based on single-ports. Although our trial is not the first one in constructing a concurrent system based on multi-ports, ours is unique in that it is only extended in terms of multi-ports. This simplicity makes it possible to control self-communication of processes. Besides, it is an extension of the π-calculus, because a single-port can be expressed as a restriction in our system. These suggest that the concept of multi-ports is natural. Furthermore, it is more expressive than other calculi including the original π-calculus in spite of this simplicity. Even the strong call-by-name λ-calculus can be embedded into our system with respect to convergence and divergence, while it has not been successfully done into the original π-calculus.

1 Introduction

The π-calculus was invented by Milner et al. as a model for expressing concurrent computation [11]. It has been studied actively in the field of concurrency due to its simplicity. As a result, it has turned out that it can be extended in various directions and that it is far more expressive than initially considered. In this paper we propose a new concurrent system, which is built on the notion of name-passing as in the original π-calculus. However, it is essentially different from previous approaches for extending the π-calculus. We claim that our system is more fundamental than the original one. The reason is that it is not only an extension of the original π-calculus but it can express the original one as a *syntax sugar*. This is different from other approaches, which tend to complicate the original π-calculus by adding extra rules.

The most distinguishing feature of our system is that it is based on the concept of *multi-ports*. To make this point clear, we explain computation of the original π-calculus. In the original π-calculus, a process transits to another by consuming a prefix of the process. For instance,

$$\overline{x}y.P \xrightarrow{\overline{x}y} P \ .$$

Informally, $\overline{x}y.P$ means "send the name y along the link named x, and then enact P". Here, $\overline{x}y.P$ is said to be an *output process*, and $\overline{x}y$ an *output action*. Similarly, $x(y).P$ means "receive some name z along the link named x, and then enact $[z/y]P$". Here,

$[z/y]P$ denotes the result of replacing occurrences of y with z in P. We call $x(y).P$ an *input process*, and $x(y)$ an *input action*.

Computation of the original π-calculus is realized as *interaction*. An output process and an input process which possess the same link name interact. The rule which expresses interaction is as follows:

$$\frac{P \overset{\bar{x}z}{\to} P' \qquad Q \overset{x(y)}{\to} Q'}{P|Q \overset{\tau}{\to} P'|[z/y]Q'} \ .$$

Here, $P|Q$ stands for the parallel composition of two processes P and Q. The process $P|Q$ can transit as P or Q, and when the transition occurs in P, it is independent of Q, and vice versa. Moreover, interaction between P and Q can occur when one is an output process and the other is an input process which possess the same link name. In the case of internal interaction, we use $\overset{\tau}{\to}$, where τ means an internal action. In the above rule, P can transit to P' sending the message z along the link named x, and Q can transit to $[z/y]Q'$ receiving the message z along the link named x. Therefore, interaction can occur in $P|Q$, and $P|Q$ itself can transit to $P'|[z/y]Q'$.

Let us now go back to the input processes, in which our system essentially differs from the original π-calculus. Milner explained the meaning of $x(y).P$ as "receive any name along the link named x, and then enact $[z/y]P$" [9]. However, one may observe that another meaning is implicitly attached to it. That is temporal precedence. In addition to Milner's explanation, it is implicitly assumed that the $x(y).P$ *does nothing* until it receives something along the link named x. In other words, in the original π-calculus a prefix of a process can be interpreted as *capsuling* the process inside as in Figure 1, where double lines denote interactions. The interaction along the link named v strips

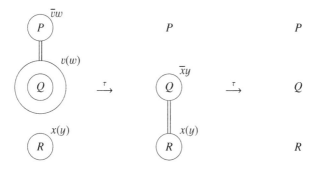

Fig. 1. Capsuling

the outermost layer $v(w)$ of the process $v(w).\bar{x}y.Q$, and the layer $\bar{x}y$ appears. Once $\bar{x}y$ becomes observable, an interaction occurs between $\bar{x}y.Q$ and $x(y).R$. Syntactically,

$$\bar{v}w.P|v(w).\bar{x}y.Q|x(y).R \overset{\tau}{\to} P|\bar{x}y.Q|x(y).R \overset{\tau}{\to} P|Q|R \ .$$

We claim that this idea restricts behavior of processes and interaction between processes. In the above example, the interaction along the link named x does not affect the interaction along the link named v if w is neither x nor y. There exists no a priori reason why we have to impose the restriction that the interaction of v should be ahead of that of x. However, there exist indeed some occasions where we *have to* impose an ordering on prefixes. A typical situation is when a prefix binds a name occurring in some succeeding prefixes: for instance, consider the process $x(y).\bar{y}z.\mathbf{0}$ where the first prefix binds a name in the second prefix. In this case, it is impossible to have interaction for the second prefix first. This kind of precedence is essential.

We improve this point and design a new concurrent system, where the temporal precedence in the original π-calculus is replaced by causal dependency. In our system, interaction does not depend on the order of prefixes; interaction may occur as long as the causality condition is satisfied. Interpreting a prefix of a process as a port along which it can interact, we regard the original π-calculus as a concurrent system in which a process has *only one* port. On the other hand, our system allows a process to have several ports, each of which can interact. In this sense, processes in our system can be seen as multi-ported.

Let us now illustrate causality of prefixes visually. For instance, consider the process

$$u(v){:}w(x){:}x(y){:}\bar{z}x.\mathbf{0}$$

in our system, where the names u, w, z, v, and x are distinct from one another. We use *colon* notation $x(y){:}P$ as an input prefix instead of *dot* notation $x(y).P$ to stress that our input prefix is different from that of Milner et al. It incorporates the capsuling facility intrinsically. Figure 2 illustrates the causality relation among the prefixes of this process, where causality of prefixes is denoted by edges. As a matter of fact, both

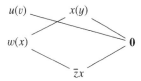

Fig. 2. Causality

$u(v)$ and $w(x)$ are considered to be outermost prefixes while $u(v)$ is the only prefix in its counterpart of the original π-calculus: $u(v).w(x).x(y).\bar{z}x.\mathbf{0}$. Returning to the process $\bar{v}w.P|v(w){:}\bar{x}y.Q|x(y){:}R$, we can see that an interaction along the port x can precede one along the port v while capsuling interpretation cannot be realized as in Figure 1.

Causal dependency might be reminiscent of the notion of *delayed input* [17, 8], which is different from ours in terms of self-communication. For instance, the delayed input process $x(y){:}\bar{x}z.P$ can transit to $[z/y]P$ while it cannot in our system. However, we can express any delayed input process, i.e., a process which can perform self-communication in different way as described in Section 3. As a result, our system has the advantage that we can control permission of self-communication.

In this paper, we also show that our system is more expressive than the original one. Although it is known that the call-by-name λ-calculus, the call-by-value λ-calculus, and the strong call-by-value λ-calculus[1] can be embedded into the original π-calculus [9], we prove the fact that not only those but also the strong call-by-name λ-calculus can be embedded into our system naturally. In particular, it is remarkable that our embedding of the strong call-by-name λ-calculus is complete with respect to convergence and divergence.

We use the following notation throughout this paper, for convenience. For any relation $\mathcal{R}$, the relations $\mathcal{R}^*$, $\mathcal{R}^?$, and $\mathcal{R}^+$ denote the reflexive and transitive closure, the reflexive closure, and the transitive closure of $\mathcal{R}$, respectively. For any relations $\mathcal{R}$ and $\mathcal{S}$, the relation $\mathcal{RS}$ is defined as follows:

$$\{ (P, R) \mid \text{there exists } Q \text{ such that } (P, Q) \in \mathcal{R} \text{ and } (Q, R) \in \mathcal{S} \} \ .$$

Furthermore, we often use an infix notation for short, e.g., $P \rightarrow P'$ denotes $(P, P') \in \rightarrow$.

2   Syntax and Semantics

In this section, we introduce a concurrent system called Mπ-calculus. The Mπ-calculus is a modification of the π-calculus, which is meant to capture the notion of multi-ports. The main difference from the π-calculus is that single-ported input prefixes of the π-calculus are replaced by the multi-ported ones.

The Mπ-calculus is a concurrent system where processes interact through passing names just as the π-calculus. We presuppose an infinite set N of *names*, and that $x, y, \ldots$ range over N. The Mπ-calculus consists of a set $\mathcal{P}$ of processes. We use $P, Q, \ldots$ to range over $\mathcal{P}$. The set $\mathcal{P}$ of processes is defined as follows:

$$P ::= M \mid P|P \mid (\nu x)P \mid !P \qquad \text{(process)}$$
$$M ::= \mathbf{0} \mid \tau.P \mid \overline{x}y.P \mid x(y){:}P \mid M + M \qquad \text{(summation)}$$

where τ is a special constant which is distinct from the others. Unary connectives bind more strongly than binary ones.

A process transits to another by consuming a prefix of the process. For instance,

$$\overline{x}y.P \xrightarrow{\overline{x}y} P \ .$$

Let us regard $\overline{x}y.P$ as a process which sends the name y along the link named x, and then enact P. The process $\overline{x}y.P$ is said to be an *output process*, and $\overline{x}y$ an *output prefix* of the output process. Symmetrically, let us regard $x(y){:}P$ as a process which receives some name z along the link named x, and then enact $[z/y]P$. Here, $[z/y]P$ denotes the result of replacing occurrences of y with z in P. We give the formal definition after we define substitution of names. We call $x(y){:}P$ an *input process*, and $x(y)$ an *input prefix* of the input process. Since the occurrences of y in P of $x(y){:}P$ only point at the locations into which a name received along x passes, they are defined to be bound in $x(y){:}P$.

---

[1]   Called the *weak* call-by-value λ-calculus in the paper [9], in which evaluation strategy is more loose than that of the call-by-value λ-calculus.

The connective | composes two processes in parallel in the Mπ-calculus. Two processes connected by the parallel composition connective transit independently, and can interact if one is an output process and the other is an input process which possess the same link name.

We explain the other connectives below. The process $\tau.P$ transits to P by performing an unobservable action τ. The connective + denotes nondeterministic choice between two processes. The process $(vx)P$ is a process P whose port (or message) x is closed (or localized). Since this name x only points at the port (or message) which should be closed (or localized), the xs in P are bound just as in an input process. The process $!P$ is a process which is allowed to be copied arbitrarily many times.

The set of *actions* is defined as follows:

$$\alpha ::= \tau \mid \overline{x}y \mid \overline{x}(y) \mid x(y) \ .$$

We define *free names*, and *bound names of an action*:

$$\begin{aligned}
&\text{fn}(\tau) = \emptyset && \text{fn}(\overline{x}y) = \{x, y\} && \text{fn}(\overline{x}(y)) = \{x\} && \text{fn}(x(y)) = \{x\} \\
&\text{bn}(\tau) = \emptyset && \text{bn}(\overline{x}y) = \emptyset && \text{bn}(\overline{x}(y)) = \{y\} && \text{bn}(x(y)) = \{y\} \ .
\end{aligned}$$

The set $n(\alpha)$ of names, called *names of α*, is defined as $\text{fn}(\alpha) \cup \text{bn}(\alpha)$. The set $\text{fn}(P)$ consists of free names of P out of the scopes of input prefixes and restriction connectives. A function σ from names to names is said to be a substitution if its support, written $\text{supp}(\sigma) = \{x \mid \sigma x \neq x\}$, is finite. The cosupport of a substitution, written $\text{cosupp}(\sigma)$, is defined as the image of its support. The set $n(\sigma)$ of names is $\text{supp}(\sigma) \cup \text{cosupp}(\sigma)$. Naturally, any substitution can be extended on an action. Formally,

$$\sigma(\tau) = \tau \qquad \sigma(\overline{x}y) = \overline{\sigma x}\sigma y \qquad \sigma(\overline{x}(y)) = \overline{\sigma x}(y) \qquad \sigma(x(y)) = \sigma x(y) \ .$$

In a similar way, a substitution replaces *free* occurrences in a process such that a new binding does not occur. We define a relation on processes, written $\xrightarrow{\alpha}$, which we consider to be a transition. For instance, $P \xrightarrow{\alpha} P'$ denotes that P transits to P' by invoking an action α. We define this by the notion of inference. Transition rules are in Table 1. The annotation on a transition arrow is the action which is performed. The output action $\overline{x}(y)$ is invoked by the process P when y is bound in P. The notion of output actions of bound names realizes a natural interaction such that:

$$\frac{\overline{x}y.P \xrightarrow{\overline{x}y} P \qquad x \neq y \qquad y \notin \text{fn}(P) \setminus \{y\}}{(vy)\overline{x}y.P \xrightarrow{\overline{x}(y)} P} \qquad \frac{y \notin \text{fn}(P) \setminus \{y\} \cup \{x\}}{x(y):Q \xrightarrow{x(y)} Q}$$

$$\frac{}{(vy)\overline{x}y.P \mid x(y):Q \xrightarrow{\tau} (vy)(P\mid Q)} \ .$$

Let us consider the process $v(w):x(y):\overline{w}y.\mathbf{0}$ where the names are distinct from one another, in order to see that computation in our system differs from that of the original π-calculus. The two prefixes $v(w)$ and $x(y)$ in this process are independent. This process receives a name along the link v as a name of its port and another name along the link x as a message along the link not named yet. It is, therefore, natural that the order of interactions does not depend on the denotation: $v(w):x(y):\overline{w}y.\mathbf{0}$. Indeed, our system allows a transition on the basis of causal dependency such that:

$$\frac{y \notin (\{w, y\} \setminus \{y\}) \cup \{x\}}{x(y){:}\overline{w}y.\mathbf{0} \overset{x(y)}{\to} \overline{w}y.\mathbf{0} \qquad v \neq y \qquad w \notin \{x, y\}}{v(w){:}x(y){:}\overline{w}y.\mathbf{0} \overset{x(y)}{\to} v(w){:}\overline{w}y.\mathbf{0}}$$.

Proposition 1. *Suppose that* $P \overset{\alpha}{\to} P'$.

1. $\mathrm{bn}(\alpha) \cap \mathrm{fn}(P) = \emptyset$ *and* $(\mathrm{fn}(P') \setminus \mathrm{bn}(\alpha)) \cup \mathrm{fn}(\alpha) \subseteq \mathrm{fn}(P)$.
2. *If* $\alpha = \overline{x}(y)$ *and* $z \notin \mathrm{n}(P)$, *then* $P \overset{\overline{x}(z)}{\to} [z/y]P'$.
3. *If* $\alpha = x(y)$ *and* $z \notin \mathrm{n}(P)$, *then* $P \overset{x(z)}{\to} [z/y]P'$.

Table 1. The transition rules

$$\tau.P \overset{\tau}{\to} P \qquad\qquad\qquad \overline{x}y.P \overset{\overline{x}y}{\to} P$$

$$\frac{z \notin (\mathrm{fn}(P) \setminus \{y\}) \cup \{x\}}{x(y){:}P \overset{x(z)}{\to} [z/y]P} \qquad \frac{P \overset{\alpha}{\to} P' \qquad x \notin \mathrm{bn}(\alpha) \qquad y \notin \mathrm{n}(\alpha)}{x(y){:}P \overset{\alpha}{\to} x(y){:}P'}$$

$$\frac{M \overset{\alpha}{\to} M' \qquad \mathrm{bn}(\alpha) \cap \mathrm{fn}(N) = \emptyset}{M + N \overset{\alpha}{\to} M'} \qquad \frac{M \overset{\alpha}{\to} M' \qquad \mathrm{bn}(\alpha) \cap \mathrm{fn}(N) = \emptyset}{N + M \overset{\alpha}{\to} M'}$$

$$\frac{P \overset{\overline{x}y}{\to} P' \qquad x \neq y \qquad z \notin \mathrm{fn}(P) \setminus \{y\}}{(\nu y)P \overset{\overline{x}(z)}{\to} [z/y]P'} \qquad \frac{P \overset{\alpha}{\to} P' \qquad x \notin \mathrm{n}(\alpha)}{(\nu x)P \overset{\alpha}{\to} (\nu x)P'}$$

$$\frac{P \overset{\alpha}{\to} P' \qquad \mathrm{bn}(\alpha) \cap \mathrm{fn}(Q) = \emptyset}{P|Q \overset{\alpha}{\to} P'|Q} \qquad \frac{P \overset{\alpha}{\to} P' \qquad \mathrm{bn}(\alpha) \cap \mathrm{fn}(Q) = \emptyset}{Q|P \overset{\alpha}{\to} Q|P'}$$

$$\frac{P \overset{\overline{x}z}{\to} P' \qquad Q \overset{x(y)}{\to} Q'}{P|Q \overset{\tau}{\to} P'|[z/y]Q'} \qquad \frac{P \overset{\overline{x}z}{\to} P' \qquad Q \overset{x(y)}{\to} Q'}{Q|P \overset{\tau}{\to} [z/y]Q'|P'}$$

$$\frac{P \overset{\overline{x}(y)}{\to} P' \qquad Q \overset{x(y)}{\to} Q'}{P|Q \overset{\tau}{\to} (\nu y)(P'|Q')} \qquad \frac{P \overset{\overline{x}(y)}{\to} P' \qquad Q \overset{x(y)}{\to} Q'}{Q|P \overset{\tau}{\to} (\nu y)(Q'|P')}$$

$$\frac{P \overset{\alpha}{\to} P'}{!P \overset{\alpha}{\to} P'|!P} \qquad\qquad \frac{P \overset{\alpha}{\to} P'}{!P \overset{\alpha}{\to} !P|P'}$$

$$\frac{P \overset{\overline{x}z}{\to} P' \qquad P \overset{x(y)}{\to} P''}{!P \overset{\tau}{\to} P'|[z/y]P''|!P} \qquad \frac{P \overset{\overline{x}z}{\to} P' \qquad P \overset{x(y)}{\to} P''}{!P \overset{\tau}{\to} [z/y]P''|P'|!P}$$

$$\frac{P \overset{\overline{x}(y)}{\to} P' \qquad P \overset{x(y)}{\to} P''}{!P \overset{\tau}{\to} (\nu y)(P'|P'')|!P} \qquad \frac{P \overset{\overline{x}(y)}{\to} P' \qquad P \overset{x(y)}{\to} P''}{!P \overset{\tau}{\to} (\nu y)(P''|P')|!P}$$

We can obtain the above results by induction on the inference of the hypothesis. Two processes are syntactically identified if they are α-equivalent: they only differ from each other in the choice of bound names.

Proposition 2. *If $P \xrightarrow{\alpha} P'$ and* $\mathrm{bn}(\alpha) \cap (\mathrm{fn}(\sigma P) \cup \mathrm{n}(\sigma)) = \emptyset$, *then* $\sigma P \xrightarrow{\sigma\alpha} \sigma P'$.

We define an equational relation between processes that we would like to identify in the concurrent system. The set of *contexts* is defined as follows:

$$C ::= P \mid [\cdot] \mid M \mid C|P \mid P|C \mid (vx)C \mid !C \qquad \text{(context)}$$
$$M ::= \tau.C \mid \overline{x}y.C \mid x(y){:}C \mid M + M \mid M + M \qquad \text{(summation context)}$$

where $[\cdot]$ is a symbol which denotes a hole of processes. When C is a context and P is a process, $C[P]$ denotes the result of substituting P for the hole $[\cdot]$ in C.

Definition 3. A relation $\mathcal{R}$ on processes is said to be *compatible* if $(P, Q) \in \mathcal{R}$ implies $(C[P], C[Q]) \in \mathcal{R}$ for every context C. An equivalence relation $\mathcal{R}$ on processes is said to be a *congruence relation* if $\mathcal{R}$ is compatible.

The structural congruence relation, written $\equiv$, is defined as the smallest congruence relation that satisfies

1. $M + \mathbf{0} \equiv M$, $M + N \equiv N + M$, $(L + M) + N \equiv L + (M + N)$,
2. $P|\mathbf{0} \equiv P$, $P|Q \equiv Q|P$, $(P|Q)|R \equiv P|(Q|R)$,
3. $(vx)(P|Q) \equiv P|(vx)Q$ if $x \notin \mathrm{fn}(P)$, $(vx)\mathbf{0} \equiv \mathbf{0}$, $(vx)(vy)P \equiv (vy)(vx)P$,
4. $!P \equiv P|!P$.

Namely, there exists a process $\mathbf{0}$ which is disregarded by $+$ and $|$, and the two connectives $+$ and $|$ satisfy commutativity and associativity. In addition, the order of closing ports are ignored, and closing a port is done only where the port exists. The rule 4. means that the process $!P$ is a process P which is allowed to be copied arbitrarily many times, as already described.

3   Conservativeness

In the previous section, we constructed a concurrent system based on the notion of causality. In this section, we see that it does not abandon temporal precedence. First, we define a concurrent system by replacing input processes and their two rules with the ones whose form are $x(y).P$ and the following rule:

$$\frac{z \notin (\mathrm{fn}(P) \setminus \{y\}) \cup \{x\}}{x(y).P \xrightarrow{x(z)} [z/y]P} .$$

It turns out that this system is just the original π-calculus. Second, a translation $\langle\!\langle \cdot \rangle\!\rangle$ from π-processes to Mπ-processes is defined as in Table 2, which clearly preserves the free names of a process, and commutes with substitution, that is, $\langle\!\langle \sigma P \rangle\!\rangle$ and $\sigma\langle\!\langle P \rangle\!\rangle$ are α-equivalent. Third, the relation $\mapsto$ is defined as the reflexive and transitive closure of the smallest compatible relation that satisfies

Table 2. The translation from π-processes to Mπ-processes

$$\langle\!\langle \mathbf{0} \rangle\!\rangle = \mathbf{0} \qquad\qquad\qquad \langle\!\langle M + N \rangle\!\rangle = \langle\!\langle M \rangle\!\rangle + \langle\!\langle N \rangle\!\rangle$$

$$\langle\!\langle \tau.P \rangle\!\rangle = \tau.\langle\!\langle P \rangle\!\rangle \qquad\qquad\qquad \langle\!\langle P|Q \rangle\!\rangle = \langle\!\langle P \rangle\!\rangle | \langle\!\langle Q \rangle\!\rangle$$

$$\langle\!\langle \overline{x}y.P \rangle\!\rangle = \overline{x}y.\langle\!\langle P \rangle\!\rangle \qquad\qquad\qquad \langle\!\langle (\nu x)P \rangle\!\rangle = (\nu x)\langle\!\langle P \rangle\!\rangle$$

$$\langle\!\langle x(y).P \rangle\!\rangle = (\nu u)(x(y):\overline{u}y.\langle\!\langle P \rangle\!\rangle | u(y):\mathbf{0}) \text{ where } u \text{ is fresh} \qquad \langle\!\langle !P \rangle\!\rangle = !\langle\!\langle P \rangle\!\rangle$$

1. $P|\mathbf{0} \mapsto P, \mathbf{0}|P \mapsto P,$
2. $(\nu x)P \mapsto P$ if $x \notin \text{fn}(P)$.

The relation $\mapsto$ is a trivial relation contained properly by the structural congruence relation $\equiv$. Finally, we give some notion. It turns out that any internal transition $\xrightarrow{\tau}$ is produced by a primitive action τ or an interaction through a port. Now we annotate τ which is produced by an interaction through a port x as in $x\tau$. Moreover, $\langle\!\langle P \rangle\!\rangle \tau$ is defined as the set of fresh names produced by $\langle\!\langle P \rangle\!\rangle$. Sometimes, $\langle\!\langle P \rangle\!\rangle \tau$ denotes some element of $\langle\!\langle P \rangle\!\rangle \tau$ for short.

Theorem 4. *If* $P \xrightarrow{\alpha} P'$, *then* $\langle\!\langle P \rangle\!\rangle \xrightarrow{\alpha} \xrightarrow{\langle\!\langle P \rangle\!\rangle \tau^?} \mapsto \langle\!\langle P' \rangle\!\rangle$.

This claims that the Mπ-calculus is an extension of the original π-calculus. Furthermore, we can know the extension to be conservative by the following theorem.

Lemma 5. *If* $\langle\!\langle P \rangle\!\rangle \xrightarrow{\alpha} P'$, *then there exists* P'' *such that* $P \xrightarrow{\alpha} P''$ *and* $P' \xrightarrow{\langle\!\langle P \rangle\!\rangle \tau^?} \mapsto \langle\!\langle P'' \rangle\!\rangle$.

Lemma 6. *If* $P \mapsto\xrightarrow{\tau} P'$, *then* $P \xrightarrow{\tau}\mapsto P'$.

Theorem 7. *If* $\langle\!\langle P \rangle\!\rangle \xrightarrow{\alpha_1} Q_1 \xrightarrow{\alpha_2} \cdots \xrightarrow{\alpha_n} Q_n$, *then there exist* $P \xrightarrow{\alpha_1^?} P_1 \xrightarrow{\alpha_2^?} \cdots \xrightarrow{\alpha_n^?} P_n$ *and* $u_1, \ldots, u_n \in \langle\!\langle P \rangle\!\rangle \tau$ *such that* $Q_i \xrightarrow{u_i\tau^?} \mapsto \langle\!\langle P_i \rangle\!\rangle$ *for any i.*

These two theorems show that a process which has temporal precedence can be expressed in the Mπ-calculus up to internal transitions and the relation $\mapsto$.

Fu [5], Parrow and Victor [12, 13], and others studied causality of processes, in particular van Breugel [17], and Merro and Sangiorgi [8] dealt with modifications of the π-calculus. Input processes can make the same transition as ours in their system. However, their systems have a rule which corresponds to the rule:

$$\frac{P \xrightarrow{\overline{x}z} P' \qquad y \notin \{x, z\}}{x(y):P \xrightarrow{\tau} [z/y]P'}.$$

This rule amounts to admitting self-communication of processes. Such an input process is said to be a *delayed input* process. We cannot understand why they expressed causal dependency by delayed input, since we do not know why self-communication is primitive and whether the delayed input can express a process without self-communication whose outermost prefixes have the same link name. Here, we claim that our formalization of input processes is more natural than delayed input for the following reasons. First, consider the case where two identical processes on network are serving each other (as in peer-to-peer applications). In our system, they can be naturally expressed as $x(y):\overline{x}z.P$. Since self-communication is forbidden, the parallel composition

$x(y){:}\overline{x}z.P|x(y){:}\overline{x}z.P$ can only transit to $\overline{x}z.[z/y]P|x(y){:}P$ (or the symmetric one) and then to $[z/y]P|[z/y]P$. On the other hand, in Merro and Sangiorgi's system the problem is that $x(y){:}\overline{x}z.P$ can transit to $[z/y]P$, that is, the process serves itself since self-communication is primitive. In the case where each of the processes is also allowed to serve itself, they can be expressed as $x(y){:}P|\overline{x}z.\mathbf{0}$ in our system (and also in Merro and Sangiorgi's system). These examples suggest that our system is more expressive than Merro and Sangiorgi's, because self-communication can be controlled by the form of processes. Second, we express a process which can interact through outermost ports named x as $x(y).P|\overline{x}z.\mathbf{0}$ in our system (using the translation in Table 2). This fact suggests that our system has delayed input processes. Finally, Merro and Sangiorgi discovered that a delayed input process could be expressed as a syntax sugar in the localized asynchronous π-calculus [8]. This fact claims that the localized asynchronous π-calculus has causal dependency now that they realize causal dependency by delayed input. However, it appears that self-communication is admitted as a by-product—that a process based on the notion of a single-port is forced to be multi-ported. In contrast, our system has the advantage that we ourselves can choose whether to allow self-communication or not.[2] On the basis of these discussions, we cannot escape the conclusion that our formalization of input processes is more natural than that of delayed input.

4   Equivalence on Processes

In this section we introduce a notion of equivalence on processes. Our notion of equivalence amounts to the so-called open bisimilarity though presented in a different way.

The notion of equivalence is very important. For instance, let us think about the case where one part of a process needs to be replaced. Although it goes without saying that we can replace it with the same one, there exist several situations where we would like to replace it with something else which is equivalent to the original one, namely which has the same capability as the original one. In order to formalize the notion of equivalence of processes properly, we must consider what it means for two processes to have the same capability. Our solution here is that two processes have the same capability when they behave in the same way. The equivalence which we define in this section is based on this intuition; it is surely an equivalence on processes (i.e., a congruence relation on processes) as we prove later.

Definition 8. A relation $\mathcal{R}$ on processes is a *hypersimulation* whenever

1. $\mathcal{R}$ is closed under substitution,
2. $P \xrightarrow{\alpha} P'$, $\mathrm{bn}(\alpha) \cap (\mathrm{fn}(P) \cup \mathrm{fn}(Q)) = \emptyset$, and $(P, Q) \in \mathcal{R}$ imply that there exists Q' such that $Q \xrightarrow{\alpha} Q'$ and $(P', Q') \in \mathcal{R}$.

---

[2] Controlling self-communication of processes is one of the reasons that we do not construct a concurrent system built on the notion of *abstractions* and *concretions*, for such a system forces $x(y).(P|Q) \equiv P|x(y).Q$ whenever $y \notin \mathrm{fn}(P)$. Then, it is natural that the process $x(y).\overline{x}z.\mathbf{0}$ can be related to $\mathbf{0}|\mathbf{0}$ by the relation $\rightarrow$ mentioned in Section 5. Such a system is, therefore, not suitable for controlling self-communication of processes.

A relation $\mathcal{R}$ on processes is said to be a *hyperbisimulation* if $\mathcal{R}$ is a hypersimulation and so is $\mathcal{R}^{-1}$. Two processes P and Q are said to be *hyperbisimilar*, written $P \sim Q$, if $(P, Q) \in \mathcal{R}$ for some hyperbisimulation $\mathcal{R}$.

The following fact ensures that the relation $\sim$ is less of a trivial one.

Proposition 9. *The relation $\equiv$ is a hyperbisimulation.*

Obviously, $\sim$ itself is a hyperbisimulation. It is, therefore, the greatest hyperbisimulation. In contrast, the following notion of bisimulation is well-known.

Definition 10. A relation $\mathcal{R}$ on processes is said to be an *open simulation* if σ is a substitution, $\sigma P \xrightarrow{\alpha} P'$, $(P, Q) \in \mathcal{R}$, and $\mathrm{bn}(\alpha) \cap (\mathrm{fn}(\sigma P) \cup \mathrm{fn}(\sigma Q)) = \emptyset$, then there exists Q' such that $\sigma Q \xrightarrow{\alpha} Q'$ and $(P', Q') \in \mathcal{R}$.

A relation $\mathcal{R}$ on processes is said to be an *open bisimulation* if $\mathcal{R}$ is an open simulation and so is $\mathcal{R}^{-1}$. Two processes P and Q are said to be *open bisimilar*, written $P \sim_o Q$, if $(P, Q) \in \mathcal{R}$ for some open bisimulation $\mathcal{R}$.

The notion of hyperbisimulation is different from that of open bisimulation; although any hyperbisimulation is an open bisimulation, the converse does not hold, as we have a counter-example $\{(\overline{xy}.\mathbf{0}, \overline{xy}.\mathbf{0}), (\mathbf{0}, \mathbf{0})\}$. It is, however, not our intention to introduce a new notion of equivalence. Indeed, it turns out that the notion of the hyperbisimilarity, which is the greatest hyperbisimulation, coincides with that of the open bisimilarity:

Proposition 11. $P \sim Q$ *if and only if* $P \sim_o Q$.

By using a useful method: up-to technique of Sangiorgi and Milner [15, 14], we have

Main Theorem 12. *The relation $\sim$ is a congruence relation.*

Sangiorgi and Milner's up-to technique is not applicable to the open bisimilarity on its own. This is why we needed Proposition 11. As a result, the open bisimilarity turns out to be a congruence relation.

We have succeeded in defining a notion of equivalence on processes with causal dependency. Thus $v(w){:}x(y){:}P \sim x(y){:}v(w){:}P$ claims that these two input prefixes are independent. Remarkably, two processes identified under considering causal dependency are exactly equivalent.

Next, we show an important property for concurrent systems. The following statement is called *the replication theorem*:

$$(vx)(P|Q|!x(y).R) \sim (vx)(P|!x(y).R)|(vx)(Q|!x(y).R) \ .$$

This statement is intuitively interpreted as follows. Let R be a resource which is used by other processes. It is natural to think of R as replicable since it is expected to be invoked out arbitrarily many times. On the left-hand side, P and Q share R, while on the right-hand side, P and Q have their own copies of R. The above statement thus claims that whenever a resource is shared by two processes, the resource may be distributed to each of the processes. However, this does not hold in general. Typically it does not hold when the processes involved send x as message. Since the name x is expected to serve as a "guard" for a resource R, we restrict it used only for the purpose. This is also why we do not use colon prefixes but dot prefixes.

A process P is said to be x-*negative* if x occurs in P only in the form $\bar{x}y$. A process which is α-convertible to an x-negative process is also considered to be x-negative.

Theorem 13. *Let P, Q, and R be x-negative.*

1. $(vx)(P|Q|!x(y).R) \sim (vx)(P|!x(y).R)|(vx)(Q|!x(y).R)$.
2. $(vx)(!P|!x(y).R) \sim !(vx)(P|!x(y).R)$.

Theorem 13 is used in the later sections, where we consider convergence and divergence of processes. In those sections, resources are considered to be environments in which a program is evaluated.

So far, we have been mainly interested in symmetric relations. However, the following relation, which may also be considered to be a sort of "equivalence" in some weak sense, is asymmetric. More precisely, it is a hypersimulation and the inverse of it is a hypersimulation up to internal actions.

Definition 14. A relation $\mathcal{R}$ is an *expansion* if $\mathcal{R}$ is closed under substitution and whenever $(P, Q) \in \mathcal{R}$ and $\text{bn}(\alpha) \cap (\text{fn}(P) \cup \text{fn}(Q)) = \emptyset$,

1. $P \xrightarrow{\alpha} P'$ implies that there exists Q' such that $Q \xRightarrow{\alpha} Q'$ and $(P', Q') \in \mathcal{R}$,
2. $Q \xrightarrow{\alpha} Q'$ implies that there exists P' such that $P \xrightarrow{\widehat{\alpha}} P'$ and $(P', Q') \in \mathcal{R}$,

where $\Rightarrow$ and $\xrightarrow{\widehat{\tau}}$ denote $\xrightarrow{\tau}{}^* \xrightarrow{\alpha} \xrightarrow{\tau}{}^*$ and $\xrightarrow{\tau}{}^?$ respectively, and $\xrightarrow{\widehat{\alpha}}$ denotes $\xrightarrow{\alpha}$ for $\alpha \neq \tau$.

We say that Q *expands* P, written $Q \geq P$, if $(P, Q) \in \mathcal{R}$ for some expansion $\mathcal{R}$.

Definition 15. A reflexive and transitive relation $\mathcal{R}$ on processes is said to be a *precongruence relation* if $\mathcal{R}$ is compatible.

Theorem 16. *The relation $\geq$ is a precongruence relation.*

5   The Strong Call-by-Name λ-Calculus

The call-by-name λ-calculus and the call-by-value λ-calculus are λ-calculi whose evaluation strategies are fixed. It is important to gain knowledge of these since strictness of their evaluation strategies makes them pragmatic. Milner discovered that the call-by-name λ-calculus, the call-by-value λ-calculus, and the strong call-by-value λ-calculus can be embedded into his original π-calculus with the construction [9]. Here, it is of theoretical interest to bring up the strong call-by-name λ-calculus whose evaluation strategy is more loose than that of the call-by-name λ-calculus, for the following facts are well-known: (1) functions which are λ-definable in the λ-calculus with full reductions are computable and vice versa; (2) the definition of λ-definable, i.e., computable, depends on whether can be reached a normal form in the λ-calculus with full reductions; and (3) a term which has a normal form in the λ-calculus with full reductions has one in the strong call-by-name λ-calculus but not in other three calculi. In the following sections, our goal is that not only the three calculi as described but also the strong call-by-name λ-calculus can be embedded into the Mπ-calculus.

In fact, it is obvious that the call-by-name λ-calculus, the call-by-value λ-calculus, and the strong call-by-value λ-calculus can be embedded into our system with respect to convergence and divergence between reactions and reductions, since Milner has already shown that these three calculi can be embedded into his original π-calculus and we have already proved that our system is conservative to the original π-calculus in Section 3. Therefore, only the strong call-by-name λ-calculus remains.

Terms and rules in the strong call-by-name λ-calculus are defined as follows:

$$M ::= x \mid \lambda x.M \mid MM$$

$$(\lambda x.M)N \to_\lambda [N/x]M \qquad \frac{M \to_\lambda M'}{\lambda x.M \to_\lambda \lambda x.M'} \qquad \frac{M \to_\lambda M'}{MN \to_\lambda M'N} .$$

The difference from the call-by-name λ-calculus is the existence of the second rule. The rule permits a function to reduce to one which returns the same output as it for any input, that is, it enforces extensionality of functions. We prove the following lemma by induction on λ-reduction in advance since we use later.

Lemma 17. *If $M \to_\lambda M'$, then $[N/x]M \to_\lambda [N/x]M'$.*

Next, we introduce a translation from λ-terms to Mπ-processes. This translation reflects the λ-reduction to the relation $\overset{\tau}{\to}$ up to the structural congruence relation $\equiv$, which is called *reaction* and denoted by $\to$. To show this, we assume that the Mπ-calculus has polyadicity, that is, it permits a fixed number of names along one port, and was first formalized in [10]. For instance,

$$\overline{x}yz.P|x(vw):Q \to P|[y/v, z/w]Q$$

where it is assumed that $[y/v, z/w]$ is not sensitive to the order of substitutions.

We give a translation from λ-terms to Mπ-processes:

$$[\![x]\!]_u = \overline{x}u.\mathbf{0}$$
$$[\![\lambda x.M]\!]_u = u(xv):[\![M]\!]_v$$
$$[\![MN]\!]_u = (vv)([\![M]\!]_v|(vv')(\overline{v}v'u|[\![v' := N]\!]))$$
$$[\![v' := N]\!] = !v'(v'').[\![N]\!]_{v''}$$

which is a modification of Milner's call-by-name translation [9]. This translation is based on the notion that functions are programs and arguments are environments in which they are evaluated. This translation makes a function (i.e., a body of a program) an input process and arguments its resources. We often omit an index of translations when it is clear from the context. The following is checked easily by induction on λ-reduction. This fact leads us an idea introduced in next sections.

Theorem 18. *If $M \to_\lambda M'$, then $[\![M]\!] \to^{\geq} [\![M']\!]$.*

For convenience, we adopt the following notation. A term M is said to be a *normal form*, written $M \not\to_\lambda$, if there exists no term to which M reduces. A term M *converges on* M', written $M \downarrow_\lambda M'$, if M reduces to M' in arbitrary finite steps and M' is a normal form. A term M *converges* if there exists a term on which M converges. A term M *diverges* if there exists an infinite reduction sequence from M. We also use similar terminology and notation for processes and reactions $\to$.

The above definitions immediately derive the following simple proposition as a corollary of Theorem 18.

Corollary 19. *If M diverges, then $[\![M]\!]$ also diverges.*

This corollary claims that the strong call-by-name λ-calculus to be sound to the Mπ-calculus in divergence. Although this says nothing in convergence, we have:

Theorem 20. *If M is a normal form, so is $[\![M]\!]$.*

There exists a correspondence once it becomes a normal form. It is, therefore, natural that we introduce a relationship between reductions and reactions connected more directly. This is done in Section 7.

6   Explicit Environment

In this section we give a translation by dividing reductions of the λ-calculus into generating environments and evaluating a function in environments.

A function f receives an argument a for a parameter x in f, and becomes an output itself. In more detail, when it is decided that f receives a for x, an environment that evaluate x in f as a is constructed, and f is evaluated in the environment until an output is needed. A λ-calculus in which these are built is said having *explicit environment*, and was first considered by Abadi et al. [1]. Many λ-calculi have been considered since that of Abadi et al. For instance, λexp, λxgc, λs, λv, and $\lambda \varepsilon$, see [6, 3], [4], [7], [2], and [16] respectively.

We define the simplest strong call-by-name λ-calculus with explicit environment as follows:

$$M ::= x \mid \lambda x.M \mid MM \mid \{M/x\}M$$

$$(\lambda x.M)N \to_\beta \{N/x\}M \qquad \frac{M \to_\beta M'}{\lambda x.M \to_\beta \lambda x.M'} \qquad \frac{M \to_\beta M'}{MN \to_\beta M'N}$$

$$\{N/x\}x \to_\varepsilon N \qquad \frac{x \notin \{y\} \cup \mathrm{fv}(N)}{\{N/y\}\lambda x.M \to_\varepsilon \lambda x.\{N/y\}M}$$

$$\{N/x\}(M_1 M_2) \to_\varepsilon \{N/x\}M_1\{N/x\}M_2 \qquad \frac{x \notin \mathrm{fv}(M)}{\{N/x\}M \to_\varepsilon M}$$

$$\frac{M \to_\varepsilon M'}{\lambda x.M \to_\varepsilon \lambda x.M'} \qquad \frac{M \to_\varepsilon M'}{MN \to_\varepsilon M'N} \qquad \frac{M \to_\varepsilon M'}{NM \to_\varepsilon NM'} \; .$$

Ordinary λ-calculi with explicit environment have reductions for environment, e.g. for combining two environments into one environment. Here, explicit environments are used only as a buffer between λ-reducible terms. It is, therefore, obvious that there exists no infinite sequence of $\rightarrow_\varepsilon$. Notice that $\{N/x\}M$ is not $[N/x]M$ but *one expression* of such a form. We extend the previous translation for a term with environment:

$$[\![\{N/x\}M]\!]_u = (\nu x)([\![M]\!]_u|[\![x := N]\!]) \ .$$

These notions divide Theorem 18 into the following two theorems.

Theorem 21. *If $M \rightarrow_\beta M'$, then $[\![M]\!] \rightarrow [\![M']\!]$.*

Theorem 22. *If $M \rightarrow_\varepsilon M'$, then $[\![M]\!] \geq [\![M']\!]$.*

Since we regard a reaction as a transition performed automatically in the concurrent system, the former theorem suggests that the Mπ-calculus has a mechanism that assigns an argument to an address of a function. However, we consider $\geq$ to be a meta-relation on processes. The Mπ-calculus, therefore, distinguishes a function with an environment from the result of evaluating the function in the environment.

7   Full Correspondence

In Section 5, we gave the translation $[\![\cdot]\!]$ from λ-terms to Mπ-processes. In Section 6, we extended it to one from λ-terms with explicit environment to Mπ-processes. Notice that we can rewrite a λ-term to some λ-terms with explicit environment equal to it; for instance, $\lambda x.y$ can be expressed as $[y/z](\lambda x.z)$, $[\lambda x.y/z]z$, and so on. Therefore, the translation $[\![\cdot]\!]$ from λ-terms to Mπ-processes can be extended to a multi-valued function. Formally, $[\![M]\!]_u$ is defined as the set:

$$\{ (\nu x)([\![M']\!]_u|[\![x := N]\!]) \mid \text{fv}(N_i) \cap \{x_1, \ldots, x_i\} = \emptyset \text{ for } 1 \leq i \leq n, \text{ and } [N/x]M' = M \}$$

where (νx), $[\![x := N]\!]$, and $[N/x]M$ denote $(\nu x_1)\cdots(\nu x_n)$, $[\![x_1 := N_1]\!]|\cdots|[\![x_n := N_n]\!]$, and $[N_n/x_n]\cdots[N_1/x_1]M$ respectively. In the sequel, when we say $[\![M]\!]$, we refer to some element of $[\![M]\!]$.

Lemma 23. *Let L be a λ-term, and P be an Mπ-process.*

1. *If $[\![L]\!] \sim P$ and $L \rightarrow_\lambda L'$, then $P \rightarrow^+\sim [\![L']\!]$.*
2. *Let α be the first action except τ with which $[\![L]\!]_u$ transits. Then u belongs to $\text{fn}(\alpha)$. Moreover if L is not an abstraction, then α is an output action.*
3. *If $[\![L]\!] \rightarrow P$, then $L \rightarrow^*_\lambda L'$ and $[\![L']\!] = P$ for some L'.*
4. *If $[\![L]\!] \sim P$ and $L \nrightarrow_\lambda$, then $P \downarrow P'$ for some P'.*

Proof. We prove only 3. due to space limitations. Let L be $[N/x]M$. By induction on the inference of $[\![L]\!] \rightarrow P$.

Case 1: Suppose that M is $\lambda x_0.M_0$. Then P is $(\nu x)(u(x_0v):P_0|[\![x := N]\!])$ where $[\![M_0]\!]_v \rightarrow P_0$ by 2. By induction hypothesis, there exists L_0 such that $M_0 \rightarrow^*_\lambda L_0$ and $[\![L_0]\!]_v = P_0$. By Lemma 17, we have $L \rightarrow^*_\lambda [N/x]\lambda x_0.L_0$. It is sufficient since $[\![[N/x]\lambda x_0.L_0]\!]_u = P$.

Case 2: Suppose that M is M_1M_2 and P is $(\nu x)((\nu v)(P_1|(\nu v')(\overline{v}v'u|[\![v' := M_2]\!]))|[\![x := N]\!])$ where $[\![M_1]\!]_v \rightarrow P_1$. By induction hypothesis, there exists L_1 such that $M_1 \rightarrow^*_\lambda L_1$ and $[\![L_1]\!]_v = P_1$. The rest is similar to Case 1.

Case 3: Suppose that M is $(\lambda x_0.M_0)M_2$ and P is $(\nu x)((\nu x_0)(\llbracket M_0 \rrbracket_u | \llbracket x_0 := M_2 \rrbracket) | \llbracket x := N \rrbracket)$. We have $L \to_\lambda [N/x][M_2/x_0]M_0$ by applying Lemma 17 to $(\lambda x_0.M_0)M_2 \to_\lambda [M_2/x_0]M_0$. It is sufficient since $x_0 \notin \mathrm{fn}(N)$ implies $\llbracket [N/x][M_2/x_0]M_0 \rrbracket_u = P$.

Case 4: Suppose that M is $x_i M_1 \cdots M_m$ $(m \geq 1)$ and P is

$$(\nu x)((\nu v_m)(\cdots(\llbracket N_i \rrbracket_{v_1} | \cdots | (\nu v_m')(\overline{v_m} v_m' u | \llbracket v' := M_m \rrbracket))) | \llbracket x := N \rrbracket) \ .$$

Since L is also $[N/x](N_i M_1 \cdots M_m)$, we have $\llbracket L \rrbracket_u = P$. This suffices to check this case.

Case 5: Suppose that M is x. It is similar to Case 4 since this case is the one of $m = 0$ in Case 4.   □

Main Theorem 24. *Let L be a λ-terms, and P be an Mπ-process.*

1. *If $L \downarrow_\lambda L'$, then for each element P of $\llbracket L \rrbracket$ there exists P' such that $P \downarrow P'$.*
2. *If $\llbracket L \rrbracket \downarrow P$, then $L \downarrow_\lambda L'$ for some L'.*
3. *L converges if and only if $\llbracket L \rrbracket$ does.*
4. *L diverges if and only if $\llbracket L \rrbracket$ does.*

Notice that all the processes which belong to $\llbracket L \rrbracket$ coincide in terms of termination property, and as a result L and $\llbracket L \rrbracket$ in Section 5 converge or diverge simultaneously. It is, however, not surprising since we have extended Milner's call-by-name translation to the multi-valued function for this purpose.

The accordance in convergence and divergence claims that the Mπ-calculus contains the strong call-by-name λ-calculus as a subsystem. Moreover, we can give an intuitive explanation to Milner's call-by-name translation, because extensionality of λ-terms is translated into optimization of Mπ-processes, i.e.,

$$\frac{M \to_\lambda M'}{\lambda x.M \to_\lambda \lambda x.M'} \quad \text{corresponds to} \quad \frac{\llbracket M \rrbracket \xrightarrow{\tau} \llbracket M' \rrbracket \quad x \notin \emptyset \quad y \notin \emptyset}{x(y){:}\llbracket M \rrbracket \xrightarrow{\tau} x(y){:}\llbracket M' \rrbracket} \ .$$

In addition, generality of the Mπ-calculus enables it to have various λ-calculi: three calculi except the strong call-by-name λ-calculus as described in Section 5. We conclude that the Mπ-calculus is not only simple and natural but also expressible and general.

Fu [5], Merro and Sangiorgi [8], Parrow and Victor [12, 13], and various other researchers have given sound embeddings of the strong call-by-name λ-calculus into their systems, and most of them have not showed their embeddings to be complete. In contrast, Parrow and Victor designed a concurrent system called *fusion calculus* using unique ideas, and showed that their embedding is not only sound but also complete to the strong call-by-name λ-calculus [13]. Their system is based on the notion of equations of names, and properly includes the π-calculus. Their system also has an advantage in the way that they deal with names. In their system, there exists no concept of binding names on input actions. As a result, it can avoid troublesome procedures for dealing with bound names, which can become tedious. Certainly, their system is simple and expressive. However, their study on concurrency does not directly give insights into the π-calculus, the de facto standard concurrent system, since their system is quite unique. On the other hand, our system is directly connected to the π-calculus which many researchers are familiar with. We could thus give them a lot of intuitive ideas. For instance, we can claim that "environments in functional languages are resources in a concurrent system" in Section 6 and that "a concurrent system can have the notion of application and extensionality of functions" in this section.

8   Conclusion and Future Work

We have introduced a concurrent system based on the concept of multi-ports, and have defined various equivalences on processes. Our system is an extension of the π-calculus, in the sense that the π-calculus can be obtained from ours by restricting the number of ports. It is noteworthy that we extend the π-calculus to our system not by adding but by replacing a rule, and that a process with only one port can be expressed as a syntax sugar for a multi-ported process. Moreover, our system has the advantage that we can control permission of self-communication as described in detail in Section 3. Although we have given examples of this, it is left as future work to find various useful applications of multi-ported processes which cannot communicate with themselves.

Our system is more expressive than the original π-calculus. As a witness, even the strong call-by-name λ-calculus can be embedded into our system, while Milner embedded only λ-calculi which do not have the extensional rule into the original π-calculus. We treated reductions of λ-calculi carefully in this paper. As a consequence, our embedding of the strong call-by-name λ-calculus has resulted in a complete one with respect to convergence and divergence. To our knowledge, our system is the first one that is a natural extension of the π-calculus and that achieves completeness of the above kind.

Although we have succeeded in giving a complete embedding of the strong call-by-name λ-calculus, it remains an open question whether it is possible to give a complete embedding of the λ-calculus with full reductions. Our success is partly due to the fact that there exists no reduction which applies to arguments:

$$\frac{M \to_\lambda M'}{NM \to_\lambda NM'}$$

in the strong call-by-name λ-calculus. Since our translation translates arguments into resources, it is necessary to add a rule which corresponds to optimization of resources in the π-calculus. A candidate for such a rule would be the following:

$$\frac{P \overset{\tau}{\to} P'}{!P \overset{\tau}{\to} !P'}$$

as some researchers indicate (and write off). However, it does not seem to be easy to introduce a notion of equivalence on processes in this system since this transition, that a process of finite copying transits to an optimized one trained infinitely, is essentially different from the others. We could think behavioral equivalence up to *infinite* internal transitions as a candidate of equivalence.

Acknowledgments

I would like to express my deepest gratitude to Masami Hagiya, Daisuke Kimura, Takafumi Sakurai, Izumi Takeuti, Makoto Tatsuta, Kazushige Terui, and Mitsuharu Yamamoto, who have worked closely with me on this paper. I am also very grateful to Carl Christian Frederiksen, Masahito Hasegawa, Kohei Honda, Yoshihiko Kakutani, Akitoshi Kawamura, and Richard Potter for providing useful advice.

Finally, I thank the anonymous referees for suggesting a number of improvements.

References

[1] M. Abadi, L. Cardelli, P.-L. Curien, and J.-J. Lévy. Explicit substitutions. In *Proceedings of POPL'90: the 17th ACM SIGPLAN-SIGACT symposium on Principles of programming languages*, pages 31–46, 1990.

[2] Z.-E.-A. Benaissa, D. Briaud, P. Lescanne, and J. Rouyer-Degli. λv, a calculus of explicit substitutions which preserves strong normalisation. *Journal of Functional Programming*, 6(5):699–722, 1996.

[3] R. Bloo. Preservation of strong normalisation for explicit substitution. Computer Science Report 95-08, Eindhoven University of Technology, 1995.

[4] R. Bloo and K. H. Rose. Preservation of strong normalisation in named lambda calculi with explicit substitution and garbage collection. In *Proceedings of CSN'95: Computer Science in the Netherlands*, 1995.

[5] Y. Fu. A proof-theoretical approach to communication. In *Proceedings of ICALP'97: the 24th International Colloquium on Automata, Languages, and Programming*, volume 1256 of *Lecture Notes in Computer Science*, pages 325–335. Springer-Verlag, 1997.

[6] F. Kamareddine and R. Nederpelt. On stepwise explicit substitution. *International Journal of Foundations of Computer Science*, 4(3):197–240, 1993.

[7] F. Kamareddine and A. Rios. A lambda-calculus à la De Bruijn with explicit substitutions. In *Proceedings of PLILP'95: the 7th International Symposium on Programming Languages, Implementations, Logics, and Programs*, volume 982 of *Lecture Notes in Computer Science*, pages 45–62. Springer-Verlag, 1995.

[8] M. Merro and D. Sangiorgi. On asynchrony in name-passing calculi. In *Proceedings of ICALP'98: the 25th International Colloquium on Automata, Languages, and Programming*, 1998.

[9] R. Milner. Functions as processes. *Journal of Mathematical Structures in Computer Science*, 2(2):119–141, 1992.

[10] R. Milner. The polyadic π-calculus: a tutorial. In F. L. Bauer, W. Brauer, and H. Schwichtenberg, editors, *Logic and Algebra of Specification*, pages 203–246. Springer-Verlag, 1993.

[11] R. Milner, J. Parrow, and D. Walker. A calculus of mobile processes. *Information and Computation*, 100(1):1–77, 1992.

[12] J. Parrow and B. Victor. The update calculus. In *Proceedings of AMAST'97: the 6th International Conference on Algebraic Methodology and Software Technology*, volume 1349 of *Lecture Notes in Computer Science*, pages 409–423. Springer-Verlag, 1997.

[13] J. Parrow and B. Victor. The fusion calculus: Expressiveness and symmetry in mobile processes. In *Proceedings of LICS'98: the 13th IEEE Symposium on Logic in Computer Science*, 1998.

[14] D. Sangiorgi. On the bisimulation proof method. *Journal of Mathematical Structures in Computer Science*, 8(5):447–479, 1998.

[15] D. Sangiorgi and R. Milner. The problem of 'weak bisimulation up to'. In *Proceedings of CONCUR'92: the 3rd International Conference on Concurrency Theory*, volume 630 of *Lecture Notes in Computer Science*, pages 32–46. Springer-Verlag, 1992.

[16] M. Sato, T. Sakurai, and R. M. Burstall. Explicit environments. In *Proceedings of TLCA'99: the 4th International Conference on Typed Lambda Calculi and Applications*, volume 1581 of *Lecture Notes in Computer Science*, pages 340–354. Springer-Verlag, 1999.

[17] F. van Breugel. A labelled transition system for π_ϵ-calculus. In *Proceedings of TAPSOFT'97: the 7th International Joint Conference on the Theory and Practice of Software Development*, volume 1214 of *Lecture Notes in Computer Science*, pages 312–336. Springer, 1997.

Concurrency Combinators for Declarative Synchronization

Paweł T. Wojciechowski

EPFL, School of Computer and Communication Sciences,
1015 Lausanne, Switzerland
Pawel.Wojciechowski@epfl.ch

Abstract. Developing computer systems that are both *concurrent* and *evolving* is challenging. To guarantee consistent access to resources by concurrent software components, some synchronization is required. A synchronization logic, or policy, is at present entangled in the component code. Adding a new component or modifying existing components, which may require a change of the (global) synchronization policy, is therefore subjected to an extensive inspection of the complete code. We propose a calculus of *concurrency combinators* that allows a program code and its synchronization policy to be expressed separately; the policies include true parallelism, sequentiality, and isolation-only transactions. The calculus is equipped with an operational semantics and a type system. The type system is used to verify if a synchronization policy declared using combinators can be satisfied by program execution.

1 Introduction

Our motivating example of evolving systems are web services [26], i.e. software components which process html or XML data documents received from the network. Due to efficiency and networking reasons, various data fragments may be processed by concurrent services, with possible dependencies on other services. To provide data consistency, transactions or barrier synchronization are required. Unfortunately, a given composition of service components may often change in order to adapt to a new environment or changing requirements, thus making programming of such components a difficult task. We therefore study declarative synchronization, which assumes separation of an object's functional behaviour and the synchronization constraints imposed on it. Such approach enables to modify and customize synchronization policies without changing the code of service components, thus making programming easier and less error-prone.

While some work on such separation of concerns exists (see [11, 8, 23, 19] among others), there are few efforts that formalized languages with declarative synchronization in mind. There are also many open questions: How to know when it is safe to spawn a new thread or call a method, so that the synchronization policy is not invalidated? Or, conversely, how can we build programs that are synchronization safe by construction? How should synchronization itself be implemented? What new language features are required?

W.-N. Chin (Ed.): APLAS 2004, LNCS 3302, pp. 163–178, 2004.
© Springer-Verlag Berlin Heidelberg 2004

In this paper, we present a small language with the goal of understanding the underlying foundations of declarative synchronization. The language allows the programmer to group expressions (methods, objects, etc.) into services, and to express an arbitrary synchronization policy that will constrain the concurrent execution of services at runtime. Our basic synchronization policies include true parallelism, sequentiality, and the combination of these two policies called isolation, which is analogous to the isolation non-interference property known from multithreaded transactions [9, 3]. Isolated services can be assumed to execute serially, without interleaved steps of other services, which significantly simplifies both programming and reasoning about program correctness.

The synchronization policy is expressed abstractly using concurrency combinators, i.e. compositional policy operators which take as arguments service names. They introduce a new problem, however. Separation of synchronization and the functional code of a program gives a way of expressing synchronization schemes which may not be satisfied by the program's execution, leading to problems such as deadlock. Any given program can only be executed for some range of synchronization schemes; the synchronization policies must be matched accordingly. In this paper, we propose a type system that can verify if the matching of a policy and program is correct. Typable programs are guaranteed to satisfy the declared synchronization policy and make progress.

The paper is organized as follows. §2 gives a small example. §3 introduces our calculus, describing its syntax and types. §4 defines the operational semantics. §5 describes the type system and main results. §6 contains related work, and §7 concludes.

2   Example

We begin with an example. Below is a term of the concurrency combinators calculus (or the CK-calculus, in short) showing how a synchronization policy can be expressed. The program expression is defined using the call-by-value λ-calculus [22], extended with service binders and typing.

$$
\begin{aligned}
&D = \texttt{rule } B \texttt{ followed } A \\
&\texttt{rule } D \,;\, C \\
&\texttt{let } r = \texttt{ref } 0 \texttt{ in} \\
&\texttt{let } f_A = \lambda^{\{A\},\{A\}} x : t.\, A \,\#\, (r := x;\; ()) \texttt{ in} \\
&\texttt{let } f_B = \lambda^{\{B\},\{B,A\}} y : t.\, B \,\#\, (\texttt{fork } (f_A \; y);\; !r) \texttt{ in} \\
&\texttt{let } f_C = \lambda^{\{C\},\{C\}} z : t.\, C \,\#\, z \texttt{ in} \\
&\texttt{in} \\
&(f_C \; (f_B \; 1))\quad (\text{* this returns } 0,\text{ never } 1 \text{ *})
\end{aligned}
$$

The program declares a synchronization rule $(B \texttt{ followed } A)\,;\, C$, which orders services A, B and C to be executed, so that: (1) A runs simultaneously with B but the overall result of their concurrent execution must be equivalent to an (ideal) serial execution in which A commences after B has completed; (2) service C can commence only after both A and B have completed.

The service names A, B and C are bound (using #) to functions, respectively f_A, f_B, and f_C. The function f_A updates a shared reference cell r (which initially contains 0), function f_B spawns a new thread (using fork) for updating the cell (by invoking f_A) in parallel with reading the current content of r. The last function, f_C, only returns its argument. Functions are decorated with a pair of service names that can be bound by a thread calling a function until the function returns, and service names that (also) can be bound by threads spawned as the effect of calling the function, e.g. f_B is decorated with $(\{B\}, \{B, A\})$.

The main expression of the program (following function declarations) calls function f_C with its argument being the result of f_B's call.

The synchronization rule defines a synchronization policy, which constrains creation and interleaving of threads by the runtime system, so that only program executions that match the policy are possible. For instance, our program with the synchronization rule removed, can return either 0 or 1, depending on how the thread spawned inside function f_B is interleaved with the main program thread. The synchronization rule ensures, however, that each execution of this program returns 0, never 1; i.e. assignment $r := x$ by service A (where $x = 1$) must block until service B has read the content of r with $!r$.

One may notice that the nested function calls in the main expression (see the last line of the program) impose some ordering on services. This means that some synchronization rules may not be satisfied. A synchronization rule can be satisfied by a program if there exists a deadlock-free execution of the program that satisfies the rule. We go back to this issue in §5, where we define a type system which is able to verify combinator satisfiability statically.

3   Language

3.1   Syntax

The syntax of the CK calculus is in Fig. 1. The main syntactic categories are concurrency combinators and expressions. We also assume the existence of reference cells, with the standard semantics of dereference ($!r$) and assignment ($:=$) operations.

Services. Services are expressions that are bound to service names, ranged over by A, B, C. We assume that service expressions are themselves deadlock-free. A composite service is a collection of services, called subservices, whose (possibly) concurrent execution is controlled by a collection of combinator declarations (explained below). A service completes if it returns a value. A composite service completes if all its subservices return a value. Below we confuse services and composite services unless stated otherwise.

Concurrency Combinators. Concurrency combinators are special functions with no free variables, ranged over by a, b, which are used to define fine-grain concurrency control over the execution of concurrent services. Formal parameters of combinators are service names. We have four basic combinators: $A \parallel B$, $A \, ; \, B$, A isolated B, and A followed B, where A and B are service names:

Variables	$x, y \in Var$	
Service names	$A, B \in Mvar$	
Packages	$p \in 2^{Mvar} \times 2^{Mvar}$	
Combinators	a, b	$::= A \mid a \parallel b \mid a \, ; b \mid a \text{ isolated } b \mid a \text{ followed } b$
Types	t	$::= \text{Unit} \mid t \rightarrow^p t'$
Values	$v, w \in Val$	$::= () \mid \lambda^p x : t. e$
Declarations	K	$::= \text{rule } a \mid A = \text{rule } a \mid K \, K$
Expressions	$e \in Exp$	$::= x \mid v \mid e \, e \mid \text{let } x = e \text{ in } e \mid \text{fork } e \mid A \, \# \, e$
Program terms	P	$::= K \, e$

We work up to alpha-conversion of expressions throughout, with x binding in e in expressions $\lambda^p x : t. e$ and $\text{let } x = e'$ in e.

Fig. 1. λ-calculus with concurrency combinators

- the "parallel" combinator ($A \parallel B$) declares services bound to formal parameters of the combinator to be arbitrarily interleaved by separate threads;
- the "sequence" combinator ($A \, ; B$) declares services bound to formal parameters of the combinator to be executed sequentially, i.e. the service bound to B can commence only after the service bound to A has completed (the condition is however ignored if B is part of A, executed by the same thread).
- the A isolated B combinator allows threads of services bound to formal parameters of the combinator to be interleaved, with fine-grain parallelism, but their concurrent execution must satisfy the isolation property, i.e. be equivalent to some serial execution of A and B (as defined in §4);
- some applications may impose an order on the operations of isolated services: the A followed B combinator is like the previous combinator, with an extra requirement that the runtime system must order the low-level operations as specified, i.e. the comparable (ideal) serial run would be "A followed by B".

Combinator Declarations. Concurrency combinators can be declared using synchronization rules, ranged over by K, which are terms of the form rule a and $A = \text{rule } a$. Complex combinators $A_0 \, op_0 \, ... \, op_{n-1} \, A_n$ are equivalent to a conjunction of n binary combinators $A_i \, op_i \, A_{i+1}$, where $i = 0..n - 1$ and op_i is one of the combinator names, i.e. $\parallel$ ("parallel"), $;$ ("sequence"), isolated and followed. For instance, rule $A \, ; B$ isolated C declares a combinator which ensures that service B can commence only after A has completed, and the execution of B is isolated from any concurrent execution of service C.

Service Composition. Combinators can be arguments of other combinators. For instance, a combinator declaration $A = \text{rule } a$ both declares a combinator a and also defines a fresh service name A, which binds a combinator a. The name A can then be used in the declaration of other combinators of composite services. (We adopt such syntax since it is convenient to express the semantics rules; the concrete syntax would use parentheses instead.)

Types. Types include the base type Unit of unit expressions and the type $t \to^p t'$ of functions. It would be routine to add subtyping on types to the calculus definition. To verify combinator satisfiability in function abstractions, the type of functions is decorated with a service package $p = (p_r, p_s)$, where p_r is a set of all service names which can be bound by a thread calling a function until the function returns, and p_s is the same as p_r but also includes service names bound by any threads spawned as the effect of calling the function. We assume that a programmer can provide information on services bound by functions explicitly, and leave type inference as an open problem.

Values. A value is either an empty value () of type Unit, or function abstraction $\lambda^p x : t. e$ (decorated with service package p). All values in the CK-calculus are first-class programming objects, i.e. they can be passed as arguments to functions and returned as results and stored in data structures.

Expressions. Basic expressions are mostly standard, including variables, values, function applications, and let-binders. The CK language allows multithreaded programs by including the expression fork e, which spawns a new thread for the evaluation of expression e. This evaluation is performed only for its effect; the result of e is never used. To bind a service name to an expression, we provide service binders of the form $A \# e$, which allow an expression e to be bound to a (non-composite) service name A. In programs, the service expression $A \# e$ is usually a body of a function. We use syntactic sugar $e_1; e_2$ for let $x = e_1$ in e_2 (for some x, where x is fresh).

Programs. A program is a pair (SP, $K e$) of a synchronization policy SP and the program expression $K e$. A synchronization policy (or a policy in short) is a set of binary combinators A op B and bindings of the form $A = B_0$ op_0 ... op_{n-1} B_n, that are extracted from declarations K, where op_i are combinator names, describing operations $\|$ ("parallel"), ; ("sequence"), isolated and followed.

We assume that every policy SP is logically consistent, i.e. (1) if A and B in SP are related by operation op (possibly via names of composite services whose A or B are subservices) then neither A and B nor B and A are related by $op' \neq op$, and (2) if A and B are related by an asymmetric operation (i.e. followed or ;) then B and A are not related. For instance, a policy $C = A \| B$ and $C; A$ is not consistent (both conditions are not satisfied). We leave consistency verification as an open problem.

Given the above requirement of consistency, a policy can be easily identified with a sequence of combinator declarations. For instance, in case of our program in §1, SP $= \{D = B$ followed A, $D; C$, B followed $A\}$.

4   Operational Semantics

We specify the operational semantics using the rules defined in Fig. 2 and 3. A state S is a collection of expressions, which are organized as a sequence $T_0, ..., T_n$, where each T_i in the sequence represents a thread. We use T, T' (with comma) to denote an unconstrained execution of threads T and T', and $T; T'$ (with

State Space:

$$
\begin{aligned}
S \in \textit{State} \quad &= \quad \textit{ThreadSeq} \\
T, c \in \textit{ThreadSeq} \quad &::= \quad f \mid T, T' \mid T; T' \mid (T) \\
f \in \textit{Exp}_{ext} \quad &::= \quad x \mid v \mid f\ e \mid v\ f \mid \texttt{let}\ x = f\ \texttt{in}\ e \mid \texttt{let}\ x = v\ \texttt{in}\ f \mid \texttt{fork}\ e \mid \\
&\qquad A\ \#\ e \mid A\{c\}
\end{aligned}
$$

Evaluation and Service Contexts:

$$
\begin{aligned}
\mathcal{E} &= [\,] \mid \mathcal{E}\ e \mid v\ \mathcal{E} \mid \texttt{let}\ x = \mathcal{E}\ \texttt{in}\ e \mid A\{\mathcal{E}\} \mid \mathcal{E}, T \mid T, \mathcal{E} \mid \mathcal{E}; T \mid v; \mathcal{E} \mid (\mathcal{E}) \\
\mathcal{C} &= [\,] \mid \overline{A\ op}\ \mathcal{C}\ \overline{op'\ A'} \qquad\qquad op \in \{\texttt{isolated}, \texttt{followed}, \|, ; \} \\
A_{\mathcal{E}\,T}\{c\} &= \mathcal{E}[A\{c\}]; T \qquad\qquad\qquad \text{for some } T
\end{aligned}
$$

Structural Congruence Rules:

$$
\begin{array}{ll}
T, T' \equiv T', T & \text{(C-Sym)} \\
T \circ () \equiv T \quad \text{where } \circ \text{ is } , \text{ or } ; & \text{(C-Nil)} \\
(); T \equiv T & \text{(C-Seq)} \\
a \parallel b \equiv b \parallel a & \text{(C-Prl)} \\
a\ \texttt{isolated}\ b \equiv b\ \texttt{isolated}\ a & \text{(C-Isol)}
\end{array}
\qquad
\dfrac{T \longrightarrow T'}{\mathcal{E}[T] \longrightarrow \mathcal{E}[T']} \ \text{(C-Expr)}
$$

Fig. 2. The CK-calculus: Operational semantics

semicolon) to denote that T' can commence only when T has completed, and (T) for grouping threads. We write $T \circ T'$ to mean either T, T' or $T; T'$.

The expressions f are written in the calculus presented in §3.1, extended with a new construct $A\{c\}$, which denotes a sequence of threads c that is part of service A. The construct is not part of the language to be used by programmers; it is just to explain semantics.

We define a small-step evaluation relation $e \longrightarrow e'$ read "expression e reduces to expression e' in one step". We also use $\longrightarrow^*$ for a sequence of small-step reductions, and a "meta" relation $\twoheadrightarrow$ (defined below) for many reduction steps with the isolation guarantee. Reductions are defined using evaluation context $\mathcal{E}$ for expressions and threads, and context $\mathcal{C}$ for synchronization policy rules. Context application is denoted by $[\,]$, as in $\mathcal{E}[e]$. We write $\overline{A\ op}$ as shorthand for a possibly empty sequence $A\ op \ldots A'\ op'$ (and similarly for $\overline{op\ A}$).

We also use an abbreviation $A_{\mathcal{E}\,T}\{c\}$ for $\mathcal{E}[A\{c\}]; T$ — i.e., "a context $\mathcal{E}$ of service A, followed by a (possibly empty) thread T or a group of threads T that are blocked until A will complete". To lighten semantics rules, we usually omit T and write $A_{\mathcal{E}}\{c\}$.

Structural congruence rules are defined in Fig. 2. They can be used to rewrite thread expressions and synchronization policy rules whenever needed.

The evaluation of a program $(\text{SP}, K\ e)$ starts in an initial state with a single thread that evaluates the program's expression e. Evaluation then takes place according to the transition rules in Fig. 3. The rules specify the behaviour of the constructs of our calculus. The evaluation terminates once all threads have been reduced to values, in which case the value v of the initial, first thread T_0

Evaluator:

$$eval \subseteq Exp \times Val$$
$$eval(e, v) \Leftrightarrow e \longrightarrow^* T_0 \circ \ldots \circ T_n \text{ and } \dot{T_0} = v,\ T_{j \neq 0} = ()$$

Transition Rules:

$$S + S' \longrightarrow S \text{ or } S + S' \longrightarrow S' \qquad\qquad \text{(R-Choice)}$$

$$\lambda x.\, e\ v \longrightarrow \{v/x\}e \qquad\qquad \text{(R-App)}$$

$$\texttt{let } x = v \texttt{ in } e \longrightarrow \{v/x\}e \qquad\qquad \text{(R-Let)}$$

$$A \,\texttt{\#}\, e \longrightarrow A\{\,e\,\} \qquad\qquad \text{(R-Bind)}$$

$$A\{\,v\,\} \longrightarrow v \qquad\qquad \text{(R-Compl)}$$

$$\mathcal{E}[\texttt{fork } e] \longrightarrow \mathcal{E}[()], e \qquad\qquad \text{(R-Fork)}$$

$$A\{\,c\,\}; T, A\{\,c'\,\}; T' \longrightarrow A\{\,c, c'\,\}; (T, T') \qquad\qquad \text{(R-Join)}$$

$$\frac{A = \mathcal{C}[\,B \ op \ \mathcal{C}'[\,C\,]\,] \in \mathrm{SP} \quad \mathcal{E}''[\,c''\,] \neq \mathcal{E}'''[\,A\{\,c''\,\}\,]}{\mathcal{E}''[\,B_{\mathcal{E}}\{\,c\,\} \circ C_{\mathcal{E}'}\{\,c'\,\}\,] \longrightarrow \mathcal{E}''[\,A\{\,B_{\mathcal{E}}\{\,c\,\} \circ C_{\mathcal{E}'}\{\,c'\,\}\,\}\,]} \qquad \text{(R-Fold)}$$

$$\frac{\begin{array}{c} A, B \text{ are innermost services of redex} \\ A = B_1 \ op \ \ldots \ op' \ B_n \in \mathrm{SP} \quad B \neq B_i \quad i = 1..n \end{array}}{A\{\,T \circ B_{\mathcal{E}}\{\,c\,\}, T'\,\} \longrightarrow A\{\,T, T'\,\} \circ B_{\mathcal{E}}\{\,c\,\}} \qquad \text{(R-Unfold)}$$

$$\frac{A\,;\, B \in \mathrm{SP}}{A_{\mathcal{E}}\{\,c\,\}, B_{\mathcal{E}'}\{\,c'\,\} \longrightarrow A_{\mathcal{E}}\{\,c\,\}; B_{\mathcal{E}'}\{\,c'\,\}} \qquad \text{(R-Seq)}$$

$$\frac{\begin{array}{c} A \texttt{ followed } B \in \mathrm{SP} \\ \mathcal{E}''[\,A_{\mathcal{E}}\{\,c\,\}; B_{\mathcal{E}'}\{\,c'\,\}\,] \longrightarrow^* S \end{array}}{\mathcal{E}''[\,A_{\mathcal{E}}\{\,c\,\}, B_{\mathcal{E}'}\{\,c'\,\}\,] \twoheadrightarrow S} \qquad \text{(R-Foll)}$$

$$\frac{\begin{array}{c} A \texttt{ isolated } B \in \mathrm{SP} \\ \mathcal{E}''[\,A_{\mathcal{E}}\{\,c\,\}; B_{\mathcal{E}'}\{\,c'\,\}\,] \longrightarrow^* S \\ \mathcal{E}''[\,B_{\mathcal{E}'}\{\,c'\,\}; A_{\mathcal{E}}\{\,c\,\}\,] \longrightarrow^* S' \end{array}}{\mathcal{E}''[\,A_{\mathcal{E}}\{\,c\,\}, B_{\mathcal{E}'}\{\,c'\,\}\,] \twoheadrightarrow S + S'} \qquad \text{(R-Isol)}$$

To lighten notation, we write $A_{\mathcal{E}}\{\,c\,\}$ instead of $A_{\mathcal{E}\,T}\{\,c\,\}$.

We assume that if SP has $A; B$ or $A \texttt{ followed } B$ for some A, then evaluation of $B\{\,c\,\}$ (or $B_i\{\,c_i\,\}$ and $i = 1..n$, if $B = B_1 \ op \ \ldots \ op' \ B_n$) is blocked till rules (R-Seq) or (R-Foll) are applied to A and B, unless no other redex is available.

Fig. 3. The CK-calculus: Operational semantics

is returned as the program's result. (A typing rule for fork will ensure that other values are empty values.) The execution of unconstrained threads can be arbitrarily interleaved. Since different interleavings may produce different results, the evaluator $\mathsf{eval}(e, v)$ is therefore a relation, not a partial function. Below we describe the evaluation rules.

Nondeterministic choice (R-Choice) between states S and S', denoted $S + S'$, can lead to either S being evaluated and S' discarded, or opposite.

The next two evaluation rules are the standard rules of a call-by-value λ-calculus [22]. Function application $\lambda x.\, e\ v$ in rule (R-App) reduces to the function's body e in which a formal argument x is replaced with the actual argument v. The (R-Let) rule reduces $\mathsf{let}\ x = v\ \mathsf{in}\ e$ to the expression in which variable x is replaced by value v in e. We write $\{v/x\}e$ to denote the capture-free substitution of v for x in the expression e.

Service binder $A \# e$ in rule (R-Bind) marks an expression e with the service name A bound to e; it reduces to the expression $A\{\,e\,\}$. The marking information will allow concurrency control rules (described below) to identify expressions that are part of a given service, and apply to them all relevant synchronization rules while evaluating the expressions.

The mark $A\{\,e\,\}$ will be erased when expression e evaluates to a value v (see (R-Compl)). Then, we say that service A has completed.

Evaluation of expression fork e creates a new thread which evaluates e (see (R-Fork)). A value returned by expression e will be discarded. Note that threads spawned by a (non-composite) service A will not be part of service A, unless the expression spawned by the new thread is explicitly bound to A.

4.1   Concurrency Combinators

The rules at the bottom half of Fig. 3, beginning from (R-Join), define the semantics of concurrency control. Programs evaluated using the rules must be first checked if the rules can be actually applied for a given synchronization policy. In §5, we present a type system that can verify this condition.

The first rule, (R-Join), groups two concurrent subexpressions of the same service. The rule (R-Fold) encloses two concurrent services that are part of a composite service A with the name A. The rule (R-Unfold) removes service B (together with any threads blocked on B) outside the scope of a composite service A whose B is not part of. Note that abbreviations $A_{\mathcal{E}}\{\,c\,\}$ and $A_{\mathcal{E}'}\{\,c'\,\}$ allow contexts $\mathcal{E}$ and $\mathcal{E}'$ to be multithreaded, if needed by reduced expressions.

The rule (R-Seq) blocks a thread (or threads) of service B until service A would complete. To explain other rules, we need to introduce a few definitions.

Isolation Property. By concurrent execution, we mean a sequence of small-step reductions in which the reduction steps can be taken by threads with possible interleaving. Two (possibly multithreaded) services are executed serially if one service commences after another one has completed.

A result of evaluating a service expression bound to A is any state S, that does not have a context $\mathcal{E}[\,A\{\,..\,\}\,]$. Note that states subsume the content of reference cells, represented with stores (the details are omitted in Fig. 3 as our main focus in this paper is on verification of combinators). An effect is any change to the content of stores.

We define isolation to mean that the effects of one service are not visible to other services executing concurrently—from the perspective of a service, it appears that services execute serially rather than in parallel.

The operational semantics of combinators A isolated B and A followed B, is captured using rules (R-Isol) and (R-Foll). The rules define the "isolated evaluation" relation ($\twoheadrightarrow$). They specify that the actual term which contains services A and B (in the conclusion of each rule) should be evaluated by the single-step reduction ($\longrightarrow$) using all evaluation rules but (R-Isol) and (R-Foll). However, the order of applying the rules must be now constrained, so that any result S or S' of such concurrent evaluation of the term, could be also obtained by evaluating a less concurrent term – given in the premises of rules (R-Isol) and (R-Foll) – in which services A and B are executed serially.

The combinator A followed B restricts the (ideal) serial execution to "A followed by B", while combinator A isolated B does not specify the order.

We assume that if SP has $A; B$ or A followed B for some A, then evaluation of $B\{\,c\,\}$ (or $B_i\{\,c_i\,\}$ and $i = 1..n$, if $B = B_1$ op ... op' B_n) is blocked till rules (R-Seq) or (R-Foll) are applied to A and B, unless no other redex is available.

Implementation of Isolation. An implementation of concurrency combinators should schedule threads of well-typed expressions so that the SP policy is effectuated. The most interesting case is the runtime support for isolation of composite services which are themselves concurrent. In our previous work [27], we have designed several fine-grain concurrency control algorithms that provide a deadlock-free implementation of such type of scheduling. They have been used to implement SAMOA — a library package in Java for developing modular network protocols, in which different network and application messages can be processed by isolated, possibly multithreaded services. We have used our package to implement example protocols for server replication. The isolated construct of SAMOA made programming of protocols easier [27], especially those with many threads. The isolation property ensures that each message is always processed using a consistent set of session and message-specific data.

5   Typing for Combinator Satisfiability

Writing down the evaluation rules for concurrency combinators, which initially seemed straightforward, appeared to be more subtle. Generally speaking, we had to decide if the combinators should be considered as powerful typing, or as directives for the runtime system to schedule operations, or maybe both, and if both, then to which degree we could depend on static analysis, and what may have to be supported by the runtime tools. Below we describe our solution.

Judgments:

$\Gamma; b; p \vdash e : t$ e is a well-typed expression of type t in Γ, bound to service names in $b = (b_r, b_s)$ of service package $p = (p_r, p_s)$

Expression Typing:

$$\frac{x : t \in \Gamma}{\Gamma; b; p \vdash x : t} \quad \text{(T-Var)}$$

$$\frac{\Gamma, x : t; \emptyset; p \vdash e : t'}{\Gamma; b; p' \vdash \lambda^p x : t. e : t \to^p t'} \quad \text{(T-Abs)}$$

$$\frac{\begin{array}{c} \Gamma; b; p \vdash e : t \\ (\Gamma, x : t); b'; p' \vdash e' : t' \\ b \subseteq b' \quad p \subseteq p' \end{array}}{\Gamma; b'; p' \vdash \text{let } x = e \text{ in } e' : t'} \quad \text{(T-Let)}$$

$$\frac{}{\Gamma; b; p \vdash () : \text{Unit}} \quad \text{(T-Unit)}$$

$$\frac{\Gamma; (\emptyset, b_s); (\emptyset, p_s) \vdash e : t}{\Gamma; b; p \vdash \text{fork } e : \text{Unit}} \quad \text{(T-Fork)}$$

$$\frac{\begin{array}{c} \Gamma; b; p' \vdash e : t' \to^p t \\ \Gamma; b'; p'' \vdash e' : t' \quad b \subseteq b' \quad p' \subseteq p'' \\ \forall A \in p_r \ \nexists B \in b'_r. \ (A, B) \text{ prl} \\ \forall A \in p_s \ \nexists B \in b'_s. \ (A, B) \text{ seq} \end{array}}{\Gamma; b' \cup p; p'' \cup p \vdash e \ e' : t} \quad \text{(T-App)}$$

$$\frac{\begin{array}{c} \Gamma; b \cup \{A\}; p \vdash e : t \\ A \in p_r \quad A \in p_s \\ \nexists B \in b_r. \ (A, B) \text{ prl} \\ \nexists B \in b_s. \ (A, B) \text{ seq} \end{array}}{\Gamma; b \cup \{A\}; p \vdash A \ \# \ e : t} \quad \text{(T-Bind)}$$

Auxiliary Definitions:

$$\frac{A \parallel B \in \text{CS or } B \parallel A \in \text{CS}}{(A, B) \ \text{prl}} \quad \text{(T-Prl)}$$

$$\frac{\begin{array}{c} A; B \in \text{CS} \\ \text{or } A \text{ followed } B \in \text{CS} \end{array}}{(A, B) \ \text{seq}} \quad \text{(T-Seq)}$$

$x \cup p = (x_r \cup p, x_s \cup p)$ $x \subseteq x' \equiv x_r \subseteq x'_r \text{ and } x_s \subseteq x'_s$ where $x = b$ or $x = p$

Fig. 4. The CK-calculus: Typing expressions

Preferably, all rules constraining components could and should be verified statically. Programs which cannot satisfy a given rule simply would not compile.

Consider our example program in §2, with a new policy $D = B$ **followed** A and $C ; D$. Unfortunately, all possible executions of the program can no longer satisfy the latter rule. The new policy requires that service C, which binds function f_C, must return before services A and B can commence. With such a policy, the program is not able to begin its execution since the function f_C is expected to be called with an argument returned by the call of f_B. However, according to the new policy, function f_B cannot be called before f_C returns. So, we have a deadlock situation. In this section, we define a type system that can verify statically combinator satisfiability, and so detect the possibility of deadlock.

Satisfiability of Combinators. The semantics can be used to formalize the notion of combinator satisfiability, as follows. A thread T binds a service name A if there exists some evaluation context $\mathcal{E}$ such that $T = \mathcal{E}[A\{f\}]$ for some expression f. A state S does not satisfy combinator $A \parallel B$ if its thread sequence contains a thread that binds both service names A and B. A state S does not satisfy combinator $A\,;B$ and also combinator A followed B, if its thread sequence contains either a term $\mathcal{E}[B\{f\}]$ such that $f = \mathcal{E}'[A\;\#\;e]$ (possibly $f = \mathcal{E}'[\texttt{fork}\;\mathcal{E}''[A\;\#\;e]]$) or a term $\mathcal{E}[B\{c\}];T$ and $T = \mathcal{E}'[A\{c'\}]$, for some contexts $\mathcal{E}$, $\mathcal{E}'$ and $\mathcal{E}''$ and expressions f, e, c and c'. In all other cases, the above combinators are satisfied. Finally, combinator A isolated B can be satisfied at runtime by all execution states. This is because any sequential evaluation of services A and B (i.e. A and B evaluated by the same thread) ensures the isolation property trivially. Otherwise, if A and B are evaluated by different threads, then rule (R-Isol) is applied to scheduling threads accordingly.

An execution run $S \longrightarrow^* S'$ does not satisfy a combinator a if it may yield a state that does not satisfy a, i.e. if there exists a state S'' in the run (including S and S') such that S'' does not satisfy a. Otherwise, we say that the run $S \longrightarrow^* S'$ satisfies combinator a.

Typing for Combinator Satisfiability. We define the type system using one judgment for expressions. The judgment and the static typing rules for reasoning about the judgment are given in Fig. 4. The typing judgment has the form $\Gamma; b; p \vdash e : t$, read "expression e has type t in environment Γ with bound service names b of service package p", where an environment Γ is a finite mapping from free variables to types. A package $p = (p_r, p_s)$ is defined by all service names which may be bound while evaluating expression e, either by the current thread only (p_r) or by all threads evaluating e (p_s); if e is single-threaded then $p_r = p_s$.

Our intend is that, given a policy SP if the judgment $\Gamma; b; p \vdash e : t$ holds, then expression e can satisfy all concurrency combinators in SP, and yields values of type t, provided the current thread binds services described in b, it may bind at most services described in p, and the free variables of e are given bindings consistent with the typing environment Γ.

The core parts of typing rules for expressions are fairly straightforward and typical for the λ-calculus with threads evaluated only for their side-effects. The only unusual rule is (T-Bind); it type checks service binders of the form $A\;\#\;e$, and requires the type of the whole expression to be e's type. To support modular design of services, service binders are typable only if they are inside a function.

The main novelty is verifying if expressions satisfy combinators. For this, we check if expressions do not invalidate any constraints imposed by the policy rules. A set of constraints CS is constructed recursively from a set of binary combinators copied from the policy SP (we assume a fixed policy for each program). For each binding rule $C = A_1\;op\;...\;op'\;A_n$ in SP, replace every combinator c of the form $X\;op\;Y$ where $X = C$ or $Y = C$, by n constraints c_i, such that c_i is exactly the same as c but the name C (on a given position) is replaced by A_i, e.g. in case of our example program in §2, CS = $\{B$ followed $A,\ B;C,\ A;C\}$.

During typechecking, an expression is evaluated for a given constraint set CS in the context of a package p, and a pair $b = (b_r, b_s)$ of service names that are bound explicitly (using #) by the current thread (b_r), and all service names that are bound by the current thread, including bindings inherited from parent threads at the time when the thread has been spawned (b_s).

For instance, consider typing the operation of binding a new service name A. The (T-Bind) rule checks if no constraint among those that define relations (A, B) prl and (A, B) seq (see in the bottom of Fig. 4) appeared in CS, where B is any service bound so far by the current thread (i.e. before A is bound). If at least one such constraint is in CS, then the program is not typable since the constraint cannot be satisfied by any execution of the program. This is because either A and B are bound in a wrong order (thus violating combinators $A; B$ and A followed B) or they are bound by the same thread (thus disabling true parallelism and so violating combinator $A \parallel B$).

A package $p = (p_r, p_s)$ decorates a function type and definition, representing all services that may be bound while evaluating the function by the current thread T only (p_r) and by T and also any other threads that are spawned as the effect of calling the function (p_s). The rule (T-App) checks if relations (A, B) prl and (A, B) seq do not hold, where A is any service in the package implemented by a function, and B is any service bound by a thread calling the function.

The rule (T-Fork) requires the type of the whole expression to be Unit; this is correct since threads are evaluated only for their side effects. Note that the forked expression is evaluated with b_r and p_r nulled since verification of the $A \parallel B$ combinator requires that any spawned threads do not inherit service bindings from their parent thread (as we only check if A and B are not single-threaded).

In a semantically richer language (with conditionals) the type system could be extended with verification of dead code branches. Otherwise, some declared policies would be rejected, even if all program executions may satisfy them.

Well-Typed Programs Satisfy Combinators. The fundamental property of the type system is that well-typed programs satisfy the declared synchronization policy, expressed using concurrency combinators. The first component of the proof of this property is a type preservation result stating that typing is preserved during evaluation. To prove this result, we extend typing judgments from expressions in Exp to states in State as shown in Fig. 5. The judgment $\vdash S : t$ says that S is a well-typed state yielding values of type t.

Lemma 1 (Type Preservation). If $\Gamma; b; p \vdash S : t$ and $S \longrightarrow S'$, then $\Gamma; b; p \vdash S' : t$.

Lemma 2 states that a program typable for some synchronization policy SP is reducible to states that satisfy all combinators in SP.

Lemma 2 (Combinator Preservation). Suppose $\Gamma; \emptyset; \emptyset \vdash S : t$ for some synchronization policy SP. If $S \longrightarrow^* S'$, then run $S \longrightarrow^* S'$ satisfies all combinators in SP up to state S'.

Type preservation and combinator preservation "up to a state" ensure that if we start with a typable expression for some policy SP, then we cannot reach an untypable expression through any sequence of reductions, and the reduced expression satisfies combinators in SP. This by itself, however, does not yield type soundness. Lemma 3 states that evaluation of a typable expression cannot get stuck, i.e. either the expression is a value or there is some reduction defined.

Judgments:

$$\vdash S : t \quad S \text{ is a well-typed state of type } t$$

Rules:

$$\frac{\begin{array}{c}|T| > 0 \quad \Gamma; \emptyset; \emptyset \vdash T_i : t_i \\ \text{for all } i < |T|\end{array}}{\vdash T : t_0} \text{ (T-State)}$$

$$\frac{\Gamma; b; p \vdash f_i : t_i \quad \Gamma; b'; p' \vdash f'_j : t_j \quad i < j}{\Gamma; b; p \vdash f_i \circ f'_j : t_i} \text{ (T-Thread)}$$

$$\frac{\vdash S : t_0 \quad \vdash S' : t_0}{\vdash S + S' : t_0} \text{ (T-Choice)}$$

$$\frac{\Gamma; b; p \vdash c : t}{\Gamma; b; p \vdash A\{c\} : t} \text{ (T-InService)}$$

Fig. 5. Additional judgments and rules for typing states

Lemma 3 (Progress). Suppose S is a closed, well-typed state (that is, $\vdash S : t$ for some t and policy SP). Then either S is a value or else, there is some state S' with $S \longrightarrow S'$.

We conclude that for a given policy SP, well-typed programs satisfy combinators in SP. An expression e is a well-typed program if it is closed and it has a type t in the empty type environment, written $\vdash e : t$.

Theorem 1 (Combinator Satisfiability). Given a policy SP, if $\vdash e : t$, then all runs $e \longrightarrow^* v_0$, where v_0 is some value, satisfy combinators in SP.

6 Related Work

There have been recently many proposals of concurrent languages with novel synchronization primitives, e.g. Polyphonic C# [2] and JoCaml [5], which are based on the join-pattern abstraction [7]; and Concurrent Haskell [14], Concurrent ML [20], and (Nomadic) Pict [21, 24] which have synchronization constructs based on channel abstractions. They enable to encode complex concurrency control more easily than when using standard constructs, such as monitors and locks.

Flow Java [4] extends Java with single assignment variables, which allow programmers to defer binding of objects to these variables. Threads accessing an unbound variable are blocked, e.g. the method call c.m() will block until c has been bound to an object (by other thread). This mechanism can be used to implement barrier synchronization in concurrent programs.

The above work is orthogonal to the goals of this paper. We are primarily focused on a declarative way of encoding and verifying synchronization through separation of concerns (see [11, 16, 8, 23, 18, 19] among others), with higher-level transactional facilities that provide automatic concurrency control. Below we discuss example work in these two areas.

Separation of Concurrency Aspects. The previous work, which set up goals close to our own is by Ren and Agha [23] on separation of an object's functional behaviour and the timing constraints imposed on it. They propose an actor-based language for specifying and enforcing at runtime real-time relations between events in a distributed system. Their work builds on the earlier work of Frølund and Agha [8] who developed language support for specifying multi-object coordination, expressed in the form of constraints that restrict invocation of a group of objects.

For a long time, the object-oriented community has been pointing out, under the term inheritance anomaly [17], that concurrency control code interwoven with the application code of classes can represent a serious obstacle to class inheritance, even in very simple situations. Milicia and Sassone [18, 19] address the inheritance anomaly problem, and present an extension of Java with a linear temporal logic to express synchronization constraints on method calls. This approach is similar to ours however we are focused on verifying static constraints between code fragments.

The Aspect Oriented Programming (AOP) approach is based on separately specifying the various concerns of a program and some description of their relationship, and then relying on the AOP tools to weave [12] or compose them together into a coherent program. Hürsch and Lopes [11] identify various concerns, including synchronization. Lopes [16] describes a programming language D, which allows thread synchronization to be expressed as a separate concern. More recently, the AOP tools have been proposed for Java, such as AspectJ [15]; they allow aspect modules to be encoded using traditional languages, and weaved at the intermediate level of Java bytecode.

We are not aware of much work on formalizing combinator-like operations. Achermann and Nierstrasz [1] describe Piccola, which allows software components to be composed (although not isolated) using connectors, with rules governing their composition.

Isolation-Only Transactions. A number of researchers describe a way to decompose transactions, and provide support of the isolation property in common programming. For instance, Venari/ML [9] implements higher-order functions in ML to express modular transactions, with concurrency control factored out into a separate mechanism that the programmer could use to ensure isolation.

Flanagan and Qadeer's [6] developed a type system for specifying and verifying the atomicity of methods in multithreaded Java programs (the notion of "atomicity" is equivalent to isolation in this paper). The type system is a synthesis of Lipton's theory of left and right movers (for proving properties of parallel programs) and type systems for race detection.

Harris and Fraser [10] have been investigating an extension of Java with atomic code blocks that implement Hoare's conditional critical regions (CCRs). However, both Flanagan and Qadeer's atomic methods and Harris and Fraser's atomic blocks must be sequential, while our isolated (composite) services can themselves be multithreaded.

Black et al. [3] defined an equation theory of atomic transaction operators, where an operator corresponds to an individual ACID (Atomicity, Consistency, Isolation, and Durability) property. The operators can be composed, giving different semantics to transactions. The model is however presented abstractly, without being integrated with any language or calculus.

Vitek et al. [25] (see also Jagannathan and Vitek [13]) have recently proposed a calculi-based model of (standard) ACID transactions. They formalized the optimistic and two-phase locking concurrency control strategies.

7   Conclusions

Our small, typed calculus may be a useful basis for work on different problems of declarative synchronization. One problem that we have identified in this paper, and solved using a type system, is satisfiability of combinators and scheduling policies. Such combination of static typing with runtime support would be helpful to implement concurrency combinators. It may be also worthwhile to investigate algorithms for inferring the typing annotations.

We have focused on the simplest language that allows us to study the core problem of §1, rather than attempting to produce an industrial-strength language. We think however that analogous work could be carried out for other languages, too. We hope that having abstractions similar to our concurrency combinators in the mainstream programming languages would facilitate the development of concurrent, service-oriented systems, especially those that need to deal with unanticipated evolution.

Acknowledgments. Research supported by the Swiss National Science Foundation under grant number 21-67715.02 and Hasler Stiftung under grant number DICS-1825.

References

1. F. Achermann and O. Nierstrasz. Applications = Components + Scripts – A Tour of Piccola. In M. Aksit, editor, *Software Architectures and Component Technology*, pages 261–292. Kluwer, 2001.
2. N. Benton, L. Cardelli, and C. Fournet. Modern concurrency abstractions for C#. In *Proc. ECOOP '02*, LNCS 2374, June 2002.
3. A. P. Black, V. Cremet, R. Guerraoui, and M. Odersky. An equational theory for transactions. In *Proc. FSTTCS '03 (23rd Conference on Foundations of Software Technology and Theoretical Computer Science)*, Dec. 2003.
4. F. Drejhammar, C. Schulte, P. Brand, and S. Haridi. Flow Java: Declarative concurrency for Java. In *Proc. ICLP '03 (Conf. on Logic Programming)*, 2003.
5. F. L. Fessant and L. Maranget. Compiling join-patterns. In *Proc. HLCL '98 (Workshop on High-Level Concurrent Languages)*, 1998.
6. C. Flanagan and S. Qadeer. A type and effect system for atomicity. In *Proc. PLDI '03 (Conf. on Programming Language Design and Implementation)*, June 2003.
7. C. Fournet, G. Gonthier, J.-J. Lévy, L. Maranget, and D. Rémy. A calculus of mobile agents. In *Proc. of CONCUR '96*, LNCS 1119, Aug. 1996.
8. S. Frølund and G. Agha. A language framework for multi-object coordination. In *Proc. ECOOP '93*, LNCS 627, July 1993.

9. N. Haines, D. Kindred, J. G. Morrisett, S. M. Nettles, and J. M. Wing. Composing first-class transactions. *ACM TOPLAS*, 16(6):1719–1736, Nov. 1994.
10. T. Harris and K. Fraser. Language support for lightweight transactions. In *Proc. OOPSLA '03*, Oct. 2003.
11. W. Hursch and C. Lopes. Separation of concerns. Technical Report NU-CCS-95-03, College of Computer Science, Northeastern University, Feb. 1995.
12. R. Jagadeesan, A. Jeffrey, and J. Riely. A calculus of untyped aspect-oriented programs. In *Proc. ECOOP 2003*, LNCS 2743, July 2003.
13. S. Jagannathan and J. Vitek. Optimistic concurrency semantics for transactions in coordination languages. In *Proc. COORDINATION '04*, Feb. 2004.
14. S. P. Jones, A. Gordon, and S. Finne. Concurrent Haskell. In *Proc. POPL '96 (23rd ACM Symposium on Principles of Programming Languages)*, Jan. 1996.
15. G. Kiczales, E. Hilsdale, J. Hugunin, M. Kersten, J. Palm, and W. Griswold. Getting started with AspectJ. *Communications of the ACM*, 44(10):59–65, Oct. 2001.
16. C. V. Lopes. *D: A Language Framework for Distributed Programming*. PhD thesis, College of Computer Science, Northeastern University, Dec. 1997 (1998).
17. S. Matsuoka and A. Yonezawa. Analysis of inheritance anomaly in object-oriented concurrent programming languages. In *Research Directions in Concurrent Object-Oriented Programming*, pages 107–150. MIT Press, 1993.
18. G. Milicia and V. Sassone. Jeeg: A programming language for concurrent objects synchronization. In *Proc. ACM Java Grande/ISCOPE Conference*, Nov. 2002.
19. G. Milicia and V. Sassone. Jeeg: Temporal constraints for the synchronization of concurrent objects. Tech. Report RS-03-6, BRICS, Feb. 2003.
20. P. Panangaden and J. Reppy. The Essence of Concurrent ML. In F. Nielson, editor, *ML with Concurrency: Design, Analysis, Implementation, and Application*, pages 5–29. Springer, 1997.
21. B. C. Pierce and D. N. Turner. Pict: A programming language based on the pi-calculus. In G. Plotkin, C. Stirling, and M. Tofte, editors, *Proof, Language and Interaction: Essays in Honour of Robin Milner*. MIT Press, 2000.
22. G. D. Plotkin. Call-by-name, call-by-value and the λ-calculus. *Theoretical Computer Science*, 1:125–159, 1975.
23. S. Ren and G. A. Agha. RTsynchronizer: Language support for real-time specifications in distributed systems. In *Proc. ACM Workshop on Languages, Compilers, & Tools for Real-Time Systems*, 1995.
24. P. Sewell, P. T. Wojciechowski, and B. C. Pierce. Location-independent communication for mobile agents: A two-level architecture. In *Internet Programming Languages*, LNCS 1686, pages 1–31, 1999.
25. J. Vitek, S. Jagannathan, A. Welc, and A. L. Hosking. A semantic framework for designer transactions. In *Proc. ESOP '04*, Mar./April 2004.
26. W3C. *Web Services Architecture*, 2004. http://www.w3.org/TR/ws-arch/.
27. P. Wojciechowski, O. Rütti, and A. Schiper. SAMOA: A framework for a synchronisation-augmented microprotocol approach. In *Proc. IPDPS 2004 (18th International Parallel and Distributed Processing Symposium)*, Apr. 2004.

A Uniform Reduction Equivalence for Process Calculi*

Zining Cao

Department of Informatics, School of Mathematical Sciences,
Peking University, Beijing 100871, P. R. China
caozn@tsinghua.org.cn

Abstract. We present a new uniform definition of reduction-based semantics for different process calculi, called indexed reduction equivalence (or congruence). We prove that early bisimulation coincides with indexed reduction equivalence for π-calculus, context bisimulation coincides with indexed reduction equivalence for higher order π-calculus and indexed reduction congruence is strictly finer than contextual barbed congruence for Safe Mobile Ambients.

1 Introduction

The studies of π-calculus started from Milner, Parrow and Walker's paper in 1992 [7]. Roughly speaking, the π-calculus is an extension of CCS where channels can be exchanged along channels. Several notions of bisimulations were proposed to describe the equivalence of processes in π-calculus [10], such as early bisimulation, late bisimulation, open bisimulation and so on. In Sangiorgi's Ph.D dissertation [8], higher order π-calculus and some interesting equivalences, such as context bisimulation, normal bisimulation and barbed equivalence, were presented.

Recently, several new process calculi have been proposed which allow us to describe the mobility of software. Among them, a famous one is Mobile Ambients (MA) [2], whose computational model is based on the notion of movement. In [4], Levi and Sangiorgi argued that the basic operational semantics for Mobile Ambients led to the phenomenon of 'grave interference'. Grave interference makes reasoning on programming much more difficult [4]. To solve this problem, a variant calculus of Mobile Ambients was proposed in [4], called Safe Mobile Ambients (SA). For SA, the concept of co-action was introduced, and a reduction is executed by the cooperation of action and co-action.

Unlike π-calculus, the operational semantics of SA was firstly given by reduction system, therefore the definition of equivalence for SA cannot be given as usual style of labeled bisimualtion in π-calculus. Several researchers studied labeled translation system for SA. In [5], a labeled translation system based

---

* This work was supported by the National Science Fund of China.

W.-N. Chin (Ed.): APLAS 2004, LNCS 3302, pp. 179–195, 2004.
© Springer-Verlag Berlin Heidelberg 2004

operational semantics for SA and a labeled bisimulation based equivalence were given. Another labeled translation system based operational semantics was given in [6], and the notions of late bisimulation and early bisimualtion were also presented.

Up to now, all proposed labeled translation systems for SA seem somewhat complicated, which makes the labeled bisimualtion for SA not very convenient for application. On the other hand, barbed equivalence is an equivalence based on reduction semantics, so it seems more natural for SA than labeled bisimualtions. Some works on comparing barbed congruence between labeled bisimulation based equivalence have also been studied. In [5], a labeled bisimulation was proved to coincide with contextual barbed congruence. In [6], the notions of late bisimulation and early bisimualtion were proved to be equivalent to contextual barbed congruence. In [11], the authors defined different formulations of barbs, and by following Honda and Yoshida's approach [3], the authors proved that these different formulations lead to the same contextual barbed congruence in the context of SA.

In this paper, we want to give another notion of reduction based semantics for mobile process, named indexed reduction equivalence/congruence. Like barbed equivalence/congruence, indexed reduction equivalence/congruence is also suitable for several famous calculi such as π-calculus, higher order π-calculus and SA. The new notion improves barbed equivalence/congruence in several aspects:

First, indexed reduction equivalence coincides with early bisimulation for π-calculi with or without match prefix. On the contrary, in [10], a counterexample shows that in the case of π-calculus without match prefix, weak barbed equivalence does not coincide with weak early bisimulation.

Second, for SA if we take into account the interactions inside of nested ambients, the contextual barbed congruence seems extremely coarse: only top-level free ambients can be observed, but the weakness of this approach is that the contents of an ambient may not be observed because of the lack of co-capabilities inside it. On the contrary, indexed reduction congruence can keep track about what happens internally in an ambient by using the indices, which allows us to distinguish some processes which are viewed to be equivalent with respect to contextual barbed congruence. To see the difference between them for SA, let us consider the two following SA processes: $m[\overline{in}\ m.p[\overline{in}\ p.0]]$ and $m[\overline{in}\ m.q[\overline{in}\ q.0]]$. Intuitively, $m[\overline{in}\ m.p[\overline{in}\ p.0]]$ is different from $m[\overline{in}\ m.q[\overline{in}\ q.0]]$ if we care the interactions inside of nested ambients, because testing process $n[in\ m.in\ p.0]$ can enter ambients m and p of the first process, but can only enter ambient m of the second one. However, from the view of contextual barbed congruence the two processes are equivalent (See Lemma 2). On the other hand, we prove that indexed reduction congruence can distinguish these two processes, so indexed reduction congruence is finer than contextual barbed congruence.

Third, for π-calculus and higher order π-calculus, the meaning of 'barb' is 'channel'; but for SA, the meaning of 'barb' is 'ambient'. Hence the intuitive meaning of barbed equivalence/congruence is actually changed in different calculi. Whereas in the definition of indexed reduction equivalence/congruence, the concept of index, which can be viewed as the name or location of components, is uniform for various calculi.

This paper is organized as follows: In Section 2 we introduce the corresponding syntax and labeled transition system for indexed π-calculus and present the notion of indexed reduction equivalence. We prove that the indexed reduction equivalence coincides with early bisimulation for π-calculus. In Section 3 we present indexed higher order π-calculus and its indexed reduction equivalence. We prove that indexed reduction equivalence is equivalent to context bisimulation for higher order π-calculus. In Section 4, we introduce the syntax and reduction system of the "indexed version" of SA, and present the notion of indexed reduction congruence for SA. At last, we prove that indexed reduction congruence is strictly finer than contextual barbed congruence for SA. The paper is concluded in Section 5.

2 π-Calculus

In this section, a new notion called "indexed reduction equivalence" for π-calculus is presented, and the equivalence between indexed reduction equivalence and early bisimulation is proved. We first briefly review π-calculus.

2.1   Syntax and Labeled Transition System of π-Calculus

We use $a, b, c,..., x, y, z,...$ to range over the class of names. The class Pr_π of the π-calculus processes is built up using the operators of prefixing, sum, parallel composition, restriction and replication in the grammar below:

$$P ::= 0 \mid x(y).P \mid \overline{x}\langle y\rangle.P \mid \tau.P \mid P_1 + P_2 \mid P_1|P_2 \mid (\nu x)P \mid !P$$

The actions are given by

$$\alpha ::= x\langle y\rangle \mid \overline{x}\langle y\rangle \mid (\nu y)\overline{x}\langle y\rangle \mid \tau$$

We write bn(α) for the set of names bound in α, which is y if α is $(\nu y)\overline{x}\langle y\rangle$ and $\oslash$ otherwise. n(α) denotes the set of names of α.

In each process of the form $(\nu y)P$ or $x(y).P$ the occurrence of y is a bound within the scope of P. An occurrence of y in a process is said to be free iff it does not lie within the scope of a bound occurrence of y. The set of names occurring free in P is denoted fn(P). An occurrence of a name in a process is said to be bound if it is not free, we write the set of bound names as bn(P). Process P and Q are α-convertible, $P \equiv_\alpha Q$, if Q can be obtained from P by a finite number of changes of bound names.

The operational semantics of π-calculus is presented in Table 1. We have omitted the symmetric versions of the rules of summation, parallelism and communication.

Table 1.

$$ALP: \frac{P \xrightarrow{\alpha} P'}{Q \xrightarrow{\alpha} Q'} P \equiv_\alpha Q, P' \equiv_\alpha Q' \qquad TAU: \tau.P \xrightarrow{\tau} P$$

$$OUT: \overline{x}\langle y\rangle.P \xrightarrow{\overline{x}\langle y\rangle} P \qquad IN: x(y).P \xrightarrow{x\langle z\rangle} P\{z/y\}$$

$$SUM: \frac{P \xrightarrow{\alpha} P'}{P+Q \xrightarrow{\alpha} P'} \qquad PAR: \frac{P \xrightarrow{\alpha} P'}{P|Q \xrightarrow{\alpha} P'|Q} bn(\alpha) \cap fn(Q) = \varnothing$$

$$COM1: \frac{P \xrightarrow{\overline{x}\langle y\rangle} P' \quad Q \xrightarrow{x\langle y\rangle} Q'}{P|Q \xrightarrow{\tau} P'|Q'}$$

$$COM2: \frac{P \xrightarrow{(\nu y)\overline{x}\langle y\rangle} P' \quad Q \xrightarrow{x\langle y\rangle} Q'}{P|Q \xrightarrow{\tau} (\nu y)(P'|Q')} y \notin fn(Q)$$

$$RES: \frac{P \xrightarrow{\alpha} P'}{(\nu x)P \xrightarrow{\alpha} (\nu x)P'} x \notin n(\alpha) \qquad OPEN: \frac{P \xrightarrow{\overline{x}\langle y\rangle} P'}{(\nu y)P \xrightarrow{(\nu y)\overline{x}\langle y\rangle} P'} x \neq y$$

$$REP: \frac{P|!P \xrightarrow{\alpha} P'}{!P \xrightarrow{\alpha} P'}$$

2.2 Syntax and Labeled Transition System of Indexed π-Calculus

This paper presents a uniform behaviour equivalence for π-calculus, higher order π-calculus and Safe Mobile Ambients, based on indexed labeled transition systems. Indices are added to the labels of the transition system. Those indices are used in the indexed reduction bisimulation, equivalence and congruence to identify between which components (tested process, testing processes) a transition takes place.

In order to give indexed reduction equivalence, we first introduce the notion of indexed process. Given an index set I, w.l.o.g., let I be the set of natural numbers, the class of the first order indexed processes IPr_π is built similar to Pr_π, expect that every prefix is assigned to an index:

$$M ::= 0 \mid \{x(y)\}_i.M \mid \{\overline{x}\langle y\rangle\}_i.M \mid \{\tau\}_i.M \mid M_1 + M_2 \mid M_1|M_2 \mid (\nu x)M \mid !M,$$

here $i \in I$.

In the following, we need the notation $\{P\}_i$ which denotes indexed process with the same index i on every prefix in its scope. The formal definition can be given inductively as follows:

$$\{0\}_i ::= 0; \quad \{x(y).P\}_i ::= \{x(y)\}_i.\{P\}_i; \quad \{\overline{x}\langle y\rangle.P\}_i ::= \{\overline{x}\langle y\rangle\}_i.\{P\}_i;$$
$$\{\tau.P\}_i ::= \{\tau\}_i.\{P\}_i; \quad \{P_1 + P_2\}_i ::= \{P_1\}_i + \{P_2\}_i; \quad \{P_1|P_2\}_i ::= \{P_1\}_i|\{P_2\}_i;$$
$$\{(\nu x)P\}_i ::= (\nu x)\{P\}_i; \quad \{!P\}_i ::= !\{P\}_i.$$

Intuitively, the index set I can be viewed as set of names of components or set of locations, then correspondingly, $\{P\}_i$ denotes a process P whose name is i or a process P located at i.

The indexed actions are given by

$$I\alpha ::= \{x\langle y\rangle\}_i \mid \{\overline{x}\langle y\rangle\}_i \mid \{(\nu y)\overline{x}\langle y\rangle\}_i \mid \{\tau\}_{i,j}$$

Similar to Table 1, we give the operational semantics of indexed processes in Table 2. The main difference between Table 1 and Table 2 is that the label $I\alpha$ on the transition arrow is of the form $\{\alpha\}_i$ or $\{\tau\}_{i,j}$, here α is an input or output action, i and j are indices. If we adopt the distributed view, $\{\alpha\}_i$ can be regarded as an input or output action performed by component i, and $\{\tau\}_{i,j}$ can be regarded as a communication between components i and j. In the following, we view $\{\alpha\}_i$ as a distributed input or output action, and $\{\tau\}_{i,j}$ a distributed communication.

Table 2.

$$ALP : \frac{M \xrightarrow{I\alpha} M'}{N \xrightarrow{I\alpha} N'} M \equiv_\alpha N, M' \equiv_\alpha N' \qquad TAU : \{\tau\}_i.M \xrightarrow{\{\tau\}_{i,i}} M$$

$$OUT : \{\overline{x}\langle y\rangle\}_i.M \xrightarrow{\{\overline{x}\langle y\rangle\}_i} M \qquad IN : \{x(y)\}_i.M \xrightarrow{\{x\langle z\rangle\}_i} M\{z/y\}$$

$$SUM : \frac{M \xrightarrow{I\alpha} M'}{M + N \xrightarrow{I\alpha} M'} \qquad PAR : \frac{M \xrightarrow{I\alpha} M'}{M|N \xrightarrow{I\alpha} M'|N} bn(I\alpha) \cap fn(N) = \varnothing$$

$$COM1 : \frac{M \xrightarrow{\{\overline{x}\langle y\rangle\}_i} M' \quad N \xrightarrow{\{x\langle y\rangle\}_j} N'}{M|N \xrightarrow{\{\tau\}_{i,j}} M'|N'}$$

$$COM2 : \frac{M \xrightarrow{\{(\nu y)\overline{x}\langle y\rangle\}_i} M' \quad N \xrightarrow{\{x\langle y\rangle\}_j} N'}{M|N \xrightarrow{\{\tau\}_{i,j}} (\nu y)(M'|N')} y \notin fn(N)$$

$$RES : \frac{M \xrightarrow{I\alpha} M'}{(\nu x)M \xrightarrow{I\alpha} (\nu x)M'} x \notin n(I\alpha) \qquad OPEN : \frac{M \xrightarrow{\{\overline{x}\langle y\rangle\}_i} M'}{(\nu y)M \xrightarrow{\{(\nu y)\overline{x}\langle y\rangle\}_i} M'} x \neq y$$

$$REP : \frac{M|!M \xrightarrow{I\alpha} M'}{!M \xrightarrow{I\alpha} M'}$$

Remark. Since $\{\tau\}_{i,j}$ and $\{\tau\}_{j,i}$ have the same meaning: a communication between components i and j, hence in the above transition system, $\{\tau\}_{i,j}$ and $\{\tau\}_{j,i}$ are considered as the same label, i.e., $M \xrightarrow{\{\tau\}_{i,j}} M'$ is viewed to be same as $M \xrightarrow{\{\tau\}_{j,i}} M'$.

2.3   Indexed Reduction Equivalence for π-Calculus

In the following, we propose a new uniform framework to define equivalence on processes, based on the move of messages among indexed processes rather than observables such as barbs.

Definition 1. Strong indexed reduction bisimulation

Let $K, L \in IPr_\pi$, we write $K \sim^i_{red} L$, if there is a symmetric relation R, s.t. whenever $K R L$ then for any indexed process M, $K|M \xrightarrow{\{\tau\}_{i,j}} K'$ implies $L|M \xrightarrow{\{\tau\}_{i,j}} L'$ for some L' with $K' R L'$.

Definition 2. Strong indexed reduction equivalence

Let P, $Q \in Pr_\pi$, we write $P \sim_{red} Q$ if $\{P\}_l \sim_{red}^i \{Q\}_l$ for some index l.

From a distributed view, P and Q are said to be strong indexed reduction equivalent if we locate P and Q at location l, then any distributed communication $\{\tau\}_{i,j}$ between $\{P\}_l$ and indexed testing process M can be matched by the same distributed communication $\{\tau\}_{i,j}$ between $\{Q\}_l$ and M, where $\{\tau\}_{i,j}$ denotes the communication between locations i and j.

Before giving the weak indexed reduction equivalence, let us compare communication $\{\tau\}_{i,i}$ with $\{\tau\}_{i,j}$ firstly. In [1], a distributed variant of CCS is proposed, where the τ-transitions are considered, as usual, to be invisible. Hence this view takes $\{\tau\}_{i,i}$ and $\{\tau\}_{i,j}$ as the same. For weak indexed reduction equivalence, we adopt another view where $\{\tau\}_{i,i}$ is regarded as different from $\{\tau\}_{i,j}$, since for an observer who can distinguish between sites, $\{\tau\}_{i,i}$ is an internal communication at location i, and $\{\tau\}_{i,j}$ represents external communication between two different locations i and j. In other words, we regard $\{\tau\}_{i,i}$ as a private event at location i, and $\{\tau\}_{i,j}$ as a visible event between locations i and j.

Now we give the weak indexed reduction equivalence which neglect $\{\tau\}_{i,i}$ since from a distributed view $\{\tau\}_{i,i}$ happens internally in location i.

Definition 3. Weak indexed reduction bisimulation

Let K, $L \in IPr_\pi$, we write $K \approx_{red}^i L$, if there is a symmetric relation R, s.t. whenever K R L then for any indexed process M, (1) $K|M \xrightarrow{\{\tau\}_{i,i}} *K'$ implies $L|M \xrightarrow{\{\tau\}_{i,i}} *L'$ for some L' with K' R L', here $\xrightarrow{\{\tau\}_{i,i}} *$ is the reflexive and transitive closure of $\xrightarrow{\{\tau\}_{i,i}}$; (2) $K|M \xrightarrow{\{\tau\}_{i,j}} K'$, here $i \neq j$, implies $L|M \xrightarrow{\{\tau\}_{i,j}} L'$ for some L' with K' R L'.

Definition 4. Weak indexed reduction equivalence

Let P, $Q \in Pr_\pi$, we write $P \approx_{red} Q$ if $\{P\}_l \approx_{red}^i \{Q\}_l$ for some index l.

2.4   Indexed Reduction Equivalence Coincides with Early Bisimulation

In this section, we study the relation between indexed reduction equivalence and early bisimulation. For the sake of space, we only discuss the case of weak bisimulation, and the same proposition holds for strong bisimulation.

We first review the definition of weak early bisimulation.

Definition 5. A symmetric relation $R \in Pr_\pi \times Pr_\pi$ is a weak early bisimulation if whenever P R Q, (1) $P \xrightarrow{\tau} *P'$ implies there exists Q' s.t. $Q \xrightarrow{\tau} *Q'$ and P' R Q'; here $\xrightarrow{\tau} *$ is the reflexive and transitive closure of $\xrightarrow{\tau}$; (2) $P \xrightarrow{\alpha} P'$ with $bn(\alpha) \cap fn(P,Q) = \oslash$ and $\alpha \neq \tau$ implies there exists Q' s.t. $Q \xrightarrow{\alpha} Q'$ and P' R Q'.

We write $P \approx_e Q$ if P and Q are weak early bisimilar.

Now we can give the equivalence between weak early bisimulation and weak indexed reduction equivalence as follows:

Proposition 1. For any P, $Q \in Pr_\pi$, $P \approx_e Q \Leftrightarrow P \approx_{red} Q$.

Proof. See Appendix A.

Remark. For the π-calculus obtained by omitting the match prefixes, weak early bisimulation is not equivalent to weak barbed equivalence, an example was given in [10, page 102, Exercise 2.4.30] as follows:

Let $P = \overline{a}\langle x \rangle | E_{x,y}$, $Q = \overline{a}\langle y \rangle | E_{x,y}$, here $E_{x,y} =!x(z).\overline{y}\langle z \rangle | !y(z).\overline{x}\langle z \rangle$, then $\neg(P \approx_e Q)$ but for each context C of the π-calculus without the match prefixes, $C[P]$ and $C[Q]$ are weak barbed bisimilar.

Since Proposition 1 holds, this example indicates that weak indexed reduction equivalence is different from weak barbed equivalence for π-calculus without match prefixes. In fact, Proposition 1 can be extended to π-calculus with match prefixes. Because of space limitation, we do not give the detailed proofs.

3   Higher Order π-Calculus

In this section, we first review the syntax and labeled transition system of the higher order π-calculus, then extend it by introducing the notion of "index". The definitions and propositions in the following are parallel with the case of π-calculus.

3.1   Syntax and Labeled Transition System of Higher Order π-Calculus

In this section we briefly recall the syntax and labeled transition system of the higher order π-calculus. We only focus on a second-order fragment of the higher order π-calculus [9], i.e. there is no abstraction in this fragment.

We assume a set N of names, ranged over by $x, y, z,...$ and a set Var of process variables, ranged over by $X, Y, Z, U, ...$ We use $E, F, P, Q,...$ to stand for processes. The class of processes is denoted as Pr_{HO}.

The grammar for the higher order π-calculus processes are given by

$$P ::= 0 \mid U \mid x(U).P \mid \overline{x}\langle Q \rangle.P \mid \tau.P \mid P_1|P_2 \mid (\nu x)P \mid !P$$

A restriction $(\nu x)P$ binds the free occurrences of x in P. Higher order input prefix $x(U).P$ binds all free occurrences of U in P. The set of names occurring free in P is denoted as $\mathrm{fn}(P)$. Alpha conversion relates expressions which are syntactically identical modulo renaming of bound names and bound variables. A process is closed if it has no free variable. Pr_{HO}^c is the set of all closed processes. We write $\mathrm{bn}(\alpha)$ for the set of names bound in action α, which is $\{\widetilde{y}\}$ if α is $(\nu\widetilde{y})\overline{x}\langle E \rangle$ and $\oslash$ otherwise. $\mathrm{n}(\alpha)$ denotes the set of names that occur in α.

The operational semantics of higher order process is given in Table 3.

3.2   Syntax and Labeled Transition System of Indexed Higher Order π-Calculus

We firstly introduce the concept of indexed process. Given an index set I, w.l.o.g., let I be the set of natural numbers, the class of the indexed processes IPr_{HO} is built similar to Pr_{HO}, except that every prefix is assigned to an index. We usually use K, L, M, N to denote indexed processes.

Table 3.

$$ALP: \frac{P \xrightarrow{\alpha} P'}{Q \xrightarrow{\alpha} Q'} P \equiv_\alpha Q, P' \equiv_\alpha Q' \qquad TAU: \tau.P \xrightarrow{\tau} P$$

$$OUT: \overline{x}\langle E\rangle.P \xrightarrow{\overline{x}\langle E\rangle} P \qquad IN: x(U).P \xrightarrow{x\langle E\rangle} P\{E/U\}$$

$$PAR: \frac{P \xrightarrow{\alpha} P'}{P|Q \xrightarrow{\alpha} P'|Q} bn(\alpha) \cap fn(Q) = \emptyset$$

$$COM: \frac{P \xrightarrow{(\nu \widetilde{y})\overline{x}\langle E\rangle} P' \quad Q \xrightarrow{x\langle E\rangle} Q'}{P|Q \xrightarrow{\tau} (\nu\widetilde{y})(P'|Q')} \widetilde{y} \cap fn(Q) = \emptyset$$

$$RES: \frac{P \xrightarrow{\alpha} P'}{(\nu x)P \xrightarrow{\alpha} (\nu x)P'} x \notin n(\alpha) \qquad REP: \frac{P|!P \xrightarrow{\alpha} P'}{!P \xrightarrow{\alpha} P'}$$

$$OPEN: \frac{P \xrightarrow{(\nu \widetilde{z})\overline{x}\langle E\rangle} P'}{(\nu y)P \xrightarrow{(\nu y,\widetilde{z})\overline{x}\langle E\rangle} P'} x \neq y, y \in fn(E) - \widetilde{z}$$

The formal definition of indexed process is given as follows:

$M ::= 0 \mid U \mid \{x(U)\}_i.M \mid \{\overline{x}\langle K\rangle\}_i.M \mid \{\tau\}_i.M \mid M_1|M_2 \mid (\nu x)M \mid !M$, here $i \in$ index set I and K is an indexed process.

In each process of the form $(\nu x)M$ the occurrence of x is a bound within the scope of M. An occurrence of x in a process is said to be free iff it does not lie within the scope of a bound occurrence of x. The set of names occurring free in M is denoted as fn(M), and the set of bound names is denoted as bn(M). Indexed input prefix $\{x(U)\}_i.M$ binds all free occurrences of U in M. An indexed process is closed if it has no free variable. IPr^c_{HO} is the set of all closed indexed processes. Process M and N are α-convertible, $M \equiv_\alpha N$, if N can be obtained from M by a finite number of changes of bound names and bound variables.

We use $\{P\}_i$ to denote indexed process with the same given index i on every prefix in its scope. The formal definition can be given inductively as follows:

$\{0\}_i ::= 0; \quad \{U\}_i ::= U; \quad \{\tau.P\}_i ::= \{\tau\}_i.\{P\}_i; \quad \{x(U).P\}_i ::= \{x(U)\}_i.\{P\}_i;$
$\{\overline{x}\langle E\rangle.P\}_i ::= \{\overline{x}\langle\{E\}_i\rangle\}_i.\{P\}_i; \quad \{P_1|P_2\}_i ::= \{P_1\}_i|\{P_2\}_i; \quad \{!P\}_i ::=!\{P\}_i;$
$\{(\nu x)P\}_i ::= (\nu x)\{P\}_i.$

The indexed actions are given by

$I\alpha ::= \{x\langle K\rangle\}_i \mid \{\overline{x}\langle K\rangle\}_i \mid \{(\nu\widetilde{y})\overline{x}\langle K\rangle\}_i \mid \{\tau\}_{i,j}$

We write bn($I\alpha$) for the set of names bound in $I\alpha$, which is $\{\widetilde{y}\}$ if $I\alpha$ is $\{(\nu\widetilde{y})\overline{x}\langle K\rangle\}_i$ and $\oslash$ otherwise. n($I\alpha$) denotes the set of names that occur in $I\alpha$. The operational semantics of indexed processes is given in Table 4.

3.3   Indexed Reduction Equivalence for Higher Order π-Calculus

The definition of strong and weak indexed reduction equivalence for higher order π-calculus is same as Definition 1-4 in the case of π-calculus. For the limitation of space, we only discuss weak bisimulation and equivalence.

Table 4.

$$ALP : \frac{M \xrightarrow{I\alpha} M'}{N \xrightarrow{I\alpha} N'} M \equiv_\alpha N, M' \equiv_\alpha N' \qquad TAU : \{\tau\}_i.M \xrightarrow{\{\tau\}_{i,i}} M$$

$$OUT : \{\overline{x}\langle K\rangle\}_i.M \xrightarrow{\{\overline{x}\langle K\rangle\}_i} M \qquad IN : \{x(U)\}_i.M \xrightarrow{\{x\langle K\rangle\}_i} M\{K/U\}$$

$$PAR : \frac{M \xrightarrow{I\alpha} M'}{M|N \xrightarrow{I\alpha} M'|N} bn(I\alpha) \cap fn(N) = \emptyset$$

$$COM : \frac{M \xrightarrow{\{(\nu\widetilde{y})\overline{x}\langle K\rangle\}_i} M' \quad N \xrightarrow{\{x\langle K\rangle\}_j} N'}{M|N \xrightarrow{\{\tau\}_{i,j}} (\nu\widetilde{y})(M'|N')} \widetilde{y} \cap fn(N) = \emptyset$$

$$RES : \frac{M \xrightarrow{I\alpha} M'}{(\nu x)M \xrightarrow{I\alpha} (\nu x)M'} x \notin n(I\alpha) \qquad REP : \frac{M|!M \xrightarrow{I\alpha} M'}{!M \xrightarrow{I\alpha} M'}$$

$$OPEN : \frac{M \xrightarrow{\{(\nu\widetilde{z})\overline{x}\langle K\rangle\}_i} M'}{(\nu y)M \xrightarrow{\{(\nu\widetilde{y,z})\overline{x}\langle K\rangle\}_i} M'} x \neq y, y \in fn(K) - \widetilde{z}$$

Definition 6. Weak indexed reduction bisimulation

Let K, $L \in IPr_{HO}^c$, we write $K \approx_{red}^i L$, if there is a symmetric relation R, s.t. whenever $K \, R \, L$ then for any indexed process M, (1) $K|M \xrightarrow{\{\tau\}_{i,i}} *K'$ implies $L|M \xrightarrow{\{\tau\}_{i,i}} *L'$ for some L' with $K' \, R \, L'$; (2) $K|M \xrightarrow{\{\tau\}_{i,j}} K'$, here $i \neq j$, implies $L|M \xrightarrow{\{\tau\}_{i,j}} L'$ for some L' with $K' \, R \, L'$.

Definition 7. Weak indexed reduction equivalence

Let P, $Q \in Pr_{HO}^c$, we write $P \approx_{red} Q$ if $\{P\}_l \approx_{red}^i \{Q\}_l$ for some index l.

3.4   Indexed Reduction Equivalence Coincides with Context Bisimulation

In this section we give the equivalence between context bisimulation and indexed reduction equivalence for higher order π-calculus. We first review the definition of context bisimulation.

Definition 8. A symmetric relation R is a weak context bisimulation if $P \, R \, Q$ implies: (1) whenever $P \xrightarrow{\tau} *P'$, then there exists Q' such that $Q \xrightarrow{\tau} *Q'$ and $P' \, R \, Q'$; (2) whenever $P \xrightarrow{x\langle E\rangle} P'$, there exists Q' s.t. $Q \xrightarrow{x\langle E\rangle} Q'$ and $P' \, R \, Q'$; (3) whenever $P \xrightarrow{(\nu\widetilde{b})x\langle E\rangle} P'$, there exist Q', F, $\widetilde{c}$, s.t. $Q \xrightarrow{(\nu\widetilde{c})x\langle F\rangle} Q'$ and for all $C(U)$ with $fn(C(U)) \cap \{\widetilde{b}, \widetilde{c}\} = \emptyset$, $(\nu\widetilde{b})(P'|C\langle E\rangle) \, R \, (\nu\widetilde{c})(Q'|C\langle F\rangle)$.

We write $P \approx_{ct} Q$ if P and Q are weak context bisimilar.

The following proposition shows that weak indexed reduction equivalence coincides with weak context bisimulation.

Proposition 2. For any P, $Q \in Pr_{HO}^c$, $P \approx_{ct} Q \Leftrightarrow P \approx_{red} Q$.

The proof of this proposition includes two steps: firstly an indexed version of context bisimulation is proved to be equivalent to indexed reduction equivalence;

secondly, the equivalence between this indexed version of context bisimulation and the original context bisimulation is proved. For the limitation of space, we do not give the detail proof.

4   Safe Mobile Ambients

For π-calculus, we have proved that the indexed reduction equivalence coincides with the early bisimulation. For higher order π-calculus, the equivalence between context bisimulation and indexed reduction equivalence is proved. But things are different for the Safe Mobile Ambients. For this formalism, the indexed reduction congruence is strictly finer than the contextual barbed congruence.

4.1   Syntax and Reduction System of Safe Mobile Ambients

The class Pr_{SA} of the safe ambients is built using the operators of prefixing, parallel composition, ambient, restriction and recursion in the grammar below:
$P ::= 0 \mid \alpha.P \mid P_1|P_2 \mid n[P] \mid (\nu n)P \mid X \mid recX.P$, here $n \in$ set N of names, $X \in$ set Var of process variables.

α is called capability and of one of the following forms:

$\alpha ::= in\ n \mid \overline{in}\ n \mid out\ n \mid \overline{out}\ n \mid open\ n \mid \overline{open}\ n$

Recursive operator $recX.P$ binds all free occurrences of X in P. A process is closed if it has no free variable; it is open if it may have free variables. Pr_{SA}^c is the set of all closed processes.

A context is a term with a hole $[]$ in it:
$C ::= [] \mid \alpha.C \mid C|P \mid P|C \mid n[C] \mid (\nu n)C \mid recX.C$
The operational semantics of Safe Mobile Ambients is reported in Table 5.

Table 5.

$$STRUC : \frac{P \longrightarrow P'}{Q \longrightarrow Q'} P \equiv Q, P' \equiv Q'$$

$$IN : n[in\ m.P_1|P_2]|m[\overline{in}\ m.Q_1|Q_2] \longrightarrow m[n[P_1|P_2]|Q_1|Q_2]$$

$$OUT : m[n[out\ m.P_1|P_2]|\overline{out}\ m.Q_1|Q_2] \longrightarrow n[P_1|P_2]|m[Q_1|Q_2]$$

$$OPEN : open\ n.P|n[\overline{open}\ n.Q_1|Q_2] \longrightarrow P|Q_1|Q_2$$

$$PAR : \frac{P \longrightarrow P'}{P|Q \longrightarrow P'|Q} \qquad RES : \frac{P \longrightarrow P'}{(\nu n)P \longrightarrow (\nu n)P'}$$

$$AMB : \frac{P \longrightarrow P'}{n[P] \longrightarrow n[P']} \qquad REC : \frac{P\{recX.P/X\} \longrightarrow P'}{recX.P \longrightarrow P'}$$

Structural congruence is a congruence relation including the following rules:

$P|Q \equiv Q|P;\ (P|Q)|R \equiv P|(Q|R);\ P|0 \equiv P;\ (\nu n)0 \equiv 0;\ (\nu m)(\nu n)P \equiv (\nu n)(\nu m)P;\ (\nu n)(P|Q) \equiv P|(\nu n)Q$ if $n \notin fn(P);\ (\nu n)(m[P]) \equiv m[(\nu n)P]$ if $n \neq m$.

4.2   Syntax and Reduction System of Indexed Safe Mobile Ambients

The class IPr_{SA} of the indexed processes is built similar to Pr_{SA}, expect that an index is assigned to every prefix:

$$M ::= 0 \mid I\alpha.M \mid M_1|M_2 \mid n[M] \mid (\nu n)M \mid X \mid recX.M, \text{ here } n \in N, \ X \in Var.$$

$I\alpha$ is called indexed capability and is one of the following forms.

$$I\alpha ::= \{in\ n\}_i \mid \{\overline{in}\ n\}_i \mid \{out\ n\}_i \mid \{\overline{out}\ n\}_i \mid \{open\ n\}_i \mid \{\overline{open}\ n\}_i, \text{ here}$$
$i \in$ set I of indices.

Operator $recX.M$ binds all free occurrences of X in M. An indexed process is closed if it has no free variable. IPr_{SA}^c is the set of all closed indexed processes.

We need the notation $\{P\}_i$ which denotes indexed process with the same index i on every capability in its scope. The formal definition is given inductively as follows:

$$\{0\}_i ::= 0; \ \{\alpha.P\}_i ::= \{\alpha\}_i.\{P\}_i; \ \{P_1|P_2\}_i ::= \{P_1\}_i|\{P_2\}_i; \ \{n[P]\}_i ::=$$
$n[\{P\}_i]; \ \{(\nu n)P\}_i ::= (\nu n)\{P\}_i; \ \{recX.P\}_i ::= recX.\{P\}_i.$

The formal definition of indexed context is given below:

$$C ::= [] \mid I\alpha.C \mid C|M \mid M|C \mid n[C] \mid (\nu n)C \mid recX.C$$

The operational semantics of indexed processes is given in Table 6.

Table 6.

$$STRUC : \frac{M \xrightarrow{i,j} M'}{N \xrightarrow{i,j} N'} M \equiv N, M' \equiv N'$$

$$IN : n[\{in\ m\}_i.M_1|M_2]|m[\{\overline{in}\ m\}_j.N_1|N_2] \xrightarrow{i,j} m[n[M_1|M_2]|N_1|N_2]$$

$$OUT : m[n[\{out\ m\}_i.M_1|M_2]|\{\overline{out}\ m\}_j.N_1|N_2] \xrightarrow{i,j} n[M_1|M_2]|m[N_1|N_2]$$

$$OPEN : \{open\ n\}_i.M|n[\{\overline{open}\ n\}_j.N_1|N_2] \xrightarrow{i,j} M|N_1|N_2$$

$$PAR : \frac{M \xrightarrow{i,j} M'}{M|N \xrightarrow{i,j} M'|N} \qquad RES : \frac{M \xrightarrow{i,j} M'}{(\nu n)M \xrightarrow{i,j} (\nu n)M'}$$

$$AMB : \frac{M \xrightarrow{i,j} M'}{n[M] \xrightarrow{i,j} n[M']} \qquad REC : \frac{M\{recX.M/X\} \xrightarrow{i,j} M'}{recX.M \xrightarrow{i,j} M'}$$

Remark. Similar to the case of π-calculus, $M \xrightarrow{i,j} M'$ is viewed to be same as $M \xrightarrow{j,i} M'$.

Structural congruence for indexed processes is similar to the one for original Safe Mobile Ambients, and we do not give the formal definition here.

Example: For indexed process $\{p[\overline{in}\ p.P]\}_0|\{q[in\ p.Q]\}_1$, indices 0 and 1 can be viewed as names of components $p[in\ p.P]$ and $q[in\ p.Q]$ respectively and

$\{p[\overline{in}\ p.P]\}_0|\{q[in\ p.Q]\}_1 \xrightarrow{0,1} p[q[\{Q\}_1]|\{P\}_0]$ represents the reduction between components 0 and 1.

4.3   Indexed Reduction Congruence for Safe Mobile Ambients

In fact, the contextual barbed congruence is considered appropriate if we do not have to care about what happens inside of nested ambients. But when we take into account the interactions inside of nested ambients, contextual barbed congruence seems too coarse. In this section, we give the concept of indexed reduction congruence for SA and show that this equivalence can distinguish processes which have different behaviours inside of nested ambients but are considered to be same with respect to contextual barbed congruence.

Let us first review the definition of contextual barbed congruence for SA in [5, 11]:

Definition 9. Contextual barbed congruence
A symmetric relation $R \subseteq Pr_{SA}^c \times Pr_{SA}^c$ is a contextual barbed bisimulation if whenever $P\ R\ Q$ then for any context C:

(1) Whenever $C[P] \longrightarrow^* P'$ then $C[Q] \longrightarrow^* Q'$ and $P'\ R\ Q'$, here $\longrightarrow^*$ is the reflexive and transitive closure of $\longrightarrow$;
(2) For each ambient n, if $C[P] \Downarrow n$, then also $C[Q] \Downarrow n$. Here $P \Downarrow n$ means $\exists P',\ P \longrightarrow^* P',\ P' \equiv (\nu\widetilde{m})(n[\mu.Q_1|Q_2]|Q_3)$ where $\mu \in \{\overline{in}\ n, \overline{open}\ n\}$ and $n \notin \widetilde{m}$.

Two closed processes P and Q are contextual barbed congruent, written as $P \approx_{sa} Q$, if there is a contextual barbed bisimulation R, $P\ R\ Q$.

A difference between π-calculus and Safe Mobile Ambients is that if a testing process interact with a π-calculus process, the interaction must happen at the top-level of process, whereas for Safe Mobile Ambients, the interaction may happen between the inner processes that are located in nested ambients. Therefore in the case of π-calculus, barbed testing reflect the interaction capability of process with context, but for Safe Mobile Ambients, barbed testing is not enough if we care the behaviour of testing process inside of nested ambients. On the contrary, by using indices, indexed reduction congruence can provide more information about what happens internally in ambients.

Definition 10. Weak indexed reduction bisimulation
Let $K,\ L \in IPr_{SA}^c$, we write $K \approx_{red}^i L$, if there is a symmetric relation R, s.t. whenever $K\ R\ L$ then for any indexed context M, (1) $M[K] \xrightarrow{i,i}^* K'$ implies $M[L] \xrightarrow{i,i}^* L'$ for some L' with $K'\ R\ L'$; (2) $M[K] \xrightarrow{i,j} K'$, here $i \neq j$, implies $M[L] \xrightarrow{i,j} L'$ for some L' with $K'\ R\ L'$.

Definition 11. Weak indexed reduction congruence
Let $P,\ Q \in Pr_{SA}^c$, we write $P \approx_{red} Q$ if $\{P\}_l \approx_{red}^i \{Q\}_l$ for some index l.

4.4 Comparison Between Indexed Reduction Congruence and Contextual Barbed Congruence

Now we show that indexed reduction congruence is strictly finer than contextual barbed congruence for SA.

Proposition 3. For any $P, Q \in Pr_{SA}^c$, $P \approx_{red} Q \Rightarrow P \approx_{sa} Q$.

Proof. See Appendix B.

To show that the inverse proposition does not hold, let us see two processes: $m[\overline{in}\ m.p[\overline{in}\ p.0]]$ and $m[\overline{in}\ m.q[\overline{in}\ q.0]]$.

Lemma 1. $\neg(m[\overline{in}\ m.p[\overline{in}\ p.0]] \approx_{red} m[\overline{in}\ m.q[\overline{in}\ q.0]])$.

Proof. Let indexed context $M[] = n[\{in\ m\}_1.\{in\ p\}_2.0]|[]$, then it is clear that $M[m[\{\overline{in}\ m\}_0.p[\{\overline{in}\ p\}_0.0]]] \xrightarrow{0,1} \xrightarrow{0,2} m[p[n[0]]]$, and $M[m[\{\overline{in}\ m\}_0.\ q[\{\overline{in}q\}_0.0]]] \xrightarrow{0,1} m[q[\{\overline{in}\ q\}_0.0]|n[\{in\ p\}_2.0]]$, but $m[q[\{\overline{in}\ q\}_0.0]|n[\{in\ p\}_2]]$ can not perform reduction $\xrightarrow{0,2}$.

On the contrary, from the view of contextual barbed congruence, these two processes are equivalent.

Lemma 2. $m[\overline{in}\ m.p[\overline{in}\ p.0]] \approx_{sa} m[\overline{in}\ m.q[\overline{in}\ q.0]]$.

Proof. See Appendix C.

The key point in proof of Lemma 2 is that after cooperating with capability $in\ m$ of context $E[]$, $m[\overline{in}\ m.p[\overline{in}\ p.0]]$ and $m[\overline{in}\ m.q[\overline{in}\ q.0]]$ reduce to $F[m[n[S]|p[\overline{in}\ p.0]]]$ and $F[m[n[S]|q[\overline{in}\ q.0]]]$ respectively. Since there is no capability $\overline{open}\ m$, $\overline{in}\ m$ or $\overline{out}\ m$ in ambient m, we have $F[m[n[S]|p[\overline{in}\ p.0]]] \Downarrow k$ iff $F[m[n[S]|q[\overline{in}\ q.0]]] \Downarrow k$ for any ambient k. Hence $m[\overline{in}\ m.p[\overline{in}\ p.0]] \approx_{sa} m[\overline{in}\ m.\ q[\overline{in}\ q.0]]$.

From the above Lemma 1 and 2, we have:

Proposition 4. For some $P, Q \in Pr_{SA}^c$, $P \approx_{sa} Q$ does not imply $P \approx_{red} Q$.

5 Conclusions

In this paper, a notion of bisimulation equivalence called "indexed reduction equivalence/congruence" is presented, in terms of "indexed contexts" where components of a context can be given indices which represent "components" of communications. This approach is a unifying treatment of equivalences on process calculi. Its relationship with existing notions of equivalences on the π-calculus, higher order π-calculus and Safe Mobile Ambients are studied. Other "uniform" formulation is [3], which does not use barbs. Perhaps that is the only one which can be related to the present work as a uniform approach, though it is quite different, both in conception and in formal nature. The idea of indexed reduction equivalence/congruence can also be extended to other process calculi.

References

1. G. Boudol, I. Castellani, M. Hennessy and A. Kiehn. Observing localities, Theoretical Computer Science, 114: 31-61 1993.
2. L. Cardelli and A. D. Gordon. Mobile Ambients. Theoretical Computer Science, 240(1):177-213, 2000.
3. K. Honda and N. Yoshida. On reduction-based process semantics. Theoretical Computer Science, 152(2): 437-486 1995.
4. F. Levi and D. Sangiorgi. Controlling interference in Ambients. In Proc. POPL'00, pages 352–364, Boston, Massachusetts, Jan. 19-21, 2000.
5. M. Merro and M. Hennessy. Bisimulation congruences in Safe Ambients. Computer Science Report 5/01. An extended abstract appear in Proc. POPL'02.
6. M. Merro and F. Zappa Nardelli. Bisimulation proof methods for Mobile Ambients. Technical Report COGS 01:2003.
7. R. Milner, J. Parrow, and D. Walker. A calculus of mobile processes, (Part I and II). Information and Computation, 100:1-77, 1992.
8. D. Sangiorgi. Expressing mobility in process algebras: first-order and higher-order paradigms, Ph.D thesis, Department of Computer Science, University of Einburgh, 1992.
9. D. Sangiorgi. Bisimulation in higher-order calculi, Information and Computation, 131(2), 1996.
10. D. Sangiorgi, D. Walker. The π-calculus: a theory of mobile processes, Cambridge University Press, 2001.
11. M. G. Vigliotti and I. Phillips. Barbs and congruences for Safe Mobile Ambients. In: Foundations of Wide Area Network Computing, July 2002.

Appendix A. Proof of Proposition 1

Proposition 1. For any P, $Q \in Pr_\pi$, $P \approx_e Q \Leftrightarrow P \approx_{red} Q$.

Proof. $\Rightarrow$ It is easy.

$\Leftarrow$ Let $R = \{(P, Q) : \{P\}_0 \approx_{red}^i \{Q\}_0\}$.

Suppose $(P, Q) \in R$, we consider the following cases:

(1) $P \xrightarrow{\tau} {}^* P'$; (2) $P \xrightarrow{x\langle y\rangle} P'$; (3) $P \xrightarrow{\overline{x}\langle y\rangle} P'$; (4) $P \xrightarrow{(\nu y)\overline{x}\langle y\rangle} P'$.

Case (1): $P \xrightarrow{\tau} {}^* P'$. For indexed process $\{0\}_1$, we have $\{P\}_0 | \{0\}_1 \xrightarrow{\{\tau\}_{0,0}} {}^* \{P'\}_0 | \{0\}_1$. Since $\{P\}_0 \approx_{red}^i \{Q\}_0$, $\{Q\}_0 | \{0\}_1 \xrightarrow{\{\tau\}_{0,0}} {}^* \{Q'\}_0 | \{0\}_1$ and $\{P'\}_0 \approx_{red}^i \{P'\}_0 | \{0\}_1 \approx_{red}^i \{Q'\}_0 | \{0\}_1 \approx_{red}^i \{Q'\}_0$. Hence $Q \xrightarrow{\tau} {}^* Q'$ and $(P', Q') \in R$.

Case (2): $P \xrightarrow{x\langle y\rangle} P'$. Since $\{P\}_0 | \{\overline{x}\langle y\rangle.0\}_1 \xrightarrow{\{\tau\}_{0,1}} \{P'\}_0 | \{0\}_1$ and $\{P\}_0 \approx_{red}^i \{Q\}_0$, we have $\{Q\}_0 | \{\overline{x}\langle y\rangle.0\}_1 \xrightarrow{\{\tau\}_{0,1}} \{Q'\}_0 | \{0\}_1$ and $\{P'\}_0 \approx_{red}^i \{Q'\}_0$. By the construction of $\{\overline{x}\langle y\rangle.0\}_1$, we have $Q \xrightarrow{x\langle y\rangle} Q'$, and $(P', Q') \in R$.

Case (3): $P \xrightarrow{\overline{x}\langle y\rangle} P'$. Since $\{P\}_0 | \{x(w).\overline{w}\langle t\rangle.0\}_1 \xrightarrow{\{\tau\}_{0,1}} \{P'\}_0 | \{\overline{y}\langle t\rangle.0\}_1$, by the definition of $\approx_{red}^i$, we have $\{Q\}_0 | \{x(w).\overline{w}\langle t\rangle.0\}_1 \xrightarrow{\{\tau\}_{0,1}} \{Q'\}_0 | \{\overline{z}\langle t\rangle.0\}_1$ and $\{P'\}_0 | \{\overline{y}\langle t\rangle.0\}_1 \approx_{red}^i \{Q'\}_0 | \{\overline{z}\langle t\rangle.0\}_1$. Furthermore $\{P'\}_0 | \{\overline{y}\langle t\rangle.0\}_1 | \{y(w)\}_2 \xrightarrow{\{\tau\}_{1,2}}$

$\{P'\}_0$, by the definition of $\approx_{red}^i$, we have $\{Q'\}_0|\{\overline{z}\langle t\rangle.0\}_1|\{y(w)\}_2 \xrightarrow{\{\tau\}_{1,2}} \{Q'\}_0$
and $\{P'\}_0 \approx_{red}^i \{Q'\}_0$. Hence $y = z$, $Q \xrightarrow{\overline{x}\langle y\rangle} Q\prime$ and $(P', Q') \in R$.

Case (4): $P \xrightarrow{(\nu y)\overline{x}\langle y\rangle} P'$. Since $\{P\}_0|\{x(w).\overline{w}\langle t\rangle.0\}_1 \xrightarrow{\{\tau\}_{0,1}} (\nu y)(\{P'\}_0|\{\overline{y}\langle t\rangle.0\}_1)$
for any w, t, by the definition of $\approx_{red}^i$, we have $\{Q\}_0|\{x(w).\overline{w}\langle t\rangle.0\}_1 \xrightarrow{\{\tau\}_{0,1}} QC$ and $(\nu y)(\{P'\}_0|\{\overline{y}\langle t\rangle.0\}_1) \approx_{red}^i QC$. So Q must perform an output action
through channel x, and there are two cases: $Q \xrightarrow{(\nu y)\overline{x}\langle y\rangle} Q'$ or $Q \xrightarrow{\overline{x}\langle y\rangle} Q'$.

Now we prove the former case holds, suppose not, $Q \xrightarrow{\overline{x}\langle y\rangle} Q'$.
Since $(\nu y)(\{P'\}_0|\{\overline{y}\langle t\rangle.0\}_1)|\{z(s).0\}_2$ can not perform $\{\tau\}_{1,2}$ for any z, we
have $QC|\{z(s).0\}_2$ can not perform $\{\tau\}_{1,2}$ for any z. But since $Q \xrightarrow{\overline{x}\langle y\rangle} Q'$, we have
$\{Q\}_0|\{x(w).\overline{w}\langle t\rangle.0\}_1|\{y(s).0\}_2 \xrightarrow{\{\tau\}_{0,1}} \{Q'\}_0|\{\overline{y}\langle t\rangle.0\}_1|\{y(s).0\}_2 \xrightarrow{\{\tau\}_{1,2}} \{Q'\}_0$, here
$\{Q'\}_0|\{\overline{y}\langle t\rangle.0\}_1|\{y(s).0\}_2$ can perform $\{\tau\}_{1,2}$.

It is contrary to $\{P\}_0 \approx_{red}^i \{Q\}_0$, so $Q \xrightarrow{(\nu y)\overline{x}\langle y\rangle} Q'$. Hence $\{Q\}_0|\{x(w).\overline{w}\langle t\rangle.0\}_1$
$\xrightarrow{\{\tau\}_{0,1}} (\nu y)(\{Q'\}_0|\{\overline{y}\langle t\rangle.0\}_1)$ and $(\nu y)(\{P'\}_0|\{\overline{y}\langle t\rangle.0\}_1) \approx_{red}^i (\nu y)(\{Q'\}_0|\{\overline{y}\langle t\rangle.0\}_1)$
which implies $\{P'\}_0 \approx_{red}^i \{Q'\}_0$, hence we have $(P', Q') \in R$.

Appendix B. Proof of Proposition 3

Definition B1. Let C be a context (or process if disregarding hole $[]$), we say
that M is an indexed context (or indexed process) w.r.t. C if one of the following
cases holds:

(1) $C = []$ and $M = []$.
(2) $C = 0$ and $M = 0$.
(3) $C = X$ and $M = X$.
(4) $C = \alpha.C_1$ and $M = \{\alpha\}_i.M_1$, here M_1 is an indexed context w.r.t. C_1.
(5) $C = C_1|C_2$ and $M = M_1|M_2$, here M_1 (M_2) is an indexed context w.r.t.
C_1 (C_2).
(6) $C = n[C_1]$ and $M = n[M_1]$, here M_1 is an indexed context w.r.t. C_1.
(7) $C = (\nu n)C_1$ and $M = (\nu n)M_1$, here M_1 is an indexed context w.r.t. C_1.
(8) $C = recX.C_1$ and $M = recX.M_1$, here M_1 is an indexed context w.r.t. C_1.

Example: $m[\{\overline{in}\ m.0\}_1.p[\{\overline{in}\ p.0\}_2]]|\{open\ n.0\}_1$ is an indexed process w.r.t.
$m[\overline{in}\ m.0.p[\overline{in}\ p.0]]|open\ n.0$.

Definition B2. Let $P \longrightarrow P'$ be an one-step reduction from P to P', and
IP (IP') is indexed process w.r.t. P (P'), then we say that $IP \xrightarrow{i,j} IP'$ is a
corresponding one-step indexed reduction w.r.t. $P \longrightarrow P'$ if one of the following
cases holds:

(1) $P = n[in\ m.P_1|P_2]|m[\overline{in}\ m.Q_1|Q_2] \longrightarrow m[n[P_1|P_2]|Q_1|Q_2] = P'$ and
$IP = n[\{in\ m\}_i.IP_1|IP_2]|m[\{\overline{in}\ m\}_j.IQ_1|IQ_2] \xrightarrow{i,j} m[n[IP_1|IP_2]|IQ_1|IQ_2] = IP'$, here IP_1 (IP_2, IQ_1, IQ_2) is an indexed process w.r.t. P_1 (P_2, Q_1, Q_2).

(2) $P = m[n[out\ m.P_1|P_2]|\overline{out}\ m.Q_1|Q_2] \longrightarrow n[P_1|P_2]|m[Q_1|Q_2] = P'$ and $IP = m[n[\{out\ m\}_i.IP_1|IP_2]|\{\overline{out}\ m\}_j.IQ_1|IQ_2] \xrightarrow{i,j} n[IP_1|IP_2]|m[IQ_1|IQ_2] = IP'$, here IP_1 (IP_2, IQ_1, IQ_2) is an indexed process w.r.t. P_1 (P_2, Q_1, Q_2).

(3) $P = open\ n.P_1|n[\overline{open}\ n.Q_1|Q_2] \longrightarrow P_1|Q_1|Q_2 = P'$ and $IP = \{open\ n\}_i.IP_1|n[\{\overline{open}\ n\}_j.IQ_1|IQ_2] \xrightarrow{i,j} IP_1|IQ_1|IQ_2 = IP'$, here IP_1 (IQ_1, IQ_2) is an indexed process w.r.t. P_1 (Q_1, Q_2).

(4) $IQ \xrightarrow{i,j} IQ'$ is a corresponding one-step indexed reduction w.r.t. $Q \longrightarrow Q'$, here $P \equiv Q$, $P' \equiv Q'$, $IP \equiv IQ$, $IP' \equiv IQ'$.

(5) $P = R|Q \longrightarrow R'|Q = P'$, $IR \xrightarrow{i,j} IR'$ is a corresponding one-step indexed reduction w.r.t. $R \longrightarrow R'$, IQ is an indexed process w.r.t Q and $IP = IR|IQ \xrightarrow{i,j} IR'|IQ = IP'$.

(6) $P = (\nu n)Q \longrightarrow (\nu n)Q' = P'$, $IQ \xrightarrow{i,j} IQ'$ is a corresponding one-step indexed reduction w.r.t. $Q \longrightarrow Q'$ and $IP = (\nu n)IQ \xrightarrow{i,j} (\nu n)IQ' = IP'$.

(7) $P = n[Q] \longrightarrow n[Q'] = P'$, $IQ \xrightarrow{i,j} IQ'$ is a corresponding one-step indexed reduction w.r.t. $Q \longrightarrow Q'$ and $IP = n[IQ] \xrightarrow{i,j} n[IQ'] = IP'$.

(8) $P = recX.Q \longrightarrow Q' = P'$, $IQ\{recX.IQ/X\} \xrightarrow{i,j} IQ'$ is a corresponding one-step indexed reduction w.r.t. $Q\{recX.Q/X\} \longrightarrow Q'$ and $IP = recX.IQ \xrightarrow{i,j} IQ' = IP'$.

Definition B3. We say that $M_1 \xrightarrow{i_1,j_1} M_2 \xrightarrow{i_2,j_2} ... \xrightarrow{i_{n-1},j_{n-1}} M_n$ is a corresponding indexed reduction w.r.t. $P_1 \longrightarrow P_2 \longrightarrow ... \longrightarrow P_n$, if for every k, M_k is an indexed process w.r.t. P_k and $M_k \xrightarrow{i_k,j_k} M_{k+1}$ is a corresponding one-step indexed reduction w.r.t. $P_k \longrightarrow P_{k+1}$.

Proposition 3. For any $P, Q \in Pr_{SA}^c$, $P \approx_{red} Q \Rightarrow P \approx_{sa} Q$.

Proof. Let $R = \{(P,Q) : IP \approx_{red}^i IQ$, here IP (IQ) is an indexed process w.r.t. P $(Q)\}$. We need to prove that for any context C, (1) if $C[P]\ R\ C[Q]$ and $C[P] \longrightarrow^* P'$, then $C[Q] \longrightarrow^* Q'$ and $P'\ R\ Q'$; (2) if $C[P]\ R\ C[Q]$ and $C[P] \Downarrow n$ then $C[Q] \Downarrow n$.

(1): For any context C, if $C[P] \longrightarrow^* P'$, then we have a corresponding indexed reduction w.r.t. $C[P] \longrightarrow^* P'$ as follows: $IC[IP] \xrightarrow{i_1,j_1} ... \xrightarrow{i_n,j_n} IP'$, here IP' is an indexed process w.r.t. P'.

Since $IP \approx_{red}^i IQ$, we have $IC[IQ] \xRightarrow{\widehat{i_1 j_1}} ... \xRightarrow{\widehat{i_n j_n}} IQ'$ and $IP' \approx_{red}^i IQ'$, here $\xRightarrow{\widehat{i,j}}$ means $\xrightarrow{i_1,i_1} \xrightarrow{i,j} ... \xrightarrow{i_n,i_n}$ if $i \neq j$, otherwise $\xrightarrow{i_1,i_1} ... \xrightarrow{i_n,i_n}$. Therefore there is Q' s.t. $C[Q] \longrightarrow^* Q'$ and $P'\ R\ Q'$.

(2): For arbitrary context C, if $C[P] \Downarrow n$, then $C[P] \longrightarrow^* P'$, $P' \equiv (\nu\widetilde{k})(n[\mu.P_1 |P_2]|P_3)$ where $\mu \in \{\overline{in}\ n, \overline{open}\ n\}$ and $n \notin \{\widetilde{k}\}$.

(a) Suppose $P' \equiv (\nu\widetilde{k})(n[\overline{in}\ n.P_1|P_2]|P_3)$, we have a corresponding indexed reduction w.r.t. $C[P]|m[in\ n.0] \longrightarrow^* P'|m[in\ n.0] \longrightarrow (\nu\widetilde{k})(n[m[0]|P_1|P_2]|P_3)$:

$IC[IP]|m[\{in\ n\}_i.0] \xrightarrow{i_1,j_1}...\xrightarrow{i_n,j_n} (\nu\tilde{k})(n[\{\overline{in}\ n\}_j.IP_1|IP_2]|IP_3)|m[\{in\ n\}_i.0]$
$\xrightarrow{i,j} (\nu\tilde{k})(n[m[0]|IP_1|IP_2]|IP_3)$, here IP_1 (IP_2, IP_3) is an indexed process w.r.t.
P_1 $(P_2,\ P_3)$, index i is different from indices in IC and IP.

Since $IP \approx^i_{red} IQ$, we have $IC[IQ]|m[\{in\ n\}_i.0] \overset{\widehat{i_1,j_1}}{\Longrightarrow} ... \overset{\widehat{i_n,j_n}}{\Longrightarrow} N' \overset{\widehat{i,j}}{\Longrightarrow} N''$.
Since the unique occurrence of index i is in $m[\{in\ n\}_i.0]$, by the reduction
from N' to N'', we have $N' \xrightarrow{k_1,k_1} ... \xrightarrow{k_n,k_n} (\nu\tilde{k})(n[\{\overline{in}\ n\}_j.IQ_1|IQ_2]|m[\{in\ n\}_i.0]$.
Therefore $C[Q] \Downarrow n$.

(b) Suppose $P' \equiv (\nu\tilde{k})(n[\overline{open}\ n.P_1|P_2]|P_3)$, then we have a corresponding
indexed reduction w.r.t. $C[P]|open\ n.0 \longrightarrow^* P'|open\ n.0 \longrightarrow (\nu\tilde{k})(P_1|P_2|P_3|0)$:

$IC[IP]|\{open\ n\}_i.0 \xrightarrow{i_1,j_1}...\xrightarrow{i_n,j_n} (\nu\tilde{k})(n[\{\overline{open}\ n\}_j.IP_1|IP_2]|IP_3)|\{open\ n\}_i.0$
$\xrightarrow{i,j} (\nu\tilde{k})(IP_1|IP_2|IP_3|0)$, here IP_1 $(IP_2,\ IP_3)$ is an indexed process w.r.t. P_1
$(P_2,\ P_3)$, index i is different from indices in IC and IP.

Since $IP \approx^i_{red} IQ$, we have $IC[IQ]|\{open\ n\}_i.0 \overset{\widehat{i_1,j_1}}{\Longrightarrow} ... \overset{\widehat{i_n,j_n}}{\Longrightarrow} N' \overset{\widehat{i,j}}{\Longrightarrow} N''$.
Since the unique occurrence of index i is in $\{open\ n\}_i.0$, by the reduction from
N' to N'', we have $N' \xrightarrow{k_1,k_1} ... \xrightarrow{k_n,k_n} (\nu\tilde{k})(n[\{\overline{open}\ n\}_j.IQ_1|IQ_2]|\{open\ n\}_i.0$.
Therefore $C[Q] \Downarrow n$.

Appendix C Proof of Lemma 2

Lemma 2. $m[\overline{in}\ m.p[\overline{in}\ p.0]] \approx_{sa} m[\overline{in}\ m.q[\overline{in}\ q.0]]$.

Proof. Let $R = \{(C[m[\overline{in}\ m.p[\overline{in}\ p.0]]], C[m[\overline{in}\ m.q[\overline{in}\ q.0]]])$: here C is an arbitrary context$\} \cup \{(C[m[s_1[S_1]|...|s_i[S_i]]], C[m[t_1[T_1]|...|t_j[T_j]]])$: here C is an arbitrary context, $S_1, ..., S_i, T_1, ..., T_j$ are arbitrary processes and $s_1, ..., s_i, t_1, ..., t_j$ are arbitrary ambients$\}$.

We want to prove that R is a contextual barbed bisimulation, i.e., if $P\ R\ Q$ then for any context D, (1) $D[P] \longrightarrow^* P'$ implies $D[Q] \longrightarrow^* Q'$ and $P'\ R\ Q'$; (2) For each ambient n, $D[P] \Downarrow n$ implies $D[Q] \Downarrow n$.

We only prove claim (1), proof of claim (2) is similar.

Given an arbitrary context D, let $E[] \equiv D[C[]]$.

Case (a): If $E[] \longrightarrow^* E'[]$, then $E[m[\overline{in}\ m.p[\overline{in}\ p]]] \longrightarrow^* E'[m[\overline{in}\ m.\ p[\overline{in}\ p]]]$ implies $E[m[\overline{in}\ m.q[\overline{in}\ q]]] \longrightarrow^* E'[m[\overline{in}\ m.q[\overline{in}\ q]]]$ and $E'[m[\overline{in}\ m.\ p[\overline{in}\ p]]]\ R$ $E'[m[\overline{in}\ m.q[\overline{in}\ q]]]$.

Case (b): If $E[] \longrightarrow^* F[n[in\ m.S_1|S_2]|[]]$, then we have $E[m[\overline{in}\ m.p[\overline{in}\ p]]] \longrightarrow^*$ $F[m[n[S']|p[\overline{in}\ p]]]$, which implies $E[m[\overline{in}\ m.q[\overline{in}\ q]]] \longrightarrow^* F[m[n[S']|q[\overline{in}\ q]]]$ and $F[m[n[S']|p[\overline{in}\ p]]]\ R\ F[m[n[S']|q[\overline{in}\ q]]]$.

Case (c): If $E[] \longrightarrow^* E'[]$ and $m[s_1[S_1]|...|s_i[S_i]] \longrightarrow^* m[u_1[U_1]|...|u_e[U_e]]$, then $E[m[s_1[S_1]|...|s_i[S_i]]] \longrightarrow^* E'[m[u_1[U_1]|...|u_e[U_e]]]$ implies $E[m[t_1[T_1]|...|t_j[T_j]]] \longrightarrow^* E'[m[v_1[V_1]|...|v_f[V_f]]]$ and $E'[m[u_1[U_1]|...|u_e[U_e]]]\ R\ E'[m[v_1[V_1]|...|v_f[V_f]]]$.

Substructural Operational Semantics and Linear Destination-Passing Style (Invited Talk)

Frank Pfenning

Carnegie Mellon University,
Pittsburgh, Pennsylvania, USA
fp@cs.cmu.edu

We introduce substructural operational semantics (SSOS), a presentation form for the semantics of programming languages. It combines ideas from structural operational semantics and type theories based on substructural logics (such as linear logic) in order to obtain a rich, uniform, and modular framework.

We illustrate SSOS with a sequence of specifications, starting from a simple functional language presented in linear destination-passing style (LDPS). Next we show how to extend the first specification modularly (that is, by adding new rules for new constructs without changing earlier rules) to treat imperative and concurrent constructs. We briefly compare our means of achieving modularity with that of modular structural operational semantics [1] and contextual semantics [2].

We then discuss how structural properties of configurations (on which the operational semantics is defined) are related to structural properties of various forms of hypothetical judgments originating in the study of linear logic and type theory. Ordered, linear, affine, and unrestricted hypothetical judgments can be used to characterize and classify semantic specifications. We are currently investigating the meta-theory of SSOS, and to what extent modularity in specifications carries over to modularity in the proof of properties such as type preservation and progress.

Many SSOS specifications can be realized immediately in the concurrent logical framework (CLF). In fact, SSOS arose from the early specifications of Concurrent ML and the π-calculus in CLF [3].

References

1. Mosses, P.D.: Modular structural operational semantics. Journal of Logic and Algebraic Programming **60–61** (2004) 195–228
2. Wright, A.K., Felleisen, M.: A syntactic approach to type soundness. Information and Computation **115** (1994) 38–94
3. Cervesato, I., Pfenning, F., Walker, D., Watkins, K.: A concurrent logical framework II: Examples and applications. Technical Report CMU-CS-02-102, Department of Computer Science, Carnegie Mellon University (2002) Revised May 2003.

W.-N. Chin (Ed.): APLAS 2004, LNCS 3302, p. 196, 2004.
© Springer-Verlag Berlin Heidelberg 2004

PType System: A Featherweight Parallelizability Detector

Dana N. Xu[1], Siau-Cheng Khoo[1], and Zhenjiang Hu[2,3]

[1]School of Computing,
National University of Singapore
{xun,khoosc}@comp.nus.edu.sg
[2]University of Tokyo,
[3]PRESTO 21, Japan Science and Technology Corporation
hu@mist.i.u-tokyo.ac.jp

Abstract. Parallel programming is becoming an important cornerstone of general computing. In addition, type systems have significant impact on program analysis. In this paper, we demonstrate an automated type-based system that soundly detects parallelizability of sequential functional programs. Our type inference system discovers the *parallelizability* property of a sequential program in a modular fashion, by exploring a ring structure among the program's operators. It handles self-recursive functions with accumulating parameters, as well as a class of non-linear mutual-recursive functions. Programs whose types are inferred to be parallelizable can be automatically transformed to parallel code in a *mutumorphic* form – a succint model for parallel computation. Transforming into such a form is an important step towards constructing efficient data parallel programs.

1 Introduction

Many computational or data-intensive applications require performance level attainable only on parallel architectures. As multiprocessor systems have become increasingly available and their price/performance ratio continues to improve, interest has grown in parallel programming. While sequential programming is already a challenging task for programmers, parallel programming is much harder as there are many more issues to consider, including available parallelism, task distribution, communication overheads, and debugging. A desirable approach for parallel program development is to start with a sequential program, test and debug the sequential program and then systematically transform the program to its parallel counterpart.

In the functional programming community, functions are usually defined recursively, and it is an open problem whether a general and formal method exists to parallelize any sequential recursive definition. One practically useful approach is the skeletal approach [20, 9], where two restrictions have been imposed on function definitions:

W.-N. Chin (Ed.): APLAS 2004, LNCS 3302, pp. 197–212, 2004.
© Springer-Verlag Berlin Heidelberg 2004

1. The operators used in the higher order functions should satisfy the associative property.
2. Programs should be expressed in some restrictive recursive forms captured by the higher order functions such as map, reduce, scan, etc.

In this paper, we propose a parallelizability detection methodology that alleviates these restrictions. Specifically, we demonstrate a system, called Parallelizable Type System (PType system in short), in which parallelizability of sequential recursive code can be detected through automatic program analysis. By parallelizability, we mean that there exists a parallel code with time complexity that is of order $O(log\ m\ /\ m)$ faster than its sequential counterpart, where m is the size of the input data.

To alleviate the first restriction, we introduce a type inference system that discovers the extended-ring property of the set of operators used in a program. We show that this property ensures parallelization of a program. Through our system, users need not know how associative operators are combined to enable parallelization. This separation of concern will greatly facilitate parallelization process.

To remove the second restriction, our system accepts any first-order functional programs with strict semantics. If a program passes the type checking phase, it can be automatically converted to parallel codes. Otherwise, the program will remain as it is.

For example, consider the following polynomial function definition:

$$poly\ [a]\ c\ =\ a$$
$$poly\ (a:x)\ c\ =\ a + c \times (poly\ x\ c)$$

In the skeletal approach, we have to introduce a (non-intuitive) combining operator $comb2$ (which is associative). Thus, the revised definition of $poly$ is:

$$poly\ xs\ c\ =\ fst\ (polytup\ xs\ c)$$
$$polytup\ [a]\ c\ =\ (a, c)$$
$$polytup\ (a:x)\ c\ =\ (a, c)\ `comb2`\ (polytup\ x\ c)$$
$$where\ comb2\ (p_1, u_1)\ (p_2, u_2)\ =\ (p_1 + p_2 * u_1, u_2 * u_1)$$

As this revised definition matches the following skeleton, parallelization is thus guaranteed.

$$poly\ xs\ c\ =\ fst\ (reduce\ comb2\ (map\ (\backslash x\ \to\ (x, c))\ xs))$$

On the other hand, our PType system can detect that the sequential definition of $poly$ is parallelizable. It infers that the expression $(a + c \times (poly\ x\ c))$ has the type $R_{[+, \times]}$. This implies that $+$ and $\times$ in $R_{[+, \times]}$ exhibit an extended-ring property. The corresponding parallel code for $poly$ is as follows.

```
poly [a] c = a
poly (xl ++ xr) c = poly xl c + (prod xl c) × (poly xr c)
prod [a] c = c
prod (xl ++ xr) c = (prod xl c) × (prod xr c)
```

An algorithm that automatically transforms a well-PTyped sequential program to an efficient homomorphism, a desired parallel computation model [21], can be found in [23].

In our implementation, the system handles first-order functional programs. It is able to parallelize a wide class of recursively-defined functions with accumulating parameters and with non-linear recursion. For clarity of the presentation, we first illustrate the system without these two features in Section 4.1 and discuss them separately in Section 4.2.

The main technical contributions of this work are as follows:

1. We propose an extended ring property of operators used in sequential programs, which guarantees the parallelizability of these programs. This frees programmers from the burden of finding a skeleton form.
2. We propose a novel and featherweight type inference system for detecting parallelizability of sequential programs in a modular fashion. We believe this is the first work on capturing parallelism in a type inference context.

The outline of the paper is as follows. In the next section, we describe the syntax of the language used, and the background of our work. Section 3 provides our account of the parallelizability property. The discovery of parallelizability using a type system is described in Section 4. We illustrate the working of the PType system through examples in Section 5. Section 6 describes our implementation. Finally, we discuss the related work and conclude the paper in Section 7.

2   Background

The PType system operates on a first-order typed functional language with strict semantics. The syntax of our source language is given in Figure 1. To aid the type inference, programmers are required to provide as annotatations properties of user-defined binary operators used in a program. Such requirements are typical for achieving reduction-style parallelism. For example, the system-defined annotation $\#(Int, [+, \times], [0, 1])$ is needed for the function definition $poly$. The annotation tells the system that, for all integers, operators $+$ and $\times$ satisfy the extended-ring property with 0 and 1 as their respective identities.

Function definitions in this paper are written in Haskell syntax [15]. For the remainder of the paper, we shall discuss detection of parallelism for recursive functions of the form

$$f(a : x) = E[\langle t_i \rangle_{i=1}^m, \langle q\ x \rangle, \langle f\ x \rangle]$$

where f is inductively defined on a list and $E[\ ]$ denotes an expression context with three groups of holes, denoted by $\langle\ \rangle$. The context itself contains no occurrence of references to a, x and f. $\langle t_i \rangle_{i=1}^m$ is a group of m terms, each of which is allowed to contain occurrences of a, but not those of references to $(f\ x)$. The $\langle q\ x \rangle$ denotes

$$\begin{array}{llll}
\tau \in \mathtt{Typ} & \textbf{Types} & n \in \mathtt{Cons} & \textbf{Constants} \\
c \in \mathtt{Con} & \textbf{Data Constructors} & v \in \mathtt{Var} & \textbf{Variables} \\
\oplus \in \mathtt{Op} & \textbf{Binary Primitive Operators} & & \\
\gamma \in \mathtt{Ann} & \textbf{Annotations} & & \\
\end{array}$$

$$\gamma ::= \#(\tau, [\oplus_1, \ldots, \oplus_n], [\iota_{\oplus_1}, \ldots, \iota_{\oplus_n}])$$

$$\begin{array}{ll}
e, t \in \mathtt{Exp} & \textbf{Expressions}
\end{array}$$

$$e, t ::= n \mid v \mid c\, e_1 \ldots e_n \mid e_1 \oplus e_2 \mid \textbf{if } e_0 \textbf{ then } e_1 \textbf{ else } e_2$$
$$\mid f\, e_1 \ldots e_n \mid \textbf{let } v = e_1 \textbf{ in } e_2$$

$$\begin{array}{llll}
p \in \mathtt{Pat} & \textbf{Patterns} & \sigma \in \mathtt{Prog} & \textbf{Programs} \\
p ::= v \mid c\, v_1 \ldots v_n & & \sigma ::= \gamma_i^*, (f_i\, p_1 \ldots p_n = e)^* \,\forall\, i.\, i \geq 1 \\
& & & \text{where } f_1 \text{ is the main function.}
\end{array}$$

Fig. 1. Syntax of the source language

an application of a parallelizable auxiliary function.[1] Lastly, $\langle f\, x \rangle$ is the self-recursive call.

For example, given the function definition

$$f_1\,(a : x) = \textbf{if } a > 0 \textbf{ then } length\, x + f_1\, x \textbf{ else } 1 + f_1\, x$$

we have

$$f_1\,(a : x) = E[\langle a > 0,\, 1 \rangle, \langle length\, x \rangle, \langle f\, x \rangle]$$
$$\textbf{where } E[\langle t_1, t_2 \rangle, \langle t_3 \rangle, \langle t_4 \rangle] = \textbf{if } t_1 \textbf{ then } t_3 + t_4 \textbf{ else } t_2 + t_4$$

As our analysis focuses on the syntactic expressions consisting of recursive calls, all variables directly or indirectly referencing an expression consisting of recursive call(s) need to be traced. We call such variables references to a recursive call, which is formally defined below:

Definition 1 (Reference to a Recursive Call). A variable v is a reference to a recursive call if the evaluation of v leads to an invocation of that call.

Consider the following two function definitions:

$$f_2\,(a : x) = \textbf{let } v_2 = 1 + f_2\, x \textbf{ in } a + v_2$$
$$f_3\,(a : x) = \textbf{let } v_3 = 1 + f_3\, x \textbf{ in let } u = 2 + v_3 \textbf{ in } a + u,$$

Variable v_2 is a reference to the recursive call $(f_2\, x)$ as it names an expression which encloses a recursive call. In f_3, variables u and v_3 are references to the recursive call $(f_3\, x)$. Variable u indirectly references the recursive call since it contains v_3.

For ease of the presentation, we focus our attention on recursive function definitions that are linear self-recursive (and discuss the handling of non-linear

---

[1] It is possible to consider applications of multiple parallelizable auxiliary functions in an expression, as in $\langle q_j\, x \rangle_{j=1}^n$. These functions are examples of mutumorphism [14]. Their calls can be *tupled* to obtain a single $(q\, x)$ via the technique described in [4, 13].

and mutually recursive functions in Section 4.2.) Furthermore, we do not consider functions with self-recursive calls occurring in the test of a conditional. Parallelization of such functions requires these functions to be annotated with a special (constraint) form of the extended-ring property [6], which are not described in this paper.

Context Preservation. Our parallelization process is inspired from a program restructuring technique known as context preservation [8]. We briefly describe the technique here.

Consider the polynomial function definition again. Context preservation is performed primarily on the recursive equation of *poly*:

$$poly\ (a : x)\ c = a + c \times (poly\ x\ c)$$

A contextual function (or context, for short) will extract away the recursive subterm of the RHS of this equation. It can be written as $\lambda\ (\bullet)\ .\ \alpha + \beta \times (\bullet)$. Here, the symbol $\bullet$ denotes a recursive subterm containing an occurrence of a self-recursive call, while α and β denote subterms that do not contain any recursive call. Such a context is said to be context preserving modulo replication (or context preserving, in short) if after composing the context with itself, we can obtain (by transformation) a resulting context that has the same form as the original context. Context preservation guarantees that the underlying function can be parallelized.

Theorem 1 (Context Preservation Theorem [8, 14]). Given is a recursive function f of the form $f\ (a : x) = e$ where expression e consists of recursive call(s). If e is context preserved, then f can be parallelized.

For function *poly*, let its context be denoted by $\lambda\ (\bullet)\ .\ \alpha_1 + \beta_1 \times (\bullet))$. We compose this context with its renamed copy, $(\lambda(\bullet)\ .\ \alpha_2 + \beta_2 \times (\bullet))$, and simplify the composition through a sequence of transformation steps:

$$
\begin{aligned}
&(\lambda\ (\bullet)\ .\ \alpha_1 + \beta_1 \times (\bullet)) \circ (\lambda(\bullet)\ .\ \alpha_2 + \beta_2 \times (\bullet)) \\
&= \lambda\ (\bullet)\ .\ \alpha_1 + \beta_1 \times (\alpha_2 + \beta_2 \times (\bullet)) && \text{— function composition} \\
&= \lambda\ (\bullet)\ .\ \alpha_1 + (\beta_1 \times \alpha_2 + \beta_1 \times (\beta_2 \times (\bullet))) && \text{— } \times \text{ is distributive over } + \\
&= \lambda\ (\bullet)\ .\ (\alpha_1 + \beta_1 \times \alpha_2) + (\beta_1 \times \beta_2) \times (\bullet) && \text{— } +, \times \text{ being associative} \\
&= \lambda\ (\bullet)\ .\ \alpha + \beta \times (\bullet) \\
&\quad \text{where } \alpha = \alpha_1 + \beta_1 \times \alpha_2 \text{ and } \beta = \beta_1 \times \beta_2
\end{aligned}
$$

Since the simplified form matches the original context, *poly* is context preserving. However, this transformation process, which is informally described in [5], is more expensive than our type-based approach. Moreover, context preservation checking is not modular, and thus lack of reusability.

3   Parallelizability

Given that context preservation leads to parallelizability, we focus on detecting context preservation of sequential programs, but in a modular fashion. Our first technical contribution is to introduce an extended ring property of the operators which guarantees automatic detection of context preservation.

$sv \in$ **S–Values** $\zeta \in$ **C–Exp**

$sv ::= bv \mid \textbf{if } \zeta_a \textbf{ then } \zeta_b \textbf{ else } bv$ $\zeta ::= C[a, (q\ x)]$

$bv ::= \underline{\bullet} \mid (\zeta_1 \oplus_1 \ldots \oplus_{n-1} \zeta_n \oplus_n \underline{\bullet})$ where C is an arbitrary expression
where $[\oplus_1, \ldots, \oplus_n]$ possesses the   context not involving references to $\underline{\bullet}$
extended-ring property

Fig. 2. Skeletal Values

Definition 2. Let $S = [\oplus_1, \ldots, \oplus_n]$ be a sequence of n binary operators. We say that S possesses the extended-ring property in [2]

1. all operators are associative;
2. each operator $\oplus$ has an identity, $\iota_\oplus$, such that $\forall v : \iota_\oplus \oplus v = v \oplus \iota_\oplus = v$;
3. $\oplus_j$ is distributive over $\oplus_i \ \forall\ 1 \le i < j \le n$.

As an example, in the non-negative integer domain, operators max, $+$ and $\times$, in that order form an extended ring. Their identities are 0, 0 and 1 respectively.

We now describe a set of "skeletons" (of expressions) which are constructed using a sequence of binary operators with the extended-ring property. We will show that expressions expressible in this "skeletal" form are guaranteed to be context preserving. We call them skeletal values (or s-values, in short). These are defined in Figure 2. We use $\underline{\bullet}$ to denote a self-recursive call in a function definition.

An s-value of the form $(\zeta_1 \oplus_1 \ldots \oplus_{n-1} \zeta_n \oplus_n \underline{\bullet})$[3] is said to be composed directly by the sequence of operators $[\oplus_1, \ldots, \oplus_n]$ with the extended-ring property. An s-value of the form $\textbf{if } \zeta_0 \textbf{ then } \zeta_1 \textbf{ else } bv$ is said to be in conditional form. Its self-recursive call occurs only in its alternate branch.

The following lemma states that all s-values are context preserving. Consequently, any expression that can be normalized to an s-value can be parallelized.

Lemma 1 (S-Values Are Context Preserved). Given a recursive part of a function definition $f(a : x) = e$, if e is an s-value, then e can be context preserved.

The proof is done by a case analysis on the syntax of s-values. Details can be found in [23].

It is worth-mentioning that s-values cover a wide class of recursive function definitions that are parallelizable. In the remainder of the paper, we will provide many practical sequential programs that can be expressed in, or normalized to an s-value, and thus be directly parallelized.

---

[2] We can also extend this property to include semi-associative operators and their corresponding left or right identities. Such extension enables more sequential programs to be parallelized.

[3] By default, it is equivalent to $(\zeta_1 \oplus_1 (\cdots \oplus_{n-1} (\zeta_n \oplus_n \underline{\bullet}) \ldots))$.

4   PType System

The main focus of the PType system is a type-inference system that enables discovery of parallelizability of sequential programs. Operationally, the type system aims to deduce the extended-ring property of a sequential program in a modular fashion. To this end, it associates each sub-expression in a recursive function definition with a type term from the type language PType.

$$\rho \in \text{PType} \qquad \psi \in \text{NType} \qquad \phi \in \text{RType}$$
$$\rho ::= \psi \mid \phi \qquad \psi ::= N \qquad \phi ::= R_S$$
$$\text{where } S \text{ is a sequence of operators}$$

Fig. 3. PType Expressions

The set of PType terms are defined in Figure 3. It comprises two categories: NType and RType. We write $[\![\rho]\!]$ to denote the semantics of PType ρ. Thus,

$$[\![N]\!] \; = \; \textbf{C–Exp},$$

where **C–Exp** is defined in Figure 2.

Given that $S = [op_1, \ldots, op_n]$ with the extended-ring property, we have:

$$[\![R_S]\!] \; = \; \{e \mid e \leadsto^* e' \wedge e' \text{ is an } s\text{-value} \wedge e' \text{ is composable by operators in } S\},$$

where $\leadsto^*$ represents a normalization process that we have defined to obtain s-values. The core set of rules for the normalization process is in [23].

Since expressions of type R_S (for some S) can be normalized to an s-value, any expression containing a self-recursive call but could not be translated to an s-value is considered ill-typed in our PType system.

As an illustration, the RHS of the self-recursive equation of the following function definition has ptype $R_{[max,+,\times]}$.

$$f_6 \; (a : x) = 5 \; `max` \; (a + 2 \times (f_6 \; x)),$$

Note that in the definition of $[\![R_S]\!]$, the expression e' is said to be composable, rather than to be composed directly, by a set of operators. There are two reasons for saying that:

1. e' need not simply be an s-value of bv category; it can also include conditionals and local abstractions, but its set of operators must be limited to S.
2. As operators in S have identities, we allow e' to contain just a subset of operators in S. We can always extend e' to contain all operators in S using their respective identities.

The last point implies that the RType semantics enjoys the following subset relation:

Lemma 2. Given two sequences of operators S_1 and S_2, both with the extended-ring property, if S_1 is a subsequence of S_2, then $[\![R_{S_1}]\!] \subseteq [\![R_{S_2}]\!]$.

The above lemma leads to the following subtyping relation:

Definition 3 (Subtyping of RType). Given two sequences of operators S_1 and S_2, both with the extended-ring property, we say R_{S_1} is a subtype of R_{S_2}, denoted by $R_{S_1} <: R_{S_2}$, if and only if $S_1 \ll S_2$ (where "$S_1 \ll S_2$" means "S_1 is a subsequence of S_2").

A type assumption Γ binds program variables to their PTypes. A judgment of the PType has the form

$$\Gamma \vdash_\kappa e :: \rho$$

This states that the expression e has PType ρ assuming that any free variable in it has PType given by Γ and κ is an expression that may occur in e. κ is either a self-recursive call or a reference to such a call. It represents the currently active reference (the detail can be seen in the type-checking rule for **let**.) Before type checking the RHS of a recursive definition of f, we initialize κ to be the term $(f\ x)$. In Γ, we also assign PType N to the recursive parameters of f.

Finally, given a recursive equation of f defined by $f\ (a : x) = e$, the expression e is said to be well-PTyped if there is some PType ρ such that $\Gamma \vdash_{(f\ x)} e :: \rho$, where Γ assigns both a and x to N. Otherwise, it is said to be ill-PTyped.

4.1   PType Checking

The PType of a function f is defined as the PType of the RHS of its recursive equation. Figure 4 lists the core set of type-checking rules.

Both constants and variables not referencing any recursive call are given NType, as shown in the rules (**var-N**) and (**con**). Use of a variable has type RType if it is the currently active reference, namely κ. The self-recursive call $(f\ x)$ will also be given an RType. We note that any use of inactive references are ill-PType, as there is no corresponding rule for it.

Rule (**op**) handles a binary operation in which a recursive function call occurs in its right operand. The operation yields a RType if the right operand has RType, and the operator under investigation is part of the sequence S. The case in which the recursive call occurs in its left operand is symmetrical, and thus omitted.

In the rule (**if**), a conditional expression is of NType if both its branches are of NType. On the other hand, it is of RType if one of its branches is of RType. When both branches are of RType, the conditional will be of RType provided both branches can be coerced to the same type R_S. These constraints are expressed by the relation $\bigtriangledown_{if}$, defined by (**if-merge**), while the coercion is defined via a type subsumption (**sub**). For example, consider the following function definition:

$$\#(Int, [+, \times], [0, 1])$$
$$f_7\ [a] = a$$
$$f_7\ (a : x) = \textbf{if } a > 5 \textbf{ then } a + f_7\ x \textbf{ else } a \times f_7\ x$$

Under the type assumption $\Gamma = \{a :: N, x :: N\}$, the types for each of the branches are $R_{[+]}$ and $R_{[\times]}$. By the rules (**if-merge**) and (**sub**), the type of the conditional becomes $R_{[+, \times]}$.

$$\frac{v \neq \kappa}{\Gamma \cup \{v :: N\} \vdash_\kappa v :: N} \ (\mathbf{var - N}) \qquad \frac{v = \kappa}{\Gamma \cup \{v :: R_S\} \vdash_\kappa v :: R_S} \qquad (\mathbf{var - R})$$

$$\frac{}{\Gamma \vdash_\kappa n :: N} \quad (\mathbf{con}) \qquad\qquad \frac{}{\Gamma \vdash_{(f\,x)} (f\,x) :: R_S} \qquad (\mathbf{rec})$$

$$\frac{\Gamma \vdash_\kappa e_1 :: N \quad \Gamma \vdash_\kappa e_2 :: \rho \quad (\rho = N) \vee (\rho = R_S \wedge \oplus \in S)}{\Gamma \vdash_\kappa (e_1 \oplus e_2) :: \rho} \qquad (\mathbf{op})$$

$$\frac{\Gamma \vdash_\kappa e_0 :: N \quad \Gamma \vdash_\kappa e_1 :: \rho_1 \quad \Gamma \vdash_\kappa e_2 :: \rho_2 \quad \triangledown_{\texttt{if}} (\rho, \rho_1, \rho_2)}{\Gamma \vdash_\kappa (\mathbf{if}\ e_0\ \mathbf{then}\ e_1 \mathbf{else}\ e_2) :: \rho} \qquad (\mathbf{if})$$

$$\frac{\Gamma \vdash_\kappa e_1 :: N \quad \Gamma \cup \{v :: N\} \vdash_\kappa e_2 :: \rho}{\Gamma \vdash_\kappa (\mathbf{let}\ v = e_1\ \mathbf{in}\ e_2) :: \rho} \qquad (\mathbf{let - N})$$

$$\frac{\Gamma \vdash_\kappa e_1 :: R_S \quad \Gamma \cup \{v :: R_S\} \vdash_v e_2 :: R_S}{\Gamma \vdash_\kappa (\mathbf{let}\ v = e_1\ \mathbf{in}\ e_2) :: R_S} \qquad (\mathbf{let - R})$$

$$\frac{\Gamma \vdash_\kappa e :: N \quad g \notin FV(\kappa)}{\Gamma \vdash_\kappa (g\,e) :: N} \ (\mathbf{g}) \qquad \frac{\Gamma \vdash_\kappa e : \rho \quad \rho <: \rho'}{\Gamma \vdash_\kappa e :: \rho'} \qquad (\mathbf{sub})$$

$$\frac{}{\triangledown_{\texttt{if}}(\rho, \rho, \rho)} \qquad \frac{}{\triangledown_{\texttt{if}}(R_S, N, R_S)} \qquad \frac{}{\triangledown_{\texttt{if}}(R_S, R_S, N)} \qquad (\mathbf{if - merge})$$

Fig. 4. Type-Checking Rules

There are two rules for the **let**-expression. Rule **let-N** applies to an expression with no recursive-call references in e_1. Thus, the resulting type depends on the type of e_2. Rule **let-R** applies to an expression with recursive-call references occurring in e_1 and the local variable v is used in the expression e_2.

Note that in the rule (**let-R**), the deductive operator has changed from $\vdash_\kappa$ to $\vdash_v$. This means that in e_2, v is the sole active reference to the recursive function. Thus, the following two expressions will fail the **PType** check: In the first expression, the recursive call is non-linear; in the second expression, the use of v is non-linear.[4]

$$\mathbf{let}\ v = f\,x\ \mathbf{in}\ f\,x \qquad\qquad \mathbf{let}\ v = f\,x\ \mathbf{in}\ \mathbf{let}\ u = v\ \mathbf{in}\ v$$

In rule (**g**), the application of an auxiliary function g is of **NType** if its argument e is of **NType** too. Otherwise, such an application may not be effectively parallelized [10], and the application will be deemed ill-**PType**d.

The soundness of our type-checking rules is shown by relating the rules to a set of normalization rules defining $\rightsquigarrow$, as shown in [23]. The main results are listed below; we refer the reader to [23] for detail.

Theorem 2 (Progress). If $\Gamma \vdash_\kappa e :: R_S$, then either e is an s-value or $e \rightsquigarrow e'$.

---

[4] Conversion of these simple non-linear expressions to their linear counterparts can be trivially done via pre-processing. We omit the detail here.

Theorem 3 (Preservation). If $e :: R_S$ and $e \leadsto e'$, then $e' :: R_S$.

Furthermore, in [23], we define a PType inference algorithm which is both sound and complete with respect to our PType checking rules. Our algorithm adopts the idea of the type reconstruction algorithm $\mathcal{W}_{UL}$ as described in [17].

4.2   Enhancement of the PType System

In this section, we show that the PType system can be enhanced to cover broader classes of parallelizable codes. These enhancements have been included in our implementation [23].

Multiple Recursion Parameters. When a function f has multiple recursion parameters, we require f to recurse over all its recursion parameters at the same frequency. That is, f is of the following form:

$$f [a_1] \ldots [a_n] = Ctx[a_1, \ldots, a_n]$$
$$f (a_1 : x_1) \ldots (a_n : x_n) = \ldots (f\ x_1 \ldots x_n) \ldots$$

where $Ctx[\ ]$ is an arbitrary context, and the expression $\ldots (f\ x_1 \ldots x_n) \ldots$ states that any self-recursive call in the equation should be of the form $(f\ x_1 \ldots x_n)$.

Example: Polynomial Addition. The following definition of *polyadd* satisfies this requirement, and its PType is $R_{[+]}$.

$$\#(List\ Float, [+], [Nil])$$
$$polyadd\ [\,]\ [\,] = [\,]$$
$$polyadd\ [\,]\ ys = ys$$
$$polyadd\ xs\ [\,] = xs$$
$$polyadd\ (a : x)\ (b : y) = [(a + b)] +\!\!+ polyadd\ x\ y$$

For clarity, we use $\overrightarrow{x}$ to denote $x_1 \ldots x_n$. To handle multiple recursion parameters, we replace all occurrences of $(f\ x)$ with $(f\ \overrightarrow{x})$ in the type checking rules, and include $\{a_1 :: N, \ldots, a_n :: N, x_1 :: N, \ldots, x_n :: N\}$ to Γ before type checking the RHS of the equation.

Accumulating Parameters. When a function f has accumulating parameters, we shall verify the well-PTypedness of each of these parameters individually before type-checking f's body. If any one of the accumulating parameters is found to be ill-typed, we conclude that the function f is ill-typed too. Thus, given a function definition of the form

$$f (a_1 : x_1) \ldots (a_n : x_n)\ p_1 \ldots p_n = \ldots (f\ \overrightarrow{x}\ e_1 \ldots e_i \ldots e_n) \ldots,$$

where $p_1 \ldots p_n$ are accumulating parameters, the type checking proceeds as follows:

$$\frac{\forall i \in \{1, \ldots, n\} : \Gamma \cup \{a_i :: N, x_i :: N, p_i :: N\}_{i \in \{1, \ldots, n\}} \vdash_{p_i} \mathcal{C}[\![e]\!]_{p_i} :: \rho_i}{\Gamma \cup \{a_i :: N, x_i :: N, p_i :: N\}_{i \in \{1, \ldots, n\}} \vdash_{(f\ \overrightarrow{x})} e :: R_S}$$

The context derivation function $\mathcal{C}$ takes an expression e and an accumulating parameter p_i as inputs and returns an expression which is the context of the accumulating parameter p_i. Its definition is available in Figure 5.

$$\mathcal{C} :: \mathtt{Exp} \rightarrow \mathtt{Var} \rightarrow (\mathtt{Exp}, \mathtt{Bool})$$
$$\mathcal{C}[\![\, n \,]\!]_{p_i} = (n, \, True)$$
$$\mathcal{C}[\![\, v \,]\!]_{p_i} = (v, \, True)$$
$$\mathcal{C}[\![\, f \overrightarrow{x} \, e_0 \, \ldots \, e_i \, \ldots \, e_n \,]\!]_{p_i} = (e_i, \, False)$$
$$\mathcal{C}[\![\, g \, e_0 \, \ldots \, e_n \,]\!]_{p_i} = (g \, e_0 \, \ldots \, e_n, \, True)$$
$$\mathcal{C}[\![\, e_1 \oplus e_2 \,]\!]_{p_i} = let \, (e_1', \, b_1) = \mathcal{C}[\![\, e_1 \,]\!]_{p_i}$$
$$(e_2', \, b_2) = \mathcal{C}[\![\, e_2 \,]\!]_{p_i}$$
$$in \; case \; (b_1, \, b_2) \; of$$
$$(True, \; True) \rightarrow (e_1 \oplus e_2, \; True)$$
$$(True, \; False) \rightarrow (e_2', \; False)$$
$$(False, \; True) \rightarrow (e_1', \; False)$$
$$(False, \; False) \rightarrow error$$
$$\mathcal{C}[\![\, \textbf{if} \; e_0 \; \textbf{then} \; e_1 \; \textbf{else} \; e_2]\!]_{p_i} = let \, (e_1', \, b_1) = \mathcal{C}[\![\, e_1 \,]\!]_{p_i}$$
$$(e_2', \, b_2) = \mathcal{C}[\![\, e_2 \,]\!]_{p_i}$$
$$in \; case \; (b_1, \, b_2) \; of$$
$$(True, \; True) \rightarrow (\textbf{if} \; e_0 \; \textbf{then} \; e_1 \; \textbf{else} \; e_2, \; True)$$
$$(True, \; False) \rightarrow (e_2', \; False)$$
$$(False, \; True) \rightarrow (e_1', \; False)$$
$$(False, \; False) \rightarrow (\textbf{if} \; e_0 \; \textbf{then} \; e_1' \; \textbf{else} \; e_2', \; False)$$
$$\mathcal{C}[\![\, \textbf{let} \; v = e_1 \; \textbf{in} \; e_2 \,]\!]_{p_i} = let \, (e_1', \, b_1) = \mathcal{C}[\![\, e_1 \,]\!]_{p_i}$$
$$in \; if \; b_1 \; then \; let \, (e_2', \, b_2) = \mathcal{C}[\![\, e_2 \,]\!]_{p_i}$$
$$in \; if \; b_2 \; then \; (\textbf{let} \; v = e_1 \; \textbf{in} \; e_2, \; True)$$
$$else \; (\textbf{let} \; v = e_1' \; \textbf{in} \; e_2', \; False)$$
$$else \; (e_1', \; False)$$

Fig. 5. Definition of Context-Derivation Function $\mathcal{C}$

Example: Bracket Matching Problem. This is a language recognition problem which determines whether the brackets '(' and ')' occurring in a given string can be matched correctly. This problem has a straightforward linear sequential algorithm, in which the string is examined from left to right. A counter is initialized to 0, and is increased/decreased whenever an opening/closing bracket is encountered. The following definition is taken from [14].

$$\#(Bool, [\wedge], [True])$$
$$\#(Int, [+, *], [0, 1])$$
$$sbp \; x = sbp' \; x \; 0$$
$$sbp' \; [\,] \; c = c == 0$$
$$sbp' \; (a : x) \; c = if \; (a ==' \, (') \; \textbf{then} \; sbp' \; x \; (1 + c)$$
$$\textbf{else if} \; (a ==')') \; \textbf{then} \; c > 0 \; \wedge \; sbp' \; x \; ((-1) + c) \; \textbf{else} \; sbp' \; x \; c$$

Two annotations are needed to type-check this program. The annotation for operators of *Bool* is meant for type checking the function sbp', and that for operators of *Int* is for type checking the context of the accumulating parameter c. The context is computed as follows:

$$\mathcal{C}[\![\, RHS \; of \; sbp' \,]\!]_c = \textbf{if} \; (a ==' \, (') \textbf{then} \; 1 + c$$
$$\textbf{else if} \; (a ==')') \textbf{then} \; (-1) + c \; \textbf{else} \; c$$

The PType inferred are : $sbp :: N$, $c :: R_{[+]}$ and $sbp' :: R_{[\wedge]}$. Note that, when we type check the function body of sbp', the PType of c is set to N.

Non-linear Mutual Recursion. We extend the PType system to cover a subset of non-linear recursive functions with an additional requirement that the binary operators must be commutative. This additional requirement is typical for research in the parallelization of non-linear recursive functions.

To parallelize a set of non-linear mutual recursive functions, we group these functions into a tuple and type-check them together. Thus, we extend κ in $\vdash_\kappa$ to become a set of mutual-recursive calls.

Consider the following mutually defined recursive functions:

$$f_i\,(a:x) \;=\; e_i \quad \forall\, i \in \{1,\dots,m\}$$
$$\text{where } \forall\, i \in \{1,\dots,m\} : e_i \;=\; p_{i1} \oplus (p_{i2} \otimes f_1\,x) \oplus \dots \oplus (p_{im} \otimes f_m\,x)$$
$$\forall\, j \in \{1,\dots,m\} : p_{ij} \;=\; g_{ij}\,a\,(q_j\,x)$$

Here, functions g_{ij} are arbitrary functions (i.e., arbitrary contexts) involving a and $(q_j\;x)$, $\forall i,j \in \{1,\dots,m\}$. Before type checking, we group the function definitions into a tuple: $(f_1,\dots,f_m) = (e_1,\dots,e_m)$. For all $j \in \{1,\dots,m\}$, type check e_j with rules defined in Figure 4, together with the (op-RR) rule and type check the tuple $(e_1,\dots,e_m)$ using the (nonlinear) rule.

$$\frac{S = \oplus : S' \quad (length\,S) \leq 2 \quad \oplus \text{ is commutative} \quad \Gamma \vdash_{\{(f_1\,x),\dots,(f_m\,x)\}} e_1 :: R_S \quad \Gamma \vdash_{\{(f_1\,x),\dots,(f_m\,x)\}} e_2 :: R_S}{\Gamma \vdash_{\{(f_1\,x),\dots,(f_m\,x)\}} (e_1 \oplus e_2) :: R_S} \;(\text{op} - \text{RR})$$

$$\frac{\Gamma \vdash_{\{(f_1\,x),\dots,(f_m\,x)\}} e_j :: R_S \quad \forall\, j \in \{1,\dots,m\}}{\Gamma \vdash_{\{(f_1\,x),\dots,(f_m\,x)\}} (e_1,\dots,e_m) :: R_S} \;(\text{nonlinear})$$

Example: Fibonacci. For the following non-linear recursive definition of the Fibonacci function,

$$lfib\,[\,] = 1 \qquad\qquad lfib'\,[\,] = 0$$
$$lfib\,(a:x) = lfib\,x + lfib'\,x \qquad lfib'\,(a:x) = lfib\,x$$

we sketch below the type checking process:

$$\Gamma \cup \{a :: N, x :: N\} \vdash_{\{(lfib\,x),(lfib'\,x)\}} (lfib\,x + lfib'\,x) :: R_{[+]}$$
$$\Gamma \cup \{a :: N, x :: N\} \vdash_{\{(lfib\,x),(lfib'\,x)\}} (lfib\,x) :: R_{[\,]}$$
$$\vdash_{\{(lfib\,x),(lfib'\,x)\}} (lfib\,x) :: R_{[+]} \quad \text{— since } R_{[\,]} <: R_{[+]}$$
$$\Gamma \cup \{a :: N, x :: N\} \vdash_{\{(lfib\,x),(lfib'\,x)\}} ((lfib\,x + lfib'\,x),(lfib\,x)) :: R_{[+]}$$

Hence, both $lfib$ and $lfib'$ have type $R_{[+]}$.

For functions which are defined with both non-linear recursion and accumulating parameters, we first transform them into their linear recursive counterpart such that the accumulating parameters and the recursion arguments can be processed in a synchronized manner [7]. If this succeeds, the transformed functions will be amenable to parallelization.

5   Examples

In this section, we show some interesting well-PTyped sequential programs by giving their PType.

The mss Problem. Consider a sequential program that finds the maximum segment sum (mss) of a list.

$$\#(Int, [max, +], [0, 0])$$

$mis\,[a] = a$		$mss\,[a] = a$
$mis\,(a:x) = a\,`max`\,(a + mis\,x)$		$mss\,(a:x) = (a\,`max`\,(a + mis\,x))\,`max`\,mss\,x$

In the definition of function mss, function mis is called with the recursion argument x. This implies that an effective parallelization of mss requires mis to be parallelizable as well. Thus, we type check the definition of mis before that of mss. The PType inferred for both definitions are: $mis :: R_{[max,+]}$ and $mss :: R_{[max]}$ respectively.

Lists and Skeletons. We show that components of the traditional skeletons such as *scan*, *map*, and *reduce*, can be viewed as parallelizable components in our PType system. Consequently, programs constructed via these skeletons can be parallelized by our system.

An extended-ring property for lists is: $\#(List, [+\!\!+, map2], [Nil, Nil])$, where $map2$ is in turn defined as: $y\,`map2`\,z = map\,(y +\!\!+)\,z$. Function $map2$ has the following properties:

1. distributive over $+\!\!+$: $\quad y\,`map2`\,(zl +\!\!+ zr) = y\,`map2`\,zl +\!\!+ y\,`map2`\,zr$
2. semi-associative : $\quad x\,`map2`\,(y\,`map2`\,z) = (x +\!\!+ y)\,`map2`\,z$

From the following recursive definition of the function *scan*, we can infer that *scan* has type $R_{[+\!\!+,map2]}$:

$$\#(List, [+\!\!+, map2], [Nil, Nil])$$
$$scan\,[a] = [\,[a]\,]$$
$$scan\,(a:x) = [\,[a]\,] +\!\!+ ([a]\,`map2`\,(scan\,x))$$

Similarly, we can apply this methodology to obtain the ptypes of *map* and *reduce*.

Technical Indicators in Financial Analysis. Many technical indicators used in technical analysis of financial market can be parallelized with our system. Following is a program for computing exponential moving average [1]:

$$\#(Indicator\ Price, [+, \times], [0, 1])$$
$$ema\,(a:x) = (close\,a)\ :\ ema'\,(a:x)\,(close\,a)$$
$$ema'\,[\,]\,p = [\,]$$
$$ema'\,(a:x)\,p = let\,r = (0.2 \times (close\,a) + 0.8 \times p)\ in\ [r] +\!\!+ ema'\,x\,r$$

The *ema* for the first day in a price history is just its closing price. At any other day, the *ema* is computed by summing the weighted closing price of that day and the weighted moving average of the previous day. The PType of the accumulating parameter p is $R_{[+, \times]}$ and that of the function ema' is $R_{[+\!\!+]}$. Finally, the PType of the function *ema* is N.

Fractal Image Decompression. A fractal image may be encoded by a series of affine transformations (which are combinations of scalings, rotations and translations) to the coordinate axes. The decompression problem has been considered in [12]. Here, we look into the parallelization of two important functions used in the decomposition process.

$$\#(List, [+\!+], [Nil])$$
$$\#(Set, [union], [Nil])$$

$$tr \ :: \ [a \rightarrow a] \ \rightarrow a \ \rightarrow [a] \qquad\qquad k \ :: \ [[a]] \ \rightarrow [a]$$
$$tr \ [f] \ p \ = \ [f \ p] \qquad\qquad\qquad k \ [a] \ fs \ = \ nodup \ (tr \ fs \ a)$$
$$tr \ (f : fs) \ p \ = \ [f \ p] +\!+ tr \ fs \ p \qquad k \ (a : x) \ fs \ = \ nodup \ (tr \ fs \ a) \ `union` \ (k \ x)$$

Here, function tr applies a list of transformations to a pixel, and function k applies these transformations to a set of pixels with the help of tr. Function $nodup$ generates a set by removing repeated occurrences of a value from a list. Types of tr and k can be inferred to be $R_{[+\!+]}$ and $R_{[union]}$ respectively.

6   Implementation

We have implemented a prototype of the PType system in Haskell 98 [15]. We have also provided a web interface to the PType system. The URL is

> `http://loris-4.ddns.comp.nus.edu.sg/~xun.`

We have tested our system with a set of non-trivial sequential programs including applications such as matrix multiplication, inversion, and polynomial multiplication, etc. Details of these programs can be found in the above URL as well. The experiment was performed on a 2 GHz Pentium-4 CPU with 512 MB of RAM. The total times taken to do PType inference for some of the applications are shown in Table 1. In general, the time complexity of PType inference is $O(n)$ where n is the size of the sequential program. The parallel code generation has time complexity of $O(n^2)$. The time complexity for executing the resulting parallel code is typically $O(log \ m)$ where m is the size of the input data.

Table 1. Parallelization Times for Some Sequential Programs

	matrix multiplication	matrix inverse	polynomial multiplication	mss	fractal image decompression
Lines of Code	50	65	16	10	22
Time (Sec)	0.026	0.04	0.007	0.007	0.04

7   Related Works and Conclusion

Generic program schemes, such as algorithmic skeletons, have been advocated for use in structured parallel programming, both for imperative programs expressed as first-order recurrences through a classic result of [22] and for functional programs via Bird's homomorphism [20, 9]. However, most sequential specifications fail to match up directly with these schemes. To overcome this shortcoming, there have been calls to constructively transform programs to match these schemes. But these proposals [19, 12] often require deep intuition and the support of ad-hoc lemmas – making automation difficult. Another approach is to provide more specialized schemes, either statically [18] or via a procedure [14], that can be directly matched to a sequential specification.

On the imperative language (e.g. Fortran) front, there have been interests in parallelization of reduction-style loops [10, 11]. By modeling loops via functions, function-type values could be reduced (in parallel) via associative function composition. These propagated function-type values could only be efficiently combined if they have a template closed under composition. This requirement is similar to the need to find a common context under recursive call unfolding, aka., context preservation, as described in [3]. Imperative loop corresponds to tail recursion, and can be considered as a special case of the linear recursive form that we have described here.

Type-based analysis has traditionally been used to support both program safety and optimization. More recently, it has also been used to support program transformations, such as useless variable elimination [16, 2]. However, these two type systems are still based on the evaluation rules of the underlying language.

We have introduced a novel view to parallelization. To the best of our knowledge, this is the first piece of work that brings together type systems and parallelization. By bringing the two fields together, we hope to apply the formalism of type theory to yet another important application domain. The marriage of type systems and parallelization hinges on the idea of the extended-ring property. Through the PType system, we have relaxed the restrictions which have usually been imposed on parallelization (eg., restriction on specific recursive form). Furthermore, the system is able to handle recursively defined functions with accumulating parameters.

With the help of the PType inferenced, we develop an algorithm that can automatically generates parallel code from a well-PTyped sequential program. Due to space limitation, the derivation detail and its correctness proof are omitted.

All the above benefits are obtained without the need for users to know the detail mechanisms behind the parallelization process. Through a clean and simple interface, the system frees the user from the burden of performing normalization (which is required in [8]) and parallelizability checking (which is required in [14]). Users only need to provide the extended-ring property of the binary operators used in the programs. Indeed, we have provided a web interface to the system, through which users can parallelize their programs, or test run many of the non-trivial programs which are available at our website.

References

1. S. Anand, W.N. Chin, and S.C. Khoo. Charting patterns on price history. In *ACM SIGPLAN International Conference on Functional Programming*, pages 134–145. ACM Press, June 2001.
2. S. Berardi. Pruning simply-typed lambda-terms. *Journal of Logic and Computation*, 6(5):663–681, 1996.
3. W. N. Chin. Synthesizing parallel lemma. In *Proc of a JSPS Seminar on Parallel Programming Systems, World Scientific Publishing*, pages 201–217, Tokyo, Japan, May 1992.

4. W. N. Chin. Towards an automated tupling strategy. In *Proc. Conference on Partial Evaluation and Program Manipulation*, pages 119–132, Copenhagen, Denmark, June 1993.
5. W.N. Chin, J. Darlington, and Y. Guo. Parallelizing conditional recurrences. In *2nd Annual EuroPar Conference*, Lyon, France, (LNCS 1123) Berlin Heidelberg New York: Springer, August 1996.
6. W.N. Chin, S.C Khoo, Z. Hu, and M. Takeichi. Deriving parallel codes via invariants. In *International Static Analysis Symposium (SAS2000)*, Santa Barbara, California, June 2000. LNCS 1824, Springer Verlag.
7. W.N. Chin, S.C. Khoo, and T.W. Lee. Synchronisation analyses to stop tupling. In *European Symposium on Programming (LNCS 1381)*, pages 75–89, March 1998.
8. W.N. Chin, A. Takano, and Z. Hu. Parallelization via context preservation. In *IEEE Intl Conference on Computer Languages*, Chicago, U.S.A., May 1998. IEEE CS Press. http://www.comp.nus.edu.sg/~chinwn/iccl98.ps.
9. M. Cole. Parallel programming with list homomorphisms. *Parallel Processing Letters*, 5(2), 1995.
10. A.L. Fischer and A.M. Ghuloum. Parallelizing complex scans and reductions. In *ACM SIGPLAN Conference on Programming Language Design and Implementation*, pages 135–136, Orlando, Florida, ACM Press, 1994.
11. A.M. Ghuloum and A.L. Fischer. Flattening and parallelizing irregular applications, recurrent loop nests. In *3rd ACM Principles and Practice of Parallel Programming*, pages 58–67, Santa Barbara, California, ACM Press, 1995.
12. Z.N. Grant-Duff and P. Harrison. Parallelism via homomorphism. *Parallel Processing Letters*, 6(2):279–295, 1996.
13. Z. Hu, H. Iwasaki, and M. Takeichi. Tupling calculation eliminates multiple data traversals. In *ACM SIGPLAN International Conference on Functional Programming*, pages 164–175, Amsterdam, The Netherlands, June 1997. ACM Press.
14. Z. Hu, M. Takeichi, and W.N. Chin. Parallelization in calculational forms. In *25th Annual ACM Symposium on Principles of Programming Languages*, pages 316–328, San Diego, California, January 1998. ACM Press.
15. S. P. Jones, J. Hughes, and et al. Report on the programming language Haskell 98, a non-strict, purely functional language.
16. N. Kobayashi. Type-based useless variable elimination. In *ACM Workshop on Partial Evaluation and Semantics-Based Program Manipulation*, pages 84–93, Boston, Massachusett, January 2000.
17. F. Nielson, H.R. Nielson, and C. Hankin. *Principles of Program Analysis*. Springer Verlag, 1999.
18. S.S. Pinter and R.Y. Pinter. Program optimization and parallelization using idioms. In *ACM Principles of Programming Languages*, pages 79–92, Orlando, Florida, ACM Press, 1991.
19. P. Roe. *Parallel Programming using Functional Languages (Report CSC 91/R3)*. PhD thesis, University of Glasgow, 1991.
20. D. Skillicorn. Architecture-independent parallel computation. *IEEE Computer*, 23(12):38–50, December 1990.
21. D. Skillicorn. Foundations of parallel programming. In *Cambridge International Series on Parallel Computation:6*, 1994.
22. H.S. Stone. Parallel tridiagonal equation solvers. *ACM Transactions on Mathematical Software*, 1(4):287–307, 1975.
23. N. Xu. A type-based approach to parallelization. *MSc thesis, School of Computing, National University of Singapore http://www-appn.comp.nus.edu.sg/~esubmit/search/index.html*, July 2003.

A Type Theory for Krivine-Style Evaluation and Compilation*

Kwanghoon Choi and Atsushi Ohori**

School of Information Science,
Japan Advanced Institute of Science and Technology,
Tatsunokuchi, Ishikawa, Japan
{khchoi,ohori}@jaist.ac.jp

Abstract. This paper develops a type theory for Krivine-style evaluation and compilation. We first define a static type system for lambda terms where lambda abstraction is interpreted as a code to pop the "spine stack" and to continue execution. Higher-order feature is obtained by introducing a typing rule to convert a code to a closure. This is in contrast with the conventional type theory for the lambda calculus, where lambda abstraction always creates higher-order function. We then define a type system for Krivine-style low-level machine, and develops type-directed compilation from the term calculus to the Krivine-style machine. We establish that the compilation preserves both static and dynamic semantics. This type theoretical framework provides a proper basis to analyze various properties of compilation. To demonstrate the strength of our framework, we perform the above development for two versions of low-level machines, one of which statically determines the spine stack, and the other of which dynamically determines the spine stack using a run-time mark, and analyze their relative merit.

1   Introduction

The Krivine abstract machine [3] can be regarded as a system to transform a state of the form $(\mathcal{E}, \mathcal{S}, M)$ consisting of an environment $\mathcal{E}$, a stack $\mathcal{S}$, and a term M to be evaluated. An environment $\mathcal{E}$ represents the binding of the free variables in M as usual. The distinguishing feature of the Krivine machine lies in its usage of a stack $\mathcal{S}$, which maintains the application context (or spine) of the term M being evaluated. For example, for the term $(\lambda x.M)\ N_1\ N_2 \ldots N_n$, the machine causes the following transition.

$$(\mathcal{E}, \mathcal{S}, (\lambda x.M)\ N_1\ N_2 \ldots N_n) \stackrel{*}{\Longrightarrow} (\mathcal{E}, V_1 \cdot V_2 \cdot \ldots \cdot V_n \cdot \mathcal{S}, \lambda x.M)$$

---

* This work has been partially supported by Grant-in-aid for scientific research on basic research (B), no :15300006.
** The second author has also been supported in part by Grant-in-aid for scientific research on priority area "informatics" A01-08, no: 16016240.

W.-N. Chin (Ed.): APLAS 2004, LNCS 3302, pp. 213–228, 2004.
© Springer-Verlag Berlin Heidelberg 2004

where each V_i is the value denoted by N_i under $\mathcal{E}$ and $V_1 \cdot V_2 \cdot ... \cdot V_n \cdot \mathcal{S}$ is the stack obtained by pushing $V_n, \ldots, V_1$ in this order. As seen from this example, the stack $\mathcal{S}$ in the state represents the arguments to the function denoted by the term $\lambda x.M$. The evaluation step for the lambda abstraction can then be performed simply by poping the stack and binding the variable to the poped value as seen below.

$$(\mathcal{E}, V_1 \cdot V_2 \cdot ... \cdot V_n \cdot \mathcal{S}, \lambda x.M) \Longrightarrow (\mathcal{E}\{x : V_1\}, V_2 \cdot ... \cdot V_n \cdot \mathcal{S}, M)$$

where $\mathcal{E}\{x : V_1\}$ is the environment obtained from $\mathcal{E}$ by extending it with $x : V_1$. When the stack is empty, the machine converts the current execution state to a closure and returns.

As observed by Leroy [6], this mechanism avoids unnecessary closure construction in evaluating nested application such as

$$(\lambda x_1. \cdots \lambda x_n.M) \ N_1 \cdots N_n$$

and yields potentially more efficient evaluation scheme for higher-order functional languages. The ZINC machine for a strict functional language exploits this mechanism. This mechanism is also closely related to an abstract machine with "spine" for a lazy functional language, where a spine denotes the evaluation context represented by a stack.

Despite the potential significance of Krivine-style evaluation strategy, however, there does not seem to exist type theoretical account for this evaluation mechanism. As a consequence, type information has not been well integrated in this evaluation mechanism. For example, if we statically know that a lambda term $\lambda x.\lambda y.M$ only flows into a context of two nested application of the form $[\_] \ M_1 \ M_2$, then we expect that we should be able to compile the term into code that pops the spine stack without performing any runtime check of verifying that the current spine stack is not empty. We would like to establish a type theoretical framework to analyze the relationship between static structure of terms and Krivine-style operational semantics. Such a framework should be useful in verifying various desired properties such as type soundness and also in developing type-directed optimizing compiler for Krivine-style evaluation machine. This requires us to develop new type systems for both source lambda terms and for low-level code performing Krivine-style evaluation using a stack and environment.

As we have pointed out above, lambda abstraction in Krivine-style evaluation denotes an operation to pop the spine stack and to bind the lambda variable to the poped value. A closure is created at the time when no more evaluation is possible. This structure is not reflected in the conventional type theory of the lambda calculus, where lambda abstraction is interpreted as a constructor to introduce a function type $\tau \to \tau'$, whose denotation is a function closure. This suggests that there should be a new form of type discipline that provides static (abstract) interpretation of this dynamic behavior.

We first define a type system for lambda terms having the following features. First, the spine of a term to be evaluated is explicitly presented in typing judgment. Second, lambda abstraction is interpreted as a constructor to pop the spine stack and bind the lambda variable. Third, closure creation is modeled by a separate structural rule (coercion).

For this typed calculus, we define a Krivine-style operational semantics and show that the type system is sound with respect to the operational semantics. The static type information made available by the type system leads us to develop a new form of Krivine-style abstract machine that does not require any explicit mark that indicates the end of the current spine stack at runtime, nor any runtime check of emptiness of the spine stack. We develop a type system for this new form of Krivine machine, and develop a type-directed compilation algorithm. We establish that the compilation algorithm preserves both static semantics (typing) and dynamic semantics by setting up a simulation relation between the evaluation relation for the lambda terms and the reduction system of our Krivine machine.

A feature that distinguishes our Krivine machine from existing Krivine-style machines is its ability to determine a spine stack statically. This is in contrast with ZINC machine [6], which determines the spine stack dynamically by explicitly inserting a mark indicating the end of each spine stack. To make precise comparison, we also develop a type system for ZINC machine, and type-directed compilation, and show that the compilation algorithm preserves both static semantics (typing) and dynamic semantics. This result also establishes that the two machines are operationally equivalent. Moreover, our type-directed compilation and semantic correctness for these two machines clarify the difference of the two machines and the role of dynamic check performed in ZINC machine.

The rest of the paper is organized as follows. Section 2 presents a Krivine-style type system for the lambda calculus, defines its operational semantics and establishes the type soundness. Section 3 defines a Krivine abstract machine that statically determines each spine stack as a typed system, and shows the type soundness. We then develop a type-directed compilation algorithm from the source calculus to this machine and establish that the compilation preserves both typing and behavior. Section 4 establishes the results for ZINC machine parallel to those of previous section, and compares the two machines. Section 5 discusses related works, and Section 6 concludes the paper with suggestions for further investigation.

Due to lack of space, we had to omit all proofs of theorems, and we could not cover interesting issues. The proofs can be found in our accompanying technical report [2]. We intend to present a more detailed account elsewhere in future.

2   A Typed Krivine-Style Calculus

We consider the following sets of lambda terms and types

$$M ::= c^b \mid x \mid \lambda x.M \mid M\ M$$
$$\tau ::= b \mid \Delta \to \tau$$
$$\Delta ::= [\tau_1, \ldots, \tau_n]$$

$$\text{(var)}\quad \Gamma\{x:\tau\}\mid\emptyset \triangleright x:\tau \qquad\qquad \text{(abs)}\ \frac{\Gamma\{x:\tau_1\}\mid \Delta \triangleright M:\tau_2}{\Gamma\mid \tau_1\cdot\Delta \triangleright \lambda x.M:\tau_2}$$

$$\text{(closure)}\ \frac{\Gamma\mid\Delta\triangleright\lambda x.M:\tau}{\Gamma\mid\emptyset\triangleright\lambda x.M:\Delta\to\tau}\qquad \text{(install)}\ \frac{\Gamma\mid\emptyset\triangleright M:\Delta\to\tau}{\Gamma\mid\Delta\triangleright M:\tau}$$

$$\text{(app)}\ \frac{\Gamma\mid\emptyset\triangleright M_2:\tau_2 \quad \Gamma\mid\tau_2\cdot\Delta\triangleright M_1:\tau_1}{\Gamma\mid\Delta\triangleright M_1\,M_2:\tau_1}$$

Fig. 1. The type system for Krivine-style term calculus

Δ is a list of types representing the types of the spine in which the term occurs. $\Delta\to\tau$ is a type of a function that consumes Δ and produces a value of type τ, and corresponds to n-ary function type in the conventional type system.

We use the following notations for lists. If X is a list then $v\cdot X$ is a list obtained by prepending v at the top of the list. The empty list is denoted by $\emptyset$. We identify a singleton list $v\cdot\emptyset$ with v and simply write v.

A term is typed relative to a typing environment Γ, which is a function from a finite set of variables to types, and a stack type Δ. We write $\Gamma\{x:\tau\}$ for the function Γ' s.t. $dom(\Gamma')=dom(\Gamma)\cup\{x\}$, $\Gamma'(x)=\tau$, and $\Gamma'(y)=\Gamma(y)$ if $y\neq x$.

A typing judgment is of the form

$$\Gamma\mid\Delta\triangleright M:\tau$$

The set of typing rules is given in Figure 1. The intuitive meaning can be understood when one reads each rule backward. The rule (abs) indicates that $\lambda x.M$ pops the spine stack $\tau\cdot\Delta$ and binds x to the popped value. The rule (app) states that evaluation of $M_1 M_2$ proceeds by first evaluating M_2 in the empty spine stack, pushing the result on the spine stack and reducing M_1 under the stack. The rule (closure) converts the currently executing code into a closure. The rule (install) is its converse.

To see how this type system derives a typing, let us consider the following lambda term.

$$(\lambda f.(\lambda x.\lambda y.M)\ (f\ 1\ 2)\ (f\ 3))\ (\lambda w.\lambda z.N)$$

Figure 2 shows a typing derivation for this term. In this example, nested lambda abstraction and the top level nested applications in $(\lambda x.\lambda y.M)\ (f\ 1\ 2)\ (f\ 3)$ are typed without invoking the structural rules, so no closure is created for reducing this spine. On the other hand, the derivation of $(f\ 1\ 2)$ and $(\lambda w.\lambda z.N)$ involves structural rules. The extra structural rules are needed due to the implicit constraint of f occurring both in the contexts ($[\ ]\ 1\ 2$) and ($[\ ]\ 3$). Later we shall see that these structural rules are compiled to closure creation and closure installation.

It is easily shown that the typability of this system is the same as that of the simply typed lambda calculus.

Fact 1. If $\Gamma\triangleright M:\tau$ is derivable in the simple type system then $\Gamma\mid\emptyset\triangleright M:\tau$ is derivable in our type system. Conversely, if $\Gamma\mid\Delta\triangleright M:\tau$ is derivable in our type system, then $\Gamma\triangleright M:\overline{\Delta\to\tau}$ is derivable in the simple type system, where $\overline{\Delta\to\tau}$ is the completely curried type.

$$P = \cfrac{\cfrac{\cfrac{\cdots}{\Gamma_f\{x:int,y:\{int\}\to int\}\,|\,\emptyset \rhd M:int}}{\Gamma_f\{x:int\}\,|\,\{int\}\to int \rhd \lambda y.M:int}}{\Gamma_f\,|\,int\cdot\{int\}\to int \rhd \lambda x.\lambda y.M:int}$$

$$\mathcal{F} = \cfrac{\cfrac{\cfrac{\cfrac{\cfrac{\{w:int,z:int\}\,|\,\emptyset \rhd N:int}{\{w:int\}\,|\,\{int\} \rhd \lambda z.N:int}}{\{w:int\}\,|\,\emptyset \rhd \lambda z.N:\{int\}\to int}}{\emptyset\,|\,\{int\} \rhd \lambda w.\lambda z.N:\{int\}\to int}}{\emptyset\,|\,\emptyset \rhd \lambda w.\lambda z.N:\{int\}\to\{int\}\to int}}$$

$$\mathcal{P}\ \cfrac{\cfrac{\cfrac{\cfrac{\cfrac{\Gamma_f\,|\,\emptyset \rhd f:\{int\}\to\{int\}\to int}{\Gamma_f\,|\,int \rhd f:\{int\}\to int}\quad \Gamma_f\,|\,\emptyset \rhd 1:int}{\Gamma_f\,|\,\emptyset \rhd f\ 1:\{int\}\to int}}{\Gamma_f\,|\,int \rhd f\ 1:int}}{\Gamma_f\,|\,\emptyset \rhd f\ 1\ 2:int}\quad \cfrac{\Gamma_f\,|\,\emptyset \rhd 2:int\quad \cfrac{\Gamma_f\,|\,\emptyset \rhd f:\{int\}\to\{int\}\to int}{\Gamma_f\,|\,int \rhd f:\{int\}\to int}\quad \Gamma_f\,|\,\emptyset \rhd 3:int}{\Gamma_f\,|\,\emptyset \rhd f\ 3:\{int\}\to int}}{\cfrac{\Gamma_f\,|\,\{int\}\to int \rhd (\lambda x.\lambda y.M)(f\ 1\ 2):int}{\cfrac{\Gamma_f\,|\,\emptyset \rhd (\lambda x.\lambda y.M)\ (f\ 1\ 2)\ (f\ 3):int}{\cfrac{\emptyset\,|\,\{int\}\to\{int\}\to int \rhd \lambda f.(\lambda x.\lambda y.M)\ (f\ 1\ 2)\ (f\ 3):int}{\emptyset\,|\,\emptyset \rhd (\lambda f.(\lambda x.\lambda y.M)\ (f\ 1\ 2))\ (\lambda w.\lambda z.N):int}}}}\ \mathcal{F}$$

where $\Gamma_f = \{f:\{int\}\to\{int\}\to int\}$

Fig. 2. An example typing derivation in the typed Krivine calculus

We first present a simple call-by-value operational semantics that reflects the feature of Krivine abstract machine, as in Figure 3. The semantics has a set of rules to determine an evaluation relation of the form

$$\mathcal{E}, \mathcal{S} \vdash M \Downarrow V$$

indicating the fact that M evaluates to a value V under an environment $\mathcal{E}$ and a Krivine stack $\mathcal{S}$. $\mathcal{E}$ is a mapping of a variable to a value, $\mathcal{S}$ is a sequence of values, and V is given by the following syntax.

$$V ::= c^b \,|\, cls(\mathcal{E}, M) \,|\, \text{wrong}$$

wrong represents runtime error.

The type system is sound with respect to the operational semantics. To show this, we first define typing relations on semantic objects

- $\models V : \tau$ (V has type τ)
- $\models c^b : b$
- $\models cls(\mathcal{E}, \lambda x.M) : \Delta \to \tau$ if there is some Γ s.t. $\models \mathcal{E} : \Gamma$, $\Gamma\,|\,\Delta \rhd \lambda x.M : \tau$
- $\models \mathcal{E} : \Gamma$ ($\mathcal{E}$ satisfies Γ)
- if $dom(\mathcal{E}) = dom(\Gamma)$ and $\models \mathcal{E}(x) : \Gamma(x)$ for all $x \in dom(\mathcal{E})$.
- $\models \mathcal{S} : \Delta$ ($\mathcal{S}$ satisfies Δ)
- if $|\mathcal{S}| = |\Delta|$ and $\models \mathcal{S}.i : \Delta.i$ for all $1 \le i \le |\mathcal{S}|$, where $\mathcal{S}.i$ and $\Delta.i$ denote the i-th elements of $\mathcal{S}$ and Δ respectively.

Fact 2. If $\Gamma\,|\,\Delta \rhd M : \Delta_1 \to \cdots \to \Delta_n \to \tau$, $\models \mathcal{E} : \Gamma$, $\models \mathcal{S}_1 : \Delta$, $\mathcal{S}_2 = \mathcal{S}_1^2 \cdot \ldots \cdot \mathcal{S}_n^2$, $\models \mathcal{S}_i^2 : \Delta_i$, and $\mathcal{E}, \mathcal{S}_1 \cdot \mathcal{S}_2 \vdash M \Downarrow V$ then $\models V : \tau$.

We also define an alternative call-by-value operational semantics using extra continuation arguments roughly following the style of [4]. This refinement is needed to establish the semantic correctness of compilation in Section 3 and 4.

$$\mathcal{E}\{x:V\}, \emptyset \vdash x \Downarrow V \qquad \mathcal{E}, \emptyset \vdash \lambda x.M \Downarrow cls(\mathcal{E}, \lambda x.M)$$

$$\frac{\mathcal{E}_0, V_0 \cdot \mathcal{S} \vdash \lambda y.M_0 \Downarrow V}{\mathcal{E}\{x : cls(\mathcal{E}_0, \lambda y.M_0)\}, V_0 \cdot \mathcal{S} \vdash x \Downarrow V} \qquad \frac{\mathcal{E}\{x : V_0\}, \mathcal{S} \vdash M \Downarrow V}{\mathcal{E}, V_0 \cdot \mathcal{S} \vdash \lambda x.M \Downarrow V}$$

$$\frac{\mathcal{E}, \emptyset \vdash M_2 \Downarrow V_2 \quad \mathcal{E}, V_2 \cdot \mathcal{S} \vdash M_1 \Downarrow V}{\mathcal{E}, \mathcal{S} \vdash M_1\ M_2 \Downarrow V} \qquad \text{(if no other rule applies)}$$
$$\frac{}{\mathcal{E}, \mathcal{S} \vdash M \Downarrow wrong}$$

Fig. 3. A call-by-value semantics for the Krivine calculus

We let K range over evaluation continuation given by the following syntax.

$$K ::= \mathsf{retCont} \mid \mathsf{appCont}(\mathcal{E}, \mathcal{S}, M, K)$$

$\mathsf{retCont}$ is the empty context. $\mathsf{appCont}(\mathcal{E}, \mathcal{S}, M_1, K)$ represents the evaluation context of M_2 in $M_1 M_2$ under $\mathcal{E}, \mathcal{S}, K$. The new evaluation relation with continuation is given in Figure 4. This is the same as the call-by-value operational semantics defined above, but it makes the evaluation order and the flow explicit.

With respect to this refined operational semantics, we establish the soundness of the type system. We introduce a typing relation on continuation of the form

$$\models K : \tau_1 \Rightarrow \tau_2 \quad \text{a continuation } K \text{ has type } \tau_1 \Rightarrow \tau_2$$

indicating that K accepts a value of type τ_1 and yields a value of type τ_2.

- $\models \mathsf{retCont} : \tau \Rightarrow \tau$ for any τ.
- $\models \mathsf{appCont}(\mathcal{E}, \mathcal{S}_1 \cdot \mathcal{S}_2, M, K) : \tau_1 \Rightarrow \tau_2$ if there are some Γ, Δ and τ_3 such that $\models \mathcal{E} : \Gamma, \models \mathcal{S}_1 : \Delta, \mathcal{S}_2 = \mathcal{S}_1^2 \cdot ... \cdot \mathcal{S}_n^2, \models \mathcal{S}_i^2 : \Delta_i, \Gamma \mid \tau_1 \cdot \Delta \triangleright M : \Delta_1 \rightarrow \cdots \rightarrow \Delta_n \rightarrow \tau_3$, and $\models K : \tau_3 \Rightarrow \tau_2$.

We now show the following.

Theorem 1. If $\Gamma \mid \Delta \triangleright M : \Delta_1 \rightarrow \cdots \rightarrow \Delta_n \rightarrow \tau, \models \mathcal{E} : \Gamma, \models \mathcal{S}_1 : \Delta, \mathcal{S}_2 = \mathcal{S}_1^2 \cdot ... \cdot \mathcal{S}_n^2, \models \mathcal{S}_i^2 : \Delta_i, \models K : \tau \Rightarrow \tau_0$, and $\mathcal{E}, \mathcal{S}_1 \cdot \mathcal{S}_2, K \vdash M \Downarrow V$ then $\models V : \tau_0$.

This result together with Fact 1 ensures that our type system can serve as an alternative type discipline to the conventional type system of the lambda calculus. In the next section, we shall develop a typed abstract machine and type directed compilation for this calculus.

3 A Krivine Machine and Compilation

This section defines a new Krivine abstract machine and its type system, develops a type-directed compilation, and establishes the correctness of compilation. Unlike existing variants of Krivine machines, there is no runtime "mark" that delimits the end of each spine, and sequence of spines of pending computation are placed in a single spine stack. The structure of the current spine is statically determined by the type system.

$$(\text{retCont}) \qquad\qquad V : \text{retCont} \Downarrow V$$

$$(\text{appCont}) \qquad \frac{\mathcal{E}, V_1 \cdot \mathcal{S}, K \vdash M \Downarrow V_2}{V_1 : \text{appCont}(\mathcal{E}, \mathcal{S}, M, K) \Downarrow V_2}$$

$$(\text{varRet}) \qquad \frac{V_0 : K \Downarrow V}{\mathcal{E}\{x : V_0\}, \emptyset, K \vdash x \Downarrow V}$$

$$(\text{varCont}) \qquad \frac{\mathcal{E}_0, V_0 \cdot \mathcal{S}, K \vdash \lambda y.M_0 \Downarrow V}{\mathcal{E}\{x : cls(\mathcal{E}_0, \lambda y.M_0)\}, V_0 \cdot \mathcal{S}, K \vdash x \Downarrow V}$$

$$(\text{absRet}) \qquad \frac{cls(\mathcal{E}, \lambda x.M) : K \Downarrow V}{\mathcal{E}, \emptyset, K \vdash \lambda x.M \Downarrow V}$$

$$(\text{absCont}) \qquad \frac{\mathcal{E}\{x : V_0\}, \mathcal{S}, K \vdash M \Downarrow V}{\mathcal{E}, V_0 \cdot \mathcal{S}, K \vdash \lambda x.M \Downarrow V}$$

$$(\text{apply}) \qquad \frac{\mathcal{E}, \emptyset, \text{appCont}(\mathcal{E}, \mathcal{S}, M_1, K) \vdash M_2 \Downarrow V}{\mathcal{E}, \mathcal{S}, K \vdash M_1 \ M_2 \Downarrow V}$$

$$(\text{wrong}) \qquad \frac{(\text{if no other rule applies})}{\mathcal{E}, \mathcal{S}, K \vdash M \Downarrow wrong}$$

Fig. 4. A call-by-value semantics with continuation

3.1   Instruction, Machine State and Execution

The set of instructions (ranged over by I) and the set of values (ranged over by v) of our Krivine machine are given as follows.

$$I ::= \text{Acc}(x) \mid \text{Grab}(x) \mid \text{Push} \mid \text{Install} \mid \text{MkCls}(C) \mid \text{Return} \mid \text{Const}(c) \mid \text{Add}$$
$$v ::= c \mid cls(E, C) \mid wrong$$

A machine state is a 5-tuple (E, S, L, C, D) where an environment E is a function from a finite set of variables to values, a spine stack S is a list of values, a local stack L is a list of values, and a code C is a list of instructions, and a "dump" D represents suspended computation, whose syntax is as follows:

$$D ::= \emptyset \mid (E, L, C) \cdot D$$

A local stack is used for holding the return value and arguments to various primitive operation. As an example of primitive operation, we only include Add for integer addition. A spine stack S represents a series of spines, including the current spine for code C and those for the computation saved in D. As we shall comment more on this later, there is no explicit delimiter in S to separate each spine. The code is statically compiled to stop at the end of the current spine.

The behavior of this machine is defined by giving a state transition relation of the form

$$(E, S, L, C, D) \longrightarrow (E', S', L', C', D')$$

determined by the set of rules given in Figure 5. We write $(E, S, L, C, D) \Downarrow v$ if $(E, S, L, C, D) \xrightarrow{*} v$.

$$(E\{x:v\},\ S,\ L,\ \mathsf{Acc}(x)\cdot C,\ D) \longrightarrow (E\{x:v\},\ S,\ v\cdot L,\ C,\ D)$$
$$(E,\ v\cdot S,\ L,\ \mathsf{Grab}(x)\cdot C,\ D) \longrightarrow (E\{x:v\},\ S,\ L,\ C,\ D)$$
$$(E,\ S,\ v\cdot L,\ \mathsf{Push}\cdot C,\ D) \longrightarrow (E,\ v\cdot S,\ L,\ C,\ D)$$
$$(E,\ S,\ v\cdot L,\ \mathsf{Return},\ (E_0,L_0,C_0)\cdot D) \longrightarrow (E_0,\ S,\ v\cdot L_0,\ C_0,\ D)$$
$$(E,\ \emptyset,\ v\cdot L,\ \mathsf{Return},\ \emptyset) \longrightarrow v$$
$$(E,\ S,\ L,\ \mathsf{MkCls}(C_0)\cdot C,\ D) \longrightarrow (E,\ S,\ cls(E,C_0)\cdot L,\ C,\ D)$$
$$(E,\ S,\ cls(E_0,C_0)\cdot L,\ \mathsf{Install}\cdot C,\ D) \longrightarrow (E_0,\ S,\ \emptyset,\ C_0,\ (E,L,C)\cdot D)$$
$$(E,\ S,\ L,\ C,\ D) \longrightarrow wrong \text{ (if no other rule applies)}$$

Fig. 5. An operational semantics for Krivine machine

3.2   A Type System for Krivine Machine Code

We follow [9] and develop a type system for the Krivine machine code language by specifying a typing rule of the form for each instruction I

$$(\text{Rule-I})\ \ \frac{\Gamma'\,|\,\Delta'\,|\,\Pi'\rhd C:\tau}{\Gamma\,|\,\Delta\,|\,\Pi\rhd I\cdot C:\tau}$$

indicating the fact that I changes the computation state from the one represented by (Γ,Δ,Π) to the one represented by (Γ',Δ',Π'). τ indicates the type of the final result, which is determined by Return instruction. The set of typing rules is given in Figure 6.

We prove the soundness theorem for this type system with respect to the machine behavior. To do this, we define typing relations on each of machine components as below.

- Value typing:
- $\models c:b$ (for some predefined base type)
- $\models cls(E,C):\Delta\to\tau$ if there is some Γ such that $\models E:\Gamma,\ \Gamma\,|\,\Delta\,|\,\emptyset\rhd C:\tau$
- Environment Typing:
- $\models \emptyset:\emptyset$
- $\models E\{x:v\}:\Gamma\{x:\tau\}$ if $\models v:\tau$ and $\models E:\Gamma$
- Spine Stack Typing (similarly for local stack typing $\models L:\Pi$):
- $\models \emptyset:\emptyset$
- $\models v\cdot S:\tau\cdot\Delta$ if $\models v:\tau$ and $\models S:\Delta$
- Dump typing:
- $\emptyset\models\emptyset:\tau\Rightarrow\tau$ for any τ
- $S_1\cdot S_2\models (E,L,C)\cdot D:\tau_1\Rightarrow\tau_2$ if there are some Γ,Δ,Π,τ_3 such that $\models E:\Gamma,\ \models S_1:\Delta,\ \models L:\Pi,\ \Gamma\,|\,\Delta\,|\,\tau_1\cdot\Pi\rhd C:\tau_3$, and $S_2\models D:\tau_3\Rightarrow\tau_2$

Using these definitions, we can establish the following.

Theorem 2. If $\Gamma\,|\,\Delta\,|\,\Pi\rhd C:\tau,\models E:\Gamma,\models S_1:\Delta,\models L:\Pi,S_2\models D:\tau\Rightarrow\tau'$ and $(E,S_1\cdot S_2,L,C,D)\Downarrow v$ then $\models v:\tau'$.

(Return)	$\Gamma \mid \emptyset \mid \tau \rhd \mathsf{Return} : \tau$
(Acc)	$\dfrac{\Gamma\{x : \tau\} \mid \Delta \mid \tau \cdot \Pi \rhd C : \tau_0}{\Gamma\{x : \tau\} \mid \Delta \mid \Pi \rhd \mathsf{Acc}(x) \cdot C : \tau_0}$
(Grab)	$\dfrac{\Gamma\{x : \tau\} \mid \Delta \mid \Pi \rhd C : \tau_0}{\Gamma \mid \tau \cdot \Delta \mid \Pi \rhd \mathsf{Grab}(x) \cdot C : \tau_0}$
(Closure)	$\dfrac{\Gamma \mid \Delta_0 \mid \emptyset \rhd C_0 : \tau_0 \quad \Gamma \mid \Delta \mid \Delta_0 \rightarrow \tau_0 \cdot \Pi \rhd C : \tau}{\Gamma \mid \Delta \mid \Pi \rhd \mathsf{MkCls}(C_0) \cdot C : \tau}$
(Push)	$\dfrac{\Gamma \mid \tau \cdot \Delta \mid \Pi \rhd C : \tau_0}{\Gamma \mid \Delta \mid \tau \cdot \Pi \rhd \mathsf{Push} \cdot C : \tau_0}$
(Install)	$\dfrac{\Gamma \mid \Delta_2 \mid \tau \cdot \Pi \rhd C : \tau_0}{\Gamma \mid \Delta_1 \cdot \Delta_2 \mid \Delta_1 \rightarrow \tau \cdot \Pi \rhd \mathsf{Install} \cdot C : \tau_0}$

Fig. 6. The type system for Krivine machine

3.3   Type-Directed Compilation

The type system of the source Krivine calculus statically determines the spine stack of each term. This information is essential for producing efficient code. To exploit this static information, we define a compilation algorithm as an algorithm that inductively translates a given typing derivation to Krivine code. We write

$$\Gamma \mid \Delta \rhd M \leadsto_k C$$

to indicate that a typing M under Γ and Δ is compiled to C. The algorithm is given in Figure 7.

Figure 8 shows the compiled code for the example typing derivation given in Figure 2. As shown in Figure 8 the derivation of $\lambda x. \lambda y. M$ does not involve any structural rule, and therefore the compilation algorithm generates two consecutive Grab instructions without creating any closure. On the other hand, the code for $\lambda w. \lambda z. N$ contains two closure generation instructions corresponding to (closure) rule in its typing derivation.

This algorithm preserves typing as shown in the following.

Theorem 3. If $\Gamma \mid \Delta \rhd M : \tau$ and $\Gamma \mid \Delta \rhd M \leadsto_k C$ then for any C_0, Δ_0, Π_0, and τ_0, if $\Gamma \mid \Delta_0 \mid \tau \cdot \Pi_0 \rhd C_0 : \tau_0$ then $\Gamma \mid \Delta \cdot \Delta_0 \mid \Pi_0 \rhd C \cdot C_0 : \tau_0$.

3.4   Correctness of Compilation

The combination of Theorem 2 and Theorem 3 establishes the soundness of the type system of the source language with respect to the operational semantics obtained by combining the compilation to the Krivine machine followed by executing the compiled code.

This only establishes a weak form of correctness. In this subsection, we establish a stronger property ensuring that the compiled code has the same operational behavior as that of the original source calculus. We achieve this by setting up a family of correspondence relations between the semantic objects in the source calculus and those of the target Krivine machine.

$$\text{(var)} \qquad \Gamma\{x:\tau\}\,|\,\emptyset \rhd x \leadsto_k \mathsf{Acc}(x)$$

$$\text{(abs)} \qquad \frac{\Gamma\{x:\tau\}\,|\,\Delta \rhd M \leadsto_k C}{\Gamma\,|\,\tau\cdot\Delta \rhd \lambda x.M \leadsto_k \mathsf{Grab}(x)\cdot C}$$

$$\text{(app)} \qquad \frac{\Gamma\,|\,\tau\cdot\Delta \rhd M_1 \leadsto_k C_1 \quad \Gamma\,|\,\emptyset \rhd M_2 \leadsto_k C_2}{\Gamma\,|\,\Delta \rhd M_1\ M_2 \leadsto_k C_2 \cdot \mathsf{Push} \cdot C_1}$$

$$\text{(code)} \qquad \frac{\Gamma\,|\,\emptyset \rhd M \leadsto_k C}{\Gamma\,|\,\Delta \rhd M \leadsto_k C \cdot \mathsf{Install}}$$

$$\text{(val)} \qquad \frac{\Gamma\,|\,\Delta \rhd \lambda x.M \leadsto_k C}{\Gamma\,|\,\emptyset \rhd \lambda x.M \leadsto_k \mathsf{MkCls}(C \cdot \mathsf{Return})}$$

Fig. 7. Type-directed compilation for Krivine machine

- Value correspondence :
  - $\models c \sim c : b$ for any constant c of type b
  - $\models cls(\mathcal{E}, \lambda x.M) \sim cls(E, C_0 \cdot \mathsf{Return}) : \Delta \to \tau$ if there is some Γ such that $\models \mathcal{E} \sim E : \Gamma$, $\Gamma\,|\,\Delta \rhd \lambda x.M \leadsto_k C_0$.
- Context correspondence :
  - $\models \mathcal{E} \sim E : \Gamma$ if $\models \mathcal{E}:\Gamma$, $\models E:\Gamma$, and $\models \mathcal{E}(x) \sim E(x):\Gamma(x)$ for all $x \in dom(\Gamma)$.
  - $\models \mathcal{S} \sim S : \Delta$ if $\models \mathcal{S}:\Delta$, $\models S:\Delta$, and $\models \mathcal{S}.i \sim S.i : \Delta.i$ for each $1 \le i \le |\mathcal{S}|$.
- Continuation correspondence :
  - $\emptyset \models \mathsf{retCont} \sim \emptyset : \tau \Rightarrow \tau$ for any τ.
  - $S_1 \cdot S_2 \models \mathsf{appCont}(\mathcal{E}, \mathcal{S}_1 \cdot \mathcal{S}_2, M, K) \sim (E, \emptyset, \mathsf{Push} \cdot C \cdot \mathsf{Install}_1 \cdot \ldots \cdot \mathsf{Install}_n \cdot \mathsf{Return}) \cdot D : \tau \Rightarrow \tau_0$ if there are some $\Gamma, \Delta, \Delta_i, \tau', \mathcal{S}_i^2$, and S_i^2 such that $\models \mathcal{E} \sim E : \Gamma$, $\models \mathcal{S}_1 \sim S_1 : \Delta$, $\Gamma\,|\,\tau\cdot\Delta \rhd M : \Delta_1 \to \cdots \to \Delta_n \to \tau'$, $\Gamma\,|\,\tau\cdot\Delta \rhd M \leadsto_k C$, $\mathcal{S}_2 = \mathcal{S}_1^2 \cdot \ldots \cdot \mathcal{S}_n^2$, $S_2 = S_1^2 \cdot \ldots \cdot S_n^2 \cdot S_{n+1}^2$, $\models \mathcal{S}_i \sim S_i : \Delta_i$, and $S_{n+1}^2 \models K \sim D : \tau' \Rightarrow \tau_0$.

We now establish the following semantic correctness theorem.

Theorem 4. Suppose $\Gamma\,|\,\Delta \rhd M : \Delta_1 \to \cdots \to \Delta_n \to \tau$, $\Gamma\,|\,\Delta \rhd M \leadsto_k C$, $\models \mathcal{E} \sim E : \Gamma$, $\models \mathcal{S}_1 \sim S_1 : \Delta$, $\mathcal{S}_2 = \mathcal{S}_1^2 \cdot \ldots \cdot \mathcal{S}_n^2$, $S_2 = S_1^2 \cdot \ldots \cdot S_n^2 \cdot S_{n+1}^2$, $\models \mathcal{S}_i \sim S_i : \Delta_i$, and $S_{n+1}^2 \models K \sim D : \tau \Rightarrow \tau_0$. If $\mathcal{E}, \mathcal{S}_1 \cdot \mathcal{S}_2, K \vdash M \Downarrow V$ then $(E, S_1 \cdot S_2, \emptyset, C \cdot \mathsf{Install}_1 \cdot \ldots \cdot \mathsf{Install}_n \cdot \mathsf{Return}, D) \Downarrow v$ such that $\models V \sim v : \tau_0$.

4   A Dynamically Typed Krivine Machine

This section considers Leroy's ZINC machine – an existing call-by-value Krivine abstract machine. Unlike in our Krivine machine we have just developed, each spine in the ZINC machine is explicitly separated by marks and each instruction grabbing an element in the current spine dynamically checks its availability. For this machine, we develop the results on compilation and its correctness parallel to those in the previous section and the relationship with the two machines.

```
(* λw.λz.N      *) MkCls(Grab(w)·MkCls(Grab(z)·[ code for N ]·Return)·Return)·Push·
(* λf. ⋯ (f 3) *) Grab(f)·Const(3)·Push·Acc(f)·Install·Push·
(* f 1 2         *) Const(2)·Push·Const(1)·Push·Acc(f)·Install·Install·Push·
(* λx.λy.M      *) Grab(x)·Grab(y)·[ code for M ]·
(*                *) Return
```

Fig. 8. Krivine machine code generated for the typing derivation of $(\lambda f.(\lambda x.\lambda y.M)$ $(f\ 1\ 2)\ (f\ 3))\ (\lambda w.\lambda z.N)$ shown in Figure 2

4.1   Instruction, Machine State and Execution

To present type system of ZINC machine, we consider the following set of instructions (ranged over by I) and values (ranged over by v) given as follows.

$$I ::= \mathsf{Acc}(x) \mid \mathsf{Grab}(x) \mid \mathsf{Reduce}(C) \mid \mathsf{Push} \mid \mathsf{Return} \mid \mathsf{Const}(c) \mid \mathsf{Add}$$
$$v ::= c \mid cls(E, C) \mid wrong$$

Each state of the ZINC machine consists of an environment (E), a spine stack (S), a local stack (L), a code (C), and a dump stack (D). Different from the Krivine machine, a dump stack contains a spine stack, as defined below:

$$D ::= \emptyset \mid (E, S, L, C) \cdot D$$

S in the current machine state and in each dump entry corresponds to one spine i.e. an application context of the term being reduced. This structure enables the code to check dynamically in runtime if the current spine is empty. Due to this property, we regarded this form of Krivine machine "dynamically typed" with respect of the structure of spine. This is in contrast with our Krivine machine where sequence of spines are put into one stack without any delimiter.

We note that, in the Leroy's original presentation of ZINC machine [6], the machine state consists of an argument stack of the form $L_1 S_1 \bullet L_2 S_2 \bullet \cdots \bullet L_n S_n$ containing sequence of spines $S_1 S_2 \cdots S_n$ and local stacks $L_1 L_2 \cdots L_n$ separated by a special symbol called "mark" denoted here by $\bullet$, and a return stack of the form $(E_1, C_1)(E_2, C_2) \cdots (E_n, C_n)$. In this organization, the emptiness check of the current spine is performed by checking whether the top value of the argument stack is $\bullet$ or not. We can see that this original machine structure is isomorphic to the machine state defined above.

The behavior of ZINC machine is defined by a state transition relation of the form

$$(E, S, L, C, D) \longrightarrow (E', S', L', C', D')$$

determined by the set of rules given in Figure 9.

The machine starts evaluating a new application context after storing the current spine stack onto the dump stack and then making it empty by $\mathsf{Reduce}(C)$. The dynamic check precedes getting a value from the spine stack to see if some value is available by either $\mathsf{Grab}(x)$ or Return. The stored spine stack will be restored only after a probing instruction finds the current spine stack exhausted.

$$(E\{x:v\},\ S,\ L,\ \mathsf{Acc}(x)\cdot C,\ D) \longrightarrow (E\{x:v\},\ S,\ v\cdot L,\ C,\ D)$$
$$(E,\ v\cdot S,\ L,\ \mathsf{Grab}(x)\cdot C,\ D) \longrightarrow (E\{x:v\},\ S,\ L,\ C,\ D)$$
$$(E,\emptyset,L,\mathsf{Grab}(x)\cdot C,(E_0,S_0,L_0,C_0)\cdot D) \longrightarrow (E_0,S_0,cls(E,\mathsf{Grab}(x)\cdot C)\cdot L_0,C_0,D)$$
$$(E,\ \emptyset,\ L,\ \mathsf{Grab}(x)\cdot C,\ \emptyset) \longrightarrow cls(E,\mathsf{Grab}(x)\cdot C)$$
$$(E,\ S,\ v\cdot L,\ \mathsf{Push}\cdot C,\ D) \longrightarrow (E,\ v\cdot S,\ L,\ C,\ D)$$
$$(E,\ v\cdot S,\ cls(E_0,C_0)\cdot L,\ \mathsf{Return},\ D) \longrightarrow (E_0,\ v\cdot S,\ L,\ C_0,\ D)$$
$$(E,\emptyset,v\cdot L,\mathsf{Return},(E_0,S_0,L_0,C_0)\cdot D) \longrightarrow (E_0,\ S_0,\ v\cdot L_0,\ C_0,\ D)$$
$$(E,\ \emptyset,\ v\cdot L,\ \mathsf{Return},\ \emptyset) \longrightarrow v$$
$$(E,\ S,\ L,\ \mathsf{Reduce}(C_0)\cdot C,\ D) \longrightarrow (E,\ \emptyset,\ \emptyset,\ C_0,\ (E,S,L,C)\cdot D)$$
$$(E,\ S,\ L,\ C,\ D) \longrightarrow wrong \ (\text{if no other rule applies})$$

Fig. 9. An operational semantics for ZINC Machine

4.2   A Type System for ZINC Machine Code

We first define the typing relations for value, for environment, for local stack, for spine stack, and for dump stack as follows:

- Value Typing:
- $\models c : b$ (for some predefined base type)
- $\models cls(E,C) : \Delta \to \tau$ if there is some Γ such that $\models E : \Gamma$, $\Gamma\,|\,\Delta\,|\,\emptyset \rhd C : \tau$.
- Environment Typing:
- $\models \emptyset : \emptyset$
- $\models E\{x:v\} : \Gamma\{x:\tau\}$ if $\models v : \tau$ and $\models E : \Gamma$
- Spine Stack Typing (similarly for local stack typing $\models L : \Pi$):
- $\models \emptyset : \emptyset$
- $\models v\cdot S : \tau\cdot\Delta$ if $\models v : \tau$ and $\models S : \Delta$
- Dump typing:
- $\models \emptyset : \tau \Rightarrow \tau$ (for any type)
- $\models (E,S,L,C)\cdot D : \tau \Rightarrow \tau_0$ if there are some Γ, Δ, Π, and τ' such that $\models E : \Gamma$, $\models S : \Delta$, $\models L : \Pi$, $\Gamma\,|\,\Delta\,|\,\tau\cdot\Pi \rhd C : \tau'$, $\models D : \tau' \Rightarrow \tau_0$.

The set of typing rules for the instructions is given in Figure 10. Note that there are two typing rules (Grab-abs) and (Grab-clo). This captures the dynamic behavior of $\mathsf{Grab}(x)$ depending on the spine stack. (Grab-abs) applies when a spine stack is not empty; otherwise (Grab-clo) applies. These two typing rules correspond to two distinct actions performed. When the spine is not empty, it actually grabs the top element from the spine and continues. Otherwise, it creates a closure.

Similarly to $\mathsf{Grab}(x)$, Return also performs two distinct actions – invoking the current closure when the spine is not empty, and returning to the caller otherwise; (Return-ins) and (Return-ret) apply respectively.

We prove the soundness theorem for this type system with respect to the ZINC machine.

Theorem 5. If $\Gamma\,|\,\Delta\,|\,\Pi \rhd C : \tau$, $\models E : \Gamma$, $\models S : \Delta$, $\models L : \Pi$, $\models D : \tau \Rightarrow \tau_0$, and $(E,S,L,C,D) \Downarrow v$ then $\models v : \tau_0$.

(Return-ret)	$\Gamma \mid \emptyset \mid \tau \rhd \mathsf{Return} : \tau$
(Return-ins)	$\dfrac{\Gamma \mid \Delta' \mid \tau' \rhd \mathsf{Return} : \tau}{\Gamma \mid \Delta \cdot \Delta' \mid \Delta \to \tau' \rhd \mathsf{Return} : \tau}$
(Acc)	$\dfrac{\Gamma\{x : \tau\} \mid \Delta \mid \tau \cdot \Pi \rhd C : \tau'}{\Gamma\{x : \tau\} \mid \Delta \mid \Pi \rhd \mathsf{Acc}(x) \cdot C : \tau'}$
(Grab-abs)	$\dfrac{\Gamma\{x : \tau\} \mid \Delta \mid \emptyset \rhd C : \tau'}{\Gamma \mid \tau \cdot \Delta \mid \emptyset \rhd \mathsf{Grab}(x) \cdot C : \tau'}$
(Grab-clo)	$\dfrac{\Gamma \mid \Delta \mid \emptyset \rhd \mathsf{Grab}(x) \cdot C : \tau}{\Gamma \mid \emptyset \mid \emptyset \rhd \mathsf{Grab}(x) \cdot C : \Delta \to \tau}$
(Push)	$\dfrac{\Gamma \mid \tau \cdot \Delta \mid \Pi \rhd C : \tau'}{\Gamma \mid \Delta \mid \tau \cdot \Pi \rhd \mathsf{Push} \cdot C : \tau'}$
(Reduce)	$\dfrac{\Gamma \mid \emptyset \mid \emptyset \rhd C_0 : \tau_0 \quad \Gamma \mid \Delta \mid \tau_0 \cdot \Pi \rhd C : \tau}{\Gamma \mid \Delta \mid \Pi \rhd \mathsf{Reduce}(C_0) \cdot C : \tau}$

Fig. 10. The type system for ZINC machine

4.3   Type-Preserving Compilation

The compilation for ZINC machine in Figure 11, opposed to that for Krivine machine, does not exploit static information about spine stacks as the machine totally depends on the dynamic situation of the spine stacks. As we shall comment more on this later in Section 4.5, the static information on the spine stacks could lead us to develop an optimization that enables ZINC machine to avoid some of dynamic tests on spine stack.

For consistency, we simply write the same compilation judgment

$$\Gamma \mid \Delta \rhd M \leadsto_z C$$

M is compiled to C under a typing M under Γ and Δ by the algorithm shown in Figure 11. An example of compiled code is shown in Figure 12.

This compilation algorithm preserves typing as shown in the following.

Theorem 6. If $\Gamma \mid \Delta \rhd M : \tau$ and $\Gamma \mid \Delta \rhd M \leadsto_z C$ then $\Gamma \mid \Delta \mid \emptyset \rhd C : \tau$.

4.4   Correctness of Compilation

Now we will show the correctness of compilation to establish a stronger property of semantic correctness of ZINC code with respect to the Krivine-style call-by-value operational semantics with continuation in Figure 4. Each correctness property of Krivine and ZINC machines allows us to confirm that the two machines are related indirectly through the behavior of source calculus.

We define correspondence between semantic objects of source calculus and those of ZINC machine by the following relations

- Value correspondence :
  - $\models c \sim c : b$ for all constants of type b
  - $\models cls(\mathcal{E}, \lambda x.M) \sim cls(E, C) : \Delta \to \tau$ if there is some Γ such that $\models \mathcal{E} \sim E : \Gamma$ and $\Gamma \mid \Delta \rhd \lambda x.M \leadsto_z C$

$$(\text{var}) \qquad \Gamma\{x:\tau\}\,|\,\emptyset \triangleright x \leadsto_z \mathsf{Acc}(x) \cdot \mathsf{Return}$$

$$(\text{abs}) \qquad \frac{\Gamma\{x:\tau\}\,|\,\Delta \triangleright M \leadsto_z C}{\Gamma\,|\,\tau\cdot\Delta \triangleright \lambda x.M \leadsto_z \mathsf{Grab}(x)\cdot C}$$

$$(\text{app}) \qquad \frac{\Gamma\,|\,\tau\cdot\Delta \triangleright M_1 \leadsto_z C_1 \quad \Gamma\,|\,\emptyset \triangleright M_2 \leadsto_z C_2}{\Gamma\,|\,\Delta \triangleright M_1\ M_2 \leadsto_z \mathsf{Reduce}(C_2)\cdot\mathsf{Push}\cdot C_1}$$

$$(\text{code}) \qquad \frac{\Gamma\,|\,\emptyset \triangleright M \leadsto_z C}{\Gamma\,|\,\Delta \triangleright M \leadsto_z C}$$

$$(\text{val}) \qquad \frac{\Gamma\,|\,\Delta \triangleright \lambda x.M \leadsto_z C}{\Gamma\,|\,\emptyset \triangleright \lambda x.M \leadsto_z C}$$

Fig. 11. Type-preserving compilation for ZINC machine

- Context correspondence :
  - $\models \mathcal{E} \sim E : \Gamma$ if $\models \mathcal{E}:\Gamma, \models E:\Gamma$, and $\models \mathcal{E}(x) \sim E(x):\Gamma(x)$ for all $x \in dom(\Gamma)$.
  - $\models \mathcal{S} \sim S : \Delta$ if $|\mathcal{S}| = |S|$ and $\models \mathcal{S}.i \sim S.i : \Delta.i$ for all $1 \le i \le |\mathcal{S}|$
- Continuation correspondence :
  - $\models \mathsf{retCont} \sim \emptyset : \tau \Rightarrow \tau$ (for any type)
  - $\models \mathsf{appCont}(\mathcal{E},\mathcal{S},M,K) \sim (E,S,\emptyset,\mathsf{Push}\cdot C)\cdot D : \tau \Rightarrow \tau_0$ if there are some Γ, Δ, Δ_i, τ', $\mathcal{S}_i$, and S_i such that $\models \mathcal{E} \sim E : \Gamma$, $\mathcal{S} = \mathcal{S}_0\cdot\mathcal{S}_1\cdot...\cdot\mathcal{S}_n$, $S = S_0\cdot S_1\cdot...\cdot S_n$, $\models \mathcal{S}_0 \sim S_0 : \Delta$, $\models \mathcal{S}_i \sim S_i : \Delta_i$, $\models K \sim D : \tau' \Rightarrow \tau_0$, $\Gamma\,|\,\tau\cdot\Delta \triangleright M : \Delta_1 \to \cdots \to \Delta_n \to \tau'$, $\Gamma\,|\,\tau\cdot\Delta \triangleright M \leadsto_z C$.

Now we can show the semantic correctness theorem as the following.

Theorem 7. Suppose $\Gamma\,|\,\Delta \triangleright M : \Delta_1 \to \cdots \to \Delta_n \to \tau$, $\Gamma\,|\,\Delta \triangleright M \leadsto_z C$, $\models \mathcal{E} \sim E : \Gamma$, $\mathcal{S} = \mathcal{S}_0\cdot\mathcal{S}_1\cdot...\cdot\mathcal{S}_n$, $S = S_0\cdot S_1\cdot...\cdot S_n$, $\models \mathcal{S}_0 \sim S_0 : \Delta$, $\models \mathcal{S}_i \sim S_i : \Delta_i$, and $\models K \sim D : \tau \Rightarrow \tau'$. If $\mathcal{E},\mathcal{S},K \vdash M \Downarrow V$ then $(E,S,\emptyset,C,D) \Downarrow v$ s.t. $\models V \sim v : \tau'$.

4.5 Comparison of Krivine and ZINC Abstract Machines

The Krivine and ZINC machine show the opposite behavior of each other in using marks. The Krivine machine determines the range of each application statically by exploiting compile-time information from our type theory. It can avoid the whole of dynamic check, but it sometimes creates unnecessary closures due to the approximate information on application contexts. The ZINC machine determines the range of each application dynamically by exploiting runtime information. It can avoid the whole of unnecessary closure creation by runtime check.

For $\lambda x.\lambda y.M$ in Figure 2, the corresponding Krivine code will safely grab each argument with no runtime check, as shown in Figure 8 because the function has type $\{int\cdot\{int\}\} \to int\} \to int$ from our type theory. However, the corresponding ZINC code will blindly check in runtime, as shown in Figure 12. This problem could be resolved by exploiting type information from our type theory.

For $\lambda w.\lambda z.N$ in Figure 2, the corresponding Krivine code will create a closure before it takes each argument because the function has type $\{int\} \to \{int\} \to int$ from our type theory. Even in the application context $f\ 1\ 2$ where two arguments

(* $\lambda w.\lambda z.N$ *)	Reduce(Grab(w)·Grab(z)·[code for N])·
(* $\lambda f.\ \cdots\ (f\ 3)$ *)	Grab(f)·Reduce(Const(3)·Push·Acc(f)·Return)·
(* $f\ 1\ 2$ *)	Reduce(Const(2)·Push·Const(1)·Push·Acc(f)·Return)·
(* $\lambda x.\lambda y.M$ *)	Grab(x)·Grab(y)·[code for M]

Fig. 12. ZINC machine code generated for the typing derivation of $(\lambda f.(\lambda x.\lambda y.M)\ (f\ 1\ 2)\ (f\ 3))\ (\lambda w.\lambda z.N)$ shown in Figure 2

are all available, the function has to be applied by two Install instructions, as shown in Figure 8, creating an unnecessary intermediate closure. The corresponding ZINC code will avoid this creation by runtime check.

5   Related Work

Although we do not aware of any work that directly addressed issues on type system and typed compilation for Krivine-style evaluation, there have been several researches worth being mentioned in terms of each facet of our type theory.

Hannan and Hick [5] proposed a type system as an analysis for uncurrying optimization identifying static application contexts by uncurried function types, which is very similar to spine stack types. Our type system, however, deals with nested application while their type system does not.

Existing approaches for typeful low-level machines, such as the typed assembly language [7] and the logical abstract machine [9, 8], have implemented higher-order functions with dump stack. As a natural consequence, they cannot properly deal with Krivine-style evaluation well. This phenomenon seems to be due to their choice of source calculus: C P S language and A-norm al form language where both have no notion of spine stack. Our approach with the Krivine-style calculus as a source calculus perfectly fits for Krivine-style evaluation.

Choi and Han [1] proposed a type system for handling dynamic application contexts. Their type system captured dynamism through some non-standard type encoding, which made their type system complex and inflexible. Our type system for ZINC machine used nondeterministic typing rules to capture dynamism, and it remained simple and flexible.

6   Conclusions

We have investigated typing properties of Krivine-style evaluation from source lambda terms down to abstract machine codes. First, we have developed a typed term calculus that accounts for Krivine-style evaluation with "spine" stack, and have shown that the type system is sound with respect to Krivine-style operational semantics. The type system has the same expressive power as that of the conventional type system of the lambda calculus. It can therefore serve as an alternative type theoretical framework for analysis and type-based optimization of lambda terms such as uncurrying.

Second, we have designed type systems for two varieties of Krivine-style low level abstract machines – one with statically determined spine stacks and the other, similar to ZINC machine, with dynamically determined ones, and have established the type soundness property for both machines. For those Krivine abstract machines, we have developed type-directed compilation algorithms, and have shown that the algorithms preserve both typing and operational semantics. We have compared the relative merit of the two varieties of Krivine-style abstract machines within a single framework.

This is the first step toward a type theory for Krivine-style evaluation and compilation, and a number of issues remain to be investigated. First of all, we need to develop an optimal type inference algorithm that detects the longest evaluation context. Second, we need to develop a practical type-directed compilation algorithm that minimizes redundant closure creation. We are currently investigating the adaptation of the Krivine abstract machine in an ML compiler we have been developing at JAIST.

Acknowledgments

The first author would like to thank Kwangkeun Yi for his helpful comments on an earlier version of ZINC type system. The second author would like to thank René Vestergaard for insightful discussion on Krivine-style evaluation.

References

1. K. Choi and T. Han. A type system for the push-enter model. *Information Processing Letters*, 87:205–211, 2003.
2. K. Choi and A. Ohori. A type theory for Krivine-style evaluation and compilation. Technical report IS-RR-2004-014, JAIST, 2004.
3. P. Cregut. An abstract machine for the normalization of λ-terms. In *Proc. ACM Conference on LISP and Functional Programming*, pages 333–340, 1990.
4. B. Duba, R. Harper, and D. MacQueen. Typing first-class continuations in ML. In *Proc. ACM Symp. on Principles of Prog. Languages*, pages 163–73, 1991.
5. J. Hannan and P. Hicks. Higher-order uncurrying. In *Proc. ACM Symposium on Principles of Programming Languages*, 1998.
6. X. Leroy. The ZINC experiment: an economical implementation of the ML language. Technical Report 117, INRIA, 1992.
7. G. Morrisett, K. Crary, N. Glew, and D. Walker. Stack-based typed assembly language. In *Proc. Workshop on Types in Compilation, LNCS 1478*, 1998.
8. A. Ohori. A Curry-Howard isomorphism for compilation and program execution. In *Proc. Typed Lambda Calculi and Applications, LNCS 1581*, pages 258–179, 1999.
9. A. Ohori. The logical abstract machine: a Curry-Howard isomorphism for machine code. In *Proc. International Symp. on Functional and Logic Programming*, 1999.

Region-Based Memory Management for a Dynamically-Typed Language

Akihito Nagata[1], Naoki Kobayashi [2], and Akinori Yonezawa[1]

[1]Dept. of Computer Science, University of Tokyo[**]
{ganat,yonezawa}@yl.is.s.u-tokyo.ac.jp
[2]Dept. of Computer Science, Tokyo Institute of Technology
kobayasi@cs.titech.ac.jp

Abstract. Region-based memory management scheme has been proposed for the programming language ML. In this scheme, a compiler statically estimates the lifetime of each object by performing an extension of type inference (called region inference) and inserts code for memory allocation and deallocation. Advantages of this scheme are that memory objects can be deallocated safely (unlike with manual memory management using malloc/free) and often earlier than with run-time garbage collection. Since the region inference is an extension of the ML type inference, however, it was not clear whether the region-based memory management was applicable to dynamically-typed programming languages like Scheme. In this paper, we show that the region-based memory management can be applied to dynamically-typed languages by combining region inference and Cartwright et al.'s soft type system.

1   Introduction

Tofte et al. [23] proposed a static memory management scheme called region inference. In this scheme, heap space is divided into abstract memory spaces called regions. Memory is allocated and deallocated region-wise and every object generated at run-time is placed in one of the regions. A compiler statically estimates the lifetime of each region, and statically inserts code for allocating/deallocating regions.

For example, a source program:

$$\text{let } x = (1, 2) \text{ in } \lambda y. \; \#1 \; x \text{ end}$$

is translated into

$$\text{letregion } \rho_2 \text{ in}$$
$$\text{let } x = (1 \text{ at } \rho_1, 2 \text{ at } \rho_2) \text{ at } \rho_3$$
$$\text{in } \lambda y. \; \#1 \; x \text{ at } \rho_4 \text{ end}$$
$$\text{end}$$

[**] Nagata's current affiliation: OS Development Dept. R&D Div. Sony Computer Entertainment Inc.

W.-N. Chin (Ed.): APLAS 2004, LNCS 3302, pp. 229–245, 2004.
© Springer-Verlag Berlin Heidelberg 2004

Here, #1 is the primitive for extracting the first element from a pair, and ρ_i stands for a region. **letregion** ρ **in** e **end** is a construct for allocating and deallocating a region. It first creates a new region ρ, and evaluates e. After evaluating e, it deallocates ρ and returns the evaluation result. v **at** ρ specifies that the value v should be stored in the region ρ. Given the source program above, a compiler can infer that the integer 2 is used only in that expression, so that it inserts **letregion** ρ_2 **in** $\cdots$ **end**. This transformation (which inserts **letregion** ρ $\cdots$ and **at** ρ) is called region inference [23].

Region-based memory management has several advantages over conventional memory management schemes. First, it is safe, compared with manual memory management using free/malloc in C. Second, it can often deallocate memory cells earlier than conventional, pointer-tracing garbage collection (in the sense that memory cells are deallocated at the end of the letregion construct, while garbage collection is invoked only periodically). Since the original region inference is an extension of the ML type inference, however, it was not clear how to apply the region-based memory management to programming languages other than ML, especially dynamically-typed programming languages such as Scheme [14]. In this paper, we show that the region-based memory management can be applied to dynamically-typed languages by combining region inference and soft typing [5].

We explain the main idea below. First, we review ideas of the original region inference. Under region inference, ordinary types are annotated with region information. For example, the type **int** of integers is replaced by $(\mathbf{int}, \rho)$, which describes integers stored in region ρ. Similarly, the function type **int** $\to$ **int** is extended to $((\mathbf{int}, \rho_1) \xrightarrow{\varphi} (\mathbf{int}, \rho_2), \rho_3)$, which describes a function stored in region ρ_3 that takes an integer stored in ρ_1 as an argument, accesses regions in φ when it is called, and returns an integer stored in ρ_2. By performing type inference for those extended types, a compiler can statically infer in which region each value is stored and which region is accessed when each expression is evaluated. Using that information, a compiler statically inserts the **letregion** construct. For example, the expression above is given a type $(\alpha \xrightarrow{\{\rho_3\}} (\mathbf{int}, \rho_1), \rho_4)$, where α is an arbitrary type. Using this type, a compiler infers that when the function is applied at execution time, only the region ρ_3 may be accessed and an integer stored in region ρ_1 is returned. Therefore, the compiler can determine that the region ρ_2 is used only in this expression, and insert **letregion** ρ_2 **in** $\cdots$.

As described above, region inference is an extension of ML type inference, so that it cannot be immediately applied to dynamically-typed language. We solve this problem by using the idea of soft typing [5].[1] We construct a new region-

---

[1] An alternative way would be to translate scheme programs into ML by preparing the following datatype:

datatype scm_val = Int of int | Pair of scm_val * scm_val
                 | Fun of scm_val $\to$ scm_val | ...

It does not work well, since too many values are put into the same region. For example, consider (**if** a **then** $\lambda x.x + 1$ **else** 2). Then, argument and return values of $\lambda x.x + 1$ would be put into the same region as that of 2.

annotated type system which includes union types and recursive types. Using union and recursive types, for example, an expression (**if** a **then** $\lambda x.x$ **else** 1), which may return either a function or an integer, can be given a region-annotated type $(\mathbf{int}, \rho_1) \vee (\tau_1 \xrightarrow{\varphi} \tau_2, \rho_3)$, which means that the expression returns either an integer stored in ρ_1 or a function stored in ρ_3. Using this kind of type, a compiler can translate (**if** a **then** $\lambda x.x$ **else** 1)2 into:

> **letregion** ρ_1, ρ_3 **in**
> (**if** a **then** ($\lambda x.x$ **at** ρ_3) **else** 1 **at** ρ_1)(2 **at** ρ_2)

We have constructed the region-type system hinted above for a core language of Scheme, and proved its soundness. We have also implemented a prototype region inference system for Scheme. In a more general perspective, one of the main contributions of this work is to show that type-based analyses (which have originally been developed for statically-typed languages) can be applied also to dynamically-typed languages by using the idea of soft typing.

The rest of this paper is organized as follows. In Section 2, we introduce a target language of our region inference and define its operational semantics. In Sections 3 and 4, we introduce a region-type system for the target language, and prove its soundness. In Section 5, we sketch a region inference algorithm. In Section 6, we discuss extensions of our target language to deal with full Scheme. In Section 7, we report the result of preliminary experiments on our region inference system. Section 8 discusses related work. Section 9 concludes.

2   Target Language

In this section, we define the syntax and the semantics of the target language of our region inference. It is a λ-calculus extended with constructs for manipulating regions (**letregion** ρ **in** $\cdots$, **at** ρ, etc.). Note that programmers need only to write ordinary functional programs: the constructs for regions are automatically inserted by our region inference described in later sections.

2.1   Syntax

Definition 2.1 [Expressions]: The set of expressions, ranged over by e, is given by:

$$e \text{ (expressions)} ::= x \mid n \text{ at } \rho \mid \lambda x.e \text{ at } \rho \mid e_1 e_2$$
$$\mid \text{ let } f = \mathbf{fix}(f, \Lambda\varrho.(\lambda x.e_1 \text{ at } \rho)) \text{ at } \rho' \text{ in } e_2$$
$$\mid f[\boldsymbol{\rho}] \mid \mathbf{if0} \ e_1 \text{ then } e_2 \text{ else } e_3$$
$$\mid \text{ letregion } \varrho \text{ in } e$$
$$\mid v \mid v[\boldsymbol{\rho}]$$
$$v \text{ (run-time values)} ::= \langle n \rangle_\rho \mid \langle \lambda x.e \rangle_\rho \mid \langle \mathbf{fix}(f, \Lambda\varrho.(\lambda x.e \text{ at } \rho)) \rangle_{\rho'}$$
$$\rho \text{ (regions)} ::= \varrho \mid \bullet$$

Here, x ranges over a countably infinite set of variables, and n ranges over the set of integers. ϱ ranges over a countably infinite set of region variables. $\boldsymbol{\rho}$ represents a sequence $\rho_1, \ldots, \rho_n$.

The expressions given above includes those for representing run-time values (ranged over by v): they have been borrowed from the formalization of Calcagno et al. [4]. An expression n **at** ρ stores an integer n in region ρ and returns (a pointer to) the integer. A region ρ is either a live region (denoted by ϱ) or a dead region $\bullet$ (that has been already deallocated). Our type system presented in the next section guarantees that n **at** $\bullet$ is never executed. $\lambda x.e$ **at** ρ stores a closure $\lambda x.e$ in region ρ and returns a pointer to it. An expression $e_1 e_2$ applies e_1 to e_2. An expression **let** $f = \mathbf{fix}(f, \Lambda\varrho.(\lambda x.e_1$ **at** $\rho))$ **at** ρ' **in** e_2 stores in region ρ' a recursive, region-polymorphic [23] function f that takes regions and a value as an argument, binds them to ϱ and x, and evaluates e_1; it then binds f to the function and evaluates e_2. An expression $f[\rho]$ applies the region-polymorphic function f to ρ. **if0** e_1 **then** e_2 **else** e_3 evaluates e_2 if the value of e_1 is 0, and evaluates e_3 otherwise. **letregion** ρ **in** e creates a new region and binds ρ to the new region; it then evaluates e, deallocates the region ρ, and evaluates to the value of e. Run-time values $\langle n \rangle_\rho$, $\langle \lambda x.e \rangle_\rho$ and $\langle \mathbf{fix}(f, \Lambda\varrho.(\lambda x.e$ **at** $\rho)) \rangle_{\rho'}$ denote pointers to an integer, a closure, and a region-polymorphic function respectively. The difference between $\langle n \rangle_\rho$ and n **at** ρ is that the former has already been allocated, so that evaluating it does not cause any memory access, while evaluation of the latter causes an access to the region ρ.

The bound and free variables of e are defined in a customary manner: x is bound in $\lambda x.e$, f, ϱ, and x are bound in $\mathbf{fix}(f, \Lambda\varrho.(\lambda x.e_1$ **at** $\rho))$, and ϱ is bound in **letregion** ϱ **in** e. We assume that α-conversion is implicitly performed as necessary, so that all the bound variables are different from each other and from free variables.

2.2   Operational Semantics

We define the operational semantics of our target language, following the formalization of Calcagno et al. [4].

Definition 2.2 [Evaluation Contexts]: The set of evaluation contexts, ranged over by E, is given by:

$$E ::= [\,] \mid Ee \mid vE \mid \mathbf{if0}\ E\ \mathbf{then}\ e_1\ \mathbf{else}\ e_2$$
$$\mid\ \mathbf{letregion}\ \varrho\ \mathbf{in}\ E$$

We write $E[e]$ for the term obtained by replacing $[\,]$ in E with e.

Definition 2.3 [Reduction]: The reduction relation $e \longrightarrow e'$ is the least relation that satisfies the rules in Figure 1.

The relation $e \longrightarrow e'$ means that e is reduced to e' on one step. As in [4], function applications are carried out by using substitutions, so that the identity of each pointer is lost. For example, we cannot tell whether or not two occurrences of $\langle 1 \rangle_\rho$ point to the same location. This does not cause a problem in our target language, since there is no primitive for comparing or updating pointers. In the rule R-REG, region deallocation is modeled by replacement of

$$E[n \text{ at } \varrho] \longrightarrow E[\langle n \rangle_\varrho] \qquad \text{(R-INT)}$$
$$E[\lambda x.e \text{ at } \varrho] \longrightarrow E[\langle \lambda x.e \rangle_\varrho] \qquad \text{(R-ABS)}$$
$$E[\langle \lambda x.e \rangle_\varrho v] \longrightarrow E[[v/x]e] \qquad \text{(R-APP)}$$
$$E[\langle \mathbf{fix}(f, \Lambda \boldsymbol{\varrho}.(\lambda x.e \text{ at } \rho)) \rangle_{\varrho'}[\boldsymbol{\rho}]] \qquad \text{(R-RAPP)}$$
$$\longrightarrow E[\langle \lambda x.[\langle \mathbf{fix}(f, \Lambda \boldsymbol{\varrho}.(\lambda x.e \text{ at } \rho)) \rangle_{\varrho'}/f][\boldsymbol{\rho}/\boldsymbol{\varrho}]e \rangle_{[\rho/\varrho]\rho}]$$
$$E[\mathbf{let} \ f = \mathbf{fix}(f, \Lambda \boldsymbol{\varrho}.(\lambda x.e_1 \text{ at } \rho)) \text{ at } \rho' \text{ in } e_2] \qquad \text{(R-FIX)}$$
$$\longrightarrow E[[\langle \mathbf{fix}(f, \Lambda \boldsymbol{\varrho}.(\lambda x.e_1 \text{ at } \rho)) \rangle_{\rho'}/f]e_2]$$
$$E[\mathbf{if0} \ \langle 0 \rangle_\varrho \text{ then } e_1 \text{ else } e_2] \longrightarrow E[e_1] \qquad \text{(R-IFT)}$$
$$E[\mathbf{if0} \ \langle n \rangle_\varrho \text{ then } e_1 \text{ else } e_2] \longrightarrow E[e_2] \qquad \text{(if } n \neq 0\text{)} \qquad \text{(R-IFF)}$$
$$E[\mathbf{letregion} \ \varrho \text{ in } v] \longrightarrow E[[\bullet/\varrho]v] \qquad \text{(R-REG)}$$

Fig. 1. Reduction rules

a region variable with the dead region $\bullet$. Notice that in each rule, the region accessed in the reduction is denoted by the meta-variable ϱ for live regions, rather than ρ: evaluation gets stuck when the dead region $\bullet$ is accessed.

Example 2.4: Let us consider:

$$\mathbf{letregion} \ \varrho_1, \varrho_5 \text{ in } (\lambda x.(\lambda y.(\mathbf{letregion} \ \varrho_3 \text{ in } e \ x) \text{ at } \varrho_2)) \text{ at } \varrho_1)(1 \text{ at } \varrho_5)$$

where $e = (\lambda z.(2 \text{ at } \varrho_4) \text{ at } \varrho_3)$. This is the program obtained by applying region inference to the source program $(\lambda x.(\lambda y.(\lambda z.2) \ x))1$.

The above program is reduced as follows.

$$\mathbf{letregion} \ \varrho_1, \varrho_5 \text{ in } (\lambda x.(\lambda y.(\mathbf{letregion} \ \varrho_3 \text{ in } e \ x) \text{ at } \varrho_2)) \text{ at } \varrho_1)(1 \text{ at } \varrho_5)$$
$$\longrightarrow \mathbf{letregion} \ \varrho_1, \varrho_5 \text{ in } \langle \lambda x.(\lambda y.(\mathbf{letregion} \ \varrho_3 \text{ in } e \ x) \text{ at } \varrho_2)) \rangle_{\varrho_1}(1 \text{ at } \varrho_5)$$
$$\longrightarrow \mathbf{letregion} \ \varrho_1, \varrho_5 \text{ in } \langle \lambda x.(\lambda y.(\mathbf{letregion} \ \varrho_3 \text{ in } e \ x) \text{ at } \varrho_2)) \rangle_{\varrho_1} \langle 1 \rangle_{\varrho_5}$$
$$\longrightarrow \mathbf{letregion} \ \varrho_1, \varrho_5 \text{ in } \lambda y.(\mathbf{letregion} \ \varrho_3 \text{ in } e \ \langle 1 \rangle_{\varrho_5}) \text{ at } \varrho_2)$$
$$\longrightarrow \lambda y.(\mathbf{letregion} \ \varrho_3 \text{ in } e \ \langle 1 \rangle_\bullet) \text{ at } \varrho_2)$$

The result contains a value $\langle 1 \rangle_\bullet$ stored in the dead region $\bullet$, but it does not cause a problem since e does not access the value.

3 Type System

In this section, we present a type system for the target language introduced in the previous section. The type system guarantees that every well-typed program never accesses dead regions. So, the problem of region inference is reduced to that of inserting "**letregion** ρ **in** $\cdots$" and " **at** ρ" so that the resulting program is well-typed in the type system (which can be done through type inference).

3.1   Syntax of Types

Definition 3.1 [Types]: The set of types, ranged over by τ, is given by:

$$
\begin{array}{lll}
\mu \text{ (atomic types)} & ::= & (\mathbf{num}, \rho) \mid (\tau_1 \xrightarrow{\varphi} \tau_2, \rho) \\
\varphi \text{ (effects)} & ::= & \xi \mid \{\rho_1, \ldots, \rho_n\} \mid \varphi_1 \cup \varphi_2 \\
\tau \text{ (types)} & ::= & r \mid \mathbf{rec}\ r.\mu_1 \vee \cdots \vee \mu_n \\
& & \mid \mathbf{rec}\ r.\mu_1 \vee \cdots \vee \mu_n \vee \alpha \\
\pi \text{ (type schemes)} & ::= & \forall \varrho^\varphi.\forall \alpha.\forall \xi.\tau
\end{array}
$$

Here, we assume that there are two sets of type variables. One, which is ranged over by α, is the set of type variables bound by universal quantifiers, and the other, which is ranged over by r, is the set of type variables for expressing recursive types.[2] The meta-variable ξ denotes an effect variable.

An atomic type $(\mathbf{num}, \rho)$ describes an integer stored in region ρ. An atomic type $(\tau_1 \xrightarrow{\varphi} \tau_2, \rho)$ describes a function that is stored in ρ and that takes a value of type τ_1 as an argument, accesses regions in φ, and returns a value of type τ_2.

A type $\mathbf{rec}\ r.\mu_1 \vee \cdots \vee \mu_n$ describes a value whose type is one of $[(\mathbf{rec}\ r.\mu_1 \vee \cdots \vee \mu_n)/r]\mu_1, \ldots, [(\mathbf{rec}\ r.\mu_1 \vee \cdots \vee \mu_n)/r]\mu_n$. For example, a value of type $\mathbf{rec}\ r.(\mathbf{num}, \rho) \vee (r \xrightarrow{\varphi} r)$ is either an integer or a function that takes a value of type $\mathbf{rec}\ r.(\mathbf{num}, \rho) \vee (r \xrightarrow{\varphi} r)$ and returns a value of the same type. Here, as in the ordinary soft type system [5], we require that the outermost type constructors of $\mu_1, \ldots, \mu_n$ are different from each other.[3] For example, $\mathbf{rec}\ r.(\mathbf{num}, \rho) \vee (\mathbf{num}, \rho')$ is invalid. (The restriction must be respected by substitutions; for example, we disallow the substitution $[(\mathbf{num}, \rho)/\alpha]$ to be applied to $\mathbf{rec}\ r.((\mathbf{num}, \rho') \vee \alpha).)$ When r does not appear in $\mu_1, \ldots, \mu_n$, we write $\mu_1 \vee \cdots \vee \mu_n$ for $\mathbf{rec}\ r.\mu_1 \vee \cdots \vee \mu_n$. In $\mathbf{rec}\ r.\mu_1 \vee \cdots \vee \mu_n \vee \alpha$, n can be 0, so that $\mathbf{rec}\ r.\alpha$ (which is abbreviated to α) is also a valid type.

Note that union types $\mu_1 \vee \cdots \vee \mu_n$ are not annotated with regions. This is because we use a tag-on-pointer representation of data at run-time, where tags to indicate the shape of each data are embedded in pointers. If a tag is stored in the memory cell instead, the union type should be annotated with a region to express where the tag is stored.

A type scheme $\forall \varrho^\varphi \forall \alpha \forall \xi.\tau$ describes a region-polymorphic function. The effect φ is the set of regions that may be accessed when regions are passed to the region-polymorphic function.[4] For example, $\mathbf{fix}(f, \Lambda\rho_1\rho_2.(\lambda x.x\ \mathbf{at}\ \rho_2))$ has a type scheme $(\forall \rho_1 \rho_2^{\{\rho_2\}}.((\mathbf{num}, \rho_1) \xrightarrow{\emptyset} (\mathbf{num}, \rho_1), \rho_2)$ (assuming that variable x has an integer type).

---

[2] This distinction between two kinds of variables is necessary to rule out a type expression like $\mathbf{rec}\ r.((\mathbf{num}, \rho) \vee r)$.

[3] Otherwise, type inference would suffer from explosion of case analyses.

[4] Actually, φ is always a singleton set $\{\rho\}$, so that it is possible to make the effect implicit, as in the original region and effect system [23].

3.2   Typing Rules

A type judgment relation is of the form $\Gamma \vdash e : \tau$ & φ. Intuitively, it means that if e is evaluated under an environment that respects the type environment Γ, the evaluation result has type τ and regions in φ may be accessed during the evaluation. Here, a type environment Γ is a mapping from a finite set of variables to the union of the set of types and the set of pairs of the form (π, ρ) (where π is a type scheme and ρ is a region).

Typing rules are given in Figures 2 and 3. Here, the relation $\tau' \prec \forall \alpha \forall \xi. \tau$ used in T-RAPP and T-VRAPP means that there exist τ'' and φ such that $\tau' = [\tau''/\alpha][\varphi/\xi]\tau$. The relation $\mu \subseteq \tau$ means that $\tau = \mathbf{rec}\ r. \cdots \vee \mu' \vee \cdots$ and $\mu = [\tau/r]\mu'$ hold for some r and μ'. $\mathbf{fv}(\Gamma)$ and $\mathbf{fv}(\tau)$ denote the sets of free region, type, and effect variables (i.e., those not bound by $\mathbf{rec}\ r.$ or $\forall \varrho^\varphi. \forall \alpha. \forall \xi.$) appearing in Γ and τ respectively.

Note that in the rule T-APP, e_1 need not be a function, since τ_1 may be $(\mathbf{num}, \rho') \vee (\tau_2 \xrightarrow{\varphi_0} \tau_3, \rho)$. When $e_1 e_2$ is evaluated, e_1 and e_2 are first evaluated and the regions in $\varphi_1 \cup \varphi_2$ may be accessed. After that, if the value of e_1 is a function, then the function is called and the regions in $\varphi_0 \cup \{\rho\}$ may be accessed. Otherwise, the evaluation gets stuck, so that no more region is accessed. So, the effect $\varphi_0 \cup \varphi_1 \cup \varphi_2 \cup \{\rho\}$ soundly estimates the set of regions that are accessed when $e_1 e_2$ is evaluated, irrespectively of whether the value of e_1 is a function or not. Recall that we use a tag-on-pointer representation of data at run-time, so, no region is accessed when it is checked whether the value of e_1 is a function or not.

Example 3.2: The type judgment:

$\emptyset \vdash \mathbf{letregion}\ \rho_0, \rho_1, \rho_3\ \mathbf{in}$
$\quad (\mathbf{if0}\ n\ \mathbf{at}\ \rho_0\ \mathbf{then}\ (\lambda x.x\ \mathbf{at}\ \rho_3)\ \mathbf{else}\ 1\ \mathbf{at}\ \rho_1)(2\ \mathbf{at}\ \rho_2) : (\mathbf{num}, \rho_2)\ \&\ \{\rho_2\}$

is derived as follows (here, n is some integer).

First, we can obtain $\emptyset \vdash n\ \mathbf{at}\ \rho_0 : (\mathbf{num}, \rho_0)\&\{\rho_0\}$ and $x : (\mathbf{num}, \rho_2) \vdash x : (\mathbf{num}, \rho_2)\ \&\ \emptyset$ by using the rule T-INT and T-VAR. By applying rule T-ABS to the latter, we obtain

$$\emptyset \vdash \lambda x.x\ \mathbf{at}\ \rho_3 : ((\mathbf{num}, \rho_2) \xrightarrow{\emptyset} (\mathbf{num}, \rho_2), \rho_3) \vee (\mathbf{num}, \rho_1)\&\{\rho_3\}.$$

We can also obtain

$$\emptyset \vdash 1\ \mathbf{at}\ \rho_1 : ((\mathbf{num}, \rho_2) \xrightarrow{\emptyset} (\mathbf{num}, \rho_2), \rho_3) \vee (\mathbf{num}, \rho_1)\&\{\rho_1\}$$

by using T-INT. By applying T-IF and T-APP, we obtain

$$\emptyset \vdash (\mathbf{if0}\ n\ \mathbf{at}\ \rho_0\ \mathbf{then}\ (\lambda x.x\ \mathbf{at}\ \rho_3)\ \mathbf{else}\ 1\ \mathbf{at}\ \rho_1)(2\ \mathbf{at}\ \rho_2)$$
$$: (\mathbf{num}, \rho_2)\&\{\rho_0, \rho_1, \rho_2, \rho_3\}$$

Finally, by using T-REG, we obtain:

$\emptyset \vdash \mathbf{letregion}\ \rho_0, \rho_1, \rho_3\ \mathbf{in}$
$\quad (\mathbf{if0}\ n\ \mathbf{at}\ \rho_0\ \mathbf{then}\ (\lambda x.x\ \mathbf{at}\ \rho_3)\ \mathbf{else}\ 1\ \mathbf{at}\ \rho_1)(2\ \mathbf{at}\ \rho_2) : (\mathbf{num}, \rho_2)\ \&\ \{\rho_2\}.$

$$\frac{\Gamma(x) = \tau}{\Gamma \vdash x : \tau \ \& \ \emptyset} \ \text{(T-VAR)}$$

$$\frac{(\mathbf{num}, \rho) \subseteq \tau}{\Gamma \vdash n \ \mathbf{at} \ \rho : \tau \ \& \ \{\rho\}} \ \text{(T-INT)}$$

$$\frac{\Gamma + \{x \mapsto \tau_1\} \vdash e : \tau_2 \ \& \ \varphi' \qquad \varphi' \subseteq \varphi}{(\tau_1 \xrightarrow{\varphi} \tau_2, \rho) \subseteq \tau_3} \ \Gamma \vdash \lambda x.e \ \mathbf{at} \ \rho : \tau_3 \ \& \ \{\rho\}} \ \text{(T-ABS)}$$

$$\frac{\Gamma \vdash e_1 : \tau_1 \ \& \ \varphi_1 \qquad (\tau_2 \xrightarrow{\varphi_0} \tau_3, \rho) \subseteq \tau_1}{\Gamma \vdash e_2 : \tau_2 \ \& \ \varphi_2}{\Gamma \vdash e_1 e_2 : \tau_3 \ \& \ \varphi_0 \cup \varphi_1 \cup \varphi_2 \cup \{\rho\}} \ \text{(T-APP)}$$

$$\frac{\Gamma(f) = (\pi, \rho_f) \qquad \pi = \forall \varrho^\varphi \forall \alpha \forall \xi.\tau}{\tau' \prec \forall \alpha \forall \xi.[\rho'/\varrho]\tau}{\Gamma \vdash f[\rho'] : \tau' \ \& \ \{\rho_f\} \cup [\rho'/\varrho]\varphi} \ \text{(T-RAPP)}$$

$$\frac{\Gamma \vdash e_1 : \tau_1 \ \& \ \varphi_1 \qquad (\mathbf{num}, \rho) \subseteq \tau_1}{\Gamma \vdash e_2 : \tau_2 \ \& \ \varphi_2 \qquad \Gamma \vdash e_3 : \tau_2 \ \& \ \varphi_3}{\Gamma \vdash \mathbf{if0} \ e_1 \ \mathbf{then} \ e_2 \ \mathbf{else} \ e_3}{: \tau_2 \ \& \ \varphi_1 \cup \varphi_2 \cup \varphi_3 \cup \{\rho\}} \ \text{(T-IF)}$$

$$\frac{\Gamma \vdash e : \tau \ \& \ \varphi \qquad \varrho \notin \mathbf{fv}(\Gamma) \cup \mathbf{fv}(\tau)}{\Gamma \vdash \mathbf{letregion} \ \varrho \ \mathbf{in} \ e : \tau \ \& \ \varphi \setminus \{\varrho\}} \ \text{(T-REG)}$$

$$\frac{\pi = \forall \varrho^{\varphi_1} \forall \xi.\tau_1 \qquad \{\varrho, \xi, \alpha\} \cap (\mathbf{fv}(\Gamma) \cup \{\rho_f\}) = \emptyset}{\Gamma + \{f \mapsto (\pi, \rho_f)\} \vdash \lambda x.e_1 \ \mathbf{at} \ \rho_t : \tau_1 \ \& \ \varphi_1}{\pi' = \forall \varrho^{\varphi_1} \forall \alpha \forall \xi.\tau_1 \qquad \Gamma + \{f \mapsto (\pi', \rho_f)\} \vdash e_2 : \tau_2 \ \& \ \varphi_2}{\Gamma \vdash \mathbf{let} \ f = \mathbf{fix}(f, \Lambda \varrho.(\lambda x.e_1 \ \mathbf{at} \ \rho_t)) \ \mathbf{at} \ \rho_f \ \mathbf{in} \ e_2 : \tau_2 \ \& \ \{\rho_f\} \cup \varphi_2} \ \text{(T-FIX)}$$

Fig. 2. Typing rules for static expressions

$$\frac{\Gamma \vdash v : (\forall \varrho^\varphi \forall \alpha \forall \xi.\tau, \rho_f)}{\tau' \prec \forall \alpha \forall \xi.[\rho'/\varrho]\tau}{\Gamma \vdash v[\rho'] : \tau' \ \& \ \{\rho_f\} \cup [\rho'/\varrho]\varphi} \ \text{(T-VRAPP)}$$

$$\frac{(\mathbf{num}, \rho) \subseteq \tau}{\Gamma \vdash \langle n \rangle_\rho : \tau \ \& \ \emptyset} \ \text{(T-VINT)}$$

$$\frac{\Gamma + \{x \mapsto \tau_1\} \vdash e : \tau_2 \ \& \ \varphi'}{\varphi' \subseteq \varphi}{(\tau_1 \xrightarrow{\varphi} \tau_2, \rho) \subseteq \tau}{\Gamma \vdash \langle \lambda x.e \rangle_\rho : \tau \ \& \ \emptyset} \ \text{(T-VABS)}$$

$$\frac{\pi = \forall \varrho^\varphi \forall \xi.\tau}{\{\varrho, \xi, \alpha\} \cap (\mathbf{fv}(\Gamma) \cup \{\rho_f\}) = \emptyset}{\Gamma + \{f \mapsto (\pi, \rho_f)\} \vdash \lambda x.e \ \mathbf{at} \ \rho_t : \tau \ \& \ \varphi}{\pi' = \forall \varrho^{\varphi\varphi} \forall \alpha \forall \xi.\tau}{\Gamma \vdash \langle \mathbf{fix}(f, \Lambda \varrho.(\lambda x.e \ \mathbf{at} \ \rho_t)) \rangle_{\rho_f} : (\pi', \rho_f) \ \& \ \emptyset} \ \text{(T-VFIX)}$$

Fig. 3. Typing rules for dynamic expressions

Example 3.3: An expression corresponding to a source program **if0** 1 **then** $\lambda x.x$ **else** $\lambda x.2$ is typed as follows.

$$\emptyset \vdash \mathbf{letregion} \ \rho_0 \ \mathbf{in}$$
$$\mathbf{if0} \ 1 \ \mathbf{at} \ \rho_0 \ \mathbf{then} \ \lambda x.x \ \mathbf{at} \ \rho_1 \ \mathbf{else} \ \lambda x.(2 \ \mathbf{at} \ \rho_2) \ \mathbf{at} \ \rho_1 :$$
$$(((\mathbf{num}, \rho_2) \vee \alpha) \xrightarrow{\{\rho_1, \rho_2\}} ((\mathbf{num}, \rho_2) \vee \alpha), \rho_1) \ \& \ \{\rho_1\}$$

The then-part must have a type of the form $(\alpha \xrightarrow{\varphi_1} \alpha, \rho_1)$ where $\{\rho_1\} \subseteq \varphi_1$ and the else-part must have a type of the form $(\beta \xrightarrow{\varphi_2} (\mathbf{num}, \rho_2), \rho_1)$ where $\{\rho_1, \rho_2\} \subseteq \varphi_2$. The type of the whole if-expression above can be obtained by unifying those types.

4   Properties of the Type System

The soundness of the type system is guaranteed by Theorems 4.1 and 4.2 given below. Theorem 4.1 implies that a well-typed, closed (i.e., not containing free variables) expression does not access a deallocated region immediately. Theorem 4.2 implies that the well-typedness of an expression is preserved by reduction. These theorems together imply that a well-typed, closed expression never accesses a deallocated region. Our proof is based on the syntactic type soundness proof of Calcagno et al. [4], and extends it to handle union/recursive types and polymorphism.

Theorem 4.1: Suppose $\emptyset \vdash e : \tau \,\&\, \varphi$, and e is one of the following forms:

- $E[n \text{ at } \rho]$
- $E[\lambda x.e \text{ at } \rho]$
- $E[\langle\lambda x.e\rangle_\rho v]$
- $E[\langle\mathbf{fix}(f, \Lambda\varrho.(\lambda x.e \text{ at } \rho'))\rangle_\rho[\rho'']]$
- $E[\mathbf{let}\ f = \mathbf{fix}(f, \Lambda\varrho.(\lambda x.e_1 \text{ at } \rho')) \text{ at } \rho \text{ in } e_2]$
- $E[\mathbf{if0}\ \langle n\rangle_\rho \text{ then } e_1 \text{ else } e_2]$

If $\bullet \notin \varphi$, then $\rho \neq \bullet$. In the fourth case, $[\rho''/\varrho]\rho' \neq \bullet$ also holds.

Theorem 4.2 [Subject Reduction]: If $\Gamma \vdash e : \tau \,\&\, \varphi$ and $e \longrightarrow e'$, then $\Gamma \vdash e' : \tau \,\&\, \varphi'$ for some φ' such that $\varphi' \subseteq \varphi$.

Proofs of the theorems above are found in the full version of this paper [19].

Note that the type system does not guarantee that evaluation of a well-typed program never gets stuck: since the target of our study is a dynamically-typed language like Scheme, our type system does allow an expression like $\mathbf{if0}\ \langle\lambda x.e\rangle_\rho \text{ then } e_1 \text{ else } e_2$. In fact, our type system can type any source program, as stated in Theorem 4.5 below.

Definition 4.3 [Source Programs]: The set of source programs, ranged over by M, is given by:

$$M ::= x \mid f \mid n \mid \lambda x.M \mid M_1 M_2$$
$$\mid \mathbf{let}\ f = \mathbf{fix}(f, \lambda x.M_1) \text{ in } M_2 \mid \mathbf{if0}\ M_1 \text{ then } M_2 \text{ else } M_3$$

Definition 4.4 [Region Erasure]: The region erasure function $(\cdot)^\sharp$ is a partial mapping from the set of expressions to the set of source programs, defined by:

$x^\sharp = x$

$(n \text{ at } \rho)^\sharp = n$

$(\lambda x.e \text{ at } \rho)^\sharp = \lambda x.e^\sharp$

$(\text{let } f = \textbf{fix}(f, \Lambda\varrho.(\lambda x.e_1 \text{ at } \rho)) \text{ at } \rho' \text{ in } e_2)^\sharp = \text{let } f = \textbf{fix}(f, \lambda x.e_1^\sharp) \text{ in } e_2^\sharp$

$(f[\rho])^\sharp = f$

$(\text{if0 } e_1 \text{ then } e_2 \text{ else } e_3)^\sharp = \text{if0 } e_1^\sharp \text{ then } e_2^\sharp \text{ else } e_3^\sharp$

$(\textbf{letregion } \varrho \text{ in } e)^\sharp = e^\sharp$

Theorem 4.5: For any closed source program M, there exist e, τ and φ such that $\emptyset \vdash e : \tau \& \varphi$ and $e^\sharp = M$.

Proof. Let τ be $\textbf{rec } r.((\textbf{num}, \rho_G) \vee (r \xrightarrow{\{\rho_G\}} r, \rho_G))$. Let us define a function $(\cdot)^\flat$ from the set of source programs to expressions by:

$$
\begin{aligned}
x^\flat &= x \\
f^\flat &= f[\epsilon] \\
n^\flat &= n \text{ at } \rho_G \\
(\lambda x.M)^\flat &= \lambda x.e^\flat \text{ at } \rho_G \\
(\text{let } f = \textbf{fix}(f, \lambda x.M_1) \text{ in } M_2)^\flat &= \\
&\quad \text{let } f = \textbf{fix}(f, \Lambda\epsilon.(\lambda x.M_1^\flat \text{ at } \rho_G)) \text{ at } \rho_G \text{ in } M_2^\flat \\
(\text{if0 } M_1 \text{ then } M_2 \text{ else } M_3)^\flat &= \text{if0 } M_1^\flat \text{ then } M_2^\flat \text{ else } M_3^\flat
\end{aligned}
$$

Here, ϵ denotes the empty sequence of regions. The idea of the above translation is to use ρ_G as a special region that is never deallocated and where all values are stored. It is easy to check that $\emptyset \vdash M^\flat : \tau \& \varphi$ holds for either $\varphi = \{\rho_G\}$ or $\varphi = \emptyset$. (In the derivation, assign the type τ to every variable ranged over by x, and assign the polymorphic type $(\forall \epsilon^{\{\rho_G\}}.\tau, \rho_G)$ to every variable ranged over by f.)

The above theorem guarantees that for any source program, there is at least one valid (i.e., well-typed) region-annotated expression. Of course, the expression constructed in the proof above is not a good annotation, since no region is deallocated. How to find a good annotation is discussed in the next section.

5   Region Inference

In this section, we show how to perform region inference, i.e., transform a source program (without constructs for regions) into a program of the target language defined in section 2. The region inference is carried out in the following steps.

1. Based on the typing rules defined in Section 3, a standard type (types without regions and effects) is inferred for each expression. This can be carried out by using the soft type inference algorithm [5].
2. Fresh region variables and effect variables are added to the types inferred above.

3. Based on the typing rules in Section 3, the actual values of region variables and effect variables are computed. During this, some region and effect variables introduced in the previous step are unified. This can be carried out in a way similar to the ordinary region inference [22]. Finally, **letregion** is inserted in the place where the side condition of T-REG is met. (Actually, inference of regions and effects and insertion of **letregion** have to be carried out in an interleaving manner to handle region polymorphism [22].)

Note that the third step is almost the same as the original region inference algorithm. Although our typing rules are a little more complex because of union types and recursive types, that difference is absorbed in the first step, where the shape of union types and recursive types are determined. For example, after the first phase, the type τ_3 in the rule T-ABS is instantiated to a type of the form $\mathbf{rec}\ r.((\tau_1' \xrightarrow{\varphi'} \tau_2', \rho') \vee \cdots)$, so that it is sufficient to solve the unification constraint $(\tau_1 \xrightarrow{\varphi} \tau_2, \rho) = (\tau_1' \xrightarrow{\varphi'} \tau_2', \rho')$ in the third step, as in the original region inference algorithm.

Since the actual algorithm (especially, the third step: see [22]) is rather complex, we sketch it here only through examples. Please consult the full version for more details [19].

Example 5.1: Consider the expression:

$$(\mathbf{if0}\ n\ \mathbf{then}\ (\lambda x.x)\ \mathbf{else}\ 1)2.$$

Here, n is an integer. Region inference for this expression is performed as follows.

First, the standard type (without regions) of the expression is inferred as $\mathbf{num} \vee (\mathbf{num} \longrightarrow \mathbf{num})$. Then, region and effect variables are inserted, as $(\mathbf{num}, \rho_1) \vee ((\mathbf{num}, \rho_2) \xrightarrow{\emptyset} (\mathbf{num}, \rho_2), \rho_3)$. Using this type, the effect of the whole expression is inferred as $\{\rho_0, \rho_1, \rho_2, \rho_3\}$. The regions ρ_0, ρ_1 and ρ_3 do not appear in the type environment (which is empty) and the type of the returned value $(\mathbf{num}, \rho_2)$, so that **letregion** can be inserted as follows.

$$\mathbf{letregion}\ \rho_0, \rho_1, \rho_3\ \mathbf{in}$$
$$(\mathbf{if0}\ n\ \mathbf{at}\ \rho_0\ \mathbf{then}\ (\lambda x.x\ \mathbf{at}\ \rho_3)\ \mathbf{else}\ 1\ \mathbf{at}\ \rho_1)(2\ \mathbf{at}\ \rho_2)$$

Example 5.2: Let us consider a recursive function:

$$\mathbf{fix}(f, \lambda x.\mathbf{if0}\ x\ \mathbf{then}\ x\ \mathbf{else}\ f(x-1)-1).$$

(Here, we have extended the language with the operation '−'.) In the first phase, the type $\mathbf{num} \rightarrow \mathbf{num}$ is inferred. In the second phase the function is tentatively given a type[5]

---

[5] As in [22], we do not consider quantifications over secondary region and effect variables to ensure termination of the algorithm.

$$\forall \rho_1, \rho_2, \rho_3^{\{\rho_3\}}.\forall \xi.((\mathbf{num}, \rho_1) \xrightarrow{\xi} (\mathbf{num}, \rho_2), \rho_3)$$

and the program is annotated as follows.

> $\mathbf{fix}(f, \Lambda\rho_1, \rho_2, \rho_3.(\lambda x.\mathbf{if0}\ x\ \mathbf{then}\ x$
> $\quad \mathbf{else}\ (f[\rho_4, \rho_5, \rho_6](x - (1\ \mathbf{at}\ \rho_7)\ \mathbf{at}\ \rho_8) - (1\ \mathbf{at}\ \rho_9))\ \mathbf{at}\ \rho_{10})\ \mathbf{at}\ \rho_3)$

In the third phase, assuming the tentative type above for f, we perform region inference for the function body, unify some region variables and insert **letregion**. For example, from the type of the then-part and the else-part, it must be the case that $\rho_1 = \rho_2 = \rho_{10}$. From the call of f, we also have $\rho_4 = \rho_8$. From this, we obtain the following refined expression:

> $\mathbf{fix}(f, \Lambda\rho_1, \rho_3.(\lambda x.(\mathbf{if0}\ x\ \mathbf{then}\ x\ \mathbf{else}\ \mathbf{letregion}\ \rho_4, \rho_6, \rho_9\ \mathbf{in}$
> $\quad (f[\rho_4, \rho_6](\mathbf{letregion}\ \rho_7\ \mathbf{in}\ (x - (1\ \mathbf{at}\ \rho_7))\ \mathbf{at}\ \rho_4) - (1\ \mathbf{at}\ \rho_9))\ \mathbf{at}\ \rho_1)\ \mathbf{at}\ \rho_3))$

and its type: $\forall \rho_1, \rho_3^{\{\rho_3\}}.\forall \xi.((\mathbf{num}, \rho_1) \xrightarrow{\xi \cup \{\rho_1, \rho_3\}} (\mathbf{num}, \rho_1), \rho_3)$. We repeat this refinement step until the result converges. In the case above, the above program is a final one.

6   Language Extensions

In this section, we show how to extend the target language defined in Section 2 to support full Scheme.

C ons C ells. We introduce cons cells by adding a new atomic type $(\tau_1 \times \tau_2, \rho)$, which describes a cons cell that is stored in ρ and consists of a car-element of type τ_1 and a cdr-element of type τ_2. We can deal with **set-car!** and **set-cdr!** by assigning the following types to them:

$$\mathbf{set\text{-}car!} : \forall \rho_1 \rho_2 \rho_3^{\{\rho_3\}}.\forall \alpha_1 \alpha_2 \alpha_3.\forall \xi_1 \xi_2.$$
$$((\alpha_1 \times \alpha_2, \rho_1) \xrightarrow{\{\rho_2\} \cup \xi_1} (\alpha_1 \xrightarrow{\{\rho_1\} \cup \xi_2} \alpha_3, \rho_2), \rho_3)$$
$$\mathbf{set\text{-}cdr!} : \forall \rho_1 \rho_2 \rho_3^{\{\rho_3\}}.\forall \alpha_1 \alpha_2 \alpha_3.\forall \xi_1 \xi_2.$$
$$((\alpha_1 \times \alpha_2, \rho_1) \xrightarrow{\{\rho_2\} \cup \xi_1} (\alpha_2 \xrightarrow{\{\rho_1\} \cup \xi_2} \alpha_3, \rho_2), \rho_3)$$

To ensure the type soundness, polymorphic types are not assigned to cons cells. For example, $\forall \alpha.((\mathbf{num}, \rho) \times (\alpha \xrightarrow{\varphi} \alpha, \rho'), \rho'')$ is not allowed. Vector types and other complex data types can be introduced in the same way.

set! We translate **set!** into ML-like operations on reference cells and then perform region inference in the same way as that for ML [23]. To perform the translation, we first perform a program analysis to find all the variables whose values might be updated by **set!**, and then replace all the accesses to those variables with ML-like operations on reference cells. For example, (**let** $((x\ (+ a\ 1)))\ \ldots\ (\mathbf{set!}\ x\ 2))$ is translated to (**let** $((x\ (\mathbf{ref}\ (+ a\ 1))))\ \ldots\ (:=\ x\ 2))$. Here, **ref** v is a primitive for creating a reference cell storing v and returns the pointer to it, and $v_1 := v_2$ is a primitive that stores v_2 in the reference cell v_1.

call/cc It seems difficult to deal with call-with-current-continuation (**call/cc**) in a completely static manner. (In fact, the region inference system for ML does not handle **call/cc**, either.) One (naive) way to deal with **call/cc** might be, when **call/cc** is invoked at run-time, to move the contents of the stack and the heap space reachable from the stack to a global region, so that they can be only collected by standard garbage collection, not by region-based memory management. An alternative way would be to first perform CPS-transformation, and then perform the region inference.

7   Implementation

Based on the type system introduced in Section 3, we have implemented a region inference system for Scheme. Cons cells and **set!** discussed in Section 6 have been already supported, but call-with-current-continuation has not been supported yet. The system transforms a source program written in Scheme into a region-annotated program, whose core syntax has been given in Section 2, and then translates it into C language. For the experiments reported below, we have inserted instructions for monitoring memory usage in the region operation library. Our implementation is available at

http://www.yl.is.s.u-tokyo.ac.jp/~ganat/research/region/

We have tested our region inference system for several programs, and confirmed that the translated programs run correctly. For example, the following program (which computes the number of leaves of a binary tree):

```
(define (leafcount t)
  (if (pair? t) (+ (leafcount (car t)) (leafcount (cdr t))) 1))
```

has been automatically translated by our system into

```
(define leafcount
   (reglambda (r60 r57 r59 r58)
     (lambda (v2)
        (if (letregion (r62) (pair?[r57 r62] v2))
            (letregion (r67 r69 r88)
               (+[r88 r67 r59 r69]
                  (letregion (r73)
                     (leafcount[r73 r57 r88 r76]
                     (letregion (r82) (car[r57 r82] v2))))
                  (letregion (r86)
                     (leafcount[r86 r57 r88 r89]
                     (letregion (r95 ) (cdr[r57 r95] v2))))))
            1 at r59))
       at r60)
at r52)
```

Here, `reglambda` creates a region-polymorphic function. The instruction `leafcount[r73 r57 r88 r76]` applies the region-polymorphic function

leafcount to region parameters r73, r57, r88, and r76. The instruction
1 at r1 puts the number 1 into region r1. Note that during the translation,
the tree argument t above is given a type of the form **rec** $r.(r \times r, \rho_1) \vee \alpha$, which
contains recursive and union types, so that it cannot be handled by the original
region inference [23] for ML unless a programmer defines a tree type using a
datatype declaration.

The result of experiments is summarized in Table 1. The table shows execution time, the maximum heap size, and the total size of allocated memory cells.
To evaluate the effectiveness of the region-based memory management, we have
also measured the execution time and the heap size of a system with garbage
collection, by turning off the region inference phase of our complier and running
the compiled code with Boehm GC library 6.2. The executioin time and the heap
size of our region-based system are listed in the rows marked "Region," while
those of GC are listed in the rows "GC."

Table 1. Results of the Experiments

program	Program Size (Lines)	Time (msec.) Region	GC	Heap Size (KBytes) Region	GC	Total Memory Allocation (KBytes)
Fib	9	51.6	27.0	4.5	49.2	323.1
Ackermann	7	59.9	32.4	18.0	89.1	399.7
Tree	16	22.2	13.6	6.2	66.6	177.6
Array	16	347.8	196.9	280.8	287.7	2342.4
QuickSort	100	793.5	526.4	695.5	693.2	5272.1
Tak	23	428.0	255.2	465.1	66.6	3733.8
Div	54	579.3	399.6	32.2	1219.6	4085.4
Deriv	65	1018.1	680.2	3327.5	5146.6	7245.4
Destruct	72	7967.9	4432.0	10960.9	1219,6	59259.5
RayTracing	1627	2371.5	1522.8	157.8	287.7	14155.7

Programs Array, Tak, Div, Deriv, Destruct have been taken from Gabriel
Scheme benchmarks [8]. Tree is the program given above to count leafs, with
a tree of size 18 given as an input. RayTracing is a program for ray tracing.
QuickSort is a program for quick sort. Fib and Ackermann calculate Fibonacci
and Ackermann number, respectively. The difference between the maximum heap
size and the total size of allocated memory shows the effectiveness of our region
inference. For example, for RayTracing, the total size of allocated memory was
14.2 MBytes, but the required heap space was 2.4 MBytes.

As for the comparison with the GC library, for some programs, the space
efficiency of our region-based memory management is significantly better than
that of the GC library. For the program Tak, however, garbage collection works
better. These results suggest that combination of the two memory management
schemes may be attractive [12]. As for the time efficiency, our current region-based memory management cannot compete with the GC library. Optimizations

for the region-based memory management such as storage mode analysis [1, 2] would be necessary to make the region-based memory management competitive with garbage collection.

8   Related Work

Region-based memory management has been applied to programming languages other than ML [3, 6, 7, 9–11, 17, 18] but most of them rely on programmers' annotations on region instructions (such as "**letregion**" and "**at** ρ"). Only a few of them, which are discussed below, support region inference (i.e., automatic insertion of region instructions). Makholm [17, 18] studied region inference for Prolog. As in our work, his region inference algorithm is based on soft typing, but technical details seem to be quite different since Prolog does not have higher-order functions (hence no need for effects) and instead has logical variables. Deters and Cytron [7] have proposed an algorithm to insert memory allocation/deallocation instructions (similar to region instructions) for Real-Time Java. Their method is based on run-time profiling, so that there seems to be no guarantee that the instructions are inserted correctly. Grossman et al. [11] has proposed a type system for region-based memory management for Cyclone (a type-safe dialect of C). In Cyclone, programmers have to explicitly insert code for manipulating regions, but some of the region annotations are inferred using some heuristics.

The idea of applying type-based program analyses to dynamically-typed programming languages by using soft typing might be a kind of folklore. In fact, Rehof has hinted on that in 1995 [21]. To the authors' knowledge, however, our work is the first to give a concrete formalization of a type-based program analysis for dynamically-typed functional languages and prove the soundness.

9   Conclusion

We have proposed a new region-type system for a dynamically-typed language, and proved its correctness. Based on the type system, we have also implemented a prototype region inference system for Scheme and tested it for several Scheme programs.

Support for call-with-current-continuation is left for future work. To make the region-based memory management more effective, we also need to incorporate several analyses such as region size inference [2]. Combination with other type-based methods for memory management [16] would also be interesting.

The general approach of this work – using soft types to apply a type-based analysis that has been originally developed for statically-typed languages to dynamically-typed languages – seems to be applicable to other type-based analyses such as linear type systems [15, 24], exception analysis [20], and resource usage analysis [13].

References

1. A. Aiken, M. Fahndrich, and R. Levien. Better static memory management: Improving region-based analysis of higher-order languages. In *Proc. of PLDI*, pages 174–185, 1995.
2. L. Birkedal, M. Tofte, and M. Vejlstrup. From region inference to von Neumann machines via region representation inference. In *Proc. of POPL*, pages 171–183. ACM Press, January 1996.
3. C. Boyapati, A. Salcianu, W. Beebee, and J. Rinard. Ownership types for safe region-based memory management in Real-Time Java, 2003.
4. C. Calcagno, S. Helsen, and P. Thiemann. Syntactic type soundness results for the region calculus. *Info. Comput.*, 173(2):199–221, 2002.
5. R. Cartwright and M. Fagan. Soft typing. In *Proc. of PLDI*, pages 278–292, 1991.
6. K. Crary, D. Walker, and G. Morrisett. Typed memory management in a calculus of capabilities. In *Proc. of POPL*, pages 262–275, New York, NY, 1999.
7. M. Deters and R. K. Cytron. Automated discovery of scoped memory regions for real-time java. In *Proceedings of ISMM'02*, pages 25–35. ACM Press, 2002.
8. R. Gabriel. Scheme version of the gabriel lisp benchmarks, 1988.
9. D. Gay and A. Aiken. Memory management with explicit regions. In *Proc. of PLDI*, pages 313–323, 1998.
10. D. Gay and A. Aiken. Language support for regions. In *Proc. of PLDI*, pages 70–80, 2001.
11. D. Grossman, G. Morrisett, T. Jim, M. Hicks, Y. Wang, and J. Cheney. Region-based memory management in Cyclone. In *SIGPLAN Conference on Programming Language Design and Implementation*, pages 282–293, 2002.
12. N. Hallenberg, M. Elsman, and M. Tofte. Combining region inference and garbage collection. In *Proc. of PLDI*, pages 141–152. ACM Press, 2002.
13. A. Igarashi and N. Kobayashi. Resource usage analysis. To appear in *ACM Trans. Prog. Lang. Syst.* A summary appeared in Proc. of POPL, pages 331–342, 2002.
14. R. Kelsey, W. Clinger, and J. R. (Editors). Revised[5] report on the algorithmic language Scheme. *ACM SIGPLAN Notices*, 33(9):26–76, 1998.
15. N. Kobayashi. Quasi-linear types. In *Proc. of POPL*, pages 29–42, 1999.
16. O. Lee, H. Yang, and K. Yi. Inserting safe memory reuse commands into ml-like programs. In *Proceedings of SAS 2003*, volume 2694 of *LNCS*, pages 171–188, 2003.
17. H. Makholm. Region-based memory management in Prolog. Master's thesis, DIKU, University of Copenhagen, 2000.
18. H. Makholm. A region-based memory manager for Prolog. In B. Demoen, editor, *First Workshop on Memory Management in Logic Programming Implementations*, volume CW 294, pages 28–40, CL2000, London, England, 24 2000. Katholieke Universiteit Leuven.
19. A. Nagata, N. Kobayashi, and A. Yonezawa. Region-based memory management for a dynamically-typed language, 2004. Full version, available from http://www.yl.is.s.u-tokyo.ac.jp/~{}ganat/research/region/.
20. F. Pessaux and X. Leroy. Type-based analysis of uncaught exceptions. In *Proc. of POPL*, pages 276–290, 1999.
21. J. Rehof. Polymorphic dynamic typing. aspects of proof theory and inferencej. Master's thesis, DIKU, University of Copenhagen, August 1995.
22. M. Tofte and L. Birkedal. A region inference algorithm. *ACM Trans. Prog. Lang. Syst.*, 20(4):724–767, July 1998.

23. M. Tofte and J.-P. Talpin. Implementing the call-by-value lambda-calculus using a stack of regions. In *Proc. of POPL*, pages 188–201. ACM Press, January 1994.
24. D. N. Turner, P. Wadler, and C. Mossin. Once upon a type. In *Proc. of Functional Programming Languages and Computer Architecture*, pages 1–11, San Diego, California, 1995.

Protocol Specialization

Matthias Neubauer and Peter Thiemann

Institut fär Informatik, Universität Freiburg, Georges-Köhler-Allee 079,
79110 Freiburg, Germany
{neubauer,thiemann}@informatik.uni-freiburg.de

Abstract. In component-based programming, the programmer assembles applications from prefabricated components. The assembly process has two main steps: adapting a component by tweaking its configuration parameters, and connecting components by gluing output interfaces to input interfaces. While convenient, this approach may give rise to code bloat and inefficiency because prefabricated code is overly general, by necessity.

The present work addresses ways to remove unnecessary code during the deployment of a closed set of components by using program specialization. Our framework models components at the intermediate language level as systems of concurrent functional processes which communicate via channels. Each channel acts as a component connector with the interface determined by the channel's protocol. We present an analysis that determines the minimum protocol required for each process and specify the specialization of a process with respect to a desired protocol, thereby removing unnecessary code.

The resulting specialization algorithm is unique in that it processes a concurrent base language, terminates always, and is guaranteed not to expand the program beyond its original size.

1 Introduction

Component-based programming [4] changes the programmer's focus of attention from low-level algorithmic issues to high-level concerns of assembling components with matching interfaces. Components are designed for generality so that they are reusable in a number of different situations. Hence, they provide ways of adapting them to the special needs of the application, e.g., by setting configuration parameters. As is often the case, generality and programming convenience come at the price of increased demands on resources like execution time and memory. Regaining this lost efficiency requires specialization of the assembled application.

Partial evaluation [15] is a successful program specialization technique that has been applied to component adaption in the past [22, 1]. However, specialization becomes more complicated in the presence of concurrency, if components replace or enhance procedural interfaces by events and communication—as customary in component frameworks for graphical user interfaces—or if resource

W.-N. Chin (Ed.): APLAS 2004, LNCS 3302, pp. 246–261, 2004.
© Springer-Verlag Berlin Heidelberg 2004

constraints must be observed. For example, partial evaluation often leads to uncontrolled code growth and the specialization of concurrent programs has not received much attention, yet.

The goal of the present investigation is to identify a specialization methodology that achieves meaningful results under resource constraints and in the presence of communication-based interfaces. The particular scenario that we investigate is one where sequential components that run concurrently communicate with each others through bidirectional channels. Some components act as servers in that they only react to queries from other components and others act as clients. An instance of such a scenario is a wireless intranet where a company provides an internal messaging service to a range of different handheld computers. Each brand of handheld comes with a component implementing the service protocol possibly with vendor-specific extensions. Since space is at premium in a handheld, this component should be as lean as possible. Our framework provides a means of specializing the handheld components with respect to the protocol actually employed by the servers. Our specializer removes the vendor-specific extensions as well as any functionality not referred to by the server. Furthermore and unlike other specializers, our specializer is guaranteed to shrink the program so that it consumes less space.

Our investigation focuses on channel-based communication between components because it subsumes traditional procedure-based interfaces. We assume that the entire system is described by a program in Gay and Hole's concurrent functional language with session types [9] with each component modeled by one process.

The present work makes the following contributions. We simplify and streamline Gay and Hole's language to a low-level concurrent functional language. Next, we extend the language's type system with subtyping and singleton types. In Section 5, we specify a notion of slice types to formally talk about specialization opportunities on the type level. Subtyping and singleton types are essential for this step. Finally, we put the pieces together and specify the specialization algorithm. Compared to other published specializers, our algorithm has three unique features. First, it deals with a concurrent base language. Second, it is guaranteed to terminate on all inputs, and third, it guarantees that the specialized program is no larger than the original one.

The type system underlying our work relies on recursive types with singleton types and subtyping. The combination with singleton types is a novel contribution to session type systems. Linear typing is also involved for tracking the state of a communication channel.

2   An Example Protocol Specialization

From a bird's eye view, the task of protocol specialization looks simple. Just weed out the unnecessary parts and you are done! Unfortunately, identifying the unnecessary parts is not trivial and care must be taken not to increase the size of the original program in the specialization process.

Recall the messaging service scenario from the introduction with two different servers providing the same service, replicated for robustness and fault tolerance. Each server comes from a different vendor, thus each of them has vendor-specific enhancements beyond the required base protocol. For simplicity, we assume that client processes attach nondeterministically to exactly one server process. If all servers are connected, then additional clients must wait for a free server. Servers that service more than one client can be modeled in our calculus but would lead to on overly complicated example.

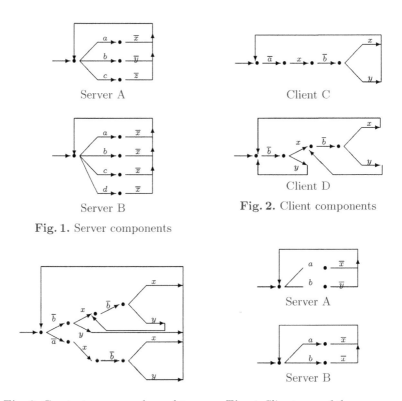

Server A

Server B

Fig. 1. Server components

Client C

Client D

Fig. 2. Client components

Server A

Server B

Fig. 3. Greatest common channel type   **Fig. 4.** Slice types of the servers

Figure 1 contains a description of the external communication behavior[1] of the two servers written as a finite automaton and Figure 5 contains sample code for server A. Each state corresponds to some internal computation at the peer and each transition corresponds to a communication operation. The annotation $a, \ldots$ on a transition denotes the ability to receive inbound messages, whereas the annotation $\overline{x}, \ldots$ denotes sent messages. Each path through an automaton corresponds to a possible behavior.

---

[1] Essentially, a graphical rendition of the channel types that will be introduced below.

```
Let p = NewPort in                        Let Rec clientC (n) =
                                              Let c = Connect (p) in
Let Rec serverA (n) =                         Let Rec clie[c] (n) =
    Let c = Listen (p) in                         Let Send c(a (n)) in
    Let Rec serv [c] (n) =                        Receive (c)
        Receive (c)                               [x (m):
        [a (m): Let n1 = Opsa (n, m) in               Let m1 = Opc (n, m) in
                Let Send c(x (n1)) in                 Let Send c (b (m1)) in
                serv [c](n1)                          Receive (c)
        ,b (m): Let n1 = Opsb (n, m) in               [x (m): Let m2 = Opcx (n, m) in
                Let Send c(y (n1)) in                          clie[c] (m2)
                serv [c](n1)                          ,y (m): Let m2 = Opcy (n, m) in
        ,c (): Let Send c(z (n1)) in                          clie[c] (m2)
                serv [c](n1)                          ]
        ]                                     in clie[c] (n)
    in serv [c](n)                        in
in
                                          serverA (0) || clientC (0)
```

Fig. 5. Code Sample for Server A and Client C Before Specialization

For example, after some initial computation, server A waits for one of the inputs a, b, or c. After receiving one of these inputs, A performs some computations and outputs $\overline{x}$, $\overline{y}$, or $\overline{z}$, respectively, then it may perform some more internal computation before it waits again for one of the inputs. The calculus in Section 3 codifies this behavior with the channel type $\mu\beta.[a : [\overline{x} : \beta], b : [\overline{y} : \beta], c : [\overline{z} : \beta]]$, which is slightly harder to read than its automata rendition in Figure 1.

Figure 2 describes the two client components (see Figure 5 for code of client C) corresponding to different brands of handheld computers. Either client is capable of communicating to either server. This may be seen by tracing each possible pair of client and server.

Assuming that A, B, C and D are the only kinds of peers involved in the intranet, it is clear that clients C and D can only ever connect to servers A and B and, vice versa, clients C and D are the only clients of servers A and B.

Since the structure of the clients is quite different, it does not make sense to tailor a server to one of the clients. Also, it would not make sense to make a fixed assignment of one server to a particular client because this assignment would defeat the robustness intended by the designer of the architecture. Hence, the first task is to find a smallest common description that subsumes the behavior of both clients and tailor both servers to this common description.

A common description of the clients' view of the channel can be constructed graphically by overlaying the two descriptions as shown in Figure 3. The general construction is more involved because client descriptions may have different loop structures that must be synchronized for constructing the common descriptions.

The common client type forms the basis for specializing both servers. However, specializing a server directly from the common client type may lead to code duplication. For example, the processing of the message b would be replicated two times in the specialized server. For that reason, we use the common client type to compute for each server a slice type which specializes the server type towards the client type while still retaining the structure of the original server type. Since the structure of the original server type closely mirrors the structure

```
    ...
Let Rec serverA (n) =
    Let c = Listen (p) in
    Let Rec serv [c] (n) =
        Receive (c)
          [ a (m): Let n1 = Opsa (n, m) in Let Send c(x (n1)) in serv [c](n1)
          , b (m): Let n1 = Opsb (n, m) in Let Send c(y (n1)) in serv [c](n1) ]
    in serv [c](n)
in
    ...
```

Fig. 6. Server A after specialization

of its implementation, we can guarantee that no code is duplicated. Figure 4 contains the slice types computed for the two servers, and Figure 6 shows the specialized code for server A.

In the example, the client components cannot be specialized, but in the general case, there might be specialization opportunities in the clients, too. The scenario is dual with the roles of clients and servers reversed. The required steps are analogous: find a common type for the servers, compute an individual slice type for each client, and then specialize the client with respect to the slice type.

Interestingly, the same framework also handles adaption with respect to configuration parameters. To see this, we have to assume that configuration parameters are presented to components via communication channels. In this scenario, each component acts as a client for its configuration channel(s) and the configuration parameters are supplied through a special configuration component. To take advantage of the actual values on these channels requires introducing singleton types into the type system. The specializer can then decide conditionals and perform primitive operations based on the additional knowledge. Specialization still does not expand the program as no unfolding of function calls takes place.

The subsequent sections first introduce a formal calculus for expressing client and server components. Then, each of the steps outlined above is put on a formal basis and it is proven that the specialization algorithm is well-defined. The soundness of the specialization follows from the soundness of subtyping in the calculus.

3   Calculus with Channel Types

This section defines the λ_{CS} calculus, a formal calculus for expressing client and server components. After presenting the syntax, a type system fixes the static semantics of λ_{CS}.

3.1   Syntax

The calculus deals with five kinds of data, first-order base type values, port values, channel values, functions, and labels. Labels have a status similar to labels in record and variant types. They occur in channel types and they can be sent and received via channels: each message consists of a value tagged with a label. Channel values must be treated linearly: during execution each channel end must have exactly one reference. Each operation on a channel changes its state and the close operation destroys the channel. In our version of the calculus channels may neither be sent nor received over a channel themselves.[2]

Labels	$l \in \text{Label}$
Variables	$x \in \text{Var}$
Channel Variables	$c \in \text{ChannelVar}$
Definitions	$d ::= x = i \mid x = \text{Op}(\tilde{x}) \mid \text{rec } x[\tilde{c}](\tilde{x}) = e \mid x = \text{NewPort}$
	$\mid\ c = \text{Connect}(x) \mid c = \text{Listen}(x) \mid \text{Send } c(\bar{l}\ x) \mid \text{Close}(c)$
Expressions	$e ::= \text{Halt} \mid \text{Let } d \text{ in } e \mid \text{If } x \text{ then } e \text{ else } e \mid x\ [\tilde{c}]\ (\tilde{x})$
	$\mid\ \text{Receive } c[g] \mid e \parallel e$
	$g ::= l(x) \to e \mid g, g$

The expressions of the calculus come in a sequentialized style reminiscent of continuation-passing style. That is, an expression e is a sequence of definitions which ends in either a Halt instruction, a conditional, a function call, a receive instruction that branches on the received label, or a concurrent execution of two expressions. All argument positions are restricted to variables. Without loss of generality, we assume that the set of labels is totally ordered, and branches of a receive instruction always occur ordered with respect to labels. The notation $\tilde{x}$ stands for $x_1, \ldots, x_n$ where n is determined by the context. Analogously, $(\tilde{x} : \tilde{\tau})$ stands for $(x_1 : \tau_1) \ldots (x_n : \tau_n)$.

A definition d is either the creation of a constant, the application of a primitive operation, the definition of a recursive function, the send operation, the creation of a new communication port, or an administrative operation on a channel: closing the channel, connecting to a channel (client connection), and listening to a channel (server connection).

3.2   Static Semantics

The following section introduces the type language for our calculus including a type language for channels, called channel types, and presents the type system.

Types	$\tau ::= b \mid [\tilde{\gamma}]\tilde{\tau} \to 0$
Channel types	$\gamma ::= \varepsilon \mid [\eta] \mid \beta \mid \mu\beta.\gamma$
	$\eta ::= \ell(\tau) : \gamma \mid \eta, \eta$
	$\ell ::= \bar{l} \mid l$
Port types	$\zeta ::= \text{Port } \gamma$
Type Environments	$\Gamma ::= \emptyset \mid \Gamma(x : \tau)$
Channel Environments	$\Theta ::= \emptyset \mid \Theta(c : \gamma)$

A type is either a base type, a function type, or a port type. Due to the sequential style, functions do not return values. Instead they must take a continuation argument. Function arguments are split in two lists, one for linear arguments carrying channel values and one for other arguments.

---

[2] Extending the calculus in this way is not hard, but not essential for the present work.

A channel type is either empty (the channel is closed), the empty word (the channel is depleted but not yet closed), a label-tagged alternative of different channel types (the value may be sent $\bar{l}(\tau)$ or received $l(\tau)$), or a type variable which is used in constructing a recursive type with the μ operator. The μ operator constructs a fixpoint, e.g., $\mu\beta.\gamma \approx \gamma[\beta \mapsto \mu\beta.\gamma]$. All uses of μ are expansive, that is, there can be no subterms of the form $\mu\beta_1 \ldots \mu\beta_n.\beta_1$.

The type system relies on two judgments, $\Theta, \Gamma \vdash e$, to check the consistency of an expression with respect to channel environment Θ and type environment Γ and $\Theta, \Gamma \vdash d \Rightarrow \Theta', \Gamma'$ to model the effect of a definition as a transformation of the environments. The rules are shown in Figures 7 and 8 respectively. For now, $\leq$ can be read as syntactic equality. Section 4 defines a suitable subtyping relation.

The **Halt** rule requires that all channels are closed. The conditional passes the environments unchanged to both branches. The let expression types the body after transforming the environment according to the definition. Applying a function requires that the function consumes all remaining channels. Receiving a tagged value eliminates a labeled alternative in the channel's type. The branches are checked with the channel type updated according to the alternative taken. For concurrent execution, the channel environment is split in two disjoint parts whereas the type environment is passed to both subexpressions.

A primitive operation has arguments and result of base type. It does not depend on the channel environment. Creating a new port guesses a port type and attaches it to a port value. Ports serve as mediators through which clients and servers can agree on a common channel type. Sending of a labeled value selects the appropriate component of the channel type for the rest of the sender expression and changes the channel environment accordingly. Function formation is independent of the current channel environment. The body of the function must be checked with the channel environment prescribed by the channels passed at the call site of the function. Closing a communication channel requires that there are no exchanges left in its type. **Listen** creates a new server channel attached to a particular port. **Connect** creates a new client channel for a port. Since the channel type registered with the port describes the communication behavior of the server, the client processes the channel using the mirrored type, $\bar{\gamma}$, with inbound and outbound labels exchanged. Mirrored types are formally defined in Figure 12. Note that mirroring a type does not affect messages.

4   Specialization Opportunities

Specialization frameworks often include a notion of binding-time analysis [15]. Such an analysis determines which values are available to specialization without actually running the program or fixing a particular value. Similar, but less permissive information can be obtained by introducing subtyping and singleton types to λ_{CS}'s type system.

$$\emptyset, \Gamma \vdash \texttt{Halt} \qquad \dfrac{\Gamma(x) \leq b \quad \Theta, \Gamma \vdash e_1 \quad \Theta, \Gamma \vdash e_2}{\Theta, \Gamma \vdash \texttt{If } x \texttt{ then } e_1 \texttt{ else } e_2}$$

$$\dfrac{\Theta, \Gamma \vdash d \Rightarrow \Theta', \Gamma' \quad \Theta', \Gamma' \vdash e}{\Theta, \Gamma \vdash \texttt{Let } d \texttt{ in } e} \qquad \dfrac{\Gamma(x) = [\bar\gamma]\bar\tau \to 0 \quad \Gamma(\bar z) \leq \bar\tau \quad \Theta \leq (\bar c : \bar\gamma)}{\Theta, \Gamma \vdash x \, [\bar c] \, \bar z}$$

$$\dfrac{\Theta(c) \leq [l_i(\tau_i) : \gamma_i]_{i=1}^n \quad (\forall i) \, \Theta(c : \gamma_i), \Gamma(x_i : \tau_i) \vdash e_i}{\Theta, \Gamma \vdash \texttt{Receive } c[l_i(x_i) \to e_i]_{i=1}^n} \qquad \dfrac{\Theta_1, \Gamma \vdash e_1 \quad \Theta_2, \Gamma \vdash e_2}{\Theta_1 + \Theta_2, \Gamma \vdash e_1 \| e_2}$$

Fig. 7. Typing rules for expressions

$$\Theta, \Gamma \vdash x = i \Rightarrow \Theta, \Gamma(x : b) \qquad \Theta, \Gamma \vdash x = \texttt{NewPort} \Rightarrow \Theta, \Gamma(x : \texttt{Port } \gamma)$$

$$\dfrac{\Gamma(x_i) \leq b}{\Theta, \Gamma \vdash x = \texttt{Op}(x_1, \dots, x_n) \Rightarrow \Theta, \Gamma(x : b)} \qquad \dfrac{\Gamma(x) \geq \texttt{Port } \gamma}{\Theta, \Gamma \vdash \texttt{Listen}(x) \Rightarrow \Theta(c : \gamma), \Gamma}$$

$$\dfrac{(\bar c : \bar\gamma), \Gamma(f : [\bar\gamma]\bar\tau \to 0)(\bar x : \bar\tau) \vdash e}{\Theta, \Gamma \vdash \texttt{rec } f[\bar c](\bar x) = e \Rightarrow \Theta, \Gamma(f : [\bar\gamma]\bar\tau \to 0)} \qquad \dfrac{\Gamma(x) = \texttt{Port } \gamma' \quad \gamma' \leq \bar\gamma}{\Theta, \Gamma \vdash c = \texttt{Connect}(x) \Rightarrow \Theta(c : \gamma), \Gamma}$$

$$\dfrac{\Gamma(x_j) \leq \tau_j \quad \gamma = [l_i(\tau_i) : \gamma_i]_{i=1}^n}{\Theta(c : \gamma), \Gamma \vdash \texttt{Send } c(l_j \, x_j) \Rightarrow \Theta(c : \gamma_j), \Gamma} 1 \leq j \leq n \quad \Theta(c : \varepsilon), \Gamma \vdash \texttt{Close } (c) \Rightarrow \Theta, \Gamma$$

Fig. 8. Typing rules for definitions

$$\dfrac{\Gamma(x) = \mathbf{S}\{i : b\} \quad i \neq 0 \quad \Theta, \Gamma \vdash e_1}{\Theta, \Gamma \vdash \texttt{If } x \texttt{ then } e_1 \texttt{ else } e_2} \qquad \dfrac{\Gamma(x) = \mathbf{S}\{0 : b\} \quad \Theta, \Gamma \vdash e_2}{\Theta, \Gamma \vdash \texttt{If } x \texttt{ then } e_1 \texttt{ else } e_2}$$

Fig. 9. Typing rules for expressions using Singleton Types

$$\Theta, \Gamma \vdash x = i \Rightarrow \Theta, \Gamma(x : \mathbf{S}\{i : b\})$$

$$\dfrac{(\forall j) \, \Gamma(x_j) = \mathbf{S}\{i_j : b\} \quad \texttt{Op}(i_1, \dots, i_n) \to i_0}{\Theta, \Gamma \vdash x = \texttt{Op}(x_1, \dots, x_n) \Rightarrow \Theta, \Gamma(x : \mathbf{S}\{i_0 : b\})}$$

Fig. 10. Typing rules for definitions introducing Singleton Types

$$(sub\text{-}s\text{-}s)\dfrac{}{\mathbf{S}\{i : b\} \leq \mathbf{S}\{i : b\}} \qquad (sub\text{-}s\text{-}b)\dfrac{}{\mathbf{S}\{i : b\} \leq b} \qquad (sub\text{-}b\text{-}b)\dfrac{}{b \leq b}$$

$$(sub\text{-}\tau\text{-}arrow)\dfrac{(\forall i) \, \gamma_i' \leq \gamma_i \quad (\forall j) \, \tau_j' \leq \tau_j}{[\bar\gamma_i]\bar\tau_j \to 0 \leq [\bar\gamma_i']\bar\tau_j' \to 0} \qquad (sub\text{-}\zeta)\dfrac{\gamma \leq \gamma'}{\texttt{Port } \gamma \leq \texttt{Port } \gamma'}$$

$$(sub\text{-}send)\dfrac{(\forall 1 \leq i \leq n) \, \tau_i' \leq \tau_i \quad \gamma_i \leq \gamma_i'}{[l_i(\tau_i) : \gamma_i]_{i=1}^{n+k} \leq [l_i(\tau_i') : \gamma_i']_{i=1}^n} \qquad (sub\text{-}recv)\dfrac{(\forall 1 \leq i \leq n) \, \tau_i \leq \tau_i' \quad \gamma_i \leq \gamma_i'}{[l_i(\tau_i) : \gamma_i]_{i=1}^n \leq [l_i(\tau_i') : \gamma_i']_{i=1}^{n+k}}$$

$$(sub\text{-}\mu\text{-}fold\text{-}right)\dfrac{\gamma \leq \gamma'[\beta \mapsto \mu\beta.\gamma']}{\gamma \leq \mu\beta.\gamma'} \qquad (sub\text{-}\mu\text{-}fold\text{-}left)\dfrac{\gamma[\beta \mapsto \mu\beta.\gamma] \leq \gamma'}{\mu\beta.\gamma \leq \gamma'}\gamma' \neq \mu\beta.\gamma''$$

Fig. 11. Subtyping

$$\bar\varepsilon = \varepsilon \qquad \bar\beta = \beta \qquad \overline{\eta, \eta} = \bar\eta, \bar\eta \qquad \bar{\bar l} = l$$

$$\overline{[\eta]} = [\bar\eta] \qquad \overline{\mu\beta.\gamma} = \mu\beta.\bar\gamma \qquad \overline{\ell(\tau) : \gamma} = \ell(\tau) : \bar\gamma \qquad \bar{\bar l} = \bar l$$

Fig. 12. Mirroring of Types

4.1   Singleton Types

Our notion of singleton types is restricted to base types. Hence, we extend the type language as follows.

$$\tau ::= \ldots \mid \mathbf{S}\{i : b\}$$

The type $\mathbf{S}\{i : b\}$ represents a particular base value, i, at the type level. Singleton types may occur wherever ordinary types are expected, also in channel types. Figures 9 and 10 show refinements of the existing typing rules facilitates by exploiting singleton types where possible. Namely, declarations of constant bindings and declarations of operator applications of statically known base values introduce singleton types. A conditional can be typed less strictly if the condition has a singleton type.

4.2   Subtyping

Following Gapeyev et al. [8], the subtype relation is the greatest fixed point of a generating function. We specify the generating function by means of inference rules shown in Figure 11. The resulting subtyping relation gives rise to a more precise instance of the typing rules in the previous section. Subtyping derives from two sources: singleton types and label-tagged alternatives occurring in channel types [20, 10].

Because a value of channel type with a sending capability as its first component can be substituted by other channels that allow "smaller" values to be transmitted instead, subtyping of outbound channel types must be contravariant. On the other hand, a channel with receiving capability can always be demoted to a type that just receives "larger" types, so subtyping for incoming channel types must be covariant.

The rule for function types extends the subtyping relation to functions in the usual way. The additional rules involving recursive μ-types explain the behavior of right and left μ-folding with respect to subtyping. The folding rules are asymmetric to makes them non-overlapping and thus invertible. Subtyping extends to port types covariantly.

5   Protocol Specialization

We divide the framework for protocol specialization into two parts. In the first subsection, we characterize slice types as potential target types for specialization. The second subsection specifies specialization with respect to a slice type.

5.1   Slice Types

As explained in the introductory section, our goal is to specialize code of a component in such a way that fragments of the code that are never used while communicating with other components of the system are removed. The relation between the actual behavior of a component, the behavior expected by all its communication partners, and the designated behavior without unreachable code is formally stated as a relation on types. Given two channel types for a channel, the one corresponding to the communication pattern of the actual implementation, and a supertype specifying the expected behavior of all communication partners, we are seeking for an intermediate channel type which only includes required communication branches and which also exhibits the same recursive structure as the channel type corresponding to the actual source code. We call intermediate channel types with such properties *slice types*.

We again define generating functions for two relations specifying lower and upper slice types by means of inference rules. In turn, the two relations are the greatest fixed points of the presented generating functions.

The relation $\gamma \trianglelefteq \gamma_s \leq \gamma'$ specifies the lower slice type relation between three channel types. It expresses two distinct features about the relation of the three types: first, all three channel types are related by the subtype relation, and second, the first channel type, γ, and the lower slice type, γ_s, exhibit the same recursive structure. The relation $\gamma \leq \gamma_s \trianglelefteq \gamma'$, specifies upper slice types. It is dual to the notion of a lower slice type by demanding that the slice type must have the same recursive structure as the upper channel type.

There are two sets of rules each defining possible lower slice types of two label-tagged alternatives, four rules for inbound channels and four rules for outbound channels, respectively. In the following, we exemplarily show the rules concerning outbound channels.

$$(\text{l-slice-}\delta\text{-send-1})\frac{\delta \leq \delta_s}{\delta \trianglelefteq \delta_s \leq []}$$

$$(\text{l-slice-}\delta\text{-send-2})\frac{l_i < l_k \leq l_j \quad \delta \trianglelefteq [\overline{l_k}(\tau^s) : \gamma^s, \delta^s] \leq [\overline{l_j}(\tau') : \gamma', \delta']}{[\overline{l_i}(\tau) : \gamma, \delta] \trianglelefteq [\overline{l_k}(\tau^s) : \gamma^s, \delta^s] \leq [\overline{l_j}(\tau') : \gamma', \delta']}$$

$$(\text{l-slice-}\delta\text{-send-3})\frac{l_i < l_j \quad \tau^s \leq \tau \quad \gamma \leq \gamma^s \quad \delta \trianglelefteq \delta^s \leq [\overline{l_j}(\tau') : \gamma', \delta']}{[\overline{l_i}(\tau) : \gamma, \delta] \trianglelefteq [\overline{l_i}(\tau^s) : \gamma^s, \delta^s] \leq [\overline{l_j}(\tau') : \gamma', \delta']}$$

$$(\text{l-slice-}\delta\text{-send-4})\frac{\tau' \leq \tau^s \trianglelefteq \tau \quad \gamma \trianglelefteq \gamma^s \leq \gamma' \quad \delta \trianglelefteq \delta^s \leq \delta'}{[\overline{l_i}(\tau) : \gamma, \delta] \trianglelefteq [\overline{l_i}(\tau^s) : \gamma^s, \delta^s] \leq [\overline{l_i}(\tau') : \gamma', \delta']}$$

To specify these rules concisely, we assume a total ordering $\leq$ on labels and also that labels are always listed in that order. Depending on the labels of the first branch of the lower and upper types, there are different possibilities to choose a first branch of a possible slice type. The subtype of an outbound alternatives may have additional alternative branches and branches starting with the same label impose a contravariant subtype relation on their transmitted values. The four rules handle different cases where the upper type does not have a branch at all, the lower and upper types start with different labels and the slice type label either corresponds to the lower label or not, or all three alternatives start with the same label.

The subtype of an inbound channel must have fewer alternative branches and the types of the incoming values behave covariantly. The rules relating singleton types and base types, function types, and port types just carry over regular subtyping to three channel types, additionally taking into account the correct alignment of the recursive structure of the slice types. The folding rules for μ-types show that a lower slice type must exactly follow the folding of the lower channel type, γ. On the other hand, folding the upper channel type γ' must not affect the slice type at all, it stays unchanged while folding the lower type and the slice type. The whole set of rules is not shown due to lack of space but may be found elsewhere [18].

The rules specifying upper slice types are analogous to the rules specifying lower slice types. The only difference is that the folding of recursive slice types—that is, slice types in the shape of μ-types—is now synchronized with the folding of the upper channel type.

5.2   Translation

Instead of stating a specific implementation for our specialization scheme, we formulate valid specialization algorithms as instances of a type-based translation relation inspired by Hughes's type specialization [14].

To this end, we specify two relations expressing valid specializations of typed expressions and definitions. The translation relation for expressions $\Theta, \Gamma \vdash e \hookrightarrow \Theta^*, \Gamma^* \vdash e^*$, specifies that the typing $\Theta^*, \Gamma^* \vdash e^*$ for a new expression e^* is a specialized version of an original expression e with $\Gamma, \Theta \vdash e$.

Only two kinds of expression may change during specialization. First, the conditional simplifies to one of the branches if the type of the condition is a singleton type. The following rule exemplarily shows the specification of valid translations for conditionals where the conditional value is known to be zero—that is, the else branch can be chosen statically.

$$\frac{\Gamma(x) = \mathbf{S}\{0 : b\} \quad \Gamma^*(x) = \mathbf{S}\{0 : b\} \quad \Theta, \Gamma \vdash e_2 \hookrightarrow \Theta^*, \Gamma^* \vdash e_2^*}{\Theta, \Gamma \vdash \mathtt{If}\ x\ \mathtt{then}\ e_1\ \mathtt{else}\ e_2 \hookrightarrow \Theta^*, \Gamma^* \vdash e_2^*}$$

Second, specialization eliminates unnecessary branches of a `Receive` expression in case the specialized channel type found in the specialized channel type environment features less alternatives than the original type.

$$\frac{\Theta(c) \leq [l_i(\tau_i) : \gamma_i]_{i=1}^n \quad \Theta^*(c) \leq [l_i(\tau_i^*) : \gamma_i^*]_{i=1}^m}{\Theta, \Gamma \vdash \mathtt{Receive}\ c[l_i(x_i) \to e_i]_{i=1}^n} \frac{(\forall 1 \leq j \leq m)\ \Theta(c : \gamma_j), \Gamma(x_j : \tau_j) \vdash e_j \hookrightarrow \Theta^*(c : \gamma_j^*), \Gamma^*(x_j : \tau_j^*) \vdash e_j^*}{\hookrightarrow \Theta^*, \Gamma^* \vdash \mathtt{Receive}\ c[l_i(x_i) \to e_i^*]_{i=1}^m} 1 \leq m \leq n$$

All the other translation rules for expressions only carry on the translation to subexpression in a compositional way leaving the actual expression context unchanged. For lack of space, we do not present the whole set of rules. The interested reader may find them elsewhere [18].

The second relation formally specifies a corresponding relation for definitions: a judgment $\Theta, \Gamma \vdash d \Rightarrow \Theta', \Gamma' \hookrightarrow \Theta^*, \Gamma^* \vdash d^* \Rightarrow \Theta'^*, \Gamma'^*$ means that a typing $\Theta^*, \Gamma^* \vdash d^* \Rightarrow \Theta'^*, \Gamma'^*$ is a valid specialization of an original definition with typing $\Theta, \Gamma \vdash d \Rightarrow \Theta', \Gamma'$. There is one nontrivial specialization rule for definitions. A primitive operation where all arguments have singleton types specializes to a constant assignment.

$$\frac{\Gamma(x_i) = \Gamma^*(x_i) = i_i \qquad \mathtt{Op}(i_1, \ldots, i_n) \to i_0}{\Theta, \Gamma \vdash x = \mathtt{Op}(x_1, \ldots, x_n) \Rightarrow \Theta, \Gamma(x : \mathbf{S}\{i_0 : b\})}$$
$$\hookrightarrow \Theta^*, \Gamma^* \vdash x = i_0 \Rightarrow \Theta^*, \Gamma^*(x : \mathbf{S}\{i_0 : b\})$$

Three rules affect the channel types found in the original program. Instead of introducing just one port type, γ, for each $\mathtt{NewPort}$ declaration, the typing of the specialized definition introduces two additional port types, γ' and γ'', one below the original type and one above it in the subtyping ordering. The idea is that the lower type γ' is the least upper bound of the server types connecting to the port whereas the upper type γ'' is the greatest lower bound of the (swapped) client types. The invariant for a type $\mathtt{Port}\ (\gamma', \gamma, \gamma'')$ is $\gamma' \le \gamma \le \gamma''$.

$$\frac{\gamma' \le \gamma \le \gamma''}{\Theta, \Gamma \vdash x = \mathtt{NewPort} \Rightarrow \Theta, \Gamma(x : \mathtt{Port}\ \gamma)}$$
$$\hookrightarrow \Theta^*, \Gamma^* \vdash x = \mathtt{NewPort} \Rightarrow \Theta^*, \Gamma^*(x : \mathtt{Port}\ (\gamma', \gamma, \gamma''))$$

When specializing the beginning of a connection to a server ($\mathtt{Connect}$), or when specializing a $\mathtt{Listen}$ to a channel, we use slice types to substitute the original channel type describing the original program behavior by specialized versions. In case of a $\mathtt{Listen}$, a possible slice type γ_s substituted for γ must both follow the recursive structure of γ and also sit between the original channel type and the channel type describing all possible communication partners.

$$\frac{\Gamma(x) \ge \mathtt{Port}\ \gamma \qquad \Gamma^*(x) \ge \mathtt{Port}\ (\gamma', \gamma, \gamma'') \qquad \gamma'' \le \gamma_s \trianglelefteq \gamma}{\Theta, \Gamma \vdash \mathtt{Listen}(x) \Rightarrow \Theta(c : \gamma), \Gamma \hookrightarrow \Theta^*, \Gamma^* \vdash \mathtt{Listen}(x) \Rightarrow \Theta^*(c : \gamma_s), \Gamma^*}$$

The situation for $\mathtt{Connect}$ commands is reversed. We again allow to use slice types as specialized versions of the original channel type γ. Here, the lower channel type used for splicing is the second channel type registered as port type, because we are now handling the other ends of the communication channels.

$$\frac{\Gamma(x) = \mathtt{Port}\ \gamma_0 \qquad \overline{\gamma_0} \le \gamma \qquad \Gamma^*(x) \ge \mathtt{Port}\ (\gamma', \overline{\gamma_0}, \gamma'') \qquad \gamma' \le \gamma_s \trianglelefteq \gamma}{\Theta, \Gamma \vdash c = \mathtt{Connect}(x) \Rightarrow \Theta(c : \gamma), \Gamma}$$
$$\hookrightarrow \Theta^*, \Gamma^* \vdash c = \mathtt{Connect}(x) \Rightarrow \Theta^*(c : \gamma_s), \Gamma^*$$

All the other translation rules again only carry on the translation to subexpression [18].

5.3 Properties of Translation

The first result states that valid translations of expressions and definitions imply that the original syntactic objects are already typeable.

Lemma 1.

(i) If $\Theta, \Gamma \vdash e \hookrightarrow \Theta^*, \Gamma^* \vdash e^*$, then $\Theta, \Gamma \vdash e$.

(ii) If $\Theta, \Gamma \vdash d \Rightarrow \Theta', \Gamma' \hookrightarrow \Theta^*, \Gamma^* \vdash d^* \Rightarrow \Theta'^*, \Gamma'^*$, then $\Theta, \Gamma \vdash d \Rightarrow \Theta', \Gamma'$.

The same property holds for results of valid translations, where $\widehat{\Gamma^*}$ denotes the type environment resulting from a Γ^* by removing lower subtypes and upper supertypes for each assigned port type.

Lemma 2.

(i) If $\Theta, \Gamma \vdash e \hookrightarrow \Theta^*, \Gamma^* \vdash e^*$, then $\Theta^*, \widehat{\Gamma^*} \vdash e^*$.

(ii) If $\Theta, \Gamma \vdash d \Rightarrow \Theta', \Gamma' \hookrightarrow \Theta^*, \Gamma^* \vdash d^* \Rightarrow \Theta'^*, \Gamma'^*$,
    then $\Theta^*, \widehat{\Gamma^*} \vdash d^* \Rightarrow \Theta'^*, \widehat{\Gamma'^*}$.

We further show that valid translations induce two simulation properties. To be able to state those, an additional dynamic semantics for λ_{CS}, given as a reduction relation $\rightarrow$ on expressions, is assumed. The dynamic semantics for λ_{CS} has been given and invariance of typing under structural rearrangement of terms and type preservation have been proven elsewhere [18], but they are left here out due to space restrictions. Full type soundness cannot be proven because the type system is not strong enough to detect deadlocks.

Each evaluation step of a program can be simulated by zero or one evaluation step of translated program.

Lemma 3.
If $\emptyset, \emptyset \vdash e \hookrightarrow \emptyset, \emptyset \vdash e^*$ and $e \rightarrow e'$, then $\emptyset, \emptyset \vdash e' \hookrightarrow \emptyset, \emptyset \vdash e'^*$ and $e^* \rightarrow^{0,1} e'^*$.

For each evaluation step of a translated program, we find a finite number of evaluation steps for the original state simulating the single evaluation step.

Lemma 4.
If $\emptyset, \emptyset \vdash e \hookrightarrow \emptyset, \emptyset \vdash e^*$ and $e^* \rightarrow^{0,1} e'^*$, then $\emptyset, \emptyset \vdash e' \hookrightarrow \emptyset, \emptyset \vdash e'^*$ and $e \rightarrow^+ e'$.

The translation is terminating because the specialized expression is smaller than the original expression. This fact can be determined by examination of the translation rules.

6   Related Work

Session types [9] have emerged as an expressive typing discipline for heterogeneous, bidirectional communication channels. In such a channel, each message may have a different type with the possible sequences of messages determined by the channel's session type. Such a type discipline subsumes typings for datagram communication as well as for homogeneous channels. Session types have been used to describe stream-based Internet protocols such as POP3 [9, 10].

Session types have also been proposed by Nierstrasz [19] for describing the behavior of active objects. The main idea is that a regular language on atomic communication actions describes the sequence of messages on each channel. The session type specifies this language with a fixpoint expression. Each operation peels off the outermost action from the channel type so that each operation changes the channel's type.

Program specialization has been explored in a number of linguistic contexts from functional languages, logical and imperative languages, to object-oriented languages [15, 12, 24]. However, specialization for languages with concurrency has proved not very fruitful thus far and the main effort has been directed towards the removal of communication and nondeterminism. The most recent reference deals with a highly specialized area, concurrent constraint languages [7]. Marinescu and Goldberg [17] treat a simple CSP-like language and Gengler and Martel [11] consider the π-calculus. Unfortunately, both of them have technical problems. Hosoya et al [13] consider partial evaluation for HACL, an ML subset with channel-based communication.

Component adaptation by partial evaluation is not a new idea. Consel [2] proposed it for programs in general and Schultz [23] proposes a research agenda with desiderata for specialization of components. Interestingly, Schultz poses a question similar to the one we are investigating in the present paper in his conclusion: "Is it possible to unify the specialization needs that arise when the same component in a single application is used by several different components, possibly each through a unique interface?" We believe our techniques are applicable—with slight modifications—to this problem.

Bobeff and Noyé [1] also argue for a combination of partial evaluation and program slicing to perform component adaptation. Their approach requires the component provider to specify specialization scenarios and to perform the program analyses to support those scenarios. A component is then deployed as a component generator that creates specialized instances for each of the specified scenarios. While we are also relying on a program analysis, our goal is not a program generator but rather a specializer working on intermediate code.

The idea of specialization with respect to an inferred type is inspired by Hughes's type specializer [14]. However, our work is in a call-by-value setting with concurrency and communication whereas Hughes's work is in the context of the applied call-by-name lambda calculus.

None of the cited works guarantees terminating specialization and a guarantee that programs does not expand. Furthermore, in none of the works the specialization algorithm is type driven as is the case for our algorithm. The only type-driven specialization algorithms that we know of are Hughes's type specialization [14] and constructor specialization by Dussart and others [6]. But those specializers have different goals and target functional languages without concurrency.

Program slicing [16, 25] and application extraction [26] are transformations which are in spirit related to the effect of our specialization effort. The main difference is that we achieve the extraction with a pure specialization approach. While the relation between program specialization and program slicing has been subject of some study [21], our work gives further indication of a deep relation between both techniques.

While the inspiration for our calculus comes from the work on calculi for communication as outlined in the introduction, the actual formulation is inspired by the capability calculus by Walker and others [27]. Our calculus may be viewed as a specialized instance of the capability calculus, first, with respect to the typing discipline (simple types instead of polymorphism) and, second, with respect to the application area, channel-based communication.

7   Conclusion

We have defined a framework for component adaption and specialization based on an intermediate language with concurrent functional processes. The framework allows removal of dead code by specializing conditionals. We have proved the soundness of the specialization algorithm. The specialization algorithm terminates always and never expands a source program beyond its original size.

References

1. Gustavo Bobeff and Jacques Noyé. Molding components using program specialization techniques. In *WCOP 2003, Eighth International Workshop on Component-Oriented Programming*, Darmstadt, Germany, July 2003.
2. Charles Consel. Program adaptation based on program transformation. *ACM Computing Surveys*, 28(4es):164, 1996.
3. Charles Consel, editor. *Proceedings of the 1997 ACM SIGPLAN Symposium on Partial Evaluation and Semantics-Based Program Manipulation*, Amsterdam, The Netherlands, June 1997. ACM Press.
4. Clemens Czyperski. *Component Software, Beyond Object-Oriented Programming*. Addison-Wesley, 1998.
5. Olivier Danvy, Robert Glück, and Peter Thiemann, editors. *Dagstuhl Seminar on Partial Evaluation 1996*, number 1110 in Lecture Notes in Computer Science, Schloß Dagstuhl, Germany, February 1996. Springer-Verlag.
6. Dirk Dussart, Eddy Bevers, and Karel De Vlaminck. Polyvariant constructor specialization. In William Scherlis, editor, *Proc. ACM SIGPLAN Symposium on Partial Evaluation and Semantics-Based Program Manipulation PEPM '95*, pages 54–63, La Jolla, CA, USA, June 1995. ACM Press.
7. Sandro Etalle and Maurizio Gabbrieli. Partial evaluation of concurrent constraint languages. *ACM Comput. Surv.*, 30(3es):11, 1998.
8. Vladimir Gapeyev, Michael Y. Levin, and Benjamin C. Pierce. Recursive subtying revealed. *Journal of Functional Programming*, 12(6):511–548, November 2002.
9. Simon Gay and Malcolm Hole. Types and subtypes for client-server interactions. In Doaitse Swierstra, editor, *Proceedings of the 1999 European Symposium on Programming*, number 1576 in Lecture Notes in Computer Science, pages 74–90, Amsterdam, The Netherlands, April 1999. Springer-Verlag.
10. Simon Gay, Vasco Vasconcelos, and Antonio Ravara. Session types for inter-process communication. Technical Report TR-2003-133, Department of Computing Science, University of Glasgow, 2003.

11. Marc Gengler and Matthieu Martel. Self-applicable partial evaluation for the pi-calculus. In Consel [3], pages 36–46.
12. John Hatcliff, Torben Æ. Mogensen, and Peter Thiemann, editors. *Partial Evaluation—Practice and Theory. Proceedings of the 1998 DIKU International Summerschool*, number 1706 in Lecture Notes in Computer Science, Copenhagen, Denmark, 1999. Springer-Verlag.
13. Haruo Hosoya, Naoki Kobayashi, and Akinori Yonezawa. Partial evaluation scheme for concurrent languages and its correctness. In L. Bougé et al., editors, *Euro-Par'96 - Parallel Processing*, number 1123 in Lecture Notes in Computer Science, pages 625–632, Lyon, France, 1996. Springer-Verlag.
14. John Hughes. Type specialisation for the λ-calculus; or, a new paradigm for partial evaluation based on type inference. In Danvy et al. [5], pages 183–215.
15. Neil Jones, Carsten Gomard, and Peter Sestoft. *Partial Evaluation and Automatic Program Generation*. Prentice-Hall, 1993.
16. Naoki Kobayashi. Useless code elimination and programm slicing for the pi-calculus. In Atsushi Ohori, editor, *Proceedings of the First Asian Symposium on Programming Languages and Systems*, number 2895 in Lecture Notes in Computer Science, pages 55–72, Beijing, China, November 2003. Springer-Verlag.
17. Mihnea Marinescu and Benjamin Goldberg. Partial-evaluation techniques for concurrent programs. In Consel [3], pages 47–62.
18. Matthias Neubauer and Peter Thiemann. Protocol specialization. Technical Report 212, Institut für Informatik, University of Freiburg, Germany, August 2004.
19. Oscar Nierstrasz. Regular types for active objects. In *Proceedings OOPSLA '93*, pages 1–15, October 1993.
20. Benjamin C. Pierce and Davide Sangiorgi. Typing and subtyping for mobile processes. In *Proc. of the 8th Annual IEEE Symposium on Logic in Computer Science*, pages 376–385. IEEE Computer Society Press, 1993.
21. Thomas Reps and Todd Turnidge. Program specialization via program slicing. In Danvy et al. [5], pages 409–429.
22. Ulrik Schultz, Julia Lawall, Charles Consel, and Gilles Muller. Toward automatic specialization of Java programs. In *13th European Conference on Object-Oriented Programming (ECOOP '99)*, Lisbon, June 1999. Springer-Verlag.
23. Ulrik P. Schultz. Black-box program specialization. In *WCOP'99, Fourth International Workshop on Component-Oriented Programming*, Lisbon, Portugal, June 1999.
24. Ulrik P. Schultz, Julia L. Lawall, and Charles Consel. Automatic program specialization for java. *ACM Transactions on Programming Languages and Systems (TOPLAS)*, 25(4):452–499, 2003.
25. Frank Tip. A survey of program slicing techniques. *Journal of Programming Languages*, 3(3):121–189, 1995.
26. Frank Tip, Peter F. Sweeney, Chris Laffra, Aldo Eisma, and David Streeter. Practical extraction techniques for Java. *ACM Transactions on Programming Languages and Systems*, 24(6):625–666, November 2002.
27. David Walker, Carl Crary, and Greg Morrisett. Typed memory management via static capabilities. *ACM Transactions on Programming Languages and Systems*, 22(4):701–771, July 2000.

Automatic Generation of
Editors for Higher-Order Data Structures

Peter Achten, Marko van Eekelen, Rinus Plasmeijer, and Arjen van Weelden

Nijmegen Institute for Information and Computer Science,
Nijmegen University, Toernooiveld 1, 6525 ED Nijmegen, The Netherlands
{peter88, marko, rinus, arjenw}@cs.kun.nl

Abstract. With generic functional programming techniques, we have
eased GUI programming by constructing a programming toolkit with
which one can create GUIs in an abstract and compositional way, using type-directed Graphical Editor Components (*GEC*s). In this toolkit,
the programmer specifies a GUI by means of a *data model* instead of
low-level GUI programming. In earlier versions of this toolkit, the data
model must have a *first-order* type. In this paper we show that the programming toolkit can be extended in two ways, such that the data model
can contain *higher-order data structures*. We added support for dynamic
polymorphic higher-order editors using the *functional shell Esther*. By
combining the earlier developed techniques of *generic GECs, abstract editors*, we also added statically typed higher-order editors. In principle this
solution extends our GUI programming toolkit with the full expressive
power of functional programming languages.

1   Introduction

In the last decade, Graphical User Interfaces (GUIs) have become the standard
for user interaction. Programming these interfaces can be done without much effort when the interface is rather static, and for many of these situations excellent
tools are available. However, when there is more dynamic interaction between
interface and application logic, such applications require tedious manual programming in any programming language. Programmers need to be skilled in the
use of a large programming toolkit.

The goal of the G raphical E ditor project is to obtain a concise programming
toolkit that is abstract, com positional, and type-directed. Abstraction is required
to reduce the size of the toolkit, compositionality reduces the effort of putting
together (or altering) GUI code, and type-directed automatic creation of GUIs
allows the programmer to focus on the data model. In contrast to visual programming environments, programming toolkits can provide ultimate flexibility,
type safety, and dynamic behavior within a single framework. We use a pure
functional programming language (Clean [20]) because functional programming
languages have proven to be very suited for creating abstraction layers on top of
each other. Additionally, they have strong support for type definitions and type
safety.

W.-N. Chin (Ed.): APLAS 2004, LNCS 3302, pp. 262–279, 2004.
© Springer-Verlag Berlin Heidelberg 2004

Our programming toolkit utilizes the Graphical Editor Component (GEC) [6] as universal building block for constructing GUIs. A GEC$_t$ is a graphical editor for values of any monomorphic ■rst-order type t. This type-directed creation of GECs has been obtained by generic programming techniques [8, 17, 16]. Generic programming is extremely beneficial when applied to composite custom types. With generic programming one defines a family of functions that depend on the structure of types. Although one structural element is the function type constructor ($\rightarrow$), it is fundamentally impossible to define a generic function that edits these higher-order values directly, because pure functional programs cannot look inside functions without losing referential-transparency (for instance by distinguishing $\lambda x \rightarrow x+1$ from $\lambda x \rightarrow 1+x$).

In this paper we extend the GEC toolkit in two ways, such that it can construct higher-order value editors. The first extension uses run-time dynamic typing [1, 19], which allows us to include them in the GEC toolkit, but this does not allow type-directed GUI creation. It does, however, enable the toolkit to use polymorphic higher-order functions and data structures. The second extension uses compile-time static typing, in order to gain monomorphic higher-order type-directed GUI creation of abstract types. It uses the abstraction mechanism of the GEC toolkit [7].

Both extensions require a means of using functional expressions, entered by the user, as functional values. Instead of writing our own parser/interpreter/type inference system we use the functional Esther shell [22], which provides type checking at the command line and can use compiled functions from disk. These functions can have arbitrary size and complexity, and even interface with the imperative world. Esther makes extensive use of dynamic types. Dynamic types turn arbitrary (polymorphic, higher-order) data structures (for instance of type [Int $\rightarrow$ Int] or (Tree a) $\rightarrow$ a) into a ■rst-order data structure of type Dynamic without losing the original type.

Contributions of this paper are:

- We provide type-safe expression editors, which are needed for higher-order value editors.
  We obtain, as a bonus, the ability to edit first-order values using expressions. Another bonus: within these expressions one can use compiled functions from disk, incorporating realworld functionality.
- The programming toolkit can now create polymorphic dynamically typed, and monomorphic statically typed, higher-order value editors.
- The programming toolkit is type-safe and type-directed.

This paper is structured as follows. Section 2 contains an overview of the first-order GEC toolkit. In Sect. 3 we present the first extension, in which we explain how Esther incorporates expressions as functional values using dynamic types. We present in Sect. 4 the second extension, and explain how we obtain higher-order type-directed GUI creation using the abstraction mechanism of the GEC toolkit. Section 5 gives examples of the new system that illustrate its expressive power. We discuss related work in Sect. 6 and conclude in Sect. 7.

Finally, a note on the implementation and the examples in this paper. The project has been realized in Clean. Familiarity with Haskell [18] is assumed, relevant differences between Haskell and Clean are explained in footnotes. The GUI code is mapped to Object I/O [4], which is Clean's library for GUIs. Given sufficient support for dynamic types, the results of this project can be transferred to Generic Haskell [12], using the Haskell [18] port of Object I/O [3]. The complete code of all examples (including the complete G EC implementation in Clean) can be downloaded from http://www.cs.kun.nl/~clean/gec.

2   The GEC Programming Toolkit

With the G EC programming toolkit [6], one constructs GUI applications in a compositional way using a high level of abstraction. The basic building block is the Graphical Editor Component (G EC). It is generated by a generic function, which makes the approach type-directed.

Before explaining G ECs in more detail, we need to point out that Clean uses an explicit multiple environment passing style [2] for I/O programming. As G ECs are integrated with Clean Object I/O, the I/O functions that are presented in this paper are state transition functions on the program state (PSt ps). The program state represents the external world of an interactive program, tailored for GUI operations. In this paper the identifier env is a value of this type. The uniqueness type system [9] of Clean ensures single threaded use of the environment. To improve the readability, uniqueness type attributes that actually appear in the type signatures are not shown. Furthermore, the code has been slightly simplified, leaving out a few details that are irrelevant for this paper.

Graphical Editor Components. A G EC$_t$ is an editor for values of type t. It is generated with a generic function [16, 8]. A generic function is a meta function that works on a description of the structure of types. For any concrete type t, the compiler is able to automatically derive an instance function of this generic function for the type t. The power of a generic scheme is that we obtain an editor for free for any monomorphic data type. This makes the approach particularly suited for rapid prototyping.

The generic function gGEC creates G ECs. It takes a definition (GECDef t env) of a G EC$_t$ and creates the G EC$_t$ object in the environment. It returns an interface (GECInterface t env) to that G EC$_t$ object. The environment env is in this case (PSt ps), since gGEC uses Object I/O.

generic[1] gGEC t :: (GECDef t (PSt ps)) (PSt ps)
$$\to (\text{GECInterface t (PSt ps), PSt ps})[2]$$

The (GECDef t env) consists of three elements. The first is a string that identifies the top-level Object I/O element (window or dialog) in which the editor

---

[1] **generic** $f\,t :: T(t)$ introduces a generic function f with type scheme $T(t)$. Keywords are type-set in **bold**.

[2] Clean separates function arguments by whitespace, instead of ->.

must be created. The second is the initial value of type t of the editor. The third is a callback function of type $t \to env \to env$. This callback function tells the editor which parts of the program need to be informed of user actions. The editor uses this function to respond to changes to the value of the editor.

```
::³ GECDef t env :=⁴ (String,t,CallBackFunction t env)
::   CallBackFunction t env := t → env → env
```

The (GECInterface t env) is a record that contains all m ethods of the newly created G EC_t.

```
:: GECInterface t env = { gecGetValue :: env → (t,env)
                        , gecSetValue :: t → env → env }⁵
```

The gecGetValue method returns the current value, and gecSetValue sets the current value of the associated G EC_t object. Programs can be constructed combining editors by tying together the various gecSetValues and gecGetValues. We are working on an arrow combinator library that abstracts from the necessary plumbing [5]. For the examples in this paper, it is sufficient to use the following tying function:

```
selfGEC :: String (t → t) t (PSt ps) → (PSt ps) |⁶ gGEC{|*|} t
selfGEC s f v env = env1
where ({gecSetValue},env1) = gGEC{|*|} (s,f v,λx → gecSetValue (f x)) env
```

Given an f of type $t \to t$ on the data model of type t and an initial value v of type t, selfGEC gui f v creates the associated G EC_t using gGEC (hence the context restriction). selfGEC creates a feedback loop that sends every edited output value back as an input to the same editor, after applying the function f.

Example 1: The standard appearance of a G EC is given by the following program that creates an editor for a self-balancing binary tree:

```
module Editor
import StdEnv, StdIO, StdGEC

Start :: *World → *World
Start world = startIO MDI Void myEditor world

myEditor :: (PSt ps) → (PSt ps)
myEditor = selfGEC "Tree" balance (Node Leaf
           1 Leaf)

:: Tree a = Node (Tree a) a (Tree a) | Leaf
```

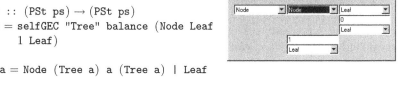

In this example, we create a G EC_{Tree Int} which displays the indicated initial value Node Leaf 1 Leaf (upper screen shot). The user can manipulate this

---

³ Type definitions are preceded by ::.
⁴ := introduces a synonym type.
⁵ $\{f_0 :: t_0, \ldots, f_n :: t_n\}$ denotes a record with field names f_i and types t_i.
⁶ In a function type, | introduces all overloading class restrictions.

value in any desired order, producing new values of type `Tree Int` (e.g., turning the upper `Leaf` into a `Node` with the pull-down menu). Each time a new value is created or edited, the feedback function `balance` is applied. `balance` takes a argument of type `Tree a` and returns the tree after balancing it. The shape and lay-out of the tree being displayed adjusts itself automatically. Default values are generated by the editor when needed.

Note that the only things that need to be specified by the programmer are the initial value of the desired type, and the feedback function. In all remaining examples, we only modify `myEditor` and the type for which an instance of `gGEC` is derived.

The tree example shows that a G EC$_t$ explicitly reflects the structure of type t. For the creation of GUI applications, we need to model both specific GUI elements (such as buttons) and layout control (such as horizontal, vertical layout). This has been done by specializing `gGEC` [6] for a number of types that either represent GUI elements or layout. Here are the types and their `gGEC` specialization that are used in the examples in this paper:

```
:: Display a = Display a    // a non-editable GUI: e.g., Hello World .
:: Hide     a = Hide     a  // an invisible GUI, useful for state.
:: UpDown     = UpPressed | DownPressed | Neutral  // a spin button: .
```

3   Dynamically Typed Higher-Order GECs

In this section we show how to extend G EC s with the ability to deal with functions and expressions. Because functions are opaque, the solution requires a means of interpreting functional expressions as functional values. Instead of writing our own parser/interpreter/type inference system we use the E sther shell [22] (Sect. 3.1).

Esther enables the user to enter expressions (using a subset of Clean) that are dynamically typed, and transformed into values and functions using compiled code. It is also possible to reuse earlier created functions, which are stored on disk. Its implementation relies on the dynamic type system [1, 19, 23] of Clean.

The shell uses a text-based interface, and hence it makes sense to create a special string-editor (Sect. 3.2), which converts any string into the corresponding dynamically typed value. This special editor has the same power as the Esther command interpreter and can deliver any dynamic value, including higher-order polymorphic functions.

3.1   Dynamics in Clean

A dynamic is a value of static type `Dynamic`, which contains an expression as well as a representation of its static type, e.g., **dynamic** 42 :: `Int`, **dynamic** `map fst` :: ∀a b: [(a, b)] → [a]. Basically, dynamic types turn every (first and higher-order) data structure into a first-order structure, while providing run-time access to the original type and value.

Function alternatives and case patterns can match on values of type `Dynamic`. Such a pattern match consists of a value pattern and a type pattern, e.g., [4 , 2] :: [Int]. The compiler translates a pattern match on a type into a run-time type unification. If the unification is successful, type variables in a type pattern are bound to the offered type. Applying dynamics at run-time will be used to create an editor that changes according to the type of entered expressions (Sect. 3.2, Example 2).

```
dynamicApply :: Dynamic Dynamic → Dynamic
dynamicApply (f :: a → b) (x :: a) = dynamic f x      :: b
dynamicApply      df           dx  = dynamic "Error" :: String
```

dynamicApply tests if the argument type of the function f, inside its first argument, can be unified with the type of the value x, inside the second argument. dynamicApply can safely apply f to x, if the type pattern match succeeds. It yields a value of the type that is bound to the type variable b by unification, wrapped in a dynamic. If the match fails, it yields a string in a dynamic.

Type variables in type patterns can also relate to type variables in the static type of a function. A ˆ behind a variable in a pattern associates it with the same type variable in the static type of the function.

```
matchDynamic :: Dynamic → t | TC t
matchDynamic (x :: tˆ) = x
```

The static type variable t, in the example above, is determined by the static context in which it is used, and imposes a restriction on the actual type that is accepted at run-time by matchDynamic. The function becomes overloaded in the predefined TC (type code) class. This makes it a type dependent function [19].

The dynamic run-time system of Clean supports writing dynamics to disk and reading them back again, possibly in another program or during another execution of the same program. This provides a means of type safe communication, the ability to use compiled plug-ins in a type safe way, and a rudimentary basis for mobile code. The dynamic is read in lazily after a successful run-time unification. The amount of data and code that the dynamic linker links is, therefore, determined by the evaluation of the value inside the dynamic.

```
writeDynamic :: String Dynamic env → (Bool,env) | FileSystem env
readDynamic  :: String env → (Bool,Dynamic,env) | FileSystem env
```

Programs, stored as dynamics, have Clean types and can be regarded as a typed file system. We have shown that dynamicApply can be used to type check any function application at run-time using the static types stored in dynamics. Combining both in an interactive 'read expression – apply dynamics – evaluate and show result' loop, already gives a simple shell that supports the type checked run-time application of programs to documents. The composeDynamic function below, taken from the Esther shell, applies dynamics and infers the type of an expression.

```
composeDynamic    :: String env → (Dynamic,env) | FileSystem env
showValueDynamic :: Dynamic → String
```

composeDynamic *expr env* parses *expr*. Unbound identifiers in *expr* are resolved by reading them from the file system. In addition, overloading is resolved. Using the parse tree of *expr* and the resolved identifiers, the dynamicApply function is used to construct the (functional) value v and its type τ. These are packed in a **dynamic** v :: τ and returned by composeDynamic. In other words, **if** $env \vdash expr :: \tau$ and $[\![expr]\!]_{env} = v$ **then** composeDynamic *expr env* = (v :: τ, env). The showValueDynamic function yields a string representation of the value inside a dynamic.

3.2   Creating a GEC for the Type Dynamic

With the composeDynamic function, an editor for dynamics can easily be constructed. This function needs an appropriate environment to access the dynamic values and functions (plug-ins) that are stored on disk. The standard (PSt ps) environment used by the generic gGEC function (Sect. 2) is such an environment. This means that we can simply use composeDynamic in a specialized editor to offer the same functionality as the command line interpreter. Instead of Esther's console we use a String editor as interface to the application user. In addition we need to convert the provided string into the corresponding dynamic. We therefore define a composite data type DynString and a specialized gGEC-editor for this type (a G EC $_{\text{DynString}}$) that performs the required conversions.

```
:: DynString = DynStr Dynamic String
```

The choice of the composite data type is motivated mainly by simplicity and convenience: the string can be used by the application user for typing in the expression. It also stores the original user input, which cannot be extracted from the dynamic when it contains a function.

Now we specialize gGEC for this type DynString. The complete definition of gGEC{|DynString|} is given below.

```
gGEC{|DynString|} (gui,DynStr _ expr,dynStringUpdate) env
    ♯⁷(stringGEC,env) = gGEC{|*|} (gui,expr,stringUpdate dynStringUpdate) env
    = ({ gecSetValue = dynSetValue stringGEC.gecSetValue
       , gecGetValue = dynGetValue stringGEC.gecGetValue },env)
where dynSetValue stringSetValue (DynStr _ expr) env
        = stringSetValue expr env
      dynGetValue stringGetValue env
        ♯ (nexpr,env) = stringGetValue env
        ♯ (ndyn, env) = composeDynamic nexpr env
        = (DynStr ndyn nexpr,env)
      stringUpdate dynStringUpdate nexpr env
        ♯ (ndyn,env) = composeDynamic nexpr env
        = dynStringUpdate (DynStr ndyn nexpr) env
```

The created G EC $_{\text{DynString}}$ displays a box for entering a string by calling the standard generic gGEC{|*|} function for the value expr of type String, yielding a

---

[7] This is Clean's 'do-notation' for environment passing.

stringGEC. The DynString-editor is completely defined in terms of this String-editor. It only has to take care of the conversions between a String and a DynString. This means that its gecSetValue method dynSetValue simply sets the string component of a new DynString in the underlying String-editor. Its gecGetValue method dynGetValue retrieves the string from the String-editor, converts it to the corresponding Dynamic by applying composeDynamic, and combines these two values in a DynString-value. When a new string is created by the application user, the callback function stringUpdate is evaluated, which invokes the callback function dynStringUpdate (provided as an argument upon creation of the DynString-editor), after converting the String to a DynString.

It is convenient to define a constructor function mkDynStr that converts any input $expr$, that has value v of type τ, into a value of type DynString guaranteeing that if $v :: \tau$ and $[\![expr]\!] = v$, then (DynStr $(v::\tau)$ $expr$) :: DynString.

```
mkDynStr :: a → DynString | TC a
mkDynStr x = let dx = dynamic x in DynStr dx (showValueDynamic dx)
```

Example 2: We construct an interactive editor that can be used to test functions. It can be a newly defined function, say $\lambda x \to x\verb|^|2$, or any existing function stored on disk as a Dynamic. Hence the tested function can vary from a small function, say factorial, to a large complete application.

```
:: MyRecord = { function :: DynString
             , argument :: DynString
             , result   :: DynString }
myEditor = selfGEC "test" guiApply (initval id 0)
where
    initval f v = { function = mkDynStr f
                  , argument = mkDynStr v
                  , result   = mkDynStr (f v) }
    guiApply  r=:⁸{ function = DynStr (f::a → b) _
                  , argument = DynStr (v::a)      _ }
              = {r &⁹ result = mkDynStr (f v)}
    guiApply  r = r
```

The type MyRecord is a record with three fields, function, argument, and result, all of type DynString. The user can use this editor to enter a function definition and its argument. The selfGEC function will ensure that each time a new string is created with the editor "test", the function guiApply is applied that provides a new value of type MyRecord to the editor. The function guiApply tests, in a similar way as the function dynamicApply (see Sect. 3.1), whether the type of the supplied function and argument match. If so, a new result is calculated. If not, nothing happens.

This editor can only be used to test functions with one argument. What happens if we edit the function and the argument in such a way that the result is not a plain value but a function itself? Take, e.g., as function the twice function

---
⁸ $x =: e$ binds x to e.
⁹ $\{r$ & $f_0=v_0, \ldots, f_n=v_n\}$ is a record equal to r, except that fields f_i have value v_i.

λf x → f (f x), and as argument the increment function ((+) 1). Then the result is also a function λx → ((+) 1) ((+) 1 x). The editor displays <function> as result. There is no way to pass an argument to the resulting function.

With an editor like the one above, the user can enter expressions that are automatically converted into the corresponding Dynamic value. As in the shell, unbound names are expected to be dynamics on disk. Illegal expressions result in a Dynamic containing an error message.

To have a properly higher-order dynamic application example, one needs an editor in which the user can type in functions of arbitrary arity, and subsequently enter arguments for this function. The result is then treated such that, if it is a function, editors are added dynamically for the appropriate number of arguments. This is explained in the following example.

Example 3: We construct a test program that accepts arbitrary expressions and adds the proper number of argument editors, which again can be arbitrary expressions. The number of arguments cannot be statically determined and has to be recalculated each time a new value is provided. Instead of an editor for a record, we therefore create an editor for a list of tuples. Each tuple consists of a string used to prompt to the user, and a DynString-value. The tuple elements are displayed below each other using the predefined list editor vertlistAGEC and access operator ^^, which will be presented in Sect. 4.1. The selfGEC function is used to ensure that each change made with the editor is tested with the guiApply function and the result is shown in the editor.

```
myEditor = selfGEC "test" (guiApply o (^^))
                (vertlistAGEC [show "expression " 0])
where
    guiApply [f=:(_,(DynStr d _)):args]
      = vertlistAGEC [f:check (fromDynStr d) args]
    where
        check (f::a → b) [arg=:(_,DynStr (x::a) _):args]
          = [arg : check (dynamic f x) args]
        check (f::a → b) _ = [show "argument " "??"]
        check (x::a)     _ = [show "result "    x]

    show s v = (Display s,mkDynStr v)
```

The key part of this example is formed by the function check which calls itself recursively on the result of the dynamic application. As long as function and argument match, and the resulting type is still a function, it will require another argument which will be checked for type consistency. If function and argument do not match, "??" is displayed, and the user can try again. As soon as the resulting type is a plain value, it is evaluated and shown using the data constructor Display, which creates a non-editable editor that just displays its value. With this editor, any higher-order polymorphic function can be entered and tested.

4   Statically Typed Higher-Order *GEC*s

The editors presented in the previous section are flexible because they deliver a
Dynamic (packed into the type DynString). They have the disadvantage that the
programmer has to program a check, such as the check function in the previous
example, on the type consistency of the resulting Dynamics.

In many applications it is statically known what the type of a supplied function must be. In this section we show how the run-time type check can be replaced
by a compile-time check, using the abstraction mechanism for G EC s. This gives
us a second solution for higher-order data structures that is statically typed,
which allows, therefore, type-directed generic GUI creation.

4.1   Abstract Graphical Editor Components

The generic function gGEC derives a GUI for its instance type. Because it is a
function, the appearance of the GUI is completely determined by that type. This
is in some cases much to rigid. One cannot use different visual appearances of the
same type within a program. For this purpose abstract G EC s (AG EC) [7] have
been introduced. An instance of gGEC for AG EC has been defined. Therefore, an
AG EC$_d$ can be used as a G EC$_d$, i.e., it behaves as an editor for values of a certain
domain, say of type d. However, an AG EC$_d$ never displays nor edits values of
type d, but rather a view on values of this type, say of type v. Values of type v
are shown and edited, and internally converted to the values of domain d. The
view is again generated automatically as a G EC$_v$. To makes this possible, the
ViewGEC d v record is used to define the relation between the domain d and the
view v.

```
:: ViewGEC d v
 = { d_val        :: d                    // initial domain value
   , d_oldv_to_v  :: d → (Maybe v) → v    // convert domain value to view value
   , update_v     :: v → v                // correct view value
   , v_to_d       :: v → d }              // convert view value to domain value
```

It should be noted that the programmer does not need to be knowledgeable
about Object I/O programming to construct an AG EC$_d$ with a view of type v.
The specification is only in terms of the involved data domains. The complete
interface to AG EC s is given below.

```
:: AGEC d                               // abstract data type
mkAGEC        :: (ViewGEC d v) → AGEC d | gGEC{|*|} v
(^^)          :: (AGEC d) → d           // Read current domain value
(^=) infixl :: (AGEC d) d → AGEC d      // Set new domain value
```

The ViewGEC record can be converted to the abstract type AGEC, using the
function mkAGEC above. Because AG EC is an abstract data type we need access
functions to read (^^) and write (^=) its current value. AG EC s allow us to define
arbitrarily many editors gec$_i$ :: AG EC$_d$ that have a private implementation of
type G EC$_{v_i}$. Because AG EC is abstract, code that has been written for editors
that manipulates some type containing AG EC$_d$, does not change when the value

of type $AGEC_d$ is exchanged for another $AGEC_d$. This facilitates experimenting with various designs for an interface without changing any other code.

We built a collection of functions creating abstract editors for various purposes. Below, we summarize only those functions of the collection that are used in the examples in this paper:

```
vertlistAGEC :: [a] → AGEC [a] | gGEC{|*|} a // all elements displayed in a column
counterAGEC  :: a  → AGEC  a  | gGEC{|*|}, IncDec a // a special number editor
hidAGEC      :: a  → AGEC  a              // identity, no editor
displayAGEC  :: a  → AGEC  a  | gGEC{|*|} a // identity, non-editable editor
```

The counter editor [0   ⇄] below is a typical member of this library.

```
counterAGEC :: a → AGEC a | gGEC{|*|}, IncDec a
counterAGEC j = mkAGEC { d_val = j, d_oldv_to_v = λi _ → (i,Neutral)
                       , update_v = updateCounter, v_to_d = fst      }
where updateCounter (n,UpPressed)   = (n+one,Neutral)
      updateCounter (n,DownPressed) = (n-one,Neutral)
      updateCounter (n,Neutral)     = (  n  ,Neutral)
```

A programmer can use the counter editor as an integer editor, but because of its internal representation it presents the application user with an edit field combined with an up-down, or spin, button. The `updateCounter` function is used to synchronize the spin button and the integer edit field. The right part of the tuple is of type `UpDown` (Sect. 2), which is used to create the spin button.

4.2   Adding Static Type Constraints to Dynamic GECs

The abstraction mechanism provided by $AGEC$s is used to build type-directed editors for higher-order data structures, which check the type of the entered expressions dynamically. These statically typed higher-order editors are created using the function `dynamicAGEC`. The full definition of this function is specified and explained below.

```
dynamicAGEC :: d → AGEC d | TC d
dynamicAGEC x = mkAGEC { d_val=x            , d_oldv_to_v=toView
                       , update_v=updView x, v_to_d=fromView x  }
where toView newx Nothing  = let dx = mkDynStr newx in (dx,hidAGEC dx)
      toView _ (Just oldx) = oldx

      fromView :: d (DynString,AGEC DynString) → d | TC d
      fromView _ (_,oldx) = case ^^oldx of DynStr (x::d^) _ → x

      updView :: d (DynString,AGEC DynString)
               → (DynString,AGEC DynString) | TC d
      updView _ (newx=:(DynStr (x::d^) _),_) = (newx,hidAGEC newx)
      updView _ (_,oldx)                     = (^^oldx,oldx)
```

The abstract `Dynamic` editor, which is the result of the function `dynamicAGEC` initially takes a value of some statically determined type d. It converts this value into a value of type DynString, such that it can be edited by the application user as explained in Sect. 3.2. The application user can enter an expression of arbitrary type, but now it is ensured that only expressions of type d are approved.

The function updView, which is called in the abstract editor after any edit action, checks, using a type pattern match, whether the newly created dynamic can be unified with the type d of the initial value (using the ^-notation in the pattern match as explained in Sect. 3.1). If the type of the entered expression is different, it is rejected[10] and the previous value is restored and shown. To do this, the abstract editor has to remember the previously accepted correctly typed value. Clearly, we do not want to show this part of the internal state to the application user. This is achieved using the abstract editor hidAGEC (Sect. 4.1), which creates an invisible editor, i.e., a store, for any type.

Example 5: Consider the following variation of Example 2:

```
:: MyRecord a b = { function :: AGEC (a → b)
                  , argument :: AGEC a
                  , result   :: AGEC b }
myEditor = selfGEC "test" guiApply (initval ((+) 1.0) 0.0)
where
    initval f v = { function = dynamicAGEC f
                  , argument = dynamicAGEC v
                  , result   = displayAGEC (f v) }
    guiApply myrec=:{ function = af, argument = av }
       = {myrec & result = displayAGEC ((^^af) (^^av))}
```

The editor above can be used to test functions of a certain statically determined type. Due to the particular choice of the initial values ((+) 1.0 :: Real → Real and 0.0 :: Real), the editor can only be used to test functions of type Real → Real applied to arguments of type Real. Notice that it is now statically guaranteed that the provided dynamics are correctly typed. The dynamicAGEC-editors take care of the required checks at run-time and they reject ill-typed expressions. The programmer therefore does not have to perform any checks anymore. The abstract dynamicAGEC-editor delivers a value of the proper type just like any other abstract editor.

The code in the above example is not only simple and elegant, but it is also very flexible. The dynamicAGEC abstract editor can be replaced by any other abstract editor, provided that the statically derived type constraints (concerning f and v) are met. This is illustrated by the next example.

Example 6: If one prefers a counter as input editor for the argument value, one only has to replace dynamicAGEC by counterAGEC in the definition of initval:

---

[10] There is currently no feedback on *why* the type is rejected. Generating good error messages as in [15] certainly improves the user interface.

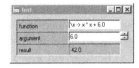

```
initval f v = { function = dynamicAGEC f
              , argument = counterAGEC v
              , result   = displayAGEC (f v) }
```

The `dynamicAGEC` is typically used when expression editors are preferred over value editors of a type, and when application users need to be able to enter functions of a statically fixed monomorphic type.

One can create an editor for any higher-order data structure τ, even if it contains polymorphic functions. It is required that all higher-order parts of τ are abstracted, by wrapping them with an AGEC type. Basically, this means that each part of τ of the form $a \to b$ must be changed into AGEC $(a \to b)$. For the resulting type τ' an edit dialog can be automatically created, e.g., by applying `selfGEC`. However, the initial value that is passed to `selfGEC` must be monomorphic, as usual for any instantiation of a generic function. Therefore, editors for polymorphic types cannot be created automatically using this statically typed generic technique. As explained in Sect. 3.2 polymorphic types can be handled with dynamic type checking.

5   Applications of Higher-Order *GEC*s

The ability to generate editors for higher-order data structures greatly enhances the applicability of G EC s. Firstly, it becomes possible to create applications in which functions can be edited as part of a complex data structure. Secondly, these functions can be composed dynamically from earlier created compiled functions on disk. Both are particular useful for rapid prototyping purposes, as they can add real-life functionality.

In this section we discuss one small and one somewhat larger application. Even the code for the latter application is still rather small (just a few pages). The code is omitted in this paper due to space limitations, but it can be found at http://www.cs.kun.nl/~clean/gec. Screen shots of the running applications are given in Appendix A.

An Adaptable Calculator. In the first example we use G EC to create a 'more or less' standard calculator. The default look of the calculator was adapted using the aforementioned A G EC customization techniques. Special about this calculator is that its functionality can be easily extended at run-time: the application user can add his or her own buttons with a user defined functionality. In addition to the calculator editor, a G EC editor is created, which enables the application user to maintain a list of button definitions consisting of button names with corresponding functions. Since the type of the calculator functions are statically known, a statically typed higher-order G EC is used in this example. The user can enter a new function definition using a lambda expression, but it is also possible to open and use an earlier created function from disk. Each time the list is changed with the list editor, the calculator editor is updated and adjusted accordingly. For a typical screen shot see Fig. 1.

A Form Editor. In the previous example we have shown that one can use one editor to change the look and functionality of another. This principle is also used in a more serious example: the form editor. The form editor is an editor with which electronic forms can be defined and changed. This is achieved using a meta-description of a form. This meta-description is itself a data structure, and therefore, we can generate an editor for it. One can regard a form as a dedicated spreadsheet, and with the form editor one can define the actual shape and functionality of such a spreadsheet. With the form editor one can create and edit fields. Each field can be used for a certain purpose. It can be used to show a string, it can be used as editor for a value of a certain basic type, it can be used to display a field in a certain way by assigning an abstract editor to it (e.g., a counter or a calculator), and it can be used to calculate and show new values depending on the contents of other fields. For this purpose, the application user has to be able to define functions that have the contents of other fields as arguments. The form editor uses a mixed mode strategy. The contents of some fields can be statically determined (e.g., a field for editing an integer value). But the form editor can only dynamically check whether the argument fields of a specified function are indeed of the right type. The output of the form editor is used to create the actual form in another editor which is part of the same application. By filling in the form fields with the actual value, the application user can test whether the corresponding form behaves as intended. For a typical screen shot see Fig. 2.

6   Related Work

In the previous sections we have shown that we can create editors that can deal with higher order data structures. We can create dynamically typed higher-order editors, which have the advantages that we can deal with polymorphic higher order data structures and overloading. This has the disadvantage that the programmer has to check type safety in the editor. The compiler can ensure type correctness of higher-order data structures in statically typed editors, but they can only edit monomorphic types. Related work can be sought in three areas:

Grammars Instead of Types: Taking a different perspective on the type-directed nature of our approach, one can argue that it is also possible to obtained editors by starting from a grammar specification instead of a type. Such toolkits require a grammar as input and yield an editor GUI as result. Projects in this flavor are for instance the recent Proxima project [21], which relies on XML and its DTD (Document Type Definition language), and the Asf+Sdf Meta-Environment [10] which uses an Asf syntax specification and Sdf semantics specification. The major difference with such an approach is that these systems need both a grammar and some kind of interpreter. In our system higher-order elements are immediately available as a functional value that can be applied and passed to other components.

GUI Programming Toolkits: From the abstract nature of the G EC toolkit it is clear that we need to look at GUI toolkits that also offer a high level of abstraction. Most GUI toolkits are concerned with the low level management of widgets in an imperative style. One well-known example of an abstract, compositional GUI toolkit based on a combinator library is Fudgets [11]. These combinators are required for plumbing when building complex GUI structures from simpler ones. In our system far less plumbing is needed. Most work is done automatically by the generic function gGEC. The only plumbing needed in our system is for combining the G EC-editors themselves. Furthermore, the Fudget system does not provide support for editing function values or expressions.

Because a G EC$_t$ is a t-stateful object, it makes sense to have a look at object oriented approaches. The power of abstraction and composition in our functional framework is similar to m ixins [13] in object oriented languages. One can imagine an OO GUI library based on compositional and abstract mixins in order to obtain a similar toolkit. Still, such a system lacks higher-order data structures.

Visual Programming Languages: Due to the extension of the G EC programming toolkit with higher-order data structures, visual programm ing languages have come within reach as application dom ain. One interesting example is the Vital system [14] in which Haskell-like scripts can be edited. Both systems allow direct manipulation of expressions and custom types, allow customization of views, and have guarded data types (like the selfGEC function). In contrast with the Vital system, which is a dedicated system and has been implemented in Java, our system is a general purpose toolkit. We could use our toolkit to construct a visual environment in the spirit of Vital.

7   Conclusions

With the original G EC-toolkit one can construct GUI applications without much programming effort. This is done on a high level of abstraction, in a fully compositional manner, and type-directed. It can be used for any monomorphic first-order data type. In this paper we have shown how the programming toolkit can be extended in such a way that G ECs can be created for higher-order data structures. We have presented two methods, each with its own advantage and disadvantage.

We can create an editor for higher-order data structures using dynamic typing, which has as advantage that it can deal with polymorphism and overloading, but with as disadvantage that the programmer has to ensure type safety at runtime. We can create a editor for higher-order data structures using the static typing such that type correctness of entered expressions or functions is guaranteed at compile-time. In that case we can only cope with monomorphic types, but we can generate type-directed GUIs automatically.

As a result, applications constructed with this toolkit can manipulate the same set of data types as modern functional programming languages can. The system is type-directed and type safe, as well as the GUI applications that are constructed with it.

References

1. M. Abadi, L. Cardelli, B. Pierce, G. Plotkin, and D. Rèmy. Dynamic typing in polymorphic languages. In *Proceedings of the ACM SIGPLAN Workshop on ML and its Applications*, San Francisco, June 1992.
2. P. Achten. *Interactive Functional Programs - models, methods, and implementations*. PhD thesis, University of Nijmegen, The Netherlands, 1996.
3. P. Achten and S. Peyton Jones. Porting the Clean Object I/O library to Haskell. In M. Mohnen and P. Koopman, editors, *Proceedings of the 12th International Workshop on the Implementation of Functional Languages, IFL'00, Selected Papers*, volume 2011 of *LNCS*, pages 194–213. Aachen, Germany, Springer, Sept. 2001.
4. P. Achten and R. Plasmeijer. Interactive Functional Objects in Clean. In C. Clack, K. Hammond, and T. Davie, editors, *Proc. of the 9th International Workshop on the Implementation of Functional Languages, IFL 1997, Selected Papers*, volume 1467 of *LNCS*, pages 304–321. St.Andrews, UK, Springer, Sept. 1998.
5. Achten, Peter and van Eekelen, Marko and Plasmeijer, Rinus and van Weelden, Arjen. Arrows for Generic Graphical Editor Components. 2004. Under Submission; available as Nijmegen Technical Report NIII-R0416, http://www.niii.kun.nl/research/reports/full/NIII-R0416.pdf.
6. Achten, Peter, van Eekelen, Marko and Plasmeijer, Rinus. Generic Graphical User Interfaces. In Greg Michaelson and Phil Trinder, editors, *Selected Papers of the 15th Int. Workshop on the Implementation of Functional Languages, IFL03*, LNCS. Edinburgh, UK, Springer, 2003. To appear: draft version available via ftp://ftp.cs.kun.nl/pub/Clean/papers/2004/achp2004-GenericGUI.pdf.
7. Achten, Peter, van Eekelen, Marko and Plasmeijer, Rinus. Compositional Model-Views with Generic Graphical User Interfaces. In *Practical Aspects of Declarative Programming, PADL04*, volume 3057 of *LNCS*, pages 39–55. Springer, 2004.
8. A. Alimarine and R. Plasmeijer. A Generic Programming Extension for Clean. In T. Arts and M. Mohnen, editors, *The 13th International workshop on the Implementation of Functional Languages, IFL'01, Selected Papers*, volume 2312 of *LNCS*, pages 168–186. Älvsjö, Sweden, Springer, Sept. 2002.
9. E. Barendsen and S. Smetsers. *Graph Rewriting Aspects of Functional Programming*, chapter 2, pages 63–102. World scientific, 1999.
10. M. v. d. Brand, A. van Deursen, J. Heering, H. de Jong, M. de Jonge, T. Kuipers, P. Klint, L. Moonen, P. Olivier, J. Scheerder, J. Vinju, E. Visser, and J. Visser. The Asf+Sdf Meta-Environment: a Component-Based Language Development Environment. In R. Wilhelm, editor, *Compiler Construction 2001 (CC'01)*, pages 365–370. Springer-Verlag, 2001.
11. M. Carlsson and T. Hallgren. FUDGETS - a graphical user interface in a lazy functional language. In *Proceedings of the ACM Conference on Functional Programming and Computer Architecture, FPCA '93*, Kopenhagen, Denmark, 1993.
12. D. Clarke and A. Löh. Generic Haskell, Specifically. In J. Gibbons and J. Jeuring, editors, *Generic Programming. Proceedings of the IFIP TC2 Working Conference on Generic Programming*, pages 21–48, Schloss Dagstuhl, July 2003. Kluwer Academic Publishers. ISBN 1-4020-7374-7.
13. M. Flatt, S. Krishnamurthi, and M. Felleisen. Classes and mixins. In *The 25TH ACM SIGPLAN-SIGACT Symposium on Principles of Programming Languages (POPL98)*, pages 171–183, San Diego, California, 1998. ACM, New York, NY.
14. K. Hanna. Interactive Visual Functional Programming. In S. P. Jones, editor, *Proc. Intnl Conf. on Functional Programming*, pages 100–112. ACM, October 2002.

15. B. Heeren, J. Jeuring, D. Swierstra, and P. Alcocer. Improving type-error messages in functional languages. Technical Report UU-CS-2002-009, Utrecht University, Institute of Information and Computing Sciences, 2002.

16. R. Hinze. A new approach to generic functional programming. In *The 27th Annual ACM SIGPLAN-SIGACT Symposium on Principles of Programming Languages*, pages 119–132. Boston, Massachusetts, January 2000.

17. R. Hinze and S. Peyton Jones. Derivable Type Classes. In G. Hutton, editor, *2000 ACM SIGPLAN Haskell Workshop*, volume 41(1) of *ENTCS*. Montreal, Canada, Elsevier Science, 2001.

18. S. Peyton Jones and Hughes J. et al. *Report on the programming language Haskell 98*. University of Yale, 1999. http://www.haskell.org/definition/.

19. M. Pil. Dynamic types and type dependent functions. In D. Hammond and Clack, editors, *Implementation of Functional Languages (IFL '98)*, LNCS, pages 169–185. Springer Verlag, 1999.

20. R. Plasmeijer and M. van Eekelen. *Concurrent CLEAN Language Report (version 2.0)*, December 2001. http://www.cs.kun.nl/~clean/contents/contents.html.

21. M. Schrage. *Proxima, a presentation-oriented XML editor*. PhD thesis, University of Utrecht, 2004 (to appear).

22. A. van Weelden and R. Plasmeijer. A functional shell that dynamically combines compiled code. In P. Trinder and G. Michaelson, editors, *Selected Papers Proceedings of the 15th International Workshop on Implementation of Functional Languages, IFL'03*. Heriot Watt University, Edinburgh, Sept. 2003. To appear; draft version available via ftp://ftp.cs.kun.nl/pub/Clean/papers/2004/vWeA2004-Esther.pdf.

23. M. Vervoort and R. Plasmeijer. Lazy dynamic input/output in the lazy functional language Clean. In R. Peña and T. Arts, editors, *The 14th International Workshop on the Implementation of Functional Languages, IFL'02, Selected Papers*, volume 2670 of *LNCS*, pages 101–117. Springer, Sept. 2003.

A   Screen Shots of Example Applications

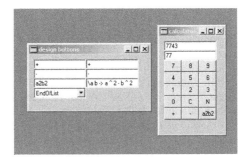

Fig. 1. A screen shot of the adaptable calculator. Left the editor for defining button names with the corresponding function definitions. Right the resulting calculator editor

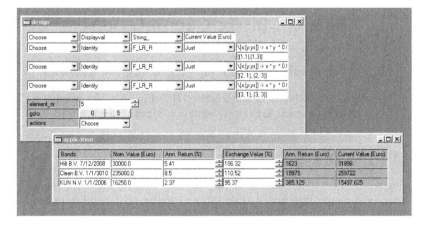

Fig. 2. A screen shot of the form editor. The form editor itself is shown in the upper left window, the corresponding editable spreadsheet-like form is shown in the other

A MATLAB-Based Code Generator for Sparse Matrix Computations

Hideyuki Kawabata, Mutsumi Suzuki, and Toshiaki Kitamura

Department of Computer Engineering, Hiroshima City University
{kawabata,suzuki,kitamura}@arch.ce.hiroshima-cu.ac.jp

Abstract. We present a matrix language compiler CMC which translates annotated MATLAB scripts into Fortran 90 programs. Distinguishing features of CMC include its applicability to programs with sparse matrix computations and its capability of source-level optimization in MATLAB language. Different from other existing similar translators, CMC has an ability to generate codes based on information on the shape of matrices such as triangular and diagonal. Integrating these functionalities, CMC provides the user with a simple way to develop fast large-scale numerical computation codes beyond prototyping. Experimental results show that the programs of SOR and CG methods generated by CMC can run several times as fast as the original MATLAB scripts.

1   Introduction

The MATLAB system [15] is one of the most popular matrix computation environments for rapid prototyping. The MATLAB language is typeless and equipped with a rich set of intrinsic functions, so that programs in the language tend to be compact and portable. MATLAB also has the facility to handle data structures for sparse matrices, which allows the user to execute large-scale computations in the interpreter-based environment [12].

MATLAB's execution speed on sparse computation is, however, somewhat limited due to its dynamic nature; run-time checks for types and array bounds prohibit a MATLAB code to compete with a program written in a compiled language like Fortran 90.

Among measures for alleviating MATLAB's problem of speed, translating a MATLAB script to a program in compiled language seems to be a promising approach. There are, of course, trade-offs between how well the semantics of the original MATLAB code is preserved after translation and how much run-time overhead is reduced.

The MathWorks provides the MATLAB Compiler (MCC) which can translate MATLAB codes into C [16]. Unfortunately, the run-time overhead is hardly removed by using MCC because the procedures of run-time libraries are almost the same as those invoked by interpretation. As a result, although a compiled code by MCC can be used just as a substitute for its MATLAB source script, the execution time of the code wouldn't be shortened very much, especially when a large-scale computation with sparse matrices is carried out.

W.-N. Chin (Ed.): APLAS 2004, LNCS 3302, pp. 280–295, 2004.
© Springer-Verlag Berlin Heidelberg 2004

FALCON project [8] has proposed a translation system of MATLAB programs into Fortran 90. The system translates MATLAB programs into Fortran 90 using its powerful static type inference mechanism. FALCON's optimization capability based on its symbolic analysis facility is reported to be very effective for loop-intensive codes. However, the execution time of a code can not necessarily be reduced by the translation when matrix operations by loop-free notations dominate overall execution time of the code. In addition, the FALCON system does not have a functionality to handle sparse matrix structures, which limits the applicability of the system for large-scale computations.

In this article, we present a MATLAB-based code generator for sparse matrix computations. The system aims at letting the user make the most of MATLAB's intelligible syntax for developing large-scale numerical computation codes. The compiler translates annotated MATLAB scripts into codes in a compiled language. We believe that the introduction of annotations in MATLAB scripts might not only help the translator to output highly optimized static codes, but also enhance source codes' maintainability.

We have been developed a system named CMC (a Compiler for Matrix Computations) which compiles annotated MATLAB scripts into optimized Fortran 90 programs. Like FALCON, CMC translates MATLAB scripts into Fortran 90 in order to reduce dynamic overheads. Unlike FALCON, CMC

- is able to maintain sparse matrices using several types of sparse structures,
- is capable of source-level optimizations, and
- can produce optimized codes using detailed shape information of matrices.

The rest of this paper is organized as follows: Section 2 describes basic design and details of each functionality of CMC [13]. In Section 3, we discuss issues on using multiple sparse structures. Experimental results are presented in Sect. 4. Related work and conclusions are presented in Sects. 5 and 6, respectively.

2   CMC: A Compiler for Sparse Matrix Computations

2.1   Overview of Our Approach

The code shown in Fig. 1 (a) is a complete description of a function written in MATLAB. In the code, variables r, A, b, and x are not typed and the user

```
function [r] = res(A,b,x)
r = b - A*x;
```
(a) A function written in MATLAB

```
function [r] = res(A,b,x)
%cmc integer,_auxarg:: s
%cmc real:: A(s,s)
%cmc real,_colvec:: b(s),x(s)
r = b - A*x;
```
(b) Annotated code for CMC

```
subroutine res(A,x,b,r,s)
implicit none
integer s
real*8 r(s)
real*8 A(s,s)
real*8 x(s)
real*8 b(s)
r = b - MATMUL(A,x)
end
```
(c) Translated dense code

Fig. 1. An example of dense code translation by CMC

```
function [r] = res(A,b,x)
%cmc integer,_auxarg:: s,n
%cmc real,_ccs(n):: A(s,s)
%cmc real,_colvec:: b(s),x(s)
r = b - A*x;
```

(a) Annotated code in
MATLAB

```
subroutine res(A_val,A_colptr,A_rowind,x,b,r,s,n)
implicit none
...
real*8 A_val(s*n)
integer A_colptr(s+1), A_rowind(s*n)
...
r = b
do Xk = 1, s
do Xiptr = A_colptr(Xk), A_colptr(Xk+1)-1
Xi = A_rowind(Xiptr)
r(Xi) = r(Xi) - A_val(Xiptr) * (x(Xk))
enddo
enddo
end
```

(b) Translated sparse code

Fig. 2. An example of sparse code translation by CMC

can pass values of any attribute, e.g., integer scalars or complex matrices, as arguments.

Figure 1 (b) shows an example of an annotated code for CMC. Directives are lines with %cmc at the beginning, which are taken as comment lines by the MAT-LAB interpreter. The syntax of inserted annotations is similar to that of the variable declaration statements in Fortran 90. There are newly defined declarators; these include shape declarators. _colvec means that the variables are column vectors. Other shape declarators not shown in Fig. 1 (b) include _rowvec and _diag, which indicate a row vector and a diagonal matrix, respectively.

Figure 1 (c) shows the translated subroutine in Fortran 90 from the code of Fig. 1 (b) by CMC. Variables for return values are listed following dummy arguments; call by address facility of Fortran allows to do this. Additional variables indicated by _auxarg are, if any, appended to the end of the list of arguments.

The translated code is fairly similar to the source code thanks to the fact that Fortran 90 supports some array operations, although this is not the case for sparse matrices.

Figure 2 (a) shows an example of annotations for sparse matrices. For indicating structures of variables, we use a set of structure declarators which currently consists of _ccs, _crs, and _md. _ccs indicates that each listed variable is of the CCS (Compressed Column Storage) format [3]. _ccs(n) means that the amount of memory for the matrices to be allocated is as large as n nonzero entries on each column. _crs and _md are for the CRS (Compressed Row Storage) format and the MD (multi-diagonal) format, respectively. Details of those sparse matrix structures are described in Sect. 3.

Figure 2 (b) shows the translated sparse code from Fig. 2 (a) by CMC. Matrix A is stored in CCS format using three one-dimensional arrays. Operations are paraphrased using indirect accesses of elements in loops. The fact that sparse matrix structures are not available in Fortran 90, unlike MATLAB, makes it tough to write and maintain programs which deal with sparse matrices in the language. CMC is designed to remove the burden from the user who wants to develop fast sparse Fortran 90 programs in a simple manner.

The Syntax of Annotations for CMC. Figure 3 shows the summary the syntax of annotations for the current implementation of CMC. annotation cor-

$$
\begin{aligned}
annotation &\rightarrow anno\_var \mid anno\_param \mid anno\_auxarg \\
anno\_var &\rightarrow \texttt{\%CMC}\ attribute\_list :: variable\_list \\
attribute\_list &\rightarrow attribute \mid attribute\ ,\ attribute\_list \\
attribute &\rightarrow type \mid shape \mid structure \\
type &\rightarrow \texttt{logical} \mid \texttt{integer} \mid \texttt{real} \mid \texttt{complex} \\
shape &\rightarrow \texttt{\_scalar} \mid \texttt{\_lowvec} \mid \texttt{\_colvec} \mid \texttt{\_diag} \mid \texttt{\_tril} \mid \texttt{\_triu} \mid \texttt{\_full} \\
structure &\rightarrow \texttt{\_dense} \mid \texttt{\_ccs}\ (\ cexpr\ ) \mid \texttt{\_crs}\ (\ cexpr\ ) \mid \texttt{\_md}\ (\ cexpr\ ) \\
variable\_list &\rightarrow variable \mid variable\ ,\ variable\_list \\
variable &\rightarrow identifier \mid identifier\ (\ cexpr\ ) \mid identifier\ (\ cexpr\ ,\ cexpr\ ) \\
anno\_param &\rightarrow \texttt{\%CMC}\ type\ ,\ \texttt{parameter} :: assign\_list \\
assign\_list &\rightarrow identifier\ \texttt{=}\ cexpr \mid identifier\ \texttt{=}\ cexpr\ ,\ assign\_list \\
anno\_auxarg &\rightarrow \texttt{\%CMC}\ type\ ,\ \texttt{auxarg} :: scalar\_list \\
scalar\_list &\rightarrow identifier \mid identifier\ ,\ scalar\_list
\end{aligned}
$$

Fig. 3. The syntax of annotations for CMC

responds to an annotation line in a source code. CMC supports parameters and auxiliary variables for size declarations of vectors and matrices. The former is the same as parameters of Fortran 90 and the latter is for additional arguments for generated Fortran 90 codes by CMC. In Fig. 3, $cexpr$ means an expression of constants, parameters, and auxiliary variables. Currently, CMC does not support multidimensional arrays.

2.2   On the Introduction of Annotations in MATLAB Programs

The function in Fig. 1 (a) can be used, giving a matrix and two column vectors to it, to get a residual column vector in an iterative solver for linear systems. The user can also use the code passing matrices for b and x and a scalar for A as arguments without receiving any run-time error from the MATLAB interpreter.

Although it is free for the user to use programs in any way, there could be usages for the codes which were previously unthought of by the programmer. For those cases, it is preferable for the programmer to assert the usage of the function in some way in order for the maintainability of the code, as well as for the elimination of causes for any trouble. From this viewpoint, it can be said that the introduction of annotations for the arguments of a function in MATLAB scripts might not only help CMC to generate highly optimized static codes, but also enhance source codes' maintainability.

2.3   The Structure of CMC

CMC's structure together with the flow of building a sparse executable using CMC is shown in Fig. 4. CMC reads an annotated MATLAB code and generate a Fortran 90 subroutine which can be linked with other Fortran 90 subroutines to make an executable. CMC also has a facility to output optimized code as a MATLAB function M-file. The user can enjoy CMC's ability of source-level optimization on the MATLAB interpreter.

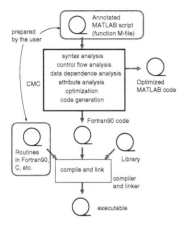

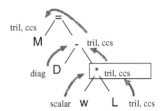

Fig. 5. Inferencing attributes for variables in the expression M=D-w*L where the attributes of D, w and L are available

Fig. 4. Building a sparse code using CMC

2.4 Attribute Inference Mechanisms of CMC

Type inference mechanisms are needed for translating a MATLAB program to an efficient Fortran 90 code. CMC follows the way of FALCON [8] on this issue, except that CMC expects arguments' attributes, such as shapes, types and sizes, to be given by the user through annotations. CMC automatically decides attributes of other variables, including intermediate ones, in the program.

CMC uses an iterative algorithm for forward data-flow analysis. For each operation in a program, the result's attributes are determined from the attributes of operands and the kind of the operation. An example is depicted in Fig. 5. When attributes of operands' are not available at some point in the course of the iterative attribute analysis, determination of the result's attributes is postponed to subsequent iterations. CMC expects programs in which all variables' attributes can be eventually determined in this way.

CMC deals with detailed shape information for matrices such as triangular and diagonal matrices as shown in Table 1. For example, parsing the expression C=A*B, where the variables A and B are matrices of upper triangular and diagonal, respectively, CMC will decide the shape of the variable C to be upper triangular. Detailed information for each matrix is used for generating efficient code. For example, diagonal matrices are treated as one-dimensional arrays. Currently, CMC does not make use of sparsity of dense triangular matrices but omits computations on zeros.

CMC also decides each variable to be sparse or dense using the rules shown in Table 2. Sparse structures are only used for matrices (not for vectors). Details on currently available sparse structures in CMC will be described in Sect. 3.

CMC generates Fortran 90 programs based on the annotations supplied by the programmer. A generated code by CMC does not support dynamic expansion of matrices and does not check array bounds at run-time. When annotations were written incorrectly, the program generated by CMC would cause run-time errors.

Table 1. Resulting shapes for binary operations between A and B. Symbols S, R, C, U, L, D, and F denote scalar, row vector, column vector, upper triangular matrix, lower triangular matrix, diagonal matrix, and full matrix, respectively

(a) shape of A*B

shape of A	S	R	C	U	L	D	F
Scalar	S	R	C	U	L	D	F
Row vec.	R	—	S	R	R	R	R
Column vec.	C	F	—	—	—	—	—
Upper tri. mat.	U	—	C	U	F	U	F
Lower tri. mat.	L	—	C	F	L	L	F
Diagonal mat.	D	—	C	U	L	D	F
Full mat.	F	—	C	F	F	F	F

(b) shape of A+B, A−B, A./B, and A.*B

shape of A	S	R	C	U	L	D	F
Scalar	S	R	C	U†	L†	D†	F
Row vec.	R	R	—	—	—	—	—
Column vec.	C	—	C	—	—	—	—
Upper tri. mat.	U†	—	—	U	F	U	F
Lower tri. mat.	L†	—	—	F	L	L	F
Diagonal mat.	D†	—	—	U	L	D	F
Full mat.	F	—	—	F	F	F	F

†: For operations + and −, resulting shape is F when the scalar value is not zero.

Table 2. Resulting structure of a binary operation between A and B

shape of A	scalar	dense	sparse
scalar	(scalar)	dense	sparse†
dense	dense	dense	dense
sparse	sparse†	dense	sparse

†: Resulting structure is dense when the operation is an addition or a subtraction.

2.5 Source-Level Optimization Mechanisms of CMC

As discussed in [17], source-level optimization is effective for matrix computation codes. CMC is equipped with the following optimization functionalities, which are simpler than those mentioned in [17] but also effective:

- classical techniques [1] such as loop-invariant code motion (LICM), copy propagation, common subexpression elimination (CSE), and dead-code elimination, and
- matrix language oriented optimizations such as strength reduction of operations considering ranks of operands.

Figures 6 and 7 show programs of the SOR method and the CG method, respectively. Figures 6 (a) and 7 (a) are source codes and Figs. 6 (b) and 7 (b) are optimized codes by CMC. The plainness of the sources compared to optimized codes are apparent even for those relatively small examples. However, the execution speed of those naively written codes are prohibitive compared to optimized codes. Unfortunately, the MATLAB system, including MCC, does not have those fairly simple optimization capabilities.

As for the strength reduction for matrix computations, CMC currently supports reordering of an associative operator *. CMC does not evaluate computational load for each matrix operation exactly; it is difficult to do that for sparse

```
function [x,i] = sor0s(A,x0,b,tol)
%cmc integer,parameter :: s=50*50
%cmc real,_ccs(5) :: A(s,s)
%cmc real,_colvec :: x0(s), b(s)
%cmc real,_scalar :: tol
w = 1.8;
D = diag(diag(A)); L = -tril(A,-1);
U = -triu(A,1);
r0 = norm(b-A*x0);
x = x0; i = 0;
while 1
i = i+1;
x = (D-w*L)\(((1-w)*D+w*U)*x+w*b);
if norm(b-A*x)/r0 <= tol, break, end
end
```
(a) A naively written SOR code

```
function [x, i] = sor0s(A, x0, b, tol)
%cmc integer,parameter :: s=50*50
%cmc real,_ccs(5) :: A(s,s)
%cmc real,_colvec :: x0(s), b(s)
%cmc real,_scalar :: tol
w = 1.8;
D = diag(diag(A)); L = -tril(A,-1);
U = -triu(A,1);
r0 = norm(b-A*x0);
x = x0; i = 0;
TMPLM00 = D-w*L;
TMPLM01 = (1-w)*D+w*U;
TMPLV02 = w*b;
while 1
i = i+1;
x = TMPLM00\(TMPLM01*x+TMPLV02);
if (norm(b-A*x)/r0<=tol), break, end
end
```
(b) The optimized SOR code

Fig. 6. Source-level optimization of SOR code in MATLAB

```
function [x,i] = cg0s(A,x0,b,tol)
%cmc integer,parameter :: s=50*50
%cmc real,_ccs(5) :: A(s,s)
%cmc real,_colvec :: x0(s), b(s)
%cmc real,_scalar :: tol
r = b-A*x0;
rn = norm(r);
x = x0; p = r; i = 0;
while 1
i = i + 1;
alpha = (r.' * r) / (p.' * A * p);
x = x + alpha * p;
rnew = r - alpha * A * p;
if norm(rnew)/rn <= tol, break, end
beta = (rnew.' * rnew) / (r.' * r);
p = rnew + beta * p;
r = rnew;
end
```
(a) A naively written CG code

```
function [x,i] = cg0s(A,x0,b,tol)
%cmc integer,parameter :: s=50*50
%cmc real,_ccs(5) :: A(s,s)
%cmc real,_colvec :: x0(s), b(s)
%cmc real,_scalar :: tol
r = b-A*x0;
rn = norm(r);
x = x0; p = r; i = 0;
TMPX00 = A * r ;
TMPS01 = r.' * r;
while 1
i = i+1;
alpha = TMPS01 / (p.' * TMPX00);
x = x + alpha * p;
rnew = r - alpha * TMPX00;
if norm(rnew)/rn <= tol, break, end
TMPS02 = rnew.' * rnew;
beta = TMPS02 / TMPS01;
p = rnew + beta * p;
r = rnew;
TMPX00 = A * p;
TMPS01 = TMPS02;
end
```
(b) The optimized CG code

Fig. 7. Source-level optimization of CG code in MATLAB

matrix computations. CMC treats each variable as dense to decide the order of multiplications, e.g., (A*B)*C or A*(B*C).

Notice that each source-level optimization might affect the applicability of other optimizations. Taking the heaviness of matrix operations into account, CMC gives CSE priority over LICM. This strategy lets the loop-invariant expression alpha*A in Fig. 7 (a) remain in the loop and the common subexpression A*p be removed, resulting in the code of Fig. 7 (b).

3   Data Structure Selection and Transformation

There are many varieties of sparse structures. It is impossible to state which structure is mostly preferable, because the speed of a code heavily depends on the combination of data structures and algorithms used in the code. The MATLAB system is adapted to a single sparse structure, CCS format, because of the simplicity of implementation and the fact that moderate efficiency has been ob-

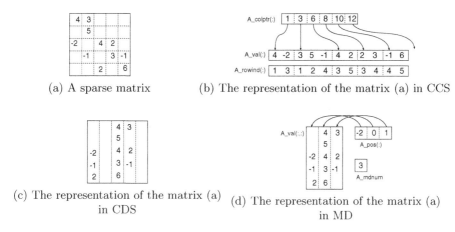

(a) A sparse matrix

(b) The representation of the matrix (a) in CCS

(c) The representation of the matrix (a) in CDS

(d) The representation of the matrix (a) in MD

Fig. 8. Data structures for sparse matrices

served for many applications by using the scheme [12]. There is another approach of automatic decision of data structures for sparse matrices [6]. Although it is mentioned that the proposed automatic heuristic selection method is practical, finding the optimal selection is shown to be NP-hard [6].

We take another simple approach: The user selects a sparse storage scheme for each sparse matrix in the dummy argument list in the source. CMC's treatment of sparse structures are as follows:

- CMC supports CCS, CRS, and MD formats as sparse storage schemes.
- Matrix computations such as addition and multiplication are done among matrices of the same scheme. When matrices of different schemes are used as operands for matrix operations, one is transformed to the other's scheme ahead of the computation. Resulting sparse structure's scheme is decided to the scheme used for the computation.

3.1   Sparse Storage Schemes

MATLAB's only sparse storage scheme is virtually the same as CCS [12] which is depicted in Fig. 8 (b). In CCS, a sparse matrix is stored using three one-dimensional arrays. Each nonzero element of a sparse matrix is stored columnwise in an array and two other integer arrays are used to store row indices and pointers for the beginning of each column. Required storage space is almost proportional to the number of nonzero elements.

CMC also supports CCS as a sparse data structure. Besides, CMC supports CRS and MD, too. CRS has almost the same characteristics as CCS since the structure is just a transpose of CCS'es.

Band matrices are often dealt with the CDS format, which is shown in Fig. 8 (c). Different from CCS and CRS, indirect addressing is not needed very often for CDS. However, for matrices with sub-/superdiagonals of zeros, CDS is not necessarily efficient in terms of storage area. CMC adopts the multi-diagonal (MD) format shown in Fig. 8 (d), instead of CDS.

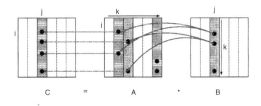

Fig. 9. Sparse matrix multiplication using CCS format. Columnwise JKI-type computation is suitable for the scheme

3.2   Computational Load of Operations Among Sparse Matrices

Thinking of using multiple sparse structures gives rise to a problem of choosing a right sparse scheme for each matrix. For high speed computation on sparse structures, it is important to avoid accesses for elements of sparse matrices by searching. Based on this, we take a simple approach; for each matrix operation, CMC forces both operands' storage scheme to be the same as well as the result's.

As an example, let us think about a matrix multiplication A*B. If A is CCS and B is CRS, it is natural to use so called an IJK-type algorithm for the multiplication, which needs inner-product computations of sparse vectors with searching for elements. On the other hand, if both A and B are CCS, a JKI-type algorithm can be used as illustrated in Fig. 9. Although both cases are of the same computational cost in terms of the number of floating-point addition and multiplication, the former needs conditional branches in the innermost loop.

Compression of data also should be taken into account when designing low-level algorithms for CCS and CRS. For example, CCS matrix product is computed column by column as shown in Fig. 9. There are two strategies to generate compressed columns one after another in the course of multiplication; both with merits and demerits:

– compress a sparse column after computing elements in the column in order
– sort a compressed column after computing elements out of order

The former is for sparse products of many nonzero entries, and the latter is for very sparse products. CMC is equipped with an adaptive mechanism, which checks the number of nonzero elements of the first column (or row in CRS case) of the computed product, to choose one of the above for storing sparse products.

CMC is equipped with storage transformation codes as library routines. Each data transformation procedure can be implemented such that the required number of (indirect) accesses for elements is almost proportional to the number of nonzero elements of the matrix. The cost for the transformation of sparse data structures would be suppressible for many matrix computation codes. An example will be shown in the next section.

3.3 Memory Allocation for Sparse Matrices

The required area for each result of operations on sparse matrices can not necessarily be decided either statically or at run-time. For a sum of sparse matrices, CMC allocates area based on the number of total nonzero elements of the operands. As for a product of sparse matrices, CMC depends on the information supplied by the user through annotations as mentioned in Sect. 2.1.

4 Numerical Experiments

Several numerical experiments were carried out to evaluate CMC's effectiveness. In this section, we discuss availability of CMC over experimental results.

4.1 The Environment of the Experiments

Experiments were done on linear system solvers. SOR and CG programs written in MATLAB were executed on following two machines:

- Fujitsu G P7000F. A SPARC64-GP machine, which is referred to as SPARC in the following sections.
- N EC SX -5. A vector computer, referred to as SX in the following.

Although both of the above systems are parallel computers, all experiments shown in this section were done on a single CPU.

Executions were timed for the following cases:

- Interpretation by M ATLAB . Programs in MATLAB were executed simply on the MATLAB interpreter of version 6.5.1.199709 R13(SP1).
- Stand-alone execution by M ATLAB C om piler (M CC).
- Stand-alone execution by CM C . Programs in Fortran 90 were generated by CMC and compiled by the vendor supplied Fortran 90 compilers.

Executions using MATLAB interpreter and MCC were done only on SPARC because the MATLAB system was not available on SX.

Each of solved linear problems was one of the following. All derived coefficient matrices are symmetric and positive definite.

- D ense problem . The linear equation $Fx = v$, where $F = (f_{i,j}) \in \mathbf{R}^{n \times n}$, $v \in \mathbf{R}^n$, s.t.

$$f_{i,j} = \begin{cases} 1 & (i = j) \\ -3^{-|i-j|} & (i \neq j), \end{cases} \quad v = (1, 0, \ldots, 0)^T$$

- Sparse problem . Laplace's equation

$$\partial^2 P / \partial x^2 + \partial^2 P / \partial y^2 = 0$$

on a plane with Dirichlet conditions, solved by five-point finite difference discretization on a square grid.

Table 3. Execution times for the sparse problem on SPARC. CCS format is used by CMC

(a) SOR

Number of unknowns	MATLAB [sec]	MCC [sec]	CMC [sec]
400	0.08	0.07	0.00932
900	0.22	0.20	0.0286
1600	0.77	0.74	0.0980
2500	1.87	1.87	0.252
4900	7.27	7.22	1.01
8100	19.9	19.4	2.68

(b) CG

Number of unknowns	MATLAB [sec]	MCC [sec]	CMC [sec]
900	0.04	0.04	0.00758
2500	0.20	0.20	0.0501
4900	0.55	0.56	0.162
8100	1.19	1.17	0.385
12100	2.31	2.19	0.716

4.2   Results on the Sparse Problem

Results on the sparse problem on SPARC are shown in Tables 3 (a) and 3 (b). The CCS format was used for sparse matrices by CMC. Executions were done on problems of broad range of complexity in terms of the number of unknowns. Tables 3 (a) and 3 (b) show that CMC outperforms MATLAB interpreter and MCC for all sizes of problems executed. CMC is about seven times and three times as fast as MATLAB for SOR and CG, respectively. It is also seen from the tables that MCC is not necessarily effective to speed up for executing those programs.

Any sparse problem could be solved using dense structures only, although it is apparently not efficient in both terms of required storage space and computational load. Figure 10 shows a comparison of speed for those cases where the sparse problem is solved by the SOR method. Notice that the execution times are shown in logarithmic scale. It is clearly seen that, whether MATLAB or CMC is used, usage of sparse structures is essential for the sparse problem.

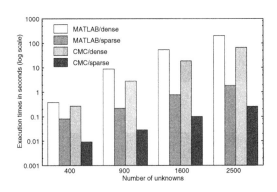

Fig. 10. Comparison between dense and sparse structures used for SOR on SPARC

Table 4. Results of the CG method on the sparse problem using three types of sparse matrix structures. Blocked algorithm was used for matrix-vector multiplication in MD

(a) Execution times on SPARC

Number of unknowns	CCS [sec]	CRS [sec]	MD [sec]
900	0.00758	0.00732	0.00599
2500	0.0501	0.0497	0.0310
4900	0.162	0.150	0.111
8100	0.385	0.354	0.277
12100	0.716	0.654	0.533

(b) Execution times on SX

Number of unknowns	CCS [sec]	CRS [sec]	MD [sec]
900	0.0477	0.0438	0.000783
2500	0.215	0.197	0.00309
4900	0.592	0.534	0.00762
8100	1.23	1.15	0.0146
12100	2.20	2.08	0.0267

4.3 Data Structure Selection and Transformation for the Sparse Problem

CMC currently supports three kinds of sparse structures, namely, CCS, CRS, and MD. Tables 4 (a) and 4 (b) show execution times of the CG method on the sparse problem using different storage scheme on SPARC and SX, respectively.

Both tables show that the MD format is preferable for the sparse problem. Although the result does not necessarily imply the superiority of MD and CRS over CCS for any sparse problem, at least it is shown that the effect of data structure selection is not negligible for sparse computations.

Data structure selection strongly affects on programs' execution speed, together with the target machines' architecture. Table 4 (b) shows an extreme example on a vector processor which gives full play to its ability on computations with direct and uniform access for memory elements in loops.

The difference of execution speed between programs on CCS and CRS is due to mainly the difference of memory access patterns. The kernel loop of CG is a scalar accumulation for CRS, while it is a vector update for CCS.

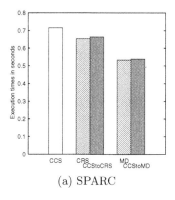

(a) SPARC

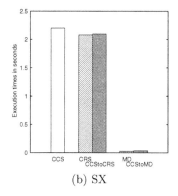

(b) SX

Fig. 11. Execution times of different storage formats. The number of unknowns were 12100 for all cases

Figures 11 (a) and 11 (b) show the execution times of the CG solver on the sparse problem where the number of unknowns is 12100 on SPARC and SX, respectively. In the figures, bars labeled 'CCS to CRS' and 'CCS to MD' are those which include times spent for data structure transformation from CCS to CRS, and CCS to MD, respectively. The figures show that the load of data structure transformation is not significant compared to that of computation. Using CMC, the user can specify any combination of data structure transformation among CCS, CRS, and MD.

4.4   Results on the Dense Problem

Tables 5 (a) and 5 (b) show the execution times for the dense problem. For computations on dense matrices, CMC just uses Fortran 90's intrinsic routines for array operations. This means that there should not be much difference of speed between executions using MATLAB and CMC. However, Table 5 (a) shows nearly twofold speed-ups by CMC against MATLAB on the SOR method. This is partly because the functionality of CMC to make the most use of detailed shape information on matrices, such as upper triangular or diagonal, in order to generate fast codes.

Table 5. Experimental results with the dense problem on SPARC

(a) SOR				(b) CG			
Number of unknowns	MATLAB [sec]	MCC [sec]	CMC [sec]	Number of unknowns	MATLAB [sec]	MCC [sec]	CMC [sec]
100	0.13	0.14	0.0718	200	0.06	0.07	0.0396
200	1.62	1.63	0.923	400	0.41	0.41	0.288
300	7.53	7.47	4.19	600	1.33	1.34	0.966
400	22.5	43.6	12.3	800	3.28	3.11	2.26

Figure 12 shows the effect of optimization based on shape information. In the SOR method, a product of a matrix and a vector is computed in each iteration. In addition, every element in a matrix is scanned to decide if direct triangular solver can be used or not. For the former case, if the translator can find out that the matrix is triangular, the amount of computation is reduced by half. For the latter, the cost of element scanning is eliminated. CMC's ability to do these favorably influenced for the SOR method as shown in Fig. 12.

4.5   Source-Level Optimizations

Figures 13 (a) and 13 (b) show the effect of CMC's source-level optimization facility. In the Figures 13 (a) and 13 (b), 'noopt' indicates that they are the results of programs in Figs. 6 (a) and 7 (a). Similarly, 'opt' indicates that they are the results of programs in Figs. 6 (b) and 7 (b). CMC's source-level optimization facility is turned off for the results of CMC/noopt in Fig. 13.

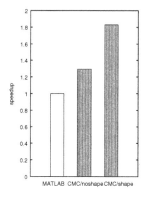

Fig. 12. The effects of code generation using shape information. The dense problem of 400 unknowns is solved by SOR on SPARC

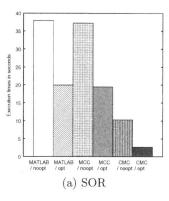
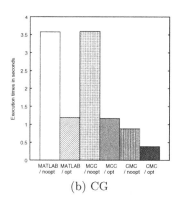

(a) SOR   (b) CG

Fig. 13. The effects of source-level optimization for linear solvers in MATLAB. The sparse problem of 8100 unknowns was solved on SPARC

Figures 13 (a) and 13 (b) imply not only that CMC's source-level optimization facility is effective for MATLAB programs, but also there are cases where CMC can speed up about 10 fold for programs even if they do not have loop-intensive elementwise computations.

5 Related Work

There are several attempts to speed up MATLAB programs [8, 17, 18, 19]. Most of them try to preserve the semantics of original MATLAB scripts. An approach to incorporate just-in-time compilation functionality to MATLAB's interactive environment [2] seems to be the extreme of the direction. Our approach basically utilizes directives by the user. As mentioned in Sect. 2, those annotations by the user could not only help CMC to generate a fast sparse code, but also promote the maintainability of the original code.

MaTX [14] and Ox [9] are freely available language processing systems for matrix computations. Unfortunately, neither of them have the facility to deal with sparse matrix structures. MaTX is a typed matrix language and the MaTX compiler can produce native executables from MaTX programs. Notice that there is a difference between typed languages' variable declaration and CMC's user directives; for CMC, the user only needs to specify attributes of variables for arguments and return values of non-builtin function calls.

There is research on adapting Fortran 90's array computation primitives for sparse matrix structures [6, 7]. This approach must be helpful for those who are used to write codes in Fortran 90. However, Fortran 90's syntax is not consistent as a matrix language. For example, the multiplication operator * can not be used for products of matrices.

As a software system aiming to aid the user in writing sparse programs, CMC could be compared to systems based on functional programming languages [11] and those based on dense descriptions in Fortran 77 [4, 5]. Although it seems to be difficult to derive any result from the comparison because of the subjective nature of user aid systems, we think MATLAB's syntax as a matrix language could be preferable.

Developing library routines for sparse matrix computations [10] seems to be the most powerful approach to help people write good sparse programs in terms of their execution speed. We think CMC can be modified to generate programs which utilize those library routines.

6   Conclusions

A MATLAB-based code generator for sparse matrix computations is presented. The code generator, named CMC, offers a way for the user to use simple and maintainable MATLAB scripts to develop programs for sparse matrix computations. Experimental results on solvers for sparse linear systems show that codes generated by CMC run several times as fast as their original scripts executed by the MATLAB interpreter.

Acknowledgments

We would like to thank Professor Emeritus Takao Tsuda of Kyoto University and Hiroshima City University and Professor Masaaki Shimasaki of Kyoto University for their fruitful comments on this research. This work was supported in part by the HCU Grant for Special Academic Research (General Studies) under Grant No. 4111, 2004.

References

1. Aho, A.V., Sethi, R., Ullman, J.D.: *Compilers — Principles, Techniques, and Tools*, Addison Wesley (1986).

2. Almasi, G., Padua, D.: MaJIC: Compiling MATLAB for Speed and Responsiveness, *Proc. PLDI'02*, pp.294–303 (2002).
3. Barrett, R., et al.: *Templates for the Solution of Linear Systems: Building Blocks for Iterative Methods*, SIAM (1994).
4. Bik, A.J.C., Wijshoff, H.A.G.: Compilation Techniques for Sparse Matrix Computations, *Proc. ICS'93*, pp.416–424 (1993).
5. Bik, A.J.C., et al.: The Automatic Generation of Sparse Primitives, *ACM Trans. Math. Softw.*, Vol.24, No.2, pp.190–225 (1998).
6. Chang, R.-G., Chuang, T.-R., Lee, J.K.: Compiler Optimizations for Parallel Sparse Programs with Array Intrinsics of Fortran 90, *Proc. Intl. Conf. Parallel Processing*, pp.103–110 (1999).
7. Chang, R.-G., Chuang, T.-R., Lee, J.K.: Efficient Support of Parallel Sparse Computation for Array Intrinsic Functions of Fortran 90, *Proc. ICS'98*, pp.45–52 (1998).
8. De Rose, L., Padua, D.: Techniques for the translation of MATLAB programs into Fortran 90, *ACM Trans. Programming Languages and Systems*, Vol.21, No.2, pp.286–323 (1999).
9. Doornik, J.A. : *Ox: Object-Oriented Matrix Language*, 4th edition, Timberlake Consultants Press (2001).
10. Duff, I.S., et al.: Level 3 Basic Linear Algebra Subprograms for Sparse Matrices: A User-Level Interface, *ACM Trans. Math. Softw.*, Vol.23, No.3, pp.379–401 (1997).
11. Fitzpatrick, S., Clint, M., Kilpatrick, P.: The Automated Derivation of Sparse Implementations of Numerical Algorithms through Program Transformation, *Tech. Rep.* 1995/Apr-SF.MC.PLK, Dept. Comput. Sci., The Queen's University of Belfast (1995).
12. Gilbert, J.R., Moler, C., Schreiber, R.: Sparse Matrices in MATLAB: Design and Implementation, *SIAM J. Matrix Anal. Appl.*, Vol.13, No.1, pp.333–356 (1992).
13. Kawabata, H., Suzuki, M.: CMC: A Compiler for Sparse Matrix Computations (in Japanese), *IPSJ Trans. Advanced Computing Systems*, to appear.
14. Koga, M.: MaTX User's Manual, http://www.matx.org/
15. The MathWorks, Inc. homepage. www.mathworks.com.
16. The MathWorks, Inc.: *MATLAB Compiler Version 3 User's Guide* (2002).
17. Menon, V., Pingali, K.: A Case for Source-Level Transformations in MATLAB, *Proc. DSL'99*, pp.53–65 (1999).
18. Ramaswamy, S., et al.: Compiling MATLAB Programs to ScaLAPACK: Exploiting Task and Data Parallelism, *Proc. IPPS'96*, pp.613–619 (1996).
19. Quinn, M.J., Malishevsky, A., Seelam, N.: Otter: Bridging the Gap between MATLAB and ScaLAPACK, *Proc. 8th IEEE Intl. Symp. High Performance Distributed Computing* (1998).

D-Fusion: A Distinctive Fusion Calculus[*]

Michele Boreale[1], Maria Grazia Buscemi[2], and Ugo Montanari[2]

[1] Dipartimento di Sistemi e Informatica, Università di Firenze, Italy
[2] Dipartimento di Informatica, Università di Pisa, Italy
boreale@dsi.unifi.it, {buscemi,ugo}@di.unipi.it

Abstract. We study the relative expressive power of Fusion and pi-calculus. Fusion is commonly regarded as a generalisation of pi-calculus. Actually, we prove that there is no uniform fully abstract embedding of pi-calculus into Fusion. This fact motivates the introduction of a new calculus, D-Fusion, with two binders, λ and ν. We show that D-Fusion is strictly more expressive than both pi-calculus and Fusion. The expressiveness gap is further clarified by the existence of a fully abstract encoding of mixed guarded choice into the choice-free fragment of D-Fusion.

1 Introduction

The design of distributed applications based on XML, like Web services [22] or business-to-business systems [6], sees the emergence of a message-passing programming style. Languages like Highwire [5] provide, in a concurrent setting, sophisticated data structures, which allow programmers to describe and manipulate complex messages and interaction patterns. If one looks for 'foundational' counterparts of these programming languages the pi-calculus [9, 10] and the Fusion calculus [16] seem very promising candidates. Both of them, indeed, convey the idea of message-passing in a distilled form, and come equipped with a rich and elegant meta-theory.

The main novelty of Fusion when compared to the pi-calculus is the introduction of *fusions*. A fusion is a name equivalence that, when applied onto a term, has the effect of a (possibly non-injective) name substitution. Fusions are ideal for representing, e.g., forwarders for objects that migrate among locations [3], or forms of pattern matching between pairs of messages [5]. Computationally, a fusion is generated as a result of a synchronisation between two complementary actions, and it is atomically propagated to processes running in parallel with the active one. This happens in much the same way as, in logic programming, term substitutions resulting from a unification step on a subgoal can be forced on the other subgoals.

If compared to pi-calculus name-passing, fusion name-passing enables a more general binding mechanism. However, differently from the pi-calculus, the binding mechanism of Fusion ignores the issue of unicity of newly generated names. One of the goals of this paper is to show that this fact limits the expressiveness of Fusion. Overcoming

---

[*] Research partially supported by FET-Global Computing projects *PROFUNDIS* and *MIKADO*.

this limitation calls for co-existence of two name binders, λ and ν: the former analogous to the only binder of Fusion, and the latter imposing unicity, like in pi-calculus. The resulting *distinctive* Fusion calculus, or *D-Fusion*, is at least as expressive as pi-calculus and Fusion separately, and in fact, we strongly argue, *more* expressive than both. However, the main motivation of the present study is not to push for adoption of yet another calculus, but rather to clarify the relationship between two fundamental concepts like binding and fusions, and propose a consistent and simple semantical framework to reason on them. A more precise account of our work follows.

The binding mechanism of pi-calculus generalises that of λ-calculus in several ways. Input prefix $a(x)$. binds like λx, and name passing takes place in pi-calculus in a way typical of functional programming, i.e., formal names are assigned their actual counterparts. The *restriction* binder ν, however, is very different from λ, as a restricted name can be exported (extruded), with the guarantee that it will never be identified to anything else.

Fusion calculus is presented in [16] as a more uniform and more expressive evolution of the pi-calculus. The main idea is to decompose input prefix $a(x)$. into a binder (x) and a prefix $a\langle x \rangle$. In the polyadic case, matching between the input list and the output list of arguments induces name unification, i.e. a fusion. The latter is propagated across processes, but one or more binders can be used to control the scope (i.e. propagation) of the fusion. Thus one achieves both a perfect symmetry between input and output and a more general name passing mechanism.

At first sight, Fusion is more general than pi-calculus. And, indeed, the pi-calculus transition system can be embedded into Fusion's, provided that one identifies restriction (νx) with the (x) binder of Fusion [16].

Our first move is to argue that this embedding breaks down if comparing the two calculi on the basis of behavioural semantics. We prove that no 'uniform' encoding exists of pi-calculus into Fusion that preserves any 'reasonable' behavioural equivalence (at least as fine as trace equivalence). Here 'uniform' means homomorphic with respect to parallel composition and name substitution, mapping (νx) to (x) and preserving (a subset of) weak traces. As hinted before, the ultimate reason for this failure is that in Fusion all names are like logical variables, i.e., unification always succeeds, which is not true in the pi-calculus.

The above considerations motivate the introduction of a new calculus, D-Fusion, with two binders, λ and ν: the first generalises input prefix, and the second corresponds to restriction. Also, any issue of symmetry between input and output is preempted, since the calculus has just one kind of prefix (no polarisation); polarised prefixes can be easily encoded, though. In D-Fusion, while lambdas are used to control the propagation of fusions, restrictions are used to possibly inhibit fusions. In logical terms, this corresponds to consider unification not only among variables, but also among variables and dynamically generated constants (that is, ν-extruded names). As expected, unification fails whenever one tries to identify two distinct constants. We show that the additional expressive power achieved in this way is relevant. Both pi-calculus and Fusion are subcalculi of D-Fusion. Moreover, the combined mechanism of restriction and unification yields additional expressive power: it allows to express a form of pattern matching which cannot be expressed in the other two calculi. As a consequence, we prove, D-Fusion cannot be uniformly encoded neither into Fusion, nor into pi-calculus.

Next, the gap between D-Fusion and Fusion/pi-calculus is explored from a more concrete perspective. First, we exhibit a simple security protocol and a related *correlation* property that are readily translated into D-Fusion. The property breaks down if uniformly translating the protocol into Fusion. The failure is illuminating: in Fusion, one has no way of declaring unique fresh names to correlate different messages of the protocol.

Palamidessi has shown [13, 14] that nondeterministic *guarded choice* cannot be simulated in the choice $(+)$ -free pi-calculus in a fully abstract way, while preserving any 'reasonable' semantics. The reason is that it is not possible to atomically perform, in the absence of $+$, an external synchronisation and an internal exclusive choice among a number of alternatives. We prove that in D-Fusion, under mild typing assumptions, guarded choice can actually be simulated in a fully abstract way in the choice-free fragment. The encoding preserves a reasonable semantics, defined in terms of barbed equivalence ([11]). Informally, branches of a choice are represented as concurrent processes. Synchronisation is performed in the ordinary way, but it forces a fusion between a λ-name global to all branches and a v-name local to the chosen branch. Excluded branches are atomically inhibited, since any progress would lead them to fusing two distinct v-names.

In the present paper, we are mainly interested in assessing the expressive power of D-Fusion compared to other calculi. The principal tool for this study will be barbed bisimilarity and the induced equivalences, as they enjoy a uniform definition based only on a reduction relation, on an observation predicate and on context-closure. We defer the study of alternative, more tractable semantics for D-Fusion, like a form of 'labelled' bisimulation, to a forthcoming work.

The rest of the paper is organised as follows. Section 2 contains a proof that the pi-calculus cannot be uniformly encoded into Fusion. In Section 3 we introduce the D-Fusion calculus, its operational semantics and barbed congruence. In Section 4 we show that D-Fusion calculus is strictly more expressive than both pi-calculus and Fusion. We further explore this expressiveness gap in Section 5, by means of an example concerning a security protocol, and in Section 6, by encoding mixed guarded choice into the choice-free calculus. Section 7 contains a brief overview of some related work and a few concluding remarks.

2   Fusion and Pi

The aim of this section is to illustrate the difference between pi-calculus and Fusion, and to show that the former cannot be uniformly encoded in the latter.

The crucial difference between the pi-calculus and Fusion shows up in synchronisations: in Fusion, the effect of a synchronisation is not necessarily local, and is regulated by the scope of the binder (x). For example, an interaction between $\bar{u}v.P$ and $ux.Q$ will result in a fusion of v and x. This fusion will also affect any further process R running in parallel, as illustrated by the example below:

$$R \,|\, \bar{u}v.P \,|\, ux.Q \xrightarrow{\{x=v\}} R \,|\, P \,|\, Q.$$

The binding operator (x) can be used to limit the scope of the fusion, e.g.:

$$R\,|\,(x)\,(\overline{u}v.P\,|\,ux.Q) \xrightarrow{\tau} R\,|\,(P\,|\,Q)[\nu\!/\!x].$$

where τ denotes the identity fusion. For a full treatment of pi-calculus and Fusion we refer to [10] and to [16], respectively.

Below, we show that there is no 'reasonably simple' encoding of the pi-calculus Π into Fusion $\mathcal{F}$. We focus on encodings $[\![\cdot]\!]$ that have certain compositional properties and preserve (a subset of) weak traces. As to the latter, we shall only require that moves of P are reflected in $[\![P]\!]$, not vice-versa. We also implicitly require that the encoding preserves arity of I/O actions (the length of tuples carried on each channel). This is sometimes not the case for process calculi encodings; however, it is easy to relax this condition by allowing names of $[\![P]\!]$ to carry *longer* tuples. We stick to the simpler correspondence just for notational convenience. Note that the encoding presented in [16] does satisfy our criterion. We shall assume here the standard pi-calculus late operational semantics [10] and, for the purpose of our comparison, we shall identify the late input pi-action $a(\widetilde{x})$ with the Fusion input action $(\widetilde{x})\,a\widetilde{x}$.

Definition 1. *A translation* $[\![\cdot]\!] : \Pi \to \mathcal{F}$ *is* uniform *if for each* $P, Q \in \Pi$ *it holds that:*

- *for each trace of actions s not containing bound outputs,* $P \xRightarrow{s}$ *implies* $[\![P]\!] \xRightarrow{s}$;
- $[\![P|Q]\!] = [\![P]\!]\,|\,[\![Q]\!]$;
- *for each* y, $[\![(\nu y)\,P]\!] = (y)[\![P]\!]$;
- *for each substitution* σ, $[\![P\sigma]\!] = [\![P]\!]\sigma$.

Note that the above notion of uniform encoding is stronger than the one introduced in [14].

The next proposition generalises an example from [16]. Below, we fix an arbitrary Π-equivalence included in trace equivalence, $\sim_\Pi$, and an arbitrary $\mathcal{F}$-equivalence which is included in trace equivalence *and* is preserved by parallel composition, $\sim_\mathcal{F}$ (like, e.g., hyperequivalence of [16]).

Proposition 1. *There is no uniform translation* $[\![\cdot]\!] : \Pi \to \mathcal{F}$ *such that for each* $P, Q \in \Pi$:

$$P \sim_\Pi Q \text{ implies } [\![P]\!] \sim_\mathcal{F} [\![Q]\!].$$

PROOF: Suppose that there exists such a translation $[\![\cdot]\!]$. Let P and Q be the following two pi-agents:

$$P = (\nu u, v)\,(\overline{a}\langle u, v\rangle\,|\,\overline{u}\,|\,v.\overline{w}) \qquad Q = (\nu u, v)\,(\overline{a}\langle u, v\rangle\,|\,(\overline{u}.(v.\overline{w}) + v.(\overline{u}\,|\overline{w})))\,.$$

Obviously, $P \sim_\Pi Q$ (e.g. they are strongly late bisimilar). Suppose $[\![P]\!] \sim_\mathcal{F} [\![Q]\!]$. Let $R = a(x, y).(\overline{c}x\,|cy)$ and A and B be as follows:

$$A = [\![P]\!]\,|\,R = (u, v)([\![\overline{a}\langle u, v\rangle]\!]\,|\,[\![\overline{u}]\!]\,|\,[\![v.\overline{w}]\!])\,|\,R$$
$$B = [\![Q]\!]\,|\,R = (u, v)([\![\overline{a}\langle u, v\rangle]\!]\,|\,[\![\overline{u}.(v.\overline{w}) + v.(\overline{u}\,|\overline{w})]\!])\,|\,R.$$

Since $\sim_\mathcal{F}$ is preserved by $|$, A and B are $\sim_\mathcal{F}$-equivalent. By uniformity of the encoding, it is easy to check that $A \xRightarrow{\overline{w}}$. On the other hand, a careful case analysis shows that $B \xcancel{\Longrightarrow}^{\overline{w}}$. This is a contradiction. $\qquad \square$

3   The Distinctive Fusion Calculus, D-Fusion

Syntax. We consider a countable set of names $\mathcal{N}$ ranged over by $a, b, \ldots, u, v, \ldots, z$. We write $\tilde{x}$ for a finite tuple $x_1, \ldots, x_n$ of names. The set $\mathcal{DF}$ of D-Fusion *processes*, ranged over by $P, Q, \ldots$, is defined by the syntax:

$$P ::= \mathbf{0} \ \big| \ \alpha.P \ \big| \ P|P \ \big| \ P+P \ \big| \ [x=y]P \ \big| \ !P \ \big| \ \lambda x P \ \big| \ (\nu x) P$$

where *prefixes* α are defined as $\alpha ::= a\tilde{\nu}$. The occurrences of x in $\lambda x P$ and $(\nu x) P$ are *bound*, thus notions of *free names* and *bound names* of a process P arise as expected and are denoted by $\mathrm{fn}(P)$ and $\mathrm{bn}(P)$, respectively. The notion of *alpha-equivalence* also arises as expected. In the rest of the paper we will identify alpha-equivalent processes. A *context* $C[\cdot]$ is a process with a hole that can be filled with any process P, thus yielding a process $C[P]$.

Note that we consider one kind of prefix, thus ignoring polarities. However, a subcalculus with polarities can be easily retrieved, as shown at the end of this section.

The main difference from Fusion is the presence of two distinct binding constructs, λ and ν. The λ-abstraction operator corresponds to the binding construct of Fusion and generalises input binding of the pi-calculus. The restriction operator (ν) corresponds to the analogous operator of the pi-calculus: it allows a process to create a fresh, new name that will be kept distinct from other names.

Definition 2 (Structural Congruence). *The structural congruence $\equiv$ is the least congruence on processes satisfying the abelian monoid laws for Summation and Composition (associativity, commutativity and $\mathbf{0}$ as identity), the scope laws*

$$(\nu x)\mathbf{0} \equiv \mathbf{0} \quad (\nu x)(\nu y)P \equiv (\nu y)(\nu x)P \quad (\nu x)(P+Q) \equiv (\nu x)P + (\nu x)Q$$
$$\lambda x\,\mathbf{0} \equiv \mathbf{0} \qquad \lambda x\lambda y P \equiv \lambda y\lambda x P \qquad \lambda x(P+Q) \equiv \lambda x P + \lambda x Q$$

plus the scope extrusion *laws*

$$(\nu x)(P|Q) \equiv P|(\nu x)Q \text{ where } x \notin \mathrm{fn}(P) \qquad \lambda x(P|Q) \equiv P|\lambda x Q \text{ where } x \notin \mathrm{fn}(P)$$

and the swapping *law*

$$\lambda x(\nu y)P \ \equiv \ (\nu y)\lambda x P \ \text{ where } \ x \neq y.$$

Operational Semantics. For R a binary relation over $\mathcal{N}$, let $R^\star$ denote the reflexive, symmetric and transitive closure of R with respect to $\mathcal{N}$. We use σ, σ' to range over substitutions, i.e. finite partial functions from $\mathcal{N}$ onto $\mathcal{N}$. Domain and co-domain of σ, denoted $\mathrm{dom}(\sigma)$, $\mathrm{cod}(\sigma)$ are defined as expected. We denote by $t\sigma$ the result of applying σ onto a term t. Given a set/tuple of names $\tilde{x}$, we define $\sigma_{|\tilde{x}}$ as $\sigma \cap (\tilde{x} \times \mathcal{N})$, and $\sigma_{-\tilde{x}}$ as $\sigma - (\tilde{x} \times \mathcal{N})$.

Below, we define fusions, that is, name equivalences that arise as the result of equating two lists of names in a synchronisation.

Definition 3 (Fusions). *We let $\phi, \chi, \ldots$ range over* fusions, *that is total equivalence relations on $\mathcal{N}$ with only finitely many non-singleton equivalence classes. We let:*

- $n(\phi)$ *denote* $\{x : x\phi y \text{ for some } y \neq x\};$
- τ *denote the identity fusion (i.e.,* $n(\tau) = \emptyset);$
- ϕ_{-z} *denote* $(\phi - (\{z\} \times \mathcal{N} \cup \mathcal{N} \times \{z\}))^\star;$
- $\{x = y\}$ *denote* $\{(x,y)\}^\star;$
- $\phi[x]$ *denote the equivalence class of* x *in* ϕ.

We now introduce a labelled transition system for D-Fusion. This will be useful in order to compare D-Fusion with other calculi and, in particular, to prove that D-Fusion cannot be encoded into pi-calculus (see Section 4). The reduction relation coincides with the identity fusion transition $\xrightarrow{\tau}$ of the labelled transition system.

Definition 4 (Labelled Transition System). *The transition relation* $P \xrightarrow{\mu} Q$, *for* μ *a label of the form* $(\nu\widetilde{x})\,\lambda\widetilde{y}\,a\widetilde{v}$ *(action) or of the form* $(\nu\widetilde{x})\,\phi$ *(effect), is defined in Table 1.*

Some notations for actions and effects. The bound names of μ are written $bn(\mu)$ and are defined as expected; when $\mu = (\nu\widetilde{x})\,\lambda\widetilde{y}\,a\widetilde{v}$ is an action we let $subj(\mu) = a$ and $obj(\mu) = \widetilde{v}$ denote the subject and object part of μ, otherwise they both denote a conventional value '$-$'. Moreover, $n(\mu)$ denotes all names in μ. We use abbreviations such as $n(\phi,\mu)$ to denote $n(\phi) \cup n(\mu)$ and $(\nu z)\,\mu$ for $(\nu\widetilde{x}z)\,\phi$, if $\mu = (\nu\widetilde{x})\,\phi$. Furthermore, we shall identify actions and effects up to reordering of the tuple $\widetilde{x}$ in $(\nu\widetilde{x})$ and $\lambda\widetilde{x}$.

The rules in Table 1 deserve some explanation. As mentioned, we have two kinds of labels, actions and effects. Apart from the absence of polarities, *actions* are governed by rules similar to those found in pi-calculus. The main difference is that on the same action one can find both ν- and λ-extruded names. On the other hand, *effects* are similar to those found in Fusion: an effect of the form ϕ can be created as a result of a communication (rule COM), and be propagated across parallel components, until a λ that binds a fused name z is encountered (rule λ-OPEN$_f$). At that point, a substitutive effect $[w/z]$ is applied onto the target process and z is discarded from the fusion (the result is ϕ_{-z}). A major difference with respect to Fusion is that our effects can also ν-extrude names. The side condition '$\phi[z] \cap \widetilde{x} = \emptyset$' in rule ν-OPEN prevents effects from equating two distinct ν-extruded names. Note that the premises of rules COM and λ-OPEN only deal with binder-free actions and effects, while λ-OPEN$_a$ only deals with ν-binder-free actions. However, structural congruence permits freely moving λ's and ν's, so the general case is covered via STRUCT.

Let us illustrate the rules with some examples. We shall write $\{\widetilde{x} = \widetilde{y}\}.P$ for $(\nu c)\,(c\widetilde{x}|c\widetilde{y}.P)$ (for a fresh name c).

Example 1.

1. Let $P = (\nu c)\,((\nu x)\,cx.P_1 \,|\, cy.P_2)$. The interaction between $cx.P_1$ and $cy.P_2$ will result into a fusion $\{x = y\}$, that causes x to be extruded:

$$P \equiv (\nu x)\,(\nu c)\,(cx.P_1 \,|\, cy.P_2) \xrightarrow{(\nu x)\,\{x=y\}} (\nu c)\,(P_1 \,|\, P_2).$$

Now consider $Q = \lambda y P$. The effect of λ-abstracting y in P is that of removing ϕ and getting the substitution $[x/y]$ applied onto the continuation:

$$Q \xrightarrow{\tau} (\nu x)\,((\nu c)\,(P_1 \,|\, P_2)[x/y]).$$

Table 1. Actions and effects transitions in D-Fusion

$$\text{(PREF)} \quad \alpha.P \xrightarrow{\alpha} P \qquad\qquad \text{(SUM)} \quad \frac{P_1 \xrightarrow{\mu} Q}{P_1 + P_2 \xrightarrow{\mu} Q}$$

$$\text{(COM)} \quad \frac{P_1 \xrightarrow{a\tilde{u}} Q_1 \quad P_2 \xrightarrow{a\tilde{v}} Q_2}{P_1 | P_2 \xrightarrow{\{\tilde{v}=\tilde{u}\}} Q_1 | Q_2} \quad |\tilde{u}| = |\tilde{v}| \qquad\qquad \text{(PAR)} \quad \frac{P \xrightarrow{\mu} Q}{P|R \xrightarrow{\mu} Q|R}$$

$$\text{(v-PASS)} \quad \frac{P \xrightarrow{\mu} Q}{(vz)\, P \xrightarrow{\mu} (vz)\, Q} \quad z \notin n(\mu) \qquad\qquad \text{(λ-PASS)} \quad \frac{P \xrightarrow{\mu} Q}{\lambda z\, P \xrightarrow{\mu} \lambda z\, Q} \quad z \notin n(\mu)$$

$$\text{(v-OPEN)} \quad \frac{P \xrightarrow{\mu} Q}{(vz)\, P \xrightarrow{(vz)\mu} Q} \qquad \begin{cases} z \in n(\mu) \\ \mu \text{ an action implies } z \neq \text{subj}(\mu) \\ \mu = (v\tilde{x})\,\phi \text{ implies } \phi[z] \cap \tilde{x} = \emptyset \end{cases}$$

$$\text{(λ-OPEN}_a) \quad \frac{P \xrightarrow{\lambda\tilde{y}\,a\tilde{v}} Q}{\lambda z\, P \xrightarrow{\lambda\tilde{y}z\,a\tilde{v}} Q} \quad z \in \tilde{v} - (\{a\} \cup \tilde{y}) \qquad\qquad \text{(λ-OPEN}_f) \quad \frac{P \xrightarrow{\phi} Q}{\lambda z\, P \xrightarrow{\phi_{-z}} Q[w/z]} \quad z\,\phi\,w, \; w \neq z$$

$$\text{(MATCH)} \quad \frac{P \xrightarrow{\mu} Q}{[a=a]P \xrightarrow{\mu} Q} \qquad\qquad \text{(STRUCT)} \quad \frac{P_1 \equiv P \quad P \xrightarrow{\mu} Q \quad Q \equiv Q_1}{P_1 \xrightarrow{\mu} Q_1}$$

Symmetric rules for (SUM) and (PAR) are not shown. Usual conventions about freshness of bound names apply.

2. Another example illustrating interplay between v-bound, λ-bound and free names:

$$\lambda z\,(vw)\,\{z, a = w, b\}.P \xrightarrow{\{a=b\}} (vw)\,P[w/z], \quad \text{but} \quad \lambda z\,(vw)\,\{z, z = w, b\}.P \xrightarrow{(vw)\{w=b\}} P[w/z].$$

Encoding I/O Polarities. We can encode input and output polarities as follows:

$$\overline{c}\langle\tilde{v}\rangle.P \stackrel{\triangle}{=} (vx)\,\lambda y\, c\tilde{v}xy.P \qquad c\langle\tilde{v}\rangle.P \stackrel{\triangle}{=} (vx)\,\lambda y\, c\tilde{v}yx.P$$

for some chosen fresh x and y. The position of the v-name x forbids fusions between actions with the same polarity and, hence, communication. For instance, the process $\overline{c}\langle\tilde{v}\rangle.P | \overline{c}\langle\tilde{u}\rangle.Q$ has no τ-transition, since the latter would force the fusion of two distinct v-names, which is forbidden by the operational rules. We denote by $\mathcal{DF}^{\text{P}}$, *polarised*

D-Fusion, the subset of $\mathcal{DF}$ in which every prefix can be interpreted as an input or output, in the above sense.

Barbed Congruence. We now define our main tools for assessing the expressive power of D-Fusion compared to other calculi, that is barbed bisimulation and barbed congruence.

Definition 5 (Barbs). *We write* $P \downarrow a$ *if and only if there exist an action* μ *and a process* Q *such that* $P \xrightarrow{\mu} Q$ *and* $\mathrm{subj}(\mu) = a$.

Definition 6 (Barbed Bisimulation). *A* barbed bisimulation *is a symmetric binary relation* $\mathcal{R}$ *between processes such that* $P \mathcal{R} Q$ *implies:*

1. *whenever* $P \xrightarrow{\tau} P'$ *then* $Q \xrightarrow{\tau} Q'$ *and* $P' \mathcal{R} Q'$;
2. *for each name a, if* $P \downarrow a$ *then* $Q \downarrow a$.

   P *is a barbed bisimilar to* Q, *written* $P \stackrel{.}{\sim} Q$, *if* $P \mathcal{R} Q$ *for some barbed bisimulation* $\mathcal{R}$.

Definition 7 (Barbed Congruence). *Two processes* P *and* Q *are* barbed congruent, *written* $P \sim Q$, *if for all contexts* $C[\cdot]$, *it holds that* $C[P] \stackrel{.}{\sim} C[Q]$.

Example 2.   1. An example of 'expansion' for parallel composition is as follows:

$$(\nu k)\,ak.\mathbf{0}|av.\mathbf{0} \sim (\nu k)\,ak.av.\mathbf{0} + av.(\nu k)\,ak.\mathbf{0} + (\nu k)\,\{k = v\}.\mathbf{0}$$

On the other side,

$$((\nu k)\,ak.ak.\mathbf{0})|av.\mathbf{0} \nsim (\nu k)\,ak.(ak.av.\mathbf{0}+av.ak.\mathbf{0}) + av.((\nu k)\,ak.ak.\mathbf{0})$$
$$+ (\nu k)\,\{k = v\}.ak.\mathbf{0},$$

since the two processes are not barbed bisimilar within a context $C[\cdot] = (\lambda x, v)([\cdot]\,|\,ax.\mathbf{0})$.
2. The following two examples show the effect of fusing a λ-abstracted name with a free name and with another λ-abstracted name, respectively:

$$\lambda v\,\{k = v\}.P \sim \tau.P[k/v] \qquad (\lambda k, v)\,\{k = v\}.P \sim \lambda k\,\tau.P[k/v].$$

On the contrary,

$$(\nu v)\,\{k = v\}.P \nsim \tau.P[k/v],$$

since the two processes are not barbed bisimilar within a context $C[\cdot] = (\nu k)\,[\cdot]$.

4   Expressiveness of D-Fusion

Pi-calculus and Fusion are subcalculi of D-Fusion, because their respective labelled transition systems are embedded into polarised D-Fusion's, under the two obvious uniform translations from Π and $\mathcal{F}$ to $\mathcal{DF}^{\mathrm{p}}$ given below. The definition of uniformity can be extended to the case of encodings from $\mathcal{F}/\Pi$ into $\mathcal{DF}^{\mathrm{p}}$ in the obvious way: in particular, by requiring that (x) and (νx) be mapped to λx and (νx), respectively.

Definition 8. *The translations $[\![\cdot]\!]_\pi : \Pi \to \mathcal{DF}^p$ and $[\![\cdot]\!]_f : \mathcal{F} \to \mathcal{DF}^p$ are defined by extending in the expected homomorphic way the following clauses, respectively:*

$$[\![\overline{a}\langle x\rangle.P]\!]_\pi = \overline{a}\langle x\rangle.[\![P]\!]_\pi \quad [\![a(x).P]\!]_\pi = \lambda x\, a\langle x\rangle.[\![P]\!]_\pi \quad [\![(\nu x)P]\!]_\pi = (\nu x)\,[\![P]\!]_\pi$$

$$[\![\overline{a}\langle x\rangle.P]\!]_f = \overline{a}\langle x\rangle.[\![P]\!]_f \quad [\![a\langle x\rangle.P]\!]_f = a\langle x\rangle.[\![P]\!]_f \quad [\![(x)P]\!]_f = \lambda x\,[\![P]\!]_f$$

As expected, inclusion in term of labelled transition systems naturally lifts to bisimulation equivalences. Let $\sim^\pi$ and $\sim^f$ denote barbed congruence, respectively, over Π ([18]) and over $\mathcal{F}$ (see [21]) (Note that, over image-finite processes, $\sim^\pi$ is pi-calculus early congruence [18], and $\sim^f$ is Fusion hyper-equivalence [21]). Also, let $\sim^{[\![\pi]\!]}$ and $\sim^{[\![f]\!]}$ be the equivalences on $\mathcal{DF}^p$ obtained by closing barbed bisimulation $\dot\sim$ only under translated pi- and Fusion-contexts, respectively (e.g., $P \sim^{[\![\pi]\!]} Q$ iff for each Π-context $C[\cdot]$, $[\![C]\!]_\pi[P] \dot\sim [\![C]\!]_\pi[Q]$).

Proposition 2.

1. *Let P and Q be two pi-calculus processes. $P \sim^\pi Q$ iff $[\![P]\!]_\pi \sim^{[\![\pi]\!]} [\![Q]\!]_\pi$.*
2. *Let P and Q be two Fusion processes. $P \sim^f Q$ iff $[\![P]\!]_f \sim^{[\![f]\!]} [\![Q]\!]_f$.*

More interesting, we now show that D-Fusion cannot be uniformly encoded into Π. The intuitive reason is that, in D-Fusion, the combined use of action prefix, fusions and restrictions allows one to express a form of pattern matching. This is not possible in Π, at least not atomically. To show this fact, we restrict our attention to polarised D-Fusion, $\mathcal{DF}^p$. The reference semantics for Π is again the late operational semantics.

Given $P \in \Pi$ and a trace of actions s, let us write $P \stackrel{\hat{s}}{\Longrightarrow}$ if $P \stackrel{s'}{\Longrightarrow}$ for some trace s' that exhibits the same sequence of subject names, with the same polarity, as s (e.g., $s = a\langle \tilde{x}\rangle \cdot \lambda \tilde{y}\overline{b}\langle \tilde{v}\rangle$ and $s' = a\langle \tilde{z}\rangle \cdot \overline{b}\langle \tilde{w}\rangle$).

Definition 9. *A translation $[\![\cdot]\!] : \mathcal{DF}^p \to \Pi$ is uniform if for each $P, Q \in \mathcal{DF}^p$:*

- *for each trace s, $P \stackrel{s}{\Longrightarrow}$ implies $[\![P]\!] \stackrel{\hat{s}}{\Longrightarrow}$;*
- *$[\![P|Q]\!] = [\![P]\!]|[\![Q]\!]$;*
- *for each y, $[\![(\nu y)P]\!] = (\nu y)\,[\![P]\!]$;*
- *for each substitution σ, $[\![P\sigma]\!] = [\![P]\!]\sigma$.*

Below, we denote by $\sim_{\mathcal{DF}^p}$ any fixed equivalence over $\mathcal{DF}^p$ which is contained in trace semantics (defined in the obvious way), and by $\sim_\Pi$ any fixed equivalence over Π which is contained in trace equivalence. Note that barbed congruence over $\mathcal{DF}^p$, $\sim$, is contained in trace equivalence.

Proposition 3. *There is no uniform translation $[\![\cdot]\!] : \mathcal{DF}^p \to \Pi$ such that $\forall P, Q \in \mathcal{DF}^p$:*

$$P \sim_{\mathcal{DF}^p} Q \Rightarrow [\![P]\!] \sim_\Pi [\![Q]\!].$$

PROOF: Suppose that there exists such a translation $[\![\cdot]\!]$. Let us consider the following two $\mathcal{DF}^p$-processes P and Q:

$$P = (\nu c, k, h)\,(c\langle k\rangle.\overline{a}.\mathbf{0}|c\langle h\rangle.\overline{b}.\mathbf{0}|\overline{c}\langle k\rangle.\mathbf{0}) \qquad Q = \tau.\overline{a}.\mathbf{0}.$$

It holds that $P \sim Q$ in $\mathcal{DF}^{\text{P}}$: the reason is that, in P, synchronisation between prefixes $c\langle h\rangle$ and $\bar{c}\langle k\rangle$, which carry different *restricted* names h and k, is forbidden (see rule V-OPEN). Thus P can only make $c\langle k\rangle$ and $\bar{c}\langle k\rangle$ synchronise, and then perform $\bar{a}$. Thus, $P \sim_{\mathcal{DF}^{\text{P}}} Q$ holds too.

On the other hand, by Definition 9, for any uniform encoding $[\![\cdot]\!]$, c and $\bar{c}$ in $[\![P]\!]$ can synchronise and, thus, $[\![P]\!] \overset{\bar{b}}{\Longrightarrow}$, while $[\![Q]\!] \overset{\bar{b}}{\not\Longrightarrow}$ (because of $b \notin \text{fn}(Q)$ and of the uniformity with respect to substitutions). Thus $[\![P]\!] \not\sim_{\Pi} [\![Q]\!]$. $\qquad\square$

Of course, it is also true that D-Fusion cannot be uniformly encoded into $\mathcal{F}$, as this would imply the existence of a uniform fully abstract encoding from Π to $\mathcal{F}$, which does not exist (Proposition 1).

The conclusion is that there is some expressiveness gap between D-Fusion on one side and the other two calculi on the other side, at least, as far as our simple notion of uniform encoding is concerned. This gap is further explored by means of more elaborate examples in the next two sections.

5   Example: Correlation

This example aims at illustrating the gap between D-Fusion and Fusion from a more concrete perspective. Consider the following simple protocol. An agent A asks a trusted server S for two keys, to be used to access two distinct services (e.g. A might be a proxy requiring remote connections on behalf of two different users). Communication between A and S takes place over an insecure public channel, controlled by an adversary, but it is protected by encryption and challenge-response nonces. Informally, the dialogue between A and S is as follows:

$$
\begin{aligned}
&1.\ A \rightarrow S : n \\
&2.\ S \rightarrow A : \{n,k\}_{k_S} \\
&1'.\ A \rightarrow S : n' \\
&2'.\ S \rightarrow A : \{n',k'\}_{k_S}
\end{aligned}
$$

Here $\{\cdot\}_{(\cdot)}$ is symmetric encryption and k_S is a secret master key shared by A and S. A simple property of this protocol is that A should never receive k and k' in the wrong order (k' and then k), even in case S accepts new requests before completing old ones. Indeed, nonces n and n' are intended to avoid confusion of distinct sessions. In other words, nonces do *correlate* each request to S with the appropriate reply of S.

Below, we show that the above small protocol and the related ordering property can be readily translated and verified in D-Fusion. Next, we show that the property breaks down when (uniformly) translating the protocol into Fusion.

D-Fusion. Encryption is not a primitive operation in D-Fusion. However, in the present case, it is sensible to model an encrypted message $\{n,k\}_{k_S}$ as an output action $\bar{k}_S\langle n,k\rangle$: only knowing the master key k_S, and further specifying a session-specific nonce, it is possible to acquire the key k (similarly for $\{n',k'\}_{k_S}$, of course). Thus, assuming A concludes the protocol with a conventional 'commit' action and that p is the public channel, A, S and the whole protocol P might be specified as follows (below, we abbreviate $\lambda \widetilde{x}\, p\langle \widetilde{x}\rangle.X$ as $p(\widetilde{x}).X$):

$$A = (\nu n)\left(\overline{p}\langle n\rangle.\mathbf{0}|\lambda y\,k_S\langle n,y\rangle.(\nu n')\left(\overline{p}\langle n'\rangle.\mathbf{0}|\lambda y'\,k_S\langle n',y'\rangle.\overline{commit}\langle y,y'\rangle.\mathbf{0}\right)\right)$$
$$S = p(x).\left(\overline{k_S}\langle x,k\rangle.\mathbf{0}|p(x').\overline{k_S}\langle x',k'\rangle.\mathbf{0}\right)$$
$$P = (\nu k_S)\,(A|S).$$

Let A_{spec} be the process defined like A, except that the $\overline{commit}\langle y,y'\rangle$ action is replaced by $\overline{commit}\langle k,k'\rangle$, and let $P_{\text{spec}} = (\nu k_S)\,(A_{\text{spec}}|S)$. The property that A should never receive k and k' in the wrong order is stated as: $P \sim P_{\text{spec}}$.

Informally, equivalence holds true because the second input action in A/A_{spec}, that is $\lambda y'\,k_S\langle n',y'\rangle$, can only get synchronised with the second output action in S, that is $\overline{k_S}\langle x',k'\rangle$. In fact, n' can be extruded only *after* x has been received, hence fusion of x and n' is forbidden. Note that the above protocol specification would not be easily translated in pi-calculus, because in A the input prefix $k_S\langle n,y\rangle$ has a ν-bound name n.

Fusion. Suppose P^f and P^f_{spec} are obtained by some uniform encoding of P and P_{spec} above into Fusion. It is not difficult to show that P^f can be 'attacked' by an adversary R that gets n and n' and fuse them together, $R = p(x).\left(\overline{p}\langle x\rangle.\mathbf{0}|p(y).\overline{p}\langle y\rangle.\mathbf{0}\right)$. Formally, for $\alpha = \overline{commit}\langle k',k\rangle$,

$$P^f|R \stackrel{\alpha}{\Longrightarrow} \text{ and, thus, } P^f|R \not\sim^{\text{he}} P^f_{\text{spec}}|R,$$

which proves that P^f and P^f_{spec} are not hyper-equivalent.

This example illustrates the difficulty of modelling fresh, indistinguishable quantities (nonces) in Fusion. This makes apparent that Fusion is not apt to express security properties based on correlation.

6   Encoding Guarded Choice

In this section we show how the combined mechanisms of fusions and restrictions can be used to encode different forms of guarded choice *via* parallel composition, in a clean and uniform way. Informally, different branches of a guarded choice will be represented as concurrent processes. The encodings add pairs of extra names to the object part of each action: these extra names are used as 'side-channels' for atomic coordination among the different branches. We start by looking at a simple example.

Example 3. Consider the guarded choice $A = \lambda x\,(\nu n)\,a\langle xn\rangle.P + \lambda x\,(\nu m)\,a\langle xm\rangle.Q$. Its intended 'parallel' implementation is the process:

$$B = \lambda x\left((\nu n)\,a\langle xn\rangle.P\,|\,(\nu m)\,a\langle xm\rangle.Q\right)$$

(here, $x,n,m \notin fn(a,P,Q)$). Assume a channel discipline by which output actions on channel a must carry two identical names. In B, the parallel component that first consumes any such message, forces fusion of x either to n or to m, and consequently inhibits the other component. E.g.:

$$\lambda u\overline{a}\langle uu\rangle|B \stackrel{\tau}{\to}\sim (\nu n)\,(P\,|\,(\nu m)\,a\langle mn\rangle.Q) \quad\sim\quad P\,|\,(\nu n,m)\,a\langle mn\rangle.Q.$$

Under the mentioned assumption, $(\nu m,n)\,a\langle mn\rangle.Q$ is equivalent to $\mathbf{0}$, because there is no way of fusing m and n. Thus the process on the right of $\sim$ is equivalent to P. In other words, choice between P and Q has been resolved atomically.

The above line of reasoning can be formalised in two ways. One way is considering a new 'disciplined' equivalence $\sim^d$, obtained by closing barbed bisimilarity only with respect to contexts $C[\cdot]$ obeying the mentioned channel discipline (i.e. for each $\overline{c}\langle\widetilde{v}\rangle$ in $C[\cdot]$ with $|\widetilde{v}| \geq 2$, $\widetilde{v} = \widetilde{w}uu$, for some $\widetilde{w}$ and u). The other way is keeping standard barbed congruence $\sim$, but inserting processes inside a 'firewall' that filters out $\overline{a}$-messages not respecting the given channel discipline. The latter can be easily defined in D-Fusion relying on 'non-linear' inputs:

$$\mathsf{F}_{a,a'}[\cdot] = (\nu a')\left(\lambda z\, azz.\overline{a'}\langle zz\rangle.\mathbf{0}|[\cdot]\right).$$

We state the result in both forms below.

Proposition 4. *Let A and B be as in Example 3.*

1. $A \sim^d B$;
2. *Let A' and B' be the processes obtained from A and B, respectively, by replacing the outermost occurrences of a with a fresh a'. Then $\mathsf{F}_{a,a'}[A'] \sim \mathsf{F}_{a,a'}[B']$.*

Note that the result above exploits in a crucial way features of both Fusion (non-linearity of input actions, in the firewall, and sharing of input variable x, in B) and of D-Fusion (restricted input).

Proposition 4 can be generalised to fully abstract encodings of different forms of guarded choice. For the sake of simplicity, we will state the results in terms of 'disciplined' equivalences. We believe the results can also be stated in terms of ordinary barbed congruence, at the cost of breaking uniformity of the encoding and of introducing more sophisticated forms of 'firewalls'. We examine two cases, input-guarded choice and mixed choice.

Input-Guarded (ig) Choice. Let us fix, as a source language the fragment of polarised D-Fusion with guarded choice, $\mathcal{DF}^{\mathrm{p,ig}}$. In this language, input prefix and summation $+$ are replaced by input-guarded choice $\sum_{i\in I} a_i\langle\widetilde{x}_i\rangle.P_i$. The target language is the fragment of polarised D-Fusion with no form of summation. The relevant clauses of the encoding are:

$$[\![\sum_{i\in i} a_i\langle\widetilde{x}_i\rangle.P_i]\!]_{\mathrm{ig}} = \lambda z\, \Pi_{i\in I}(\nu n)\,\lambda\widetilde{x}_i\, a_i\langle\widetilde{x}_i zn\rangle.[\![P_i]\!]_{\mathrm{ig}} \qquad [\![\overline{a}\langle\widetilde{v}\rangle.P]\!]_{\mathrm{ig}} = \lambda z\, \overline{a}\langle\widetilde{v}zz\rangle.[\![P]\!]_{\mathrm{ig}},$$

where $\Pi_{i\in I}X_i$ denotes the parallel composition of all X_i's. The encoding acts as a homomorphism over the remaining operators. Below, we denote by $\sim^{\mathrm{p,ig}}$ barbed congruence over $\mathcal{DF}^{\mathrm{p,ig}}$, and denote by $\sim^{[\![\mathrm{p,ig}]\!]}$ the equivalence over D-Fusion obtained by closing barbed bisimulation under translated contexts (i.e. $P \sim^{[\![\mathrm{p,ig}]\!]} Q$ iff for each $\mathcal{DF}^{\mathrm{p,ig}}$-context $C[\cdot]$, it holds $[\![C]\!]_{\mathrm{ig}}[P] \sim [\![C]\!]_{\mathrm{ig}}[Q]$); note that both equivalences are *reasonable* semantics in the sense of [13]. The proof of the following theorem is straightforward, given that there is a 1-to-1 correspondence between reductions and barbs of R and of $[\![R]\!]_{\mathrm{ig}}$, for any R, and given that the encoding is compositional, in particular, for any context $C[\cdot]$, it holds $[\![C]\!]_{\mathrm{ig}}[[\![P]\!]_{\mathrm{ig}}] = [\![C[P]]\!]_{\mathrm{ig}}$.

Theorem 1 (Full Abstraction for ig Choice). *Let $P, Q \in \mathcal{DF}^{\mathrm{p,ig}}$. It holds that $P \sim^{\mathrm{p,ig}} Q$ if and only if $[\![P]\!]_{\mathrm{ig}} \sim^{[\![\mathrm{p,ig}]\!]} [\![Q]\!]_{\mathrm{ig}}$.*

Of course, the above theorem also yields a fully abstract encoding of input-guarded choice for pi-calculus, which may be viewed as a sub-calculus of $\mathcal{DF}^{\mathrm{p,ig}}$.

Mixed Choice in a Sorted pi-Calculus. As a source language we fix here a sorted version of polyadic pi-calculus [9] with 'mixed' choice, Π^{mix}. In this language, prefixes and $+$ are replaced by mixed summation, $\sum_{i\in I} a_i(\tilde{x}_i).P_i + \sum_{j\in J} \overline{b_j}\langle \tilde{v}_j\rangle.Q_j$. The target language is again the fragment of polarised D-Fusion with no summation at all. The encoding is a bit more complex than in the previous case, as it implies adding *two* pairs of extra names to coordinate different branches. The relevant clause is:

$$\llbracket \sum_{i\in I} a_i(\tilde{x}_i).P_i + \sum_{j\in J} \overline{b_j}\langle v_j\rangle.Q_j\rrbracket_{\text{mix}} =$$
$$(\lambda z, u)\,(\,\Pi_{i\in I}(\nu n)\,\lambda\tilde{x}_i\,a_i\langle\tilde{x}_i znuu\rangle.\llbracket P_i\rrbracket_{\text{mix}} \mid \Pi_{j\in J}(\nu n)\,\overline{b_j}\langle\tilde{v}_j uuzn\rangle.\llbracket Q_j\rrbracket_{\text{mix}}\,).$$

Note that the relative positions of ν-names correctly forbid communication between branches of opposite polarities within the same choice (no 'incestuous' communication, according to the terminology of [12]). The encoding acts as a homomorphism over the remaining operators of Π^{mix}.

Below, $\sim^{\text{mix}}$ denotes barbed congruence over Π^{mix}, and $\sim^{\llbracket\text{mix}\rrbracket}$ the equivalence over D-Fusion obtained by closing barbed bisimulation under translated Π^{mix}-contexts. Both equivalences are reasonable semantics in the sense of [13]. The proof of the following theorem is again straightforward by correspondence on reductions and barbs, and by compositionality of the encoding.

Theorem 2 (Full Abstraction for Mixed Choice). *Let $P, Q \in \Pi^{\text{mix}}$. It holds that $P \sim^{\text{mix}} Q$ if and only if $\llbracket P\rrbracket_{\text{mix}} \sim^{\llbracket\text{mix}\rrbracket} \llbracket Q\rrbracket_{\text{mix}}$.*

In a pi-calculus setting, it is well-known that mixed choice cannot be encoded into the choice-free fragment, if one requires the encoding be uniform and preserve a reasonable semantics [13, 14, 12]. The theorem above shows that pi-calculus mixed choice *can* be implemented into the choice-free fragment of D-Fusion. The encoding is uniform, deadlock- and divergence-free, and preserves a reasonable semantics. This is yet another evidence of the expressiveness gap between D-Fusion and pi-calculus.

7   Conclusions and Future Work

We have proposed the D-Fusion calculus, an extension of the fusion calculus where two distinct binders coexist, one analogous to the (x) binder in fusion, the other imposing name freshness. We have shown that D-Fusion is strictly more expressive than both Fusion and pi-calculus.

Our expressiveness results seem to suggest that the design of an efficient distributed implementation of D-Fusion might be nontrivial. This design would probably involve the introduction of a distributed model of the calculus, including, e.g., explicit fusions [4] for broadcasting fusions asynchronously and rollback mechanisms for handling fusion failures. We leave this task for future work. For the time being, we just note that distributed implementations of pi/fusion-like calculi do exist (e.g., the fusion machine of [3]) and may represent a good starting point for distributed implementations of D-Fusion.

Another point that deserves further study is characterization of D-Fusion barbed congruence in terms of a more tractable, labelled bisimulation, which would avoid universal quantification on all contexts. Preliminary results indicate that definition of this equivalence would require a (nontrivial) integration of *substitutive effects* à la fusion calculus [16], i.e. name substitutions resulting from fusions, with *distinctions* à la open pi-calculus [19].

We also plan to extend the D-Fusion calculus by generalising name fusions to substitutions over an arbitrary signature of terms. It would be interesting to compare the expressive power of this extended D-Fusion to systems of Concurrent Constraint or Logic Programming that allow creation of fresh names, such as lambda-Prolog [8], and CCP [17, 20].

In [7] Merro gives an encoding from asynchronous Chi calculus (a variant of Fusion, indipendently introduced by Fu, [2]) to (asynchronous) pi-calculus. However, no result on the other direction is proven. Here, we have proved that pi-calculus cannot be encoded into Fusion.

In [1] the synchronisation mechanism of the pi-calculus is extended to allow for polyadic synchronisation, where channels are vectors of names. The expressiveness of polyadic synchronisation, matching and mixed choice is compared.

Acknowledgments. The authors wish to thank Bjorn Victor for stimulating discussions. The anonymous referees provided valuable suggestions.

References

1. M. Carbone and S. Maffeis. On the Expressive Power of Polyadic Synchronisation in Pi-Calculus. To appear in *Nordic Journal of Computing*.
2. Y. Fu. A Proof Theoretical Approach to Communication. In *Proc. of ICALP '97*, LNCS 1256. Springer-Verlag, 1997.
3. P. Gardner, C. Laneve, and L. Wischik. The fusion machine (extended abstract). In *Proc. of CONCUR '02*, LNCS 2421. Springer-Verlag, 2002.
4. P. Gardner and L. Wischik. Explicit Fusions. *Theoretical Computer Science*. To appear.
5. L. G. Meredith, S. Bjorg, and D. Richter. Highwire Language Specification Version 1.0. Unpublished manuscript.
6. Microsoft Corp. Biztalk Server - http://www.microsoft.com/biztalk.
7. M. Merro. On the Expressiveness of Chi, Update, and Fusion calculi. In Proc. of EXPRESS '98, ENTCS 16(2), Elsevier Science, 1998.
8. D. Miller. Unification under a mixed prefix. *Journal of Symbolic Computation*,14(4):321–358, 1992.
9. R. Milner. The Polyadic pi-Calculus: a Tutorial. Technical Report, Computer Science Dept., University of Edinburgh, 1991.
10. R. Milner, J. Parrow, and D. Walker. A calculus of mobile processes (parts I and II). *Information and Computation*, 100(1):1–77, 1992.
11. R. Milner and D. Sangiorgi. Barbed Bisimulation. In *Proc. of ICALP '92*, LNCS 623, Springer-Verlag, 1992.
12. U. Nestmann and B. C. Pierce. Decoding choice encodings. *Information and Computation*, 163(1):1–59, 2000.
13. C. Palamidessi. Comparing the Expressive Power of the Synchronous and the Asynchronous pi-calculus. In *Conf. Rec. of POPL'97*, 1997.
14. C. Palamidessi. Comparing the Expressive Power of the Synchronous and the Asynchronous pi-calculus. *Mathematical Structures in Computer Science*, 13(5):685–719, 2003.

15. J. Parrow and B. Victor. The Update Calculus. In *Proc. of AMAST'97*, LNCS 1349, Springer-Verlag, 1997.
16. J. Parrow and B. Victor. The Fusion Calculus: Expressiveness and Symmetry in Mobile Processes. In *Proc. of LICS'98*. IEEE Computer Society Press, 1998.
17. E. Shapiro. The Family of Concurrent Logic Programming Languages. *ACM Computing Surveys*, 21(3):413-510, 1989.
18. D. Sangiorgi. Expressing Mobility in Process Algebras: First-Order and Higher-Order Paradigms. PhD thesis, Department of Computer Science, University of Edinburgh, 1992.
19. D. Sangiorgi. A Theory of Bisimulation for the pi-Calculus. *Acta Informatica*, 33(1): 69-97, 1996.
20. V. Saraswat. Concurrent Constraint Programming. The MIT Press, 1993.
21. B. Victor. The Fusion Calculus: Expressiveness and Symmetry in Mobile Processes. PhD thesis, Department of Computer Systems, Uppsala University, 1998.
22. World Wide Web Consortium (W3C) - http://www.w3.org/TR/wsdl12.

A Functional Language for Logarithmic Space

Peter Møller Neergaard*

Mitchom School of Computer Science,
Brandeis University,
Waltham, MA 02454, USA
turtle@achilles.linearity.org

Abstract. More than being just a tool for expressing algorithms, a well-designed programming language allows the user to express her ideas efficiently. The design choices however effect the efficiency of the algorithms written in the languages. It is therefore important to understand how such choices effect the expressibility of programming languages.

The paper pursues the very low complexity programs by presenting a first-order function algebra BC_ε^- that captures exactly LF, the functions computable in logarithmic space. This gives insights into the expressiveness of recursion.

The important technical features of BC_ε^- are (1) a separation of variables into safe and normal variables where recursion can only be done over the latter; (2) linearity of the recursive call; and (3) recursion with a variable step length (course-of-value recursion). Unlike formulations of LF via Turing machines, BC_ε^- makes no references to outside resource measures, e.g., the size of the memory used. This appears to be the first such characterization of LF-computable functions (not just predicates).

The proof that all BC_ε^--programs can be evaluated in LF is of separate interest to programmers: it trades space for time and evaluates recursion with at most one recursive call without a call stack.

1 Introduction

Let thy speech be short, comprehending much in a few words.
From the Aprocrypha

Programmers are used to ask "how fast is my algorithm?", but an equally important question is "how fast is my programming language?". While Church-Turing thesis states that all general-purpose programming languages can solve the same problems, they do not necessarily do so equally efficiently. For instance, Pippenger [19] proves that LISP with assignments is asymptotically faster than pure LISP for a particular online permutation problem. And for typed languages increasingly complex intersection types allow increasingly larger classes of problems to be solved as investigated by Kfoury et al. [10, 15].

* Supported by the Danish Research Agency grants 1999-114-0027 and 642-00-0062 and the NSF grant CCR-9806718.

W.-N. Chin (Ed.): APLAS 2004, LNCS 3302, pp. 311–326, 2004.
© Springer-Verlag Berlin Heidelberg 2004

Starting with seminal papers by Immerman [8] and Bellantoni and Cook [2], the field of implicit computational complexity has blossomed providing—to paraphrase Landin—the next 700 languages for (mainly) polynomial time. Such languages capture their respective complexity class through internal limitations rather than external measures. While these languages in most cases are cumbersome to program, they provide precise insights into how programming constructs affect complexity. For instance, the present paper gives a language, BC_ε^-, for the functions computable in logarithmic space (LF) through a syntactic restriction on course-of-value recursion combined with linearity. This suggests duplicate recursive calls as a potential way for programs to break out of LF.

These characterizations can also be useful for complexity theory: A particular notorious line of research is the separation problem asking whether there, for instance, are functions computable in polynomial time (PF) that are not in LF, or functions in non-deterministic polynomial time (NPF) that are not in PF. While everybody would believe so—and for instance trust the security of their ATM cards on it—sadly nothing has been proved yet.

Characterizing complexity classes via Turing machines is appealing to programmers: the model is easy to understand and standard programming tricks can be used. An external measure is however like splitting coal from diamonds by the look: the job gets done, but you gain no insight to why the two are different.

In contrast, comparing the present characterization of LF with the characterization B of PF due to Bellantoni and Cook [2],[1] reveals linearity as the key difference between PF and LF. The much, much harder (and much more interesting) question is of course whether any function in PF truly needs nonlinearity.

1.1 BC_ε^- in a Nutshell

On surface, BC_ε^- is a slight (hence the ε in the name) generalization of the function algebra BC^- developed by Murawski and Ong [16]. Its merits are that it highlights the limitations of LF, shows linearity as a potential distinction between LF and PF, and is less cumbersome to use as course-of-value recursion is more natural than primitive recursion.

Recursion in BC_ε^- is a boiled down version of primitive recursion which we (for lack of a shorter name) call safe affine course-of-value recursion: (1) in the recursive step, recursion over the recursive value is prohibited (safe recursion), (2) the recursive value can be used only once in the recursive step function (affinity), but (3) we can skip steps in the recursive chain (course-of-value recursion). Point (1) is accomplished through an idea due to Bellantoni and Cook [2]: We divide the function arguments into normal and safe arguments (syntactically divided by :); recursion can only be done over normal arguments and the recursive value is provided to the step function as a safe argument.

---

[1] B uses a more restricted recursion principle than BC_ε^-. One can however use the recursion principle of BC_ε^- without breaking the PF soundness or completeness of B.

In effect, BC_ε^- has a very limited course-of-values as a different step length is allowed at each step of the recursion, e.g., we can recurse through[2] $f(10001111 :)$, $f(1000 :), f(10 :), f(1 :), f(0 :)$ where the step length is $4, 2, 1, 1$. This is accomplished by a separate function which computes the step length from the normal arguments. Syntactically, we express the recursion principle as follows

$$f(n, \boldsymbol{x} : \boldsymbol{y}) = \begin{cases} g(\boldsymbol{x} : \boldsymbol{y}) & \text{if } n = 0 \\ h_b(x', \boldsymbol{x} : f(x' \gg |d_b(x', \boldsymbol{x} :)|, \boldsymbol{x} : \boldsymbol{y})) & \text{if } n = 2x' + b \end{cases}$$

where $n \gg i$ right shifts n by i, i.e., drops the bottom i bits of n. Standard primitive recursion arises by simply choosing $d_b(x', \boldsymbol{x}) = 0$.

As primitive recursion corresponds to right folding, BC_ε^- programs can be seen as functional programs written only using a generalized right fold function.

1.2   Related Work

Bellantoni and Cook's B [2] captures exactly the functions computable in polynomial time. BC⁻ is an affine version of B developed by Murawski and Ong [16] in work connecting B with Girard's characterization of PF through light logic [4]. While Ong and Mairson in unpublished work establish that BC⁻ can be evaluated in LF, it is unknown whether BC⁻ is LF complete. This is solved by BC_ε^- which is both LF-complete and sound. We reuse the basic idea of Ong and Mairson for soundness, but make it clearer by establishing a connection to tail recursion.

The difference between BC_ε^- and BC⁻ is the recursion principle. BC_ε^- uses course-of-value recursion, while BC⁻ uses the more restricted primitive recursion. Combined with affinity this is a true party-killer as it imposes a quantum effect on the recursive value: you can ask for its value, but in doing so you loose the value. Thus, only one bit of the recursive value can determine the control in the next step of the recursion. This seems to prevent BC⁻ from being LF-complete.

The reader might faint and think "why another characterization?" when the literature already contains a plethora characterizations of the LF-computable predicates or, at best, size-bounded functions:

(1) Bellantoni [3] shows that restricting B to unary numbers is exactly the non-size increasing LF-computable functions. This in particular includes all LF-computable predicates. The result stems from unary numbers using only logarithmic space when represented binary. In my view this is a trick of representation which does not cast any light on the difference between PF and LF.

(2) Goerdt [5] characterizes LF-predicates (and other complexity classes) in finite model theory. Jones [9] recasts the results in terms of read-only (cons-less) functional program using only fold to do iteration. Unlike BC_ε^- they cannot produce big output (being read-only).

---

[2] Here, and throughout, function arguments for BC_ε^- are given in binary.

(3) Voda [20] and Kristiansen [11] have characterizations of the LF-computable predicates based on restricted imperative programs with loops.

This is however all characterization of predicates where BC_ε^- with simple restrictions goes further and characterize the full class of computable functions: after all most people use computers for more than yes/no-questions.

Finally a comparison should be made to the standard approach to separation through complete problems, i.e., problems that are provably the hardest within a complexity class. Like characterizations through implicit computational complexity complete problems say something intrinsic about the nature of the complexity class. They do however not necessarily tell how the computation is limited; this is why I find implicit characterizations more appealing.

A full version of this extended abstract is available as part of my dissertation [14] with SML implementations of the programs [13].

2   Preliminaries and BC_ε^-

We assume that the reader is familiar with standard complexity theoretic notions like complexity classes, hardness, and complete problems [17]. We also assume working knowledge of standard ML [18]. Being computer scientists, the concrete representation of numbers is important. We use $\mathbb{N}_1$ to denote the natural numbers in unary, i.e., a string of 1s with length n, and $\mathbb{N}_2$ for natural numbers in binary. In both cases, we use ε to explicitly denote the empty string corresponding to 0. We write bitstrings of the bits $b_1, \ldots, b_k$ as $b_k \cdots b_1$ with b_k the most significant bit. The length function on numbers is $|\cdot|$. We use $\mathbb{N}^{k,l}$ for $\mathbb{N}^k \times \mathbb{N}^l$.

We first introduce our LF-language BC_ε^-. It is given as a function algebra. We divide the function arguments into normal and safe arguments (syntactically distinguished by a :) where recursion is only possible over the former and the latter can be used at most once.

Definition 1. We use $\mathbb{N}_2$ as our input and output domain.

(1) We define the set of base functions to be the functions: $0(:) = \varepsilon$; $p(: \varepsilon) = \varepsilon$ and $p(: yb) = y$; $\pi_j^{m,n}(x_1, \ldots, x_m : x_{m+1}, \ldots, x_{m+n}) = x_j$ with $1 \leq j \leq m + n$; $s_0(: y) = y0$; $s_1(: y) = y1$; and $c(: y_11, y_2, y_3) = y_2$ and $c(: y_1, y_2, y_3) = y_3$ otherwise.

(2) Let the following functions be given: $f : \mathbb{N}_2^{M,N} \to \mathbb{N}_2$, $g_1, \ldots, g_M : \mathbb{N}_2^{m,0} \to \mathbb{N}_2$, and $h_1 : \mathbb{N}_2^{m,n_1} \to \mathbb{N}_2, \ldots, h_N : \mathbb{N}_2^{m,n_N} \to \mathbb{N}_2$. Let $n \geq n_1 + \cdots + n_N$ and define safe and ne composition of the functions as the following function in $\mathbb{N}_2^{m,n} \to \mathbb{N}_2$:

$$(f \circ \langle g_1, \ldots, g_M : h_1, \ldots, h_N \rangle)(x_1, \ldots, x_m : y_1, \ldots, y_n) =$$
$$f(g_1(\boldsymbol{x} :), \ldots, g_M(\boldsymbol{x} :) : h_1(\boldsymbol{x} : \boldsymbol{y}_1), \ldots, h_N(\boldsymbol{x} : \boldsymbol{y}_N))$$

where $\boldsymbol{x} = x_1, \ldots, x_m$ and $\boldsymbol{y}_1, \ldots, \boldsymbol{y}_n$ is a division of the variables $y_1, \ldots, y_n$ such that each y_i occurs at most once in any of the vectors $\boldsymbol{y}_1, \ldots, \boldsymbol{y}_n$.

(3) Given functions $g : \mathbb{N}_2^{m,n} \to \mathbb{N}_2$, $h_0, h_1 : \mathbb{N}_2^{m+1,1} \to \mathbb{N}_2$, $d_0, d_1 : \mathbb{N}_2^{m+1,0} \to \mathbb{N}_2$, we define the safe affine course-of-value recursion of the functions, written $\mathtt{rec}(g, h_0, \delta_0, h_1, \delta_1)$, to be the function $f : \mathbb{N}_2^{m+1,n} \to \mathbb{N}_2$ defined as follows:

$$
f(n, \boldsymbol{x} : \boldsymbol{y}) = \begin{cases} g(\boldsymbol{x} : \boldsymbol{y}) & \text{if } n = \varepsilon \\ h_{b_1}(b_k \cdots b_2, \boldsymbol{x} : f(b_k \cdots b_{2+\delta}, \boldsymbol{x} : \boldsymbol{y})) & \text{if } n = b_k \cdots b_1, \, k \geq 1, \\ & \delta = |d_{b_1}(b_k \cdots b_2, \boldsymbol{x} :)| \end{cases}
$$

(4) The function algebra $\mathrm{BC}_\varepsilon^-$ is the least set of functions over the integers $\mathbb{N}_2$ containing the base functions and closed under safe affine composition and safe affine course-of-value recursion.

Remark 1. Bellantoni and Cook's function algebra B [2] is obtained by dropping the affinity in the composition and recursion scheme, i.e., by using

$$
(f \circ \langle g_1, \ldots, g_M : h_1, \ldots, h_N \rangle)(\boldsymbol{x} : \boldsymbol{y}) = \\ f(g_1(\boldsymbol{x} :), \ldots, g_M(\boldsymbol{x} :) : h_1(\boldsymbol{x} : \boldsymbol{y}), \ldots, h_N(\boldsymbol{x} : \boldsymbol{y}))
$$

and letting $f = \mathtt{rec}(g, h_0, d_0, h_1, d_1)$ be

$$
f(n, \boldsymbol{x} : \boldsymbol{y}) = \begin{cases} g(\boldsymbol{x} : \boldsymbol{y}) & \text{if } n = \varepsilon \\ h_{b_1}(b_k \cdots b_2, \boldsymbol{x} : \boldsymbol{y}, f(b_k \cdots b_{2+\delta}, \boldsymbol{x} : \boldsymbol{y})) & \text{if } n = b_k \cdots b_1, \, k \geq 1 \\ & \delta = |d_{b_1}(b_k \cdots b_2, \boldsymbol{x} :)| \ . \end{cases}
$$

Notation 1. When f is nullary (i.e., a constant), we write f for $f \circ \langle : \rangle : \mathbb{N}^{m,n} \to \mathbb{N}$ for any m and n. We write $\mathtt{rec}(g, h, \delta)$ for $\mathtt{rec}(g, h, \delta, h, \delta)$.

The syntactic restrictions impose a bound on the size of the output.

Lemma 1 ([2, Lem. 4.1]). *Let $f \in BC_\varepsilon^-$ be function. There is a monotone polynomial q_f such that $|f(\boldsymbol{x} : \boldsymbol{y})| \leq q_f(|\boldsymbol{x}|) + \max_i |y_i|$.*

3   LF Completeness

We will now show that $\mathrm{BC}_\varepsilon^-$ is complete for LF-computations. We do so by showing that given any LF Turing machine we can define the following function in $\mathrm{BC}_\varepsilon^-$:

$T(t, s, w, i, j) = $ "the output tape in reverse and preceded by a 1 after t iterations starting in state s with the work tape w, the head of the read-only input tape in position i, and the head of the work tape in position j."

Before giving the definition of the function T it seems appropriate to state exactly what we mean by a LF Turing machine in this paper; after all every author has her own slightly different definition of Turing Machine.

Notation 2. We consider Turing machines with a read-only input tape (denoted I) of length n, a work tape (denoted W) with $O(\log n)$ symbols, and a write-only output tape (denoted O) infinite to the right. We assume that the program will never try to move beyond the limits of the tapes. The machine's program consists of labeled instructions $l : I$ consecutively numbered as $0, \ldots, S-1$ where I is one of the following: left_I, left_W, right_I, right_W, if_I then l' else l'', if_W then l' else l'', and $\text{write}_W b$ and $\text{write}_O b$ with $b = 0, 1$. We assume that the program idles on a single state when there is no more output.

It should (hopefully) be clear that these conventions do not differ essentially from the reader's favorite definition of a Turing machine.

We can now turn to the function T; the function is presented in pseudo-code in Fig. 1. The remainder of this section is devoted to showing that the function can be encoded in $\mathrm{BC}_\varepsilon^-$. This has two parts: (1) representing the functions in Fig. 1 in $\mathrm{BC}_\varepsilon^-$, (2) turning the recursion over multiple variables into a recursion over a single variable. Starting with the last point, we observe the following bounds: $0 \leq s < S$, $0 \leq i < n$, $0 \leq j < \log_2 n \leq n$. Moreover, the work tape is bound by $c \log_2 n$ for some constant c; this gives $2^{c \log_2 n} = n^c$ different configurations of the work tape. Since the Turing machine cannot twice be in the same configuration without doing an infinite loop, the maximum number of steps the machine can take before looping infinitely is $N = S \cdot n \cdot n \cdot n^c = S \cdot n^{c+2}$. We can encode the tuple (t, s, w, i, j) uniquely as the number: $t \cdot N + (((w \cdot n) + i) \cdot n + j) \cdot S) + s$. Consequently, each step is represented by decreasing the encoding with $N + ((((w - w') \cdot n) + (i - i')) \cdot n + (j - j')) \cdot S) + (s - s')$ where w', i', j', and s' represent the new state. By using unary representation this corresponds to a simple right shift—easily caught with the course-of-value recursion scheme.[3] We therefore show how to do the functions in Fig. 1 using unary numbers.

Proposition 1. Let m and n by numbers in binary. Right shift $\text{shift}^R(m : n)$ of m by $|n|$ and selection of bit $|n|$ from m are definable in $\mathrm{BC}_\varepsilon^-$.

Proposition 2. Let b be either 0 or 1. The following function is representable in $\mathrm{BC}_\varepsilon^-$:

$$\text{set}_b(m, b_k \cdots b_0 :) = \begin{cases} b_k \cdots b_{|m|+1} b b_{|m|-1} \cdots b_1 & \text{when } k \geq |m| + 1 \\ b b_{k-1} \cdots b_0 & \text{otherwise} \end{cases}.$$

Note that set_b does not change the length of the output. We then continue with arithmetic:

Proposition 3. Let m and n be integers in unary notation. Then the following functions are representable in $\mathrm{BC}_\varepsilon^-$: (1) $\text{plus}(m : n) = m + n$, (2) $\text{minus}(n : m) = \max(m - n, 0)$, (3) $\text{mult}(m, n :) = m \cdot n$, (4) $\text{div}(m, n :) = \lfloor m/n \rfloor$ where $n \neq 0$, (5) $\text{mod}(m, n :) = m \bmod n$ where $n \neq 0$, (6) $\text{zero?}(m :) = 1$ if, and only if, $m = 0$, and (7) $\text{<?}(m, n :) = 1$ if, and only if, $m < n$.

---

[3] Note that binary representation will not work as the difference between two numbers is not necessarily a string of most significant bits.

$$\mathrm{T}(-1, s, w, i, j, x :) = 1$$

$$\mathrm{T}(t, s, w, i, j, x :) = \mathtt{let}\ b_{\mathrm{I}} = \mathrm{bit}(i : x)\ \mathtt{in}$$
$$\mathtt{let}\ b_{\mathtt{w}} = \mathrm{bit}(j : \mathrm{unary2bin}(w :))\ \mathtt{in}$$
$$\mathrm{O}(\mathrm{T}(t - 1, \mathrm{S}(b_{\mathtt{w}}, b_{\mathrm{I}}, s :), \mathrm{W}(w, j, s :), \mathrm{I}(i, s :), \mathrm{J}(j, s :), x :), s :)$$

$$\mathrm{O}(t, s :) = \begin{cases} s_b(t) & \text{if } I_s = \mathtt{write}_0\ b \\ t & \text{otherwise} \end{cases}$$

$$\mathrm{S}(b_{\mathtt{w}}, b_{\mathrm{I}}, s :) = \begin{cases} l' & \text{if } I_T = \mathtt{if}_T\ \mathtt{then}\ l'\ \mathtt{else}\ l''\ \text{and } b_T = 1 \\ l'' & \text{if } I_s = \mathtt{if}_T\ \mathtt{then}\ l'\ \mathtt{else}\ l''\ \text{and } b_T = 0 \\ s + 1 & \text{otherwise} \end{cases}$$

$$\mathrm{W}(w, j, s :) = \begin{cases} \mathrm{bin2unary}(\mathrm{set}_b(j, \mathrm{unary2bin}(w :) :) :) & \text{if } I_s = \mathtt{write}_{\mathtt{w}}\ b \\ w & \text{otherwise} \end{cases}$$

$$\mathrm{I}(i, s :) = \begin{cases} i + 1 & \text{if } I_s = \mathtt{right}_{\mathrm{I}} \\ i - 1 & \text{if } I_s = \mathtt{left}_{\mathrm{I}} \\ i \end{cases}$$

$$\mathrm{J}(j, s :) = \begin{cases} j + 1 & \text{if } I_s = \mathtt{right}_{\mathtt{w}} \\ j - 1 & \text{if } I_s = \mathtt{left}_{\mathtt{w}} \\ j \end{cases}$$

$$\mathrm{set}_b(m, b_k \cdots b_0 :) = \begin{cases} b_k \cdots b_{|m|+1} bb_{|m|-1} \cdots b_0 & \text{when } 0 \le k \le |m| \\ bb_{k-1} \cdots b_0 & \text{otherwise} \end{cases}$$

Fig. 1. The function T simulating a LF Turing machine

While the representations are straightforward, it is worth noticing how $\mathrm{BC}_\varepsilon^-$ allows a simpler definition of division than primitive recursion:

$$\mathrm{div}(m, n :) = \mathrm{div}'(m + 1, n :) - 1$$

$$\mathrm{div}'(m, n :) = \begin{cases} 0 & \text{when } m \le 0 \\ 1 + \mathrm{div}'(m - n, n :) & \text{when } m \ge n \end{cases}$$

An unfortunate limitation of the syntactic restrictions of $\mathrm{BC}_\varepsilon^-$ is that the two branches cannot share any safe arguments. In a recursion this prevents using a conditional to choose between two different actions on the recursive result. At the cost of having the conditional controlled by a normal variable, we regain a conditional that shares the variables of the two branches:

Lemma 2. Let $f, g : \mathbb{N}^{0,1} \to \mathbb{N}$ be two functions representable in $\mathrm{BC}_\varepsilon^-$. Then the following function is representable in $\mathrm{BC}_\varepsilon^-$: $\mathrm{COND}_{f,g}(m : n) = f(: n)$ when $m \bmod 2 = 1$ and $\mathrm{COND}_{f,g}(m : n) = g(: n)$ when $m \bmod 2 = 0$.

Another useful function is reversing a bit string. Since we are working with numbers, not bit vectors, we do not necessarily have $\mathrm{rev}(\mathrm{rev}(x :) :) = x$.

Lemma 3. There is a BC_ε^- function $\mathrm{rev} : \mathbb{N}_2 \times \mathbb{N}_1 \to \mathbb{N}$ that reverses a bit string, i.e., given a number n in unary $\mathrm{rev}(b_k \cdots b_0, n :) = b_0 b_1 \cdots b_{k-n}$.

Even though we are using unary numbers in the recursion, updating the work tape is simpler to describe if the work tape is in binary. We therefore introduce functions to convert between binary and unary notation. This involves computing the logarithm which I have failed to represent in BC^-.

Lemma 4. Let m be an integer in unary notation. Then there is a BC_ε^--function $\log(m :) = \lfloor \log_2 m \rfloor + 1$ when $m \geq 0$ and $\log(0 :) = 0$.

Proof. We implement log as follows:

$$\log(m :) = \begin{cases} 0 & \text{when } m = 0 \\ 1 + \log(m \div 2 :) & \text{when } m > 0 \end{cases}$$

which has the following representation as a BC_ε^- program:

$$\log(m :) = \mathtt{rec}(0,0,0,\mathtt{s}_1 \circ \langle : \pi_2^{1,1} \rangle, \mathtt{div} \circ \langle \pi_1^{1,0}, 2_1 : \rangle) \ . \qquad \Box$$

It should be noted how the course-of-value recursion allows us to recurse to $m \div 2$.

In converting from binary to unary we need the powers of 2. It is generally not possible to do exponentation in BC_ε^- as it would break the bound in Lemma 1. We can however test whether a number is a power and two. By searching all the numbers between $0, \ldots, m$ we find the largest power of 2 smaller than m. This is captured in the following lemma:

Lemma 5. Let $m, n \in \mathbb{N}$ be integers coded in unary representation. The following functions are representable in BC_ε^-: (1) $\mathrm{power}?(m, n :) = 1$ if, and only if, m is a power of n. (2) $\mathrm{largest\_power}(m, n :) = \max(\{n^i \leq m \mid i \in \mathbb{N}\} \cup \{0\})$.

We now have the tools to code the functions converting between the two representations of integers. When converting from binary to unary, the output might grow exponentially. This obviously violates the bound in Lemma 1 and we therefore have to provide an extra argument limiting the size.

Proposition 4.

(1) The function $\mathrm{unary2bin} : \mathbb{N}_1 \to \mathbb{N}_2$ is representable in BC_ε^-.
(2) Let $\mathrm{bin2unary}(m, n :)$ be the unary representation of m provided that $m \leq n$. The function $\mathrm{bin2unary} : \mathbb{N}_2 \times \mathbb{N}_1 \to \mathbb{N}_1$ is representable in BC_ε^-.

Proof. As for turning a number in unary into binary we simply use the standard algorithm for finding the representation of number in a given radix. The only problem is that the straightforward implementation provides the bits in the wrong order. Consequently, we first convert the number and then reverse it.

As for bin2unary, we use largest_power to find the highest power of 2 so we can find the most significant bit to query for:

$$\text{bin2unary}(m, n :) = \text{bin2unary}'(\text{largest\_power}(n, 2 :), m :)$$

$$\text{bin2unary}'(p, m :) = \begin{cases} 0 & \text{when } p = 0 \\ \text{plus}(\text{c}(: \text{bit}(\log(p :) - 1 : m), p, 0) : & \text{when } p = p' + 1 \\ \quad \text{bin2unary}'(p \div 2, m :) \end{cases}$$

Correctness follows by induction on m. □

Proposition 5. The function T given in Fig. 1 is representable in BC_ε^-.

Proof. Except for the step functions S, W, I, J, and O, we have seen how to represent the functions in Fig. 1 in BC_ε^-. We have also seen how to turn the multivariable recursion into recursion over one variable.

As for the functions S, W, I, J, and O, the conditions, e.g., "$I_s = \text{right}_I$" can all statically be turned into comparisons on the numerical value of s using $<?$. In W we exploit that the number of configurations of the work tape is $2^{c \cdot \log_2 n} = n^c$. We augment W with a fourth argument, the input tape x. Taking w' to be the updated work tape $\text{set}_b(j, \text{unary2bin}(w :) :)$, we can therefore compute its unary representation as

$$\overbrace{\text{bin2unary}(w', n^c :) = \text{bin2unary}(w', \text{mult}(|x|, \text{mult}(|x|, \cdots \text{mult}(|x|, |x| :) :) :) :)}^{c - 1 \text{ mults}}$$

$$= \text{bin2unary} \circ \langle \text{set}_b \circ \langle \pi_2^{4,0}, \text{unary2bin} \circ \langle \pi_1^{4,0} : \rangle \rangle,$$

$$\text{mult} \circ \langle \pi_4^{4,0}, \cdots \text{mult} \circ \langle \pi_4^{4,0}, \pi_4^{4,0} \rangle \rangle \rangle$$

We obtain T through affine composition. □

We conclude with the following corrolary:

Corollary 1. For any LF Turing Machine T, there is BC_ε^- function $f_T : \mathbb{N}^{1,0} \to \mathbb{N}$ computing the same function: T on input x produces the output tape y if, and only if, $f_T(x :) = 1y$.

The function f_T is constructible in time $O(S^2)$ and space $O(\log S)$ whereas the input can be transduced in time $O(|x|)$ and space $O(1)$.

It is not an issue that we use logarithmic space to compile between the Turing machine and BC_ε^- as it is the logarithmic in the size of the program.

Proof. The function f_T is constructed immediately as $\text{T}(S \cdot |x|^{c+2}, 0, 0, 0, 0, x :)$.

Precise time and space bounds of course depend on how the BC_ε^- are represented; we consider only outputting their textual representation. An inspection of the construction in the proof shows that S, W, I, and J can be output with one scan over the program. For each instruction we need to output the unary representation of the instruction number. (In the case of S we might also need to output the unary representation of the label.) This can be done in time $O(S^2)$. The $O(\log S)$ space uses arises from keeping track of the instruction.

4   LF **Soundness**

Having shown that BC_ε^- is LF complete, we continue to show that it is also
LF sound. We reuse an unpublished construction by Ong and Mairson. The
construction depends on two facts:

(1) The output and all intermediate values are bound by Lemma 1.[4] We therefore
    need only a counter of size $O(\log|\boldsymbol{x};\boldsymbol{y}|)$ to iterate over the bits of the output.
(2) One bit of the output can be produced storing only one bit of the safe
    arguments and a constant number of bits from the normal arguments. This
    is straightforward except for the case of safe affine recursion.

    For safe affine recursion we use computational amnesia and evaluate the
    recursion without storing the call stack until we can produce a bit at some re-
    cursion level. We cache the bit and—as there is no stack of return addresses—
    restart the recursion from the top. With a cached bit we can produce a bit
    at higher level. Repeating this, we can eventually produce the bit a recursion
    depth 0. We illustrate this with the parity function $P = \mathtt{rec}(g, h_0, h_1)$:

$$g(:) = 0 \qquad h_0(x:r) = \mathtt{co}\langle\, : r, 1, 0\rangle \qquad h_1(x:r) = \mathtt{co}\langle\, : r, 0, 1\rangle.$$

A standard evaluation of $P(\mathtt{10111} :)$ would result in the following unwinding

$$P(\mathtt{10111} :) = h_1(\mathtt{1011} : h_1(\mathtt{101} : h_1(\mathtt{10} : h_0(\mathtt{1} : h_1(\varepsilon : 0))))).$$

With the computational amnesia we go through

$$P(\mathtt{10111} :), P(\mathtt{1011} :), P(\mathtt{101} :), P(\mathtt{10} :), P(\mathtt{1} :), P(\varepsilon :) = 0.$$

We remember the result (and its recursion depth, 5) and restart the computation of $P(\mathtt{10111} :)$. We now only need to go through the calls

$$P(\mathtt{10111} :), P(\mathtt{1011} :), P(\mathtt{101} :), P(\mathtt{10} :), P(\mathtt{1} :) = h_1(\varepsilon : P(\varepsilon :)) = h_1(\varepsilon : 0) = 1$$

as we can look up the stored value of $P(\varepsilon :)$. We remember that the value 1
was found at recursion depth 4. We restart the computation and keep repeating until we eventually find $P(\mathtt{10111} :) = 0$.

The affinity of BC_ε^- is crucial for the correctness of this approach: two recursive calls would require two bits from the first level, 4 from the second etc. This
is illustrated by the following function which is directly representable in B, but
not in BC_ε^-:

$$f(0, m :) = m \qquad f(ni, m :) = \mathtt{c}(: f(n, m :), \mathtt{p}(f(n, m :)), \mathtt{p}(\mathtt{p}(f(n, m :)))).$$

After determining the conditional using computational amnesia, the wrong
bit for $f(n, m :)$ is cached in either branch. This must be queried through computational amnesia, but when this succeeds the cache no longer holds bit 0
controlling the conditional.

---

[4] Bellantoni and Cook [2, Lemma 4.1] only state the inequality as a bound on the
output. As their proof is compositional, it is also a bound on the intermediate values.

```
type bit = int option
type input = int -> bit
type program-m-n = input -> ··· -> input -> int -> bit
                   ‾‾‾‾‾‾‾‾‾‾‾‾‾‾‾‾‾‾‾‾‾‾‾‾
                           m + n times
fun zero (bt : int) = NONE
fun succ0 (y1 : input) (bt : int) =
    if bt = 0 then SOME 0 else y1 (bt - 1))
fun succ1 (y1 : input) (bt : int) =
    if bt = 0 then SOME 1 else y1 (bt - 1))
fun pred (y1 : input) (bt : int) = y1 (bt + 1)
fun cond (y1 : input) (y2 : input) (y3 : input) (bt : int) =
    let fun boolFromBit NONE = false
          | boolFromBit (SOME b) = (b = 1)
    in if boolFromBit (y1 0) then y2 bt else y3 bt
    end
(* Translation of π_j^{m,n}; first when j≤m and then when m > j *)
fun proj-m-n-j (x1 : input) ... (xm : input)
               (y1 : input) ... (yn : input) (bt : int) = xj bt
fun proj-m-n-j (x1 : input) ... (xm : input)
               (y1 : input) ... (yn : input) (bt : int) = y(j − m) bt
```

Fig. 2. Translations of each of the base constructors into a SML function

In this section we detail idea outlined above and prove that it stays within LF. The core is to show that we in LF can find any given bit of the output by only storing a fixed number of bits of the inputs to each subexpression. We do this by translating each BC_ε^--expression into an SML-expression that finds any given bit of the output by querying individual bits of the input.

The translation of the base constructors is in Fig. 2. A function with m normal arguments and n safe arguments gives a function of type program-m-n. The base constructors take the normal and safe arguments and the index of the bit requested. They either return the bit or marks that the bit is non-existing; this is caught in the type bit. The arguments are given as second-order functions that returns a bit of the input upon request. The translation of safe affine composition is given in Fig. 3 and is also straightforward.

Finally, the translation of safe affine course-of-value recursion is given in Fig. 4. The function saferec starts computing the requested bit at depth 0. If there is a request for a bit from the recursive call, recursiveCall updates the goal and restarts the computation by raising the exception Restart$n$ (where n is a unique identifier). When a goal bit eventually has been computed—either because the base case was reached or because the recursive call was cached—the cache kept in result is updated. The function saferec keeps restarting the search from depth 0 until it successfully computes the bit at depth 0. Finally, we notice that we can find the length of the displacement function by simply querying for bits 0, 1, 2, etc. until the index reaches a non-existing bit.

```
fun comp (f : program-M-N)
         (g1 : program-m-0) ⋯ (gM : program-m-0)
         (h1 : program-m-n₁) ⋯ (hN : program-m-nN)
         (x1 : input) ⋯ (xm : input)
         (y1 : input) ⋯ (yn : input) (bt : int) =
    let fun X1 bt = g1 x1 ... xm bt
        ⋮
        fun XM bt = gM x1 ... xm bt
        fun Y1 bt = h1 x1 ... xm yi₁,₁ ... yi₁,ₗ₁ bt
        ⋮
        fun YN bt = hN x1 ... xm yiN,1 ... yiN,ₗN bt
    in f X1 ... XM Y1 ... YN bt
    end
```

Fig. 3. Translation of safe affine composition into an SML function. The division of the variables $y1, \ldots, yn$ between the functions $h1, \ldots, hN$ computing safe arguments is given by the vectors of indices $i_1, \ldots, i_N$. They satisfy the relation $\{i_{1,1}, \ldots, i_{1,l_1}, i_{2,1}, \ldots, i_{N-1,l_{N-1}}, i_{N,1}, \ldots, i_{L,l_N}\} \subseteq \{1, \ldots, n\}$ and that there is at most one $i_{j,j'}$ for any given number in $\{1, \ldots, n\}$

Definition 2. Let f be a function of BC_ε^- with m normal and n safe arguments. The ML function $\lceil f \rceil$ of type program-m-n is defined inductively based on Figs. 2–4: $\lceil 0 \rceil = $ zero, $\lceil s_b \rceil = $ succb, $\lceil p \rceil = $ pred, $\lceil c \rceil = $ cond, $\lceil \pi_j^{m,n} \rceil = $ proj-m-n-j, $\lceil rec(g, h_0, \delta_0, h_1, \delta_1) \rceil = $ saferec $\lceil g \rceil$ $\lceil h_0 \rceil$ $\lceil \delta_0 \rceil$ $\lceil h_1 \rceil$ $\lceil \delta_1 \rceil$, and $\lceil f \circ \langle g_1, \ldots, g_M : h_1, \ldots, h_N \rangle \rceil = $ comp $\lceil g_1 \rceil$ $\cdots$ $\lceil g_M \rceil$ $\lceil h_1 \rceil$ $\cdots$ $\lceil h_N \rceil$.

In the following we establish correctness through the following facts:

- The functions are tail recursive. Consequently there is a fixed maximal depth of the stack for any program.
- Each stack entry is representable in logarithmic space on the inputs.
- The function succeeds and returns the correct bit provided that the input functions are correct and succeed without raising an exception Restart$n$.

We conclude from the first two facts that the program is LF. From the last fact we conclude that the algorithm is correct.

Notation 3. We adapt the convention of Barendregt [1] and use $\equiv$ for the syntactic equivalence of functions.

We assign an abstraction label a to each function abstraction; we write fn^a x => e. We refer to abstraction labels as pairs of the function name and the parameter, e.g., succ0 above has two abstraction labels: $\langle$succ0, y1$\rangle$ and $\langle$succ0, bit$\rangle$.

We recall that when evaluating the program every function applied—even when it is the result of evaluating an expression—is constructed by one of the abstraction occurrences fn^a x => e in the program.

```
exception Restartn
val NORESULT = { depth = ~1, res = NONE, bt=~1 }

fun saferec (g : program-(m − 1)-n)
            (h0 : program-m-1) (d0 : program-m-0)
            (h1 : program-m-1) (d1 : program-m-0)
            (x1 : input) ... (xm : input)
            (y1 : input) ... (yn : input) (bt : int) =
    let val result = ref NORESULT
        val goal = ref ({ bt=bt, depth=0 })
        fun loop1 body = if body () then () else loop1 body
        fun loop2 body = if body () then () else loop2 body
        fun findLength (z : input) =
            let fun search i = if z i <> NONE then search (i + 1) else i
            in search 0
            end
        fun x' (bt : int) = x1 (1 + bt + #depth (!goal))
        fun recursiveCall (d : program-m-0) (bt : int) =
            let val delta = 1 + findLength (d x' x2 ... xm)
            in if #depth (!goal) + delta = #depth (!result)
                    andalso #bt (!result) = bt
               then #res (!result)
               else
                    goal := { bt=bt, depth = #depth (!goal) + delta };
                    raise Restartn
            end
    in
    ( loop1 (fn () =>    (* Loops until we have the bit at depth 0 *)
      ( goal := { bt=bt, depth=0 };
        loop2 (fn () => (* Loops while the computation is restarted *)
          let val res =
            case x1 (#depth (!goal)) of
              NONE => g x2 ... xm y1 ... yn (#bt (!goal))
            | SOME b =>
              let val (h, d) = if b=0 then (h0,d0) else (h1,d1)
              in h x' x2 ... xm (recursiveCall d) (#bt (!goal))
              end
          in ( result := { depth = #depth (!goal),
                           res = res,
                           bt = #bt (!goal) };
               true )
          end handle Restartn => false
        0 = #depth (!result) ));
      #res (!result))
    end
```

Fig. 4. Translation of safe affine recursion

We follow Jones [9] in defining tail recursion slightly more liberal than usual: the call stack can grow, but there are never two stack entries for the same abstraction.

Definition 3 (Tail Recursion).

(1) An occurrence of expression e in e_0 is in tail position of e_0 if (a) $e_0 \equiv e$, (b) $e_0 \equiv$ if e_1 then e_2 else e_3 and e is in tail position of e_2 or e_3, (c) $e_0 \equiv$ case e_0' of p_1 => e_1 $\cdots$ p_l => e_l and e is in tail position of e_i for some $i = 1, \ldots, l$. (d) $e_0 = e_1; \ldots; e_l$ and e is in tail position of e_l. (e) $e_0 =$ let val $v_1 = e_1$ $\cdots$ val $v_l = e_l$ in e_{l+1} end and e is in tail position of e_{l+1}.
(2) An expression e is tail recursive if there is a partial order $\succeq$ on e's abstraction labels such that: For every abstraction $\texttt{fn}^{a_0}$ x => e_0 in e, and every abstraction $\texttt{fn}^{a_1}$ x => e_1' that can result from evaluating the function part e_1 of any application e_1 e_2 occurring in e_0, we have either (a) $a_0 \succ a_1$ or (b) $a_0 = a_1$ and the application is in tail position.

The partial order in the above definition ensures that the program can be evaluated without having more than one entry per abstraction on the call stack. Rather than a fully formal proof based on the formal definition of ML [12], we rely on an informal understanding of ML evaluation. Furthermore, we make the following idealized assumptions: (1) Arithmetic can be done with arbitrary precision. In particular none of the functions, +, -, *, =, and <>, raise any exceptions. (2) The memory is arbitrarily large. In particular, the function $\texttt{ref}$ will never raise an exception. (3) The basic functions are implemented tail recursively, i.e, +, -, *, =, <>,#,!, and $\texttt{ref}$ are all tail recursive.

We can now establish that the functions used in the construction fulfill the conditions for tail recursion.

Proposition 6. Let $F \in \mathbb{N}^{m,n}$ be a function of BC_ε^-. Its encoding into an SM L expression is $\lceil F \rceil \equiv$ $\texttt{fn}^{a_1}$ inp1 => $\cdots$ => $\texttt{fn}^{a_n}$ inp$n$ => $\texttt{fn}^{a_{n=1}}$ bt => e of type program-m-n. W e consider an application P = $\lceil F \rceil$ exp1 $\cdots$ exp$l$ where $l = m + n$. Each of the argument expressions exp$i$ can evaluate to abstractions with abstraction labels in the set A_i. Furthermore, none of the abstraction labels in $A_1 \cup \cdots \cup A_l$ occurs in P. There exists a partial order $\succeq$ on the abstraction labels with the following properties:

(1) Consider any abstraction $\texttt{fn}^{a'}$ x => e' in P and any application e_1' e_2' occurring in e'. For any abstraction $\texttt{fn}^{a_1'}$ x => e_1'' that e_1' can evaluate to, we have either (a) $a' \succ a_1'$ or (b) $a' = a_1'$ and the application is in tail position.
(2) There is an abstraction label $\top_\succeq$ that is the successor of all other abstraction labels that occur in $\lceil F \rceil$ and $A_1 \cup \cdots \cup A_l$.
(3) It holds that $a_1 \succ \cdots \succ a_{l+1}$.
(4) None of the elements $a_i' \in A_i$ for $1 \leq i \leq l$ has a predecessor in $\succeq$.

Proof. We use induction on the structure of F inspecting each case. $\square$

Proposition 7. Given any BC_ε^--function $F \in \mathbb{N}^{M,N}$, its SML-encoding $\lceil F \rceil$ can be evaluated in logarithmic space, i.e., for any $x_1, \ldots, x_M, y_1, \ldots, y_N \in \mathbb{N}$ we can compute $F(x_1, \ldots, x_M : y_1, \ldots, y_N)$ using only logarithmic workspace.

Proof. This is accomplished by iteratively (and therefore tail recursively) query $\lceil F \rceil$ bit by bit. Using Prop. 6 the full program is tail recursive.   □

It is not hard to realize the correctness of the functions zero, succ0, succ1, pred, cond, proj-m-n-j, and comp. We omit the gory details of the correctness proof for saferec (it can be found in the full version) as the intuition has been presented above. The proof relies on establishing that (1) within a call to saferec, the calls to recursiveCall correspond to the recursive calls done in a standard evaluator, and (2) every time loop2 is started, it takes fewer loops until the cached bit is found.

We notice that the encoding can be produced by scanning over the BC_ε^--expression keeping a pointer on where we are in the expression and a counter on the number of safe recursions. We conclude the following.

Theorem 1. For any function definable in BC_ε^-, there is a Turing Machine evaluating the function in LF. The Turing Machine can be constructed from the function expression in logarithmic space in the size of the BC_ε^--expression.

5   Conclusion and Future Work

We have presented the first implicit characterization of the LF-computable functions. The characterization is appealing because it with two simple measures, affinity and a division into safe and normal arguments, obtains a well-known complexity class. When compared to Bellantoni and Cook's B it highlights linearity as a potential distinction between LF and PF.

Existing work on automatic analysis of resource usage, only derives pure polynomial bounds. It is likely that BC_ε^- could serve as a first step toward a more realistic analysis. A first step would be to allow the conditional to share arguments between the branches. This could be achieved through a resource conscious type system in the style of Hofmann [6] with an additive type operator.

Another line of research is to continue the investigation of the connection to linear logic. A first question is whether there is a direct encoding into light linear logic [4] of safe affine course-of-value recursion. This would suggest a lighter than light fragment of linear logic corresponding to logarithmic space.

Acknowledgments

I am indebted to my advisor Harry Mairson for his encouragement and inspiration, as well as his willingness to comment on all stages of the work. I deeply appreciate the very detailed comments I received from Olivier Danvy and Steve Homer. I thank Alan Bawden, Jakob Grue Simonsen, Assaf Kfoury, and Sebastian Skalberg for the general support and Peter Clote, Neil Jones, Steven Lindell, and Stan Wainer for persistently and patiently answering my questions on LF.

References

[1] H. P. Barendregt. *The Lambda Calculus: Its Syntax and Semantics*. North-Holland, revised edition, 1984.

[2] S. Bellantoni and S. A. Cook. A new recursion-theoretic characterization of the polytime functions. *Computational Complexity*, 2:97–110, 1992.

[3] S. J. Bellantoni. *Predicative Recursion and Computational Complexity*. Ph.D. thesis, University of Toronto, Sept. 30 1992.

[4] J.-Y. Girard. Light linear logic. *Inform. & Comput.*, 143:175–204, 1998.

[5] A. Goerdt. Characterizing complexity classes by higher type primitive recursive definitions. *Theoret. Comput. Sci.*, 100(1):45–66, June 1992.

[6] M. Hofmann. Linear type and non-size-increasing polynomial time computation. In *Proc. 14th Ann. IEEE Symp. Logic in Comput. Sci.*, July 1999.

[7] *Proc. Workshop on Implicit Computational Complexity*, July 2002.

[8] N. Immerman. Languages that capture complexity classes. *SIAM Journal of Computing*, 16(4):760–778, Aug. 1987.

[9] N. D. Jones. The expressive power of higher-order types, or life without CONS. *J. Funct. Programming*, 11(1):55–94, Jan. 2001.

[10] A. J. Kfoury, H. G. Mairson, F. A. Turbak, and J. B. Wells. Relating typability and expressibility in finite-rank intersection type systems. In *Proc. 1999 Int'l Conf. Functional Programming*, pp. 90–101. ACM Press, 1999.

[11] L. Kristiansen. New recursion-theoretic characterizations of well-knwon complexity classes. In ICC '02 [7].

[12] R. Milner, M. Tofte, R. Harper, and D. B. MacQueen. *The Definition of Standard ML (Revised)*. MIT Press, 1997.

[13] P. Møller Neergaard. An example SML implemenation of a LOGSPACE linear BC evaluator, 2003–2004.

[14] P. Møller Neergaard. *Complexity Aspects of Programming Language Design—From Logspace to Elementary Time via Proofnets and Intersection Types*. Ph.D. thesis, Brandeis University, Oct. 2004.

[15] P. Møller Neergaard and H. G. Mairson. Types, potency, and impotency: Why nonlinearity and amnesia make a type system work. In *Proc. 9th Int'l Conf. Functional Programming*. ACM Press, Sept. 2004.

[16] A. S. Murawski and C.-H. L. Ong. Can safe recursion be interpreted in light logic? In *2nd International Workshop on Implicit Computational Complexity*, June 2000.

[17] C. H. Papadimitriou. *Computatational Complexity*. Addison-Wesley, Reading, Mass., 1994.

[18] L. C. Paulson. *ML for the Working Programmer (2nd ed.)*. Cambridge University Press, 1996.

[19] N. Pippenger. Pure versus impure lisp. In *Conf. Rec. POPL '96: 23rd ACM Symp. Princ. of Prog. Langs.*, pp. 104–109, 1996.

[20] P. J. Voda. Two simple intrinsic characterizations of main complexity classes. In ICC '02 [7].

Build, Augment and Destroy, Universally

Neil Ghani[1], Tarmo Uustalu[2], and Varmo Vene[3]

[1] Dept. of Math. and Comp. Sci., University of Leicester,
University Road, Leicester, LE1 7RH
N.Ghani@mcs.le.ac.uk

[2] Institute of Cybernetics, Tallinn Univ. of Technology,
Akadeemia tee 21, EE-12618 Tallinn, Estonia
tarmo@cs.ioc.ee

[3] Dept. of Computer Science, University of Tartu,
Liivi 2, EE-50409 Tartu, Estonia
varmo@cs.ut.ee

Abstract. We give a semantic footing to the FOLD/BUILD syntax of programming with inductive types, covering shortcut deforestation, based on a universal property. Specifically, we give a semantics for inductive types based on limits of algebra structure forgetting functors and show that it is equivalent to the usual initial algebra semantics. We also give a similar semantic account of the AUGMENT generalization of BUILD and of the UNFOLD/DESTROY syntax of coinductive types.

1 Introduction

The beauty of the IN/FOLD and OUT/UNFOLD syntax for programming with inductive and coinductive types [13, 21] is thanks to the fact that it is based directly on the semantic interpretation of such types as initial algebras and final coalgebras. Apart from the clarity provided by this close match between syntax and semantics, there are practical benefits for the programmer. For example, in the case of inductive types, (i) the constructors IN form the structure map of the initial algebra which, as an isomorphism, supports pattern matching in function definitions; (ii) the mediating algebra map to any other algebra gives rise to a canonical recursion combinator usually called FOLD to aid structured programming; (iii) β-equality (also called computational rules) is derived from the fact that the mediating map is an algebra map; and (iv) η-equality and permutative equality (also called extensionality rules), which provide the correctness for program transformations such as FOLD fusion, are derived from the uniqueness of the mediating map. In essence, all the fundamental properties of an inductive type can be derived systematically from its semantics as an initial algebra. The same can be said about coinductive types and their final coalgebra semantics.

Recently there has been a significant amount of work starting with Gill et al.'s [10] which proposes an alternative approach to programming with inductive types based on using the FOLD-combinator in interaction with a new

W.-N. Chin (Ed.): APLAS 2004, LNCS 3302, pp. 327–347, 2004.
© Springer-Verlag Berlin Heidelberg 2004

constructor called BUILD. This is related to deforestation [35] or semantics-preserving program transformation to eliminate intermediate datastructures. Use of intermediate datastructures should in principle be encouraged in functional programming as it gives well-structured programs, but the resulting programs are also inefficient, thus the need for automated deforestation. There exist several deforestation methods, but probably the most successful is Gill's shortcut deforestation where removal of intermediate datastructures is achieved by repeated application of very simple rewrite rules, but which requires that programming with inductive intermediate datastructures is done in terms FOLD and BUILD.

Despite the proliferation of this interesting work described, the semantic foundations of the FOLD/BUILD paradigm are not so clear. Thus, for example, various program transformations have to be derived and justified in a relatively ad-hoc manner. We would rather prefer to be able to automatically derive the essential properties of the FOLD/BUILD style of programming from similar principles to the initial algebra semantics underpinning the IN/FOLD style of programming.

This paper achieves this. Our key insight is that initial algebras are an instance of a more general concept of *universal properties* which are pervasive throughout programming language semantics. Thus we give a characterization of initial algebras via an alternative universal property from which the syntax and equational properties of the FOLD/BUILD paradigm arise in the manner described above. The suitable universal property turns out to be rather simple and, moreover, intuitive. It is that of being the limit of a functor forgetting algebra structure or, intuitively, the largest object with a fuseable fold-like operation.

The benefits of our approach are not just to provide semantic clarity by placing the FOLD/BUILD-style of programming on the same universal footing that other programming language constructions have. Indeed, as with all good semantics, we use our universal characterization of FOLD/BUILD to derive a number of other concrete deliverables. Thus, the key contributions of this paper are:

- We give a categorical foundation to the FOLD/BUILD approach to inductive types which replaces the more ad-hoc foundations in the literature with universal constructions. This extracts the properties that BUILD must have in order validate shortcut deforestation and provides a categorical justification to the encoding of inductive types using type quantification.
- Implicit in this is a proof of the equi-expressiveness of the FOLD/BUILD syntax and the usual IN/FOLD syntax. In particular, the FOLD/BUILD constructions suffice to define the IN/FOLD syntax validating all IN/FOLD axioms.
- The flexibility of this semantic approach is demonstrated by the ease with which we extend it to cover the FOLD/AUGMENT fusion of Gill [11] and the UNFOLD/DESTROY paradigm of programming with coinductive types. (As a matter of fact, helped by the transparency of the framework, we have found that a useful AUGMENT combinator is definable not only for free algebras, but for a far more wide class of parameterized inductive types. For space reasons, we will publish that result separately elsewhere, only giving some hints here.)

The paper, appealing both to functional programmers and semanticists, is organized as follows: Sect. 2 begins by a demonstration of how the classical infrastructure for programming and reasoning with inductive types arises from the initial algebra semantics. It continues with an exposition of our alternative and equivalent semantics where the BUILD combinator is a primitive construction and FOLD/BUILD fusion is axiomatic. This alternative semantics is based on a kind of cones that from the functional programming perspective are polymorphic functions required to meet a non-trivial coherence condition; we conclude the section by showing that it is a condition of strong dinaturality. In Sect. 3, we give a justification of Gill's AUGMENT generalization of BUILD in our framework. Sect. 4 is an exposition of the dual development for the semantics of coinductive types. In Sect. 5, we give a condensed orientation about relating work and, in Sect. 6, we conclude, pointing out a number of directions for future work.

From the reader, we assume only the most basic definitions from category theory, in particular those of category, functor and natural transformations. Familiarity with limits and colimits will be helpful, but they are defined in the text. We work with a base category about which we make no or very mild assumptions, but the concrete examples to keep in mind are categories most relevant for programming semantics, like **Set** and **CPO**. Throughout the text, we use Haskell for examples, but this is purely illustrative; we are not discussing the semantics of Haskell or any particular language in this paper.

2   Inductive Types and Build

2.1   Inductive Types as Initial Algebras

The customary structured approach to list programming equips the type [a] of lists over a with constructors [] and (:) (for nil and cons) and a destructor foldr. In Haskell, this is accomplished as follows:

```
data [a] = [] | a : [a]

foldr :: (a -> x -> x) -> x -> [a] -> x
foldr c n [] = n
foldr c n (a : as) = c a (foldr c n as)
```

The syntax thus outlined derives directly from the categorical semantics of lists over type A as a chosen initial algebra of the functor $1 + A \times -$.

Algebras and the property of an algebra being initial are defined as follows:

Definition 1 ((Initial) Algebra). *Let $\mathcal{C}$ be a category and $F : \mathcal{C} \to \mathcal{C}$ be a functor. An F-algebra is an object X in $\mathcal{C}$ together with a map $\varphi : FX \to X$ in $\mathcal{C}$. An F-algebra map $(X, \varphi) \to (Y, \psi)$ is a map $f : X \to Y$ such that $f \circ \varphi = \psi \circ Ff$. An initial F-algebra is an initial object in the category F-**alg** of F-algebras, i.e., an F-algebra with a unique map from it to any F-algebra.*

We agree to denote a chosen initial F-algebra by $(\mu F, \mathsf{in}_F)$, and the unique map from it to an F-algebra (X, φ) by $\mathsf{fold}_{F,X}\varphi$.

By the definition, an algebra for the functor $1 + A \times -$ is an object X and a map $\varphi : 1 + A \times X \to X$. The latter is of course equivalent to a pair of maps $\varphi_0 : 1 \to X$ and $\varphi_1 : A \times X \to X$ giving interpretations of [] and (:). Maps from an algebra (X, φ) to an algebra (Y, ψ) are just maps from X to Y which preserve the interpretations of [] and (:) in the algebras. This is of course exactly what a *model* and *model homomorphism* are taken to be in universal algebra. We are interested in a specific algebra, namely the one where [] is interpreted as nil and (:) as the cons operation (of the given implementation of lists). This means that lists over A are really modelled by an *initial algebra* of $1 + A \times -$.

Note how characterizing lists as a chosen initial algebra provides all the syntax and equalities we need to program and reason with: i) the structure map of the initial algebra provides the constructors nil and cons which, taken together, form an isomorphism, supporting pattern matching:

$$\mathsf{in}_F : F(\mu F) \to \mu F$$

ii) the mediating map provides the FOLD-combinator `foldr`:

$$\frac{(X, \varphi) \in F\text{-}\mathbf{alg}}{\mathsf{fold}_{F,X}\varphi : \mu F \to X}$$

iii) that the FOLD combinator constructs an algebra map gives the equation

$$\frac{(X, \varphi) \in F\text{-}\mathbf{alg}}{\mathsf{fold}_{F,X}\varphi \circ \mathsf{in}_F = \varphi \circ F\mathsf{fold}_{F,X}\varphi}$$

which defines the computational rules of β-equality or FOLD cancellation; and iv) the uniqueness of the mediating map provides the following extensionality rules

$$\mathsf{fold}_{F,F(\mu F)}\mathsf{in}_F = \mathsf{id}_{\mu F} \qquad \frac{f : (X, \varphi) \to (Y, \psi) \in F\text{-}\mathbf{alg}}{f \circ \mathsf{fold}_{F,X}\varphi = \mathsf{fold}_{F,Y}\psi}$$

The first rule is often taken to be η-equality "lite" while the second rule of permutative conversion provides the soundness of FOLD fusion. As with all initial objects, initial algebras are defined up to isomorphism, which means, e.g., that any initial algebra of $1 + A \times -$ will be isomorphic to the type of lists over A. Thus the initial algebra semantics defines our list type up to isomorphism, which really means that we can program with it independently of how it is implemented.

2.2   Universal Constructions, Limits

That so much of the infrastructure to program with lists and inductive types in general is explained by the single concept of an initial algebra is very elegant. Initial algebras are instances of the more general concept of universal constructions which arise in numerous other places in the semantics of programming languages. We will not give the definition of a universal construction here; this can be found in any standard reference, such as [20]. Informally, a universal property states that, for some objects and maps which satisfy some properties, there is a unique map (called the mediating map) between this structure and any other structure satisfying the same properties. Universal properties define structures up to isomorphism. Other examples are, e.g., (categorical) products, which model product types, and general limits, which we will use in this paper.

Products are an instructive familiar example where again the universal property provides all the information we need to program and reason with product types. The fact that the product (final span) is a span gives the projections while pairing arises as the mediating map from any other span. The fact that pairing is a map of spans is precisely β-equality while the uniqueness of the mediating map is the usual η-equality. We can see that all universal properties have an implicit syntax with associated computational and extensionality rules.

We will shortly need the concept of a limit and record here the definition.

Definition 2 (Limit). *A cone for a functor $J : \mathcal{C} \to \mathcal{D}$ is a pair (C, γ) consisting of an object C in $\mathcal{D}$ and, for each object X in $\mathcal{C}$, a map $\gamma_X : C \to JX$ in $\mathcal{D}$ such that, for every map $f : X \to Y$ in $\mathcal{C}$, we have $Jf \circ \gamma_X = \gamma_Y$. A map of cones $(C, \gamma) \to (D, \delta)$ is a map $h : C \to D$ in $\mathcal{D}$ such that, for each object X in $\mathcal{C}$, we have $\delta_X \circ h = \gamma_X$. A limit of J is a final object in the category J-**cone** of J-cones.*

2.3   Building Build

The initial algebra semantics based syntax for inductive types is elegant and useful in many ways, but the structure it imposes on programs leads often to inefficiency.

Consider the task of programming the sum of the squares of a list of integers. The following is a modular and well-structured program:

```
sumSq m = sum (map square [1..m])
```

Unfortunately, it uses two intermediate datastructures, which of course implies inefficiency. The methodology of shortcut deforestation [10] proposes reprogramming summation, mapping and list generation in terms of foldr and a new combinator build as follows:

```
build :: (forall x. (a -> x -> x) -> x -> x) -> [a]
build theta = theta (:) []

sum = foldr (+) 0
map f xs = build (\ c n -> foldr (\ x ys -> f x 'c' ys) n xs)
upto i1 i2 = build (\ c n -> upto' c n i1 i2)
upto' c n i1 i2 = if i1 > i2 then n else i1 'c' upto' c n (i1 + 1) i2
```

The point of build is to abstract over the constructor occurrences in a list to provide foldr with direct access to their positions which motivates the foldr/build fusion rule

```
foldr c n (build theta) == theta c n
```

Applying this rewrite rule twice, we get a monolithic (and thus not so programmer-friendly) but efficient version:

```
sum . map square
== \ xs -> foldr (+) 0
            (build (\ c n -> foldr (\ x ys -> square x 'c' ys) n xs))
== foldr (\ x ys -> square x + ys) 0

foldr (\ x ys -> square x + ys) 0 (upto 1 m)
== foldr (\ x ys -> square x + ys) 0 (build (\ c n -> upto' c n 1 m))
== upto' (\ x ys -> square x + ys) 0 1 m

sumSq m = sumSq' 1 m
sumSq' i1 i2 = if i1 > i2 then 0 else square i1 + sumSq' (i1 + 1) i2
```

This paper explains shortcut deforestation or FOLD/BUILD fusion via an alternative semantics of inductive types which matches the FOLD/BUILD rather than the IN/FOLD syntax but is still equivalent to the initial algebra semantics.

Given a category $\mathcal{C}$ and functor $F : \mathcal{C} \to \mathcal{C}$, let us write $U_F : F\text{-alg} \to \mathcal{C}$ for the functor forgetting F-algebra structure, i.e., the functor which maps an algebra (X, φ) to X and an F-algebra map $f : (X, \varphi) \to (Y, \psi)$ to $f : X \to Y$.

Our alternative semantics for the inductive type given by a functor F will be the limit of U_F. Let us spell out what U_F-cones are and what a U_F-limit is. By Definition 2, a U_F-cone is an object C in $\mathcal{C}$ and, for any F-algebra (X, φ), a map $\Theta_X\varphi : C \to X$ in $\mathcal{C}$, such that (*) for any F-algebra map $f : (X, \varphi) \to (Y, \psi)$, we have $f \circ \Theta_X\varphi = \Theta_Y\psi$. A U_F-cone map $h : (C, \Theta) \to (D, \Xi)$ is a map $h : C \to D$ in $\mathcal{C}$ such that, for any F-algebra (X, φ), we have $\Xi_X\varphi \circ h = \Theta_X\varphi$. A U_F-limit is a U_F-cone to which there is a unique map from any other U_F-cone. Let us write $(\mu^* F, \text{fold}_F^*)$ for a chosen U_F-limit and $\text{build}_{F,C}^* \Theta$ for the mediating map from (C, Θ), hinting towards the propositions we will present in a moment. Intuitively, a U_F-cone is an object with an operation which types as a fold operation from that object and is fuseable; the U_F-limit is the greatest such object.

The general idea of deriving syntax from universal properties suggests that we may consider introducing a type $\mu^* F$ and a destructor fold_F^* and constructor build_F^* with typing rules

$$\frac{(X, \varphi) \in F\text{-alg}}{\text{fold}_{F,X}^* \varphi : \mu^* F \to X} \quad \frac{f : (X, \varphi) \to (Y, \psi) \in F\text{-alg}}{f \circ \text{fold}_{F,X}^* \varphi = \text{fold}_{F,Y}^* \psi} \quad \frac{(C, \Theta) \in U_F\text{-cone}}{\text{build}_{F,C}^* \Theta : C \to \mu^* F}$$

As the β-conversion rule, we get

$$\frac{(C, \Theta) \in U_F\text{-cone} \quad (X, \varphi) \in F\text{-alg}}{\text{fold}_{F,X}^* \varphi \circ \text{build}_{F,C}^* \Theta = \Theta_X\varphi}$$

and the η- and permutative conversion rules are

$$\text{id}_{\mu^* F} = \text{build}_{F,\mu^* F}^* \text{fold}_F^* \qquad \frac{h : (C, \Theta) \to (D, \Xi) \in U_F\text{-cone}}{\text{build}_{F,D}^* \Xi \circ h = \text{build}_{F,C}^* \Theta}$$

We see that an U_F-limit provides almost exactly the syntax made use of in FOLD/BUILD fusion: if one ignores the coherence condition (*) of an U_F-cone,

fold_F^* and build_F^* type as FOLD and BUILD should and, moreover, the β-conversion rule is the FOLD/BUILD fusion law. The next proposition shows that an initial F-algebra is, in fact, a U_F-limit.

Proposition 1. *Let $\mathcal{C}$ be a category and $F : \mathcal{C} \to \mathcal{C}$ be a functor. If there is an initial F-algebra $(\mu F, \mathrm{in}_F)$, then μF is the vertex of an U_F-limit.*

Proof. We make use of the definition and properties of an initial F-algebra. We begin by observing that $(\mu F, \mathrm{fold}_F)$ is a U_F-cone, since, for any F-algebra map $f : (X, \varphi) \to (Y, \psi)$, we have $f \circ \mathrm{fold}_{F,X} \varphi = \mathrm{fold}_{F,Y} \psi$. We prove that $(\mu F, \mathrm{fold}_F)$ is the final U_F-cone by showing that, given any U_F-cone (C, Θ), the required mediating U_F-cone map is $\mathrm{build}_{F,C} \Theta =_{\mathrm{df}} \Theta_{\mu F} \, \mathrm{in}_F : C \to \mu F$.

To see that $\mathrm{build}_{F,C} \Theta$ is a U_F-cone map from (C, Θ) to $(\mu F, \mathrm{fold}_F)$, we note that, for any F-algebra (X, φ), the map $\mathrm{fold}_{F,X} \varphi : \mu F \to X$ is an F-algebra map $(\mu F, \mathrm{in}_F) \to (X, \varphi)$, and hence, $\mathrm{fold}_{F,X} \varphi \circ \Theta_{\mu F} \, \mathrm{in}_F = \Theta_X \, \varphi$. To see that $\mathrm{build}_{F,C} \Theta$ is unique, consider any U_F-cone map $h : (C, \Theta) \to (\mu F, \mathrm{fold}_F)$. As $(\mu F, \mathrm{in}_F)$ is an F-algebra, we have $\mathrm{fold}_{F,\mu F} \mathrm{in}_F \circ h = \Theta_{\mu F} \, \mathrm{in}_F$. From this, as $\mathrm{fold}_{F,\mu F} \mathrm{in}_F = \mathrm{id}_{\mu F}$, we get $h = \Theta_{\mu F} \, \mathrm{in}_F$ as required.[1] $\square$

On the basis that inductive types are limits of functors forgetting algebra structure, and that the syntax suggested by this universal property includes a combinator exhibiting all that is expected from BUILD (in particular FOLD/BUILD fusion), although posing a coherence condition on its argument, we take this universal property to constitute the specification of BUILD. The usual FOLD/BUILD fusion will be correct, if coherence is automatic for actual invocations of BUILD. We will touch upon this question in the next subsection.

We have shown that, if F has an initial algebra, it has a final U_F-cone, i.e., that the initial algebra modelling of an inductive type is at least as strong as the limit of forgetful functor modelling: from the IN/FOLD-syntax, we can define the FOLD/BUILD-syntax. But, in fact, the reverse is also true, the two notions are equi-expressive.

Proposition 2. *If there is a U_F-limit $(\mu^* F, \mathrm{fold}_F^*)$, then $\mu^* F$ is the carrier of an initial F-algebra.*

Proof. Define, for any F-algebra (X', φ'), a map $\mathrm{infold}_{F,X'}^* \varphi' : F(\mu^* F) \to X'$ by

$$\mathrm{infold}_{F,X'}^* \varphi' =_{\mathrm{df}} \varphi' \circ F \, (\mathrm{fold}_{F,X'}^* \, \varphi')$$

For any F-algebra map $f : (X', \varphi') \to (Y', \psi')$, we have

$$\begin{aligned}
f \circ \mathrm{infold}_{F,X'}^* \varphi' &= f \circ \varphi' \circ F \, (\mathrm{fold}_{F,X'}^* \, \varphi') \\
&= \psi' \circ F \, (f \circ \mathrm{fold}_{F,X'}^* \, \varphi') \\
&= \psi' \circ F \, (\mathrm{fold}_{F,Y'}^* \, \psi') \\
&= \mathrm{infold}_{F,Y'}^* \, \psi'
\end{aligned}$$

---

[1] Shorter: An initial object is a limit of the identity functor, so an initial F-algebra is a $\mathrm{Id}_{F\text{-}\mathbf{alg}}$-limit. By the preservation of limits by right adjoints, its carrier is a U_F-limit.

This tells us that $(F(\mu^*F), \text{infold}_F^*)$ is a U_F-cone.

Define now a map $\text{in}_F^* : F(\mu^*F) \to \mu^*F$ by

$$\text{in}_F^* =_{\text{df}} \text{build}_{F,F(\mu^*F)}^* \text{infold}_F^*$$

Obviously (μ^*F, in_F^*) is an F-algebra. We prove that it is initial by showing that, given any F-algebra (X, φ), the map $\text{fold}_{F,X}^* \varphi : \mu^*F \to X$ is the required unique mediating F-algebra map.

To see that $\text{fold}_{F,X}^* \varphi$ is an F-algebra map $(\mu^*F, \text{in}_F^*) \to (X, \varphi)$, we invoke that $(F(\mu^*F), \text{infold}_F^*)$ is a U_F-cone to observe that

$$\begin{aligned}
\text{fold}_{F,X}^* \, \varphi \circ \text{in}_F^* &= \text{fold}_{F,X}^* \, \varphi \circ \text{build}_{F,F(\mu^*F)}^* \text{infold}_F^* \\
&= \text{infold}_{F,X}^* \, \varphi \\
&= \varphi \circ F \, (\text{fold}_{F,X}^* \, \varphi)
\end{aligned}$$

It remains to verify that $\text{fold}_{F,X}^* \varphi$ is unique.

We have just seen that $\text{fold}_{F,X'}^* \, \varphi'$ is an F-algebra map $(\mu^*F, \text{in}_F^*) \to (X', \varphi')$ for any F-algebra (X', φ'), hence $\text{fold}_{F,X'}^* \, \varphi' \circ \text{fold}_{F,\mu^*F}^* \, \text{in}_F^* = \text{fold}_{F,X'}^* \, \varphi'$. It follows that $\text{fold}_{F,\mu^*F}^* \, \text{in}_F^*$ is a U_F-cone map from the U_F-limit $(\mu^*F, \text{fold}_F^*)$ to itself, therefore $\text{fold}_{F,\mu^*F}^* \, \text{in}_F^* = \text{id}_{\mu F}$.

Now consider any F-algebra map $f : (\mu^*F, \text{in}_F^*) \to (X, \varphi)$. We have $f = f \circ \text{fold}_{F,\mu^*F}^* \, \text{in}_F^* = \text{fold}_{F,X}^* \, \varphi$, which completes the uniqueness proof.   □

This proposition assures us that the FOLD/BUILD paradigm is no weaker than the customary IN/FOLD. Everything we can program with IN/FOLD, we can also do with FOLD/BUILD. E.g., we may implement natural numbers as follows:

```
data Nat = BuildN (forall x . x -> (x -> x) -> x)
```

```
foldN :: x -> (x -> x) -> Nat -> x
foldN z s (BuildN theta) = theta z s
```

Now, the zero and successor constructors and, in fact, all numbers are definable:

```
zeroN :: Nat
zeroN = BuildN (\ z _ -> z)
```

```
succN :: Nat -> Nat
succN n = BuildN (\ z s -> s (foldN z s n))
```

```
toN :: Int -> Nat
toN n = BuildN (\ z s -> ntimes n s z)
```

```
ntimes n f = if n == 0 then id else f . ntimes (n - 1) f
```

We see that what we get are the Church numerals. How FOLD/BUILD fusion for natural numbers works is therefore intuitively very clear: By abstracting out the occurrences of the zero and successor constructors in a numeral, we obtain direct access to their positions, and it is exactly these constructor occurrences that folds replace. More generally, we have constructed a categorical version of the type quantification based encoding of inductive types of [19, 3].

2.4   Strong Dinatural Transformations

We now turn to the question about the coherence condition of U_F-cones. It is rather well-behaved: we will shortly see that it is a strong dinaturality condition.

Dinatural transformations and strongly dinatural transformations are two generalizations of the concept of natural transformation for mixed-variant functors. Standard dinaturality, as introduced by Dubuc and Street [4], is fairly well known, but, for reference, we record the definition.

Definition 3 (Dinaturality). *Let $H, K : \mathcal{C}^{op} \times \mathcal{C} \to \mathcal{D}$ be functors. A* dinatural *transformation $\Theta : H \to K$ is a family of maps $\Theta_X : H(X, X) \to K(X, X)$ in $\mathcal{D}$ for all objects X in $\mathcal{C}$ such that, for every map $f : X \to Y$ in $\mathcal{C}$, the following hexagon commutes:*

$$
\begin{array}{ccccc}
 & & H(X,X) \xrightarrow{\;\;\Theta_X\;\;} K(X,X) & & \\
 & \overset{H(f,X)}{\nearrow} & & \overset{K(X,f)}{\searrow} & \\
H(Y,X) & & & & K(X,Y) \\
 & \underset{H(Y,f)}{\searrow} & & \underset{K(f,Y)}{\nearrow} & \\
 & & H(Y,Y) \xrightarrow{\;\;\Theta_Y\;\;} K(Y,Y) & &
\end{array}
$$

A major deficiency of standard dinatural transformations is that they do not generally compose. Strongly dinatural transformations address and solve exactly this problem. They appeared in Mulry's paper [23], but the exact authorship is unclear: in the beautiful in-depth account [24], they are attributed to Barr, personal communication.

Definition 4 (Strong Dinaturality). *Let $H, K : \mathcal{C}^{op} \times \mathcal{C} \to \mathcal{D}$ be functors. A* strongly dinatural *transformation $\Theta : H \to K$ is a family of maps $\Theta_X : H(X, X) \to K(X, X)$ in $\mathcal{D}$ for all objects X in $\mathcal{C}$ such that, for every map $f : X \to Y$ in $\mathcal{C}$, object W and maps $p_0 : W \to H(X, X)$, $p_1 : W \to H(Y, Y)$ in $\mathcal{D}$, if the square in the following diagram commutes, then so does the hexagon:*

$$
\begin{array}{ccccc}
 & & H(X,X) \xrightarrow{\;\;\Theta_X\;\;} K(X,X) & & \\
 & \overset{p_0}{\nearrow} & \overset{H(X,f)}{\searrow} & & \overset{K(X,f)}{\searrow} \\
W & & H(X,Y) & \Rightarrow & K(X,Y) \\
 & \underset{p_1}{\searrow} & \overset{H(f,Y)}{\nearrow} & & \overset{K(f,Y)}{\nearrow} \\
 & & H(Y,Y) \xrightarrow{\;\;\Theta_Y\;\;} K(Y,Y) & &
\end{array}
$$

If $\mathcal{D}$ is a category with pullbacks such as, e.g., **Set**, one can equivalently require that, for every map $f : X \to Y$ in $\mathcal{C}$, the outer hexagon of the above diagram commutes for (W, p_0, p_1) the chosen pullback of $H(X, f)$ and $K(f, Y)$.

It is easy to see that every strongly dinatural transformation is also dinatural, but the converse does not hold in general.

We will need strongly dinatural transformations between $H, K : \mathcal{C}^{op} \times \mathcal{C} \to \mathcal{D}$ for the special case where $\mathcal{C}$ is locally small (meaning that all homcollections $\mathrm{Hom}(A, B)$ are sets), $\mathcal{D} = \mathbf{Set}$ and $H = \mathrm{Hom}(F\,-, G\,-) : \mathcal{C}^{op} \times \mathcal{C} \to \mathbf{Set}$ for some functors $F, G : \mathcal{C} \to \mathcal{C}$. In this situation, the difference between dinaturality and strong dinaturality is especially apparent. A dinatural transformation $\Theta : H \to K$ is a family of functions $\Theta_X : \mathrm{Hom}(F\ X, G\ X) \to K\ X$ such that, for any maps $f : X \to Y, \xi : F\ Y \to G\ X, \varphi : F\ X \to G\ X, \psi : F\ Y \to G\ Y$, if the two triangles

$$
\begin{array}{ccc}
F\,X & \xrightarrow{\ \varphi\ } & G\,X \\
{\scriptstyle F\,f}\downarrow & \overset{\xi}{\nearrow} & \downarrow{\scriptstyle G\,f} \\
F\,Y & \xrightarrow[\ \psi\ ]{} & G\,Y
\end{array}
$$

commute, then $K\ (X, f)\ (\Theta_X\ \varphi) = K\ (f, Y)\ (\Theta_Y\ \psi)$. For a strongly dinatural transformation, in contrast, the condition is: for any maps $f : X \to Y, \varphi : F\ X \to G\ X, \psi : F\ Y \to G\ Y$, if the square

$$
\begin{array}{ccc}
F\,X & \xrightarrow{\ \varphi\ } & G\,X \\
{\scriptstyle F\,f}\downarrow & & \downarrow{\scriptstyle G\,f} \\
F\,Y & \xrightarrow[\ \psi\ ]{} & G\,Y
\end{array}
$$

commutes, then $K\ (X, f)\ (\Theta_X\ \varphi) = K\ (f, Y)\ (\Theta_Y\ \psi)$. Clearly the second one of the two implications is stronger because of its weaker antecedent.

Comparing the unwinding of the definition of strong dinaturality and our ealier unwinding of the definition of limit, we arrive at the following observation.

Proposition 3. *Let $\mathcal{C}$ be a locally small category and $F : \mathcal{C} \to \mathcal{C}$ a functor. A U_F-cone structure with vertex C is the same thing as a strong dinatural transformation from $\mathrm{Hom}(F\ -, -)$ to $\mathrm{Hom}(C, -)$.*

Proof. Both U_F-cone structures and strong dinatural transformations from $\mathrm{Hom}(F-, -)$ to $\mathrm{Hom}(C, -)$ are families of maps $\Theta_X : \mathrm{Hom}(FX, X) \to \mathrm{Hom}(C, X)$ such that, for any maps $f : X \to Y, \varphi : FX \to X, \psi : FY \to Y$, if $f \circ \varphi = \psi \circ Ff$, then $f \circ \Theta_X \varphi = \Theta_Y \psi$. □

The proposition tells us that the typing rule for BUILD can be rewritten as

$$
\frac{\Theta \in \mathsf{SDinat}(\mathsf{Hom}(F\ -, -), \mathsf{Hom}(C, -))}{\mathrm{build}_{F,C}\Theta : C \to \mu F}
$$

We may ask now when a term $\Theta : \forall X. (FX \Rightarrow X) \Rightarrow C \Rightarrow X$ is guaranteed to be a strongly dinatural transformation. The answer depends on the specifics of the language and model under scrutiny and, in particular, on the semantics assigned to type quantification. This is a subtle and technical topic that we wish to discuss separately and in detail elsewhere. For this paper, we note however that in parametric models of polymorphic languages terms of type $\forall X. (FX \Rightarrow X) \Rightarrow C \Rightarrow X$ define strong dinaturals. From a practical point of view, it is then possible to get strong dinaturality for free.

We finish the discussion of BUILD by arguing that it makes perfect sense to separate language-specific questions such as when a term is strong dinatural from questions about basic semantic constructions appropriate for modelling some general phenomenon, e.g. the question of what BUILD is. We do not, for example, ask when a type constructor is a functor in a discussion of the initial algebra semantics. Certainly there exist simple sufficient syntactic conditions for functoriality, e.g., positivity, but the definition of any such condition and the proof of its sufficiency is specific to the language and model used. The situation with strong dinaturality of a term is completely analogous.

3   Augmenting Build

BUILD presentations of producers do not always suffice for deforestation. Consider the definition of the `append` function for lists as a `foldr`:

```
append as bs = foldr (:) bs as
```

Abstracting the constructors, we get the following attempt of a definition of `append` in terms of `build`:

```
append as bs = build theta
   where theta c n = foldr c bs as
```

Unfortunately however, this attempt is incorrect, as the type of `theta` is not general enough. The problem is that the constructor occurrences in the list `bs`, while being part of the final result of `append`, are not abstracted in `theta`. So, one solution for the problem would be to replace the list `bs` with a traversal which uniformly replaces its constructor occurrences:

```
append as bs = build theta
   where theta c n = foldr c (foldr c n bs) as
```

Although this is indeed a correct definition of `append`, it introduces an extra traversal of the list `bs` and there is no guarantee that this traversal can be removed by subsequent fusion.

As a better solution, Gill [11] introduced a new combinator `augment` which generalizes `build` by abstracting out the nil-constructor position in a list:

```
augment :: (forall x. (a -> x -> x) -> x -> x) -> [a] -> [a]
augment theta bs = theta (:) bs
```

In terms of `augment`, `append` is easily expressed as follows:

```
append as bs = augment (\ c n -> foldr c n as) bs
```

Note, that `build` is just a special case of `augment`:

```
build theta == augment theta []
```

and `foldr`/`build` fusion or shortcut deforestation for lists generalizes to

```
foldr c n (augment theta bs) == theta c (foldr c n bs)
```

The same idea can be easily extended to arbitrary inductive types by abstracting over non-recursive constructors, to obtain a version of shortcut deforestation tailored specifically for functions that graft. This has been done by Johann [15]. We present however a slightly more general version and, following our general methodology, derive it from a unique existence situation.

Let $H : \mathcal{C} \to \mathcal{C}$ be a functor and let $T' : \mathcal{C} \to [\mathcal{C}, \mathcal{C}]$ be the functor given by $T'AX =_{df} A + HX$. Then, if an initial $T'A$-algebra (= a free H-algebra over A) exists for every object A of $\mathcal{C}$, we can get a functor $T : \mathcal{C} \to \mathcal{C}$ by defining $TA =_{df} \mu(T'A)$. This models an inductive type parameterized in non-recursive constructors. Decompose, each map $\mathsf{in}_{T'A}$ into two maps $\eta_A : A \to TA$ and $\tau_A : H(TA) \to TA$ by setting

$$\eta_A =_{df} \mathsf{in}_{T'A} \circ \mathsf{inl}_{A,H(TA)}$$
$$\tau_A =_{df} \mathsf{in}_{T'A} \circ \mathsf{inr}_{A,H(TA)}$$

Define, finally, for any map $f : A \to TB$, a map $f^\star : TA \to TB$ by

$$f^\star =_{df} \mathsf{fold}_{T'A,TB}[\,f, \tau_B\,]$$

Conceptually, η packages the non-recursive constructors of the parameterized type, τ packages the recursive constructors, and $()^\star$ is substitution for non-recursive constructors. It is standard knowledge the data $(T, \eta, ()^\star)$ so constructed constitute a monad which, more specifically, is the free monad over H, but we will not make deep use of this fact in this paper. With the stage set, we can now proceed to a proposition which supplies the parameterized inductive type T with an AUGMENT combinator.

Proposition 4. *Let $\mathcal{C}$ be a category, $H : \mathcal{C} \to \mathcal{C}$ a functor such that initial algebras of all functors $T'A =_{df} A + H-$ exist. Let T, η, τ, $()^\star$ be defined as above. Then, for any map $f : A \to TB$ and $U_{T'A}$-cone (C, Θ) there exists a unique map $h : C \to TB$ such that, for any $T'B$-algebra $(X, [\varphi_0, \varphi_1])$, it holds that*

$$\mathsf{fold}_{T'B,X}[\varphi_0, \varphi_1] \circ h = \Theta_X([\,\mathsf{fold}_{T'B,X}[\varphi_0, \varphi_1] \circ f, \varphi_1\,])$$

We denote the unique map by $\mathsf{augment}_{T',C}(\Theta, f)$.

Proof. We prove that

$$\mathsf{augment}_{T',C}(\Theta, f) = \Theta_{TB}[\,f, \tau_B\,]$$

It is easy to see that $\mathsf{fold}_{T'B,X}[\varphi_0, \varphi_1] : TB \to X$ is a $T'A$-algebra map from $(TB, [\,f, \tau_B\,])$ to $(X, [\mathsf{fold}_{T'B,X}[\varphi_0, \varphi_1] \circ f, \varphi_1])$. Hence from (C, Θ) being a $U_{T'A}$-cone,

$$\mathsf{fold}_{T'B,X}[\varphi_0, \varphi_1] \circ \Theta_{TB}[\,f, \tau_B\,] = \Theta_X[\mathsf{fold}_{T'B,X}[\varphi_0, \varphi_1] \circ f, \varphi_1\,]$$

as needed.

Assume now that there is a map $h : C \to TB$ such that, for any $T'B$-algebra $(X, [\varphi_0, \varphi_1])$, it holds that

$$\mathsf{fold}_{T'B,X}[\varphi_0, \varphi_1] \circ h = \Theta_X[\mathsf{fold}_{T'B,X}[\varphi_0, \varphi_1] \circ f, \varphi_1]$$

Then

$$h = \mathsf{fold}_{T'B,TB}[\eta_B, \tau_B] \circ h$$
$$= \Theta_{TB}[\mathsf{fold}_{T'B,X}[\eta_B, \tau_B] \circ f, \tau_B]$$
$$= \Theta_{TB}[f, \tau_B]$$

so we also have uniqueness. □

On the level of syntax, the proposition proved justifies the introduction of a combinator $\mathsf{augment}_{T'}$ with a typing rule

$$\frac{(C, \Theta) \in U_{T'A}\text{-}\mathbf{cone} \quad f : A \to TB}{\mathsf{augment}_{T',C}(\Theta, f) : C \to TB}$$

and β-conversion rule

$$\frac{(C, \Theta) \in U_{T'A}\text{-}\mathbf{cone} \quad f : A \to TB \quad (X, [\varphi_0, \varphi_1]) \in T'B\text{-}\mathbf{alg}}{\mathsf{fold}_{T'B,X}[\varphi_0, \varphi_1] \circ \mathsf{augment}_{T',C}(\Theta, f) = \Theta_X[\mathsf{fold}_{T'B,X}[\varphi_0, \varphi_1] \circ f, \varphi_1]}$$

which is fusion of FOLD and AUGMENT. One also gets the following conversion rules relating to the monad structure on T:

$$\frac{(C, \Theta) \in U_{T'A}\text{-}\mathbf{cone} \quad f : A \to TB}{\mathsf{augment}_{T',C}(\Theta, f) = f^\star \circ \mathsf{build}_{T'A,C}\Theta} \qquad \frac{(C, \Theta) \in U_{T'A}\text{-}\mathbf{cone}}{\mathsf{build}_{T'A,C}\Theta = \mathsf{augment}_{T',C}(\Theta, \eta_A)}$$

$$\frac{(C, \Theta) \in U_{T'A}\text{-}\mathbf{cone} \quad f : A \to TB \quad g : B \to TC}{g^\star \circ \mathsf{augment}_{T',C}(\Theta, f) = \mathsf{augment}_{T',C}(\Theta, g^\star \circ f)}$$

Johann [15] describes essentially the same combinator, but in a restricted form where the type of non-recursive constructors is fixed (so that $B = A$). (The reason must be that, in the prototypical case of lists, the type of non-recursive constructors is constantly 1; normally, one does not consider the possibility of supporting multiple nil's drawn from a parameter type.) Unfortunately, this restriction hides the rather important role of the monad structure on T.

As an example, we may consider the parameterized type of binary leaf labelled trees, Haskell-implementable as follows:

```
data BLTree a = Leaf a | Bin (BLTree a) (BLTree a)

foldB :: (a -> x) -> (x -> x -> x) -> BLTree a -> x
foldB l b (Leaf a) = l a
foldB l b (Bin as0 as1) = b (foldB l b as0) (foldB l b as1)
```

The BUILD and AUGMENT combinators are implementable as follows:

```
buildB :: (forall x. (a -> x) -> (x -> x -> x) -> x) -> BLTree a
buildB theta = theta Leaf Bin

augmentB :: (forall x. (a -> x) -> (x -> x -> x) -> x)
                              -> (a -> BLTree b) -> BLTree b
augmentB theta f = theta f Bin
```

The shortcut deforestation laws say that

```
foldB l b (buildB theta) == theta l b

foldB l b (augmentB theta f) == theta (foldB l b . f) b
```

Elsewhere we will show that there is no reason to stop at AUGMENT for free monads. A similar combinator is possible for any monad obtained from a parameterized monad via initial algebras as described in [32]. Some parameterized inductive types covered by this more general construction are, e.g., finitely branching node labelled trees and inductive hyperfunctions [17].

4   Coinductive Types and Destroy

Since coinductive types are dual to inductive types, it is clear that, if inductive types admit a universal characterization with BUILDS as the mediating maps, then there must be a universal characterization of coinductive types centered around a dual combinator. We now turn to this characterization.

In the standard modelling, a coinductive type is a chosen final coalgebra of a functor.

Definition 5 ((Final) Coalgebra). *Let C be a category and $F : C \to C$ be a functor. An F-coalgebra is an object X together with a map $\varphi : X \to F\,X$. An F-coalgebra map $(X, \varphi) \to (Y, \psi)$ is a map $f : X \to Y$ such that $\psi \circ f = Ff \circ \varphi$. A final F-coalgebra is a final object in the category F-**coalg** of F-coalgebras, i.e., an F-coalgebra with a unique map to it from any F-coalgebra.*

We agree to denote a chosen final F-coalgebra by $(\nu F, \mathsf{out}_F)$, and the unique map to it from an F-coalgebra (X, φ) by $\mathsf{unfold}_{F,X}\varphi$. The final coalgebra semantics justifies the well-known syntax of coinductive types which is given by a type νF, a destructor out_F and a constructor unfold_F subjected to the following typing and conversion rules:

– typing rules:

$$\mathsf{out}_F : \nu F \to F(\nu F) \qquad \frac{(X, \varphi) \in F\text{-}\mathbf{coalg}}{\mathsf{unfold}_{F,X}\varphi : X \to \nu F}$$

– β-conversion rule (= cancellation law for UNFOLD):

$$\frac{(X, \varphi) \in F\text{-coalg}}{\mathsf{out}_F \circ \mathsf{unfold}_{F,X}\varphi = F(\mathsf{unfold}_{F,X}\varphi) \circ \varphi}$$

– η- and permutative conversion rules (= identity and fusion laws for UNFOLD):

$$\mathsf{id}_{\nu F} = \mathsf{unfold}_{F,F(\nu F)}\mathsf{out}_F \qquad \frac{f : (X, \varphi) \to (Y, \psi) \in F\text{-coalg}}{\mathsf{unfold}_{F,Y}\psi \circ f = \mathsf{unfold}_{F,X}\varphi}$$

To give some examples, the type of streams over a given type A can be modelled by a final coalgebra of functor $A \times -$, the type of colists (possibly infinite lists) over A by a final coalgebra of the functor $1 + A \times -$ etc.

A Haskell implementation of the final coalgebra view of streams based on the β-conversion rule would be the following:

```
data Str a = forall x . UnfoldS (x -> a) (x -> x) x

hdS :: Str a -> a
hdS (UnfoldS h t x) = h x

tlS :: Str a -> Str a
tlS (UnfoldS h t x) = UnfoldS h t (t x)
```

The usual implementation of streams, which avoids rank-2 type signatures, exploits the fact that the final coalgebra structure map is an isomorphism.

```
data Str a = MkStr { hd :: a, tl :: Str a }

unfoldS :: (x -> a) -> (x -> x) -> x -> Str a
unfoldS h t x = MkStr { hd = h x, tl = unfoldS h t (t x) }
```

Colists are Haskell-implemented, e.g., by Haskell's (lazy) lists and `unfoldr`:

```
unfoldr :: (x -> Maybe (a, x)) -> x -> [a]
unfoldr phi x = case phi x of
                  Nothing   -> []
                  Just (a,x') -> a : unfoldr phi x'
```

(Recall that Haskell is semantically based on **CPO** where inductive and coinductive types coincide.)

Our alternative modelling of the coinductive type given by a functor F views it as a colimit of the forgetful functor $V_F : F\text{-coalg} \to \mathcal{C}$. We recall the definition of a colimit of a functor.

Definition 6 (Colimit). *A* cocone *for a functor $J : \mathcal{C} \to \mathcal{D}$ is a pair (C, γ) consisting of an object C in $\mathcal{D}$ and, for each object X in $\mathcal{C}$, a map $\gamma_X : JX \to C$ in $\mathcal{D}$ such that, for every map $f : X \to Y$ in $\mathcal{C}$, we have $\gamma_Y \circ Jf = \gamma_X$. A map of cocones $(C, \gamma) \to (D, \delta)$ is a map $h : C \to D$ in $\mathcal{D}$ such that, for each object X in $\mathcal{C}$, we have $h \circ \gamma_X = \delta_X$. A* colimit *of J is an initial object in the category of J-**cocone** of J-cocones.*

By this definition, a cocone of V_F is given by an object C and, for any F-coalgebra (X, φ), a map $\Theta_X \, \varphi : X \rightarrow C$, such that, for any F-coalgebra morphism $f : (X, \varphi) \rightarrow (Y, \psi)$, we have $\Theta_Y \, \psi \circ f = \Theta_X \, \varphi$ (which is to say that Θ is a strongly dinatural transformation from $\mathrm{Hom}(-, F \, -)$ to $\mathrm{Hom}(-, C)$). A V_F-cocone map $(C, \Theta) \rightarrow (D, \Xi)$ is a map $h : C \rightarrow D$ such that, for any F-coalgebra (X, φ), we have $h \circ \Theta_X \, \varphi = \Xi_X \, \varphi$. A V_F-colimit is a V_F-cocone with a unique map to every V_F-cocone. We denote a chosen V_F-colimit by $(\nu^* F, \mathsf{unfold}^*_F)$ and the unique V_F-cocone map from a given V_F-cocone (C, Θ) by $\mathsf{destroy}^*_{F,C} \Theta$. Intuitively, a V_F-cocone is an object with a fuseable unfold-like operation and the V_F-limit is the smallest such.

The syntax derived from the alternative semantics consists of a type $\nu^* F$ along with a destructor unfold_F and constructor $\mathsf{destroy}_F$ plus these rules:

- typing rules:

$$\frac{(X, \varphi) \in F\text{-}\mathbf{coalg}}{\mathsf{unfold}^*_{F,X} \, \varphi : C \rightarrow \nu^* F} \qquad \frac{f : (X, \varphi) \rightarrow (Y, \psi) \in F\text{-}\mathbf{coalg}}{\mathsf{unfold}^*_{F,Y} \, \psi \circ f = \mathsf{unfold}^*_{F,X} \varphi} \qquad \frac{(C, \Theta) \in V_F\text{-}\mathbf{cocone}}{\mathsf{destroy}^*_{F,C} \Theta : \nu^* F \rightarrow C}$$

- β-conversion rule:

$$\frac{(C, \Theta) \in V_F\text{-}\mathbf{cocone} \quad (X, \varphi) \in F\text{-}\mathbf{coalg}}{\mathsf{destroy}^*_{F,C} \Theta \circ \mathsf{unfold}^*_{F,X} \, \varphi = \Theta_X \, \varphi}$$

- η- and permutative conversion rules:

$$\mathsf{id}_{\nu^* F} = \mathsf{destroy}^*_{F, \nu^* F} \mathsf{unfold}^*_F \qquad \frac{h : (C, \Theta) \rightarrow (D, \Xi) \in V_F\text{-}\mathbf{cocone}}{h \circ \mathsf{destroy}^*_{F,C} \Theta = \mathsf{destroy}^*_{F,D} \Xi}$$

The equivalence of the two semantics is established by the following proposition dualizing Propositions 1, 2.

Proposition 5. *Let $\mathcal{C}$ be a category and $F : \mathcal{C} \rightarrow \mathcal{C}$ a functor. Then, (a) if there is a final F-coalgebra $(\nu F, \mathsf{out}_F)$, then νF is the vertex of a V_F-colimit, and (b) if there is a V_F-colimit $(\nu^* F, \mathsf{unfold}^*_F)$, then $\nu^* F$ is the carrier of a final F-coalgebra.*

Proof (Constructions). The statements are immediate by duality from Propositions 1, 2. But to show the constructions, we sketch an explicit dual proof.

(a) Set, for any V_F-cocone (C, Θ), $\mathsf{destroy}_{F,C} \Theta =_{\mathrm{df}} \Theta_{\nu F} \, \mathsf{out}_F$. Check that $(\nu F, \mathsf{unfold}_F, \mathsf{destroy}_F)$ is a V_F-colimit.

(b) Set, for any F-coalgebra (X, φ), $\mathsf{unfoldout}^*_{F,X} \, \varphi =_{\mathrm{df}} F \, \mathsf{unfold}^*_{F,X} \, \varphi \circ \varphi$. Set $\mathsf{out}^*_F =_{\mathrm{df}} \mathsf{destroy}^*_{F,F \, (\nu^* F)} \mathsf{unfoldout}^*_F$. Check that $(\nu^* F, \mathsf{out}^*_F, \mathsf{unfold}^*_F)$ is a final F-coalgebra. $\qquad \square$

From (a), we get a new combinator for coinductive types, DESTROY, and a new shortcut deforestation law: the DESTROY combinator is derived from a final coalgebra being a colimit of the functor forgetting coalgebra structure, and the shortcut deforestation or UNFOLD/DESTROY fusion law is just the corresponding β-conversion rule. For streams, in particular, we get a DESTROY combinator with the following Haskell implementation:

```
destroyS :: (forall x . (x -> a) -> (x -> x) -> x -> c) -> Str a -> c
destroyS theta = theta hdS tlS
```

For possibly infinite lists, we obtain the following combinator:

```
destroyL :: (forall x . (x -> Maybe (a, x)) -> x -> c) -> [a] -> c
destroyL theta = theta OutL
         where OutL [] = Nothing
               OutL (a : as) = Just (a, as)
```

Shortcut deforestation for streams says

```
destroyS theta . unfoldS h t == theta h t
```

while for colists it says

```
destroyL theta . unfoldr phi == theta phi
```

The DESTROY combinator and shortcut deforestation for colists appear in Gill [11] and Svenningsson [29]. In fact, they speak of Haskell's lists, but to have the transformation correct, it is essential that the type is coinductive.

Part (b) of the proposition gives an alternative arrangement of syntax for programming with coinductive types where DESTROY rather than OUT is primitive. For streams, a possible complete Haskell implementation is this:

```
data Str a = forall x . UnfoldS (x -> a) (x -> x) x

destroyS :: (forall x . (x -> a) -> (x -> x) -> x -> c) -> Str a -> c
destroyS theta (UnfoldS h t x) = theta h t x
```

The usual head and tail destructors, which constitute the OUT destructor for streams, are non-primitive in this implementation. They are definable functions:

```
hdS :: Str a -> a
hdS = destroyS (\ h _ -> h)

tlS :: Str a -> Str a
tlS = destroyS (\ h t -> UnfoldS h t . t)
```

As an example, we could program stream indexing as follows:

```
fromS :: Int -> Str a -> a
fromS n = destroyS (\ h t -> h . ntimes n t)
```

We find that the terms fromS n deserve to be called *Church indexicals*.

Just as the BUILD combinator for inductive types admits a generalization to an AUGMENT combinator for monadic parameterized inductive types, a dual generalization of DESTROY is possible for comonadic parameterized coinductive types. We will not spell out the details here.

5   Related Work

Programming and reasoning about inductive and coinductive types with combinators derived from the initial algebra and final coalgebra semantics was first explored by Hagino [13]. To the functional programming community, this idea was introduced in [21, 22, 28] and became very popular then. The method to encode inductive types via type quantification (the "impredicative encoding") was first described in [19, 3]. Shortcut deforestation for lists was proposed by Gill et al. [11, 10]. For general inductive types, it was defined in [30, 18].

The landmark works on parametricity are Reynold's and Wadler's papers [26, 27, 34], categorical studies on the semantics of polymorphism based on dinaturality and strengthenings include [12, 2, 8]. Some discussions of the implications of parametricity for (co)inductive types are [36, 14, 1]. Strong dinaturality, most probably first introduced in [23], has recently been studied closely in [5, 6].

Most closely related to the work reported here, Johann [16, 15] has given a thorough proof of the correctness of FOLD/BUILD and FOLD/AUGMENT fusion via parametricity of contextual equivalence. Pavlovic [25] has analyzed FOLD/BUILD fusion in terms of "paranatural" transformations which are essentially the same as strong dinaturals.

6   Conclusions

We have shown that besides the initial algebra semantics inductive types admit an alternative but equivalent semantics in terms of limits of forgetful functors. This equivalent semantics matches nicely the FOLD/BUILD syntax that has been invented for the purpose of program transformations. In particular, it gives a language-independent axiomatic specification of BUILD where the correctness of shortcut deforestation is an axiom. This separation between the general semantics of inductive types and parametricity theorems for specific languages and their models is, to our view, good and helpful, because of the modularity and clarity it brings.

As future work we intend to give an account of rational types (essentially non-wellfounded trees with finitely many distinct subtrees) based on the general theory put forward in Ghani et al. [9] in order to systematically study disciplines for programming with rational types such as the "cycle therapy" of Turbak and Wells [31]. We also plan to achieve a similar account for the vanish combinators à la Voigtländer [33]. A further topic will be parametricity in terms of strong dinaturals for languages supporting interleaved inductive and coinductive types.

Acknowledgments. The authors are thankful to Patricia Johann and John Launchbury for useful comments.

All three authors benefitted from the support from the EU FP5 IST programme via the APPSEM II project and from the Royal Society ESEP programme within joint research project No. 15642. The second and third author were also partially supported by the Estonian Science Foundation under grant No. 5567.

References

1. T. Altenkirch. Logical relations and inductive/coinductive types. In G. Gottlob, E. Grandjean, and K. Seyr, eds., *Proc. of 12th Int. Wksh. on Computer Science Logic, CSL'98*, v. 1584 of *Lecture Notes in Computer Science*, pp. 343–354. Springer-Verlag, 1999.

2. E. S. Bainbridge, P. J. Freyd, A. Scedrov, and P. J. Scott. Functorial polymorphism. *Theoretical Computer Science*, 70(1):35–64, 1990. Corrigendum, ibid., 71(3):431, 1991.

3. C. Böhm and A. Berarducci. Automatic synthesis of typed Λ-programs on term algebras. *Theoretical Computer Science*, 39(2–3):135–154, 1985.

4. E. Dubuc and R. Street. Dinatural transformations. In S. M. Lane, ed., *Reports of the Midwest Category Seminar IV*, v. 137 of *Lecture Notes in Mathematics*, pp. 126–137. Springer-Verlag, 1970.

5. A. Eppendahl. Parametricity and Mulry's strong dinaturality. Technical Report 768, Dept. of Computer Science, Queen Mary and Westfield College, London, 1999.

6. A. Eppendahl. *Categories and Types for Axiomatic Domain Theory*. PhD thesis, Queen Mary, University of London, 2003.

7. L. Fegaras. Using the parametricity proposition for program fusion. Technical report CSE-96-001, Dept. of Computer Science and Engineering, Oregon Graduate Institute, Portland, OR, 1996.

8. P. J. Freyd. Structural polymorphism. *Theoretical Computer Science*, 115(1):107–129, 1993.

9. N. Ghani, C. Lüth, and F. D. Marchi. Coalgebraic monads. In L. S. Moss, ed., *Proc. of 5th Wksh. on Coalgebraic Methods in Computer Science, CMCS'02*, v. 65(1) of *Electronic Notes in Theoretical Computer Science*. Elsevier, 2002.

10. A. Gill, J. Launchbury, and S. L. P. Jones. A short cut to deforestation. In *Conf. Record of 6th ACM SIGPLAN-SIGARCH Int. Conf. on Functional Programming Languages and Computer Architecture, FPCA'93*, pp. 223–232. ACM Press, 1993.

11. A. J. Gill. *Cheap Deforestation for Non-strict Functional Languages*. PhD thesis, Univ. of Glasgow, 1996.

12. J.-Y. Girard, A. Scedrov, and P. J. Scott. Normal forms and cut-free proofs as natural transformations. In Y. N. Moschovakis, ed., *Logic from Computer Science*, v. 21 of *Mathematical Sciences Research Institute Publications*, pp. 217–241. Springer-Verlag, 1991.

13. T. Hagino. A typed lambda calculus with categorical type constructors. In D. H. Pitt, A. Poigné, and D. E. Rydeheard, eds., *Proc. of 2nd Int. Conf. on Category Theory and Computer Science, CTCS'87*, v. 283 of *Lecture Notes in Computer Science*, pp. 140–157. Springer-Verlag, 1987.

14. R. Hasegawa. Categorical data types in parametric polymorphism. *Mathematical Structures in Computer Science*, 4(1):71–109, 1994.

15. P. Johann. A generalization of short-cut fusion and its correctness proof. *Higher-Order and Symbolic Computation*, 15(4):273–300, 2002.

16. P. Johann. Short-cut fusion is correct. *Journal of Functional Programming*, 13(4):797–814, 2003.

17. S. Krstić, J. Launchbury, and D. Pavlović. Categories of processes enriched in final coalgebras. In F. Honsell and M. Miculan, eds., *Proc. of 4th Int. Conf. on Found. of Software Science and Computation Structures, FoSSaCS'01*, v. 2030 of *Lecture Notes in Computer Science*, pp. 303–317. Springer-Verlag, 2001.

18. J. Launchbury and T. Sheard. Warm fusion: Deriving build-catas from recursive definitions. In *Conf. Record 7th ACM SIGPLAN-SIGARCH Int. Conf. on Functional Programming Languages and Computer Architecture, FPCA'95*, pp. 314–323. ACM Press, 1995.

19. D. Leivant. Reasoning about functional programs and complexity classes associated with type disciplines. In *Proc. of 24th Annual IEEE Symp. on Foundations of Computer Science, FOCS'83*, pp. 460–469. IEEE CS Press, 1983.

20. S. Mac Lane. *Categories for the Working Mathematician*, v. 5 of *Graduate Texts in Mathematics*, 2nd ed. Springer-Verlag, 1997. (1st ed., 1971).

21. G. Malcolm. Data structures and program transformation. *Science of Computer Programming*, 14(2–3):255–279, 1990.

22. E. Meijer, M. Fokkinga, and R. Paterson. Functional programming with bananas, lenses, envelopes and barbed wire. In J. Hughes, ed., *Proc. of 5th ACM Conf. on Functional Programming Languages and Computer Architecture, FPCA'91*, v. 523 of *Lecture Notes in Computer Science*, pp. 124–144. Springer-Verlag, 1991.

23. P. S. Mulry. Strong monads, algebras and fixed points. In M. P. Fourman, P. T. Johnstone, and A. M. Pitts, eds., *Applications of Categories in Computer Science*, v. 177 of *London Math. Society Lecture Note Series*, pp. 202–216. Cambridge University Press, 1992.

24. R. Paré and L. Román. Dinatural numbers. *Journal of Pure and Applied Algebra*, 128(1):33–92, 1998.

25. D. Pavlovic. Logic of build fusion. Technical Report KES.U.00.9, Kestrel Institute, 2000.

26. J. C. Reynolds. Towards a theory of type structure. In B. Robinet, ed., *Proc. of Programming Symp. (Colloque sur la programmation)*, v. 19 of *Lecture Notes in Computer Science*, pp. 408–425. Springer-Verlag, 1974.

27. J. C. Reynolds. Types, abstraction and parametric polymorphism. In R. E. A. Mason, ed., *Proc. of 9th IFIP World Computer Congress, Information Processing '83*, pp. 513–523. North-Holland, 1983.

28. T. Sheard and L. Fegaras. A fold for all seasons. In *Proc. of 6th ACM SIGPLAN/SIGARCH Int. Conf. on Functional Programming Languages and Computer Architecture, FPCA'93*, pp. 233–242. ACM Press, 1993.

29. J. Svenningsson. Shortcut fusion for accumulating parameters & zip-like functions. In *Proc. of 7th ACM SIGPLAN Int. Conf. on Functional Programming, ICFP'02*, v. 37(9) of *SIGPLAN Notices*, pp. 124–132. ACM Press, 2002.

30. A. Takano and E. Meijer. Shortcut deforestation in calculational form. In *Conf. Record 7th ACM SIGPLAN/SIGARCH Int. Conf. on Functional Programming Languages and Computer Architecture, FPCA'95*, pp. 306–313. ACM Press, 1995.

31. F. Turbak and J. B. Wells. Cycle therapy: A prescription for fold and unfold on regular trees. In *Proc. of 3rd Int. ACM SIGPLAN Conf. on Principles and Practice of Declarative Programming, PPDP'01*, pp. 137–149. ACM Press, 2001.

32. T. Uustalu. Generalizing substitution. *Theoretical Informatics and Applications*, 37(4):315–336, 2003.

33. J. Voigtländer. Concatenate, reverse and map vanish for free. In *Proc. of 7th ACM SIGPLAN Int. Conf. on Functional Programming, ICFP'02*, v. 37(9) of *SIGPLAN Notices*, pp. 14–25. ACM Press, 2002.

34. P. Wadler. Theorems for free! In *Proc. of 4th Int. Conf. on Funct. Prog. Languages and Computer Arch., FPCA'89*, pp. 347–359. ACM Press, 1989.
35. P. Wadler. Deforestation: Transforming programs to eliminate trees. *Theoretical Computer Science*, 73(2):231–248, 1990.
36. P. Wadler. Recursive types for free! Draft manuscript, 1990.

Free Σ-Monoids:
A Higher-Order Syntax with Metavariables

Makoto Hamana

Department of Computer Science, Gunma University, Japan
hamana@cs.gunma-u.ac.jp

Abstract. The notion of Σ-monoids is proposed by Fiore, Plotkin and
Turi, to give abstract algebraic model of languages with variable binding
and substitutions. In this paper, we give a free construction of Σ-monoids.
The free Σ-monoid over a given presheaf serves a well-structured
term language involving binding and substitutions. Moreover, the free
Σ-monoid naturally contains interesting syntactic objects which can be
viewed as "metavariables" and "environments". We analyse the term language of the free Σ-monoid by relating it with several concrete systems,
especially the λ-calculus extended with contexts.

1 Introduction

In theory of programming languages, we often use some extension of the λ-
calculus. When we develop such a theory, we usually use a formal language
consisting of both λ-calculus and its meta-language. For example, when we write
like "for a term $\lambda x.M \cdots$", this "M" is a *metavariable* denoting some λ-term
and is not a (object) variable of the λ-calculus. Since we can also instantiate
this M by substitution at the meta-level, we can see that an operation similar to
the β-reduction also happens at the meta-level. Sato et al. proposed a series of
λ-calculi that formalises both the object-level and such a notion of meta-levels
[SSB99, SSK01, SSKI03].

A natural question is what is a good semantics of such a kind of calculus,
and clearly existing semantics of the λ-calculus has not covered this object/meta
features. This is an interesting mathematical problem. We also expect that it may
be a step to theoretical foundation of meta-programming features considered
in the traditional declarative languages (such as Lisp's quote and backquote,
Prolog's assert) and also revisited recently in the modern programming languages
(such as MetaML, FreshML, Boost C++ Library etc.)

This paper shows that the notion of *free Σ-monoids* can provide an unified
view of the structure of object and meta-levels in syntax. The structure of Σ-
monoids is an abstract algebraic model of syntax with variable binding and
substitutions proposed by Fiore, Plotkin and Turi [FPT99]. Although the notion
of meta-level was originally not considered for Σ-monoids, we will see that the
free construction of them explored here can naturally induce the notions of object
and meta-levels. Moreover, the syntax extracted from the free Σ-monoids can be

W.-N. Chin (Ed.): APLAS 2004, LNCS 3302, pp. 348–363, 2004.
© Springer-Verlag Berlin Heidelberg 2004

used to analyse and relate existing work on extensions of λ-calculus enriched by several new constructs: contexts, metavariables, and environments.

Organisation and Results. Our contribution of this paper is summarised as follows.

i. To give an explicit free construction M_Σ of Σ-monoid (Sect. 3), and show it is a monad (Sect. 4).
ii. To show the free Σ-monoid $M_\Sigma X$ naturally has two-level substitution structure (Sect. 5.1):
    - the Σ-monoid multiplication β gives capture-avoiding substitution, and
    - the monad multiplication μ gives possibly capturing substitution.
iii. The generators X of the free Σ-monoid can be seen as "metavariables" in the sense of Sato et al. [SSKI03]. (Sect. 5.1).
iv. To show a link between Plotkin's staged variables [Plo00] and variables decorated with substitutions in contextual calculi [Tal93, Mas99, HO01, San98, SSK01] via a Kan extension (Sect. 5.2, 5.3).
v. The construct $\lceil x \rceil \langle t_1, \ldots, t_l \rangle$ in the free Σ-monoid which is naturally arisen by the free construction can be seen as an "explicit environment" in the sense of Sato, Sakurai and Burstall [SSB99] (Sect. 5.4).

How to Read the Paper. This paper is based on the work on semantics of abstract syntax with variable binding by Fiore el al. [FPT99] in the framework of categorical algebra. Basic knowledge of category theory is assumed for reading Sect. 2-4, especially monoids, monads and algebras (e.g. [Mac71] Chap. VI, VII). But the construction of free Σ-monoid (Sect. 3.1 (I)) is purely syntactic, so one can understand it without the knowledge of category theory. Also, in Sect. 5, we see how the notion of Σ-monoids gives a unifying point of view on various syntactic manipulations and constructs, as variable binding, holes of contexts, explicit environments, and substitution of object and meta-variables by terms. So, the reader who is interested in these syntactic aspect can start from Sect. 5 after the preliminaries of Sect. 2.

2   Preliminaries

2.1   Matavariables and Object Variables

In this paper, we precisely distinguish "object-level variables" and "meta-level variables". Before going to the main part, we firstly explain this distinction to avoid confusion.

For example, consider the following λ-term in a certain mathematical context:

$$\lambda a.\lambda b.M a$$

where M is a λ-term. At the level of text, this M is a meta-level variable "M". The variable a itself is an actual object-level variable "a" [1]. Moreover, there is also an important difference between metavariables and object variables in view of substitutions. If we substitute a term bb for the (object) variable a in the above term, this is actually impossible because usually we assume "capture-avoiding substitutions" in the λ-calculus, i.e.

$$(\lambda a.\lambda b.Ma)[a := bb] = (\lambda a'.\lambda b.Ma')[a := bb] = \lambda a'.\lambda b.Ma'.$$

But the situation in the case of metavariables differs. If we want to substitute a term bb for M, we have

$$(\lambda a.\lambda b.Ma)\{M \mapsto bb\} = \lambda a.\lambda b.(bb)a$$

where $\{- \mapsto -\}$ denotes a meta-level substitution. In this case, although the (object) variable b is *captured* by the binder, usually it does not matter.

If we view these phenomena at the extra meta-level (i.e. meta-meta-level), these two classes of variables are classified by the distinction of substitutions: capture-avoiding and possibly capturing. We use the notions of "object variables" and "metavariables" in this sense (cf. [SSKI03]) and use the following terminology: *metavariable* or simply *variable* for the notion of metavariable, and *object variable* for the notion of object-level variable.

We do not call "object variable" simply variable except for a particular case in this paper.

2.2 Binding Algebras

Now we are going to technical preliminary. We review the notion of binding algebras by Fiore, Plotkin, and Turi. For detail, see [FPT99].

A *binding signature* Σ is consisting of a set Σ of function symbols with an arity function $a : \Sigma \to \mathbb{N}^*$. A function symbol of arity $\langle n_1, \ldots, n_l \rangle$, denoted by $f : \langle n_1, \ldots, n_l \rangle$, has l arguments and binds n_i variables in the i-th argument $(1 \le i \le l)$.

Example 1. The signature of the λ-calculus has a function symbol λ of arity $\langle 1 \rangle$, *viz.* λ-abstraction with one argument and binding one variable, and function symbol @ of arity $\langle 0, 0 \rangle$, *viz.* application with two arguments and binding no variables. Hereafter, we refer to this signature as "the signature of the λ-calculus".

The free Σ-monoid we will give in this paper consists of terms constructed by this kind of binding signature. For example, by using the construction rules (I) in Sect. 3.1, the term $\lambda([1]\mathsf{ovar}(1))$ can be constructed. This is an encoding of the λ-term $\lambda x.x$ by the method of de Bruijn levels [FPT99], where [-] denotes a binder and $\mathsf{ovar}(i)$ an object variable i.

---

[1] Indeed, this can also be seen as a metavariable a denoting some object-level variable. But assuming a itself is an object variable is simpler and there is no difference in reasoning about them (cf. [Pit03]).

Let $\mathbb{F}$ be the category which has finite cardinals $n = \{1, \ldots, n\}$ (n is possibly 0) as objects, and all functions between them as arrows $m \to n$. This is the category of object variables by the method of de Bruijn levels (i.e. natural numbers) and their renamings. The functor category $\mathbf{Set}^{\mathbb{F}}$ plays an central role in this paper. The objects of it are functors $\mathbb{F} \to \mathbf{Set}$ and the arrows are natural transformations between them. An object $A \in \mathbf{Set}^{\mathbb{F}}$ is often called a *presheaf*.

We define the functor $\delta : \mathbf{Set}^{\mathbb{F}} \to \mathbf{Set}^{\mathbb{F}}$ as follows: for $L \in \mathbf{Set}^{\mathbb{F}}, n \in \mathbb{F}, \rho \in$ arr $\mathbb{F}$,

$$(\delta L)(n) = L(n+1), \quad (\delta L)(\rho) = L(\rho + \mathrm{id}_1).$$

To a binding signature Σ, we associate the *signature functor* $\Sigma : \mathbf{Set}^{\mathbb{F}} \to \mathbf{Set}^{\mathbb{F}}$ given by

$$\Sigma A \triangleq \coprod_{f:\langle n_1, \ldots, n_l \rangle \in \Sigma} \prod_{1 \leq i \leq l} \delta^{n_i} A.$$

A Σ-*binding algebra* (or simply Σ-*algebra*) is a pair (A, α) consisting of a presheaf $A \in \mathbf{Set}^{\mathbb{F}}$ and a map[2] $\alpha = [f_A]_{f \in \Sigma} : \Sigma A \longrightarrow A$ called *algebra structure*, where f_A is an *operation*

$$f_A : \delta^{n_1} A \times \ldots \times \delta^{n_l} A \longrightarrow A$$

defined for each function symbol $f : \langle n_1, \ldots, n_l \rangle \in \Sigma$.

Define the presheaf $V \in \mathbf{Set}^{\mathbb{F}}$ by

$$V(n) = n; \quad V(\rho) = \rho \quad (\rho : m \to n \in \mathbb{F}).$$

In [FPT99], this V is called "the presheaf of variables". More precisely, this V means the presheaf of *object variables*.

Proposition 2. *([**FPT99**]) $(\mathbf{Set}^{\mathbb{F}}, \bullet, V)$ forms a monoidal category [Mac71], where the monoidal product is defined as follows. For presheaves A and B,*

$$(A \bullet B)(n) \triangleq (\coprod_{m \in \mathbb{N}} A(m) \times B(n)^m) / \approx \tag{1}$$

where $\approx$ is the equivalence relation generated by

$$(t; u_{\rho 1}, \ldots, u_{\rho m}) \sim (A(\rho)(t); u_1, \ldots, u_l)$$

for $\rho : m \to l \in \mathbb{F}$. The arrow part of $A \bullet B$ is defined by

$$(A \bullet B)(\rho)(t; u_1, \ldots, u_l) \triangleq (t; B(\rho)(u_1), \ldots, B(\rho)(u_l))$$

for $\rho : n \to k \in \mathbb{F}$. This is certainly well-defined because the equivalence relation $\approx$ is preserved by the map $(A \bullet B)(\rho)$.

Here and throughout this paper, we use the following notation.

Notation 3. An element of $A(m) \times B(n)^m$ is denoted by $(t; u_1, \ldots, u_m)$ where $t \in A(m)$ and $u_1, \ldots, u_m \in B(m)$. A representative of an equivalence class in $A \bullet B(n)$ is also denoted by this notation.

---

[2] $[\,]$ denotes a copair of coproducts.

3   Free Σ-monoids

Definition 4. Let Σ be a signature functor with strength st defined by a binding signature. A Σ-*monoid* consists of a *monoid object* [Mac71] $M = (M, \eta : \mathrm{V} \to M, \mu : M \bullet M \to M)$ in the monoidal category $(\mathbf{Set}^{\mathbb{F}}, \bullet, \mathrm{V})$ with a Σ-binding algebra $\alpha : \Sigma M \to M$ such that

$$
\begin{array}{ccc}
\Sigma(M) \bullet M & \xrightarrow{\;st\;} \Sigma(M \bullet M) \xrightarrow{\;\Sigma\mu_M\;} \Sigma M \\
{\scriptstyle \alpha \bullet M} \downarrow & & \downarrow {\scriptstyle \alpha} \\
M \bullet M & \xrightarrow[\quad\mu_M\quad]{} & M
\end{array}
$$

A morphism of Σ-monoids $(M, \alpha) \longrightarrow (M', \alpha')$ a morphism in $\mathbf{Set}^{\mathbb{F}}$ which is both Σ-algebra homomorphism and monoid morphism. This defines the category Σ-**Mon** of Σ-monoids.

Theorem 5. *([**FPT99**]) A free Σ-algebra* TV *over* V *is an initial Σ-monoid.*

A natural question is an existence of a *free Σ-monoid*. This means whether is there a Σ-monoid which is freely generated from a given *arbitrary* $X \in \mathbf{Set}^{\mathbb{F}}$ and has universality. TV is an example of it but is not a full answer because this Σ-monoid is only generated[3] from a *particular* presheaf.

Now, our aim is to give a free Σ-monoid, denoted by $M_\Sigma X$, generated from arbitrary $X \in \mathbf{Set}^{\mathbb{F}}$. In the following, we explicitly construct it with substitution monoidal structure as a "language" equipped with the feature of variable binding and substitutions. In contrast to V of the presheaf of object variables, we will show that the presheaf X of generators is regarded as the presheaf of *metavariables*, which was not considered in [FPT99]. The actual situation will be clear in Sect. 5.

Remark 6. Notice that the relationship between the notions of free Σ-algebra and free Σ-monoid is *not* a simple implication. Namely, although TV is a free Σ-algebra over V (equivalently, an initial V + Σ-algebra), it is *not* a free Σ-monoid *over* V. Correctly, TV is a free Σ-monoid *over* $0 \in \mathbf{Set}^{\mathbb{F}}$ of the empty set functor, i.e. in our notation, TV $= M_\Sigma 0$. This is easily checked because the explicit construction of TV ([FPT99] Sect. 2) is the same as the construction (I) of $M_\Sigma X$ without using the rule ($\blacklozenge$) (because of $X = 0$) below.

3.1   Construction

Let Σ be a binding signature and X an arbitrary presheaf in $\mathbf{Set}^{\mathbb{F}}$. We construct the Σ-monoid $M_\Sigma X$ by the following four steps and show that it is free.

---

[3] See Remark 6.

(I) The Presheaf $M_\Sigma X$. First we define the set $\bar{M}_\Sigma X(n)$ indexed by $n \in \mathbb{N}$ by the following construction rules (by starting from the first rule).

$$\frac{i \in V(n)}{\mathsf{ovar}(i) \in \bar{M}_\Sigma X(n)}\ \nu(n)$$

$$\frac{f : \langle i_1, \ldots i_l \rangle \in \Sigma \quad t_1 \in \bar{M}_\Sigma X(n+i_1) \quad \cdots \quad t_l \in \bar{M}_\Sigma X(n+i_l)}{f([n+1,\ldots,n+i_1]t_1,\ldots,[n+1,\ldots,n+i_l]t_l) \in \bar{M}_\Sigma X(n)}\ f_{M_\Sigma X}(n)$$

$$\frac{x \in X(l) \quad t_1,\ldots,t_l \in \bar{M}_\Sigma X(n)}{\lceil x \rceil \langle t_1,\ldots,t_l \rangle \in \bar{M}_\Sigma X(n)}\ \sigma(n) \qquad (\blacklozenge)$$

Note that any $l \in \mathbb{N}$ with $X(l) \neq \varnothing$ is possible to apply the rule $(\blacklozenge)$ because X is a functor $\mathbb{F} \to \mathbf{Set}$. So, l is possibly 0, i.e. if $x \in X(0)$, $\lceil x \rceil \langle \rangle \in \bar{M}_\Sigma X(n)$ for all $n \in \mathbb{N}$.

Notation 7. We often simply write $\lceil x \rceil$ for $\lceil x \rceil \langle \mathsf{ovar}(1),\ldots,\mathsf{ovar}(l) \rangle$. Since the binders are clear from the arity of function symbol $f \in \Sigma$, we often abbreviate $f([n+1,\ldots,n+i]t_1,\ldots,[n+1,\ldots,n+l]t_l)$ as just $f(t_1,\ldots,t_l)$.

Define the equivalence relation $\doteq$ on $\bar{M}_\Sigma X(n)$ generated by context (by function symbols in Σ) closure of "the axiom"

$$\lceil x \rceil \langle t_{\rho 1},\ldots,t_{\rho l} \rangle \ \doteq\ \lceil X(\rho)(x) \rceil \langle t_1,\ldots,t_m \rangle \tag{2}$$

for every $\rho : l \to m \in \mathbb{F}, x \in X(l), t_1,\ldots,t_m \in \bar{M}_\Sigma X(n)$ (so, for example, $f(\lceil x \rceil \langle t_2, t_1 \rangle) \doteq f(\lceil X(\rho)(x) \rceil \langle t_1, t_2 \rangle))$. The presheaf $M_\Sigma X \in \mathbf{Set}^{\mathbb{F}}$ is defined by $M_\Sigma X(n) \triangleq \bar{M}_\Sigma X(n) / \doteq$, and for $\rho : n \to n' \in \mathbb{F}$, the arrow part is defined by structural induction (see Remark 8):

$$M_\Sigma X(\rho)(\mathsf{ovar}(i)) = \mathsf{ovar}(\rho(i))$$
$$M_\Sigma X(\rho)(f(t_1,\ldots,t_l)) = f(M_\Sigma X(\rho)(t_1),\ldots,M_\Sigma X(\rho)(t_l))$$
$$M_\Sigma X(\rho)(\lceil x \rceil \langle t_1,\ldots,t_l \rangle) = \lceil x \rceil \langle M_\Sigma X(\rho)(t_1),\ldots,M_\Sigma X(\rho)(t_l) \rangle.$$

The most important point of this construction is the invention of the rule $(\blacklozenge)$, and the related construct $\lceil x \rceil \langle t_1,\ldots,t_n \rangle$ and axiom (2). Syntactic meanings of this construct will be discussed in detail in Sect. 5. The idea of rule $(\blacklozenge)$ comes from a construction of free symmetric multicategory. If the reader is familiar with categorical type theory, this rule may be able to be understood as the (formal) composition of arrows with the principle of "substitution as composition".

(II) Σ-algebra. $M_\Sigma X$ has the $V + \Sigma$-algebra structure

$$[\,\nu, [f_{M_\Sigma X}]_{f \in \Sigma}\,] : V + (\Sigma M_\Sigma X) \longrightarrow M_\Sigma X$$

where the maps $\nu, f_{M_\Sigma X}$ are defined by the construction rule of the presheaf $\bar{M}_\Sigma X$ (the mappings from the upper to the lower in the construction rules). Moreover, it has the $(X + X \bullet -)$-algebra structure $[\eta, \sigma]$. The naturality of algebra structures is straightforward.

Remark 8. When we define a map (say ϕ) whose domain is $M_\Sigma X$ in this paper, we always define it by *structural induction* on terms of the initial $V + X \bullet - + \Sigma$-algebra $(\bar{M}_\Sigma X, [\nu, \sigma, [f_{M_\Sigma X}]_{f \in \Sigma}])$. This way is possible only when the map ϕ respects the equivalence relation $\doteq$ (i.e. $s \doteq t \Rightarrow \phi(s) = \phi(t)$) and in our case, the map ϕ to be defined is always so. Notice that $M_\Sigma X$ is *not* an initial algebra, so *in general* the structural induction is not available to deal with elements in $M_\Sigma X$. Rather than a simple initial algebra, $M_\Sigma X$ is an equational variety using the "axiom" (2).

(III) Monoid. We construct the monoid $(M_\Sigma X, \nu, \beta)$ in the monoidal category $(\mathbf{Set}^{\mathbb{F}}, \bullet, V)$. The unit $\nu : V \to M_\Sigma X$ is already defined in (I). The multiplication $\beta : M_\Sigma X \bullet M_\Sigma X \to M_\Sigma X$ is defined inductively as follows.

$$\beta(n) : \coprod_m M_\Sigma X(m) \times M_\Sigma X(n)^m / \sim \ \longrightarrow \ M_\Sigma X(n)$$

$$(\mathsf{ovar}(i); \vec{t}\,) \longmapsto t_i$$

$$(f(s_1, \ldots, s_l); \vec{t}\,) \longmapsto f(\beta(n+i_1)(s_1; \mathsf{up}_{i_1}(\vec{t}\,)), \ldots, \beta(n+i_l)(s_l; \mathsf{up}_{i_l}(\vec{t}\,)))$$

$$(\lceil x \rceil \langle s_1, \ldots, s_l \rangle; \vec{t}\,) \longmapsto \lceil x \rceil \langle \beta(n)(s_1; \vec{t}\,), \ldots, \beta(n)(s_l; \vec{t}\,) \rangle \quad (x \in X(l))$$

where $f : \langle i_1, \ldots, i_l \rangle \in \Sigma$ and $\vec{t}$ denotes $t_1, \ldots, t_m$, and the weakening map from $M_\Sigma X(n)$ to $M_\Sigma X(n+i)$ is defined by $\mathsf{up}_i \triangleq M_\Sigma(\mathsf{id}_n + \mathsf{w}_i)$ where $\mathsf{w}_i : 0 \to i$. This is well-defined, and the naturality of β follows from the definitions of $M_\Sigma X(\rho)$. The isomorphisms $V \bullet M_\Sigma X \cong M_\Sigma X$, $M_\Sigma X \bullet V \cong M_\Sigma X$, $(M_\Sigma X \bullet M_\Sigma X) \bullet M_\Sigma X \cong M_\Sigma X \bullet (M_\Sigma X \bullet M_\Sigma X)$ of monoid are defined by

$$(i; \vec{t}\,) \mapsto u_i \ , (t; 1, \ldots, l) \mapsto t$$

$$((s; \vec{t}\,); \vec{u}\,) \mapsto (s; (t_1; \vec{u}\,), \ldots, (t_l; \vec{u}\,))$$

The inverse mappings are obvious except for $u : M_\Sigma X \to V \bullet M_\Sigma X$. This u is defined by $t \mapsto (1; t)$ because in $V \bullet M_\Sigma X(n) = \coprod_m m \times M_\Sigma X(n)^m / \approx$, always

$$(i; t_1, \ldots, t_l) \sim (1; t_i)$$

holds by taking $\rho : 1 \to m, 1 \mapsto i$ in the definition of $\sim$; thus u is an isomorphism. The monoid laws are proved by induction on the terms in $M_\Sigma X$.

Notice that the associative law in this case is "substitution lemma" by considering that β is "performing substitution" (Sect. 5.2).

(IV) Σ-monoid. The remaining task is to show that the monoid $(M_\Sigma X, \nu, \beta)$ makes the following diagram of Σ-monoid law commutative. The strength st is the one defined in [FPT99].

$$
\begin{array}{ccc}
\Sigma(M_\Sigma X) \bullet M_\Sigma X \xrightarrow{\ st\ } \Sigma(M_\Sigma X \bullet M_\Sigma X) \xrightarrow{\ \Sigma\beta\ } \Sigma M_\Sigma X \\
{\scriptstyle \alpha \bullet M_\Sigma X} \downarrow \qquad\qquad\qquad\qquad\qquad\qquad\qquad \downarrow {\scriptstyle \alpha} \\
M_\Sigma X \bullet M_\Sigma X \xrightarrow{\qquad\qquad\qquad \beta \qquad\qquad\qquad} M_\Sigma X
\end{array}
$$

Instantiating this diagram at $n \in \mathbb{F}$ and chasing an element, this eventually becomes the equality

$$\beta(n)(f(s_1, \ldots, s_l); \vec{t}\,) = f(\beta(n+i_1)(s_1; \mathsf{up}_{i_1}(\vec{t}\,)), \ldots, \beta(n+i_l)(s_l; \mathsf{up}_{i_l}(\vec{t}\,))).$$

In fact, this is true because it is nothing but the equation (3.1) in the definition of β. Hence, we have the following.

Proposition 9. $(M_\Sigma X, \nu, \beta)$ *is a Σ-monoid.*

3.2   Universality

Definition 10. An *assignment* $\phi : X \to A$ is a morphism of $\mathbf{Set}^{\mathbb{F}}$ whose target A has a Σ-monoid structure $(A, \tilde{\nu}, \tilde{\beta})$.

Then, this is extended to a Σ-monoid morphism $\phi^* : M_\Sigma X \to A$ as follows.

$$
\begin{aligned}
M_\Sigma X(n) &\longrightarrow A(n) \\
\mathsf{ovar}(i) &\longmapsto \tilde{\nu}(n)(i) \\
f(t_1, \ldots, t_l) &\longmapsto f_A(\phi^*(n+i_1)(t_1), \ldots, \phi^*(n+i_l)(t_l)) \\
\lceil x \rceil \langle t_1, \ldots, t_l \rangle &\longmapsto \tilde{\beta}(n)(\phi(l)(x); \phi^*(n)(t_1), \ldots \phi^*(n)(t_l))
\end{aligned}
$$

where $f : \langle i_1, \ldots, i_l \rangle \in \Sigma$. Checking this is certainly a Σ-monoid morphism is straightforward.

Lemma 11.
Let $\phi : X \to A$ and $\psi : X \to B$ be assignments. For a Σ-monoid morphism $h : B \to A$ such that $\phi = h \circ \psi$ in $\mathbf{Set}^{\mathbb{F}}$, the right diagram commutes in Σ-$\mathbf{Mon}$.

$$
\begin{array}{ccc}
M_\Sigma X & \xrightarrow{\psi^*} & B \\
 & \searrow{\scriptstyle \phi^*} & \downarrow{\scriptstyle h} \\
 & & A
\end{array}
$$

Proof. Instantiating the diagram at $n \in \mathbb{F}$, use induction on the structure of terms. □

Finally, we show the Σ-monoid $M_\Sigma X$ has the following universality, which means freeness.

Proposition 12.
Let A be a Σ-monoid and $\phi : X \to A$ an assignment. Then, there exists a unique Σ-monoid morphism $\hat{\phi}$ that makes the right diagram commutative where $\eta_X(n)$ maps x to $\lceil x \rceil$.

$$
\begin{array}{ccc}
X & \xrightarrow{\eta_X} & M_\Sigma X \\
{\scriptstyle \phi}\downarrow & \swarrow{\scriptstyle \hat{\phi}} & \\
A & &
\end{array}
$$

Proof. Actually, such $\hat{\phi}$ exists by taking $\hat{\phi} = \phi^*$. For uniqueness, take $B = M_\Sigma X$ in Lemma 11. □

Theorem 13. $(M_\Sigma X, \nu, \beta)$ *is the free Σ-monoid over $X \in \mathbf{Set}^{\mathbb{F}}$.*

This universality can be rephrased as an adjunction:

Corollary 14. *The functor* $U : \Sigma\text{-}\textbf{Mon} \rightarrow \textbf{Set}^{\mathbb{F}}$ *that forgets the* Σ*-monoid structure has the left adjoint* M_Σ, *i.e. there is an adjunction*

$$\textbf{Set}^{\mathbb{F}} \xrightarrow[\quad U \quad]{\overset{M_\Sigma}{\quad\perp\quad}} \Sigma\text{-}\textbf{Mon}$$

4 Free Σ-Monoid Construction is a Monad

By Corollary 14 and the basic theorem of category theory (every adjunction gives a monad [Mac71]), we know that $U M_\Sigma$ gives a monad on $\textbf{Set}^{\mathbb{F}}$. We state this with the usual identification regarding M_Σ as the endofunctor $U M_\Sigma$ on $\textbf{Set}^{\mathbb{F}}$.

Theorem 15. (M_Σ, η, μ) *is a monad on* $\textbf{Set}^{\mathbb{F}}$.

It is valuable to concretely describe this monad and show the theorem to know the internal structure of the language given by the free Σ-monoid. So, in this section, we explicitly show that M_Σ gives a monad on $\textbf{Set}^{\mathbb{F}}$.

Functor. First, we describe the functor $M_\Sigma : \textbf{Set}^{\mathbb{F}} \rightarrow \textbf{Set}^{\mathbb{F}}$. In Sect. 3.1 (I), we have defined the object part of M_Σ by giving the construction of the free Σ-monoid over a presheaf X. Now, we define the arrow part: for $\phi : X \rightarrow Y \in$ arr $\textbf{Set}^{\mathbb{F}}$, $M_\Sigma(\phi) : M_\Sigma X \rightarrow M_\Sigma Y$ is defined as follows:

$$M_\Sigma\phi(n)(\mathsf{ovar}(i)) = \mathsf{ovar}(i)$$
$$M_\Sigma\phi(n)(f(t_1, \ldots, t_l)) = f(M_\Sigma\phi(n + i_1)(t_1), \ldots, M_\Sigma\phi(n + i_l)(t_l))$$
$$M_\Sigma\phi(n)(\lceil x \rceil \langle t_1, \ldots, t_l \rangle) = \lceil \phi(n)(x) \rceil \langle M_\Sigma\phi(n)(t_1), \ldots, M_\Sigma\phi(n)(t_l) \rangle$$

where $f : \langle i_1, \ldots, i_l \rangle \in \Sigma$.

Unit. The unit $\eta : \mathsf{Id} \rightarrow M_\Sigma$ is defined by $\eta_X(n) : X(n) \rightarrow M_\Sigma X(n)$, $x \mapsto \lceil x \rceil$.

Multiplication. The multiplication $\mu : M_\Sigma \circ M_\Sigma \rightarrow M_\Sigma$ is defined by

$$\mu_X(n) : M_\Sigma(M_\Sigma X)(n) \longrightarrow M_\Sigma X(n)$$
$$\mathsf{ovar}(i) \longmapsto \mathsf{ovar}(i)$$
$$f(t_1, \ldots, t_l) \longmapsto f(\mu_X(n + i_1)(t_1), \ldots, \mu_X(n + i_l)(t_l))$$
$$\lceil s \rceil \langle t_1, \ldots, t_l \rangle \longmapsto \beta(n)(s; \mu_X(n)(t_1), \ldots \mu_X(n)(t_l))$$

where $f : \langle i_1, \ldots, i_l \rangle \in \Sigma$, and $s \in M_\Sigma X(m)$, $t_1, \ldots, t_l \in M_\Sigma M_\Sigma X(n)$.

Monad Laws. We write M for M_Σ for simplicity. The unit laws of the monad is proved straightforwardly by induction of terms in $MX(n)$. The associative law of the monad is also proved by induction, but more cumbersome. The associative law at $X \in \mathbf{Set}^{\mathbb{F}}$ and $n \in \mathbb{F}$ is

$$
\begin{array}{ccc}
MMMX(n) & \xrightarrow{\ M\mu_X(n)\ } & MMX(n) \\[4pt]
{\scriptstyle \mu_{MX}(n)}\Big\downarrow & & \Big\downarrow{\scriptstyle \mu_X(n)} \\[4pt]
MMX(n) & \xrightarrow[\ \mu_X(n)\ ]{} & MX(n)
\end{array}
$$

Namely, we need to prove the equation

$$
\mu_X(n) \circ M\mu_X(n)\ (w) = \mu_X(n) \circ \mu_{MX}(n)\ (w) \tag{3}
$$

for all $w \in MMMX(n)$. We proceed by induction on the structure of w. The cases $w = \mathsf{ovar}(i), f(\vec{t}\,)$ are straightforward chasing. The case $w = \lceil s \rceil \langle \vec{t}\,\rangle$ is again cumbersome. For simplicity, hereafter we omit subscripts and the component parameter n of the natural transformations μ, β. By using $M\mu$ as an arrow part of the functor M_Σ defined above, the equation (3) becomes

$$
\begin{aligned}
\text{lhs} &= \mu(M\mu(\lceil s \rceil \langle \vec{t}\,\rangle)) = \mu(\lceil \mu(s) \rceil \langle M\mu(\vec{t}\,)\rangle) \\
&= \beta(\mu(s);\ \mu(M\mu(\vec{t}\,))) \overset{\text{I.H.}}{=} \beta(\mu(s);\ \mu\mu(\vec{t}\,)), \\
\text{rhs} &= \mu(\beta(s;\ \mu(\vec{t}\,))).
\end{aligned}
$$

So, we need to prove

$$
\beta(\mu(s);\ \mu\mu(\vec{t}\,)) = \mu(\beta(s;\ \mu(\vec{t}\,))). \tag{4}
$$

Conceptually, this means a commutation of the monoid multiplication β and the monad multiplication μ. This point will be discussed with a relationship to contextual calculi in Sect. 5.2. The equation (4) is proved again by induction on the structure of $s \in MMX(n)$. The case $s = u\langle \vec{v}\,\rangle$ is the most complicated case, but a careful equational calculation shows it. Hence, we have shown Th. 15.

A structure similar to this monoid M_Σ and monoid $M_\Sigma X$ is also considered by Ghani and Uustalu [GU03] from the viewpoint of combination of two signatures. They used finitary monads in the category $[\mathbf{Set}, \mathbf{Set}]_f$ of finitary functors, instead of monoids in $\mathbf{Set}^{\mathbb{F}}$, to model substitutions. This finitary monad approach is equivalent to monoid approach in $\mathbf{Set}^{\mathbb{F}}$ used here because the equivalence of categories $[\mathbf{Set}, \mathbf{Set}]_f \simeq \mathbf{Set}^{\mathbb{F}}$. Hence, our M_Σ can also be seen as a structure having monads in two-levels, i.e. it induces the monads on $[\mathbf{Set}, \mathbf{Set}]_f$ and on $\mathbf{Set}$.

5   Analysis on the Term Language of Free Σ-Monoids

5.1   Multiplications as Substitution Operations

An intuition of the multiplication μ of the monad M_Σ is the operation that "erases" (or "collapse") all the outermost brackets "$\lceil - \rceil$". This operation can also be considered as a substitution. Because, for example, performing the multiplication

$$\mu_X(n)(f(\lceil t \rceil)) = f(t)$$

can be rewritten as "applying a substitution"

$$\mu_X(n)(\ f(\lceil * \rceil)\{* \mapsto t\}\ ) = f(t)$$

Here, the notation $f(\lceil \_ \rceil)\{\_ \mapsto \_\}$ is another representation of an element of $M_\Sigma \circ M_\Sigma$, which is a syntactic form of (suspended) substitution. Although we can more rigorously define this identification, we keep this informal for simplicity.

There are two important properties of μ as substitution by this understanding. We state this:

i. μ performs a substitution of *metavariables*.
ii. μ performs a *possibly capturing* substitution.

The above examples shows (i). Why this is metavariable substitution is that the construct $\lceil t \rceil$ is considered as a metavariable in $M_\Sigma(M_\Sigma X)$ (or $*, t$ are metavariables in $M_\Sigma X$). In this case, the generators $M_\Sigma X$ is considered as metavariables.

Interestingly and importantly, we see that μ has the property (ii). For example, we have

$$\mu_X(0)(\ \lambda([1]\lceil \mathsf{ovar}(1) \rceil)\ ) = \lambda([1]\mathsf{ovar}(1))$$

by using the signature of the λ-calculus given in Example 1. Here, the object variable 1 is *captured* by the binder "[1]".

Notice that this kind of capturing cannot happen in the case of the Σ-monoid multiplication $\beta : M_\Sigma X \bullet M_\Sigma X \to M_\Sigma X$. Consider a similar try:

$$\beta(\ \lambda([1]\mathsf{ovar}(1)); \mathsf{ovar}(2)\ ).$$

This expresses that we want to replace the object variable $\mathsf{ovar}(a)$ inside λ with the free object variable $\mathsf{ovar}(b)$. But actually the term is not well-formed, i.e.

$$(\lambda([1]\mathsf{ovar}(1)); \mathsf{ovar}(2)) \notin M_\Sigma X \bullet M_\Sigma X(2).$$

Hence, we state the following by the definition of β and this observation:

iii. β performs a substitution of *object variables*.
iv. β performs a *capture-avoiding* substitution.

5.2   Staged Variables and a Construction of a Presheaf of Metavariables

We have obtained a construction of the free Σ-monoid $M_\Sigma X$ over $X \in \mathbf{Set}^{\mathbb{F}}$ and shown that M_Σ is a monad. As a consequence, we can think of X as a kind of "variables" as in the case of first-order universal algebra.

But what is a presheaf X of variables? In the case of first-order universal algebra, elements in the set X of generators can be just considered as syntactic constants of variables. In the case of binding algebra, this is not so simple, because X itself is a presheaf. One may guess that the component $X(n)$ for each n is a set of variables. This seems feasible but what is a concrete meaning of a "variable" x in a particular component $X(n)$ is still not clear, especially we should know the meaning of the index n. Also, since X must be a functor, we need to consider the functoriality of X.

A hint to answer this problem can be found in Plotkin's "Metalanguage for programming with bound object variables" [Plo00]. He considered the notion of "staged variables" for this metalanguage. Let us see this notion by adapting it for our term language. A variable x has a "stage" n that is a set $\{1, \ldots, n\}$ of object variables, and it is denoted by $x : n$. A typing judgment

$$x : n \vdash t : n$$

means that as usual, t depends on a variable x, and also the term t depends only *on object variables* in n. A staged variable $x : n$ is a variable which means that it is only instantiated by a term having free object variables from 1 to n. The staged variables forms an ℕ-indexed set X by setting $x \in X(n)$ iff $x : n$.

An ℕ-indexed set X is "almost" a presheaf in $\mathbf{Set}^{\mathbb{F}}$. But clearly it is not sufficient because it lacks the arrow part. So, we need to seek some canonical way of constructing a presheaf $X' \in \mathbf{Set}^{\mathbb{F}}$ from an ℕ-indexed set X of staged variables.

Fortunately, there is a construction for it. The category of ℕ-index sets can be expressed as the presheaf category $\mathbf{Set}^{\mathbb{N}}$ (by considering ℕ as a discrete category). Thus, this problem can be abstracted to that of finding a construction of a presheaf in $\mathbf{Set}^{\mathbb{F}}$ from a given presheaf in $\mathbf{Set}^{\mathbb{N}}$. This can be obtained by a Kan extension. Namely, for the inclusion functor J, we have the left Kan extension:

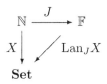

We write this extension as $\hat{X} \in \mathbf{Set}^{\mathbb{F}}$ and calculate it as follows. By the coend formula of the left Kan extension (where "·" denotes a copower) [Mac71] and discreteness of ℕ, we have

$$\hat{X}(n) = (\mathrm{Lan}_J X)(n) = (\int^{k \in \mathbb{N}} \mathbb{F}(Jk, -) \cdot X(k))(n) = \coprod_{k \in \mathbb{N}} \mathbb{F}(k, n) \times X(k)$$

with the obvious arrow part. We use the last coproduct formula as a *definition* of $\hat{X}$ for a given ℕ-indexed set X of *staged variables*.

5.3   Variables Decorated with Substitutions

Next, we consider syntactic meaning of "variables" in $\hat{X}(n)$. Now we know that an element of $\hat{X}(n)$ is a pair (ξ, x) where $x : k$ (i.e. $x \in X(k)$) and $\xi : k \to n \in \mathbb{F}$. So, we use the notation

$$x^\xi \in \hat{X}(n)$$

and call this syntactic construct *a variable with renamer* [Ham01, Ham03] where ξ is a renamer, because ξ is a renaming function on object variables.

By the term construction rule in Sect. 3.1 (I), the above variable with renamer x^ξ becomes the term

$$\lceil x^\xi \rceil = \lceil x^\xi \rceil \langle 1, \ldots, n \rangle \doteq \lceil x \rceil \langle \mathsf{ovar}(\xi 1), \ldots, \mathsf{ovar}(\xi k) \rangle \in M_\Sigma \hat{X}(n)$$

where we are using "the axiom" (2). (In particular, if $\xi : 0 \to n$, $\lceil x^\xi \rceil \doteq \lceil x \rceil \langle \rangle \in M_\Sigma \hat{X}(n)$). Hence, a variable with renamer is merely a particular form of the construct $\lceil x \rceil \langle \cdots \rangle$. Or, one may call it a variable decorated with substitution.

One may seem that this is merely a semantically derived object, or this has no actual computational usefulness. However, it is not true. The same syntactic construct, a variable decorated with substitution, has appeared in several extended λ-calculus for computing with *contexts* [Tal93, Mas99, HO01, San98, SSK01] (also, the same construct is appeared in the series of work based on Nominal Logic [Pit03], e.g. "suspension" construct in [UPG03]). Their extensions of λ-calculus with contexts have the feature of "hole variables" meaning holes of contexts. In these calculi, the notion of "holes decorated with substitutions" plays an essential role to ensure *commutativity of β-reduction and hole-filling operation*. This problem will be clear by the following argument by Sands [San98] on failure of naive extension of the λ-calculus with holes. Later, we will see that this relates to the free Σ-monoid.

Consider the λ-calculus extended with the hole $\square$ syntactically. If we consider this extended λ-calculus naively, we have the following kind of reduction:

$$(\lambda x.\square)y \to_\beta \square.$$

But this is not adequate, since filling the hole with x does not commute with this β-reduction:

$$
\begin{array}{ccc}
(\lambda x.\square)I & \xrightarrow{\ \beta-\text{red.}\ } & \square \\
\text{fill with } x \Big\downarrow & & \Big\downarrow \text{fill with } x \\
(\lambda x.x)I \xrightarrow{\ \beta-\text{red.}\ } I & \not\equiv & x
\end{array}
\qquad (5)
$$

Notice that the operation of filling a hole allows the capture of the variable x by the binder, which is the main feature of contextual calculi. The problem of the above non-commutativity is due to the fact that the reduction step "forgets" the term I. So, the solution in contextual calculi is to syntactically decorate holes with explicit substitutions, so that e.g.

$$(\lambda x.\square)I \to_\beta \square^{\{I/x\}}. \qquad (6)$$

Then, by using this modified β-reduction, the above diagram commutes because the both reductions go to I.

Interestingly, the above diagram has already appeared in this paper. In the proof of monad law in Sect. 4, we encountered the equation (4)

$$\beta(\,\mu(s);\,\mu\mu(\vec{t}\,)\,) = \mu(\,\beta(s;\,\mu(\vec{t}\,))\,).$$

This is diagrammatically,

$$
\begin{array}{ccc}
(s;\,\mu(\vec{t}\,)) \in MMX \bullet MMX & \xrightarrow{\ \ \beta\ \ } & MMX \\[4pt]
{\scriptstyle \mu \bullet \mu} \downarrow & & \downarrow {\scriptstyle \mu} \\[4pt]
MX \bullet MX & \xrightarrow[\ \ \beta\ \ ]{} & MX
\end{array}
$$

and we have proved that it commutes. We claim that *this is nothing but the commutativity of the diagram (5)*. The reason is as follows. We have seen that our metavariables allow possibly capturing substitution in Sect. 5.1. Namely, our metavariables behave exactly the same as holes in contextual calculi. This means that the substitution operation μ of metavariables can be seen as the operation of filling holes. And since β-reduction is a replacement of object-level variables, it corresponds to the substitution of object variables by the monoid multiplication β. Hence, the commutativity (4) of β and μ is the same as the diagram (5)[4]. This means the diagram (5) is an instance of monad law of the free Σ-monoid.

More concretely, Sands' discussion can be formulated in our term language. Assume the beta-axiom of the λ-calculus by using the binding signature of λ-calculus:

$$\lambda([1]\lceil M\rceil)@\lceil N\rceil = \beta(\lceil M\rceil;\lceil N\rceil)$$

where metavariables $M \in X(1)$ and $N \in X(0)$. Then, using the metavariable $* \in X(1)$, we have

$$\lambda([1]\lceil *\rceil)@I = \beta(\lceil *\rceil;I) = \lceil *\rceil\langle I\rangle.$$

By regarding the bound object variable 1 as x and the metavariable $\lceil *\rceil$ as $\square$, this *precisely* corresponds to the reduction (6).

This is an interesting link between the notions appeared in the different areas. We have seen that Plotkin's notion of staged variables naturally induces the notion of decorated variables that has been used for computing with contextual holes.

5.4 Explicit Environments

As we have seen, we can consider the Σ-monoid $M_\Sigma X$ as a "language" having the features of binding, substitutions, and metavariables. It is not only practically

---

[4] So, our implicit intension of naming β the Σ-monoid multiplication is this similarity to β-reduction. Notice also that β-reduction is a substitution of object-level variables.

shown, but also theoretically justified, i.e. it has the desired universal property (Th. 12). Hence, we summarise it formally:

Definition 16. A *higher-order syntax with metavariables* is specified by

- a given binding signature Σ, and
- an indexed set $X(n)$ of staged variables[5] for each $n \in \mathbb{N}$.

The presheaf $M_\Sigma \hat{X}$ of terms is constructed by the construction rules (I) in Section 3.1 where $\hat{X}(n) = \coprod_{k \in \mathbb{N}} \mathbb{F}(k, n) \times X(k)$. Then, terms are expressed as the following BNF:

$$M_\Sigma \hat{X}(n) \ni \quad t ::= \mathsf{ovar}(i) \mid f(t_1, \ldots, t_l) \mid \lceil x \rceil \langle t_1, \ldots, t_l \rangle$$
$$X(n) \ni \quad x$$

where $i \in n$.

This syntax is standard[6] except for the seemingly exotic construct $\lceil x \rceil \langle t_1, \ldots, t_l \rangle$. We call this construct an *explicit environment* which follows the terminology in Sato, Sakurai and Burstall's λ-calculus with "explicit environments" [SSB99]. Namely, $\lceil x \rceil \langle t_1, \ldots, t_l \rangle$ can be seen as a first-class representation of an environment (i.e. a list of (variable,value)-pairs).

Because the sequence part always means substitutes of object variables from 1 to l, informally a term $\lceil x \rceil \langle t_1, \ldots, t_l \rangle$ means

$$\lceil x \rceil \langle 1 \mapsto t_1, \ldots, l \mapsto t_l \rangle.$$

This is a "suspended" substitution because the substitution process does not happen before instantiating the variable x. Our understanding is that a term $\lceil x \rceil \langle t_1, \ldots, t_l \rangle$ is an explicit environment having a "placeholder" $[\_]$ that is named "x" and it waits for an actual term to evaluate (by the multiplication μ) under the environment $\langle t_1, \ldots, t_l \rangle$.

Acknowledgments. The discussion with Masahiko Sato on the role of metavariables in "calculi of metavariables" was an important step of this work; I would like to thank him. I also thank Neil Ghani, and the anonymous referees for useful comments. This work is supported by the JSPS Grant-in-Aid for Scientific Research (16700005).

References

[FPT99]   M. Fiore, G. Plotkin, and D. Turi. Abstract syntax and variable binding. In *Proc. 14th Annual Symposium on Logic in Computer Science*, pages 193–202, 1999.

---

[5] These are metavariables.

[6] By regarding $\mathsf{ovar}(i)$ as an object variable.

[GU03]   N. Ghani and T. Uustalu. Explicit substitutions and higher order syntax. In *Proceedings of 2nd ACM SIGPLAN Workshop on Mechanized Reasoning about Languages with Variable Binding, MERLIN'03*, pages 135–146, 2003.

[Ham01]   M. Hamana. A logic programming language based on binding algebras. In *4th International Symposium on Theoretical Aspects of Computer Software (TACS 2001)*, LNCS 2215, pages 243–262, 2001.

[Ham03]   M. Hamana. Term rewriting with variable binding: An initial algebra approach. In *Fifth ACM-SIGPLAN International Conference on Principles and Practice of Declarative Programming (PPDP2003)*. ACM Press, 2003.

[HO01]   M. Hashimoto and A. Ohori. A typed context calculus. *Theoretical Computer Science*, 266:249–271, 2001.

[Mac71]   S. Mac Lane. *Categories for the Working Mathematician*, volume 5 of *Graduate Texts in Mathematics*. Springer-Verlag, New York, 1971.

[Mas99]   Ian A. Mason. Computing with contexts. *Higher-Order and Symbolic Computation*, 12(2):171–201, 1999.

[Pit03]   A. M. Pitts. Nominal logic, a first order theory of names and binding. *Information and Computation*, 186:165–193, 2003.

[Plo00]   G. Plotkin. Another meta-language for programming with bound names modulo renaming. In *Winter Workshop in Logics, Types and Rewriting*, Heriot-Watt University, February 2000. Lecture slides.

[San98]   D. Sands. Computing with contexts: A simple approach. In *Second Workshop on Higher-Order Operational Techniques in Semantics (HOOTS II)*, volume 10 of *Electronic Notes in Theoretical Computer Science*, 1998.

[SSB99]   M. Sato, T. Sakurai, and R. Burstall. Explicit environments. In *In Proceedings of TLCA'99*, LNCS 1581, pages 340–354, 1999.

[SSK01]   M. Sato, T. Sakurai, and Y. Kameyama. A simply typed context calculus with first-class environments. In *5th International Symposium on Functional and Logic Programming (FLOPS 2001)*, LNCS 2024, pages 359–374, 2001.

[SSKI03] M. Sato, T. Sakurai, Y. Kameyama, and A. Igarashi. Calculi of metavariables. In *Computer Science Logic and 8th Kurt Gödel Colloquium (CSL'03 & KGC)*, LNCS 2803, pages 484–497, 2003.

[Tal93]   C. L. Talcott. A theory of binding structures and applications to rewriting. *Theoretical Computer Science*, 112(1):99–143, 1993.

[UPG03]   C. Urban, A. M. Pitts, and M. J. Gabbay. Nominal unification. In *Computer Science Logic and 8th Kurt Gödel Colloquium (CSL'03 & KGC)*, LNCS 2803, pages 513–527, 2003.

The Scala Experiment – Can We Provide Better Language Support for Component Systems?

Martin Odersky

École Polytechnique Fédérale de Lausanne,
1015 Lausanne, Switzerland
`martin.odersky@epfl.ch`

True component systems have been an elusive goal of the software industry. Ideally, software should be assembled from libraries of pre-written components, just as hardware is assembled from pre-fabricated chips. In reality, large parts of software applications are written "from scratch", so that software production is still more a craft than an industry.

Components in this sense are simply software parts which are used in some way by larger parts or whole applications. Components can take many forms; they can be modules, classes, libraries, frameworks, processes, or web services. Their size might range from a couple of lines to hundreds of thousands of lines.

At least to some extent, the lack of progress in component software is due to shortcomings in the programming languages used to define and integrate components. Most existing languages offer only limited support for component abstraction and composition. This holds in particular for statically typed languages such as Java and C# in which much of today's component software is written.

Scala[1] has been developed between 2001 and 2004 in the programming methods laboratory at EPFL. It stems from a research effort to develop better language support for component software. There are two hypotheses that we would like to validate with the Scala experiment. First, we postulate that a programming language for component software needs to be *scalable* in the sense that the same concepts can describe small as well as large parts. Therefore, we concentrate on mechanisms for abstraction, composition, and decomposition rather than adding a large set of primitives which might be useful for components at some level of scale, but not at other levels. Second, we postulate that scalable support for components can be provided by a programming language which unifies and generalizes object-oriented and functional programming.

To validate our hypotheses, Scala needs to be applied in the design of components and component systems. Only serious application by a user community can tell whether the concepts embodied in the language really help in the design of component software. To ease adoption by users, the new language needs to integrate well with existing platforms and components. Scala has been designed to work well with Java and C#. It adopts a large part of the syntax and type systems of these languages. At the same time, progress can sometimes only be achieved by throwing over board some existing conventions. This is why Scala is

W.-N. Chin (Ed.): APLAS 2004, LNCS 3302, pp. 364–365, 2004.
© Springer-Verlag Berlin Heidelberg 2004

not a superset of Java or C#. Some features are missing, others are re-interpreted to provide better uniformity of concepts.

While Scala's syntax is intentionally conventional, its type system breaks new ground in at least three areas. First, abstract type defininitions and *path-dependent types* apply the νObj calculus [2] to a concrete language design. Second, *symmetric mixin composition* combines the advantages of mixins and traits. Third, *views* enable component adaptation in a modular way.

In this talk, I give an overview of Scala and demonstrate how it helps solving some hard problems in the construction of component systems.

References

1. M. Odersky and al. The Scala Language Specification. Technical report, EPFL Lausanne, Switzerland, Jan. 2004. Available online `http://scala.epfl.ch`.
2. M. Odersky, V. Cremet, C. Röckl, and M. Zenger. A nominal theory of objects with dependent types. In *Proc. ECOOP'03*, Springer LNCS 2743, July 2003.

Pointcuts as Functional Queries

Michael Eichberg, Mira Mezini, and Klaus Ostermann

Software Modularity Lab, Department of Computer Science,
Darmstadt University of Technology, Germany
{eichberg,mezini,ostermann}@informatik.tu-darmstadt.de

Abstract. Most aspect-oriented languages provide only a fixed, built-in set of pointcut designators whose denotation is only described informally. As a consequence, these languages do not provide operations to manipulate or reason about pointcuts beyond weaving. In this paper, we investigate the usage of the functional query language XQuery for the specification of pointcuts. Due to its abstraction and module facilities, XQuery enables powerful composition and reusability mechanisms for pointcuts.

1 Introduction

Join points and pointcuts are pivotal concepts of aspect-oriented programming (AOP for short). *Join points* are points in the code (static join point) and/or execution (dynamic join point) of a program. A *pointcut* is a set of join points that share common properties, e.g., the set of all execution points of a certain program, where one would like to control access rights. Pointcuts are defined by means of *pointcut designators* - predicates on join points. Once a pointcut is specified, semantic effect at the referenced join points can be defined in a uniform way, e.g., implementing a certain access control policy.

AspectJ-like languages come with a set of predefined pointcut designators, such as e.g., `call` and `get`, that are used as predicates over join points. One disadvantage of this approach is that there is no general-purpose mechanism in AspectJ to relate different join points, only some special-purpose predicates such as `cflow` allow pointcuts to go beyond a single join point. To convey an intuition of this limitation, let us consider identifying all join points where the value of a variable is changed that is previously read in the control flow of a method `display`, the goal being that we would like to recall `display` at any such point. Assuming a hypothetical AspectJ compiler that employs some static analysis techniques to predict control flows, one can write a pointcut `p1` that selects all getters in the predicted control flow of `display`. However, it is not possible to combine `p1` with another pointcut `p2` which takes the result of `p1` as a parameter, retrieves the names of the variables read in the join points selected by `p1`, and then selects the set of join points where one of these variables is changed. What we need is the ability to reason about join points in `p1` and `p2` *simultaneously*.

In this paper we argue that a pointcut language should have a general purpose mechanism to define predicates that relate different join points. In order to show

W.-N. Chin (Ed.): APLAS 2004, LNCS 3302, pp. 366–381, 2004.
© Springer-Verlag Berlin Heidelberg 2004

the value and the feasibility of such AO languages we have implemented an AOP model in which pointcuts are sets of nodes in a tree representation of the program's modular structure, and such sets are selected by queries on node attributes written in a query language and can be passed around to other query functions as parameters.

These concepts are exemplified in the Java context, as follows. We have created an XML-to-class file assembler/disassembler that can be used to create an XML representation of a class file and convert an XML file back into a class file on the basis of our BAT [1] bytecode framework. On top of this XML representation of the program structure, we use XQuery, a standard functional XML query language as our pointcut language. The choice for XML and XQuery is not conceptual, though; the decision was mainly a matter of reusing existing tools - it would have also been possible to define the query language directly on class files but then we could not reuse existing XQuery implementations.

Pointcuts specified as functional queries over some representation of a program have three main benefits. First, queries enable to write *precise specifications of pointcuts*. In current languages, pointcuts are only described informally and have a complicated, imperative implementation. Formal specifications of AspectJ-like pointcut languages exist but the implementation of the poincuts is separated from their specification. On the contrary, queries allow a short and precise specification of the meaning of a pointcut construct (assuming that the semantics of the XQuery primitives themselves is clear – in the case of XQuery, this is backed up by the existence of a formal semantics [19]). Second, poincuts as functional queries enable *open pointcut languages* in a very natural way. By means of our query language users can extend the pointcut language with their own pointcuts: It becomes possible to create libraries of domain-specific pointcuts, e.g., for synchronization, or for optimizations.

Last but not least, a pointcut query language allows to create more *semantic pointcut mechanisms* [6, 10]. Since we consider the support for more semantic pointcuts an important goal of our work, let us clarify what we mean by a semantic pointcut mechanism. We will use for this purpose the display updating example, basically an instantiation of the observer pattern [5], used as a canonical example for AspectJ [10]. In the example, graphical objects of type FigureElement, such as Points and Lines are shown on a singleton Display object (the classes involved are shown in Fig. 1). Furthermore, it is required that any change on the part of the state of the graphical objects which is read during the execution of FigureElement.draw() should trigger an update of the display object by calling the method Display.update().

An example implementation of the display updating functionality in AspectJ is shown in Listing 1.1. The aspect modularizes the decisions about (a) where to trigger the update of the display object, as well as, (b) how the triggering should be performed. The "how" is to call Display.update() after any element of the "where" set. The "where" consists of invocations of methods whose name starts with set declared in FigureElement+ ("+" denotes subclasses FigureElement), or of the method FigureElement.moveBy(int,int).

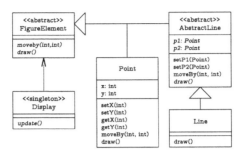

Fig. 1. UML diagram of the FigureElement example

While nicely modularizing the decision about where to trigger the display updating functionality[1], the pointcut in Listing 1.1 is problematic in terms of modular composition of the aspect and the graphical objects [6, 10]. Instead of expressing our intention to *"select points in the execution that modify variables previously read within the control flow of the method* `FigureElement+.draw()`*"*, the pointcut actually relies on implementation details of how the interesting points actually appear in the program code. The problem with such a specification is that it makes the pointcut fragile w.r.t. changes in graphical object classes. E.g., if one adds a new field that does not have a setter method, but is actually read in the control flow of any method `FigureElement+.draw`, changes to this field would escape the aspect, if the latter is not accordingly modified.

Listing 1.1. Display Updating in AspectJ

```
1 FigureElement+.set*(..)) ||
2         call(void FigureElement.moveBy(int, int)) { Display.update(); }
```

To convey the intuition behind more semantic pointcut mechanisms Kiczales [10] gives the example of the `pcflow` pseudo-pointcut[2] shown in Listing 1.2. The pointcut is meant to say: *" (a) predict the control flow of* `FigureElement+.draw()` *and find field reading execution points within it, (b) retrieve the set of the fields being read (denoted by* `<displayState()>`*), and (c) trigger a display update at any execution point where a field contained in* `<displayState()>` *is modified"*. This specification describes the set of the join points we want to select by their semantics - it describes "what" the interesting points are, rather than "how" they are implemented. We call this an *implementation-shy* pointcut[3]. As such, it remains stable toward changes in the implementation mentioned above. One can conclude that implementation-shy pointcut mechanisms make AOP more useful, more principled, more robust.

---

[1] In an object-oriented solution, the programmer would have to spread the code for triggering the update of the display around the classes **Point** and **Line**.

[2] The "*" after the keyword **pointcut** stands for "pseudo".

[3] This is in analogy to the notion of structure-shy behavior supported by traversal strategies in Demeter [13].

Listing 1.2. PCFlow Pseudo-Code

```
1 pointcut* displayState(): pcflow(execution(void FigureElement+.draw()))
2                                          && get(* FigureElement+.*);
3 after set(<displayState()>)(): { Display.update(); }
```

Unfortunately, implementation-shy pointcuts are not properly supported by AOP languages so far. As we already mentioned, the key problem is that with current technology there is no general-purpose support to relate different join points. However, the pseudo-notation `<displayState()>` stands for a reification of the result produced by the `displayState` pointcut, so that the names of the accessed fields can be retrieved and passed as a parameter to the `set` pointcut. We will demonstrate how pointcuts as the one in Listing 1.2 can be expressed as queries.

In this paper, we focus only on static pointcuts, i.e., pointcuts that correspond directly to locations in the source-code/byte-code, also called *join point shadows* in the terminology introduced in [14]. AspectJ's dynamic pointcuts such as `target`, `this`, and `cflow` are not in the focus of this paper. The reason is that these pointcuts do not by themselves define new shadows and are implemented by the AspectJ compiler by inserting conditional logic at shadows selected by static pointcuts [7]. Our focus on static pointcuts is due to the use of the static structure of the program as the data over which to run queries. Also, one of the first usages of this pointcut language is in the context of our XIRC tool [4], whose purpose is to visualize crosscutting structure in the code. However, we think that the notion of pointcuts as functional queries can be applied to any representation of a program, e.g., a representation of the dynamic control flow. This would allow to express dynamic join points more elegantly but is also challenging to implement efficiently. The generalization of our approach to queries on the dynamic call graph is actually the next step in our future work.

The reminder of this paper is structured as follows. In Sec. 2 we give an overview of our representation of class files as XML trees. In Sec. 3, we give a short introduction to XQuery and show how basic and advanced pointcuts can be implemented as queries. In addition, we present first performance results of our implementation, indicating that an efficient implementation is feasible. Sec. 4 presents related work. Sec. 5 concludes.

2   Data Model

The data model on top of which pointcut queries are formulated is closely related, although not identical (see below), to Java bytecode. As mentioned before, all pointcut queries operate on an XML representation of a class file. This XML representation is generated by analyzing the bytecode of a class and can always be transformed back into bytecode. The `BAT2XML` tool is used for this purpose[4]. Representing a class file as an XML document, i.e., as a tree structure, is a very natural thing to do: A class defines methods and fields and each method in turn

---

[4] The tool can be downloaded from: http://www.st.informatik.tu-darmstadt.de/BAT

defines its functionality by an ordered sequence of (bytecode) instructions. If necessary, sub-sequences of instructions can be further grouped.

The meta-structure of the generated XML representation is shown in Fig. 2. A top-level `all` node represents a program space for which we want to determine shadows corresponding to a pointcut designator[5]. All classes belonging to the program space at hand are represented by the children of `all`. The children of a class node, in turn, define the inherited classes and interfaces as well as the declared fields and methods. While a class node can have many `field` and `method` children it can have at most one `inherits` child node. The `inherits` node can have one `class` node and an arbitrary number of `interface` children. A `field` node basically defines the `name` and the `type` of a field. A `method` node represents a method declaration, consisting of two children, the node representing the `signature` of the method and the node representing its `code`. If the method is native or abstract the `code` child does not exist. However, if it exists, it has one to many children representing the `instructions` of the method.

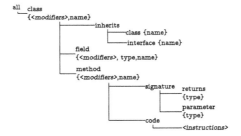

Fig. 2. The meta structure of the XML representation of a program.

The `<modifiers>` of a class, method or field are represented by attributes with boolean values, i.e., if a class is abstract the corresponding node has an attribute `abstract` with the boolean value `true`. The visibility modifiers (`public`, `protected` and `private`) are represented by the `visibility` attribute the value of which is the name of the visibility identifier. E.g., the XML representation of the field definition `private final int length` would be:

```
1 <field visibility="private" final="true" type="int" name="length"/>
```

Our XML representation abstracts over some details of Java bytecode to make the XML representation accessible to a query writer at a higher-level of abstraction. For instance, a field read access is represented in Java bytecode either as a `getfield` or as a `getstatic` instruction, depending on whether the field is static or not. In the XML representation both bytecode instructions are uniformly represented by a `get` node with an attribute indicating whether or not the field is static. The `declaringClassName` and the `fieldName` are the attributes of every `get` or `put` instruction, as shown below:

---

[5] Several strategies similar to those employed in AspectJ, (e.g., `.lst` files) can be used to determine this scope.

```
1 <get declaringClassName="AbstractLine" fieldName="p1"
2          static="false" type="Point" />
```

In a similar way, there are different invocation operations in Java byte-code for virtual and static methods. All `invoke` bytecode instructions are represented by one `invoke` node. The attributes of an `invoke` instruction are the name of the invoked method, the name of the declaring class, and the `signature` of the method including its return type, as shown below:

```
1 <invoke declaringClassName="FigureElement" methodName="moveBy">
2   <signature>
3    <returns type="void"/><parameter type="int"/><parameter type="int"/>
4   </signature>
5 </invoke>
```

All in all, the XML presentation of the byte code is roughly equivalent to an abstract syntax tree of the source code, modulo some peculiarities of the byte-code format[6].

Note that the introduced abstraction does not lead to loss of expressiveness in writing queries. For most queries (especially queries to express AspectJ pointcuts) the only information we need is that a certain field is read/written by a `get/put` instruction, or that a method is invoked. The abstraction brings our data model a little closer to the structure of the source code. Nevertheless, we do not fully abstract from bytecode details, e.g., there are no explicit `get`, `invoke` instructions in source code.

For illustration, listing 1.3 shows the XML representation generated for the following Java source code:

```
1 abstract class AbstractLine extends FigureElement {
2     Point p1 = new Point(); Point p2 = new Point();
3     FigureElement(){ super(); }
4     void setP1(Point point) {this.p1 = point;}
5     void setP2(Point point) {this.p2 = point;}
6     void moveBy(int x,int y){
7         this.p1.moveBy(x, y); this.p2.moveBy(x, y);
8     }
9     abstract void draw();
10 }
```

Listing 1.3. XML Representation of the Java class `AbstractLine`

```
1 <class abstract="true" name="AbstractLine">
2     <inherits><class name="FigureElement"/></inherits>
3     <field type="Point" name="p1"/>
4   <field type="Point" name="p2"/>
5   <method name="<init>">
6     <signature><returns type="void"/></signature>
7     <code>...</code>
8   </method>
9   <method name="setP1">
10     <signature> <returns type="void"/>
11         <parameter type="Point"/>
12     </signature>
13     <code>
14       <load index="0"/>
```

---

[6] For example, exception handling in byte code can in general not be mapped back to the original *try-catch-finally* form.

```
15      <load index="1"/>
16      <put declaringClassName="AbstractLine" fieldName="p1"/>
17      <return/>
18    </code>
19  </method>
20  <method name="setP2">... as "setP1" but setting p2 </method>
21  <method name="moveBy">
22    <signature> <returns type="void"/>
23        <parameter type="int"/><parameter type="int"/>
24    </signature>
25    <code>...</code>
26  </method>
27  <method abstract="true" name="draw">
28    <signature><returns type="void"/></signature>
29  </method>
30 </class>
```

The XML representation defines the same methods (line 9,20,21,27) and fields (line 3,4) as the source code. The constructor is represented by the method `<init>` (line 5) with return type `void` (line 6). The code of the constructor (line 7,27) and the `moveBy` methods are omitted for brevity. To understand the representation of the `setP1` method it is important to know that the Java Virtual Machine (JVM) is a stack machine. The instruction `<load index="0"/>` (line 14) puts the value stored in the local variable with index 0 onto the stack. This value is `this` and is always stored in the local variable with index 0 at the beginning of an instance method. The parameters passed to a method are stored in the following local variables. In this case, the instance of `Point` that will be assigned to the field `p1` is stored in the local variable with index 1 (line 15) and is also put onto the stack. The `put` instruction (line 16) pops both values from the stack and assigns the top value to the field `p1` of the instance referenced by the 2nd top-most value. Finally, the return instruction terminates the method.

3   Queries

We will first introduce XQuery. Subsequently, we show how AspectJ's primitive pointcuts, such as `execution, call, and within`, as well as pattern matching on signatures can be expressed in XQuery. The goal is to give the reader an intuition of the pointcuts-as-queries metaphor by the relation to something known. The remaining static pointcuts of AspectJ, such as `staticinitialization`, `set`, and `get`, can be expressed in a similar way, and will not be discussed for brevity reasons. Finally, we will demonstrate the power of our approach by a more sophisticated pointcut example and discuss weaving and performance issues.

3.1   XQuery

XQuery [18] is a query language for Extensible Markup Language (XML) data sources. While XQuery is a fully functional language comprised of several kinds of expressions that can be nested and composed with full generality, we will only elaborate on the parts that are relevant to the purpose of this paper. For our purposes, the most important part of XQuery is the notion of *path expressions*. In a nutshell, a path expression selects nodes in a (XML-)tree. For example, the path expression `$all/class/method` selects all method nodes of the tree corresponding to the XML document from listing 1.3. In general, a path expression consists of a series of *steps*, separated by the slash character. The path expression above has two steps: the *child* steps `class` and `method`. The result of each path expression is a sequence of nodes; in this case all `method` nodes from Listing 1.3.

XQuery supports different directions in navigating through a tree, called *axes*. In the path expression above we have seen the *child* axis. Other axes relevant for this paper are the *descendant axis* (denoted by "`//`"), the *parent axis* (denoted by "`..`"), and the *attribute axis* (denoted by "`@`"). Using the descendants axis rather than the child axis means that one step may traverse multiple levels of the hierarchy. For example, the above query could be rewritten as `$all//method`. The attribute axis selects an attribute of the given context node, whereas the parent axis selects the parent of a given node. For example, the path expression `$all//code/../@name` selects all `name` attributes of all method nodes that have a `code` child, i.e., which are not abstract or native methods. Another important feature of XQuery is its notion of *predicates* - (boolean) expressions enclosed in square brackets, used to filter a sequence of values. For example, the query `$all//method[@name="setP1"]` selects all methods whose name is `setP1`.

One can bind the result of an expression to a variable by means of a `let` expression. Variables in XQuery are marked with the `$` character. As already mentioned, we will use the variable name `$all` for the root element node containing all classes on which we want the queries to operate. XQuery also offers a number of set operators to combine sequences of nodes, namely `union`, `intersect`, and `except`, with the usual set-theoretic denotation, except that the result is again a sequence in document order. The last important feature of XQuery used in this paper is its notion of a function definition. The following function definition subtracts the results of two pointcuts passed to it as parameters. Note that all selection operations in XQuery work on *sequences* of selected nodes: `$p1, $p2` being of type `element()*` means that they are *sequences* of selected elements. Hence, it is possible to pass the result of another pointcut query to this function.

```
declare function diff($p1 as element()*,$p2 as element()*) as element()*
{ $p1/.. except $p2/.. }
```

3.2   Method Execution and Pattern Matching

Let us start with the `execution` pointcut designator (PCD) in AspectJ. As an example, consider finding executions of the method `void setX(int i)` declared in class `Point`. In AspectJ, this would be expressed by the PCD `execution(* Point.setX(..))`. The same semantics can be expressed in our approach by the query `$all/class[@name="Point"]/method[@name="setX"]`. We start with the set of all nodes (`$all`), search from there for class nodes with the `name` attribute `Point` (recall that the `@` operator selects attributes) and select direct method sub-nodes of the latter with the `name` attribute equal to `setX`.

Note how AspectJ's notion of wild cards corresponds to specifying or omitting additional query constraints. E.g., to find all methods named `setX` in *all* classes (corresponding to execution(* *.setX(..)) in AspectJ), we would write: $all//method[@name="setX"]. Constraints on the signature can be expressed by appropriate conditions. For example, the query

$all//method/signature/parameter[1][@type="int"]/../..

selects methods whose first parameter is of type int. Note that /../.. selects the ancestor method node of the int parameter node at hand. Similarly, one can select based on return types or modifiers.

XQuery provides a rich library of functions for pattern matching on names. E.g., $all/class[@name="Point"])/method[starts-with(@name,"set")] selects all methods whose name starts with set in class Point (corresponding to execution(* Point.set*(..)) in AspectJ), whereby starts-with is a library function of XQuery. Similarly, other name patterns can be expressed by appropriate calls to these library functions.

3.3   Method Calls and Subtype Predicates

Another important category of pointcuts are method calls, corresponding to AspectJ's call PCDs. For such slightly more sophisticated pointcuts, it makes sense to define a reusable XQuery function. This is illustrated by the function call below, which given a set of nodes from which to select, denoted by $all, and a set of (previously selected) method nodes, $meths, passed to it as parameters, selects from $all any call instruction to one of the methods in $meths. The = operator in XQuery is implicitly existentially quantified if it is used on sets/sequences of values: If *there exists* a node in the set $meths whose name is the same as @methodName the condition evaluates to *true*.

```
declare function call($all element(), $meths as element()*) as element()* {
    $all//invoke[(@methodName = $meths/@name) and
                 (@declaringClassName = $meths/../@name)]
}
```

Given the definition of call, the following expression selects all calls to any method whose first parameter is of type int (corresponding to the PCD call(* *.*(int, ..)) in AspectJ). This usage of the call query function demonstrates the idea of relating different join points: The query parameter passed to the call function is itself a pointcut.

```
call($all,$all//method/signature/parameter[1][@type="int"]/../..)
```

An important operation in the context of method calls is the ability to reason about all subtypes of a given type. This is important for expressing predicates of the kind *"calls to a method m of class C or any of its subclasses"*, corresponding to PCDs of the form call(* *.C+.m(..)) in AspectJ. All subtypes of a given set $types of previously selected classes can be retrieved by the recursive function definition subtypes below. This function computes the direct subtypes of $types in $s. If $s is empty, then $types is already the result, otherwise the result is the union of $types with the result of the recursive call subtypes($all, $s).

```
1  declare function subtypes($all as element()*, $types as element()*)
2          as element()* {
3     let $s := $all/class[./inherits//@name = $types/@name]
4     return if (empty($s)) then $types else $types union subtypes($all, $s)
5  }
```

For illustration, the function `subtypes` is used in the following query to select calls to methods in class `FigureElement` or any of its subclasses, whose
name starts with the string `set` (PCD `call(* FigureElement+.set*(..))` in
AspectJ).

```
1  call($all,subtypes($all,$all/class[@name="FigureElement"])
2                          /method[starts-with(@name,"set")])
```

3.4 Lexical Restrictions and PCD Composition

Lexical predicates on join points such as *"within the code of class X"*, expressed
by the primitive pointcut `within` in AspectJ, can be expressed in two different
ways as queries, which we will illustrate by AspectJ's PCD `within(Line) &&
get(* *.p1)`. One way is to select by the name of the unit (class or method) serv-
ing as the lexical scope. E.g., `$all//class[@name="Line"]//get[@name="p1"]`
selects all field read instructions accessing a field `p1` inside the code of the class
`Line`. The same PCD can be expressed by `$all//class[@name="Line"]//*
intersect $all//get[@name="p1"]`, using the path selection operation `//*`,
which selects all sub-nodes of a given node.

Note the use of XQuery's set operation `intersect` above. Together with the
path selection operation, it enables to combine lexical restrictions with any other,
arbitrary sophisticated, query. For illustration, consider the following query,
which corresponds to AspectJ's PCD `within(Line) && call(* Point.getX(
..))`. The same semantics would be hard to express by the approach to lexical
restrictions based on predicates on the name of the lexical element.

```
1  let $c := call($all,$all//class[@name="Point"]/method[@name="getX"])
2  $all//class[@name="Line"]//* intersect $c
```

The example just discussed brings us to the issue of composing queries. The
logical PCD composition operations from AspectJ, *or* (`||`), *and* (`&&`) and *not*
(`!`) can be very naturally expressed in our approach by the corresponding set
operators of XQuery, as shown below.

```
1  pc1 && pc2   <-->   pc1 intersect pc2
2  pc1 || pc2   <-->   pc1 union pc2
3  !pc1         <-->   $all except pc1
```

3.5 Advanced Pointcuts

In the introduction, we discussed the need to support more abstract pointcuts
and discussed a pointcut designator proposed by Kiczales [10] that predicts the
control flow of methods. We presented such a semantic-based pointcut in the
introduction and argued that in order to support it, support for relating different

join points is needed. In the following we show how the desired semantic can be expressed by pointcut queries.

A very simple (and not very precise) mechanism of predicting the control flow of a set of methods $m is specified by the following query. The local variable $pcflow1 selects all methods that are called inside $m. If this set is empty, then $m is already the result, otherwise we compute the next level of methods that are not yet contained in the predicted control flow. The condition `except $m//method` guarantees that the function terminates in the presence of cyclic call structures.

```
1  declare function pcflow($all as element()*, $m as element()*)
2       as element()* {
3     let $pcfl1 := $all//method[@name = $m//invoke/@method] except $m//method
4     return if (empty($pcfl1)) then $m else pcflow($all, $m union $pcfl1)
5  }
```

This algorithm for predicting the control flow is not very precise because it considers only method names and not subtyping restrictions or control flow/data flow analysis inside method bodies. Of course, we could define more sophisticated predictions using control- and dataflow techniques, but this is not in the scope of this paper[7]. The purpose of the example is primarily to illustrate the generality and expressiveness of our queries. To serve this purpose, let us take a look at how this function can be used in our observer example focusing on how it can be used to make the pointcut specification more robust. The following query selects all assignment instructions to fields that are read in the predicted control flow of the method `FigureElement+.draw()`, thereby expressing the `pcflow` pseudo PCD from the introduction.

```
1  $all//put[@name = pcflow($all,
2                  subtypes($all,$all/class[@name="FigureElement"])
3                                    /method[@name="draw"])//get/@name ]
```

Note how an aspect that defines an advice (e.g., to call `Display.update()`) with this pointcut as a parameter abstracts over the control flow between **Figure-Element** and **Display** objects. The advice would be "control flow shy", which means that it will not be affected by changes in the implementation of the base software other than changing the name of the class `FigureElement`, or of the methods `draw` and `update`, hence enhancing modular reasoning supported by aspect modularity.

3.6   Weaving

The language to specify pointcuts is largely independent from the question on how to use a pointcut. It can be used for different purposes, e.g., weaving of advice code, generation of error/warning messages, visualization, support for refactoring etc. In order to create a complete system we have implemented a primitive weaving engine on top of our pointcut language that weaves calls to a central aspect dispatcher before and after every join point of a query result.

---

[7] We have implemented a more precise version of `pcflow` that takes subtyping into account but we do not present it here due to space reasons.

At runtime, advices can be registered for a pointcut via a corresponding API. Context information (caller, receiver, arguments etc.) can be received via API calls. It would be straightforward to integrate advices like in AspectJ directly into a programming language on top of this API.

3.7   Performance

Query	Time in sec.

`1` `let $field := //field[@visibility="protected"]`
`2` `return //get[@declaringClassName = $field/../@name`
`3` `            and @fieldName = $field/@name]`
 	
get(protected *.*)
	0.81
	(273 nodes)
	
	2.15

`1` `//invoke[@declaringClassName="de.tud.BytecodePointcut"`
`2` `         and @methodName="getFilter"]`
 	
call(de.tud.BytecodePointcut.getFilter(..))
	0.45
	(5 nodes)
	
	2.14

`1` `$all/class[starts-with(@name, "de.tud.")]`
`2` `   //invoke[@declaringClassName="de.tud.BytecodePointcut"`
`3` `            and @methodName="getFilter"]`
 	
call(de.tud.BytecodePointcut.getFilter(..)) && within (de.tud..*)
	0.06
	(5 nodes)
	
	2.32

`1` `let $types :=`
`2` `    subtypes($all/class[@name="de.tud.Instruction"])/@name`
`3` `return //invoke[@methodName="toString" and`
`4` `                @declaringClassName = $types]`
 	
call(de.tud.Instruction+.toString(..))
	0.66
	(26 nodes)
	
	4.78

`1` `pcflow(//method[@name="toString" and not(.//parameter[1])])`
`2` `  //put`
 	
set(*.*) withincode <pcflow(*.toString())>
	10.64
	(14 nodes)

In order to show that our approach can be implemented with reasonable performance we made an initial performance evaluation of pointcuts as queries. We have measured the time needed to evaluate some pointcut queries using the BAT toolkit itself as the code base [8], which has 704 class files (roughly 1.5MB of uncompressed class files). The following table shows the evaluated queries along with an equivalent AspectJ PCD (if possible) and the time required to evaluate them together with the number of selected nodes. To measure the times for AspectJ we have used an instrumented variant of the weaving class loader in order to isolate the time to evaluate a pointcut as much as possible. We simply used a `declare warning` statement such that no actual weaving took place[9]. However, this should not be considered a hard, fair comparison because the time to load the XML representation takes longer than reading the binary representation of a class and more memory is required (roughly 3-4 times) to

---

[8] Time measured on an AthlonXP 2600, 512MB Ram, WindowsXP and Sun JDK 1.5.0beta1

[9] We used AspectJ version 1.2 for comparison.

hold the XML representation. Further, the time measured for the AspectJ weaver includes the time to create its internal representation out of an in-memory byte array, whereas in our case the input is parsed XML which does not need to be further transformed. The purpose of these numbers is merely to indicate that the performance does not explode in our system for queries that resemble AspectJ's pointcut designators. Indeed, they indicate that the performance is reasonable and that the architecture can be used to prototype new queries and will deliver comparable numbers. Note that for queries, such as e.g., the `pcflow` query, it is necessary to further investigate if they can be implemented efficiently enough for every day usage.

These preliminary measurements are very encouraging and show that the usage of a full-fledged query pointcut language can be considered.

4   Related Work

The most relevant related works are approaches that propose crosscut languages based on logic query languages [9, 6]. In these approaches, pointcuts are specified as logic queries in Prolog or Prolog-like languages. JQuery [9] is a browser which allows users to select views of the program and to define how the selected program elements should be ordered on the browser. The logic query pointcut language proposed in [6] operates on top of a reification of static and/or dynamic properties of Smalltalk programs.

The goal of these languages is quite similar to ours, the main difference being the usage of a logic versus a functional query language. The pointcut language of [6] can directly express dynamic join points, while the pointcut language discussed in this paper can only express patterns relating static join points. However, we think that this difference is mainly due to the different data model on which the languages operate.

A more important difference is that, by the usage of unification, one gets a powerful mechanism to retrieve context information from join points for free. This is more complicated in our approach, where context information has to be explicitly retrieved. On the other hand, in our approach one gets the advantage of a statically-typed functional language with a powerful module system for free. The possibility of creating user-defined pointcut libraries as in our approach is not mentioned in [6]. We cannot yet give a final answer to the question which of these approaches is better suited to express pointcuts, but we think that at least our work provides a good basis for a comparison.

Josh [2] is an AspectJ-like language with an extensible pointcut mechanism built on top of Javassist [3]. The Josh compiler takes an aspect as input and produces a special weaver – a Java program that uses Javassist to perform the weaving. The generated weaver iterates over all elements of a program that are exposed as meta-objects by Javassist, such as classes, fields, constructors and method objects, and adds the advice code if the element at hand represents a join point shadow [11] that matches the pointcut designator of the advice. To realize matching, the compiler generates calls to static methods corresponding to pointcut designators provided by Josh. Such methods are implemented by a developer in the process of extending Josh with new PCDs[10].

There are significant differences between Josh and our approach. Especially, Josh does not support declarative pointcut specifications. New PCDs are implemented as meta-programs in Josh using the Javassist library. Josh basically suffers from the problems of a meta-programming approach, especially with respect to the composability of the PCDs implemented as meta-programs. In the introduction, we claimed the precise specification of pointcuts as one of the benefits of the pointcuts-as-queries approach as compared to current AOP languages, where pointcuts have complicated, imperative semantics. This is worse in Josh, where such complicated imperative meta-programming semantics can be written by the developer.

Masuhara and Kawauchi presented in [15] a pointcut which selects join points based on the flow of data. To be precise, the proposed `dflow` pointcut designator selects join points with a specific value, if the value originated from a location selected by a pointcut. We think that our query language would be a good basis for specifying these kinds of pointcuts in a general-purpose framework, so this is part of our future work.

We view our approach as contributing to the definition of an AOP language capable to accommodate different join point models of different AOP approaches. In this respect, it is related to the *Concern Manipulation Environment* [8] (CME) which is intended to be an extensible, reusable, open, and customizable platform on which AOSD tool developers can build and integrate tools. Opposed to CME's goal to provide a query engine as one of the components (tools) of a concern manipulation environment, we argue for having crosscuts be first-class constructs of an aspect-oriented language and for having built-in language expressions that operate on these values. However, we also investigated the usage of queries over the program in an IDE in the context of the XIRC tool [4], which can be used to visualize crosscutting structure specified as a functional query.

We believe that an aspect-oriented language with a pointcut language such as our query language is general enough to express a wide range of very different pointcut models. Hyper/J [17] and Demeter [13, 16, 12] are two approaches to AOP that have a very different pointcut model than AspectJ. Since Hyper/J uses only static composition rules, we think that these rules can be directly expressed as queries. For example, a composition rule such as *mergeByName* boils down to finding methods/classes with the same name, which can easily be expressed as a query.

Demeter is related in that both approaches use a notion of path expressions, called *traversal strategies* in the context of Demeter. The aim is different, however. In Demeter, path expressions are used to find traversal paths in the object graph whose edges are association and inheritance links, while we use path ex-

---

[10] In addition to pointcut matching, the methods also take care of injecting dynamic checks as well as code needed for exposing context information at a join point to the advice code.

pressions over the program tree for selecting arbitrary sets of related join points. Nevertheless, we think that it is possible to use a query to find traversal paths in the sense of Demeter. We plan to create a query library for traversal strategies in the future. In [?], Lieberherr tries to establish a common framework for relating pointcut expressions a la AspectJ and traversal strategies as they are used in Demeter, stating that in his view, both can be described by a two level graph structure, with a selection language as the top-level. The work presented here makes this relation very explicit.

5   Summary

In this paper, we have investigated the usage of the functional query language XQuery for the specification of pointcuts. We have shown that XQuery enables powerful composition and reusability mechanisms for pointcuts. While we have investigated this approach only in terms of a static representation of the program, we think that the general idea can be generalized to arbitrary representations of the program semantics.

The aim and achievements of our work are similar to other approaches using logic query languages. To a degree, a comparison between these approaches boils down to a comparison between the respective paradigms, logic programming versus functional programming. We hope that our approach will be a good basis to conduct this debate in terms of the specific requirements of a pointcut language.

References

1. Christoph Bockisch and Michael Eichberg. BAT. http://www.st.informatik.tu-darmstadt.de/bat, 2004.
2. Shigeru Chiba and Kiyoshi Nakagawa. Josh: An Open AspectJ-like Language. In *Proceedings of AOSD 2004*, Lancaster, England. ACM Press.
3. Shigeru Chiba and Muga Nishizawa. An Easy-to-Use Toolkit for Efficient Java Bytecode Translators. In *Proceedings of GPCE '03*, Lecture Notes in Computer Science, pages 364–376. Springer.
4. M. Eichberg, M. Mezini, K. Ostermann, and T. Schäfer. XIRC: A kernel for cross-artifact information engineering in software development environments. In *Proceedings of 11th IEEE Working Conference on Reverse Engineering (to appear)*, 2004.
5. Erich Gamma, Richard Helm, Ralph Johnson, and John Vlissides. *Design Patterns: Elements of Reusable Object-Oriented Software*. Professional Computing Series. Addison Wesley, 1995.
6. Kris Gybels and Johan Brichau. Arranging Language Features for More Robust Pattern–Based Crosscuts. In *Proceedings of AOSD 2003*, pages 60–69, Boston, Massachusetts. ACM Press.
7. Erik Hilsdale and Jim Hugunin. Advice Weaving in AspectJ. In *Proc. of AOSD 2004*. ACM Press.
8. IBM Watson Research Center. Concern manipulation environment (CME): A flexible, extensible, interoperable environment for AOSD. http://www.eclipse.org/cme/.

9. Doug Janzen and Kris De Volder. Navigating and querying code without getting lost. In *Proceedings of the 2nd international conference on Aspect-oriented software development*, pages 178–187. ACM Press, 2003.

10. Gregor Kiczales. Keynote talk at AOSD 2003. http://www.cs.ubc.ca/~gregor/.

11. Gregor Kiczales, Erik Hilsdale, Jim Hugunin, Mik Kersten, Jeffry Palm, and William G. Griswold. An Overview of AspectJ. In *Proceedings of ECOOP 2001*, volume 2072 of *Lecture Notes in Computer Science*, pages 327–355, Budapest,Hungary. Springer.

12. Karl Lieberherr, Doug Orleans, and Johan Ovlinger. Aspect-Oriented Programming with Adaptive Methods. *Communications of the ACM*, 44(10):39–41, 2001.

13. Karl J. Lieberherr. *Adaptive Object-Oriented Software: The Demeter Method with Propagation Patterns*. PWS Publishing Company, Boston, 1996. ISBN 0-534-94602-X.

14. Hidehiko Mashuhara, Gregor Kiczales, and Chris Dutchyn. Compilation semantics of aspect-oriented programs. In *Foundations of Aspect-Oriented Languages Workshop at AOSD '02*, 2002.

15. Hidehiko Masuhara and Kazunori Kawauchi. Dataflow Pointcut in Aspect-Oriented Programming. In *Proceedings of APLAS'03*, Lecture Notes in Computer Science, pages 105–121, Bejing, China.

16. Doug Orleans and Karl Lieberherr. DJ: Dynamic adaptive programming in Java. In *Reflection 2001: Meta-level Architectures and Separation of Crosscutting Concerns*, Kyoto, Japan, September 2001. Springer Verlag. 8 pages.

17. Harold Ossher and Peri Tarr. Hyper/J: Multi-dimensional separation of concerns for Java. In *Proc. of ICSE '00*. ACM Press, 2000.

18. World Wide Web Consortium. XQuery 1.0: An XML query language, W3C working draft Jun 7, 2001, http://www.w3.org/tr/xquery/, 2001.

19. World Wide Web Consortium. XQuery 1.0 formal semantics, http://www.w3.org/tr/query-semantics, 2001.

Formal Design and Verification of Real-Time Embedded Software

Pao-Ann Hsiung[†] and Shang-Wei Lin

Department of Computer Science and Information Engineering,
National Chung-Cheng University, Chiayi, Taiwan–621, ROC
[†]hpa@computer.org

Abstract. Currently available application frameworks that target at
the automatic design of real-time embedded software are poor in integrating functional and non-functional requirements. In this work, we
reveal the internal architecture and design flow of a newly proposed
framework called *Verifiable Embedded Real-Time Application Framework*
(VERTAF), which integrates three techniques namely software
component-based reuse, formal synthesis, and formal verification. Component reuse is based on a formal UML real-time embedded object
model. Formal synthesis employs quasi-static and quasi-dynamic scheduling with multi-layer portable efficient code generation, which can output
either RTOS-specific application code or automatically-generated real-
time executive with application code. Formal verification integrates a
model checker kernel from SGM, by adapting it for embedded software.
The proposed architecture for VERTAF is component-based which allows
plug-and-play for the scheduler and the verifier. The architecture is also
easily extensible because reusable hardware and software design components can be added. Application examples developed using VERTAF
demonstrate significantly reduced relative design effort as compared to
design without VERTAF, which also shows how high-level reuse of software components combined with automatic synthesis and verification
increase design productivity.

Keywords: application framework, code generation, real-time embedded software, formal synthesis, formal verification, scheduling, software
components, UML modeling.

1   Introduction

With the proliferation of embedded systems in all aspects of human life, we are
making greater demands on these systems, including more complex functionalities such as pervasive computing, mobile computing, embedded computing,
and real-time computing. Currently, the design of real-time embedded software
is supported partially by modelers, code generators, analyzers, schedulers, and
frameworks [2], [5], [8]-[12], [13]-[16], [19], [22]-[27], [29], [30]. Nevertheless, the
technology for a completely integrated design and verification environment is still

W.-N. Chin (Ed.): APLAS 2004, LNCS 3302, pp. 382–397, 2004.
© Springer-Verlag Berlin Heidelberg 2004

relatively immature. Furthermore, the methodologies for design and for verification are also poorly integrated relying mainly on the experiences of embedded software engineers. Motivated by the above status-quo, this work demonstrates how the integration of software engineering techniques such as software component reuse, formal software synthesis techniques such as scheduling and code generation, and formal verification technique such as model checking can be realized in the form of an integrated design environment targeted at the acceleration of real-time embedded software construction.

Several issues are encountered in the development of an integrated design environment. First and foremost, we need to decide upon an architecture for the environment. Since our goal is to integrate reuse, synthesis, and verification, we need to have greater control on how the final generated application will be structured, thus we have chosen to implement the environment as an object-oriented application framework [6], which is a "semi-complete" application, where users fill in application specific objects and functionalities. A major feature is "inversion of control", that is the framework decides on the control flow of the generated application, rather than the designer. Other issues encountered in architecting an application framework for real-time embedded software are as follows.

1. To allow software component reuse, how do we define the syntax and semantics of a reusable component? How can a designer uniformly and guidedly specify the requirements of a system to be designed? How can the existing reusable components with the user-specified components be integrated into a feasible working system?
2. What is the control-data flow of the automatic design and verification process? When do we verify and when do we schedule?
3. What kinds of model can be used for each design phase, such as scheduling and verification?
4. What methods are to be used for scheduling and for verification? How do we automate the process? What kinds of abstraction are to be employed when system complexity is beyond our handling capabilities?
5. How do we generate portable code that not only crosses real-time operating systems (RTOS) but also hardware platforms. What is the structure of the generated code?

Briefly, our solutions to the above issues can be summarized as follows.

1. Software Component Reuse and Integration: A subset of the Unified Modeling Language (UML) [21] is used with minimal restrictions for automatic design and analysis. Precise syntax and formal semantics are associated with each kind of UML diagram. Guidelines are provided so that requirement specifications are more error-free and synthesizable.
2. Control Flow: A specific control flow is embedded within the framework, where scheduling is first performed and then verification because the complexity of verification can be greatly reduced after scheduling [9].

3. System Models: For scheduling, we use variants of Petri Nets (PN) [11], [12] and for verification, we use Extended Timed Automata (ETA) [1], [12], both of which are automatically generated from user-specified UML models that follow our restrictions and guidelines.
4. Design Automation: For synthesis, we employ quasi-static and quasi-dynamic scheduling methods [11], [12] that generate program schedules for a single processor. For verification, we employ symbolic model checking [3], [4], [20] that generates a counterexample in the original user-specified UML models whenever verification fails for a system under design. The whole design process is automated through the automatic generation of respective input models, invocation of appropriate scheduling and verification kernels, and generating reports or useful diagnostics. For handling complexity, abstraction is inevitable, thus we apply model-based, architecture-based, and function-based abstractions during verification.
5. Portable Efficient Multi-Layered Code: For portability, a multi-layered approach is adopted in code generation. To account for performance degradation due to multiple layers, system-specific optimization and flattening are then applied to the portable code. System dependent and independent parts of the code are distinctly segregated for this purpose.

In summary, this work illustrates how an application framework may integrate all the above proposed design and verification solutions. Our implementation has resulted in a Verifiable Embedded Real-Time Application Framework (VERTAF) whose features include formal modeling of real-time embedded systems through well-defined UML semantics, formal synthesis that guarantees satisfaction of temporal as well as spatial constraints, formal verification that checks if a system satisfies user-given properties or system-defined generic properties, and code generation that produces efficient portable code.

The article is organized as follows. Section 2 describes the design and verification flow in VERTAF along with an illustration example. Section 3 presents the experimental results of an application example. Section 4 gives the final conclusions with some future work.

2   Design and Verification Flow in VERTAF

Before going into the component-based architecture of VERTAF, we first introduce the design and verification flow. As shown in Figure 1, VERTAF provides solutions to the various issues introduced in Section 1.

In Figure 1, the control and data flows of VERTAF are represented by solid and dotted arrows, respectively. Software synthesis is defined as a two-phase process: a machine-independent software construction phase and a machine-dependent software implementation phase. This separation helps us to plug-in different target languages, middleware, real-time operating systems, and hardware device configurations. We call the two phases as front-end and back-end phases. The front-end phase is further divided into three sub-phases, namely

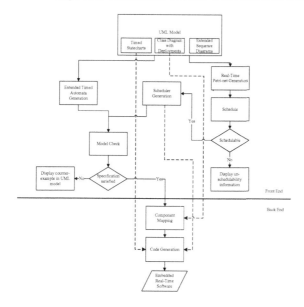

Fig. 1. Design and Verification Flow of VERTAF

UML modeling phase, real-time embedded software scheduling phase, and formal verification phase. There are two sub-phases in the back-end phase, namely component mapping phase and code generation phase. We will now present the details of each phase in the rest of this section illustrated by a running example called Entrance Guard System (EGS). EGS is an embedded system that controls the entrance to a building by identifying valid users through a voice recognition IC and control software that runs on a StrongARM 1100 microprocessor.

2.1   UML Modeling

UML [21] is one of the most popular modeling and design languages in the industry. It standardizes the diagrams and symbols used to build a system model. After scrutiny of all diagrams in UML, we have chosen three diagrams for a user to input as system specification models, namely class diagram, sequence diagram, and statechart. These diagrams were chosen such that information redundancy in user specifications is minimized and at the same time adequate expressiveness in user specifications is preserved. UML is a generic language and its specializations are always required for targeting at any specific application domain. In VERTAF, the three UML diagrams are both restricted as well as enhanced along with guidelines for designers to follow in specifying synthesizable and verifiable system models (just as synthesizable HDL code for hardware designs).

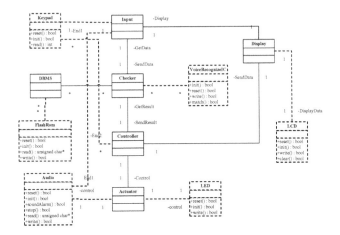

Fig. 2. Class Diagram with Deployment for Entrance Guard System

The three UML diagrams extended for real-time embedded software specification are as follows.

- *Class Diagrams with Deployment*: A deployment relation is used for specifying a hardware object on which a software object is deployed. There are two types of methods, namely event-triggered and time-triggered that are used to model real-time behavior.
- *Timed Statecharts*: UML statecharts are extended with real-time clocks that can be reset and values checked as state transition triggers.
- *Extended Sequence Diagrams*: UML sequence diagrams are extended with control structures such as concurrency, conflict, and composition, which aid in formalizing their semantics and in mapping them to formal Petri net models that are used for scheduling.

For our running EGS example, some of the above diagrams are shown in Figures 2, 3, and 4, respectively.

UML is well-known for its informal and general-purpose semantics. The enhancements described above are an effort at formalizing semantics preciseness such that there is little ambiguity in user-specified models that are input to VERTAF. Furthermore, design guidelines are provided to a user such that the goal of correct-by-construction can be achieved. Typical guidelines are given here.

- Hardware deployments are desirable as they reflect the system architecture in which the generated real-time embedded software will execute and thus generated code will adhere to designer intent more precisely.

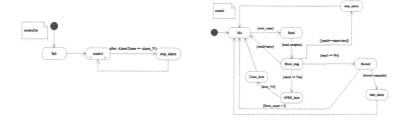

Fig. 3. Timed Statecharts for Controller in Entrance Guard System

- If the behavior of an object cannot be represented by a simple statechart that has no more than four levels of hierarchy, then decompose the object.
- To maximize flexibility, a sequence diagram can represent one or more use-case scenarios. Overlapping behavior among scenarios often results in significant redundancy in sequence diagrams, hence either control structures may be used in a sequence diagram or a set of non-overlapping sequence diagrams may be inter-related with precedence constraints.
- Ensure the logical correctness of the relationships between class diagram and statecharts and between statecharts and sequence diagrams. The former relationship is represented by actions and events in statecharts that correspond to object methods in class diagram. The latter relationship is represented by state-markers in sequence diagrams that correspond to statechart states.

The set of UML diagrams input by a user, including a class diagram with deployments, a timed statechart corresponding to each class, and a set of extended sequence diagrams, constitutes the requirements for the real-time embedded software to be designed and verified by VERTAF. The formal definition of a system model is as follows.

Definition 1. Real-Time Embedded Software System Model
Given a class diagram $D_{class} = \langle C, \delta \rangle$, a statechart $D_{schart}(c) = \langle Q, q_0, \tau \rangle$ for each class c in C, and a set of sequence diagrams $\{D_{seq} | D_{seq} = \langle C', M \rangle, C' \subseteq C\}$, where C is a set of classes, δ is the mapping for inter-class relationships and deployments, Q is a set of states, q_0 is an initial state, τ is a transition relation between states, and M is a set of messages, a real-time embedded software system S is defined as a set of objects as specified in D_{class}, the behavior of which is represented by the individual statecharts $D_{schart}(c)$, and which interact with each other by sending/receiving messages $m \in M$ as specified in the set of sequence diagrams $\{D_{seq}\}$. A formal behavior model of the system S is defined as the parallel composition of the set of statecharts along with the behavior represented by the sequence diagrams. Notationally, $D_{schart}(c_0) \times \ldots \times D_{schart}(c_{|C|}) \times B(D^1_{seq}, \ldots, D^k_{seq})$ denotes the system behavior semantics, where B is the scheduler ETA as formalized in Section 2.2.

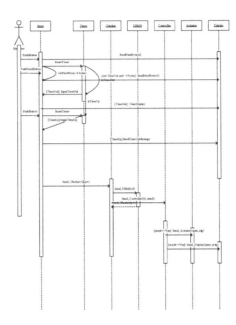

Fig. 4. An Extended Sequence Diagram for Entrance Guard System

2.2   Real-Time Embedded Software Scheduling

There are two issues in real-time embedded software scheduling, namely how are memory constraints satisfied and how are temporal specifications such as deadlines satisfied. Based on whether the system under design has an RTOS specified or not, two different scheduling algorithms are applied to solve the above two issues.

- *Without RTOS*: *Quasi-dynamic scheduling* (QDS) [11], [12] is applied, which requires *Real-Time Petri Nets* (RTPN) as system specification models. QDS prepares the system to be generated as a single real-time executive kernel with a scheduler.
- *With RTOS*: *Extended quasi-static scheduling* (EQSS) [28] with real-time scheduling [18] is applied, which requires *Complex Choice Petri Nets* (CCPN) and set of independent real-time tasks as system specification models, respectively. EQSS prepares the system to be generated as a set of multiple threads that can be scheduled and dispatched by a supported RTOS such as MicroC/OS II or ARM Linux.

In order to apply the above scheduling algorithms, we need to map the user-specified UML models into Petri nets, RTPN or CCPN. RTPN enhances the standard Petri net with code execution characteristics associated with transitions. Given a standard Petri net $N = \langle P, T, \phi \rangle$, where P is a set of places,

T is a set of transitions, and ϕ is a weighted flow relation between places and transitions, $N_R = \langle N, \chi, \pi \rangle$ is an RTPN, where χ maps a transition t to its worst-case execution time α_t and deadline β_t and π is the period for N_R. CCPN allows non-free choices at transitions [28], but does not allow the computations from a branch place to synchronize at some later place. Further, CCPN only allows a loop that has at least a single token in some place along the loop. These restrictions imposed by CCPN also apply to RTPN and are set mainly for synthesizability. Here, we briefly describe how RTPN and CCPN models are generated automatically from user-specified UML sequence diagrams, through a case-by-case construction.

1. A message in a sequence diagram is mapped to a set of Petri net nodes, including an incoming arc, a transition, an outgoing arc, and a place. If it is an initial message, no incoming arc is generated. If a message has a guard, the guard is associated to the incoming arc.
2. For each set of concurrent messages in a sequence diagram, a fork transition is first generated, which is then connected to a set of places that lead to a set of message mappings as described in Step (1) above.
3. If messages are sent in a loop, the Petri-nets corresponding to the messages in the loop are generated as described in Step (1) and connected in the given sequential order of the messages. The place in the mapping of the last message is identified with the place in the mapping of a message that precedes the loop, if any. This is called a branch place. The loop iteration guard is associated with the incoming arc of the first message in the loop, which is also an outgoing arc of the branch place. Another outgoing arc of the branch place points to a transition outside the loop, which corresponds to the message that succeeds the loop.
4. Different sequence diagrams are translated to different Petri-nets. If a Petri net has an ending transition which is the same as the initial transition of another Petri net, they are concatenated by merging the common transition.
5. Sequence diagrams that are inter-related by precedence constraints are first translated individually into independent Petri nets, which are then combined with a connecting place, that may act as a branch place when several sequence diagrams have a similar precedent.
6. An ending transition is appended to each generated Petri-net because otherwise there will be tokens that are never consumed resulting in infeasible scheduling.

By applying the above mapping procedure, all user-specified sequence diagrams are translated and combined into a compact set of Petri nets. All kinds of temporal constraints that appear in the sequence diagrams such as time-out, time interval between two events (sending and receiving of messages), periods and deadlines associated with a message, and timing guards on messages are translated into guard constraints on arcs in the generated Petri nets. This set of RTPN or CCPN is then input to QDS or EQSS, respectively, for scheduling. Details on the scheduling procedures can be found in [11], [12], and [28]. The basic strategy is to decompose each Petri net into conflict-free components that are scheduled individually for satisfaction of memory constraints. A conflict-free component is a reduction of a Petri net into one without any branch place. This is EQSS. QDS applies EQSS first and then because the resulting memory satisfying schedules may have some sequencing flexibilities, they are taken advantage of for satisfaction of temporal constraints. Finally, we have a set of feasible schedules, each of which corresponds to a particular behavior configuration of the system. A behavior configuration of a system is a feasible computation that results from the concurrent behaviors of the conflict-free components of its constituent Petri nets. For example, a system with two Petri nets, N_1 and N_2, which have two conflict-free components each, namely N_{11}, N_{12}, and N_{21}, N_{22}, can have totally at most four different behavior configurations: $N_{11}||N_{21}, N_{12}||N_{21}, N_{11}||N_{22}$, and $N_{12}||N_{22}$.

For systems without RTOS, we need to automatically generate a scheduler that controls the system according to the set of transition sequences generated by QDS. In VERTAF, a scheduler is constructed as a separate class that observes and controls the status of each object in the system. Temporal constraints are monitored by the scheduler class using a global clock. Further, for verification purposes, an extended timed automaton is also generated by following the set of transition sequences. For uniformity, this scheduler automaton can be viewed as a timed statechart for the generated scheduler class and thus the scheduler is just another object in the system. Code generation becomes a lot easier with this uniformity.

For our running EGS example, a single Petri net is generated from the user-specified set of statecharts, which is then scheduled using QDS. In this example, scheduling is required only for the timers associated with the actuator, the controller, and the input object. After QDS, we found that EGS is schedulable.

2.3   Formal Verification

VERTAF employs the popular model checking paradigm for formal verification of real-time embedded software. In VERTAF, formal ETA models are generated automatically from user-specified UML models by a flattening scheme that transforms each statechart into a set of one or more ETA, which are merged, along with the scheduler ETA generated in the scheduling phase, into a state-graph. The verification kernel used in VERTAF is adapted from *State Graph Manipulators* (SGM) [29], which is a high-level model checker for real-time systems that operate on state-graph representations of system behavior through manipulators, including a state-graph merger, several state-space reduction techniques, a dead state checker, and a TCTL model checker. There are two classes of system properties that can be verified in VERTAF: (1) system-defined properties including dead states, deadlocks, livelocks, and syntactical errors, and (2) user-defined properties specified in the *Object Constraint Language* (OCL) as defined by OMG in its UML specifications. All of these properties are automatically translated into TCTL specifications for verification by SGM.

Automation in formal verification of user-specified UML models of real-time embedded software is achieved in VERTAF by the following implementation mechanisms.

1. User-specified timed statecharts are automatically mapped to a set of ETA.
2. User-specified extended sequence diagrams are automatically mapped to a set of Petri nets that are scheduled and then a scheduler ETA is automatically generated.
3. Using the state-graph merge manipulator in SGM, all the ETA resulting from the above two steps are merged into a single state-graph representing the global system behavior.
4. User-specified OCL properties and system-defined properties are automatically translated into TCTL specification formulas.
5. The system state-graph and the TCTL formulas obtained in the previous two steps are then input to SGM for model checking.
6. When a property is not satisfied, SGM generates a counterexample, which is then automatically translated into a UML sequence diagram representing an erratic trace behavior of the system. This approach provides a seamless interface to VERTAF users such that the formal models are all hidden and the users need to interact only with what they have specified in UML models.

Design complexity is a major issue in formal verification, which leads to unmanageable and exponentially large state-spaces. Both engineering paradigms and scientific techniques are applied in VERTAF to handle the state-space size explosion issue. The applied techniques include (1) Model Construction Guidelines, (2) Architectural Abstractions, (3) Functional Abstractions, and (4) State-Space Reductions. Due to page-limit, we have not elaborated on the individual techniques.

For our running EGS example, the ETA for each statechart were generated and then merged with the scheduler ETA. For illustration, we show in Figure 5 the ETA that is generated by VERTAF corresponding to the controller statechart of Figure 3. The other 6 ETA are omitted due to page-limit. All ETA were input to SGM and AGR was applied. Reduction techniques were then applied to each state-graph obtained from AGR. OCL constraints were then translated into TCTL and verified by the SGM model checker kernel.

2.4   Component Mapping

This is the first phase in the back-end design of VERTAF and starts to be more hardware dependent. All hardware classes specified in the deployments of the class diagram are those supported by VERTAF and thus belong to some existing class libraries. The component mapping phase then becomes simply the configuration of the hardware system and operating system through the automatic generation of configuration files, make files, header files, and dependency files. The corresponding hardware class API will be linked in during compilation.

The main issue in this phase occurs when a software class is not deployed on any hardware component or not deployed on any specific hardware device type,

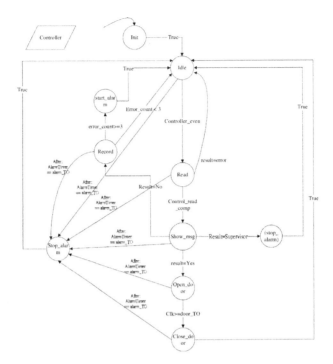

Fig. 5. ETA for Controller in EGS

for example the type of microcontroller to be used is not specified. Currently, VERTAF adopts an interactive approach whereby the designer is warned of this lack of information and he/she is requested to choose from a list of available compatible device types for the deployment. An automatic solution to this issue is not feasible because estimates are not easy without further information about the non-deployed software classes.

Another issue in this phase is the possible conflicts among hardware devices specified in a class diagram such as interrupts, memory address ranges, I/O ports, and bus-related characteristics such as device priorities. Users are also warned in case of such conflicts.

2.5   Code Generation

There are basically three issues in this phase including hardware portability, software portability, and temporal correctness. We adopt a 3-tier approach for code generation: a hardware abstraction layer, an OS with middleware layer, and a scheduler with temporal monitor, which solves the above three issues, respectively. Currently supported underlying hardware platforms include ARM-based, StrongARM-based, 8051-based, and Lego RCX-based Mindstorm systems. For hardware abstraction, VERTAF supports MicroHAL and the embedded version of POSIX. For OS, VERTAF supports MicroC/OS, Linux, and eCOS. For

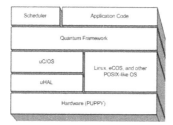

Fig. 6. Multi-Tier Code Architecture

middleware, VERTAF is currently based on the Quantum Framework [38]. For scheduler, VERTAF creates a custom ActiveObject according to the Quantum API. Included in the scheduler is a temporal monitor that checks if any temporal constraints are violated. As shown in Figure 6, this multi-tier approach decouples application code from the OS through the middleware and from the hardware platform through the OS and hardware abstraction layer.

Each ETA that is generated either from UML statecharts or from the scheduled Petri nets (sequence diagrams) is implemented as an ActiveObject in the Quantum Framework. The user-defined classes along with data and methods are incorporated into the corresponding ActiveObject. The final program is a set of concurrent threads, one of which is a scheduler that can control the other objects by sending messages to them after observing their states. For systems without an OS, the scheduler also takes the role of a real-time executive kernel.

For our running example, the final application code consisted of 6 activeobjects derived from the statecharts and 1 activeobject representing the scheduler. Makefiles were generated for linking in the API of the 6 hardware classes and configuration files were generated for the StrongARM microprocessor with MicroC/OS II and embedded Linux. There were totally 2,300 lines of C code, out of which the designer had to write only around 300 lines of code.

3   AICC Cruiser Application

An application developed with VERTAF is AICC (Autonomous Intelligent Cruise Controller) system application [7], which had been developed and installed in a Saab automobile by Hansson et al. The AICC system can receive information from road signs and adapt the speed of the vehicle to automatically follow speed limits. Also, with a vehicle in front cruising at lower speed the AICC adapts the speed and maintains safe distance. The AICC can also receive information from the roadside (e.g. from traffic lights) to calculate a speed profile which will reduce emission by avoiding stop and go at traffic lights. The system architecture consisting of both hardware (HW) and software (SW) is shown in Figure 7. The software development methodology used in [7] is based on sets of interconnected so-called software circuits. Each software circuit has a set of input connectors where data are received and a set of output connectors where data

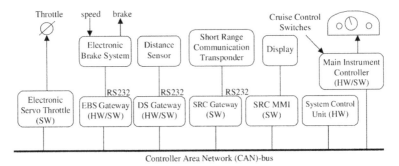

Fig. 7. AICC System Architecture

are produced. We model the software circuits in [7] as active application domain objects in VERTAF.

As shown in Figure 8, there are five domain objects specified by the designer of AICC for implementing a Basement system. Basement is a vehicle's internal real-time architecture developed in the Vehicle Internal Architecture (VIA) project [7], within the Swedish Road Transport Informatics Programme. As observed in Figure 8, each object may correspond (map) to one or more tasks. The tasks and the Call-Graph are as shown in Table 1 and Figure 8, respectively. There are totally 12 tasks performed by 5 application domain objects. There were 21 application framework objects specified by the designer. Totally, 26 objects were in the final program code generated. The average integration time per object was 0.5 day and the average learning time was amortized as 0.1 day for each designer using the framework. Without using the framework, the average integration time was 2 days for each object. This application took 5 days for 3 real-time system designers using VERTAF. The same application took the same designers 20 days to complete development a second time. The significant decrease in design time was due to the high degree of automation in VERTAF.

4   Conclusion

An object-oriented component-based application framework, called VERTAF, was proposed for real-time embedded systems application development. It was a result of the integration of three different technologies: software component reuse, formal synthesis, and formal verification. Starting from user-specified UML models, automation was provided in model transformations, scheduling, verification, and code generation. VERTAF can be easily extended since new specification languages, scheduling algorithms, etc. can easily be integrated into it. Future extensions will include support for share-driven scheduling algorithms. More applications will also be developed using VERTAF. VERTAF will be enhanced in the future by considering more advanced features of real-time applications, such as: network delay, network protocols, and on-line task scheduling. Performance

Table 1. AICC Tasks

Index	Task Description	Object	p	e	d
1	Traffic Light Info	SRC	200	10	400
2	Speed Limit Info	SRC	200	10	400
3	Proceeding Vehicle Estimator	ICCReg	100	8	100
4	Speed Sensor	ICCReg	100	5	100
5	Distance Control	ICCReg	100	15	100
6	Green Wave Control	ICCReg	100	15	100
7	Speed Limit Control	ICCReg	100	15	100
8	Coordination & Final Control	Final_Control	50	20	50
9	Cruise Switches	Supervisor	100	15	100
10	ICC Main Control	Supervisor	100	20	100
11	Cruise Info	Supervisor	100	20	100
12	Speed Actuator	EST	50	5	50

SRC: Short Range Communication, ICCReg: ICC Regulator, EST: Electronic Servo Throttle,
p: period, e: execution time, d: deadline

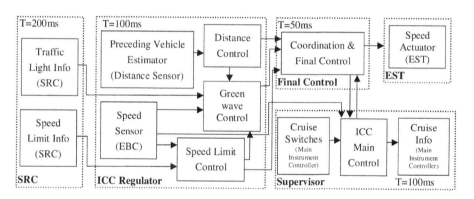

Fig. 8. AICC Call-Graph

related features such as context switch time and rate, external events handling, I/O timing, mode changes, transient overloading, and setup time will also be incorporated into VERTAF in the future.

References

1. R. Alur and D. Dill, "Automata for modeling real-time systems," Theoretical Computer Science, Vol. 126, No. 2, pp. 183-236, April 1994.
2. T. Amnell, E. Fersman, L. Mokrushin, P. Petterson, and W. Yi, "TIMES: a tool for schedulability analysis and code generation of real-time systems," in Proceedings of the 1st International Workshop on Formal Modeling and Analysis of Timed Systems (FORMATS, Marseille, France), September 2003.

3. E. M. Clarke and E. A. Emerson, "Design and synthesis of synchronization skeletons using branching time temporal logic," in Proceedings of the Logics of Programs Workshop, LNCS Vol. 131, pp. 52-71, Springer Verlag, 1981.

4. E. M. Clarke, O. Grumberg, and D. A. Peled, Model Checking, MIT Press, 1999.

5. B. P. Douglass, Doing Hard Time: Developing Real-Time Systems with UML, Objects, Frameworks, and Patterns, Addison Wesley Longman, Inc., Reading, MA, USA, November 1999.

6. M. Fayad and D. Schmidt, "Object-oriented application frameworks," Communications of the ACM, Special Issue on Object-Oriented Application Frameworks, Vol. 40, October 1997.

7. H. A. Hansson, H. W. Lawson, M. Stromberg, and S. Larsson, "BASEMENT: A distributed real-time architecture for vehicle applications," Real-Time Systems, Vol. 11, No. 3, pp. 223-244, 1996.

8. P.-A. Hsiung, "RTFrame: An object-oriented application framework for real-time applications," in Proceedings of the 27th International Conference on Technology of Object-Oriented Languages and Systems (TOOLS'98), pp. 138-147, IEEE Computer Society Press, September 1998.

9. P.-A. Hsiung, "Embedded software verification in hardware-software codesign," Journal of Systems Architecture - the Euromicro Journal, Vol. 46, No. 15, pp. 1435-1450, Elsevier Science, November 2000.

10. P.-A. Hsiung and S.-Y. Cheng, "Automating formal modular verification of asynchronous real-time embedded systems," in Proceedings of the 16th International Conference on VLSI Design, (VLSI'2003, New Delhi, India), pp. 249-254, IEEE CS Press, January 2003.

11. P.-A. Hsiung and C.-Y. Lin, "Synthesis of real-time embedded software with local and global deadlines," in Proceedings of the 1st ACM/IEEE/IFIP International Conference on Hardware-Software Codesign and System Synthesis (CODES+ISSS'2003, Newport Beach, CA, USA), pp. 114-119, ACM Press, October 2003.

12. P.-A. Hsiung, C.-Y. Lin, and T.-Y. Lee, "Quasi-dynamic scheduling for the synthesis of real-time embedded software with local and global deadlines," in Proceedings of the 9th International Conference on Real-Time and Embedded Computing Systems and Applications (RTCSA'2003, Tainan, Taiwan), February 2003.

13. A. Knapp, S. Merz, and C. Rauh, "Model checking timed UML state machines and collaboration," in Proceedings of the 7th International Symposium on Formal Techniques in Real-Time and Fault-Tolerant Systems, LNCS Vol. 2469, pp. 395-414, Springer Verlag, September 2002.

14. T. Kuan, W.-B. See, and S.-J. Chen, "An object-oriented real-time framework and development environment," in Proceedings OOPSLA'95 Workshop #18, 1995.

15. S. Kodase, S. Wang, and K. G. Shin, "Transforming structural model to runtime model of embedded software with real-time constraints," in Proceedings of Design, Automation and Test in Europe Conference, Munich, Germany, pp. 170-175, March 2003.

16. L. Lavazza, "A methodology for formalizing concepts underlying the DESS notation," Software Development Process for Real-Time Embedded Software Systems, EUREKA-ITEA project (http://www.dess-itea.org), D 1.7.4, December 2001.

17. W.-S. Liao and P.-A. Hsiung, "FVP: A formal verification platform for SoC," in Proceedings of the 16th IEEE International SoC Conference, Portland, Oregon, USA, IEEE CS Press, September 2003.

18. C. Liu and J. Layland, "Scheduling algorithms for multiprogramming in a hard-real time environment," Journal of the Association for Computing Machinery, Vol. 20, pp. 46-61, January 1973.

19. D. de Niz and R. Rajkumar, "Time Weaver: A software-through-models framework for embedded real-time systems," in Proceedings of the International Workshop on Languages, Compilers, and Tools for Embedded Systems, San-Diego, California, USA, pp. 133-143, June 2003.

20. J.-P. Queille and J. Sifakis, "Specification and verification of concurrent systems in CESAR," in Proceedings of the International Symposium on Programming, LNCS Vol. 137, pp. 337-351, Springer Verlag, 1982.

21. J. Rumbaugh, G. Booch, and I. Jacobson, The UML Reference Guide, Addison Wesley Longman, 1999.

22. M. Samek, Practical Statecharts in C/C++ Quantum Programming for Embedded Systems, CMP Books, 2002.

23. D. Schmidt, "Applying design patterns and frameworks to develop object-oriented communication software," Handbook of Programming Languages, Vol. I, 1997.

24. W.-B. See and S.-J. Chen, "Object-oriented real-time system framework," in Domain-Specific Application Frameworks (M. E. Fayad and R. E. Johnson, eds.), ch. 16, pp. 327-338, John Wiley, 2000.

25. B. Selic, "Modeling real-time distributed software systems," in Proceedings of the 4th International Workshop on Parallel and Distributed Real-Time Systems, pp. 11-18, 1996.

26. B. Selic, "An efficient object-oriented variation of the statecharts formalism for distributed real-time systems," in Proceedings of the IFIP Conference on Hardware Description Languages and Their Applications, 1993.

27. B. Selic, G. Gullekan, P. T. Ward, Real-time Object Oriented Modeling, John Wiley and Sons, Inc., 1994.

28. F.-S. Su and P.-A. Hsiung, "Extended quasi-static scheduling for formal synthesis and code generation of embedded software," in Proceedings of the 10th IEEE/ACM International Symposium on Hardware/Software Codesign (CODES'02, Colorado, USA), pp. 211-216, ACM Press, May 2002.

29. F. Wang and P.-A. Hsiung, "Efficient and user-friendly verification," IEEE Transactions on Computers, Vol. 51, No. 1, pp. 61-83, January 2002.

30. S. Wang, S. Kodase, and K. G. Shin, "Automating embedded software construction and analysis with design models," in Proceedings of International Conference of Euro-uRapid, Frankfurt, Germany, December 2002.

McJava – A Design and Implementation of Java with Mixin-Types

Tetsuo Kamina and Tetsuo Tamai

University of Tokyo,
3-8-1, Komaba, Meguro-ku, Tokyo, 153-8902, Japan
{kamina,tamai}@graco.c.u-tokyo.ac.jp

Abstract. A programming construct *mixin* was invented to implement uniform extensions and modifications to classes. Although mixin-based programming has been extensively studied both on the methodological and theoretical point of views, relatively few attempts have been made on designing *real* programming languages that support mixins. In this paper, we address the issue of how to introduce a feature of declaring a mixin that may also be used as a type to nominally typed object-oriented languages like Java. We propose a programming language McJava, an extension of Java with mixin-types. To study type-soundness of McJava, we have formulated the core of McJava with typing and reduction rules, and proved its type-soundness. We also describe a compilation strategy of McJava that translates McJava programs to Java programs thus eventually making it runnable on standard Java virtual machines.

1 Introduction

Object-oriented programming languages like Java and C# offer class systems that provide a simple and flexible mechanism for reusing collections of program pieces. Using inheritance and overriding, programmers may derive a new class by specifying only the elements that are extended and modified from the original class. However, a pure class-based approach lacks a mechanism of abstracting uniform extensions and modifications to multiple classes.

A programming construct *mixin* (also known as *abstract subclass*) was invented to implement modules that provide such uniform extensions and modifications [20]. This construct provides much reusability because a mixin makes it possible to add common features (that will be duplicated in a single inheritance hierarchy) to a variety of classes. Mixin-based programming, popularized by CLOS [17], has been studied both on the methodological and theoretical point of views [8, 9, 4, 7, 12]. Small core languages that support mixins or *mixin modules* are also proposed [13, 11, 16]. Despite the existence of these extensive studies, relatively few attempts are made on designing *real* programming languages that support mixins with notable exception of the language Jam [3] that integrates mixins with Java.[1]

---

[1] We will note differences between Jam and our approach in section 5.

W.-N. Chin (Ed.): APLAS 2004, LNCS 3302, pp. 398–414, 2004.
© Springer-Verlag Berlin Heidelberg 2004

In many cases, a mixin is considered as a means for providing uniform extension to classes; however, some mixin-based systems also allow a mixin to be composed with other mixins (e.g. [13]). Composition of two mixins produces another mixin that has both features of its constituents. It can be regarded as a kind of inheritance in the form of mixin composition, which enhances the reusability of mixins still further.

In this paper, we address how to add *mixin-types*, a mechanism of declaring a mixin that may also be used as a type, to nominally typed, mainstream object-oriented languages like Java. We present a programming language Mc-Java.[2] McJava has the following features; (1) mixins are explicitly supported as a language feature, and mixin names are used as types; (2) *higher order mixins* (mixins composed with other mixins) are supported, and flexible subtyping rules among subsequences of composition are provided, that promotes much flexible code reuse; (3) mixin composition is a subject to type-checking.

To study type-soundness of McJava, we have developed Core McJava, a small calculus for McJava that is based on FJ [15], a tiny subset of Java. Because Core McJava is very small, it is suitable for focusing on type-checking issues. We have proved the type-soundness theorem of Core McJava, that provides an assurance that McJava type system is sound.

Because McJava is designed as an extension of Java, it is desirable that Mc-Java programs may run on the standard JVM; however, owing to its flexibility of subtyping, how to compile McJava programs to JVM is not so straightforward. Because Java does not allow a class to inherit from multiple classes, McJava subtyping must be *linearized* in the compilation. This linearization imposes unnecessarily deep inheritance chains to the compiled program. In this paper, we also present a compilation strategy of McJava, and show an optimization algorithm by eliminating unused types from the inheritance chains. Based on this strategy, we implemented a prototype version of McJava compiler that type-checks McJava programs and translates them into Java programs thus making it runnable on the standard JVM.

We summarize the contributions of this paper:

- Introducing mixins into a mainstream, statically-typed language.
- Including higher order mixins and mixin-based subtyping.
- Establishing the soundness of the type system.
- Devising a compilation strategy and optimization.

2   An Overview of McJava

Mixin Declarations and Mixin-Types. To demonstrate how a mixin is declared in McJava, we start with a very simple example. Figure 1 shows a declaration of mixin `Color`. This mixin provides "color" feature that is intended to be composed with widget classes.

---

[2] Mixin-based **C**ompositions for **Java**.

```
interface WidgetI { void paint(Graphics g); }
mixin Color requires WidgetI {
  int color;
  void paint(Graphics g) {
    g.setColor(this);
    super.paint(g);
    ... }
  void setColorValue(int color) { this.color=color; }
  int getColorValue() { return this.color; }
}
```

Fig. 1. A color mixin

A statement beginning with a keyword `mixin` is a *mixin declaration*. A mixin declaration has the following form:

mixin X [requires I] { ... }

where X denotes the name of mixin and I denotes the interface that the mixin *requires*. This means that classes that implement interface I can be composed with mixin X. For example, both class `Label` and class `TextField`, declared as

```
class Label implements WidgetI { void paint(Graphics g) { .. }}
class TextField { void paint(Graphics g) { ... } }
```

can be composed with mixin `Color`, as they implement interface `WidgetI`. Note that, it is not necessary for these classes to explicitly declare that they implement interface `WidgetI`, as shown by class `TextField`. A class that implicitly implements a `paint` method (i.e. a class that has a `void paint()` method without declaring `implements WidgetI`) may also be composed with mixin `Color`.[3]

When a required interface is declared in a mixin, methods are to be imported to the mixin from a class to be composed. For example, the `paint` method in mixin `Color` invokes `super.paint(g)` that results in invocation of `paint` declared in `Color`'s "superclass". McJava also allows an anonymous interface to appear in `requires` clause for more handy syntax:

mixin Color requires { void paint(graphics g); } { ... }

If a mixin requires *no* interfaces (i.e. a mixin that imports no methods), we may omit the `requires` clause.

A composition of mixin `Color` and class `Label` is written as `Color::Label`. This composition is regarded as a subclass that is derived from the parent `Label` class, with subclass body declarations being the same as the body of mixin

---

[3] Note that the `requires` clause of a mixin declaration is quite different from `implements` clause of ordinary class declarations in that a required interface in mixin declaration is not used as a type but used as a *constraint*. In fact, there is no subtype relation between mixin `Color` and interface `WidgetI`.

```
interface WidgetI { void paint(Graphics g); }
mixin Font requires WidgetI {
  String font;
  void paint(Graphics g) {
    g.setFont(this);
    super.paint(g);
    ... }
  void setFontName(String font) { this.font=font; }
  String getFontName() { return this.font; }
}
```

Fig. 2. A Font mixin

Color. Similarly, a composition `Color::TextField` is regarded as a subclass of `TextField`. In this sense, a mixin is a uniform extension of classes that may be applied to many different parent classes.

Besides this modularity, McJava also provides the useful feature of mixin-types, which means a declared mixin is also used as a type. It is to be noted that using a mixin as a type is often useful to abstract all the results of composing the mixin with other classes and mixins. We may write the name `Color`, for example, in a formal parameter of a method declaration that results in a method that takes an instance of all the results of composing mixin `Color` with composable classes as an argument.

As an abstract class in Java cannot be instantiated, it is forbidden to create an instance of an abstract subclass (i.e. a mixin) in McJava.

Higher Order Mixins and Subtyping. In McJava a mixin may also be composed with a mixin. For example, the previous mixin `Color` may be composed with mixin `Font` declared in Figure 2. This composition, written as `Color::Font`, is regarded as a mixin that has both features of `Color` and `Font`.

A mixin `Color` may also be composed with a composition `Font::Label` resulting in a new composition `Color::Font::Label`. The composition operator `::` is associative, that is a result of composing a mixin `Color` with a composition `Font::Label`, written `Color::(Font::Label)`, is the same as `(Color::Font)::` `Label`, a result of composing `Color::Font` with `Label` (recall that a composition of a mixin and another mixin is also regarded as a mixin).

A composition `Color::Font::Label` provides all the methods declared in `Color`, `Font`, and `Label`. In McJava, the order of method lookup for compositions is well-defined. If a method `paint` is searched on `Color::Font::Label`, for instance, `Color` is searched first, then `Font`, followed by `Label`. Because the order of method lookup controls the *behavior* [18] of mixin compositions, the composition operator `::` is not commutative. For instance, `Color::Font` is not the same type as `Font::Color`, because the behavior of each composition may be different.

One of the novel features of McJava is the flexibility of its subtype relation over compositions. In McJava, a composition is a subtype of all its constituent.

For example, `Color::Font::Label` is a subtype of `Label`, `Font`, and `Color`. It is also a subtype of its subsequences, `Font::Label`, `Color::Font` and (maybe somewhat surprisingly) `Color::Label`. Because the operator `::` is not commutative, the order of composition is significant (i.e. `Color::Font` is not a subtype of `Font::Color`). The further reason of this restriction is, if we do not require respecting order in subtyping between sequences, `Color::Font` is a subtype of `Font::Color` that is a subtype of `Color::Font`. This means subtype relation is no longer partial order because, as mentioned earlier, `Color::Font` $\neq$ `Font::Color`, which will confuse many Java users. However, it is interesting to investigate whether the type system remains sound with this more flexible definition of composition subtyping. This issue remains as one of our future work.

The subtyping system proposed here enhances much reusability of code. Consider the situation where we use normal Java to extend a class `Label` to `FontLabel`, then further to `ColorFontLabel`. Suppose, we also extend `Label` to `ColorLabel` independently. In Java, however, `ColorFontLabel` is not a subtype of `ColorLabel`.

Mixin Composability. Adding mixin-types to Java type system requires the type-checker to perform more sophisticated type-checking. We briefly summarize here what McJava type-checker does to check the well-typedness of mixin compositions. To ensure that compiled McJava programs run safely, the type-checker must check whether the following requirements are met:

- For all the compositions $X_1::\cdots::X_n::C$, where $X_1, \cdots, X_n$ are mixins and C is a class, the composition $X_2::\cdots::C$ must implement all the interfaces that the mixin X_1 requires.
- For all the compositions `X::T`, where X is a mixin and T is a mixin, a class, or a composition, if X declares a method m and a method m' with the same name m and the same signature is also declared in T, then the return type of m must be the same as the type of m'.

The first rule ensure that no "method not understood" error occurs at runtime. The second rule corresponds to the Java rule on overriding. In other words, if the mixin X accidentally "overrides" a method declared in T with the different return type, the compiler reports an error.

3   Core Calculus of McJava

To provide an assurance that McJava type system is sound, we have developed Core McJava, a small calculus of McJava that is suitable for proving the type soundness theorem.

The design of Core McJava is based on FJ [15], a minimum core language of Java. FJ is a very small subset of Java, focusing on just a few key constructs. For example, FJ constructors always take the same stylized form: there is one parameter for each field, with the same name as the field. FJ provides no side-effective

$T ::= \bar{X} :: C \mid \bar{X}$ $L_C ::=$ **class** C **extends** $\bar{X} :: C$ $\quad \{ \bar{T} \ \bar{f}; \ K_C \ \bar{M} \}$ $L_X ::=$ **mixin** X **requires** I $\quad \{ \bar{T} \ \bar{f}; \ K_X \ \bar{M} \}$ $L_I ::=$ **interface** $I \ \{ \ \bar{M_I}; \ \}$ $K_C ::= C(\bar{S} \ \bar{g}, \ \bar{T} \ \bar{f})$ $\quad \{$**super**$(\bar{g}); \ $**this**$.\bar{f}=\bar{f}; \}$ $K_X ::= X(\bar{T} \ \bar{f})\{ \ $**this**$.\bar{f}=\bar{f}; \}$ $M ::= T \ m(\bar{T} \ \bar{x})\{ \ $**return** $e; \}$ $M_I ::= T \ m(\bar{T} \ \bar{x})$ $e ::= x \mid e.f \mid e.m\texttt{<}\bar{T}\texttt{>}(\bar{e})$ $\quad \mid$ **new** $\bar{X} :: C(\bar{e})$	$T \ <: \ T \qquad$ (S-REFL) $T_1 :: \cdots :: T_n \ <: \ T_2 :: T_3 :: \cdots :: T_n$ $\qquad <: \ T_1 :: T_3 :: \cdots :: T_n$ $\qquad \cdots$ $\qquad <: \ T_1 :: T_2 :: \cdots :: T_{n-1}$ $\qquad\qquad\qquad\qquad$ (S-COMP) $\dfrac{T \ <: \ S \qquad S \ <: \ U}{T \ <: \ U}$ $\qquad\qquad\qquad\qquad$ (S-TRANS) $\dfrac{\texttt{class } C \texttt{ extends } \bar{X} :: D \ \{\ldots\}}{C \ <: \ \bar{X} :: D}$ $\qquad\qquad\qquad\qquad$ (S-CLASS)
Fig. 3. Core McJava syntax	**Fig. 4.** Subtype relation

operations, that means a method body always consists of **return** statement followed by an expression. Because FJ provides no side-effects, the only place where assignment operations may appear is within a constructor declaration. In FJ, all the fields are initialized at the object instantiation time. Once initialized, an FJ object never changes its state. FJ does not support modifiers of members and constructors, that means all the members and constructors of classes are public. Interfaces are also not supported by FJ.

Core McJava shares the same features of FJ explained above. In the following subsections, we present the syntax and operational semantics of Core McJava and its type soundness theorem.

Syntax. The abstract syntax of Core McJava is given in Figure 3. In this paper, the metavariables d and e range over expressions; K_C and K_X range over constructor declarations; m ranges over method names; M ranges over method declarations; C and D range over class names; X and Y range over mixin names; R, S, T, U and V range over type names; I ranges over interface names; x ranges over variables; f and g range over field names. As in FJ, we assume that the set of variables includes the special variable **this**, which is considered to be implicitly bound in every method declaration. Unlike full McJava, and as in FJ, Core McJava does not allow classes to implement interfaces; however, Core McJava provides interfaces that are used only in the **requires** clause. This is a primary feature of McJava that cannot be excluded from the core calculus.

In Core McJava, a method invocation expression $e_0.m(\bar{e})$ is annotated with the static types $\bar{T}$ of m's arguments, written $e_0.m\texttt{<}\bar{T}\texttt{>}(\bar{e})$. This annotation is necessary because, unlike FJ, Core McJava actually provides method overloading. To capture the McJava's feature of overloaded method resolution, determining which overloaded method to invoked at compile time, a method invocation expression necessarily retains the static types of its arguments. We include this feature in Core McJava, because it is crucial for the problem we are studying.[4] Because of this condition, Core McJava is not a subset of McJava whereas FJ is a subset of Java; instead, we view Core McJava as an intermediate language to which the user's programs in McJava are translated. This translation is straightforward.

We write $\bar{f}$ as a shorthand for a possibly empty sequence $f_1, \cdots, f_n$ and write $\bar{M}$ as a shorthand for $M_1 \cdots M_n$. The length of a sequence $\bar{x}$ is written as $\#(\bar{x})$. Empty sequences are denoted by $\cdot$. Similarly, we write "$\bar{T}\ \bar{f}$" as a shorthand for "$T_1\ f_1, \cdots, T_n\ f_n$"; "$\bar{T}\ \bar{f}$;" as a shorthand for "$T_1\ f_1; \cdots T_n\ f_n;$"; "this.$\bar{f} = \bar{f}$;" as a shorthand for "this.$f_1 = f_1; \cdots$this.$f_n = f_n;$"; $\bar{X}$ as a shorthand for $X_1 :: \cdots :: X_n$.

As in Figure 3, there are two kinds of types: $\bar{X}$ and $\bar{X} :: C$. The former denotes a *mixin-mixin composition* that is generated by composing mixin names, while the latter denotes *mixin-class composition* that is a result of composing mixin names (possibly empty sequence) and a class name. The former is a mixin that cannot be instantiated, while the latter is a concrete class that can be instantiated.

We write $T\ <:\ U$ when T is a subtype of U. Subtype relations between classes, mixins, and compositions are defined in Figure 4, i.e., subtyping is a reflexive and transitive relation of the immediate subclass relation given by the extends clauses in class declarations and mixin compositions.

Class Table. A Core McJava program is a pair of (CT, e) of a *class table* CT and an expression e. A class table is a map from class names and mixin names to class declarations and mixin declarations. The expression e may be considered as the main method of the "real" McJava program. The class table is assumed to satisfy the following conditions: (1) $CT(C) = $ class C ... for every $C \in dom(CT)$; (2) $CT(X) = $ mixin X ... for every $X \in dom(CT)$; (3)Object $\notin dom(CT)$; (4) $T \in dom(CT)$ for every class name and mixin name appearing in $ran(CT)$; (5) there are no cycles in the subtype relation induced by CT; (6) there are no field hidings of a class or a mixin by its subtype, whose subtyping relation is induced by CT.

In the induction hypothesis, we abbreviate $CT(C) = $ class C... and $CT(X) = $ mixin X ... as class C ... and mixin X ..., respectively.

Auxiliary Functions. For the typing and reduction rules, we need a few auxiliary definitions, given in Figure 5 and 6.

The fields of type T, given in Figure 5, written *fields*(T), is a sequence $\bar{T}\ \bar{f}$ pairing the type of each field with its name. If T is a class, *fields*(T) is a sequence for all the fields declared in class T and all of its superclasses. If T is a mixin, *fields*(T) is a sequence for all the fields declared in that mixin. If T is a composition, *fields*(T) is a sequence for all the fields declared in all of its constituent mixins and a class. For the field lookup, we also have the definition of *ftype*(f_i, T) that is a type of field f_i declared in T. In contrast with McJava, field hiding is not allowed in Core McJava.

---

[4] We have solved the overloading problem that was faced by Jam.

$$
\begin{array}{|c|c|}
\hline
\begin{array}{c}
\text{class } C \text{ extends } \bar{X} :: D \ \{\bar{T} \ \bar{f}; \ K_C \ \bar{M}\} \\
\dfrac{\mathit{fields}(\bar{X} :: D) = \bar{S} \ \bar{g}}{\mathit{fields}(C) = \bar{S} \ \bar{g}, \ \bar{T} \ \bar{f}}
\end{array}
&
\mathit{fields}(\texttt{Object}) = \cdot \\
\hline
&
\dfrac{\mathit{fields}(X) = \bar{T} \ \bar{f} \qquad \mathit{fields}(T) = \bar{S} \ \bar{g}}{\mathit{fields}(X :: T) = \bar{S} \ \bar{g}, \ \bar{T} \ \bar{f}} \\
\hline
\dfrac{\texttt{mixin } X \texttt{ requires } I \ \{\bar{T} \ \bar{f}; \ K_X \ \bar{M}\}}{\mathit{fields}(X) = \bar{T} \ \bar{f}}
&
\dfrac{\mathit{fields}(T) = \bar{T} \ \bar{f}}{\mathit{ftype}(f_i, T) = T_i} \\
\hline
\end{array}
$$

Fig. 5. Field lookup

The type of method m declared in type T with argument types $\bar{T}$ is given by $\mathit{mtype}(m, \bar{T}, T)$. The function mtype is defined in Figure 6 by S that is a result type. If T is a composition, the left operand of :: is searched first. If m with argument types $\bar{T}$ is not found in T, we define it **nil**. The type of method m in interface I is also defined in the same way. Similarly, the body of method m declared in type T with argument types $\bar{T}$, written $\mathit{mbody}(m, \bar{T}, T)$, is a pair, written $\bar{x}.e$ of a sequence of parameters $\bar{x}$ and an expression e. As mentioned earlier, in contrast with FJ, method overloading is allowed in Core McJava.

Typing. The typing rule for compositions is given in Figure 7. A composition is well-formed if (1) there are no fields declared with the same name both in the left component and the right component of the composition, (2) there is no method collision, that is, if some methods are declared with the same name and with the same argument types in the left and the right, the return type of both methods must be the same, and (3) for all the methods declared in the interface that is required by the left mixin, the right operand of the composition declares the methods named and typed as the same as the interface. Well-formedness of class types and mixin types are straightforward and omitted in this paper.

Figure 8 shows the typing rules for expressions. An environment Γ is a finite mapping from variables to types, written $\bar{x} : \bar{T}$. The typing judgment for expressions has the form $\Gamma \vdash e : T$, read "in the environment Γ, expression e has type T". These rules are syntax directed, with one rule for each form of expressions. Most of them are straightforward extension of the rules in FJ. The typing rules for constructor and method invocations check that the type of each argument is a subtype of the corresponding formal parameter. The typing rule for constructor invocation also assures that there are no instances of mixins and mixin-mixin compositions.

Figure 9 shows the typing rules for methods, classes and mixins. The type of the body of a method declaration is a subtype of the declared type, and, for a method in a class, the static type of the overriding method is the same as that of the overriden method. A class definition is well-formed if all the methods declared in that class and the constructor are well-formed. Similarly, a mixin is well-formed if all the methods declared in that mixin are well-formed.

$$\dfrac{}{mtype(m, T, \texttt{Object}) = \texttt{nil}}$$

$$\dfrac{\texttt{class } C \texttt{ extends } \bar{X} :: D\ \{\bar{T}\ \bar{f};\ K_C\ \bar{M}\} \quad S\ m(\bar{S}\ \bar{x})\{\ \texttt{return } e;\ \} \in \bar{M}}{mtype(m, \bar{S}, C) = S}$$

$$\dfrac{\texttt{class } C \texttt{ extends } \bar{X} :: D\ \{\bar{T}\ \bar{f};\ K_C\ \bar{M}\} \quad S\ m(\bar{S}\ \bar{x})\{\ \texttt{return } e;\ \} \notin \bar{M}}{mtype(m, \bar{S}, C) = mtype(m, \bar{S}, \bar{X} :: D)}$$

$$\dfrac{\texttt{mixin } X \texttt{ requires } I\ \{\bar{T}\ \bar{f};\ K_X\ \bar{M}\} \quad S\ m(\bar{S}\ \bar{x})\{\ \texttt{return } e;\ \} \in \bar{M}}{mtype(m, \bar{S}, X) = S}$$

$$\dfrac{\texttt{mixin } X \texttt{ requires } I\ \{\bar{T}\ \bar{f};\ K_X\ \bar{M}\} \quad S\ m(\bar{S}\ \bar{x})\{\ \texttt{return } e;\ \} \notin \bar{M}}{mtype(m, \bar{S}, X) = mtype(m, \bar{S}, I)}$$

$$\dfrac{\texttt{interface } I\ \{\bar{M}_I;\} \qquad T\ m(\bar{T}\ \bar{x}) \in \bar{M}_I}{mtype(m, \bar{T}, I) = T}$$

$$\dfrac{\texttt{interface } I\ \{\bar{M}_I;\} \qquad T\ m(\bar{T}\ \bar{x}) \notin \bar{M}_I}{mtype(m, \bar{T}, I) = \texttt{nil}}$$

$$\dfrac{mtype(m, \bar{T}, X) = T}{mtype(m, \bar{T}, X :: T_0) = T}$$

$$\dfrac{mtype(m, \bar{T}, X) = \texttt{nil} \quad mtype(m, \bar{T}, T_0) = T}{mtype(m, \bar{T}, X :: T_0) = T}$$

$$\dfrac{}{mbody(m, \bar{T}, \texttt{Object}) = \texttt{nil}}$$

$$\dfrac{\texttt{class } C \texttt{ extends } \bar{X} :: D\ \{\bar{T}\ f;\ K_C\ \bar{M}\} \quad S\ m(\bar{S}\ \bar{x})\{\ \texttt{return } e;\ \} \in \bar{M}}{mbody(m, \bar{S}, C) = \bar{x}.e}$$

$$\dfrac{\texttt{class } C \texttt{ extends } \bar{X} :: D\ \{\bar{T}\ f;\ K_C\ \bar{M}\} \quad S\ m(\bar{S}\ \bar{x})\{\ \texttt{return } e;\ \} \notin \bar{M}}{mbody(m, \bar{S}, C) = mbody(m, \bar{S}, \bar{X} :: D)}$$

$$\dfrac{\texttt{mixin } X \texttt{ requires } I\ \{\bar{T}\ \bar{f};\ K_X\ \bar{M}\} \quad S\ m(\bar{S}\ \bar{x})\{\ \texttt{return } e;\ \} \in \bar{M}}{mbody(m, \bar{S}, X) = \bar{x}.e}$$

$$\dfrac{\texttt{mixin } X \texttt{ requires } I\ \{\bar{T}\ \bar{f};\ K_X\ \bar{M}\} \quad S\ m(\bar{S}\ \bar{x})\{\ \texttt{return } e;\ \} \notin \bar{M}}{mbody(m, \bar{S}, X) = \texttt{nil}}$$

$$\dfrac{mbody(m, \bar{T}, X) = \bar{x}.e}{mbody(m, \bar{T}, X :: T) = \bar{x}.e}$$

$$\dfrac{mbody(m, \bar{T}, X) = \texttt{nil} \quad mbody(m, \bar{T}, T) = \bar{x}.e}{mbody(m, \bar{T}, X :: T) = \bar{x}.e}$$

Fig. 6. Method lookup

Dynamic Semantics. The reduction relation is of the form $e \longrightarrow e'$, read "expression e reduces to expression e' in one step". We write $\longrightarrow^*$ for the reflexive and transitive closure of $\longrightarrow$.

The reduction rules are given in Figure 10. There are two reduction rules, one for field access and one for method invocation. The field access reduces to the corresponding argument for the constructor. Due to the stylized form of object constructors, the constructor has one parameter for each field, in the same order as the fields are declared. The method invocation reduces to the expression of the method body, substituting all the parameter $\bar{x}$ with the argument expressions $\bar{d}$ and the special variable this with the receiver (we write $[\bar{d}/\bar{x}, e/y]e_0$ for the result of substituting x_1 by $d_1,...,x_n$ by d_n and y by e in e_0). Note that a

$$fields(X) \cap fields(T) = \emptyset$$
$$\text{\texttt{interface}}\ I\ \{\bar{M_I}\}\quad (1)\qquad (2)$$
$$\text{\texttt{mixin}}\ X\ \text{\texttt{requires}}\ I\ \{\ \dots\ \bar{M}\ \}$$
$$\overline{X :: T\ ok}$$
$$(\text{T-COMP})$$
where

$$\forall(S\ m(\bar{T}\ \bar{x})\{\dots\}) \in \bar{M}$$
$$(1) = mtype(m, \bar{T}, X) = mtype(m, \bar{T}, T)$$
$$\text{or}\ mtype(m, \bar{T}, T) = \text{\texttt{nil}}$$
If T is a composition $\bar{X} :: C$, then
$$(2) = \forall(U\ n(\bar{S}\ \bar{x})) \in \bar{M_I}$$
$$mtype(n, \bar{S}, I) = mtype(n, \bar{S}, T)$$

Fig. 7. Well-formed composition

$$\Gamma \vdash x : \Gamma(x)\qquad (\text{T-VAR})$$

$$\frac{\Gamma \vdash e_0 : S\qquad ftype(f, S) = T}{\Gamma \vdash e_0.f : T}$$
$$(\text{T-FIELD})$$

$$\frac{\Gamma \vdash e_0 : S\qquad mtype(m, \bar{S}, S) = T}{\Gamma \vdash \bar{e} : \bar{T}\qquad \bar{T} <: \bar{S}}$$
$$\overline{\Gamma \vdash e_0.m\texttt{<}\bar{S}\texttt{>}(\bar{e}) : T}$$
$$(\text{T-INVK})$$

$$\frac{fields(\bar{X} :: C) = \bar{S}\ \bar{f}\qquad \Gamma \vdash \bar{e} : \bar{T}}{\bar{T} <: \bar{S}\qquad \bar{X} :: C\ ok}$$
$$\overline{\Gamma \vdash \text{\texttt{new}}\ \bar{X} :: C(\bar{e}) : \bar{X} :: C}$$
$$(\text{T-NEW})$$

Fig. 8. Expression typing

$$\bar{x} : \bar{T}, \text{\texttt{this}} : C \vdash e_0 : U_0\qquad U_0 <: T_0$$
$$\text{\texttt{class}}\ C\ \text{\texttt{extends}}\ \bar{X} :: D\ \{\dots\}$$
$$T_0\ ok\qquad \bar{T}\ ok$$
$$\text{if}\ mtype(m, \bar{T}, \bar{X} :: D) = S_0,\ \text{then}\ S_0 = T_0$$
$$\overline{T_0\ m(\bar{T}\ \bar{x})\{\ \text{\texttt{return}}\ e_0\texttt{;}\ \}\ \text{OK IN}\ C}$$
$$(\text{T-CMETHOD})$$

$$\bar{x} : \bar{T}, \text{\texttt{this}} : X \vdash e_0 : S_0\qquad S_0 <: T_0$$
$$T_0\ ok\qquad \bar{T}\ ok$$
$$\text{\texttt{mixin}}\ X\ \text{\texttt{requires}}\ I\ \{\dots\}$$
$$\overline{T_0\ m(\bar{T}\ \bar{x})\{\ \text{\texttt{return}}\ e_0\texttt{;}\ \}\ \text{OK IN}\ X}$$
$$(\text{T-XMETHOD})$$

$$K_C = C(\bar{S}\ \bar{g},\ \bar{T}\ \bar{f})\{\ \text{\texttt{super}}(\bar{g})\texttt{;}$$
$$\text{\texttt{this}}.\bar{f}\texttt{=}\bar{f}\texttt{;}\}$$
$$\frac{fields(\bar{X} :: D) = \bar{S}\ \bar{g}\qquad \bar{M}\ \text{OK IN}\ C}{\bar{X} :: D\ ok\qquad \bar{T}\ ok}$$
$$\text{\texttt{class}}\ C\ \text{\texttt{extends}}\ \bar{X} :: D$$
$$\overline{\{\bar{T}\ \bar{f}\texttt{;}\ K_C\ \bar{M}\}\ \text{OK}}$$
$$(\text{T-CLASS})$$

$$K_X = X(\bar{T}\ \bar{f})\{\ \text{\texttt{this}}.\bar{f}\texttt{=}\bar{f}\texttt{;}\}$$
$$\frac{\bar{M}\ \text{OK IN}\ X\qquad \bar{T}\ ok}{\text{\texttt{mixin}}\ X\ \{\bar{T}\ \bar{f}\texttt{;}\ K_X\ \bar{M}\}\ \text{OK}}$$
$$(\text{T-MIXIN})$$

Fig. 9. Well-formed definitions

$$\frac{fields(\bar{X} :: C) = \bar{T}\ \bar{f}}{\text{\texttt{new}}\ \bar{X} :: C(\bar{e}).\text{\texttt{f}}_i \longrightarrow e_i}$$
$$(\text{R-FIELD})$$

$$\frac{mbody(m, \bar{T}, \bar{X} :: C) = \bar{x}.e_0}{\text{\texttt{new}}\ \bar{X} :: C(\bar{e}).m\texttt{<}\bar{T}\texttt{>}(\bar{d})}$$
$$\longrightarrow [\bar{d}/\bar{x}, \text{\texttt{new}}\ \bar{X} :: C(\bar{e})/\text{\texttt{this}}]e_0$$
$$(\text{R-INVK})$$

Fig. 10. Operational semantics

method lookup in method invocation uses static types of arguments, using type annotations $\bar{T}$.

Properties. We show that Core McJava is type sound. The proof is given in the preliminary version of this paper [16]. [5] Intuitively, the step of proving Core McJava type soundness theorem is almost the same as that of FJ, but details vary a little.

Theorem 1 (Subject Reduction). *If* $\Gamma \vdash e : T$ *and* $e \longrightarrow e'$, *then* $\Gamma \vdash e' : T'$ *for some* $T' <: T$.

---

[5] In this paper we omit type casts from [16] because they are less relevant to what we discuss in this paper.

Theorem 2 (Progress). *Suppose e is a well-typed expression.*

1. *If e includes* new $\bar{X} :: C(\bar{e}).f$ *as a subexpression, then* $\text{fields}(\bar{X} :: C) = \bar{T} \, \bar{f}$ *and* $f \in \bar{f}$ *for some* $\bar{T}$ *and* $\bar{f}$.
2. *If e includes* new $\bar{X} :: C(\bar{e}).m\mathtt{<}\bar{T}\mathtt{>}(\bar{d})$ *as a subexpression, then* $\text{mbody}(m, \bar{T},$ $\bar{X} :: C) = \bar{x}.e_0$, $\emptyset \vdash \bar{d} : \bar{S}$ *where* $\bar{S} <: \bar{T}$, *and* $\#(\bar{x}) = \#(\bar{d})$ *for some* $\bar{x}$ *and* e_0.

To state type soundness formally, we introduce a value v of an expression e by $v ::= $ new $\bar{X} :: C(\bar{e})$.

Theorem 3 (Core McJava Type Soundness). *If* $\emptyset \vdash e : T$ *and* $e \longrightarrow^* e'$ *with* e' *a normal form, then* e' *is a value v of e with* $\emptyset \vdash v : U$ *and* $U <: T$.

4   Implementing McJava

So far, we have overviewed the semantics of McJava. In this section, we show a compilation strategy from McJava programs to Java programs.

Outline of the Compilation Strategy. In order to explain the translation process, we start with a simple example code shown in Figure 11.

At the first step, the translator creates a file A.java from a class A. Then, it writes the body of class declaration into that file. At the beginning, the translator just copies the body of class A into A.java. Eventually, the translator encounters a composition type M::C that is not allowed in Java syntax. To compile this composition, the translator generates a new class M_C and replaces the occurrence of M::C with M_C. The class M_C extends a class C and implements an interface M that contains interface method declarations extracted from mixin M (Figure 12). The resulting class and interface are as follows:

```
interface M { void g(); }
class M_C extends C implements M {
  void g() { int i = new A().f((M)this); ... }}
```

Note that this, an argument of method invocation f, is type-casted to M. This casting is required, because in the translation this has type M_C that is

```
class A {
  int f(M m) { ... }
  boolean f(M::C h) { ... } }
mixin M { // mixin M requires no interfaces
  void g() {
    int i = new A().f(this);
    ... }}
class Test {
  public static void main(String args[]) {
    new M::C().g(); }}
```

Fig. 11. An example program

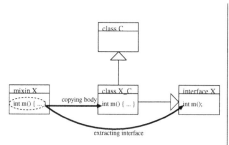

Fig. 12. Translation into Java classes

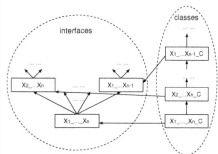

Fig. 13. Linearizing inheritance chain

subtype of both M and C, but M and C are not comparable. Without the type-cast, if class C has another method `String f(C m)`, the translated Java program will be ill-typed.

The translator also replaces the occurrence of M::C with M_C in the class `Test`:

```
class Test {
  public static void main(String args[]) {
    new M_C().g(); }}
```

So far, a simple case is explained, but McJava supports higher order mixins and flexible subtyping among them. We now describe a more general case. A composition $X_1 :: \cdots :: X_n$, where each X_i $(i \in 1 \cdots n)$ is a mixin, is translated into an interface $X_1. \cdots .X_n$ that extends all its immediate super types (shown by S-COMP in Figure 4). The body of this interface is empty. A composition $X_1 :: \cdots :: X_n :: C$, where each X_i $(\in 1 \cdots n)$ is a mixin and C is a class, is translated into a class $X_1. \cdots .X_n.C$ that implements interface $X_1. \cdots .X_n$ and extends all its immediate super types other than $X_1. \cdots .X_n$ (i.e. its immediate super types whose the rightmost operands of :: are C). Because a Java class can inherit only a single class, the class $X_1. \cdots .X_n.C$ cannot extends so many classes at once; instead, they are linearized in a single inheritance chain (Figure 13)[6]. If class C has constructors, the default constructor of C is private. In this case, the McJava compiler writes constructor declarations that just invoke **super** in all the descendant classes of C.[7]

Optimizing Compilation. The major problem of McJava compilation strategy explained above is, when we have a composition $X_1 :: \cdots :: X_n :: C$, then

---

[6] Making $X_1.C$ be a subclass of $X_2.C$ seems to be harmful, when an $X_1.C$'s method overrides an $X_2.C$'s method. To avoid this accidental overriding, the McJava compiler inserts a code that checks the type of **this** by using the **instanceof** operators, to make the appropriate body of method to be executed.

[7] Currently McJava forbids to declare a constructor for mixins.

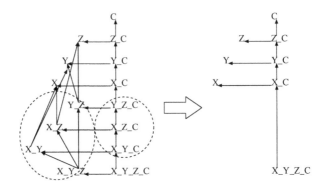

Fig. 14. Optimizing translation

we need to consider 2^n combinations that preclude a scalable compilation algorithm. Even though the situation where computing this combinations takes unacceptable ammount of time (e.g. the situation to compose more than 10 mixins at once) seems to be practically rare in the real problems, the introduction of an unnecessarily deep inheritance chain by linearization may results in critical run-time overhead. Indeed, the depth of inheritance becomes 2^n with the above algorithm.

Fortunately, type names that are not used in the source program can be removed from the inheritance chain. Assume the situation where we have a type X::Y::Z::C, but other compositions such as X::Y::C, Y::Z::C etc. are actually not used in the program (Figure 14). In this case, type names appear inside the dashed ovals can be removed from the inheritance chain, resulting in a new inheritance chain that is shown in the right hand side of Figure 14. By using this technique, almost all the overhead imposed by the linearization becomes acceptable.

The algorithm of optimization is explained below:

1. McJava compiler prepares a table $\mathcal{T}$ that contains all the type names used in the program. This process requires the whole program analysis.
2. Construct a connected graph $graph(T)$ from a composition type T. For example, $graph(X :: Y :: Z :: C)$ becomes the left hand side of Figure 14.
3. For all the *class types* $\bar{X} :: C$ that are not in $\mathcal{T}$ except the class C and compositions that are composed with exactly one mixin, do the following operations:
   (a) Delete two edges $(U, \bar{X} :: C)$ and $(\bar{X} :: C, S)$, where both U and S are class types, from $graph(T)$.
   (b) Insert a new edge (U, S) into $graph(T)$.
4. For all the *mixin types* $\bar{X}$ that are not in $\mathcal{T}$, delete all the edges $(U_i, \bar{X})$ and $(\bar{X}, S_i)$ from $graph(T)$.

Evaluating the Translation. Current McJava compiler does not support separate compilation. This does not necessarily mean that current McJava compiler is impractical. Actually there are some practical systems that do not support separate compilation such as some C++ compilers [1] and AspectJ compiler [5]. It is clear, however, that support for separate compilation is very helpful to distribute binary form of mixins. For this purpose, we are thinking of introducing a *stub generator* that compiles mixins and a *linker* that composes the binary mixins before load time.[8]

McJava compiler is backward compatible to standard Java compilers.[9] That is, every Java program that can be compiled with a standard Java compiler can also be compiled with the McJava compiler.

Implementation Status. At the moment we have developed a preliminary version of McJava compiler that has some restrictions including that it does not support access to Java standard libraries. The latest version of McJava compiler is downloadable at `http://kumiki.c.u-tokyo.ac.jp/~kamina/mcjava/`.

5   Related Work

Jam [3] is a smooth extension of Java with mixins. Jam gives semantics of mixin compositions by translation to Java that is informally expressed by the *copy principle*. Even though this semantics looks natural, it has a serious problem in method overloading resolution, especially when an overloaded method is invoked with `this` as an argument. For example, a Jam program written the same as Figure 11 is not typable. This problem never occurs in McJava. Furthermore, due to the copy principle, it is very difficult to add higher order mixins in Jam.

Another approach of implementing a mixin is to parameterize a superclass of a generic class using a type parameter [23, 27, 22, 2]. One of the restrictions of McJava that is not shared by the generic type approach is its disability to access mixin's superclass type inside the mixin, e.g.:

```
class Color<Widget extends WidgetI> extends Widget {
  Widget f;
  ... }
```

We may partially solve this problem by adopting a coding convention to make the classes composed with the mixin explicitly implement the constraint (the required interface) of that mixin. Another possible design of McJava is to impose a superclass of the mixin to explicitly implement the required interface. In other words, the superclass must be a subtype of the required interface. However, there is a tradeoff. The reason why we take the approach of structural constraint, where a superclass of mixin must be a *structural* subtype of required interface, is that it is more flexible for compositions. Mixins are often implemented *after* the implementation of possible superclasses. Imposing these classes to be a nominal

---

[8] The idea is taken from Jiazzi [19].
[9] Except that McJava reserves keywords `mixin` and `requires`.

subtype of required interface is rather restrictive, because it would require re-implementation of the original classes. Another difference between generic classes and McJava is the flexibility of subtyping. Generic classes cannot capture the full power of McJava type system, where a mixin may be used as a type, and Color::Font is a subtype of both Color and Font.

Besides the feature of structural constraints on mixin's superclasses, McJava is a *nominally typed* class-based language, that means the name of a class (or mixin) determines its subtype relationship. On the other hand, in object-oriented languages with *structural subtyping*, the subtype relation between classes is deter-mined by their structures. A core calculus of classes and mixins for structurally typed language was proposed by Bono et al.[6]. Instead, we take a nominal ap-proach, because the target language (Java) is nominally typed.

To our knowledge, a core calculus for mixin types extending Java was orig-inally developed by Flatt et al.[13]. The novel feature of this calculus, named MixedJava, is its ability to support hygienic mixins [2, 19]. Hygienic mixins use the static type information when looking up a method, avoiding the problem of method collision. This feature is achieved by changing the protocol of method lookup: in MixedJava, each reference to an object is bundled with its *view* of the object, the run-time context information. A view is represented as a chain of mixins for the object's instantiation type. It designates a specific point in the full mixin chain, the static type of that object, for selecting methods during dy-namic dispatch. Even though the proposal of hygienic mixins is useful, there is no implementation of MixedJava. However, there exists two kinds of implemen-tation of hygienic mixins [2, 19], each of them does not conform the McJava type system either; without support for hygienic mixins, McJava defines very flexible subtyping relations. For example, the subtype relation $X :: Y :: C <: X :: C$ is missing in MixedJava. Our work of adapting the implementation strategies of hygienic mixins cited above to our McJava compiler is in progress, and the result will be published in elsewhere.

Mixin modules [10], essentially motivated by the problem of interaction with recursive constructs that cross module boundaries in module systems of func-tional languages, mainly focus on facilitating reusing large scale programming constructs such as frameworks [11]. Our work, on the other hand, mainly fo-cuses on integrating mixin-types and its flexible subtyping with real program-ming languages. The work [11] sacrifices mixin subtyping in favor of allowing method renaming. MixJuice [14] is also independently proposed by Ichisugi et al. to modularize large scale compilation unit.

Schärli et al. proposed *traits* [21], fine grained reusable components as build-ing blocks for classes. Traits support method renaming that overcomes the prob-lem of method collision. When traits are composed, the members of those traits are "flattened" into one class, which also solves the ordering problem of mixins. Our work, in contrast with traits, has more focus on declaring a mixin as a type, and studying their subtype relations. We also would like to note that the order-ing of mixins is useful particularly when we "extend" a parametrized superclass with the same name of method as the superclass, and invoke it via super.m, where m is a method name.

Mixins may be used as vehicles to directly implement *roles* in terms of role modeling [24]. Epsilon [26, 25], a role-based executable model, was also proposed for this purpose. While Epsilon has a feature of dynamic object adaptation, we consider McJava and its core calculus provides a bood basis for incorporating static typing into Epsilon.

6   Conclusions

This paper reports the design and implementation of programming language McJava that is an extension of Java with mixin-types. In McJava, a mixin is a type, and a composition is a subtype of its constituents. McJava's semantics is different from Jam's copy principle; we solved a bothersome problem of using this inside mixins Jam faced, and provide a strong feature of higher order mixins and flexible subtyping. We formally present a type system and operational semantics of Core McJava, a small calculus of McJava, that gives an assurance that McJava type system is sound.

Acknowledgements. The authors would like to thank Atsushi Igarashi, Hidehiko Masuhara and Etsuya Shibayama for their very helpful comments on the earlier version of this paper. The research has been conducted under Kumiki Project, supported as a Grant-in-Aid for Scientific Research (13224087) by the Ministry of Education, Culture, Sports, Science and Technology (MEXT), Japan.

References

1. GCC home page. http://gcc.gnu.org/.
2. Eric Allen, Jonathan Bannet, and Robert Cartwright. A first-class approach to genericity. In *Proceedings of OOPSLA2003*, pages 96–114, 2003.
3. Davide Ancona, Giovanni Lagorio, and Elena Zucca. Jam – A smooth extension of java with mixins. In *ECOOP 2000*, pages 154–178, 2000.
4. Davide Ancona and Elena Zucca. A theory of mixin modules: Basic and derived operators. *Mathematical Structures in Computer Science*, 8(4):401–446, 1998.
5. AspectJ. http://www.eclipse.org/aspectj/.
6. Viviana Bono, Amit Patel, and Vitaly Shmatikov. A Core Calculus of Classes and Mixins. In *Proceedings of ECOOP'99*, LNCS 1628, pages 43–66, 1999.
7. Gilad Bracha. *The Programming Language Jigsaw: Mixins, Modularity and Multiple Inheritance*. PhD thesis, University of Utah, 1992.
8. Gilad Bracha and William Cook. Mixin-based inheritance. In *OOPSLA 1990*, pages 303–311, 1990.
9. Gilad Bracha and Gary Lindstrom. Modularity meets inheritance. In *Proceedings of the IEEE Computer Society International Conference on Computer Languages*, pages 282–290. IEEE Computer Society, 1992.
10. Dominic Duggan and Constantinous Sourelis. Mixin modules. In *ICFP'96*, pages 262–272, 1996.

11. Dominic Duggan and Ching-Ching Techaubol. Modular mixin-based inheritance for application frameworks. In *OOPSLA 2001*, pages 223–240, 2001.
12. Robert Bruce Findler and Matthew Flatt. Modular object-oriented programming with units and mixins. In *Proceedings of ICFP 1998*, pages 98–104, 1998.
13. Matthew Flatt, Shriram Krishnamurthi, and Matthias Felleisen. Classes and mixins. In *POPL 98*, pages 171–183, 1998.
14. Yuuji Ichisugi and Akira Tanaka. Difference-Based Modules: A Class-Independent Module Mechanism. In *Proceedings of ECOOP 2002*, pages 62–88, 2002.
15. Atsushi Igarashi, Benjamin Pierce, and Philip Wadler. Featherweight Java: A minimal core calculus for Java and GJ. *ACM TOPLAS*, 23(3):396–450, 2001.
16. Tetsuo Kamina and Tetsuo Tamai. A core calculus for mixin-types. In *Foundations on Object Oriented Languages (FOOL11)*, 2004. Revised version is available at `http://www.graco.c.u-tokyo.ac.jp/~kamina/papers/fool/kamina.pdf`.
17. Gregor Kiczales, Jim des Rivieres, and Daniel G. Bobrow. *The Arts of the Metaobject Protocol*. The MIT Press, 1991.
18. Barbara H. Liskov and Jeannette M. Wing. A behavioral notion of subtyping. *ACM Transactions on Programming Languages and Systems (TOPLAS)*, 16(6):1811–1841, 1994.
19. Sean McDirmid, Matthew Flatt, and Wilson C. Hsieh. Jiazzi: New-age components for old-fashioned Java. In *Proceedings of OOPSLA2001*, pages 211–222, 2001.
20. D. A. Moon. Object-oriented programming with flavors. In *OOPSLA'86 Conference Proceedings: Object-Oriented Programming: Systems, Languages, and Applications*, pages 1–8, 1986.
21. Nathanael Schärli, Stéphane Ducasse, Oscar Nierstrasz, and Andrew Black. Traits: Composable units of behavior. In *ECOOP 2003*, LNCS 2743, pages 248–274, 2003.
22. Yannis Smaragdakis and Don Batory. Implementing Layered Designs with Mixin Layers. In *Proceedings ECOOP'98*, volume 1445 of *Lecture Notes in Computer Science*, pages 550–570, 1998.
23. B. Stroustrup. *The C++ Programming Language*. Addison-Wesley, 3rd edition, 1997.
24. Tetsuo Tamai. Objects and roles: modeling based on the dualistic view. *Information and Software Technology*, 41(14):1005–1010, 1999.
25. Tetsuo Tamai. Evolvable Programming based on Collaboration-Field and Role Model. In *International Workshop on Principles of Software Evolution (IW-PSE'02)*, pages 1–5, 2002.
26. Naoyasu Ubayashi and Tetsuo Tamai. Separation of Concerns in Mobile Agent Applications. In *Metalevel Architectures and Separation of Crosscutting Conserns – Proceedings of the 3rd International Conference (Reflection 2001)*, volume 2192 of *Lecture Notes in Computer Science*, pages 89–109, 2001.
27. Michael VanHislt and David Notkin. Using C++ templates to implement role-based designs. In *JSSST International Symposium on Object Technologies for Advanced Software*, pages 22–37. Springer-Verlag, 1996.

A Relational Model for Object-Oriented Designs[*]

He Jifeng[1,**], Zhiming Liu[1,2], Xiaoshan Li[3], and Shengchao Qin[4]

[1] International Institute for Software Technology, The United Nations University
{hjf,lzm}@iist.unu.edu
[2] Department of Mathematics and Computer Science, The University of Leicester
zl2@mcs.le.ac.uk
[3] Faculty of Science and Technology, The University of Macau
xsl@umac.mo
[4] Singapore-MIT Alliance & Dept. of Computer Science, National Univ. of Singapore
qinsc@comp.nus.edu.sg

Abstract. This paper develops a mathematical characterisation of object-oriented concepts by defining an observation-oriented semantics for an object-oriented language (OOL) with a rich variety of features including subtypes, visibility, inheritance, dynamic binding and polymorphism. The language is expressive enough for the specification of object-oriented designs and programs. We also propose a calculus based on this model to support both structural and behavioural refinement of object-oriented designs. We take the approach of the development of the design calculus based on the standard predicate logic in Hoare and He's Unifying Theories of Programming (UTP). We also consider object reference in terms of object identity as values and mutually dependent methods.

Keywords: *Object Orientation, Refinement, Semantics, UTP.*

1   Introduction

Software engineering is mainly concerned with using techniques to systematically develop large and complex program suites. However, it is well known that it is hard to obtain the level of assurance of correctness for safety critical software using old fashioned programming techniques. In the search for techniques for making software cheaper and more reliable, two important but largely independent approaches have been visibly influential in recent years. They are

- object-oriented programming, and
- formal methods.

First, it becomes evident that *objects* are and will remain an important concept in software development. Experimental languages of the 1970's introduced various concepts of package, cluster, module, etc, giving concrete expression to the importance of

---

[*] The work is supported by the 211 Key Project of MoE and the 973 Project 2002CB312001 of MoST of China.

[**] On leave from Software Engineering Institute of East China Normal University.

W.-N. Chin (Ed.): APLAS 2004, LNCS 3302, pp. 415–436, 2004.
© Springer-Verlag Berlin Heidelberg 2004

modularity and encapsulation, the construction of software components hiding their state representations and algorithmic mechanisms from users, exporting only those features which are needed in order to use the components. This gives the software components a level of abstraction, separating the view of what a module does for the system from the details of how it does them. It is also clear that certain features of objects, particularly *inheritance* and the use of *object references* as part of the data stored by an object, could be used to construct large system *incrementally* and efficiently, as well as making it possible to *reuse* objects in different contexts.

At least for highly critical systems, it seems essential to give software engineering the same basis in mathematics that is the hall mark of other important engineering disciplines. In this there has good progress, resulting in three main paradigms: model-based, algebraic and process calculi. Both practitioners of formal methods and experts in object technology have investigated how formal specification can supplement object-oriented development, e.g. [21], or how it may help to clarify the semantics of object-oriented notations and concepts, e.g. [1]. Examples of such work include formalisation of the OMG's core object model [19] using Z.

Model-based formalisms have been used extensively in conjunction with object-oriented techniques, via languages such as Object-Z [8], VDM++ [12], and methods such as Syntropy [11] which uses the Z notation and Fusion [10] that is related to VDM. Whilst these formalisms are effective at modelling data structures as sets and relations between sets, they are not ideal for capturing more sophisticated object-oriented mechanisms, such as dynamic binding and polymorphism.

Using predicate transformer, Cavalcanti and Naumann defined an object-oriented programming language with subtype and polymorphism [9, 29]. Sekerinski [33, 28] defined a rich object-oriented language by using a type system with subtyping and predicate transformers. However, neither reference types nor mutual dependency between classes are tackled in those approaches. America and de Boer have given a logic for the parallel language POOL [5]. It applies to imperative programs with object sharing, but without subtyping and method overriding. Abadi and Leino defined an axiomatic semantics for an imperative, object-oriented language with object sharing [2], but it does not permit recursive object types. Poetzsch-Heffter and Müller have defined a Hoare-style logic for object-oriented programs that relaxes many of the previous restrictions [31]. However, as pointed by Leino in [23], instead of allowing the designer of a method defining its specification and then checking that implementation meet the specification, the specification of a method in the Poetzsch-Heffter and Müller logic is derived from the method's known implementation. Leino presented a logic in [23] with imperative features, subtyping, and recursive types. It allows the specification of methods of classes, but restricting inheritance and not dealing with visibility.

In this paper, we aim to develop a mathematical characterisation of object-oriented concepts, and provide a proper semantic basis essential for ensuring correctness and for the development of tool support for the use of formal techniques. We define an object-oriented language with subtypes, visibility, reference types, inheritance, dynamic binding and polymorphism. The language is sufficiently similar to Java and C++ and can be used in meaningful case studies and to capture some of the central difficulties in modelling object-oriented programs.

We build a logic of object-oriented programs as a conservative extension of the standard predicate logic [18]. In our model, both commands and class declarations are identified as predicates whose alphabets include logic variables representing the initial and final values of program variables, as well as those variables representing the contextual information of classes and their links. Our framework allows local variables to be redefined in its scope. Consequently, their states will usually comprise sequences of values. A variable of a primitive type stores a data of the corresponding type whereas a variable of an object type holds the identity or reference of an object as its value. We define the traditional programming constructs, such as conditional, sequential composition, and recursion in the exactly same way as their counterparts in an imperative programming language without reference types. This makes our approach more accessible to users who are already familiar with the existing imperative languages. For simplicity, unlike [30], we consider neither attribute domain redefinition nor attribute hiding. This assumption will be incorporated into the well-formedness condition of a declaration section in Section 3. With this assumption, the set $attr(C)$ of attributes of C contains all the attributes declared in C and those inherited from its superclasses. We simplify the model this way because our focus is program requirement specification, design and verification, whilst attribute domain redefinition and attribute hiding are languages facilities for programming around defects in the requirement specification and design or for the reuse of some classes that were not originally designed for program being developed.

After this introduction, Section 2 introduces the syntax of the language. The semantics of the language is given in Section 3, with the discussion about behavioural refinement of OO designs. In Section 4, we present some initial work towards a (structural) refinement calculus for OO design and programming. We will draw some conclusions in Section 5.

2   Syntax

In our model, an object system (or program) S is of the form $cdecls \bullet P$, where $cdecls$ is a *declaration* of a finite number of classes, and P is called the main method and is of the form (glb, c) consisting of a finite set glb of *global variables* with their types and a command c. P can be understood as the `main` method if S is taken as a Java program.

2.1   Class Declarations

A declaration $cdecls$ is of the form: $cdecls := cdecl \mid cdecls; cdecl$, where $cdecl$ is a *class declaration* of the following form

[private] class N extends M {
    private $(U_i\ u_i = a_i)_{i:1..m}$; protected $(V_i\ v_i = b_i)_{i:1..n}$; public $(W_i\ w_i = c_i)_{i:1..k}$;
    method $m_1(\underline{T}_{11}\ \underline{x}_1, \underline{T}_{12}\ \underline{y}_1, \underline{T}_{13}\ \underline{z}_1)\{c_1\}; \cdots; m_\ell(\underline{T}_{\ell 1}\ \underline{x}_\ell, \underline{T}_{\ell 2}\ \underline{y}_\ell, \underline{T}_{\ell 3}\ \underline{z}_\ell)\{c_\ell\}\}$

Note that

- A class can be declared as private or public. By default, it is assumed as public. We use a function *anno* to extract this information from a class declaration such that $anno(cdecl)$ is *true* if $cdecl$ declares a private class and *false* otherwise.

- N and M are distinct names of classes, and M is called the direct superclass of N.
- Attributes annotated with `private` are private attributes of the class, and similarly, the `protected` and `public` declarations for the protected and public attributes. Types and initial values of attributes are also given in the declaration.
- the `method` declaration declares the methods, their value parameters ($\underline{T}_{i1}\ \underline{x}_i$), result parameters($\underline{T}_{i2}\ \underline{y}_i$), value-result parameters ($\underline{T}_{i3}\ \underline{z}_i$) and bodies ($c_i$). We sometimes denote a method by $m(\underline{paras})\{c\}$, where $\underline{paras}$ is the list of parameters of m and c is the body command of m.
- The body of a method c_i is a command that will be defined later.

We will use Java convention to write a class specification, and assume an attribute `protected` when it is not tagged with `private` or `public`. We have these different kinds of attributes to show how visibility issues can be dealt with. We can have different kind of methods too for a class.

2.2   Commands

Our language supports typical object-oriented programming constructs, but we also allow some commands for the purpose of specification and refinement:

$$c ::= \ skip \mid chaos \mid \textbf{var}\ T\ \text{x=e} \mid \textbf{end}\ x \mid c; c \mid c \triangleleft b \triangleright c \mid c \sqcap c$$
$$\mid b * c \mid le.m(\underline{e}, \underline{v}, \underline{u}) \mid le := e \mid C.new(x)[\underline{e}]$$

where b is a Boolean expression, e is an expression, and le is an expression which may appear on the left hand side of an assignment and is of the form $le ::= x \mid le.a$ where x is a simple variable and a an attribute of an object. Unlike [30] that introduces "statement expressions", we use $le.m(\underline{e}, \underline{v}, \underline{u})$ to denote a call of method m of the object denoted by the left-expression le with actual value parameters $\underline{e}$ for input to the method, actual result parameters $\underline{v}$ for the return values, and value-result parameters $\underline{u}$ that can be changed during the execution of the method call and with their final values as return values too; and use the command $C.new(x)[\underline{e}]$ to create a new object of class C with the initial values of its attributes assigned to the values of the expressions in $\underline{e}$ and assign it to variable x. Thus, $C.new(x)[\underline{e}]$ uses x with type C to store the newly created object.

2.3   Expressions

Expressions, which can appear on the right hand sides of assignments, are constructed according to the rules below.

$$e ::= x \mid null \mid self \mid e.a \mid e\ \textbf{is}\ C \mid (C)e \mid f(e)$$

where $null$ represents the special object of the special class $NULL$ that is a subclass of all classes and has $null$ as its unique object, $self$ will be used to denote the active object in the current scope (some people use `this`), $e.a$ is the a-attribute of e, $(C)e$ is the type casting, $e\ \textbf{is}\ C$ is the type test.

3   Semantics

We now show how to use the basic model of the UTP to define the semantics of our language. We will adopt the convention that the semantics $[\![\mathcal{E}]\!]$ of an element $\mathcal{E}$, such as $e_1 = e_2$ or $x := e$, of the language is denoted by $\mathcal{E}$ itself in a semantic defining equation. When $\mathcal{E}$ appears on the left hand side of a defining equation, it means that its semantics is defined as the right hand side of the equation. When $\mathcal{E}$ appears on the right hand side, it denotes its *defined* semantics of $\mathcal{E}$.

3.1   Programs Are Designs

In [18], Hoare and He proposed a state-based model in which a program or a program command is identified as a *design*, represented by a pair (α, P), where α denotes the set of variables of the program, and P is a predicate of the form

$$p(x) \vdash R(x, x') =_{df} (ok \wedge p(x)) \Rightarrow (ok' \wedge R(x, x'))$$

Notice that
- we call α the *alphabet* of the design and P the *contract* of the design; α declares the *variables* (including logical ones) whose *values* form the *state* of the program at a moment of time, and the contract specifies the *behaviour* of the program in terms of what change in the state it may make.
- x and x' stand for the initial and final values of program variables x in α, respectively.
- predicate p, called the *precondition* of the program, characterises the initial states in which the activation of the program will lead its execution to termination.
- predicate R, called the *post-condition* of the program, relates the initial states of the program to its final states, and
- we describe the termination behaviour of a program by the Boolean variables ok and ok', where the former is true if the program is properly activated and the later becomes true if the execution of the program terminates successfully.

In what follows, we give formal definitions of sequential composition of designs and design refinement.

Definition 1. *For a given alphabet α and two contracts P_1 and P_2, the sequential composition $P_1; P_2$ is defined as the relation composition*

$$(P_1(x, x'); P_2(x, x')) =_{df} \exists m \cdot P_1(x, m) \wedge P_2(m, x')$$

We also define the composite design $(\alpha, P_1); (\alpha, P_2)$ by $(\alpha, P_1; P_2)$.

Within this model, the concept of refinement is defined as predicate implication.

Definition 2. (**Design Refinement**). *Design $D_2 =_{df} (\alpha, P_2)$ is a refinement of design $D_1 =_{df} (\alpha, P_1)$, denoted by $D_1 \sqsubseteq D_2$, if $\forall x, x' \ldots, z, z' \cdot (P_2 \Rightarrow P_1)$, where $x, \ldots, z$ are variables contained in α. $D_1 \equiv D_2$ if and only if $D_1 \sqsubseteq D_2$ and $D_2 \sqsubseteq D_1$.*

Definition 3. (**Data Refinement**). *Let ρ be a mapping (that can also be specified as a design) from α_2 to α_1. Design $D_2 =_{df} (\alpha_2, P_2)$ is a refinement of design $D_1 =_{df} (\alpha_1, P_1)$ under ρ, denoted by $D_1 \sqsubseteq_\rho D_2$, if $(\rho; P_1) \sqsubseteq (P_2; \rho)$.*

A program command usually modifies a subset of the program variables in α. Let V be a subset of α, the notation $V : (p \vdash R)$ denotes the (*framed*) design $p \vdash (R \wedge \underline{w}' = \underline{w})$, where $\underline{w}$ contains all variables in α but those in V. V is called the frame of the design $p \vdash R$. In examples, we often omit the frames of designs by assuming that a design only changes the value of a variable x if its primed version x' occurs in the design.

For simplicity, the above model in [18] adopts a universal data type and allows neither reference types nor nested declaration. This assumption will not be applicable to modelling OO designs anymore. However, we can still follow this classical way of defining a state-based model for a programming language and define our OOL in terms of *values, variables, states, expressions, commands, declarations and programs*.

3.2   Values, Objects, Variables and States

Each program declares a set `cname` of class names, a partial function `superclass` that maps a class name in `cname` to its *direct superclass*, a function `attr` that associates each class name $C \in$ `cname` with the set `attr`(C) of its attributes, and a function `op` that associates each $C \in$ `cname` the set `op`(C) of its methods. We use $\preceq$ to denote the reflexive and transitive closure of `superclass` and $C_1 \preceq C_2$ denotes that C_1 is a subclass of C_2.

We assume a set $\mathcal{T}$ of *primitive types* and an infinite set *REF* of *object identities* (or *references*), and *null* $\in$ *REF*. A value is either a member of a primitive type in $\mathcal{T}$ or an object identity in *REF*. Let the set of values be $VAL =_{df} \bigcup \mathcal{T} \cup REF$. An *object* o is an entity defined by the following structure $o ::= null \mid \langle ref, \text{type}, \text{state} \rangle$, where $ref \in REF$, and `type` is a class name, and `state` is a mapping from `attr(type)` to VAL. Given an object $o = \langle ref, C, \sigma \rangle$, we use *identity*$(o)$ to denote the identity ref of o, `type`(o) the type C of the object o, and `state`$(o)(a)$ the value $\sigma(a)$ of an attribute a of class C.

Let $\mathcal{O}$ be the set of all objects, including *null*. Notice that infinite recursive and looping constructions are allowed, such as $\langle r_i, C, \sigma_i \rangle$ such that $\sigma_i(a) = r_i$, where a is an attribute of C that is type of C too.

The following notations will be employed in the semantics definitions.

- Given a non-empty sequence $\underline{s} = \langle s_1, .., s_k \rangle$, we have $head(\underline{s}) = s_1$, $tail(\underline{s}) = \langle s_2, .., s_k \rangle$. We use $|\underline{s}|$ to denote the length of s, and $\pi_i(\underline{s})$ the *ith* element s_i, for $i : 1, .., k$.
- For two sets S and S_1, $S_1 \trianglerighteq S$ is the set obtained by removing elements in S_1 from S. Note that $\trianglerighteq$ has higher associativity than normal set operators like $\cup, \cap$.
- For a mapping $F : D \longrightarrow E$, $d \in D$ and $r \in E$,

$$F \oplus \{d \mapsto r\} =_{df} F' \qquad \text{where } F'(b) =_{df} \begin{cases} r, & \text{if } b = d; \\ F(b), & \text{if } b \in \{d\} \trianglerighteq D. \end{cases}$$

- For an object $o = \langle ref, C, \sigma \rangle$, an attribute a of C and a value d,

$$ref \oplus \{a \mapsto d\} =_{df} \langle ref, C, \sigma \oplus \{a \mapsto d\} \rangle$$

– For a set $S \subseteq \mathcal{O}$ of objects,

$$S \uplus \{\langle ref, C, \sigma \rangle\} =_{df} \{o \mid identity(o) = ref\} \trianglerighteq S \cup \{\langle ref, C, \sigma \rangle\}$$
$$Ref(S) =_{df} \{ref \mid ref \text{ is the identity of an object in } S\}$$

Our model describes the behaviour of an OO program as a *design* containing the logical variables given in Fig 1 as its *free variables* that form the alphabet of the program.

The semantic model will ensure that for any o_1 and o_2 in Σ, $identity(o_1) = identity(o_2)$ implies $\texttt{type}(o_1) = \texttt{type}(o_2)$ and $\texttt{state}(o_1) = \texttt{state}(o_2)$. We therefore can use identity of an object to refer to an object in Σ. In the rest of the paper, an object $o = \langle ref, C, \sigma \rangle$ means one in Σ if there is no confusion, and will use $ref.a$ to denote the value of $\texttt{state}(o)(a)$, and $\texttt{type}(ref)$ to denote $\texttt{type}(o)$ (i.e. C).

3.3   Evaluation of Expressions

The evaluation of an expression e determines its type $\texttt{type}(e)$ and its value that is a member of $\texttt{type}(e)$ if this type is primitive, and an object of the current type that is attached to e. The evaluation makes use of the state of Σ. However, an expression can only be evaluated when it is well-defined. Some well-definedness conditions are static that can be checked at compiling time, but some are dynamic. The evaluation results of expressions are given in Fig. 2.

3.4   Semantics of Commands

A typical aspect of an execution of an OO program is about how objects are to be attached to program variables (or entities [27]). An attachment is made by an assignment, the object creation or parameter passing in a method invocation. With the approach of UTP, these different cases are unified as an assignment of a value to a program variable. We shall only present the semantic definitions for assignment, object creation and method calls, due to page limit. All other programming constructs will be defined in exactly the same way as their counter-parts in a procedural language, thus are omitted here. We also present some basic refinement laws for commands.

Assignments: An assignment $le := e$ is well-defined if both le and e are well-defined and current type of e matches the declared type of le

$$\mathcal{D}(le := e) =_{df} \mathcal{D}(le) \wedge \mathcal{D}(e) \wedge \texttt{type}(e) \preceq \texttt{decltype}(le)$$

Notice that this requires dynamic type matching. However, it is *safe* to replace the condition $\texttt{type}(e) \preceq \texttt{decltype}(le)$ with $\texttt{decltype}(e) \preceq \texttt{decltype}(le)$, as the semantics will ensure the later implies the former. With the use of type test e **is** C and type casting $(C)e$, changing the dynamic type matching to the static matching will not lose expressive power either.

There are two cases of assignment. The first is to (re-)attach a value to a variable (i.e. change the current value of the variable), but this can be done only when the type of the object is consistent with the declared type of the variable. The attachment of values to other variables are not changed.

$$x := e =_{df} \{x\} : \mathcal{D}(x := e) \vdash (\overline{x}' = \langle \texttt{value}(e) \rangle \cdot tail(\overline{x}))$$

variable	representation	description
cname		the set of classes declared so far
pricname		the set of private class names
attr(C)	$\{\langle a_i : T_i, d_i\rangle\}_{i=1}^m$	T_i and d_i are the type and initial value of attribute a_i, and will be referred by decltype($C.a_i$) and initial($C.a_i$) respectively. We also abuse the notation $a \in$ attr(C) and use it to denote $\exists T, d \cdot (\langle a : T, d\rangle \in$ attr(C)). Again, we do not allow attribute hiding (or redefinition) in a subclass. We also use an attribute name to represent its value and a type name to denote the set of its legal values.
op(C)	$\{m_1 \mapsto$ $(\underline{x}_1{:}\underline{T}_{11}, \underline{y}_1{:}\underline{T}_{12}, \underline{z}_1{:}\underline{T}_{13}, D_1),$ $...,$ $m_k \mapsto$ $(\underline{x}_k{:}\underline{T}_{k1}, \underline{y}_k{:}\underline{T}_{k2}, \underline{z}_k{:}\underline{T}_{k3}, D_k)\}$	each method m_i has $\underline{x}_i, \underline{y}_i$ and $\underline{z}_i$ as its value, result and value-result parameters respectively, that are denoted by val($C.m_i$), res($C.m_i$), and valres($C.m_i$), and the behaviour of m_i is defined by the design D_i referred by Def($C.m_i$). Sometimes we simply denote each element in op(C) as $m_i \mapsto (paras_i, D_i)$. We also sometimes abuse the notation $m \in$ op(C) and use it to denote $\exists paras, D \cdot (m \mapsto (paras, D) \in$ op(C))
$\Sigma(C), \Sigma$	$\Sigma =_{df} \bigcup_{C \in \text{cname}} \Sigma(C)$	$\Sigma(C)$:the set of objects of class C that currently exist in the execution of the program. Σ: system state, also called current configuration [30]
superclass	$\{N \mapsto M, ...\}$	a partial function mapping a class (N) to its *direct* superclass (M).
glb		the set of global variables declared at the beginning of the main program
locvar	$\{(x_1, \langle T_{11}, .., T_{1m}\rangle),$ $...,$ $(x_n, \langle T_{n1}, .., T_{nk}\rangle)\}$	the set of local variables which are known to the current scope of the program. T_{i1}, for $i = 1, .., n$ is the most recently declared type of x_i
var	var = glb $\cup$ locvar	
visibleattr		the set of attributes which are visible from inside the current class, i.e. all its declared attributes plus the protected attributes of its superclasses and all public attributes. Every time before a method of an object is executed, this set is set to the attributes of the class of the object, and it will be reset after the execution of the method.
$\overline{x}$		the state of variable $x \in$ var. Since a local variable can be redeclared, its state usually comprises a nonempty finite sequence of values, whose first (head) element represents the current value of the variable. $\overline{x}$ for $x \in$ glb contains at most one value and thus we can simply use x to denote it. A primitive variable takes values of primitive type, while an object variable can store an object *name* or *identity* as its value.

Fig. 1. The Alphabet: Logical Variables

As we do not allow attribute hiding/redefinition in subclasses and semantics of assignment, the assignment to a simple variable has not side-effect, and thus the Hoare triple $\{o_2.a = 3\}$ $o_1 := o_2$ $\{o_1.a = 3\}$ is valid in our model for variables o_1 of class C_1 and

Expression	Evaluation
null	$\mathcal{D}(null) =_{df} true,$ $\texttt{type}(null) =_{df} NULL,$ $\texttt{value}(null) =_{df} null$
x	$\begin{aligned} \mathcal{D}(x) \quad &=_{df} x \in \texttt{var} \wedge (\texttt{decltype}(x) \in \mathcal{T} \vee \texttt{decltype}(x) \in \texttt{cname}) \text{ (Static)} \\ &\wedge \quad \texttt{decltype}(x) \in \mathcal{T} \Rightarrow head(\overline{x}) \in \texttt{decltype}(x) \qquad \text{(Dynamic)} \\ &\wedge \quad \texttt{decltype}(x) \in \texttt{cname} \Rightarrow \\ & \qquad head(\overline{x}) \in Ref(\varSigma(\texttt{decltype}(x))) \qquad\qquad \text{(Dynamic)} \\ \texttt{type}(x) \quad &=_{df} \begin{cases} \texttt{decltype}(x) & \texttt{decltype}(x) \in \mathcal{T} \\ \texttt{type}(head(\overline{x})) & \text{otherwise} \end{cases} \\ \texttt{value}(x) &=_{df} head(\overline{x}) \end{aligned}$
self	$\begin{aligned} \mathcal{D}(self) \quad &=_{df} self \in \texttt{locvar} \wedge \texttt{decltype}(self) \in \texttt{cname} \text{ (Static)} \\ &\wedge \quad head(\overline{self}) \in Ref(\varSigma(\texttt{decltype}(self))) \quad \text{(Dynamic)} \\ \texttt{type}(self) &=_{df} \texttt{type}(head(\overline{self})) \\ \texttt{value}(self) &=_{df} head(\overline{self}) \end{aligned}$
$x.a$	$\begin{aligned} \mathcal{D}(x.a) =_{df} \quad & \mathcal{D}(x) \\ & \wedge \texttt{decltype}(x) \in \texttt{cname} \wedge \texttt{type}(x).a \in \textbf{visibleattr} \text{ (Static)} \\ & \wedge head(\overline{x}) \neq null \\ \texttt{type}(x.a) =_{df} \quad & \texttt{type}(head(\overline{x}).a) \\ \texttt{value}(x.a) =_{df} \quad & head(\overline{x}).a \end{aligned}$
$le.a$	$\begin{aligned} \mathrm{D}(le.a) =_{df} \quad & \mathrm{D}(le) \wedge \texttt{type}(le).a \in \textbf{visibleattr} \\ \texttt{value}(le.a) =_{df} \quad & \texttt{value}(le).a \\ \texttt{type}(le.a) =_{df} \quad & \texttt{type}(\texttt{value}(le).a) \end{aligned}$
$(e \textbf{ is } C)$	$\begin{aligned} \mathcal{D}(e \textbf{ is } C) \quad &=_{df} \mathcal{D}(e) \wedge (\texttt{type}(e) \in \texttt{cname}) \wedge (C \in \texttt{cname}) \\ \texttt{type}(e \textbf{ is } C) &=_{df} Bool \\ \texttt{value}(e \textbf{ is } C) &=_{df} \texttt{value}(e) \neq null \wedge \texttt{type}(e) \preceq C \end{aligned}$
$(C)e$	$\begin{aligned} \mathcal{D}((C)e) \quad &=_{df} \mathcal{D}(e \textbf{ is } C) \wedge \texttt{value}(e \textbf{ is } C) \\ \texttt{type}((C)e) &=_{df} \texttt{type}(e) \\ \texttt{value}((C)e) &=_{df} \texttt{value}(e) \end{aligned}$
e/f	$\begin{aligned} \mathcal{D}(e/f) \quad &=_{df} \quad \mathcal{D}(e) \wedge \mathcal{D}(f) \wedge \texttt{decltype}(e) = Real \\ & \qquad \wedge \texttt{decltype}(f) = Real \wedge \texttt{value}(f) \neq 0 \\ \texttt{value}(e/f) &=_{df} \quad \texttt{value}(e)/\texttt{value}(f) \end{aligned}$

Fig. 2. Evaluation of Expressions

o_2 of C_2, where $C_2 \preceq C_1$ and C_1 has a as protected attribute of integer type. This has made the theory much simpler than the Haore-logic based semantics for OO programming in [30].

The second case is to modify the value of an attribute of an object attached to an expression. This is done by finding the attached object in the system state $\varSigma$ and modifying its state accordingly. Thus, all variables that point to the identity of this object will be updated.

$$le.a := e =_{df} \{\varSigma(\texttt{decltype}(le))\}: \mathcal{D}(le.a := e) \vdash \left(\begin{array}{l} \varSigma(\texttt{decltype}(le))' = \varSigma(\texttt{decltype}(le)) \\ \uplus (\{\texttt{value}(le)\} \oplus \{a \mapsto \texttt{value}(e)\}) \end{array} \right)$$

For example, let x be a variable of type C such that C has an attribute d of D and D has an attribute a of integer type. $x.d.a := 4$ will change state of $x = \langle 1, C, \{d \mapsto 2\}\rangle$, where reference 2 is the identity of $\langle 2, D, \{a \mapsto 3\}\rangle$ to $x = \langle 1, C, \{d \mapsto 2\}\rangle$, but the 2 is now the identity of the object $\langle 2, D, \{a \mapsto 4\}\rangle$.

This semantic definition shows the side-effect of an assignment and does reflect the OO feature pointed out by Broy in [7] that an invocation to a method of an object which contains such an assignment or an instance creation defined later on, changes the state Σ of the system.

Law 1. $(le := e; le := f(le)) \equiv (le := f(e))$

Law 2. $(le_1 := e_1; le_2 := e_2) \equiv (le_2 := e_2; le_1 := e_1)$, *provided* le_1 *and* le_2 *are distinct simple names which do not occur in* e_1 *or* e_2.

Note that the law might not be valid if le_i are composite names. For instance, the following equation is not valid when x and y have the same value:

$$x.a := 1; \; y.a := 2 \equiv y.a = 2; \; x.a = 1$$

Object Creation. The execution of $C.new(x)[\underline{e}]$ is well-defined if $C \in$ cname, the length of the list $\underline{e}$ of the expressions is the same as the number of attributes of C and the types of the expressions match those of the corresponding attributes of C, i.e.

$$\mathcal{D}(C.new(x)[\underline{e}]) =_{df} C \in \text{cname} \wedge |\underline{e}| = size(\text{attr}(C)) \wedge \forall i \cdot \text{type}(e_i) \preceq \text{decltype}(C.a_i)$$

The command (re-)declares variable x, creates a new object, attaches the object to x and attaches the initial values of the attributes to the attributes of x too.

$$C.new(x)[\underline{e}] =_{df} \{\text{var}, x, \Sigma(C)\} :$$

$$\mathcal{D}(C.new(x)[\underline{e}]) \vdash \exists ref \notin Ref(\Sigma) \cdot$$

$$\left(\begin{array}{l} (\Sigma(C)' = \Sigma(C) \cup \{\langle ref, C, \{a_i \mapsto \text{value}(e_i)\}\rangle \mid a_i \in \text{attr}(C)\}) \wedge \\ ((x \in \text{glb} \wedge (x' = ref) \\ \vee \\ (x \in \text{locvar} \wedge (\overline{x}' = \langle ref\rangle \cdot \overline{x})) \wedge (\text{locvar}' = \{x\} \trianglerighteq \text{locvar} \cup \{(x, \langle C\rangle \cdot \text{locvar}(x))\}) \\ \vee \\ (x \notin \text{var} \wedge (\overline{x}' = \langle ref\rangle) \wedge (\text{locvar}' = \text{locvar} \cup \{(x, \langle C\rangle)\}))) \end{array} \right)$$

We will use $C.new(x)$ to denote the command $C.new(x)[\underline{\text{Initial}(C.a)}]$ that creates an instance of C with the default initial values of its attributes.

Law 3. *If* x *and* y *are distinct,* x *does not appear in* $\underline{f}$ *and* y *does not appear in* $\underline{e}$,

$$C_1.new(x)[\underline{e}]; C_2.new(y)[\underline{f}] \equiv C_2.new(y)[\underline{f}]; C_1.new(y)[\underline{e}]$$

Law 4. *If* x *is not free in the Boolean expression* b, *then*

$$C.new(x)[\underline{e}]; (P \triangleleft b \triangleright Q) \equiv (C.new(x)[\underline{e}]; P) \triangleleft b \triangleright (C.new(x)[\underline{e}]; Q)$$

Method Call. Let v, r and vr be lists of expressions. The command $le.m(v, r, vr)$ assigns the values of the actual parameters v and vr to the formal value and value-result parameters of the method m of the object o that le refers to, and then executes the body of m. After it terminates, the value of the result and value-result parameters of m are passed back to the actual parameters r and vs.

$$le.m(v, r, vr) =_{df} (\mathcal{D}(le) \wedge \text{type}(le) \in \text{cname} \wedge m \in \text{op}(\text{type}(le)) \Rightarrow$$

$$\exists N \cdot (\text{type}(le) = N) \wedge \left(\begin{array}{l} \text{var } N \, self = le, T_1 \, x = v, T_2 \, y = r, T_3 \, z = vr; \\ \Psi(N.m); \; r, vr := y, z; \\ \text{end } self, x, y, z \end{array} \right)$$

where x, y, z are resp. value, result and value-result parameters of the method m of class $\text{type}(le)$, and $\Psi(N.m)$ stands for the design associated with method m of class N, that will be defined in the semantics of the whole program in Section 3.6.

3.5   Class Declarations

A class declaration *cdecl* given in Section 2.1 is well-defined if the following conditions hold.

1. N has not been declared before: $N \notin$ cname.
2. N and M are distinct: $N \neq M$.
3. The attribute names in the class are distinct.
4. The method names in the class are distinct.
5. The parameters of every method are distinct.

Let $\mathcal{D}(cdecl)$ denote the conjunction of the above conditions for class declaration *cdecl*. The class declaration *cdecl* adds the structural information of class N to the state of the program, and this role is characterised by the following design.

$cdecl =_{df}$

$\{\text{cname}, \text{pricname}, \text{superclass}, \text{pria}, \text{prota}, \text{puba}\} : \mathcal{D}(cdecl) \vdash$

$$\left(\begin{array}{l} \text{cname}' = \text{cname} \cup \{N\} \\ \wedge\ \text{pricname}' = (\text{pricname} \cup \{N\} \lhd anno(cdecl) \rhd \text{pricname}) \\ \wedge\ \text{superclass}' = \text{superclass} \oplus \{N \mapsto M\} \\ \wedge\ \text{pria}' = \text{pria} \oplus \{N \mapsto \{\langle \underline{u} : \underline{U}, \underline{a}\rangle\}\} \\ \wedge\ \text{prota}' = \text{prota} \oplus \{N \mapsto \{\langle \underline{v} : \underline{V}, \underline{b}\rangle\}\} \\ \wedge\ \text{puba}' = \text{puba} \oplus \{N \mapsto \{\langle \underline{w} : \underline{W}, \underline{c}\rangle\}\} \\ \wedge\ \text{op}' = \text{op} \oplus \{N \mapsto \{(m_1 \mapsto (\underline{paras})_1, c_1)), \cdots\cdots, (m_\ell \mapsto (\underline{paras}_\ell, c_\ell))\}\} \end{array} \right)$$

where the logical variables pria, prota and puba are introduced to record the declared attributes of N, from which the state attr can later be constructed. Similarly, the dynamic behaviour of the methods cannot be defined before the dependency relation among classes is specified. At the moment, the logical variable op(N) binds each method m_i to code c_i rather than its definition which will be calculated in the end of the declaration section.

Example. Consider a simple bank system illustrated by the UML class diagram in Figure 3. *Account* is an abstract class[1] and has two subclasses of current accounts *CA* and saving accounts *SA*.

The declaration of class *Account*, denoted by *declAccount*, is written as follows. Note that we allow specification notations (designs) to appear in methods and commands.

class *Account* {
protected : *Int aNo, Int balance*;
method : *getBal*($\emptyset$, *Int b*, $\emptyset$) {*b* := *balance*};
          withdraw(*Int x*, $\emptyset$, $\emptyset$){*balance* $\geq$ *x* $\vdash$ *balance'* = *balance* − *x*}}

The declaration *declCA* of *CA* is given as

class *CA* **extends** *Account*
method : *withdraw*(*Int x*, $\emptyset$, $\emptyset$){*balance* := *balance* − *x*}
}

---

[1] See [25] for a formal definition of an abstract class.

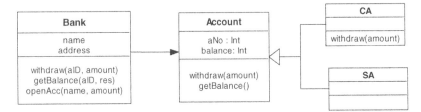

Fig. 3. A bank system

We can write the declarations of *SA* (in which method *withdraw* is just inherited the from *Account*) and *Bank* (which has a set of accounts associated with it) in the same way.

It is easy to see that both *declAccount* and *declCA* are well-formed. The semantics of *declAccount* is defined by the following design.

$$declAccount = true \vdash$$
$$\begin{pmatrix} \text{cname}' = \text{cname} \cup \{Account\} \wedge \text{prot}' = \{Account \mapsto \{\langle Int\ aNo\rangle, \langle int\ balance\rangle\}\} \wedge \\ \text{op}' = \{Account \mapsto \{getBal \mapsto (\langle\emptyset, Int\ b, \emptyset\rangle, b' = balance), \\ withdraw \mapsto (\langle Int\ x, \emptyset, \emptyset\rangle, balance \geq x \vdash balance' = balance - x)\}\} \end{pmatrix}$$

The semantics of *declCA* is the following.

$$declCA = true \vdash \begin{pmatrix} \text{cname}' = \text{cname} \cup \{CA\} \wedge \\ \text{superclass}' = \{CA \mapsto Account\} \wedge \\ \text{op}' = \{Account \mapsto \{withdraw \mapsto \\ (\langle Int\ x, \emptyset, \emptyset\rangle, balance' = balance - x)\}\} \end{pmatrix}$$

The semantics of *declSA* and *declBank* for classes *SA* and *Bank* can be defined in the same way.

A class declaration section *cdecls* comprises a sequence of class declarations. Its semantics is defined from the semantics of a single class declaration given above, and the semantics of sequential composition. However, the following well-definedness conditions need to be enforced onto a declaration section:

1. All class names used must be declared in the declaration section;
2. Any superclass of a declared class is declared too;
3. The function `superclass` does not induce circularity;
4. No attributes of a class can be redefined in its subclasses;
5. No method is allowed to redefine its signature in its subclass.

The formal definitions for these conditions are omitted here due to page limitation. In what follows we denote them as $\mathcal{D}_1, \ldots, \mathcal{D}_5$, respectively.

3.6   The Semantics of a Program

Let *cdecls* be a class declaration section and *P* main method of the form (glb, c), the meaning of a program (*cdecls* • *P*) is defined as the composition of the meaning of class declarations *cdecls* (defined in Section 3.5), the design *init*, and the meaning of command *P*:

$$cdecls \bullet P =_{df} cdecls;\ init;\ \texttt{cname}' = \texttt{pricname} \trianglerighteq \texttt{cname};\ c$$

where the design *init* performs the following tasks

1. to check the well-definedness of the declaration section,
2. to decide the values of `attr` and `visibleattr` from those of `pria`, `prota` and `puba`,
3. to define the meaning of every method body *c*,
4. to check the well-definedness of `glb`, i.e. its consistency with the class declarations:

$$\mathcal{D}(\texttt{glb}) =_{df} \forall (x : T) \in \texttt{glb} \cdot T \in (\mathcal{T} \cup (\texttt{pricname} \trianglerighteq \texttt{cname}))$$

The design *init* is formalised as:

$$init =_{df} \{\texttt{visibleattr}, \texttt{attr}, \texttt{op}\} :$$
$$\mathcal{D}_1 \wedge \mathcal{D}_2 \wedge \mathcal{D}_3 \wedge \mathcal{D}_4 \wedge \mathcal{D}_5 \wedge \mathcal{D}(\texttt{glb}) \vdash$$
$$\begin{pmatrix} \texttt{visibleattr}' = \bigcup_{N \in \texttt{cname}} \{N.a \mid a \in \texttt{puba}(N)\} \\ \wedge\ \forall N \in \texttt{cname} \cdot \texttt{attr}'(N) = \texttt{pria}(N) \cup \bigcup\{\texttt{prota}(M) \cup \texttt{puba}(M) \mid N \preceq M\} \\ \wedge\ \texttt{op}'(N) = \{m \mapsto (\overline{paras}, \Psi(N.m)) \mid (m \mapsto (\overline{paras}, c)) \in \texttt{op}(M) \wedge N \preceq M\} \end{pmatrix}$$

where the family of designs $\Psi(N.m)$ is defined in the rest of this section.

The family of designs $\Psi(N.m)$ captures the dynamic binding and is defined by a set of recursive equations, which contains for each class $N \in$ cname, each class M such that $N \preceq M$, and every method $m \in \texttt{op}(M)$ and equation

$$\Psi(N.m) = F_{N.m}(\Psi) \quad \text{where } \texttt{supercalss}(N) = M$$

where F is constructed according to the following rules:

(1) m is not defined in N, but in a superclass, i.e. $m \notin \texttt{op}(N) \wedge m \in \cup\{\texttt{op}(M) \mid N \preceq M\}$. The defining equation for this case is simply

$$F_{N.m}(\Psi) =_{df} Set(N); \phi_N(\textbf{body}(M.m)); Reset$$

where the design $Set(N)$ finds out all attributes visible to class N in order for the invocation of method m of N to be executed properly, whereas $Reset$ resets the environment to be the set of variables that are accessible to the main program only:

$$Set(N) =_{df} \{\texttt{visibleattr}\} : true \vdash$$
$$\texttt{visibleattr}' = \begin{pmatrix} \{N.a \mid a \in \texttt{pria}(N)\} \cup \bigcup_{N \preceq M}\{M.a \mid a \in \texttt{prota}(M)\} \cup \\ \bigcup_{M \in \texttt{cname}}\{M.a \mid a \in \texttt{puba}(M)\} \end{pmatrix}$$

$$Reset =_{df} \{\texttt{visibleattr}\} : true \vdash \texttt{visibleattr}' = \bigcup_{M \in \texttt{cname}}\{M.a \mid a \in \texttt{puba}(M)\}$$

The function ϕ_N renames the attributes and methods of class N in the code **body**$(N.m)$ by adding object reference *self* that represents the *active* object that is executing its method. The definition of ϕ_N is given in Fig. 4. Note that *Set* and *Reset* are used to ensure data encapsulation that is controlled by `visibleattr` and the well-formedness condition of an expression.

(2) m is a method defined in class N. In this case, the behaviour of the method $N.m$ is captured by its body **body**$(N.m)$ and the environment in which it is executed

$$F_{N.m}(\Psi) =_{df} Set(N); \phi_N(\textbf{body}(N.m)); Reset$$

P	$\phi_N(P)$	P	$\phi_N(P)$
$skip$	$skip$	$chaos$	$chaos$
$P_1 \lhd b \rhd P_2$	$\phi_N(P_1) \lhd \phi_N(b) \rhd \phi_N(P_2)$	$P_1; P_2$	$\phi_N(P_1); Set(N); \phi(P_2)$
$P_1 \sqcap P_2$	$\phi_N(P_1) \sqcap \phi_N(P_2)$	$b * P$	$\phi_N(b) * (\phi_N(P); Set(N))$
$var\ x : T = e$	$var\ x : T = \phi_N(e)$	end x	end x
$C.new(x)$	$C.new(\phi_N(x))$	$le := e$	$\phi_N(le) := \phi_N(e)$
$le.m(v,r,vr)$	$\phi_N(le).m(\phi_N(v),\phi_N(r),\phi_N(vr))$	$le.a$	$\phi_N(le).a$
$m(v,r,vr)$	$self.m(\phi_N(v),\phi_N(r),\phi_N(vr))$	$null$	$null$
$self$	$self$	$f(e)$	$f(\phi_N(e))$
x	$\begin{cases} self.x, & x \in \bigcup_{N \preceq M} \mathtt{attrname}(M) \\ x, & otherwise \end{cases}$		

Fig. 4. The Definition of ϕ_N

4   Refinement

We would like the refinement calculus to cover not only the early development stages of requirements analysis and specification but also the later stages of design and implementation. This section presents the initial results of our exploration on three kinds of refinement:

1. Refinement relation between object systems.
2. Refinement relation between declaration sections.
3. Refinement relation between commands.

From now on, we assume the main method of each program does not use direct field access, that is, expressions of the form *le.a*. This assumption actually does not reduce the expressiveness of the language, as we can always use *getField* and *setField* methods to replace direct field access where necessary. In what follows, we give formal definitions for the above-mentioned refinement relations.

Definition 4. *Let S_1 and S_2 are object programs which have the same set of global variables* glb, *let $Ivar_{S_i}$, $i = 1, 2$, be the set of all other variables that are free in P_i and $Ivar'_{S_i}$ be the set of their primed versions. S_1 is a* refinement S_2, *denoted by $S_1 \sqsupseteq_{sys} S_2$, if its behaviour is more controllable and predictable than that of S_2:*

$$S_1 \sqsupseteq_{sys} S_2 =_{df} \forall \mathtt{glb}, \mathtt{glb'} \cdot (\exists Ivar_{S_1}, Ivar'_{S_1} \cdot S_1) \Rightarrow (\exists Ivar_{S_2}, Ivar'_{S_2} \cdot S_2)$$

This indicates the external behaviour of S_1, that is, the pairs of pre- and post global states, is a subset of that of S_2.

Definition 5. *Let* cdecls$_1$ *and* cdecls$_2$ *be two declaration sections. We say* cdecls$_1$ *is a* refinement *of* cdecls$_2$, *denoted by* cdecls$_1 \sqsupseteq_{class}$ cdecls$_2$, *if the former can replace the later in any object system:*

$$\text{cdecls}_1 \sqsupseteq_{class} \text{cdecls}_2 =_{df} \forall P \cdot (\text{cdecls}_1 \bullet P \sqsupseteq_{sys} \text{cdecls}_2 \bullet P)$$

where P stands for a main method (glb, c).

Intuitively, it states that $cdecls_1$ supports at least the same set of services as $cdecls_2$.

Definition 6. *Let P_1 and P_2 be main methods with the same global variables, and c_1 and c_2 be commands. We define*

$$P_1 \sqsupseteq_{cmd} P_2 =_{df} \forall \text{cdecls} \cdot (\text{cdecls} \bullet P_1) \sqsupseteq_{sys} (\text{cdecls} \bullet P_2)$$
$$c_1 \sqsupseteq c_2 =_{df} \forall \underline{v}, \underline{v}' \cdot (c_1 \Rightarrow c_2)$$

where cdecls *is a declaration section, and* $\underline{v}$ *and* $\underline{v}'$ *are free variables in* c_1 *and* c_2.

Intuitively, it denotes that P_1 does better than P_2, i.e. ensures a stronger postcondition with a weaker precondition, under the same environment.

We have already given some refinement laws for refining program commands in Section 3.4, which are to ensure the correctness of the semantic model. In what follows, we first give a group of refinement laws that in fact formalize principles of refactoring [13]. After that, we will present three refinement laws which capture three key principles and patterns in object-oriented design, that are well known as the *Expert Pattern*, *High Cohesion Pattern* and *Low Coupling Pattern* [22, 24].

We first introduce some notations. We use $N[supc, pri, prot, pub, ops]$ to denote a well-formed class declaration that declares the class N that has *supc* as its direct superclass; *pri*, *prot* and *pub* as its sets of private, protected and public attributes; and *ops* as its set of methods. *supc* is always of either a class name M, when M is the direct superclass of N, or $\emptyset$ when N has no superclass. We may also only refer to some, or even none of M, *pri*, *prot*, *pub*, *ops* when we talk about a class declaration. For example, N denotes a class declaration for N, and $N[pri]$ a class declaration that declares the class N that has *pri* as its private attributes.

Law 5. *The order of the class declarations in a declaration section is not essential:*

$$N_1; \ldots; N_n = N_{i_1}; \ldots; N_{i_n}$$

where N_i is a class declaration and $i_1, \ldots, i_n$ is a permutation of $\{1, \ldots, n\}$.

A law like this may look utterly trivial, but it is not so obvious for a semantic definition of a class declaration to guarantee this law. For example, if the the pre-condition of the class declaration requires that the direct superclass has been declared, this law would not hold.

The next law says that more services may come from more classes.

Law 6. *If a class name N is not in* cdecls, cdecls $\sqsubseteq N[M, pri, prot, pub, ops]$; cdecls.

Introducing a private attribute has no effect.

Law 7. *If neither N nor any of its superclasses and subclasses in* cdecls *has x as an attribute* $N[pri]$; cdecls $\sqsubseteq N[pri \cup \{T\ x = d\}]$; cdecls.

Changing a private attribute into a protected one may support more services.

Law 8. $N[pri \cup \{T\ x = d\}, prot]$; cdecls $\sqsubseteq N[pri, prot \cup \{T\ x = d\}]$; cdecls.

Similarly, changing a protected attribute to a public attribute refines the declaration too.

Adding a new method can refine a declaration.

Law 9. *If m is not defined in N, let m(paras){c} be a method with distinct parameters paras and a command c. Then*

$N[ops]; \text{cdecls} \sqsubseteq N[ops \cup \{m(paras)\{c\}\}]; \text{cdecls}$

provided that there is no superclass of N in cdecls.

Law 10. *We can refine a method to refine a declaration. If $c_1 \sqsubseteq c_2$,*

$N[ops \cup \{m(paras)\{c_1\}\}]; \text{cdecls} \sqsubseteq N[ops \cup \{m(paras)\{c_2\}\}]; \text{cdecls}$

Inheritance introduces refinement.

Law 11. *If none of the attributes of N is defined in M or any superclass of M in* cdecls,

$N[\emptyset, pri, prot, pub, ops]; \text{cdecls} \sqsubseteq N[M, pri, prot, pub, ops]; \text{cdecls}$

We can introduce a superclass as given in the following law.

Law 12. *Let $C_1 = N[\emptyset, pri \cup S, prot, pub, ops]$, $C_2 = N[\{M\}, pri, prot, pub, ops]$. Assume M is not declared in* cdecls,

$C_1; \text{cdecls} \sqsubseteq C_2; M[\emptyset, \emptyset, S, \emptyset, \emptyset]; \text{cdecls}$

We can move some attributes of a class to its superclass.

Law 13. *If all the subclasses of M but N do not have attributes in S, then*

$M[prot_1]; N[\{M\}, prot \cup S]; \text{cdecls} \sqsubseteq M[prot_1 \cup S]; N[\{M\}, prot]; \text{cdecls}$

We can move the common attributes of the direct subclasses of a class to the class itself.

Law 14. *If M has $N_1, \ldots, N_k$ as its direct subclasses,*

$M[prot]; N_1[prot_i \cup S]; \ldots; N_k[prot_k \cup S]; \text{cdecls}$
$\sqsubseteq M[prot \cup S]; N_1[prot_1]; \ldots; N_k[prot_k]; \text{cdecls}$

We can move some methods of a class to its superclass.

Law 15. *Let m(paras){c} be a methods of N, but not a method of its direct superclass M. Assume that c only involves the protected attributes of M, then*

$M[ops]; N[\{M\}, ops_1 \cup \{m(\underline{paras})\{c\}\}]; \text{cdecls}$
$\sqsubseteq M[ops \cup \{m(\underline{paras})\{c\}\}]; \overline{N[\{M\}, ops_1]}; \text{cdecls}$

We can remove a redundant method from a subclass.

Law 16. *Assume that N has M as its direct superclass and $m(paras)\{c\} \in ops \cap ops_1$, and c only involves the protected attributes of M,*

$M[ops]; N[\{M\}, ops_1]; \text{cdecls} \sqsubseteq M[ops]; N[\{M\}, ops_1 \backslash \{m(\underline{paras})\{c\}\}]; \text{cdecls}$

We can remove any unused private attributes.

Law 17. *If $(T\ x)$ is a private attribute of $N[pri]$ that is not used in any command of N,*

$N[pri];$ cdecls $\sqsubseteq N[pri\backslash\{T\ x = d\}];$ cdecls

We can remove any unused protected attributes.

Law 18. *If $(T\ x = d)$ is a protected attribute of $N[prot]$ that is not used in any command of N and any subclass of N,*

$N[prot];$ cdecls $\sqsubseteq N[prot\backslash\{T\ x = d\}];$ cdecls

The expert patterns says that a class is allowed to delegate some tasks to its associated classes that contain the information for the tasks.

Law 19 (**Expert Pattern for Responsibility Assignment**). *Suppose $M[ops_1]$ is defined in cdecls, $m(paras_1)\{c_1\} \in ops_1$, and $(M\ o)$ be an attribute of N, then*

$N[ops \cup \{n(paras)\{c[\tilde{c}_1]\}\}];$ cdecls $\sqsubseteq N[ops \cup \{n(paras)\{c[o.m]\}\}];$ cdecls

Here c_1 is obtained from $\tilde{c}_1$ by replacing $o.x$ with x, that is, $c_1 = \tilde{c}_1[x/o.x]$. Notice that $\tilde{c}_1$ does not refer to any attribute of N. While $c[\tilde{c}_1]$ denotes that $\tilde{c}_1$ occurs as part of command c, and $c[o.m]$ denotes that the command obtained from $c[\tilde{c}_1]$ by substituting $o.m$ for $\tilde{c}_1$. Note also that $paras_1 \subseteq paras$.

This law is illustrated by the UML class diagram in Figure 5. It will become an equation if x is a public attribute M.

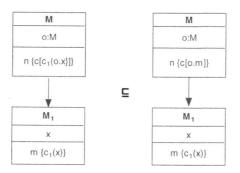

Fig. 5. Object-oriented Functional decomposition

To understand the above law, let us consider a simple example from the aforementioned bank system in Section 3.5.

Consider method *getBalance* of class *Bank*. Initially, we might have the following design for it:

getBalance(*Int aID, Int res*, $\emptyset$) $=_{df}$
$\exists a \in \Sigma(Account) \cdot a.aNo = aID \vdash \exists a \in \Sigma(Account) \cdot a.aNo = aID \Rightarrow res' = a.balance$

Note that it requires the attributes of class *Account* to be visible (public) to other classes (like *Bank*). Applying Law 19 to it, we can get the following design:

getBalance(*Int aID, Int res*, $\emptyset$) $=_{df}$
$\exists a \in \Sigma(Account) \cdot a.aNo{=}aID \vdash \exists a \in \Sigma(Account) \cdot a.aNo{=}aID \Rightarrow res'{=}a.getBalance()$

The refinement delegates the task of balance lookup to the *Account* class.

It is important to note that method invocation, or in another term, object interaction takes time. Therefore, this object-oriented refinement (and the one described in Law 21 later) usually exchanges efficiency for "simplicity", ease of reuse and maintainability, and data encapsulation.

After functionalities are delegated to associated classes, data encapsulation can be applied to increase security and maintainability. The visibility of an attribute can be changed from public to protected, or from protected to private under certain circumstances. This is captured in the following law.

Law 20 (Data Encapsulation). *Suppose $M[pri, prot, pub]$, and $(T_1\ a_1 = d_1) \in pub$, $(T_2\ a_2 = d_2) \in prot$.*

1. *If no operations of other classes have expressions of the form $le.a_1$, except for those of subclasses of M, we have*

$$M[pri, prot, pub]; cdecls \sqsubseteq M[pri, prot \cup \{T_1\ a_1 = d_1\}, pub\backslash\{T_1\ a_1 = d_1\}]; cdecls$$

2. *If no operations of any other classes have expressions of the form $le.a_2$, we have*

$$M[pri, prot, pub]; cdecls \sqsubseteq M[pri \cup \{T_2\ a_2 = d_2\}, prot\backslash\{T_2\ a_2 = d_2\}, pub]; cdecls$$

After applying Law 19 exhaustively (i.e. the expert pattern) to the class *Bank* for method *getBalance*, we can then apply Law 20 to the class diagram on the right hand side of Figure 5 to achieve the encapsulation of the attribute *balance* of the class *Account*. The attribute *aNo* can be encapsulated in a similar way.

Another principle of object-oriented design is to make classes simple and highly cohesive. This means that the responsibilities (or functionalities) of a class, i.e. its methods, should be strongly related and focused. We therefore often need to decompose a complex class into a number of associated classes, so that the system will be

- easy to comprehend
- easy to reuse
- easy to maintain
- less delicate and less effected by changes

We capture the *High Cohesion* design pattern [22] by the following refinement rule.

Law 21 (High Cohesion Pattern). *Assume $M[pri, op]$ is a well-formed class declaration, $pri = \{x, y\}$ are (or lists of) attributes of M, $m_1\{c_1(x)\} \in op$ only contains attribute x, method $m_2\{c_2[m_1]\} \in op$ can only change x by calling m_1 (or though it does not have to change it at all). Then*

1. *$M \sqsubseteq M[pri_{new}, op_{new}]; M_1[pri_1, op_1]; M_2[pri_2, op_2]$, where*
   - *$pri_{new} = \{M_1\ o_1, M_2\ o_2\}$*
   - *$op_{new} = \{m_1\{o_1.m_1\}, m_2\{o_2.m_2\}\}$*
   - *$pri_1 = \{x\}$, $op_1 = \{m_1\{c_1(x)\}\}$*
   - *$pri_2 = \{y, M_1\ o_1\}$, $op_2 = \{m_2\{c_2[o_1.m_1]\}\}$*

   such that $\forall o : M \cdot (o.o_1 = o.o_2.o_1)$ is an invariant of M. This invariant has to be established by the constructors of these three classes.
   This refinement is illustrated by the diagram in Figure 6(a).

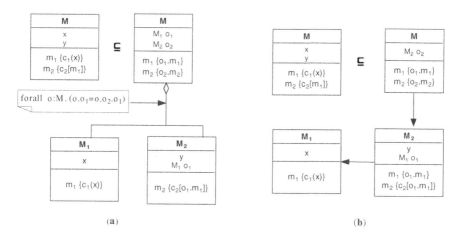

Fig. 6. Class Decomposition

2. $M \sqsubseteq M[pri_{new}, op_{new}]; M_1[pri_1, op_1]; M_2[pri_2, op_2]$, where

- $pri_{new} = \{M_2\ o_2\}$
- $op_{new} = \{m_1\{o_1.m_1\}, m_2\{o_2.m_2\}\}$
- $pri_1 = \{x\}, op_1 = \{m_1\{c(x)\}\}$
- $pri_2 = \{y, M_1\ o_1\}, op_2 = \{m_1\{o_1.m_1\}, m_2\{c_2[o_1.m_1]\}\}$

such that $p(o_1.x, y)$ is an invariant of M_2.
This refinement is illustrated by the diagram in Figure 6(b).

Notice that the first refinement in Law 21 requires that M to be coupled with both M_1 and M_2; and in the second refinement M is only coupled with M_2, but more interaction between M_2 and M_1 are needed than in the first refinement. We believe that the above three laws, together with the other simple laws for incremental programming effectively support the use-case driven and iterative RUP development process [22]. The use of the patterns for responsibility assignment in object-oriented software development is clearly demonstrated in Larman's book [22] and in the lecture notes of Liu in [24].

For each of the laws, except for Law 13 in the Appendix, let *LHS* and *RHS* denote the declarations on the left and right hand sides, respectively. For any main program P, each refinement law becomes an equational law: $LHS \bullet P \cong RHS \bullet P$, provided $LHS \bullet P$ is well-defined.

5   Conclusion

We have shown how Hoare and He's design calculus [18] is used to define an OO language. A program is represented as a predicate called a *design*, and the refinement relation between programs is defined as implication between predicates.

In [7], Broy gave an assessment of object-orientation. Our model reflects most of the features, no matter good or bad, of object-oriented designs. For example, the model does show that inheritance with attribute hiding and method overriding makes it difficult to analyse the system behaviour, and method invocation on an object may indeed change the system's global states.

Nevertheless, formal techniques for object-orientation have achieved significant advance in areas of both formal methods and object technology, e.g. [1, 2, 6, 4, 8, 29]. There are a number of recent articles on Hoare Logics for object-oriented programming (see, e.g. [30, 35, 20, 31, 23, 9]). The normal form of a program in our paper is similarly to that of [9, 30]. However, one major difference of our work is that we also provide a formal characterisation and refinement of the contextual/structural features, i.e. the declaration section, of an object program. This is motivated by our work on the formalisation and combinations of UML models [25, 26] to deal with consistency problems of different UML models. This characterisation has been proven to be very useful in defining semantics for integrated specification languages in general. For example, [32] uses this characterisation in defining a semantics of TCOZ.

The notions of different kinds of refinements in our model are very close to those in [9], though the semantics in [9] is defined in terms of the weakest precondition predicate transformer and does not deal with reference types. We take a *weak semantic* approach meaning that when the pre-condition of a contact is not satisfied in a state, the program will then behave as *chaos*, and any modification to the program, such as adding exceptional handling, will be a refinement to the program. We also describe static well-formedness conditions in the pre-condition so that any correction of any static inconsistency in a program, such as static type mismatching, missing variables, missing methods, etc. will be refinement too. This decision is required for *structural refinement calculus* of OO designs in order to treat *refactoring* [13] as refinement and properly combine it with *functional/behavioural refinement*. This combination is important for the application of the model to composing different UML models and to reasoning about their consistency [25, 26] and in giving semantics for integrated language [32]. Also our work on formal object-oriented design with UML [25, 26] has provided us with the insight of functional decomposition in the object-oriented setting and its relation with data encapsulation. The functional decomposition and data encapsulation are characterised by the refinement **laws** 6 - 7. They reflect the essential principle of object-oriented design.

The power of UTP[18] for describing different features of computing, such as state-based properties, communication, timing, higher-order computing [18, 36, 34], makes our approach ready for an extension to cope with these different aspects of object-oriented designs. Alternatively, one can also use temporal logic, such as [3], for the specification and verification of multithreading Java-like programs. However, we would like to deal with concurrency at a higher level when we extend this model for component-based software development [17, 16].

In [7], Broy also argued that the property of object identities is of too low level and implementation oriented. This is true to some extent and the use of references does cause some side-effects, making the semantics a bit more difficult. A preliminary version of the model without references can be found in [15]. However, that version is only slight simpler than this version. On the other hand, the complexity in fact mainly affects reasoning about low level design and implementation. At high level requirement analysis and design, we can simply use the identities as the objects they refer to or just talk about objects in an abstract way. In our approach for analysis of use cases [25], we mainly describe the change of system states in terms of what objects are created or deleted, what modifications are made to an object and what links between objects are formed or broken. We think that features like method overriding and attribute hiding are only useful to program around the requirement and design defects detected at the coding stage or even after, or when one tries to reuse a class with a similar template in a program that the class was not originally designed. These features cause problems in program verification and the smooth application of the notion of program refinements.

Future work includes the study of the issue of completeness of the refinement calculus, applications to more realistic case studies, and formal treatment of *patterns* [14].

References

1. M. Abadi and L. Cardeli. *A Theory of Objects*. Springer-Verlag, 1996.
2. M. Abadi and R. Leino. A logic of object-oriented programs. In M. Bidoit and M. Dauchet, editors, *TAPSOFT '97: Theory and Practice of Software Development, 7th International Joint Conference*, pages 682–696. Springer-Verlag, 1997.
3. E. Abraham-Mumm, F.S. de Boer, W.P. de Roever, and M. Steffen. Verification for Java's reentrant multithreading concept. In *Foundations of Software Science and Computation Structures, LNCS 2303*, pages 5–20. Springer, 2002.
4. P. America. Designing an object-oriented programming language with behavioural subtyping. In J. W. de Bakker, illem P. de Roever, and G. Rozenberg, editors, *REX Workshop*, volume 489 of *Lecture Notes in Computer Science*, pages 60–90. Springer, 1991.
5. P. America and F. de Boer. Reasoning about dynamically evolving process structures. *Formal Aspects of Computing*, 6(3):269–316, 1994.
6. M.M. Bonsangue, J.N. Kok, and K. Sere. An approach to object-orientation in action systems. In J. Jeuring, editor, *Mathematics of Program Construction, LNCS 1422*, pages 68–95. Springer, 1998.
7. M. Broy. Object-oriented programming and software development - a critical assessment. In A. McIver and C. Morgan, editors, *Programming Methodology*. Springer, 2003.
8. D. Carrington, *et al. Object-Z: an Object-Oriented Extension to Z*. North-Halland, 1989.
9. A. Cavalcanti and D. Naumann. A weakest precondition semantics for an object-oriented language of refinement. In *LNCS 1709*, pages 1439–1460. Springer, 1999.
10. D. Coleman, *et al. Object-Oriented Development: the FUSION Method*. Prentice-Hall, 1994.
11. S. Cook and J. Daniels. *Designing Object Systems: Object-Oriented Modelling with Syntropy*. Prentice-Hall, 1994.
12. E. Dürr and E.M. Dusink. The role of VDM^{++} in the development of a real-time tracking and tracing system. In J. Woodcock and P. Larsen, editors, *Proc. of FME'93, LNCS 670*. Springer-Verlag, 1993.
13. M. Fowler, K. Beck, J. Brant, W. Opdyke, and D. Roberts. *Refactoring: Improving the Design of Existing Code*. Addison-Wesley, 1999.
14. E. Gamma, *et al. Design Patterns*. Addison-Wesley, 1995.
15. J. He, Z. Liu, and X. Li. Towards a refinement calculus for object-oriented systems (invited talk). In *Proc. ICCI02, Alberta, Canada*. IEEE Computer Society, 2002.
16. J. He, Z. Liu, and X. Li. A component calculus. In H.D. Van and Z. Liu, editors, *Proc. Of FME03 Workshop on Formal Aspects of Component Software (FACS03), UNU/IIST Technical Report 284, UNU/IIST, P.O. Box 3058, Macao*, Pisa, Italy, 2003.
17. J. He, Z Liu, and X. Li. Contract-oriented component software development. Technical Report 276, UNU/IIST, P.O. Box 3058, Macao SAR China, 2003.

18. C.A.R. Hoare and J. He. *Unifying Theories of Programming*. Prentice-Hall, 1998.

19. I. Houston. Formal specification of the OMG core object model. Technical report, IMB, UK, Hursely Park, 1994.

20. M. Huisman and B. Jacobs. Java program verification via a Hoare logic with abrupt termination. In T. Maibaum, editor, *FASE 2000, LNCS 1783*, pages 284–303. Springer, 2000.

21. K. Lano and H. Haughton. *Object-oriented specification case studies*. Prentice Hall, New York, 1994.

22. C. Larman. *Applying UML and Patterns*. Prentice-Hall International, 2001.

23. K. Rustan M. Leino. Recursive object types in a logic of object-oriented programming. In *LNCS 1381*. Springer, 1998.

24. Z. Liu. Object-oriented software development in UML. Technical Report UNU/IIST Report No. 228, UNU/IIST, P.O. Box 3058, Macau, SAR, P.R. China, March 2001.

25. Z. Liu, J. He, X. Li, and Y. Chen. A relational model for formal requirements analysis in UML. In J.S. Dong and J. Woodcock, editors, *Formal Methods and Software Engineering, ICFEM03, LNCS 2885*, pages 641–664. Springer, 2003.

26. Z. Liu, J. He, X. Li, and J. Liu. Unifying views of UML. Research Report 288, UNU/IIST, P.O. Box 3058, Macao, 2003. Presented at UML03 Workshop on Compostional Verification of UML and submitted for the inclusion in the final proceedings.

27. B. Meyer. From structured programming to object-oriented design: the road to Eiffel. *Structured Programming*, 10(1):19–39, 1989.

28. A. Mikhajlova and E. Sekerinski. Class refinement and interface refinement in object-orient programs. In *Proc of FME'97, LNCS*. Springer, 1997.

29. D. Naumann. Predicate transformer semantics of an Oberon-like language. In E.-R. Olerog, editor, *Proc. of PROCOMET'94*. North-Holland, 1994.

30. C. Pierik and F.S. de Boer. A syntax-directed hoare logic for object-oriented programming concepts. Technical Report UU-CS-2003-010, Institute of Information and Computing Science, Utrecht University, 2003.

31. A. Poetzsch-Heffter and P. Muller. A programming logic for sequential Java. In S.D. Swierstra, editor, *Proc. Programming Languages and Systems (ESOP'99), LNCS 1576*, pages 162–176. Springer, 1999.

32. S. Qin, J.S. Dong, and W.N. Chin. A semantics foundation for TCOZ in Unifying Theories of Programming. In K. Araki, S. Gnesi, and D. Mandrioli, editors, *FME 2003: Formal Methods, LNCS 2805*, pages 321–340. Springer, 2003.

33. F. Sekerinski. A type-theoretical basis for an object-oriented refinement calculus. In *Proc. of Formal Methods and Object Technology*. Springer-Verlag, 1996.

34. A. Sherif and J. He. Towards a time model for Circus. In *ICFEM02, LNCS 2495*. Springer, 2002.

35. D. von Oheimb. Hoare logic for Java in Isabelle/HOL. *Concurrency and Computation: Practice and Experience*, 13(13):1173–1214, 2001.

36. J.C.P. Woodcock and A.L.C. Cavalcanti. A semantics of Circus. In *ZB 2002, LNCS 2272*. Springer, 2002.

Exploiting Java Objects Behavior for Memory Management and Optimizations

Zoe C.H. Yu, Francis C.M. Lau, and Cho-Li Wang

Department of Computer Science,
The University of Hong Kong,
Pokfulam Road, Hong Kong
{chyu, fcmlau, clwang}@cs.hku.hk

Abstract. We study the behavior of Java objects in order to explore potential garbage collection optimization opportunities in Java programs. Our study has led to one probable strategy for using heap buffers effectively through obtaining liveness and type information of objects. To allow examination of the Java memory, we implement a heap profiling tool by instrumenting an existing Java virtual machine. The tool records useful object events during program execution, and groups the objects according to their types. We apply the tool to different benchmarks and analyze the results. We also try to characterize the objects' behaviors and suggest that memory occupied by certain objects can be reused by other objects, leading to improved performance of the program. We implement a simple prototype to demonstrate the feasibility of the object reuse approach.

1 Introduction

Garbage collection (GC) is the automatic management of dynamically allocated storage [22]. It was first devised and used by McCarthy in late 1950s during the implementation of Lisp [26]. GC frees programmers from bookkeeping and deallocating unused memory in a program explicitly, and thus helps avoid many memory problems such as dangling references and memory leaks. An ineffective GC mechanism, however, can either degrade the overall system performance or exhaust quickly all usable memory of an application program. Hence a large number of GC algorithms and techniques have been proposed over the past 40 years or so. Basic GC algorithms include the *mark-sweep* [26], *reference counting* [11], *copying* [15, 10], and the *generational* [24, 36] methods.

Java is one of the most popular object-oriented languages, which has brought GC into the mainstream of programming practice and research. From the software engineering point of view, GC supports better abstraction and encapsulation because manual memory management requires good understanding of the program to determine the last use of an object and perform deletion which makes code reusability nearly impossible. Manual memory management also requires low-level knowledge of how memory is structured, which contradicts the concept of information hiding. However, it is difficult to devise a garbage collector which

W.-N. Chin (Ed.): APLAS 2004, LNCS 3302, pp. 437–452, 2004.
© Springer-Verlag Berlin Heidelberg 2004

is both time efficient and effective in space saving. Time efficiency certainly affects users' choice of a programming language, but the amount of memory occupied by objects should not be overlooked. In general, for reason of one kind or another, GC does not immediately reclaim those objects that have become unreachable, but intermittently. Moreover, there could also be objects in the heap that are reachable but no longer in use, which occupy the heap memory unnecessarily.

Many systems use a single GC algorithm for all applications. But because objects in different applications might behave differently, a fit-all algorithm could perform poorly for a certain kind of applications [16]. We believe that a good GC should have the ability to automatically adjust its object collection and retention policies to fit the specific execution patterns of an application. Objects' liveness (that is, the time period during which the objects are actually in used) information has been shown to be useful in early reclamation of objects [18, 19, 31]. The earlier an useless object can be reclaimed, the more space saving can be enjoyed by the program. Liveness information can also provide GC with some hints about whether an object should be retained for later use.

We set out to study the behavior of Java objects in order to explore potential GC optimization opportunities in Java programs that would lead to the implementation of improved/optimal GC strategies. To aid our study, we implement a heap profiling tool by instrumenting the baseline compiler of the Jikes RVM [2]. Using the tool, we can monitor and log all object events during a program's execution. In Section 3, we give some details on the tool and how we have used it in our experiments.

We perform postmortem analysis on the object traces obtained via our profiling tool. We focus on the objects' liveness and their types to determine if the memory occupied by one object, O_1, could be reused by another object, O_2. The reuse is possible if O_1 becomes garbage before the creation of O_2 and both O_1 and O_2 are of the same class type. If we can provide a good "caching" mechanism for such expiring/expired objects (and thus their reusable memory), we should be able to improve the space-time performance of the system. In Section 4, we show from the experimental results that in fact a considerable amount of objects created in a program can be reused. We demonstrate in Section 5 the feasibility of the approach through a preliminary prototype implementation of an object caching mechanism in the Jikes RVM. Object caching involves many issues which may affect the resulting system performance. We discuss some of these issues in Section 6.

This work makes the following contributions:

- We study the behavior of Java objects through detecting their liveness and types. And then for the analysis, the objects can be grouped into (1) immutable vs. mutable; and (2) prolific vs. non-prolific [33].
- We study the amount of space saving by applying object caching to objects of prolific types. We show that significant space saving can be achieved for certain kinds of applications.

– We study the feasibility of an actual implementation of object caching of prolific objects in a runtime memory management system. Preliminary results show that the approach is promising.

2   Related Work

Our focus is on opportunities for reusing existing objects in Java programs. Although there have been plenty of work on object reuse, most of them targeted at functional languages. To our knowledge, this is the first attempt to consider actual reuse of objects' memory to save space and redundant operations for an object-oriented language.

2.1   Memory Behavior Study for Java

Dieckman and Hölzle [13] presented an in-depth analysis of the object allocation behavior of the SPECjvm98 benchmarks [34], and confirmed the applicability of the *weak generational hypothesis* [24] to Java objects. The weak generational hypothesis states that newly created objects have higher mortality than older objects. Yang et al. [35] studied Java objects' lifespan in terms of the actual amount of CPU cycles an object spanned instead of the traditional approach where the number of bytes allocated is used. Kim and Hsu [23] analyzed the memory behavior, lifetime characteristics, temporal locality, and the effects of using fully associative caches, 2-way set associative caches, and 4-way set associative cache on the performance of several SPECjvm98 applications. They also investigated the impact on performance of GC under different heap configurations, as well as the relationship between heap size and cache miss. Shuf et al. [32] studied the distribution of different kinds of heap and field accesses and the hotness of fields and methods. They have also examined the relationship between performance and data misses in the data TLB, L1 data cache, and the L2 data cache, and suggested the co-allocation of method tables to reduce TLB misses.

There were studies on using offline profile-directed feedback approaches for various kinds of GC optimizations. Shaham et al. [29] performed postmortem analysis to study the *drag time*, the time difference between the last use time and the GC time, of Java objects. Based on that they presented an offline profiling tool that an help reduce objects' drag time [30]. Fitzgerald and Tarditi [16] investigated the use of profiling results to direct the selection of a most suitable collector for an application from a pool of available collectors. Blackburn et al. [6] presented a profile-driven approach to gather objects' liveness information for pretenuring long-lived objects to reduce the copying overhead of GC. Shuf et al. [33] suggested the use of offline profiling to detect *prolific* types which produce a large number of object instances. They also presented a *type-based* GC which uses the prolific type information to direct the garbage collector to perform frequent collection on prolific object types in order to improve the effectiveness of GC.

2.2   Reusing Existing Objects

There are two main approaches to reusing existing objects [25]. The first approach, known as *hash consing* [17], tries to coalesce two different object instances that have the same memory contents into a single one, hence saving space. The second approach tries not to construct new object instances from scratch but extend the lifetime of existing object instances so that they act as the new ones. This approach is often called *object caching*, *memoization*, or *pooling* [4, 27, 28]. Object caching is the retention of object buffers in the middleware/lower level for future reuse. In dynamic programming/functional languages, it is also called memoization which is used to cache intermediary answers for later use. While object pooling usually refers to the reuse of objects in the application layer.

Hash Consing. Basically, hash consing makes two identical objects share the same copy in the heap. This is done by checking if an identical object already exists before an object is constructed. The concept of hash consing was first used in the construction of DAGs for common subexpression elimination [14].

Appel and Gonçalves [3] have described a hash-consing GC for SML/NJ. It is a two-generational collector, where hash consing is performed only when non-updatable objects are copied from the younger to the older generation. Therefore, each immutable object residing in the older generation is guaranteed not to have a duplicated record. However, their experimental results show that only a small amount of space saving can be achieved. Their GC also exhibits performance slow-down in general, because of the more expensive memory allocation operations.

Marinov and O'Callahan [25] presented *object equality profiling* that can detect equivalent object instances for the possibility of merging for Java programs. The check for mergeability of two objects requires the inspection of two labelled graphs for isomorphism. They gave a formal definition of mergeability, and used the inspection results to direct manual code transformation in order to take advantage of mergeability opportunities in Java programs. Our analysis is similar to that of Marinov and O'Callahan in that both of us consider the reuse of existing objects to improve system performance. Unlike Marinov and O'Callahan who focus on the hash consing type of reuse, we focus on the object caching type.

Object Caching, Memoization, and Object Pooling. Object caching, memoization, and pooling are techniques to enhance performance by reducing the need to construct new objects. Caching and memoization have been used widely in functional languages such as Lisp and ML; object pooling has been used in some applications where reusing of objects can be done manually, such as the JDBC connection pooling [12] in Java.

Bonwick [8] presented a kernel memory allocator called the *slab* allocator, which can reduce the cost of allocating complex objects by retaining the initial state of these objects between their uses. The slab allocator also segregates objects according to their sizes and lifetimes to reduce internal and external fragmentation.

Acar et al. [1] presented a framework that provides user's control over equality, identification of dependencies, and space management for selective memoization in the context of ML. They do not encourage automatic support of memoization and argue that it is crucial to provide users with controls due to some possible performance issues related to equality test and cache replacement policy.

Shuf et al. [33] proposed a hypothesis which states that objects of prolific types have short lifetimes. Based on the hypothesis, they think it is possible to recycle prolific objects by placing them into a special free pool instead of a general free memory pool. However, they did not carry out the necessary performance study to confirm that possibility. Our work is to extend their work and study the amount of space saving through the reuse of prolific objects. Note that Shuf et al. also tried to reduce the space requirement of prolific objects, but instead of object caching, they used the *short type pointer* technique to eliminate unnecessary type descriptor pointers. We have implemented a simple prototype to demonstrate the feasibility and benefits of reusing object buffers, which we describe in Section 4.2.

3 Methodology

We conducted experiments to collect object traces for our analysis. In this section, we describe our experimental setup, the methodologies for object traces and their analysis, and the benchmark suite we used.

3.1 The Profiling Tool

Our heap profiling tool operates in two phases. In the first phase, the heap profiling tool runs the target Java program and logs all the object events into a file. In the second phase, objects are grouped according to their types, and object events are sorted by their liveness information. Other information such as the objects' sizes, their declaring class, etc. are also extracted from the traces. With all this, we can then explore possible opportunities for GC optimization.

Instrumentation. We instrument the baseline compiler of the Jikes RVM (v2.3.1) to emit code to trap object events during runtime. We monitor the program execution with the instrumented Jikes RVM. For each object, we record its creation time, declaring class, size in bytes, type, last access time (i.e. reads, writes, and identity-based operations), and the times at which GC is triggered. Each Java object has an object header, which holds the object's type, hash code, lock state, and GC information, etc. We expand the object header to include an object ID field for object identification, and an age field for keep tracking of the object's liveness during program execution. We measure the time at which an event is triggered in terms of the number of bytes allocated since the beginning of the program execution because that is not affected by the amount of codes instrumented. A buffer is used to log the events generated temporarily. The logged data is written into a file when the buffer is full.

We modify the baseline compiler to emit assembly codes for barriers so that the following events can be trapped during runtime:

- Allocation of objects and arrays (e.g. `new`, `newarray` etc.)
- Reading and writing an object field (e.g. `getfield`, `putfield` etc.)
- Reading and writing an array element (e.g. `aaload`, `aastore` etc.)
- Reading an array length (e.g. `arraylength`)
- Identity-based operations, including:
  - Invoking an object's method (e.g. `invokevirtual` etc.)
  - Comparing an object reference (e.g. `if_null`, `instanceof` etc.)
  - Locking and unlocking an object (e.g. `monitorenter`, `monitorexit`)

The barrier code inserted is *non-substituting*, which means that the original code sequence generated for a given operation will not be replaced by the compiler. The advantage of using a non-substituting barrier is that any optimization performed during code generation will remain intact.

As the Jikes RVM is written in Java, instrumentation of some event points can result in infinite recursion. For example, while a program event is being processed, the instrumentation causes the profiler to log the object traces into a file. This executes another instrumentation point and reenters itself. We tackle the infinite looping problem by using a preallocated buffer to record the object traces, and stay away from the non-substituting barriers by setting the memory contents of the preallocated buffer directly, with the help of the compiler. This only partially solves the problem because many internal data structures used in the Jikes RVM involve arrays. Therefore, our non-substituting barriers would not trap events generated by any Jikes RVM related class. This also has the positive side-effect of reducing the number of immortal objects recorded, which are not supposed to be garbage collected.

We do not enable the instrumentation until the `main()` method is about to be compiled, to ensure the correctness and stability of the Jikes RVM. It is because many Java virtual machines, including Jikes RVM, have to bring up all the system classes following the initialization of its threads, class loader, and memory management subsystems, all before the execution of `main()`. Therefore, performing instrumentation before these processes may result in unexpected errors. As a result, built-in objects created before the loading of `main()` are untracked.

Our instrumentation ensures thread safety through the use of the Jikes RVM's interruptibility pragma which directs the compiler to disable thread switching and stack overflow tests in method prologues. Therefore, any method calls generated are guaranteed to be atomic within the Java threads model.

Analysis. The profiling tool analyzes the object traces obtained by partitioning objects according to their types. Scalars (non-array objects) are placed in the same partition if they have the same class type. For arrays, they must have the same class type and the same length. For the object instances of each class type, we produce a sorted list of the instances' creation times and last use times, and analyze if they have non-overlapping lifetimes. We define an object's lifetime as the difference between the time at which it is created and the time it is last used. We examine the result to determine the amount of reusable objects and the times at which they become reusable. Other object information such as the number of field references is extracted during the analysis.

3.2   Benchmarks

We used the SPECjvm98 [34] benchmarks, the jolden [9] benchmarks, and five other miscellaneous Java programs for the experiments. We briefly describe these programs in the following.

We skip _201_compress of the SPECjvm98 benchmark suite because its execution time is too long using our tool. _202_jess is a Java expert shell system for puzzle solving. _205_raytrace is a ray tracer which works on a scene depicting a dinasaur. _209_db performs multiple database functions on a memory resident database. _213_javac is the Java compiler from JDK 1.0.2. _222_mpegaudio is an application for decompressing MP3 audio files. _227_mtrt is a multithreaded version of _205_raytrace. _228_jack is a Java parser generator.

Of the jolden benchmark suite, we omit the Power program because it has a similar problem as _201_compress using our heap profiling tool. BH is a Barnes & Hut N-body force computation algorithm. BiSort performs bitonic sort twice on a random set of integers. Em3D models electromagnetic waves propagation in a 3-D object. Health is a simulation of the Columbian health-care system. MST computes the minimum spanning tree of a graph. Perimeter computes the total perimeter of a region in a binary image represented by a quadtree. TreeAdd recursively traverses and sums the values in a balanced binary tree. TSP is the traveling saleman problem. Voronoi computes a voronoi diagram from a set of points stored in a balanced binary tree recursively.

The rest are some miscellaneous benchmark programs from renowned research institutes. MTSP is a multithreaded TSP program using a branch-and-bound algorithm. MTNbody is a multithreaded version of the Barnes & Hut N-body force computation algorithm. CUP [20] is a LALR parser generator. JLex [5] is a lexical analyzer generator. JFlex [21] is a fast lexical analyzer generator, a rewrite of JLex.

All the benchmarks were executed on a 2.4 GHz Intel Xeon machine with 512 KB L2 cache and 1 GB memory, running Redhat Linux 9.0.

4   Analysis of the Experimental Results

In this section, we study the heap to characterize the behavior of Java objects. We also investigate the potential amounts of space and time saving through the reuse of memory occupied by Java objects.

4.1   Objects' Behavior Due to Types

Mutable and Immutable Objects. We classify Java objects into two basic types: mutable and immutable. An object is immutable if its content cannot be

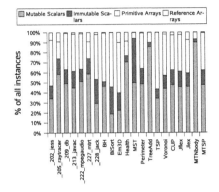

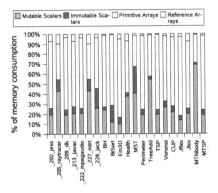

Fig. 1. Instance Counts of Mutable and Immutable Object Types

Fig. 2. Memory Consumption of Mutable and Immutable Objects

changed after construction—for example, `String` and `Integer`. In the experiments, we consider all arrays as mutable, regardless of whether they are primitive or reference arrays. Other than all primitive type class wrappers, the `String` class, the `BigInteger` class, the `BigDecimal` class, and the `Color` class, we also regard the `Class` class as an immutable type because the memory contents of `Class` objects will not be changed normally once they have been constructed.

Figures 1 and 2 show the instance counts and the memory consumption of both mutable and immutable objects created in different Java applications, respectively. It is interesting to note that every Java application creates a certain amount of immutable objects. For example, the amount of immutable objects created in MST is 43.91% of the total number of objects created. It is because MST requires a large number of `Integer` objects to maintain the distances of the nodes in the graph. Objects of immutable types, once used in a program, tend to be created in a large amount. Every time an immutable object needs to be modified, a new object instance has to be created. Thus, immutable objects could occupy a considerable amount of the heap memory, though this is not always true due to their small size. This is also depicted in Figure 2.

The detection of immutable objects can help optimizing GC to achieve space saving. We have mentioned in Section 2 the work of hash consing. In particular, [25] has carried out an object equality analysis to study the potential space saving by merging identical objects in Java programs. However, hash consing usually requires expensive equality tests, such as comparing the subtrees of two potential mergeable objects. If we only apply hash consing to instances of existing immutable classes in Java, the equality test can be cheaper, because immutable objects do not contain object references younger than themselves, and their memory contents cannot be modified once constructed. Therefore we do not need to consider if an merged object will later be modified, leading to incorrect result, because this will not happen in the immutable class objects in the Java class library. Still, we believe that hash consing can be applied to other user defined immutable classes by providing compiler with the capability to detect immutable objects through static analysis.

We can also observe from Figure 1 that all applications create a tremendous amount of primitive arrays. In particular, a large proportion of them are character arrays and byte arrays. During program execution, the Just-In-Time compiler of the Jikes RVM has to create a large number of byte arrays to maintain the code generated. The large number of character arrays is due to the large number of String objects created in the applications. Moreover, although the number of scalars created is usually more than that of primitive arrays, primitive arrays occupy more heap memory. This suggests that the size of primitive arrays created is usually larger than that of scalars. Nonetheless, most Java objects we can observe are small in size.

Diversed Types Instantiation. It is observed during profiling that an object instance tends to have long lifetime if it creates many object instances of diversed class types, because the object is usually the root, or close to the root in the object connectivity graph of an application. Although the observation is trivial, it provides a simple method to predict long-lived objects—simply detect the number of different class types of all the object instances created in an object. This is particularly useful for GC to make pretenuring decision for potentially long-lived objects. For example, in _227_mtrt, a Scene class instance, which creates object instances of more than 20 different class types, is an object of long lifetime. Another example is an OctNode class instance, which creates other object instances of more than five different class types, has a fairly long lifetime as well.

4.2   Objects' Liveness and Reusability

In this section, we analyze objects' liveness and study the potential space saving through reusing the heap memory occupied by Java objects. Figure 3 shows the age distribution of Java objects. More than 75% of the objects (of which approximately 50% are scalars, 25% are arrays) allocated are short-lived. This suggests that the weak generational hypothesis is true for Java.

Recently, Shuf et al. [33] proposed the *prolific hypothesis* which states that objects of prolific types have short lifetime. The hypothesis appears to be true with the programs we tried, as shown in Figure 4. Given that the two hypotheses are true, we can easily deduce that if two objects have non-overlapping lifetimes, and they are of the same class type, we can save the construction cost of the later object by reusing the memory occupied by the other object. This can also save space by reducing the maximal amount of memory required in the program, provided that the drag time of the reused object is small. Figure 5 shows the upper bounds of the memory saved in the Java applications when we apply object caching to objects of prolific types. Following Shuf et al., we regard an object type as prolific if the number of the object type instances created is more than 1% of the total number of objects created by an application. Also, we pick the least recently used (LRU) cached object when we need to reuse an object.

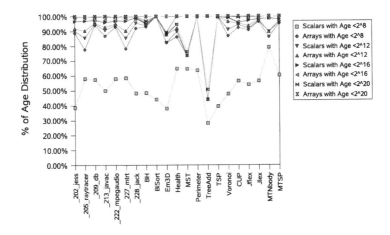

Fig. 3. Age Distribution of Java Objects

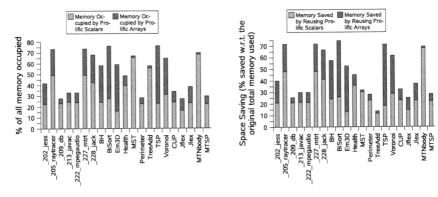

Fig. 4. Memory Occupied by Prolific Scalar and Array Objects

Fig. 5. Memory Saved by Reusing Prolific Objects

As can be seen in Figure 5 that most applications achieve a high percentage of space saving which ranges from 13.62% to 74.55%. If object caching is applied to prolific scalars only, the percentage of saving ranges from 11.67% to 68.06%. This suggests that it is more effective to apply object caching to prolific scalars than to prolific arrays. The larger amount of prolific scalars created also implies that many of them have shorter lifetime when compared with prolific arrays.

_215_javac and _222_mpegaudio of the SPEC benchmarks show a smaller percentage value in the amount of space saved. _215_javac requires some long-lived large arrays to maintain objects' type and other information inside the Java compiler. _222_mpegaudio uses several multi-dimensional arrays for maintaining and decoding MP3 audio files data. These arrays tend to be large in size, non-prolific, and long-lived. These arrays are being used throughout the entire program execution, and thus cannot be reused. _209_db, the MST, Perimeter,

and TreeAdd programs of the jolden benchmarks, and the multithreaded benchmark MTNbody do not require an array or require only a slight use of arrays in
the programs, so only a small amount of space can be saved from prolific arrays.
Applications which can have a relatively high degree of space saving from prolific
arrays usually need to create a lot of `String` objects, and hence correspondingly
a large amount of character arrays.

5   Preliminary Results of an Actual Implementation

Time efficiency is an important issue to consider in real-life applications, which
is easily perceived by the user. The impact of memory usage, however, is not so
easily felt by the user. As a result, a certain compromise between space effectiveness and time efficiency has to be made when designing a memory management
system.

In section 4.2, we study the potential amount of space saving through reusing
the memory occupied by prolific objects. This approach can improve the time
performance of a garbage collector, because fewer objects are reclaimed and returned to the memory allocation system. This approach can also improve the
time performance of the memory allocator, because the effort to allocate an
object is much reduced if reuse can be applied. To demonstrate the usefulness
of the recycling of prolific objects, we have implemented a simple prototype
of object caching, where memory space occupied by prolific objects can be
reused.

5.1   Implementation

The prototype is modified from the lazy Mark-Sweep (MS) collector in the Jikes
RVM. To support the reuse of memory consumed by prolific type objects, we
partition the heap into two regions: a recycle region and an MS region. Memory
allocated for objects residing in the recycle region may be reused by other objects
created in the future, but that in the MS region will be freed and returned to
the memory allocator.

We enhance the segregated free-list allocator [37] included in the Jikes RVM
to enable memory reuse. The original free-list allocator arranges memory into
blocks, each of which contains a free-list of memory cells for objects of a particular size. We modify the allocator so that objects of the same prolific types
are allocated in the same memory block in the recycle region. Object references
from the MS region to the recycle region are maintained using a "remembered
set". GC is applied more frequently to the recycle region. Memory blocks in the
recycle region are examined to see if they contain only objects that will no longer
be used. If that is the case, instead of freeing the memory blocks and returning
them to the normal memory free-list (FL), they are kept using another list, called
the recycle-list (RL). At memory allocation time, a simple test is performed to
check if memory buffer of a particular object class type and size is available from
RL. If yes, we simply re-initialize a memory cell in the RL by zeroing its content

and return it to the allocator; otherwise, we try to allocate a new memory cell from the FL instead.

5.2 Performance Evaluation

We compare the space-time performance of our prototype with the lazy MS collector using GCBench [7]. GCBench is a benchmark which creates binary trees of different lifetimes. It attempts to model memory allocation properties that are important to GC. We use the same hardware platform mentioned in Section 3 for the performance evaluation. The maximum and the minimum heap sizes of the Jikes RVM are set to 2 MB and 10 MB respectively. So, the heap size can be expanded if there is not enough free memory, even after the invocation of GC.

Figures 6 and 7 show the space-time performance of the MS collector and our collector, the Recycler, respectively. From the two figures, we can see that the Recycler achieves a better space-time performance. The total execution time of the Recycler is 22.41% faster than that of the MS collector. It is mainly because of the shorter instruction sequence required for memory allocation when

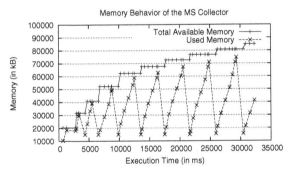

Fig. 6. The Space-Time Performance of GCBench using the MS Collector

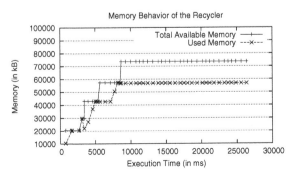

Fig. 7. The Space-Time Performance of GCBench using the Recycler

memory is obtained from RL instead of FL. In particular, the Recycler reduces the allocator's effort in splitting and coalescing free blocks repeatedly. It also reduces much GC overhead, because less GC is required for reclaiming memory blocks. The maximal space requirement of the Recycler is 31.44% smaller than that of the MS collector. It is because the memory buffers retained in the heap can be reused immediately without GC. The MS collector, on the other hand, can be faced with a large amount of newly created objects and garbage being kept in the heap before the occurrence of GC. The oscillating "Used Memory" curve in Figure 6 attests to this fact. The plateau in Figure 7 suggests that the memory buffers retained in the previous time period is enough to support future allocation.

6   Future Work

Our preliminary results presented in previous sections show that automatic object caching is a promising approach to improve the space-time performance of a memory management system. However, there are still many hurdles to overcome before we can have a Recycler that works perfectly. In this section, we address some important issues for which good future solutions could lead to a better memory allocator and collector design.

6.1   Equality Test

Any object caching scheme requires searching a table to find a match of the required object type for each object allocation. The search usually requires a test of equality. In many cases, in order to improve the performance of searching, the search involves some form of hashing. In Java, the test of equality of two objects can require the traversal of the whole object structure. The overhead of tree traversal is likely to offset the performance gain from object caching. Fortunately, equality test by tree traversal is necessary only if we would like to reuse an object in its entirety. In our case, we need only to detect if two objects are of the same class, regardless of the field values they keep. The equality test therefore becomes simple and efficient, since each object can maintain an ID for its class type so that the equality test of two object types is equivalent to comparing two integers. The only overhead is to re-initialize the memory contents of the object buffer before it can be reused. This overhead should be relatively small, and the re-initialization can be performed lazily in order to minimize its cost.

6.2   Space and Cache Management

Object caching, pooling, and hash consing share a common problem of space requirement, because they usually maintain a data structure such as a table or a list to maintain objects which will potentially be used in the future. During the course of program execution, the data structure may be expanded to use up all the memory available. Therefore, object caching should work hand-in-hand with the memory allocator and the garbage collector so that the amount of the retained object buffers can shrink or expand with the data structure as needed. This requires the support of the compiler or profile-directed feedback system etc. to provide the system with some runtime data for making the right decisions.

Since object caching extends the lifetime of objects which would have expired originally, these cached objects can reside in the heap for a long time before they are reused. This can increase the total space requirement of a program. In our prototype, the Recycler simply retains an amount of object buffers based on the amount of prolific objects allocated and reused since the last occurrence of GC. In any case, the object caching policy should probably be application specific. We believe that more understanding of object allocation patterns could help this issue.

Another problem in object cache management is the object cache selection policy. Given a pool of object buffers of the same class type, which cached object should be selected for reuse is a question. A widely used method for object cache selection should be the LRU policy. Nevertheless, different policies for object cache selection might result in different amounts of space and time saved, because of the locality effect. More study on this issue is required.

7   Conclusion

In this paper, we have studied the behavior of Java objects in order to explore potential GC optimization opportunities. We analyze the object traces produced from our heap profiling tool and study objects' liveness and types. We try to classify the objects by their being mutable or immutable, and prolific or non-prolific. Although Java programs usually create a large number of mutable objects, they produce a considerable amount of immutable objects of two particular types, `String` and `Integer`. We believe that existing techniques such as hash consing can be applied to these immutable types to achieve space saving, and yet avoiding the high cost of equality test.

We have analyzed the potential space saving in Java programs through the use of object caching on prolific objects. We find that a significant amount of space saving (more than 70%) can be achieved for certain kinds of applications.

We have implemented a prototype (the Recycler) to demonstrate that object caching is a viable approach to creating a memory management system which is both space effective and time efficient. We also address some important issues for future research.

References

1. Acar, U. A., Blelloch, G. E., and Harper, R.: Selective Memoization. Proceedings of the 30th ACM SIGPLAN-SIGACT Symposium on Principles of Programming Languages. ACM. New Orleans, Louisiana, USA (2003) 14–25

2. Alpern, B., Attanasio, C. R., Barton, J. J., Burke, M. G., Cheng, P., Choi, J.-D., Cocchi, A., Fink, S. J., Grove, D., Hind, M., Hummel, S. F., Lieber, D., Litvinov, V., Mergen, M. F., Ngo, T., Russell, J. R., Sarkar, V., Serrano, M. J., Shepherd, J. C., Smith, S. E., Sreedhar, V. C., Srinivasan, H., and Whaley, J.: The Jalapeño Virtual Machine. IBM System Journal 39. **1** (2000)
3. Appel, A. W. and Gonçalves, M. J. R.: Hash-consing Garbage Collection. Technical Report CS-TR-412-93, Princeton University (1993)
4. Bellman, R.: Dynamic Programming. Princeton University Press (1957)
5. Berk, E. J. and Ananian, C. S.: JLex: A Lexical Analyzer Generator for Java(TM). http://www.cs.princeton.edu/~appel/modern/java/JLex/
6. Blackburn, S. M., Singhai, S., Hertz, M., McKinley, K. S., and Moss, J. E. B.: Pretenuring for Java. Proceedings of the OOPSLA'01 Conference on Object Oriented Programming Systems Languages and Applications. ACM. Tampa Bay, Florida, USA (2001) 342–352
7. Boehm, H. J.: GCBench. http://www.hpl.hp.com/personal/Hans_Boehm/gc/gc_bench/
8. Bonwick, J.: The Slab Allocator: An Object-Caching Kernel Memory Allocator. USENIX Summer 1994 Technical Conference. Boston, Massachusetts, USA (1994)
9. Cahoon, B. and McKinley, K. S.: Data Flow Analysis for Software Prefetching Linked Data Structures in Java. International Conference on Parallel Architectures and Compilation Techniques (PACT'01). Barcelona, Spain (2001)
10. Cheney, C. J.: A Nonrecursive List Computing Algorithm. Commun. ACM, Vol. 13. **11** (1970) 677–678
11. Collins, G. E.: A Method For Overlapping and Erasure Of Lists. Commun. ACM, Vol. 3. **12** (1960) 655–657
12. Davis, T. E.: Build Your Own ObjectPool in Java to Boost App Speed: Increase the Speed of Your Applications while Reducing Memory Requirements. http://www.javaworld.com/javaworld/jw-06-1998/jw-06-object-pool.html
13. Dieckmann, S. and Hölzle, U.: A Study of the Allocation Behavior of the SPECjvm98 Java Benchmarks. ECOOP'99. Lecture Notes in Computer Science, Vol. 1628. Springer-Verlag, Berlin Heidelberg. Lisbon, Portugal (1999) 92–115
14. Ershov, A. P.: On Programming of Arithmetic Operations. Commun. ACM, Vol. 1. **8** (1958) 3–6
15. Fenichel, R. R. and Yochelson, J. C.: A Lisp Garbage-Collector for Virtual-Memory Computer Systems. Commun. ACM, Vol. 12. **11** (1969) 611–612
16. Fitzgerald, R. and Tarditi, D. The Case for Profile-Directed Selection of Garbage Collectors. Proceedings of the 2nd International Symposium on Memory Management. ACM. Minneapolis, Minnesota, USA (2000) 111–120
17. Goto, E.: Monocopy and Associative Algorithms in an Extended Lisp. Technical Report 74-03, Information Science Laboratory, University of Tokyo, Tokyo, Japan, May (1974)
18. Hirzel, M., Diwan, A., and Hosking, A.: On the Usefulness of Liveness for Garbage Collection and Leak Detection. ECOOP'01. Lecture Notes in Computer Science, Vol. 2072. Springer-Verlag, Berlin Heidelberg. Budapest, Hungary (2001) 181–206
19. Hirzel, M., Diwan, A., and Henkel, J.: On the Usefulness of Type and Liveness Accuracy for Garbage Collection and Leak Detection. ACM Transactions on Programming Languages and Systems, Vol. 24. **6** (2002) 593–624
20. Hudson, S. E., Flannery, F., and Ananian, C. S.: CUP Parser Generator for Java. http://www.cs.princeton.edu/~appel/modern/java/CUP/
21. Hudson, S. E.: JFlex—The Fast Scanner Generator for Java. http://jflex.de/

22. Jones, R. and Lins, R.: Garbage Collection: Algorithms for Automatic Dynamic Memory Management. John Wiley & Sons Ltd., Baffins Lane, Chichester (1996)

23. Kim, J.-S. and Hsu, Y.: Memory System Behavior of Java Programs: Methodology and Analysis. ACM SIGMETRICS Performance Evaluation Review, Vol. 28. **1** (2000) 264–274

24. Lieberman, H. and Hewitt, C.: A Real-Time Garbage Collector Based on the Lifetimes of Objects. Commun. ACM, Vol. 26. **6** (1983) 419–429

25. Marinov, D. and O'Callahan, R.: Object Equality Profiling. Proceedings of the Conference on Object-Oriented Programming, Systems, Languages, and Applications. ACM. Anaheim, California, USA (2003) 313–325

26. McCarthy, J.: Recursive Functions Symbolic Expressions and Their Computation by Machine, Part I. Commun. ACM, Vol. 3. **4** (1960) 184–195

27. Michie, D.: "Memo" Functions and Machine Learning. Nature, 218, Apr (1968)

28. Pugh, W.: An Improved Replacement Strategy for Function Caching. Proceedings of the 1988 ACM Conference on LISP and Functional Programming. ACM. Snowbird, Utah, USA (1988) 269–276

29. Shaham, R., Kolodner, E. K., and Sagiv, M.: On the Effectiveness of GC in Java. Proceedings of the 2nd International Symposium on Memory Management. ACM. Minneapolis, Minnesota, USA (2000) 12–17

30. Shaham, R., Kolodner, E. K., and Sagiv, M.: Heap Profiling for Space-Efficient Java. Proceedings of the ACM SIGPLAN'01 Conference on Programming Language Design and Implementation. ACM. Snowbird, Utah, USA (2001) 104–113

31. Shaham, R., Kolodner, E. K., and Sagiv, M.: Estimating the Impact of Heap Liveness Information on Space Consumption in Java. Proceedings of the 3rd International Symposium on Memory Management. ACM. Berlin, Germany (2002) 64–75

32. Shuf, Y., Serrano, M. J., Gupta, M., and Singh, J. P.: Characterizing the Memory Behavior of Java Workloads: A Structured View and Opportunities for Optimizations. Proceedings of the 2001 ACM SIGMETRICS International Conference on Measurement and Modeling of Computer Systems. ACM. Cambridge, Massachusetts (2001) 194–205

33. Shuf, Y., Gupta, M., Bordawekar, R., and Singh, J. P.: Exploiting Prolific Types for Memory Management and Optimizations. Proceedings of the 29th ACM SIGPLAN-SIGACT Symposium on Principles of Programming Languages. ACM. Portland, Oregon, USA (2002) 295–306

34. Standard Performance Evaluation Corporation: SPEC JVM98 Benchmarks. http://www.specbench.org/osg/jvm98/

35. Yang, Q., Srisa-an, W., Skotiniotis, T., and Chang, J. M.: Java Virtual Machine Timing Probes: A Study of Object Life Span and Garbage Collection. Proceedings of 21st IEEE International Performance, Computing, and Communications Conference. Phoenix, Arizona (2002)

36. Ungar, D.: Generation Scavenging: A Non-Disruptive High Performance Storage Reclamation Algorithm. Proceedings of the 1st ACM SIGSOFT/SIGPLAN Software Engineering Symposium on Practical Software Development Environments (1984) 157–167

37. Wilson, P. R., Johnstone, M. S., Neely, M., and Boles, D.: Dynamic Storage Allocation: A Survey and Critical Review. Proceedings of the International Workshop on Memory Management. Springer-Verlag (1995) 1–116

Author Index